PELICAN BIOGRAPHIES

TOLSTOY

Henri Troyat, member of the French Academy, was born a Russian (name: Lev Trassov), but was educated in France. In 1938 he won the Prix Goncourt. He has written many other works: biographies, an epic series of novels about Russia, other novels, short stories, historical essays and travel books. Many of these are available in English, including a life of Dostoyevsky. *Tolstoy* is being recognized as his greatest work.

HENRI TROYAT

Tolstoy

Translated from the French by
Nancy Amphoux

PENGUIN BOOKS

Penguin Books Ltd, Harmondsworth, Middlesex, England
Penguin Books Australia Ltd, Ringwood, Victoria, Australia

—

First published in France by Librairie Artheme Fayard in 1965
Published in the U.S.A. in 1967
Published in Pelican Books 1970

—

Copyright © Doubleday & Company, Inc. 1967

—

Made and printed in Great Britain
by Hazell Watson & Viney Ltd
Aylesbury, Bucks
Set in Linotype Georgian

Contents

Illustrations

PART I

—

THE TERMS OF THE PROBLEM

[1]

Before Leo Tolstoy

NAPOLEON and Alexander I might exchange sociable
letters or recall their ambassadors, promise their peoples
peace or plunge them into war, sacrifice thousands of soldiers at Eylau or embrace at Tilsit; but old Prince Nicholas
Sergeyevich Volkonsky, who had been living in retirement
on his family estate of Yasnaya Polyana since 1800, turned
a deaf ear to the clamour of a world in which he no longer
had a place. No one knew quite why he had suddenly withdrawn from public life. Some of the people who knew him
best intimated that he had too much character to remain in
the shadow of the throne: years before, he had refused to
marry young Varenka Engelhardt, niece – and mistress – of
Potemkin, the dreaded favourite of Catherine II, with the
comment, 'Whatever possessed him to imagine that I would
marry his whore?' Yet, despite this arrogant retort, or perhaps because of it, the empress had favoured him. Appointed captain in the Guards, he accompanied her to Mogi-
lev to meet Joseph II of Austria. Then, rising swiftly
through the ranks, he became ambassador extraordinary to
the king of Prussia, commander of the Azov Musketeers,
and finally general and military governor of Arkhangelsk,
on the shores of the White Sea. This little-to-be-envied post
in a glacial climate had been conferred upon him by Tsar
Paul I, who succeeded Catherine the Great, but whether as
a mark of special favour or disgrace it was impossible to tell.
In any event, Prince Volkonsky wasted no time in coming
to blows with his new sovereign, whose splenetic and capricious temperament had already terrified all Russia. When,
after some trivial professional incident, he received a letter
from the emperor omitting the traditional 'I remain your
benevolent sovereign' at the bottom of the page, he

surmised that his career was at an end and, taking the initiative, quickly asked to be relieved of active duty.

Once settled at Yasnaya Polyana,* this cultivated, dynamic and fiercely proud man resolved never to set foot outside it again. He liked to say that he needed nobody and nothing and that anyone who wanted to see him could make the trip, as his estate was only one hundred and thirty miles from Moscow.† Often, as though to convince himself of his own importance, he shut himself up in his sitting-room to pore over the family tree. The trunk, from which serpentine limbs curled out laden with illustrious names, was held by St Michael, prince of Chernigov. According to this document, the Volkonskys descended from the famous Prince Rurik, one of whose offspring had been given a holding, in the fourteenth century, in the government of Tula on the banks of the Volkona River. One Prince Volkonsky (Fyodor Ivanovich) died a hero at the battle of Kulikovo, in the war of independence with the Tatars of the Golden Horde; another (Sergey Fyodorovich) was a general in the Seven Years' War, and would have been killed but for a little icon he wore around his neck, which stopped the enemy shell.[1]

In recognition of the services rendered to the State by this great family, Prince Nicholas Sergeyevich Volkonsky had been granted the privilege of keeping two armed sentinels at Yasnaya Polyana. Day and night they paced back and forth in their shabby uniforms, guns over their left shoulders and shakos askew, between the two little towers of whitewashed brick, topped by buckler-shaped roofs, which flanked the entrance to the estate. Peasants and tradesmen, and even honoured guests, were reminded by these soldiers that although the master of the house had withdrawn from the

---

* The Russian word *yasny* means 'luminous' or 'clear' and *yasen* is an ash tree, so some translate Yasnaya Polyana by 'Clear Glade' and others, less poetic but closer to the truth, by 'Ash Glade'.

† One hundred and ninety-six versts. One verst equals 3,500 feet, or approximately ·66 mile.

world and was no longer influential at court, all in the government of Tula owed him their respect. His serfs loved and feared him. He gave them advice on cultivating the land and saw that they were decently housed, fed and clothed; he shielded them from badgering by the provincial administrative authorities, and organized festivities for them. His severity was proverbial, but his muzhiks were never beaten. At seven o'clock every morning, eight serf-musicians in wide blouses, breeches, white stockings and pumps would assemble in front of their music stands near an ancient elm. A little boy would cry out, 'He's awake!' as he went by carrying a pitcher of hot water. Thereupon the orchestra tuned up, and the opening chords of a Haydn symphony rose to the windows of the princely bed-chamber. At the end of their *aubade* the musicians dispersed, one going off to feed the pigs, another to knit stockings in the servants' hall, a third to spade in the garden.

Visitors to the house, whatever their rank, were made to await the 'Grande Levée' in the antechamber. And when the double doors of the dressing-room swung open at last, there was not one among the assembly who did not feel something akin to fear at the sight of the little, withered old man tottering stiffly towards him out of the depths of the ages, in a powdered wig above heavy black brows that shaded an expression of sparkling youth. He speedily dispatched the importunate callers and set off for a walk or drive around his estate, of which he was very proud. The grounds were extensive, overgrown and untidy, with avenues of venerable lime trees, giant lilacs, dishevelled elders, clumps of hazel and birch and dark families of larch. There were four ponds stocked with carp, a deep stream – the Voronka – an orchard and a hamlet of a dozen isbas. The master's house, built of wood and embellished by a peristyle of columns and a neo-classical pediment, was always freshly painted white. It was flanked by two pavilions. The view from the top of the hill looked out on a calm, rolling landscape crossed by the old Kiev highway, from which the monotonous creak of carts and the cries of drivers on their way to Tula could be heard during the warm season.

Prince Volkonsky loved nature, books, music and rare flowers, which he grew in his greenhouses, and he loathed hunting. He held superstition and inactivity to be the roots of all evil. He combated the former by reading the French Encyclopedists, and he warded off the latter by writing his memoirs – which he did standing at a tall desk – by studying mathematics, and by turning snuffboxes – foot on the pedal, hand guiding the gouge and eyes sparkling with glee – in a cloud of pale sawdust and curly shavings.

But most of his time was devoted to the education of his daughter and only child Marya, offspring of his marriage to Princess Katerina Dmitrievna Trubetskoy. The princess died in 1792 when Marya was just two years old.* The prince remained a widower and grew to dote upon this lack-lustre, ungainly and docile child. However, as he had a horror of emotional effusions he maintained a lofty reserve in her presence. Above all, he wanted her to have a well-furnished mind; in addition to French, which all people of good society preferred to Russian, he accordingly had her learn English, German and Italian. She had taste, played the piano prettily and was interested in the history of art. Lastly, her father himself taught her algebra and geometry, with such zest and intensity that she grew faint as he leaned over her, exuding a sour smell of pomaded decrepitude, and assailed her with questions and reprimands. Well, if he could not make a mathematician of her, at least he could hope to fashion her in his own image, give her self-control and a clear and logical mind and prepare her to sail un-ruffled through life's stormy seas. From her association with this caustic and domineering old man, Marya learned to hide her feelings; but at heart she remained an emotional girl with a penchant for daydreaming. She cared for the poor, read French novels and thought it natural to devote

* Princess Marya Nikolayevna Volkonsky was born on 10 November 1790.

her existence to the worship of her father. The idea of marriage did not even cross her mind: the prince would never consent to let her go! Besides, she was not pretty. She had her father's heavy brows, and flushed scarlet whenever anything annoyed her. Nobody was interested in her. It was as though the steely glare of Nicholas Sergeyevich Volkonsky repulsed all the young men for twenty miles around. Only one had found favour in his eyes: a son of Prince Sergey Fyodorovich Golitsin and that same Varenka Engelhardt, Potemkin's niece and mistress, whom he had refused to marry in his youth. The two men had become friends late in life and, to consolidate their mutual esteem, resolved to marry their children, without consulting them. As a first step family portraits were exchanged, painted by serfs on the two estates. Marya, to whom nobody had ever paid court, was ecstatic at the thought of this mysterious suitor whom she had hardly ever glimpsed, but whose father, begirt with the ribbon of the Order of St Andrew, and mother, opulent, red-haired and covered with jewels, already presided in effigy over the drawing-room at Yasnaya Polyana. When her excitement had reached fever pitch, a dreadful blow fell: her fiancé died of typhoid fever. For her, this was a sign from God: she was not to think of any man other than her father. She swallowed her tears as she had been taught, but looked wistfully back to this nascent love, whose purity and melancholy were so reminiscent of the romantic reading of her childhood. Now, imprisoned in her remote province, she knew she was destined to die an old maid and tried not to let the fact make her too unhappy. After all, life at Yasnaya Polyana was very pleasant. Her father had given her two young companions to entertain her. She preferred Mlle Louise Hénissienne,* a mischievous, lively young Frenchwoman but, 'I manage very well with both of them,' she wrote. 'I play music, giggle and frolic about with one, and talk of noble feelings and deplore frivolity with the other; and both of them are terribly fond of me.' [2]

* Mlle Bourienne, in *War and Peace*.

Sometimes, wearying of the cooing of these turtledoves, Marya would slip across to the outbuildings to talk to the passing pilgrims. They stopped off there to eat and sleep, unknown to the prince, who was reputed to have no patience with visionary vagabonds. Hirsute and lice-infested, their packs on their backs and their eyes full of sky, they walked from one end of Russia to the other to reach some miraculous monastery. Without believing a word of their tales, Marya marvelled at the strength of their faith. If only she, too, could break her bonds and set off to roam the world! But she was riveted to Yasnaya Polyana. And she was growing old and faded. When she compared herself with her companions, she hated her plain, prematurely old face with its heavy brows and weary mouth. 'I shall go to some town to pray,' she wrote, 'and then, before I have time to settle down and become attached to it, I shall move on. I shall walk until my feet give way beneath me, I shall lie down and die somewhere, and reach at last that eternal, peaceful haven where there are no more sorrows or sighs.'

She dreamed of ending her life, but it was her father who died. On 3 February 1821 she suddenly found herself alone in the world. She was thirty-one years old and until that day she had lived with the sole aim of coddling the master of Yasnaya Polyana in his old age. With him gone, she was cast adrift and rudderless; she could see nothing of the slightest attraction in the days ahead. Her need to dedicate herself now encountered nothing but empty space. Seeking an outlet for her surplus affection, she took it into her head to marry Louise Hénissienne's sister to one of her cousins, Prince Michael Alexandrovich Volkonsky.

The rest of the family howled 'Misalliance', but Marya stood her ground, sold one of her estates, and put the money in her companion's name to help the young couple. Bulgakov, postmaster-general of Moscow, wrote indignantly to his brother: 'After losing all hope of tasting the joys of wedlock herself, the princess, daughter of the late Prince Nicholas Sergeyevich – an ugly old maid with bushy eyebrows – has given part of her property to an Englishwoman (a Frenchwoman) who lives with her.'

Louise Hénissienne's sister and Prince Michael Alexandrovich Volkonsky were married in Moscow in April 1821. Marya made a special trip; she was the only member of the fiancé's numerous kin to attend the religious ceremony. As she watched the two young people being blessed by the priest, her heart contracted within her. Her thoughts were turning more and more often to love, marriage, motherhood. Was she really to be deprived of these simple joys, the common lot of woman?

In Moscow she lived in the family house, which, although it was much too big for her, held fewer reminders of the old prince than Yasnaya Polyana. Her friends exhorted her to go out and enjoy herself. One day in a drawing-room, she found herself face to face with a man of average height, who had wavy hair, a melancholy expression and a moustache brushed demurely downward. He wore his uniform well and spoke French correctly. He was introduced to Marya: Count Nicholas Ilich Tolstoy. Marya found him quite pleasant but, as always, allowed nothing of her feelings to show. This meeting was not an accident. The very next day negotiations with a view to matrimony got under way between the plenipotentiaries of the two parties.

To tell the truth, Count Nicholas Ilich Tolstoy was not overjoyed by the prospect of a union with a person who, in addition to being dismayingly homely, was five years older than he. But he was on the brink of bankruptcy and a rich marriage was the only thing that could save him. The great name he bore would have recommended him to any heiress in Russia. The Tolstoys claimed descendancy from a Lithuanian knight named Indris, who had settled and been baptized at Chernigov in the fourteenth century; his great-grandson was given the name of Tolstoy, or 'The Stout', by Grand Duke Basil the Blind. One Peter Andreyevich Tolstoy had been appointed ambassador to Constantinople by Peter the Great, and then head of the Secret Chancellery;

in 1724 he was raised to the nobility for his services, although this did not prevent him from ending his days in prison for plotting against Catherine II. Less ambitious than his ancestors, Ilya Tolstoy contented himself with squandering his fortune and that of his wife, née Gorchakov, by sending his laundry to be washed in Holland, having his fish shipped directly from the Black Sea, giving balls and theatrical performances on his estate near Belyev, losing substantial sums at hombre and whist – until the day when, crippled with debt, he accepted a post as governor of Kazan for want of anything better. In the meantime his son Nicholas, just eighteen years old, had gone off on a sudden impulse to join the army. The year was 1812, Napoleon was marching on Russia, the young were afire with patriotism. From standard-bearer in a regiment of hussars, Nicholas soon became an aide-de-camp to General Gorchakov – a close relative of his mother – but despite this powerful protector, he did not shine in the campaign of 1813. Shortly after the blockade of Erfurt he was taken prisoner by the French on his way back from a mission to St Petersburg. He was liberated in 1814 when the allied troops entered Paris, returned to Russia, and was made a major, then a lieutenant-colonel. Was this security at last? No; the extravagance of old Count Ilya Tolstoy in his post as governor of Kazan had assumed such proportions that there could no longer be any question of his son honourably pursuing a military career. The family was ruined, the Belyev estate mortgaged. Nicholas, smelling bankruptcy in the air, resigned his commission and went to live with his parents at Kazan. Aline and Pelagya, his two sisters, had married while he was away, the first to Count Osten-Saken and the second to V. I. Yushkov, and left home. Even without them, the household had preserved its appeal, thanks to a distant cousin – Tatyana Alexandrovna Ergolskaya, nicknamed 'Toinette'. She was a poor orphan, who had been taken in by the Tolstoys when a child and brought up with their own children. She was the same age as Nicholas, and mutely adored him. Thick brown braids framed her handsome, slightly severe face, and her brown eyes sparkled like agate. Her bearing was full of grace and energy. When her cousin first came back to Kazan, she thought he was going to ask for her hand. But for the moment, although Nicholas was aware of the discreet affection she had borne him for so many years, he was interested only in having fun. Every salon in town clamoured for him; he was the life of every party. Dancing and playing, he forgot the sorry state of the family affairs. After all, his father set a perfect example of irresponsibility: the budget of the government of Kazan was being increasingly imperilled by his mismanagement and disreputable dealings, yet old Count Ilya Tolstoy kept smiling through it all; everything, he thought, would come right in the end. A committee of investigation appointed by the Russian Senate suddenly decided to look into his accounts. Horror-stricken, he fell ill and died before he had time to write out his defence. Some people even claimed he committed suicide.

Overnight, Nicholas Tolstoy, who had scarcely given a thought to money in the past, opened his eyes upon an abyss. He auctioned off his land and moved into a modest apartment in Moscow with his cousin Toinette and his mother and, to provide for them, grudgingly accepted a post as deputy director of the Veterans' Orphanage. Toinette ran the household, and took care of her aunt – read to her, endured every whim of the spoiled, tyrannical, pernickety old woman. The dominant feature of Toinette's personality was a need to suffer for the happiness of others; her all-embracing affection encompassed both the countess, from whom she tried to hide the truth about the family's financial predicament, and the servants, with whom she was kind and firm. But her cousin Nicholas Tolstoy was always at the centre of her mind, superb and unattainable. He held no secrets for her; she did not idealize him, and cherished his very faults. He was far from being 'a paragon of virtue'. At sixteen his parents had offered him one of their servant girls, to teach him the facts of life. A child, Mishenka, was born of this liaison, and subsequently became a postilion and died a pauper.[3] While in his regiment the count had also had numerous affairs, to which he made covert allusion in Toinette's presence. She hoped that, wearying of so many different adventures and sobered by a shortage of ready cash, it would occur to him that she could make him happy. And, it was true, there were days when he looked at her so tenderly that she was thrown into a flutter of confusion. But he never talked about their future. He was accustomed to life on a grander scale and he chafed against his straitened circumstances. Having to count his money made him misanthropic. He sometimes stayed in his room for hours, smoking his pipe. The countess moaned that a good marriage was the only thing that could save them. Toinette thought back to the time when, as a little girl, she had been carried away by the story of Mucius Scaevola, and resolved to prove to her cousins that she, too, was capable of heroism, which she did by applying a red-hot iron ruler to her forearm. She did not utter a sound while her flesh smoked, and she still bore the scar; she smiled at it ruefully and thought that the time had come once again to demonstrate her strength of character. When the family began talking about this Marya Nikolayevna Volkonsky, who was so homely, almost middle-aged, with the heavy eyebrows and the great fortune, she stifled her jealousy and urged Nicholas Tolstoy to make a marriage of reason.

On 9 July 1822 Princess Marya Nikolayevna Volkonsky, heiress to the estate of Yasnaya Polyana, married Count Nicholas Ilich Tolstoy. Her dowry comprised eight hundred male peasant serfs in the government of Tula and Orel; her fiancé had nothing to offer but his name and his elegant bearing.

This loveless union proved, nevertheless, to be a harmonious one. True, Marya was not passionately in love with her husband, but she felt affection and esteem for him and something akin to gratitude. And he in turn was not long to discover a quality of integrity in his wife that far outweighed any outward graces, and acknowledged her as his moral and intellectual superior. Indeed, her self-control must have been quite remarkable, to get along with her in-laws. Now that her son's position was secure, the old countess regretted that he had not married someone more dazzling. And she was unhappy because he was neglecting her for his wife. She was jealous and showed it. And Toinette, who was also living with the young couple, silently suffered the daily torture of their wedded bliss. She spied on Marya's every move, tried to find some reason to hate her and couldn't and, subdued by the newcomer's kindly and placid nature, no longer knew whether to rejoice at Nicholas's happiness or despair because he was sharing it with someone else.

On 31 June 1823, Countess Marya gave birth to a son, Nicholas – 'Coco' – and it seemed to her that her cup was full. The child became the centre of her universe. She asked her husband to hand in his resignation and, in 1824, the entire family left Moscow to settle at Yasnaya Polyana.

Nicholas Tolstoy, who had hitherto shown scant interest in agriculture, became transformed into a country squire. A tradition-bound conservative, he spurned all newfangled methods of farming, but he was always out in the fields, chatting paternally with his serfs; he gave them advice when it was time to sow and only seldom, and reluctantly, issued orders to whip a man guilty of insubordination or negligence. In the autumn he often set off with his borzoi at dawn and did not come home until nightfall, exhausted, elated and covered with dirt. His high spirits and vivacity exploded at table. But he was also known to shut himself up in his library to read. There, Buffon consorted with the *Vaudevilles du XVIIIe siècle*, *The Travels of Young Anacharsis* stood next to Cuvier, and the *History of the Popes* alongside the *Songs of the Freemasons*. He swallowed it all pell-mell and said he would not buy any more books until he had read the ones he had. When he was obliged to leave Yasnaya Polyana and go to Moscow to deal with the numerous lawsuits which his father's creditors had brought against the estate, Marya and he exchanged epistles of restrained affection. At a time when lyrical out-pourings between married couples were the rule, Nicholas Tolstoy began his letters simply, 'My tender friend,' and his wife replied, 'My tender friend,' and signed herself, 'Your devoted Marya'. True, she made up for lost time alone in her room, composing French verses in which the prosody was approximative but the sentiments high-flown:

> O wedded love! Our hearts' most gentle bond!
> The source and nurse of our most cherished pleasures!
> With thy celestial flame, inspire our souls forever,
> And in thy peace let our desires be crowned ...
> Yes, my heart confirms it, this envied destiny
> Heaven in its goodness has kept for you and me
> And these two names now joined, Nicholas and Marie,
> Will ever signify two souls joined happily.

These exercises were interspersed with meditations on the serious problems of life. Marya liked to compose maxims, also in French, to consult in time of crisis: 'The generous impulses of youth must become the principles of adulthood ... ,' 'When we are very young we seek everything outside ourselves ... but, gradually, everything sends us back inside ... ,' 'Often, we might resist our own passions, but are swept away by those of others ...'

Before little Nicholas was three years old she had a second son, Sergey (17 February 1826). The following year, another birth: Dmitry (23 April 1827) and, one year later, a fourth heir to the great name of Tolstoy was entered in the parish records:

On August 28 1828,* in the village of Yasnaya Polyana, at the home of Count Nicholas Ilich Tolstoy, a son, Leo, was born, and

* This date, like all the others in this book, is given according to the Russian Julian calendar, which is twelve days behind the Gregorian calendar in the nineteenth century, and thirteen days in the twentieth.

baptized on the twenty-ninth by Vasily Mazhaisky, priest, assisted by the deacon Arkhip Ivanov, the sacristan Alexander Yodorov and the cantor Fyodor Grigoryev; the god-parents are Simon Ivanovich Yasikov, landowner in the district of Belyev, and Countess Pelagya Tolstoy.

After being convinced at thirty-two that she would end her days a spinster, Marya Tolstoy could not get used to the joy of finding herself, at thirty-eight, the mother of four children. She loved them more than she ever loved her father, more than she loved her husband. Leaving Toinette to manage the household, she gave herself up body and soul to her task as educator. She doted upon the last-born, Leo, 'little Benjamin'; but Nicholas, the eldest – 'Coco' – received her most ardent attention. Like her father before her, she wanted him to become a man of exceptional abilities. Every evening she recorded his words and deeds in a diary, noted his shortcomings, considered the best ways of correcting them. Her chief fear was that he should prove over-sensitive. When he was four she upbraided him for weeping over a tale of a wounded bird or the sight of a dog fight. She wanted him to be brave, 'as befits the son of a father who served his country valiantly'. To reward him for progress in reading she gave him numbered slips of paper bearing such notes as 'Very good . . .,' 'Passable . . .,' 'Very slow at the beginning, good on the following page . . .'

After a certain amount of friction, perfect harmony had been established between Marya, her mother-in-law and Toinette. On a trip, Marya wrote to the latter: 'Dear Toinette, how can you imagine that I am able to forget you or stop thinking of you just because I am in pleasant surroundings elsewhere? You know that when I love, nothing can efface those dear to me from my heart.' And elsewhere: 'You are so kind to me and so fond of my little sparrow that I feel that when I talk about him, I give as much joy to you as I do to myself.' Her sons were growing, handsome and healthy, the estate was beginning to prosper under Nicholas's management, and the future only looked more rosy

when the young woman found, in 1829, that she was once
again with child. This fifth pregnancy did not prevent her
from leading a very active life. When the children were in
bed, she would play the piano – a concerto by Field or the
Pathétique sonata – read aloud, give her cousin an Italian
lesson or discuss with her the principles of Rousseau's *Émile*.
Nicholas would join them in the drawing-room and entertain them with his hunting tales and jokes. He drew on his
pipe as he talked and peered through the windows into the
dark grounds outside – and now and then they heard the
night watchman going down the drive, striking his metal
plate. Late in February 1830 there was a great to-do in the
house. The black leather divan which Marya had adopted
for her deliveries was carried into her room [4] where, on 2
March, she gave birth to a girl, also called Marya.

Soon after, the mother's health declined. She had been
exhausted by childbearing. She ran a continual fever and
complained of violent headaches. The servants said she was
certainly going to lose her mind. After taking communion,
she asked to see her loved ones, to bid them farewell. The
family assembled around her bed. In his nurse's arms little
Leo, twenty-three months old, screamed in terror at the
sight of the livid mask whose eyes, full of tears, were fixed
upon him with unbearable tenderness. He did not recognize
his mother. He hated this strange woman. The nurse took
him back to his bedroom where he grew calm again amidst
his toys.[5] Countess Marya Nikolayevna Tolstoy died on 4
August 1830.

Left a widower, Nicholas Tolstoy fully realized how large
a place this woman he married in cold blood had occupied
in his life during the last eight years. What was to become
of the children and the house without her? Perhaps the
time had come to give a second chance to his cousin Toinette, previously rejected on financial grounds. For the sake
of appearances, he let a few years go by and then asked her
to be his wife. She was deeply touched, for she had gone on
loving him in secret, but refused out of loyalty to the de-

ceased. The evening of their conversation, she wrote on a scrap of paper, 'August 16, 1836. Today Nicholas made me a singular proposal: to be his wife and a mother to his children, and never to leave them. I refused the first and promised to fulfil the second as long as I shall live.' She put the note away in a little pearl-embroidered purse, and nothing more was ever said by her or her cousin of a project which, by bringing them together, would probably have destroyed their respect for each other.

[2]

Childhood

THE harder little Leo tried to remember his mother, the more she eluded him. He tried to identify her by questioning those who had known her, but in vain. They told him she was good, gentle, upright, proud, intelligent, and an excellent storyteller, but he could not attach a face to this assortment of qualities, and as though to deepen the mystery, there was not a single portrait of her in the house. Only a silhouette cut out of black paper, showing her at the age of ten or twelve, with a round forehead and a round chin, her hair in a veil at the nape of her neck. His whole life long Leo Tolstoy tried to instil life into this frustrating profile. He grew older, but his mother remained a little girl. Driven by his need for love, he finally came to think of her as a mythical being to whom he had recourse in times of distress and upon whom he relied for supernatural assistance. Only a few years before his death he wrote, '... I walk in the garden and I think of my mother, of Maman; I do not remember her, but she has always been an ideal of saintliness for me. I have never heard a single disparaging remark about her.'[1] And also, 'Felt dull and sad all day. Toward evening the mood changed into a desire for caresses, for tenderness. I wanted, as when I was a child, to nestle against some tender and compassionate being and weep with love and be consoled ... become a tiny boy, close to my mother, the way I imagine her. Yes, yes, my Maman, whom I was never able to call that because I did not know how to talk when she died. She is my highest image of love – not cold, divine love, but warm, earthly love, maternal. ... Maman, hold me, baby me! ... All that is madness, but it is all true.'[2]

Although Leo Tolstoy could not remember his mother,

he did remember – or thought he did – things that happened even before her death. 'I am all bound up; I want to stretch out my arms and I cannot,' he wrote in his *Reminiscences*. 'I scream and cry and I hate my own screaming, but I cannot stop. People are leaning over me – I can't remember who – and everything is shrouded in semi-darkness. There are two of them. My screaming affects them; they are anxious; but they do not release me as I want them to, and I scream still louder.' His second memory was a brighter one. He was sitting in a wooden tub, surrounded by a sourish smell, while a servant-woman rubbed his body with bran.

For the first time [he wrote in the same work] I became aware of and liked my little body with the ribs sticking out on my chest, and the dark, smooth wooden tub, and my nurse's sleeves rolled up, and the warm, steaming, agitated water and its lapping noise and, most of all, the polished feeling of the wet rim of the tub when I ran my little hands along it. It is strange and frightening to think that from the day I was born until I was three years old, all the time I was nursing and being weaned, beginning to crawl and walk and talk, however I rack my brains, I can remember nothing but these two impressions. . . . From the child of five to me there is only a step. From the embryo to the newborn child an abyss. And from non-existence to the embryo, not an abyss but the inconceivable.

Gradually, however, the shadows moving around him assumed form. He could attach names to the faces. At five he was living contentedly in his little upstairs room with his sister Marya and Dunya, a little girl the family had adopted, when the grownups decided it was time for him to join his older brothers downstairs and pass from the hands of his nurse into those of the German tutor, Fyodor Ivanovich Rössel. He was frightened to tears at the thought of this change, and Aunt Toinette tried to pacify him as she dressed him in his new clothes – a real boy's outfit, in denim, with braces. When she had finished, she kissed him. 'I remember her,' he wrote, 'being rather small and thickset, with brown hair and an expression of kindness, tenderness, compassion. ... I saw that she was feeling the same thing as I – it was sad, very sad, but it had to be.' She led him down the stairs. When he appeared, hanging back and sniffling, his brothers called him a blubber-puss. But their insults fell unheeded. He was oblivious to all but his terror of Fyodor Ivanovich Rössel, who had pale eyes behind big spectacles, an aquiline nose and a tasselled cap, and wore a quilted, flower-patterned dressing-gown that he changed for a dark blue redingote before coming to table.

This awesome-looking personage soon revealed itself to be the most good-natured and soft-hearted man alive. His German accent, when he spoke Russian, was utterly comical; sometimes he lost his temper, shouted and struck his pupils with a ruler or a pair of braces, but his tantrums inspired laughter more than tears. He was supposed to instruct the children in all subjects, but he chiefly taught them the 'language of Goethe'. Their instructor in the 'language of Voltaire' was Aunt Toinette. At five Leo Tolstoy knew the French alphabet as well as the Russian; and he said later that he often thought directly in French.

But for the time being, he was bent only on having fun with his brothers who, after teasing him, accepted him as one of their group. He loved the smile and big dark eyes and curious whims of Dmitry, closest to his own age; he looked up to Nicholas, who was five years his senior; but Sergey, two years older than he, was the one he worshipped – handsome Sergey, remote and strange, who was always singing, drew extraordinary roosters with coloured pencils, and raised chickens in secret. 'I copied him, I loved him, I wanted to be him,'[3] wrote Tolstoy. But Sergey paled before Nicholas, when it came to inventing a new game. Nicholas had such a lively imagination that he could tell fantastic or droll stories for hours on end, making them up out of thin air and embellishing them with drawings of horned and moustachioed devils. One day he told his brothers that he knew a secret, and when the secret was unveiled all sickness would vanish from the earth and love would flower in every heart, and all men, happy at last, would become Ant Brothers.* While awaiting this glorious apocalypse, the boys used to sit together under shawl-draped chairs, where, huddling in the shadows, they felt a sense of profound mystery. Little Leo in particular, cuddling into the tribal heat and smell, held his breath and listened to the beating of his own heart, and was moved to tears by the thought of the 'brotherhood of ants'. He would dearly have loved to know the chief secret thanks to which all men would become healthy and never quarrel again, but Nicholas said it was carved on a green stick, and the green stick was buried on the edge of a ravine in the old Zakaz forest. 'I used to believe,' he later wrote, 'that there was a green stick on which words were carved that would destoy all the evil in the hearts of men and bring them everything good, and I still believe today that there is such a truth, that it will be revealed to men, and will fulfil its promise.' And, remembering where the green stick was supposedly hidden, he added, 'Since my body has to be buried somewhere, I have asked that it be in that place, in memory of Nicholas.'

Another time, Nicholas promised his brothers to take them up Fanfaron Mountain. But anyone who wanted to join the expedition must first stand in a corner of the room and 'not think of the white bear'; then he must walk, without missing a step, along a crack between the floorboards; the third condition was not to have seen a hare, 'dead, alive or roasted,' for a whole year and to swear he would never tell what he learned there. If anyone passed all these trials – and others, more difficult, to be set later – his wish would come true at the top of the mountain. They all made a wish for the future: Sergey wanted to learn to model horses and hens in wax; Dmitry wanted to draw objects life-size, like real

---

* As Tolstoy observed in his *Reminiscences*, Nicholas probably meant to say 'Moravian Brothers', which was the name of a religious sect that flourished in Bohemia in the sixteenth century. The confusion in the child's mind arose from the fact that the Russian word for ant is *muravey*, which is phonetically similar to 'Moravian'.

painters did; Leo did not know what to choose and said he would like to draw the same thing, only in miniature.

On the outskirts of this enchanted world, tutelary divinities stood guard. First, in Maman's place, there was Tatyana Alexandrovna Ergolskaya, Aunt Toinette, who cherished the children of Yasnaya Polyana as though they were her own. Leo Tolstoy wrote, 'Her chief influence upon me was, from childhood, to make me feel the spiritual joy of loving. I could see and sense how happy she was to love, and I understood this happiness. Secondly, she taught me to appreciate a withdrawn and quiet life. ... The main features of this life were the absence of material cares, pleasant relations with other people ... and the absence of hurry or any sense of the passing of time.'[4] In Aunt Toinette's room there were jars full of raisins and cookies and dates and candy standing in a row. No treat was sweeter to little Leo than those she dispensed on great occasions to reward him for being good. He also loved to lie down behind her on the drawing-room sofa, breathing in her perfume, melting into her warmth, laying his cheek against the small brown hand, 'barred by an energetic vein', that hung limply down from the armrest.

Less close to the children than she, Nicholas Ilich Tolstoy appeared to his youngest son as a paragon of elegance, strength and good humour. How handsome he was as he set out for town in a redingote and narrow trousers, or went hunting amidst his playful wolfhounds, or inhaled his pipe, slowly and deeply, with eyes half-closed and a bluish haze above his head! Sometimes he came into the boys' room, quickly sketched something with a sure hand, exchanged three or four words of German with Fyodor Ivanovich Rössel, commanded Leo, his 'big pouf', to recite a poem by Pushkin – 'Farewell, free element! ...' or 'Napoleon', criticized his bombastic delivery, told a funny story, and whirled about and vanished, leaving them all entranced.

The morning hours in the classroom with the tutor passed quickly, and afterwards they could go outdoors to play. The grounds were so vast that the children found some new corner to explore every day. During the warm weather they fished for crayfish in the Voronka, tore their skin chasing each other through the brambles, went to visit the horses in the stable and the dogs in the kennel, picked mushrooms and blackberries, chattered with the ragged serf-children, tanned and shy; and in the winter there were skating parties and snowball fights. As soon as they came indoors they had to wash and change and go to the drawing-room, where Grandmother, Aunt Alexandra, Aunt Toinette, little Pashenka and Fyodor Ivanovich Rössel were waiting for Papa to emerge from his study so they could go in to dinner. There he was at last, sturdy and energetic, 'with his red neck and soft flat-heeled boots' and eyes sparkling with childish merriment. While he was kissing Grandmother's hand, the painted, dark-red double doors swung open and there in the doorway stood Foka Demidich, the major-domo, one-time second violin in the late Prince Volkonsky's orchestra. Hunched into a navy-blue redingote, he furrowed his brow and declaimed in a rusty voice that dinner was served. Everybody stood up. Papa gave his arm to grandmother, and the aunts, children, friends and tutor crowded together behind them. The family filed into the dining-room, where a footman stood behind each chair, clutching a plate to his heart. When guests were present, their own servants were posted behind their backs and served them throughout the meal. The table was covered with a coarse linen cloth, the work of local weavers, and on it stood carafes of water, jugs of kvass, old silver spoons, wooden-handled iron knives and forks and plain glasses. The soup was served in the pantry and the footmen handed out the *piroshki* that went with it, one by one. With the first mouthful the conversation became animated, crackled among the tablemates. Papa ate, joked and drank, his cheeks on fire. At every witticism the children burst out laughing. From the beginning their minds were fixed on one thing: dessert – fritters, milk pudding, fried doughnuts, cream cheese and sour cream!

Now and then Leo stole a glance at old Tikhon, former flutist in Prince Volkonsky's orchestra. Livid, waxen and shrivelled, he stood behind Grandmother's chair, clasping a plate to his bosom, and followed the master's discussion so intently that his shaved lips sometimes gaped wide and his eyes grew round in amazement.

When the meal was over, Tikhon brought the master's pipe, already lighted, and tiptoed away. But he soon re-appeared in the mirror that reflected a corner of the paternal study. Yielding to temptation, he would steal a pinch of tobacco from the soft rose-shaped leather pouch Nicholas Ilich had left on his desk. He deserved a scolding a hundred times over, but his magnanimous master merely smiled. Wild with gratitude, Leo caught hold of his father's white hand, which had a pink spot on the fleshy part of the palm, and kissed it.

In the afternoon, when the weather was fine, there were outings in the carriage with the aunts and the tutor, to the hamlet of Grumond, two miles away from Yasnaya Polyana. The canopied charabanc with its leather apron and the high-springed yellow cabriolet bounced along the rutted paths of the forest of Zakaz, in single file. The children shouted and sang, the horses flicked their ears. At the end of the road Matryona the cow-girl was waiting for them with black bread, sour cream and raw milk.

Winter evenings also had their charm. The entire family shut itself up, shivering, into the main house, isolated by snow and silence. The tile stoves crackled. Time passed with delectable slowness. Numb with contentment, little Leo told himself that no house in the whole world was more beautiful than the one in which he had been born. Yet the amenities here were primitive; apart from a few mahogany stands and one or two winged armchairs, all the furniture had been hewn and put together by the muzhiks; the only note of luxury was the gilt of the frames around the mirrors and paintings. Even the children's shoes were made by the village cobbler.

Before going to bed they said good-night to the grown-ups and kissed their hands. If they had been good, they were allowed a few extra minutes in the drawing-room. Grandmother, with a ruched bonnet on her head, laid out her eternal 'traveller's solitaire' on a little table. Beside her on the divan sat the wife of a Tula gunsmith whom she had adopted for a friend and who wore cartridge belts over her jacket. The gunsmith's wife spun wool and, now and then, she would knock her spindle against the wall, in which she had finally gouged a hole. One aunt read aloud, the other knitted or did needlepoint; Papa, his pipe between his teeth, stared absently at the cards and, curled up on a chair, Milka, his whippet, blinked and yawned.

When the grownups gave the children the order to retire, the fun was not yet over for at least one of them: it was the custom in the family for them to take turns spending the night with their grandmother, Pelagya Nikolayevna. The instant he entered her room, Leo fell into a state of ecstasy. He watched her – corpulent and white, in her nightdress and white cap – as she washed her hands. To amuse him she made soap bubbles between her wrinkled yellow fingers. An old man sat in the window bay: Leo Stepanovich, whom Prince Volkonsky had bought long ago for his gifts as a storyteller. He was blind, which was why he was also allowed to be present during Her Highness's toilette. A bowl containing some scraps from the master's meal was brought to him there. When Pelagya Nikolayevna had completed her ablutions she climbed up into her bed, Leo jumped into his, and a maid put out the candles, leaving only a vigil light burning in the corner in front of the icons. In this eerie light the matriarch, leaning back against her pillows, her head upright under her white nightcap, looked down on the world as from a throne of snow. Her shadow wavered on the wall. The blind man began his tale in a drawling voice: 'Once there was a powerful king who had an only son ...'

Leo, fascinated by this hieratic grandmother, did not listen: was she asleep, or did she hear everything that was said? He could not tell. Sometimes the bard, draped in his cloak, deferentially asked, 'Do you command me to proceed?' The reply snapped down, dictatorial, from the summit of the bed: 'Yes; go on.' And he resumed his tale, mixing Russian folklore with tales from Scheherazade. Lulled by the monotonous murmur, Leo's eyes closed, and he carried away into his dreams a mask of an ancient queen under a beribboned lace cap.

In the morning Grandmother made more soap bubbles between her fingers without losing a whit of her majesty. Sometimes she took the children to gather hazelnuts. She would climb into the famous yellow cabriolet and two servants – Petrushka and Matyusha – would harness themselves to the shafts and pull her along the paths. In the woods they reverently bent down the branches for their mistress, who chose the ripest nuts and stuffed them in a bag. Her grandsons raced around her, scavenging and squabbling. 'I remember Grandmother,' Tolstoy later wrote, 'the hazel grove, the pungent smell of its leaves, the servants, the yellow cabriolet, the sun, and they all melt together into a single impression of radiance.'[5] In reality, Pelagya Nikolayevna was a narrow-minded woman, capricious and despotic, hard on those who served her but indulgent to the point of spinelessness with her son and grandchildren.

Alexandra Ilinichna, called Aunt Aline – the sister of Nicholas Ilich Tolstoy – was a very different proposition. She had married Count Osten-Saken when she was very young, and shortly after their wedding he had gone berserk and tried to kill her. The first time he wounded her with a pistol shot; and the second time, while she was recovering, he came into her room and tried to cut out her tongue with a razor. While the maniac was being shut up in an asylum, his wife, who was pregnant, gave birth to a stillborn child. Her relatives were afraid she would not be able to bear the awful news, and gave out that the baby was alive; they brought her a girl child, Pashenka, to whom a servant, the wife of the Tolstoy cook, had just given birth. The real

mother did not dream of protesting against a decision from
such high quarters, and so Pashenka was raised in the
master's house, not learning the secret of her birth until
long afterwards. The hapless Aline must have been crushed
when she learned of the subterfuge; but she tried not to
blame anyone and to remain as fond of Pashenka as before, and sought consolation in prayer. Having lost her
husband and her home, she lived in her brother's house,
voluntarily did without comfort and service, scrupulously
observed all fasts, gave her money to the poor, read nothing
but the lives of the saints, and spent her time talking to the
pilgrims, the simpletons, monks, nuns and half-mad holy
men who stopped at the house to rest between stations on a
pilgrimage. It was said that she had been very pretty and
coquettish in her youth, that her blue eyes had turned
many young men's heads at the balls, that she had played
the harp and could recite French verse. How was one to
believe it, looking at this mummy draped in dark cloth,
who dedicated body and soul to God? Little Leo smelled a
very particular acid odour in the wake of his Aunt Aline
which was due, he thought, to the 'lack of attention the old
lady paid to her toilette'.

The odour given off by Prascovya Isayevna, the housekeeper, was one of sweetish resin: one of her duties, as
official responsible for administering enemas to the children,
was to collect their chamberpots in her room and burn
lozenges from the Far East in them. She said the lozenges,
which she called 'Ochakov essence', had been brought back
by Leo's grandfather when he went to fight the Turks, 'on
horse, on foot and every other way'. She had known this
grandfather very well; long ago, he had refused to let her
marry Tikhon, the flutist-serf; she had held Maman in her
arms; she was a hundred, a thousand, years old; nothing
could leave the cupboards, chests, cellar or storerooms without her personal authorization. ... When Nicholas Ilich
Tolstoy became engaged to Princess Marya, the princess
wanted to free Prascovya Isayevna in return for her services.

When she saw the paper containing her release, Prascovya Isayevna bristled and cried out, with tears in her eyes, 'I guess you must not like me, mistress, since you're sending me away!' And so she stayed on in the house, a servant.

Among the other servants, there was Tatyana Philippovna, the children's maid, tiny and dark-skinned; the old nursemaid Anushka, who had only one tooth in the middle of her mouth; Nicholas Philippich, the coachman, surrounded by the rich aroma of horse dung; Akim, the gardener's assistant, an inoffensive simpleton who addressed God as 'my doctor, my druggist' – in all, some thirty persons, most of whom had no specific duties and loitered about in the pantry and halls, warming themselves by the stoves, gossiping around the samovars and snoring in unused rooms. In addition to this permanent staff, there were the guests who came for a few days and forgot to go away again, poor relations and their servants, orphans and wards taken in some soft-hearted evening, Russian, French and German tutors, whose turnover was more rapid – a large floating population basking in the master's bounty, feeding at his table and singing his praises.

The number of inmates doubled at the approach of the holidays. For Christmas and the New Year, neighbours, servants and peasants dressed up in costumes and flocked into the big house, led by old Gregory scraping at his fiddle. The disguises were always the same: a bear and his trainer, bandits and Turks, muzhiks dressed as women or women dressed as muzhiks. They went from room to room, bowed low before the masters, and received small presents. The two aunts dressed the children, who were quarrelling by the costume trunk over who was to wear the gem-studded belt and who the gold-embroidered muslin jacket. Staring into the mirror, with a turban on his head and a black moustache drawn on his face with burnt cork, little Leo, paralysed with admiration, imagined that he was seeing one of those heroes whose exploits the blind storyteller related to put Grandmother to sleep. But, to his disgust, when his make-up was washed off again there was the same old baby face, with its shapeless nose and thick lips and little grey eyes. A big, fat boy, a 'patapouf', like Papa said.

When the holidays were over, a large contingent of guests lingered on in the house. Even in such a capacious residence – thirty-two rooms, counting the outbuildings* – privacy was impossible. Everyone was entangled in the joys and tribulations of everyone else. Even had one wanted to think only of one's own affairs, other faces and other troubles assailed you at every turn in the corridor, drawing-room, stable, village.

One day Prascovya Isayevna, the housekeeper, scolded Leo and rubbed his nose on a napkin he had inadvertently soiled. Choking with anger, he ran to hide on the balcony. 'By what right does that servant-woman dare to speak familiarly to me, me, her master, and strike me in the face with a wet napkin as though I were some little muzhik?'[6] he thought. But he found nothing to retort when a stableboy reprimanded him for whipping the old horse Raven to make him go. 'Ah, my little master, there's no pity in you!' Scarlet with shame, Leo slid off the horse's back and, 'kissing the animal on the neck, begged his pardon for mistreating him'.[7] Sometimes a conversation overheard among the grownups would also leave him perplexed. Temyashev, a neighbour visiting Yasnaya Polyana, told in Leo's presence how he had sent his cook to the army for twenty-five years because the fellow had taken it into his head to eat meat during Lent. Some time later, this same Temyashev was announced in the drawing-room one winter evening when the family was having its tea by the light of two candles. He strode into the room and fell to his knees; the long pipe in his hand struck the floor and sparks flew up; in the sudden illumination Leo saw his anxious face. Still prostrated, Temyashev explained to Nicholas Ilich Tolstoy that he had brought his illegitimate daughter Dunyechka to be raised by him. This little scene was part of a prearranged agreement

* And not forty-two, as Tolstoy mistakenly says in his *Reminiscences*.

between the two men: Temyashev was a confirmed bachelor, who had more money than he knew what to do with, and two illegitimate children; he wanted to bequeath part of his fortune to them, but under the law his sisters would inherit it all. To get round the difficulty, he had conceived the plan of signing a fictitious sale contract for one of his estates in the name of Nicholas Ilich Tolstoy; after his death Tolstoy would legitimize the transaction by paying back the three hundred thousand roubles he received to the orphans. The papers were signed then and there and, as a pledge of mutual trust, Dunyechka, blank-eyed and snivelling, remained behind in the house with her nursemaid Eupraxya, a thick, bony, wrinkled old woman 'whose Adam's-apple hung down and swung like a turkey gobbler's'. Inside these folds of flesh there was a hard ball, which she condescended to let the children touch.

'Childhood candour, carefree heart, need to love, and faith: shall I ever find you again?' wrote Leo Tolstoy. 'What time could be better than that when the two highest virtues, innocent joy and a limitless need to love, are the only mainsprings of life?' When he was little he believed a current of love was passing perpetually between his family and the rest of the world, even though the grownups were occasionally a disappointment to him. Curled up under the blankets in the glow of the vigil light burning below the icon, he thought, 'I love Nanny; Nanny loves me and she loves Mitya (Dmitry); I love Mitya; Mitya loves me and he loves Nanny; and Nanny loves Aunt Toinette and me and Papa; and everybody loves and everybody is happy.'[8] But if everybody was happy, how was one to explain the fact that Christ died crucified, as Aunt Toinette said?

'Auntie, why did they torture him?'

'They were wicked people.'

'But he was good, so good! ... Why did they beat him? Did it hurt him, Auntie, did it hurt him?'[9]

Nor was Christ the only one to be pitied. Hadn't he heard that gentle Fyodor Ivanovich Rössel was going to have his dog killed just because its paw had been crushed? Leo could not bear the thought of this unjust execution; his tears welled up again. His brothers began to call him 'Lyova Ryova', 'Leo Cry-Baby'. His mother, who had been such a stickler for strength of character, would certainly have been horrified by this son who had so little control over his emotions. The fact was that he felt everything more intensely than the others. A melody plunged him into morbid melancholy, the stable smells enthralled him, he thrilled to feel a dog's cold muzzle under his fingers, he wanted to drink the wind that lashed his face in the fields and eat the earth whose colour and smell in the springtime made him dizzy with joy. In *Childhood* [10] he wrote, 'The sounds of voices and hoofs and carts, the gay piercing call of quail and buzzing of insects circling round, and the smell of wormwood tufts and the straw and horses' sweat, and the thousand different shadows and colours which the burning sun set off on the pale yellow fields, the blue line of the forest and the pink-tinged white clouds, and the white gossamer floating in the air or lying on the stubble – I saw it all, I heard it, I felt it.' And thus he moved with equal zest, eyes wide open, nostrils flaring and ears cocked, from ants to plants, plants to horses and horses to men. This free and gay life would assuredly never end! However, the grownups were already saying that it was impossible to give the children a decent education at Yasnaya Polyana. The oldest boy, Nicholas, was going on fourteen, and Leo, the youngest, was eight. The lessons of good old Fyodor Ivanovich Rössel were no longer enough, they said, to fill these young minds thirsting for knowledge. They needed real professors, who would force them to study seriously. To Leo's sorrow and anxiety, his father told him in the last days of 1836 that all of them would soon be moving to Moscow.

[3]

The World Outside

ON 10 January 1837 the family and oldest servants gathered
in the drawing-room for the leave-taking prayer. Everybody
sat in a circle for a minute without speaking, then they rose
and crossed themselves facing the icon, and those who were
leaving went out on to the steps, one by one. As they passed,
weeping serfs caught at the children's hands and kissed
them on the shoulder, and Leo inhaled, with a mixture of
sadness and repulsion, the 'odour of grease' given off by the
bent heads. He had a lump in his throat. Leave the house!
To go where? Find what? Luckily, all the people he loved
were coming too. Papa, with an authority that must have
reminded him of his days of military glory, assigned them
to their places in the coaches lined up before the peristyle.
Grandmother, Aunt Toinette, Aunt Aline and her adopted
child Pashenka, the five Tolstoy children, the count's ward
Dunyechka, the tutors and, lastly, thirty servants, crowded
into the covered sledges and tarantasses. Dogs whined and
barked in the snow around the motionless teams. A groom
led the relay horses out of the stables by their bridles. A few
servants, red-nosed from the cold, lashed the baggage into
place on the coaches with heavy ropes. An order rang out,
and the convoy slowly moved off, gliding between a hedge
of muzhiks in sheepskin coats and women in striped kerchiefs, and, passing between the two towers that marked the
entrance to the estate, turned on to the road used by the rest
of the world. When he could no longer see his birthplace,
Leo nearly burst into sobs. A little later he consoled himself with the thought that he was wearing 'a new suit, with
trousers that had straps under the heel'.

One hundred and thirty miles – a surface of packed,
crusted snow going across barren plains and through frail

birch groves. At every relay they drank scalding tea at the inn, hung thick with the smell of smoke, leather and cabbage. Grandmother's coach was in the lead, hoisted up on its high wheels, as comfortable as a house. There was food inside to last for ten days, a medicine kit, dressing-case, and a night commode, so that the passengers might relieve themselves without getting out of the coach. Frozen by the wind, footmen clung to jutting platforms on either side of the box. The carriage was so monumentally big that it could not get through the archway of the post-house at Serpukhov, but apart from that, the trip went off without incident. They slept in the upstairs rooms of the inns, which were cold and full of bedbugs. The next morning – for the last lap of the journey – Papa invited each of his sons in turn to sit with him in his sledge. It was at his father's side that Leo entered Moscow at last, after a four-day voyage.

Golden cupolas blazed in the sun. The low hum of a hive rose up from the city. Bells rang out from time to time. The caravan entered the suburbs, where the snow was no longer so white. Suddenly, the twisting, narrow streets, little wooden houses, broken palisades and thronged open-air markets gave way to broad avenues, stone mansions and haughty churches with pink, blue, green or buttercup-yellow façades. The village became a city. Papa called out the names of the monuments as proudly as though he owned them. A many-coloured crowd hurried along the sidewalks: merchants in cloaks, peasants in bark shoes, uniformed officers, gentlemen dressed in 'European style', shopgirls in kerchiefs and ladies in hats. ... No one paid any attention to the travellers. This fact plunged Leo into bewilderment. At Yasnaya Polyana the Tolstoys were the centre of the earth. Why, in Moscow, did no one seem to notice them at all? Why did nobody take off his hat when they went by? 'For the first time,' he wrote in *Boyhood*, 'it became clear to me that we (our family, that is) were not the only people on earth, that all the world's interests did not converge upon us and that there was another life, that of people who had nothing in common with us, cared nothing about us and did not even know we existed.' Instead of turning away from these strangers, he became fascinated by their mystery. 'How do they live, what do they live on?' he wondered. 'How do they bring up their children? How do they punish them?'

The caravan entered the Prechistenskaya district, silent and stately, close to the centre of town, went down Plyuchi-ka Street, parallel to the river, turned into a courtyard and stopped, in front of a handsome house two and a half storeys high, with a long empire façade pierced by eleven windows.

Having spent all his life in the country, Leo could not get used to having neighbours ten feet away. One couldn't feel at home any more, in this overcrowded city that pressed in on one from all sides. The house was cold and impersonal, inhospitable. Papa often dined out and travelled a great deal. Leo's older brothers were preparing for their university entrance examinations. Leo went for walks with Fyodor Ivanovich Rössel, absentmindedly learned his lessons, and dreamed of possessing one day an imagination equal to that of the blind storyteller whom Grandmother unfortunately had had to leave behind when they came to Moscow. Very soon he convinced himself that he too had wonderful stories to tell. He had only to pick up a pen. After stitching together a notebook, he covered it with blue paper and wrote the title in fat letters on the first page: 'Grandfather's Tales'. At the bottom of the page, the publisher's name: 'The Children's Library.' Then, in a laborious hand, he began:

In the town of P . . . there lived an old man ninety years of age who had served under five emperors, who had seen more than one hundred battles, who held the rank of colonel, who had ten decorations paid for in blood for he had ten wounds and walked on crutches having only one leg, and had three scars on his forehead while one of his fingers, the middle one, had fallen at Braila. He had five children: two little lasses and three young fellows, he called them, although the eldest already had four children and four grandchildren . . .

The story went on in this vein for eighteen pages and stopped abruptly when its author wearied of his numerous heroes.

Then, too, the family atmosphere in mid-1837 may not have been conducive to creativity. For some time now, Nicholas Ilich Tolstoy had been worried about his health. He drank a good deal, coughed, spat blood. Shortly after signing the fictitious sale contract for his neighbour Temyashev's estate at Pirogovo, he learned of the latter's death. As he expected they would, the dead man's sisters immediately attacked the contract that reduced their share of the inheritance in favour of the two orphan girls. Exasperated by their pettifogging manoeuvres, Nicholas Ilich Tolstoy assembled his papers, took two servants, and set out for Tula to contend with his adversaries. He covered the distance – one hundred and five miles – in twenty-four hours, which was a feat at the time. At nine in the evening of the following day, 21 June, he fell down dead in the middle of the street, of an attack of apoplexy.*

The news filled little Leo with grief and fright. At church, however, during the first requiem mass, a sense of importance began to mingle with his sorrow; he thought that he cut an interesting figure in his mourning clothes, that everybody felt sorry for him because he was an orphan, and that he had a part to play in the world. Besides, since he had not been present when his father died, he still half-expected to see him again. He constantly thought he recognized him on the street among the passers-by. Every time he saw a stocky man whose face was a little flushed, his heart thudded with love.† 'I loved my father very much,' Leo Tolstoy

---

* As neither money nor papers were found on him, his servants were suspected of killing him; after an inquest, however, the final verdict was death through natural causes.

† Compare with the feelings of little Sergey in *Anna Karenina*, when he refuses to believe his mother's death.

wrote in his *Reminiscences*, 'but I did not learn how strong that love was until he died.'

Aunt Toinette's despair is shown by a note in her hand:

June 21 1837. A terrible day for me. . . . I have lost what was most dear to me in all the world, the only being who loved me, who always treated me with the most affectionate and sincere consideration and who has taken all my happiness away with him. The only thing that binds me to life is that now I shall live for his children.[1]

Nicholas Ilich's mother bore her bereavement with less fortitude. She wept from morning to evening and, when night came, ordered the door of her son's room opened, smiled at his ghost and held conversations with him: 'Come, little one, come closer, my sweet! I am so glad you have come! They told me you were no more! How absurd! As if you could die before me!'[2] Or she would suddenly cry out against God for dealing so harshly with her, when she had done nothing wrong. The frightened children listened from afar to her outbursts and her sobbing and hysterical laughter. They were forbidden to go near her when she was having one of her fits.

Pelagya Nikolayevna was a long time recovering her self-possession. The guardianship of the children was entrusted to Nicholas's older sister, the pious Aunt Aline. She solemnly agreed to undertake this task, but her first allegiance was to the Lord: she had no practical sense, and allowed the family affairs to go to rack and ruin because she could not bring herself to believe in human wickedness. In this unorganized household, where three women in black were vainly trying to keep life going, the children smelled medicine wherever they went, and longed for their happy years at Yasnaya Polyana. To keep up the pretence for them, or to deceive herself, the matriarch insisted upon continuing the old formal dinner tradition. As before, the children waited in silence for the moment to go in to table. A door suddenly opened, the swish of a gown was heard, and Grandmother appeared, regal and stern, her skull hidden by a lace cap with lavender ribbons. The moment she let herself sink into her armchair, the rest of the family clattered into theirs. The major-domo filled the soup plates and handed them out, making allowance for the rank and age of each. Leo's mouth watered and he squinted in impatience.

Later, to divert the children, Pelagya Nikolayevna allowed them to go to the theatre even though they were still in mourning. Dazzled by the huge red-plush and gilt nave, Leo was unable to decide where the entertainment was. Instead of watching the stage he looked at the boxes across from him; the audience interested him more than the actors. Instinctively, he turned towards truth, towards life. So many attentive, sober, mysterious faces! These strangers sitting there in rows fascinated him even more because he had hardly ever been out in society before. On Christmas Day, at the home of the vastly rich Shipov, he felt that he and his brothers had been invited out of charity, because they were orphans. And as though to prove the fact, the presents they received were a shoddy lot; the most handsome toys on the tree went to the nephews of Prince Gorchakov, former minister of war.

This humiliation paled, however, beside another that Leo had been suffering for the last few months, at the hands of a newcomer in the house: M. Prosper de St Thomas. The pedagogical competence of old Fyodor Ivanovich Rössel having proved increasingly inadequate, Grandmother decided to dismiss him and engage a Frenchman in his stead. Stunned by his disgrace, the miserable outcast began by demanding, in addition to his wages, repayment for the little gifts he had presented to various members of the family; then, dissolving in tears, he begged to be kept on without payment. Grandmother stood fast, though, and he was forced to relinquish his post to Prosper de St Thomas. While his former pupils made a poor show of dissembling their sorrow, he pointed out each of them in turn to his successor, saying, 'Sergey is a good boy, he will do well but he must be watched. ... Leo is too tender-hearted, you will get nothing out of him by threats, but everything by kindness. Please, I ask you, love them, treat them well. ...' Prosper de St Thomas commented drily: 'Be assured, *mein Herr*, that I shall find the way to bring them to heel.'[3]

Prosper de St Thomas was a short little man of twenty-five, blond, muscular and active, good-looking and with a better-than-average education, but he was full of his own importance and favoured strong-arm techniques with his pupils. Perhaps, like many of his fellow countrymen who had come to seek their fortunes in Russia, he dreamed of capturing the heart of some wealthy heiress and marrying her. In the meantime, he spent his pocket money on patent-leather boots and silk waistcoats and wore violet-scented powder; his speech was full of grace-notes and frills and he 'played his role of pedagogue to the hilt'. He was not the only tutor in the household, however. In all, the Tolstoys employed eleven teachers, not counting the dancing-master. According to Aunt Toinette's account book, these gentlemen's honoraria for 1837–8 totalled 8,304 roubles,* a very considerable sum at the time. But the executive director of studies was Prosper de St Thomas.

Beneath his stiff, sarcastic exterior, the man's judgement was not unsound. Speaking of his pupils, he said: 'Nicholas is both willing and able; Sergey is able but not willing; Dmitry is willing but not able; and Leo is neither.' And, it was true, Leo was a poor student, he did not understand problems in arithmetic and made no attempt to memorize the names and dates his masters stuffed into his head. And yet, behind his laziness, it was easy to detect a sensitivity

---

* About that time the rouble was listed at $0.52. This relation is based on the price of roubles, in terms of sterling, in St Petersburg and the price of dollars, also in terms of sterling, in New York. The value of the dollar in 1860 was about five times greater than in 1967 (using 1949 as the base year). Very approximately, then, 8,304 roubles would equal $23,500 in today's dollars. This method of calculation is used throughout.

and imagination that were altogether out of the ordinary. Prosper de St Thomas himself had to agree. 'That boy has a head,' he said one day. 'He's a young Molière.' But it required more than flattery to win the boy over. From the start he had hated this foreign schoolmaster for his self-centredness, pretentiousness and conceit. When St Thomas wanted to punish one of his pupils, he would puff up his chest, fling out one arm and cry, 'On your knees, you good-for-nothing!' 'I stood there, livid with anger,' Tolstoy wrote in *Boyhood*, 'and told myself I would die on the spot sooner than kneel in front of him; but he leaned on my shoulders with all his strength, bent my back and forced me to my knees.' The harder St Thomas worked to humiliate the boy, the more he rebelled against his teacher's heavy-handed authority. As an act of defiance, one morning he stuck out his tongue at St Thomas, who promptly grabbed him by the hand, locked him into a dark closet and threatened to use a whip on him. He did not really intend to beat the boy, knowing how strongly his family opposed corporal punishment. But Leo was already imagining himself dishonoured, debased, presenting his naked backside to his heartless, violet-scented schoolmaster. Flogged, like a muzhik. Anything but that! Seated on a chest in the darkness, his eyes brimming with tears and his throat contracted with rage, he let himself be carried away by a wild dream. He imagined himself poor, orphaned, leaving his birthplace, enlisting in the hussars, going off to war, massacring his enemies, and collapsing, covered with wounds and the single cry of 'Victory!' on his lips. Later, he recovered, was promoted to the rank of general, and was walking down the Tver Boulevard with his arm in a sling one day when he met the emperor, who congratulated him on his bravery. Leaning casually upon his sabre, he requested, as a reward for his heroic deeds, the favour of annihilating his enemy, 'the alien St Thomas'. Of course, the emperor consented, and then it was Leo's turn, towering above his ex-tutor, to bellow, 'On your knees, you good-for-nothing!' 'But suddenly,' he wrote, 'it occurs to me that the real St Jérôme [St Thomas] will come through that door any minute with the rod, and I see that I am not a general who has saved his fatherland but the most wretched, and the most pitiable of creatures.'[4] And, the moment after he was brought back to reality, he sailed off on the wings of another fancy: he was dead, lamented by all his loved ones, and beside his corpse stood St Thomas, overcome with remorse, begging forgiveness of his family. He was told: 'You are the one responsible for his loss; you terrified him; he could not bear the humiliation you inflicted upon him. Begone, dog!'[5]

It was while ruminating thus bitterly in the dark that Leo experienced his first religious doubts. If God were just, why was St Thomas not punished for his wickedness on the spot? Why go on living in a world in which might was stronger than right? It must be so pleasant to die and fly away to dwell among the pure souls! Lost in his tears, he repeated over and over in a half-whisper, 'We are flying away, higher and higher!' When he was released from his confinement twenty-four hours later, the desire to leave the earth still tormented him. He imagined that all he had to do was crouch down and hug his arms around his knees. One day he could stand it no longer and jumped out of his third-floor bedroom window. The cook found him lying senseless on the ground. By some miracle, none of his bones was broken, and all he got for his fall was a mild concussion. After eighteen hours of deep sleep, he awoke as though nothing had happened. Later, he confessed that he had jumped out the window less in an attempt to fly than to 'impress the others'. 'I remember,' he wrote, 'that I was continually pre-occupied with myself: I was always conscious, rightly or wrongly, of what people thought of me, and worried about the feelings I inspired in those around me, and this spoiled all my pleasure.' Often his self-consciousness helped him to overcome his fears. When he went to the riding school with his brothers, he demanded that the riding-master give him

a lesson, too. Once on the horse's back he took fright, but
he clenched his teeth and hung on. With every jolt he slid
inexorably earthward, but he did not utter a sound. Finally,
he fell. Would they laugh at him? Choking down his tears,
he asked to be put back in the saddle, set off at a trot, and
fell no more.

His need to attract attention by performing some spectacular deed was intensified by his certainty that nobody
could love him for his looks. He had hoped his features
would improve with time, but at nine, at ten, he still had
his cauliflower nose and little steely eyes set deep in their
sockets.* Weary of asking God, in his nightly prayers, to
make him as handsome as his brother Sergey, he decided
he would be unusual, if nothing else. Seizing a pair of
scissors he cut off his eyebrows, which he judged too thick.
But they grew back coarser than ever. No doubt about it;
the Almighty did not intend him to have any face but his
own, crude, hairy and red.

This sense of his unsightliness became more acute in the
presence of Sonya Koloshin, a distant cousin, who was also
nine years old, had silky blond hair and periwinkle eyes.
Dazzled by the vivacious little girl, he dreamed of spending
his life with her 'in a black closet'. The first time they spoke
to each other in the familiar form he felt 'a kind of intoxication'. But he was shy and did not dare tell her that he
admired and loved her. 'I could not hope she would re-
ciprocate,' he wrote in *Childhood*, 'and I did not even dream
of it: my soul did not require so much, to be ecstatically
happy. I did not see that in exchange for the love that filled
me with delight one might demand still greater happiness,
or desire anything more than that this feeling might go on
forever.' One night in bed, too agitated to sleep, he turned
to his brother Sergey and told him in a low voice, in the
dark, that he was 'terribly much in love with Sonya'; but his

---

* On 10 May 1852, when he was twenty-four, he wrote in his diary,
'Aquiline noses drive me to distraction. They seem to me to possess
all the strength of character and good fortune in the world.'

brother sneered at this platonic passion and said that in Leo's place he would 'cover the girl's fingers with kisses, and then her eyes, her lips, feet ...' Horrified, Leo hid his face in the pillow to avoid hearing any more of such 'foolishness'.[6]

Later, he became equally enamoured of little Lyubov Islavin, and once, in a fit of jealousy, he pushed her so hard that she fell off the balcony. She was injured by the fall and limped for some time afterwards.*

Leo's passion for girls did not prevent him from being attracted to certain boys of his age as well. He was subjugated by physical beauty, regardless of sex. In *The Cossacks* he wrote that there was 'something akin to love'[7] between Olenin and Lukashka; in *War and Peace* he describes the young officer Ilin, who 'tried to imitate Rostov and adored him like a woman in love';[8] and he wrote in his diary, on 29 November 1851, 'I have often been in love with a man. My first love was for the two Musin-Pushkin brothers.' He was so obsessed by these two boys, Sasha and Alyosha Musin-Pushkin, that he sometimes wept when he thought of them and prayed God to show them to him in his dreams if he had not seen them during the day.

Besides the passionate attraction I felt for him [he wrote of one of them in *Childhood*] his presence aroused in me an equal degree of terror of causing him any unhappiness, offending him, or displeasing him. Perhaps this was because he always wore such a haughty expression, or because, despising my own looks, I attached too much importance to beauty in others, or more probably – and this is an infallible sign of love – because I feared him as much as I loved him. The first time he spoke to me I was so overwhelmed for this unhoped-for good fortune that I turned pale, I blushed, I could say nothing in reply. ... No word was

---

* Lyubov Islavin later married Dr Behrs and had a daughter; and it was to this girl, Sonya, that Leo Tolstoy proposed in 1862. Thus he became the son-in-law of the woman he had loved when he was a child and had pushed off the balcony to punish her for talking to other boys.

ever spoken between us in allusion to my love, but he was conscious of his power over me and, involuntarily but tyrannically, took advantage of it in our childish relations.[9]

Most of the time the Tolstoys and the Musin-Pushkin brothers played with lead soldiers, inventing military episodes: marches, battles, bivouacs and floggings. Full-scale novels were composed there on the table and rug, in a clutter of colourful figurines and cardboard boxes.

A more singular amusement consisted in burning pieces of paper in chamberpots.

On 25 May 1838, while the children were engaged in this pursuit, they heard rapid footsteps coming down the hall. In the midst of their laughter the door flew open and Prosper de St Thomas appeared, pale, his lower jaw trembling. 'Your grandmother is dead,' he said sharply. The children were struck dumb. Leo was filled with a holy terror. For the second time in eleven months a loved one had gone out of his life. Of course, he had known Grandmother was ill for weeks; when he went to visit her, lying in her bed, he had seen that she was very pale and her hands were swollen with hydropsy; but he had supposed she could go on living like that for ages.

This time, unlike the days after his father's death, he was present throughout all the preparations for the burial. Undertakers in black coats congregated in the house early in the morning. A glass-topped coffin arrived. The boy stared at his ancestor inside the big box on the table: stretched out full length, with waxen face and hooked nose, a white bonnet on her head, her expression was stern, remote and dissatisfied. She was still listening to the blind storyteller's legends. But when Leo kissed her forehead he felt the icy skin under his lips and fled from the room with a cry. The next day, his grief undiminished, he nevertheless felt a strange thrill of joy as he put on a black mourning suit edged with white crepe and heard the visitors talking about him and his brothers in compassionate tones: 'The father is hardly cold in his grave and the grandmother goes

after him! Now they really are orphans.'[10] Leo was
obsessed by the thought of death. In the air he sniffed
smells of incense and wilted flowers that made his throat
contract. 'The inert body reminds me sharply and unpleasantly that I too shall have to die one day – a feeling
that is usually mistaken for grief,' he wrote in *Boyhood*. 'I
do not miss Grandmother, and I doubt that anyone really
does.'[11]

As long as the old lady was alive, neither Aunt Toinette
nor Aunt Aline had dared to curtail the style of living to
which she had so long been accustomed. But the moment
the funeral was over, they resolved in the interests of economy to divide the family. Of the five Tolstoy children,
only the two eldest, Nicholas and Sergey (aged fifteen and
twelve), would remain in Moscow with Aunt Aline and St
Thomas; the younger children, Dmitry, Leo and Marya
(eleven, ten and eight) would return to Yasnaya Polyana
with Aunt Toinette. A small apartment was rented for the
urbanites, and the others set out on 6 July 1838. Four
coaches, harnessed troika style, bore them southward.

Leo's satisfaction at returning to the big house of his infancy, and the meadows, trees, river and ponds, was
increased by the fact that one hundred and thirty miles
now separated him from the abhorred St Thomas. For his
lessons there was soft-hearted, ignorant Fyodor Ivanovich
Rössel, restored to favour, and then a seminarian, and later
a few unprepossessing and inoffensive tutors. But his most
profitable lessons were those he learned from the peasants.
He listened to their talk with friendly curiosity, and could
not understand their resignation in the face of poverty. One
of them – young Mitka Kopilov, who had been Count Tolstoy's coachman – was obliged to return to his aged father
and resume the hard life of a muzhik when the Tolstoy
family cut down its expenses. In one month the elegant house
servant in silken blouse and velvet coat was transformed
into a ragged bark-shod labourer. He ploughed and scythed
and sowed with laughing face and bright eyes, and never

uttered a complaint. Nor did Kuzma, the groom, complain when Andrey Ilin, the strapping steward, led him away to the barn. As the two men passed him, Leo asked them what they were going to do. Kuzma hung his head and Andrey Ilin muttered, 'I'm going to punish him.' Leo was stupified by this announcement. 'I wondered then,' he wrote in his *Reminiscences*, 'whether I was too stupid to understand the reason for it or whether it was they, the adults, who were stupid. I finally persuaded myself that the grownups knew more about everything than I did, and that this was the way things had to be.' That evening, however, when he told Aunt Toinette about the incident, she burst out, 'Why did you not prevent it?' This added to his bewilderment. He did not think it was possible for him to intervene in a matter of such consequence. Since the beginning of time there had been serfs to obey and masters to command, and a few strokes now and then had never lessened the friendship that flourished between owners and muzhiks. Besides, at Yasnaya Polyana there was never any talk of physical punishment. Hence, this was an exceptional measure. Crimson with shame, as though he himself had been whipped, Leo told himself that he had been lacking in charity. Now it was too late! Poor Kuzma must be off having ointment put on his back to ease the pain. Next time. ... The child comforted himself with long-term promises, but most often the generous impulses that sprang from his heart were throttled by the unconscious egotism of the young lord. The weather had been exceptionally dry that year, the harvest promised to be scanty, famine was threatening, and the animals' food was rationed; but he and his brother Dmitry stole into the peasants' fields to pull up oats and take them back to the stable to feed their own horses. 'My brother and I did this while there were people who had not eaten for two days, whose sole source of sustenance was those same oats. I did not feel guilty about it, it didn't occur to me that it was wrong.'[12]

When autumn came Aunt Toinette and the three orphans

returned to Moscow. They were to attend the ceremony of
the laying of the cornerstone of Holy Saviour Cathedral by
Tsar Nicholas I, and to congratulate the eldest Tolstoy son,
who had just been admitted to the Department of Philosophy at Moscow University.

During the three-day trip Leo renewed his acquaintance
with the Russia of the open roads: jingling bells, creaking
axles and the smell of moth-eaten cloth, long convoys dragging through the dust, pilgrims on foot with their sacks on
their backs, swift troikas bearing some ministerial courier,
slanting figures engraved on the mile-posts. Sometimes they
met another *calèche*, and the boy said to himself, 'In two
seconds, the faces looking at us with friendly curiosity two
lengths away will have flashed past. It seems strange that
these faces have nothing to do with me and that I may
never see them again.'[13] Or, unexpectedly, there in the
middle of the fields stood the red-roofed house of a country
squire. 'Who lives in that house?' Leo wondered. 'Are there
any children, a father and mother, a schoolmaster? Why
shouldn't we go up and meet its owners?' Too late! The
house was far behind and a village had taken its place. 'It
smelled of smoke and tar and cracknel. ... The harness
bells did not ring out as they did in the open country.
Thatched-roofed isbas filed past on either side.'[14]

In Moscow, Leo's thirst for new faces and excitement was
satisfied beyond his wildest dreams. On 10 September
1838 he saw – from a great distance, it is true – Tsar
Nicholas I laying the cornerstone of the cathedral. The
military parade that followed thrilled him to the bone. He
wanted to march in step with the music and die for his
country.

His devotion to the monarchy should by rights have been
accompanied by an equal devotion to the Church, but although he was brought up in the Orthodox religion, his
faith was not unshakable. Out of respect for the grownups
he believed what they told him about God and the saints
but, underneath it all, he was perfectly prepared to believe

the opposite, and so he was not unduly astonished when one of his comrades, Volodya Milyutin, sententiously announced that the pupils in his class at the lycée had reached the conclusion that God did not exist and that everything they had been taught about Him was 'false and made-up'. The Tolstoy brothers discussed the news among themselves and judged it to be interesting, 'perhaps even true'. Of course Nicholas, now a university student, led the debate with all the authority of his seventeen years. He had made new friends, with whom he smoked pipes, exchanged incomprehensible witticisms and laughed noisily while slapping his thighs.

Ignored by these high-powered brains from the University of Moscow, Leo sought in himself an explanation for the mysteries that surrounded him. Even Prosper de St Thomas, who had been wont to call him 'lazy' and a 'good-for-nothing', was astonished by his intellectual precocity. Lazy he still was, for studying galled him; but instead of mathematics, history and geography lessons, he explored his own conscience with a degree of insight that was uncanny in a boy of twelve. Between two games of hide-and-seek, he meditated upon his character, man's destiny, the disintegration of matter and the immortality of the soul. He was bowled over, blinded, by totally contradictory ideas. He had no sooner adopted one set of rules for life than he discovered another, still more attractive. In order to train his will-power and resist pain in the true Stoic manner, he would hold the big Tatishchev dictionary out at arm's length, or, hiding in a storeroom, tear off his shirt and scourge himself with a rope or, after scorching his hands at the stove, plunge them into the snow. The following week, it would be the Epicureans: he decided that death might come upon him unawares at any moment and that, this being the case, the only attitude possible for a man was to make the most of the present with no thought for the morrow. Implementing this conclusion, he neglected his studies, flung away his notebooks and, draped across his bed, de-

voured light novels and gingerbread until he made himself
sick. Sometimes, in a fit of wrath, he would summon God
to prove His existence by performing a miracle then and
there, and the next minute, not having received a satisfactory response, proclaimed himself an atheist. This coldly
rational decision did not prevent him from wondering,
when he looked at a circle chalked on the blackboard,
whether in view of the existence of symmetry, which is a
phenomenon pleasing to the eye, our present life must not
be preceded by another, of which we remember nothing,
and followed by a third, of which we can guess nothing.
Perhaps he had been a horse, before becoming a human.
All things considered, however, the philosophical system
that appealed to him most was scepticism. 'I imagined,' he
wrote in *Boyhood*, 'that there was nothing and nobody in
the universe except me, that objects were not objects but
appearances, visible only when I paid attention to them and
vanishing the instant I stopped thinking about them. ...
There were moments when I became so possessed by this
idée fixe that I would whirl around, hoping to ambush the
void where I was not.'

This perpetual self-analysis refined his intellect, but it
taxed his nerves. Suddenly he would ask himself, 'What am
I thinking about? I am thinking about what I am thinking! – And now what am I thinking about? – I think that
I am thinking about what I am thinking about.' His brain
began to reel and he saw a series of mirrors multiplying his
thought into infinity.

My mind broke down, beyond the limits of reason [he went on].
However, my vanity was enormously flattered by my philosophical discoveries; I often imagined myself as a great man discovering new truths for the benefit of mankind, and I contemplated
other mortals with a proud awareness of my own merit. But the
strange thing was that the moment I came into contact with
those same mortals I lost all my confidence before the lowliest
among them; and the higher I held myself in my own esteem the
less capable I was, in their presence, not only of imposing my

sense of my dignity upon them, but even of teaching myself not to be embarrassed by my simplest remark or most ordinary action.[15]

In the thick of his philosophical interrogations, he would be visited by dreams of earthly success. If he passed a general in the street, he imagined him being struck by Leo's air of intelligence and boldness, taking him under his wing, guiding him in his military career, decorating him for bravery. Or he would see himself a poet, adulated and worshipped like that Pushkin who had been killed in a duel by a Frenchman three years before. When he returned to Yasnaya Polyana with the rest of the family, he wrote a poem in five stanzas, expressing his affection for Aunt Toinette, copied it on to a sheet of fine paper and gave it to her on her name-day, 12 January 1840. These unpolished verses delighted the grownups. After reading them in Moscow, Prosper de St Thomas himself deigned to write a letter of congratulation to their author: 'I read them to Princess Gorchakov; the whole family wanted to read them too, and all were enchanted with them. Do not imagine, however, that their praise was intended for the skill with which they were written, for they contain imperfections due to your ignorance of the canons of versification; they praised you, as I did myself, for the thought, which was admirable, and hope you will not stop there; that would be a great shame.'[16]

With such encouragement, Leo launched into more ambitious literary projects. No event was too mighty for his pen; Napoleonic wars, the battle of Kulikovo, the exploits of Marfa Pozadnitsa leading the people of Novgorod; he wrote his own versions of them all in a ruled notebook. His brain was boiling over with patriotic zeal when he wrote, 'The walls of Moscow witnessed the shame and defeat of the invincible armies of Napoleon.' The fate of Pompeii, on the other hand, he evoked with melancholy: 'How fickle and unstable are all the things of this world: Pompeii, the second city of Italy at the height of its glory and splendour, is today nothing but a heap of ruins and ash. ... Thus, when God wishes to punish, he can change the rich man into a pauper in an hour.'

In those days he read a great deal. His preferences ranged from the Bible (he wept with compassion at the tale of Joseph and his brothers) to the *Thousand and One Nights*, the legends of the Russian people and Pushkin's poems. His brothers, too, were reading and writing. In 1841, they spent the summer together at Yasnaya Polyana. But Aunt Aline was not well. She was haunted by thoughts of death, and finally took refuge in the convent of Optina-Pustyn, where she quietly passed away on 30 August of that year. She was buried in the nuns' cemetery; Leo wrote an epitaph in verse which was engraved upon her tomb:

> How sweet and enviable in our dream
> Thy rest in the celestial haven does seem!

Once again there were the mourning suits and tears and family complications. With Aunt Aline gone, a new guardian had to be appointed. Legally, this honour fell to Aunt Pelagya Yushkov, sister of the deceased. Nicholas, the eldest Tolstoy child, wrote to her on behalf of them all: 'Do not abandon us, dear Aunt, you are all we have left in the world.' Aunt Pelagya arrived in Moscow forthwith, called the little tribe together and decided to 'sacrifice herself', as she put it.

In reality this 'sacrifice' gave her considerable satisfaction: if she had declined, the guardianship would have passed to Aunt Toinette as next of kin, and she hated Aunt Toinette with all her soul, and had hated her for years – Pelagya could never forget that her husband, retired colonel of the hussars Vladimir Ivanovich Yushkov, had married her as a last resort after being turned down by Toinette, with whom he had been in love. He might still be cherishing some impure feelings towards that outwardly unexciting and faded creature. One had to be so careful with men! In any event, Pelagya had been too humiliated at the time of her engagement to pass up any opportunity for revenge. In her ex-rival's presence she feigned effusive and artificial affection, but she had laid her plans. She could have accepted the guardianship and let Toinette continue to have actual custody of the children; instead, she abruptly decided to take them back to Kazan with her and send them to school there. Of course, should she so desire, Aunt Toinette would be welcome to live in her house, as a guest. Pained and dignified, the old spinster refused this humiliating proposal: 'It is a cruel and barbaric thing to separate me from the children whom I have cared for so tenderly for nearly twelve years!' she wrote, in French, to Vladimir Ivanovich Yushkov.

Hers was a strange fate: she had rejected Yushkov because she was in love with Nicholas Tolstoy, and here the children of that same Nicholas Tolstoy were being ravished from her by the woman Yushkov had married to console himself for losing her. She must have spent many an evening ruefully recalling the marriage proposal her dear cousin Nicholas had made so long ago. Had she listened to him then, no one would be able to take the orphans away from her today. As usual, she resigned herself and yielded. It was agreed that she would go to live at Pokrovskoye with her sister Elizabeth Alexandrovna Ergolskaya, widow of another Tolstoy.* The separation was heart-rending. The children wept. Little Masha wanted to run away with Auntie. At last, one misty November morning, the family left Yasnaya Polyana for Kazan, travelling by short stages. The furniture and heavy baggage had been loaded on to barges that were to go down the Oka to the Volga. The numerous household staff piled on to other barges; carpenters, tailors, harness makers, cobblers, cooks, scrubwomen, grooms, men-servants and chambermaids. The young gentlefolk travelled by road, in a closed coach. Now and then they stopped at the edge of a forest, bathed in a stream or gathered mushrooms, and the

* Peter Ivanovich Tolstoy, cousin of Nicholas Ilich Tolstoy.

gay activity and constantly changing scenery helped Leo to bear the thought that Aunt Toinette was far away and he would not see her again until the summer holiday.

At the end of two weeks in the carriage, the churches and minarets of Kazan appeared on the horizon.

[4]

Kazan

THE city was built on a range of hills above a boggy plain that was flooded every spring by the Volga and its tributary the Kazanka, and the only exotic thing about it was its legend. The mind dreamed of past glories and scenes of violence inside the crumbling Kremlin walls and under the pointed tower of Suyumbeka; the Tatar district was a quaint site with its bric-à-brac of ramshackle minarets and dusty booths; there was a certain stateliness in the neo-classical pediments of the official buildings; but a veil of boredom and lassitude floated over all. To enliven the monotony of provincial life, the people of high society entertained each other incessantly. 'At Kazan,' a contemporary wrote,[1] 'it was possible for a bachelor not to keep a table of his own, for there were at least twenty or thirty houses where people gathered for dinner without being invited. ... After the meal and after coffee and chat of this and that, they all went their separate ways home for a little nap. ... In the evening off we went again, to a reception or a ball, that always ended in a Lucullan feast. ...'

This fluttering, superficial life was that of the Yushkov family. They received the children with well-meaning effusions, lodged them and dressed them, introduced them to their acquaintances and took no further notice of them. Aunt Pelagya was very different from Aunt Aline and Aunt Toinette. A social butterfly of limited intellectual capacity, she had a kind heart, the brains of a sparrow, she harboured deep-seated resentments dating from her youth, and her aim was to enjoy herself and be popular. Sofya Andreyevna Tolstoy wrote of her, 'She doted on archbishops, monasteries, and cloth-of-gold embroideries which she made and gave to churches and convents; she also loved good food, and liked to decorate her room tastefully, giving long thought to the position of a divan, for example.' She had a strong sense of tradition, and wanted each of the Tolstoy boys to have his own personal serf, a boy of his own age – she thought this a charming custom. Her husband, Vladimir Ivanovich Yushkov, was a likeable man, unsubstantial, witty and a woman chaser, who shone in the salons, dabbled at the piano, squeezed the servant girls' waists and feared nothing so much as to be left alone with his wife, whose looks distressed him and whose prattling drove him wild. Although he was sincerely fond of his nephews, he had no more time or inclination to guide their steps than his wife had. Little Marya was boarded out and the four brothers continued their studies in their chosen subjects. Nicholas, now seventeen years old, enrolled at the University of Kazan, where Sergey and Dmitry joined him in 1843, entering the Department of Mathematics. Leo, having suddenly decided to become a diplomat, was preparing to enter the Department of Oriental Languages. From the first, the task appeared a formidable one: the requirements for the entrance examination included – in addition to history, geography, statistics, mathematics, Russian literature, logic, Latin, French, German and English – an elementary knowledge of Arabic and Turko-Tatar. While slogging reluctantly away at these unappetizing subjects, he endeavoured to improve his external appearance and cultivate a distinguished bearing. Awed by his elder brother Nicholas, who, by virtue of his age and learning, was almost an adult, he nevertheless felt much closer to Sergey, whose good looks, high spirits and elegance had always impressed him. In order to become more like Sergey, and also to acquire the proper Yushkov tone, he endeavoured to observe the proprieties in all things. Unfortunately, when he looked at himself in a mirror, he found himself still more ugly and common than when he had been a child: 'The most vulgar, coarse and ugly features,' he confessed, 'little grey eyes that looked more stupid than clever. ... My face was that of a common muzhik, and so were my big hands and feet.'[2] But it ought to be possible to counterbalance them with a cultivated mind and distinguished manners. With this as his point of departure, he resolved that his goal in life would be to become, no longer a general, scholar or poet, but a man of distinction – *comme il faut*.* Society thereafter ceased to be divided into rich and poor, good and bad, clever and stupid, civilian and military, healthy and sick: there were only people *comme il faut* and people not *comme il faut*. 'My way of being *comme il faut* [he wrote] consisted first of all in the perfect mastery of the French language and, in particular, the proper accent. A man who pronounced French badly aroused in me a feeling of contempt. ... The second requirement for being *comme il faut* was to have fingernails that were long, well-shaped and clean; the third was to be able to bow, dance and converse; the fourth (very important) was to appear indifferent, to wear a certain air of distinguished and disdainful boredom at all times.'[3]

The code of behaviour which Leo invented proved more difficult to apply than he would have supposed. He was straining to become a fashion plate; yet, whatever he tried, all he achieved was a caricature of Sergey. On the other hand, he deemed himself far more advanced than his other brother Dmitry, a sober, pensive, determined boy who paid scant attention to his appearance, did not go out into society, did not dance and, winter and summer alike, wore a student's coat and a cravat that was too tight for him, obliging him to stick out his neck from time to time to disengage it. Even his friends were peculiar. His brothers had made friends among the aristocracy, but Dmitry went round with Poluboyarinov, a poor student, who was so dirty and threadbare that the servants were embarrassed when he came to the door. And what was one to think of his attach-

---

Comme il faut was the French term Tolstoy used; its chief meaning is a combination of 'proper, respectable, gentlemanly'; for him, of course, it meant something more than 'what was done' or 'the thing', as opposed to 'not quite the thing'. (Tr. note.)

ment to Lyubov Sergeyevna, a girl the family had taken in out of charity? She was timid, mild and vague, and her face was swollen as though by bee-stings. Her eyes were scarcely visible between two folds of fat, and her pale scalp showed through thin black hair in patches. When the flies settled on her face in the summer, she did not even feel them. She never opened the windows or the transom in her room, and the smell was suffocating. Dmitry, literally fascinated by such ugliness, developed a great affection for Lyubov Sergeyevna, regularly went to see her in her lair, read to her and listened to her tales of woe. Aunt Pelagya was afraid he might marry the wretched creature. But he paid no heed to teasing or chiding. Imperturbable and placid, he continued to behave as though the world outside did not exist and the soul were the only thing that counted. Occasionally, he mistreated Vanyusha, the little serf Aunt Pelagya had given him, but he repented the next moment and begged pardon of the boy, who gaped at such kindness. For Leo and Sergey, going to church was a custom to be respected but not taken seriously, but Dmitry went to every service and prayed with a fervour that could scarcely have been less *comme il faut*. On Orthodox holy days, he dragged the whole family to the prison church where the service was very long and very beautiful. In the nave, a glass partition with a door in it separated the faithful free from the faithful unfree. Once, one of the latter wanted to give some money to the sacristan to buy a candle. As none of the good people around would carry out his request, Dmitry pushed his way up to the partition and did what the convict had asked. He was reprimanded because it was forbidden to have any contact with the prisoners. He said nothing, but, feeling he had done no more than his duty, he repeated his gesture on the following days. This obstinacy irritated Leo, who saw it as a lack of *savoir vivre*. He made fun of Dmitry, said he was crazy, called him Noah in public and choked with delight when a trustee of the University of Kazan tried to persuade the young man to dance by explaining, in deadly earnest, that David had done no less before the Ark. And yet, in his heart, he envied his impossible brother for having found his way and refusing to relinquish it in the face of scoffs and taunts. Perhaps, to merit the respect of others, and especially of oneself, it was not enough to be *comme il faut*. As the date for his university entrance examinations drew near, Leo became increasingly convinced of the need for moral improvement.

During Holy Week he was hurrying to finish reviewing his lessons, for the examinations took place immediately after Easter. He was sixteen, and Lenten fasting and rapid growth had overtaxed his strength. His eyes continually strayed from his book to stare out of the window at the blue sky and trees covered with shiny buds and the new grass coming up between the paving stones. A servant in shirtsleeves rolled up, wearing an apron, came to remove the putty and bend back the nails in the double casements. When the window was opened, the fresh-scented air flooded the room and Leo, dizzy with joy, could scarcely keep from crying out in wonder. 'Everything spoke to me of beauty, happiness, virtue! ... Everything told me that beauty and happiness and virtue were all one!'[4]

Then and there he resolved to change his life. He would go to mass every Sunday, read the Gospels one hour every day, give two and a half roubles a month to the poor – without telling anyone – clean his room himself, oblige no one to wait on him, always go to the University on foot – and if his family gave him a coach of his own he would sell it without a twinge and offer the money to some needy family. As for his studies, he would confound his professors by his application, win two gold medals, become a lecturer, a doctor of philosophy, one of the greatest scholars in Russia. This would not prevent him from keeping in top physical condition, so that he could compete with the famous athlete Rappo in strength and skill. When he had reached the height of his powers, She would enter his life. She: the ideal woman – who was, Tolstoy later wrote, 'a little like

Sonya, a little like Basil's wife, Masha, used to be when she was washing our linen in a tub, and a little like the woman with a white throat and pearl necklace I saw once at the theatre in a box next to us'. And if some upstart should take it into his head to offend this adorable creature, he would pluck him off the ground like a feather, just to frighten him, and then magnanimously let him go. Everybody would admire and love him. At the sound of his name hundreds of strangers would commune in ecstasy. He would be rich, honoured, respected. ... From these dizzy heights he plummeted back to earth with a jolt that restored him to his senses in a flash, showing him all his old shortcomings, and he fell to loathing himself, body and soul, with morbid delight. A few days before his examinations he decided to write down in a notebook the 'Rules of Life' he would follow in the future. He divided them into three categories: duties to oneself, duties to one's neighbour, duties to God. He began to list them, lost count, gave up and went back to the first page to set down the title: 'Rules of Life.' But his pen would not move smoothly across the page, the letters kept running together, the whole thing was illegible. 'Why is everything so beautiful and clear inside,' he asked, 'and so formless on paper and in my life in general?'[5] A servant interrupted him to announce that the priest had come to confess the family before Easter communion. He quickly hid his notebook, took a glance in the mirror (that hideous nose, lumpish, red!), brushed his hair upwards – he fancied this gave him 'a pensive air' – and went down to the sitting-room where an icon and lighted tapers had been placed on a cloth-covered table. The confessor, an old monk with white hair and a severe countenance, did not appear at all shattered by Leo's revelations and concluded with the words, 'the blessing of the Heavenly Father be upon thee, my son, and may He ever preserve thee in faith, meekness, and humility. Amen.' Purified and relieved, Leo no longer doubted that God looked upon him with special favour and would, in any event, help him through his exams.

The truth is that in his state of unpreparedness, aid from such a source would not have been unwelcome; and during the first question periods, he might well have believed that Providence had indeed singled him out: in religious instruction he got four out of five, five in German, Arabic, Turko-Tatar; five-plus in French, four in algebra, arithmetic, English and Russian literature; but he answered very badly in history and geography, statistics, Latin ... ones and twos rained down upon the examiners' cards. Hoping to rescue the candidate, the trustee of the University of Kazan who was a friend of the Tolstoy family asked him an easy question: 'Name the French seaports.' Leo's mind went blank. From the North Sea to the Mediterranean he saw nothing but barren coastline. With a premonitory shudder, he realized that France would be his downfall: one out of five. He flunked.

Swallowing his humiliation, he decided to take the exams over again in September. His holidays were ruined by academic anxiety. No trip to Yasnaya Polyana. Instead of his favourite authors – Pushkin, Dickens, Schiller, Dumas – he had to dig his way back into the dim, grey mist of his textbooks. At last he passed, and could don the student's uniform he had been coveting for months. Dark-blue tunic with brass buttons, three-cornered cocked hat, patent-leather boots and a sword at his side – the first time he went out on the street in this garb, he was conscious that he was no longer little Leo: he was Count Leo Tolstoy. 'I felt,' he wrote, 'against my will, an oozing, radiant, idiotically self-satisfied smile spreading across my face and I noticed that this smile communicated itself even to the people I was talking to.'[6]

His first contacts with the academic world increased his feeling of his own singularity. Dozens of boisterous students shoved into him without noticing him, exchanged rough handshakes, evil-sounding comments and unintelligible jokes. At first it seemed out of the question for him to join any of his fellow students' groups. Some he found poor and vulgar, not at all *comme il faut*; the others, the aristocratic clan, displayed a shocking degree of doltish pretentiousness; and the professors rattled off their lectures without conviction. An outpouring of empty words, a Niagara of platitudes! ... Gradually, however, he grew so used to this fraternal community that he could no longer live without it. He even came to love the atmosphere of the lecture halls, with the speaker's monotonous voice droning on and on, the jostling in the corridors, the glasses of vodka tossed off on the sly in some nearby tavern, the easy-going, interchangeable companions, who distracted him from his work. He could, of course, have made up for lost time at home, after classes were over. But then there were the temptations of society. As grandson of a former governor of the town, nephew of the Yushkovs who had such a wide circle of friends, and the bearer in his own right of a considerable name, Leo Tolstoy was much sought after in the salons, despite his youth. Kazan was one long series of parties, winter and summer. The marshal of nobility, governor of the province, trustee of the University of Kazan, principal of the Rodyonov School for Young Ladies, notables, wealthy merchants, senior civil servants, all took turns arranging balls, suppers, masquerades, *tableaux-vivants*. These gatherings of the 'gilded youth' amused Leo Tolstoy, he would have been grief-stricken to miss a single one, and yet, as soon as he found himself among other people, he became paralysed by a morbid shyness. Deafened by the blare of the music, blinded by the chandeliers and the young ladies' glances, agitated by a thousand subtle scents given off by the waltzing gowns, he lost every semblance of poise, did not dare open his mouth, and wished himself invisible. While his fellow students were flirting with the ladies, he took refuge in a corner, brows beetling, hands hidden behind his back, and mutely admired the inaccessible beauties beyond. On the rare occasions when he invited one of them to dance, he was so distraught that he got his feet mixed up, blushed, apologized and speedily led her back to her place. 'My dear

Leo, you are nothing but a sack of flour!' exclaimed (in French) the principal of the Rodyonov School for Young Ladies, not at all pleased with his deportment. The young ladies whispered among themselves that he was 'a boring partner'.[7]

In spite of his dread of appearing ridiculous, he agreed to act in two amateur theatricals being given in February 1845. 'To which of the actors shall we give the palm?' wrote a local chronicler of mellifluous pen. 'We are hard put to say, for each played his part so excellently that in many places the audience forgot it was a stage play they were observing and not nature itself.'[8] One member of the company was a young man named Dmitry Dyakov (Mitya), to whom Leo was immediately attracted. He was also struck by Dmitry's sister, Alexandra. But she was so pretty that, whenever he looked at her, he was overcome by his own ugliness. Mitya, who had a gentle face, a fine small mouth and wavy blonde hair, was less intimidating. In their long conversations together, the two friends agreed that man's destiny was to progress towards moral perfection and that it was for each person, in his small sphere of influence, to discourage vice by setting an example of virtue. 'Our souls,' Tolstoy later related, 'were so well attuned that any chord struck in one, no matter how lightly, echoed in the other.'[9] Sometimes they descended from the clouds to talk of their future, military service, art, marriage, how to bring up children. They both considered it absurd to look for beauty in a woman; any self-respecting man should marry a person who was 'able, above all else, to help him improve himself'.[10] Metaphysical problems intoxicated them like fumes of opium. 'I used to love,' Tolstoy wrote, 'the moment when ideas, flowing faster and faster, growing more and more abstract, finally became so nebulous that one could no longer find any words to express them and, believing one was saying what one meant, said something quite different. I loved the instant when, after rising higher and higher into the realms of thought, one suddenly sensed the immen-

sity beyond and recognized the impossibility of going any
further.'[11] Tolstoy was unmistakably intimidated by Mitya
Dyakov, who was five years his senior. He wished to hide
nothing from this incomparable, irreplaceable friend. 'I always say exactly what I am most ashamed to admit, but only
to people I am sure of!' he proudly declared one day.[12]

Other friends, the two Zybin brothers, temporarily communicated to him their passion for music. With his customary single-minded zealousness, Tolstoy practised scales on
the piano, tried to loosen up his 'big fingers' by keeping
them constantly in motion, on his knees at the dinner table,
or on his pillow in bed, and in the end, he even wrote a
waltz.* While engaged in these artistic pursuits, he was not
above joining his fellow students in one of their shabby
'carouses' in an atmosphere of smoke, sweat and pomaded
hair. He banged his glass against theirs, laughed, sang and
felt his mounting fatigue and disgust, and was convinced
that the others were having no more fun than he, but that a
rule of honour required them all to pretend they were wildly
gay. He came home with a heavy conscience and a woolly
mouth. In those days he stared at women and talked about
them with a lack of restraint that made a poor cover for
his inexperience. His passion suddenly settled upon a ladies'
maid at the Yushkovs', big Matryona, who was twenty-five
years old, had a pretty round face, a quantity of white skin
and provocative manners. He had noticed one of the footmen in the house pursuing her assiduously; then he surprised
his own brother Sergey scuffling with her on the stairs. She
pushed the young gentleman away with a laugh and whispered, 'Really, watch where you're putting your hands, you
should be ashamed of yourself.'[13] At first he was terrified
by Sergey's boldness; then Leo dreamed of usurping his
place in the girl's favours. A hundred times he crouched in
the corridor listening to the flutter in the women-ser-

---

* He never forgot it, and played it at Yasnaya Polyana in 1906. He
himself admitted that he had only sketched out the melody, and one
of the Zybin brothers did the arrangement.

vants' room and erecting foolproof schemes for conquest, but he never had the courage to push open the door. 'What would I say, with my cabbage nose and my tufts of hair sticking up in the air, if she asked me what I wanted?'[14]

It was not long afterwards, no doubt, that he lost his virginity, in the most commonplace and tawdry way; barely sixteen years old, a liquor-sodden girl, a brothel bedroom. Later, he told his secretary, N. N. Gusev: 'The first time my brothers dragged me to a brothel and I performed that act, I sat down afterwards at the foot of the woman's bed and cried.'[15] The hero of his short story, *Memoirs of a Billiard-marker*, also weeps and rages at his friends after they have forced him to sleep with a prostitute. 'You think it's funny, but I am sad,' he says. 'Why did I do it? I won't forgive you for it and I won't forgive myself as long as I live.'* The memory of this distasteful body-to-body skirmish with a total stranger long prevented Leo Tolstoy from taking another woman in his arms. He preferred poetic elucubrations and solitary relief to the sordid pleasures of possession.

The end-of-term examinations found him unprepared. His marks were so poor that the board of examiners would not allow him to sit for the end-of-the-year examinations. Their decision, dated 26 April 1845, was accompanied by the following commentary: 'Insufficient attendance in class and total failure in history.' Mortified by this censure, Tolstoy blamed it on the hatred of Ivanov, his history professor, who had quarrelled with his family a short time before. He shut himself up in his room and indulged in a three-day bout of tears, rage and curses. He envied his brother Nicholas, who was going to enlist in the army the following month. He dreamed of going with him, fighting in the Caucasus, dying a hero, or possibly committing suicide. Then, picking up the notebook in which he had first written his 'Rules of Life', he opened it and felt a momentary rush

* The hero of the tale *A Holy Night* (1853) also cries 'like a baby' in the same circumstances.

of remorse and nostalgia. 'When I recovered, I decided to revise my rules of life,' he wrote, 'convinced that this time I would never do anything wrong again, would never spend one second in idleness and would never violate the principles I had laid down for myself.' [16]

Filled with these noble resolutions, he set off out for Yasnaya Polyana with his brothers. Aunt Toinette was there, with her warm eyes and little blue-veined hands. The moment he entered the drawing-room he felt 'the gentle caress of the old house'. 'How,' he wondered, 'have the house and I managed to live so long without each other?' [17] The windowpanes reflected memories of his childhood, he ran to bathe in the swift, merry water of the Voronka, stretched out in the shade of a birch grove, opened a book, read a few lines, drank in the shimmering, layered transparence of the leaves and felt coursing through him 'the same force of life, fresh and young, that filled Nature around me'.[18] Then, closing his book, he went to pick apples in the orchard or plunged into the dark, moist forest, filled with the smell of rotting fruit, moss and raspberries. In the evening, after supper, he settled himself to sleep on the terrace, heedless of the clouds of mosquitoes that vibrated in the shadows. One by one the last lamps emigrated from the ground floor to the rooms above, voices were lowered, the lights went out, the whole house sank into sleep and the night watchman began his rounds, stumping down the avenue striking his iron plate.

Then everything took on a different meaning for Leo Tolstoy: the silver-frosted sprays of poplar, the soft creaking of two birches against each other, the leaping frogs 'which sometimes climbed up the steps of the terrace, their backs gleaming greenish in the moonlight ...' [19] Surrounded by shadows and the eerie phosphorescence, he dreamed of the ideal woman, with one black braid lying over her shoulder and provocative breasts. 'But,' he wrote, 'something told me that S H E, with her bare arms and searing embrace, was by no means all the happiness in the

world and that even my love for HER was by no means
the only good. The longer I stared up at the moon, high in
the sky, the more it seemed to me that true beauty and true
happiness were still higher, more pure, closer to Him, the
source of all that is good and beautiful, and tears of joy, an
unfulfilled, straining sort of joy, came to my eyes. ... It
seemed to me then that Nature, the moon and I were one
and the same.' [20]

These nocturnal meditations were supplemented during
the day by the study of the philosophers. He was not satisfied by Descartes' 'I think, therefore I am' and proposed, in
its stead, 'I want, therefore I am'. Dazzled by this discovery,
he even outlined a theory, beginning with the words: 'If
man did not desire, there would be no man.' [21] And, after
finding fault with Descartes, he came in due course to Rousseau. The *Confessions* thundered through his brain like an
earthquake. He learned that he was not alone to harbour a
writhing mass of sordid instincts, that all men were probably equally cowardly, covetous, lying, envious and cruel, but
that it required great strength of character to own up to it.
As for the theory of the benefits of a primitive life as opposed to the evils of civilization: he might have invented
it himself. 'I thought I was reading my own mind and
simply added a few details here and there,' he said in
Youth.

These reflections inspired him to withdraw into himself
and flee his fellows; and Aunt Toinette, watching him wander through the grounds – gazing at nothing, slack-jawed,
conversing with some imaginary partner – began to worry.
When addressed, he came back from another world, assuming an expression at once dazed and condescending. He,
who formerly took such pains with his dress in order to
appear *comme il faut* at all times, now preached simplicity
of attire and began to neglect his appearance. With his own
hands, he sewed a dressing-gown of coarse linen, which he
wore in the day as he meditated and, by means of an ingenious system of flaps which could be unbuttoned and

folded back, used at night as bed and blanket. No more shirt, no cravat, no hose: slippers, over bare feet. He did not even change for company. When Aunt Toinette rebuked him for this get-up, he angrily retorted that he was above such 'vain contingencies'. However, the new Diogenes of Yasnaya Polyana was hard put to overcome the emotions women aroused in him. 'I always watched most attentively as the ladies' gowns – especially pink ones – came and went around the pond, across the meadow or in front of the house,'[22] he wrote. And he alternated his philosophical investigations with romanesque readings which were disturbing in quite another way: Eugène Sue, Alexandre Dumas and Paul de Kock were his revenge upon reality. 'Not only did I not dare suspect the author of lying,' he wrote, 'but the author himself did not exist for me, and the characters, real and living events, sprang up before my eyes, straight off the printed page. ... I discovered in myself all the passions they described, and I resembled all the characters, both heroes and villains, in every novel, just as a hypochondriac discovers every symptom of every conceivable disease in himself when he reads a treatise on medicine.' When his imagination had become white-hot, he closed his book and confronted a void. Not one woman in his life. How long could he be content with the solitary pleasures so dear to Rousseau?

In mid-August, he left Yasnaya Polyana with his brothers, returned to Kazan and, rather than repeat his first year in the Department of Oriental Languages, asked to be transferred to the Law Department.

I do not know whether this will please you or not [he wrote to Aunt Toinette on 25 August 1845], but I have changed departments and become a student of law. I personally find this science more easy and natural to apply to our private lives than any other and I am consequently very pleased with the change. Now I am going to tell you my plans and the kind of life I want to live. I won't go out in society at all. I will divide my time equally between music, drawing, languages and my courses at the University. May God grant me the determination to carry out my intentions.

On his way through Moscow he had seen his brother Nicholas, attached as a cadet, or 'junker',* to the 14th Artillery Brigade which was stationed not far from the city.

'Poor fellow, he's having a miserable time in the camp, especially as he hasn't a cent, one must find it extremely hard,' he exclaimed in the same letter. 'And the others! Good God, what yokels, if ever there were any! You need only one glimpse of camp life at first hand to lose all desire for a career in the army.'

His decision was already taken: he would be neither officer nor diplomat, but jurist! However, his first law courses did not provide the intellectual stimulus he had expected from them. He continued to receive poor marks, and was even put into confinement once, for unexplained absence from Professor Ivanov's history lectures. (Him again!) In the vaulted cell with its barred window, he found a fellow law student and undertook to explain to him, with passion, that history was nothing but a 'heap of myths and useless, trivial details, sprinkled with dates and names!'

The future author of *War and Peace* railed on until nightfall against official historians and the 'temple of the false science', lighted from below by a tallow candle, gesticulating, his cap in his eyes and his coat unbuttoned, across from his companion who was dropping with sleep.

Despite his relative diligence at his studies, he miraculously scraped through the end-of-year examinations and departed, elated, for Yasnaya Polyana, determined to turn his hand to estate management during the summer months. Soon after his arrival, he wrote to his brother Nicholas, who had meanwhile been transferred to the Caucasus:

I have been at Yasnaya with the whole family,† which is just as it should be, for two weeks now, and yet I shall not begin to live

---

*A young man from the upper classes serving a sort of military apprenticeship before receiving his officer's commission. (Tr. note.)

†That is, Aunt Toinette, Dmitry, Sergey and Marya Tolstoy.

according to my rules until tomorrow. This 'tomorrow' will make you laugh, yet I still have hope! I must tell you that I am up to my neck in estate management: *primo*, it keeps me busy and *secundo*, it amuses me – I am inventing all sorts of machines and improvements. I don't know whether I have told you about the three books I am writing: one is called *Miscellany*, another *What Is Needed for the Welfare of Russia? and Studies of Russian Customs*, and the third is *Observations on Property Management*. ... My *Miscellany* will be filled with poetry, philosophy and in general things that are not pretty but are amusing to write.

Thus, even before he knew he was going to be a writer, Tolstoy was preoccupied by the three areas he spent the rest of his life exploring: storytelling, educating his fellow men and organizing life on a country estate.

At the level of mental maturity he had now reached, it seemed absurd that he should still be required to live in the home of his guardian, Aunt Pelagya. His brothers Dmitry and Sergey agreed, and so, when they returned to Kazan, they took their leave of the Yushkov household and moved together into a six-room cottage, rented for seven hundred roubles a year. During his second year in the Law Department Leo Tolstoy, as flighty, unstable and unconcentrated as ever, nevertheless expressed some interest in Professor Vogel's discussions on the death penalty and deigned to attend a few of Professor Meyer's lectures on the history of civil law. His private studies waxed as his class attendance waned. Every minute he stole from the Department was spent in reading and exalting discourse: 'Gogol, Rousseau, Pushkin, Goethe's *Faust*, Hegel. . . .' Since January 1847 he had been keeping a diary of his thoughts and actions, and especially of his resolutions. His *idée fixe* was to perfect his famous 'Rules of Life'. It seemed to him that the more clearly he defined perfection, the more chance he had of attaining it. His recipes for virtue covered whole pages. 'Get up early (five o'clock), go to bed early (nine to ten o'clock). ... Eat little and avoid sweets. ... Try to do everything by yourself. ... Have a goal for your whole life, a goal for one section of your life, a goal for a shorter period and a goal for the year; a goal for every month, a goal for every week, a goal for every day, a goal for every hour and for every minute, and sacrifice the lesser goal to the greater. . . .' 'Keep away from women. . . .' 'Kill desire by work. . . .' 'Be good, but try to let no one know it. . . .' 'Always live less expensively than you might. . . .' 'Change nothing in your style of living even if you become ten times richer. . . .'[23] Setting down these aphorisms with the glowing conviction of his eighteen years, Leo Tolstoy believed he would remain true to them until death. But, at his present degree of intellectual ebullition, the notes in his diary were no longer enough. He drafted a commentary on Rousseau's philosophy, formulated in passing a few caustic remarks about history, 'the most backward science of all', outlined an essay on the immortality of the soul, and another in French on the second chapter of Bruyère's *Characters*: and, counselled by Professor Meyer, began a comparative study of the *Directives* of Catherine II and Montesquieu's *Spirit of the Laws*. He became enthused by this at-first-glance forbidding task. But then he fell ill; was he going to have to give up all literary activity, perhaps for days? Fortunately, it was nothing serious, and at eighteen his vitality was such that the fever itself was fuel for his meditations. Admitted to the university clinic on 11 March 1847, he looked forward happily to a period of uninterrupted study far from academic obligations and worldly temptation. In the calm of the big white hall, he seriously applied his mind, for the first time, to the problem of the lawfulness of power. He accepted the imperial government as a necessity, but he had doubts as to the fate of freedom and justice for the individual under such a system; and he was opposed to capital punishment but advocated the assimilation of enacted law to natural law. 'The *Directives* brought more glory to Catherine than benefit to Russia,' he wrote.

At the same time, he continued his diary with impassioned solemnity. 'It has become plain to me,' he wrote, 'that the irregular behaviour which most people of fashion take to be a consequence of youth is nothing more than an expression of premature spiritual depravity. ... If a man but leave society and withdraw into himself, a little thought will cause the glasses he has been wearing, through which he saw everything in a false light, to drop from his eyes. ...' And further on, 'I am beginning to feel a passion for study growing within me. ... I should be the unhappiest man alive if I did not have a purpose in life....'

He had a sudden revelation that he could not go on taking courses in the Law Department. He had been too happy working by himself to go back to the tedious discipline of the University. 'Strange as it may seem,' he wrote later, 'my work on the *Directives* and Montesquieu's *Spirit of the Laws* opened up a new field of intellectual activity to me, whereas the University, with all its rules and regulations, not only did not help me to study but actually prevented me from doing so.'[24] He also said, 'Men of genius are incapable of studying when they are young, because they unconsciously feel that they must learn everything differently from the mass.'[25]

When he left the clinic he already knew that his true professors were not Ivanov, Meyer and Vogel, but Montesquieu and Rousseau.

On 12 April 1847, without waiting to take his examinations, he asked the rector for permission to withdraw from the University, for reasons of health – any excuse would do. His request was granted. On 23 April, leaving his brothers Sergey and Dmitry to carry on docilely with their studies, he collected his books and papers together and packed his trunks. According to his habit, he outlined his life for the next two years at Yasnaya Polyana: 'Study the entire law course, practical medicine and part of medical theory; also French, Russian, German, English, Italian and Latin, and agriculture, both theory and practice; also history, geography, statistics; and mathematics – (high-school course);

write a thesis; reach an average degree of perfection in
music and painting; write rules of life.'[26] His friends from
the University accompanied him as far as the ford in the
Kazanka River, which was rising. Handshakes, kisses,
thumps on the shoulders ... the coachman was growing
restive. The young man climbed up again, looked across to
the opposite bank and smiled confidently at the future.

At the University, an inscription scratched with a knife in
an iron desk – 'Count Leo Tolstoy' – was the only trace of
the five and a half years he had spent in Kazan.

[5]

Wild Oats

THE first thing Leo did upon arriving at Yasnaya Polyana was to invite Aunt Toinette back under his roof. At nineteen he was no longer subject to any guardian's dictates and might choose whom he liked to manage his household. The old spinster saw that her moment of revenge upon the intriguer, Pelagya Ivanovna Yushkov, was at hand. She gratefully resumed possession of her two ground-floor rooms, hung up her icons in a corner and put out her tins of dates, candies, cookies and raisins on her dresser. Soon afterwards Sergey and Dmitry also came back to the old house, after passing their university examinations, and Nicholas joined them, having obtained a special furlough for 'family affairs'. All the Tolstoy sons were now their own masters and the inheritance could be divided up. According to the Russian law of that time, daughters were entitled to only one fourteenth of the movable goods and one eighth of the real property of their parents' estate, the remainder being divided equally among the sons. The boys considered these provisions unjust and decided that their sister Marya should receive a fifth of the whole, like themselves. They had discussed the allocation of the land the previous year. Nicholas, the eldest son, had chosen Nikolskoye; Sergey, who was a great horse-fancier, took the estate and stud farm of Pirogovo: Marya was given 2,440 acres of land and 150 peasants on the same estate; Dmitry received Sherbatchevka in the government of Kursk; and Leo inherited Yasnaya Polyana and a few neighbouring hamlets – a total of approximately 4,000 acres of land and 330 peasants. When Sergey Tolstoy was asked why his brother Leo had preferred Yasnaya Polyana to all the other lots, he answered, 'It was considered the least profitable share of the entire estate.' The deed of settlement was signed on 11 July 1847 and the brothers separated immediately afterwards, each going off to prospect his claim. Marya did not stay long, either: in November of that year she married her cousin Valerian Petrovich Tolstoy and settled on the Pokrovskoye estate with him.

Now sole and absolute master of Yasnaya Polyana and its inhabitants, Leo Tolstoy began to plumb the extent of his responsibilities a little more every day. First, he decided to modernize the farming methods, and ordered a mechanical threshing machine built to his own specifications. At its inaugural demonstration for the peasants, the contraption throbbed, whistled, wheezed and threshed nothing. Deflated, Tolstoy moved on from technology to welfare. From afar, the thought of the reformation he would carry out on his land had positively intoxicated him. Close up, he was less sure of his theories. The stewards heard him out with obsequious smiles as he expounded his projects for social reform, and when he had finished talking they presented him with accounts which were so entangled that he no longer knew whether they were all crooks or himself a hopeless fool. He was too unsure of himself to argue, shout and throw the riff-raff out of his office, and so in the end, battle-weary, he grudgingly endorsed what he would rather have damned. Similarly, when he tried to give the muzhiks a vision of a more elevated and prosperous way of life, he felt he was infringing upon their time-worn ways. They met his exhortations and his benevolent concern with a staggering force of inertia. Centuries of serfdom had atrophied their brains. Cringing and blinking, their faces baked by sun and dirt, they refused to abandon their status as beasts of burden for a better life. 'Master, our young master!' they respectfully murmured. And when his back was turned they called him a madman.

Ivan Churis's isba was on the very verge of collapse, but when the master, appalled at such destitution, offered to build him a new one, the fellow pleaded to be allowed to stay on in his old hovel, with his filth and his eccentricities.

Yukhvanka wanted to sell his horse, claiming it was too old to work; but when Leo went to buy the animal, just to do the man a favour, he saw that there was nothing the matter with it: the muzhik only wanted to get rid of it because he was too lazy to farm his field. Karp, the coachmaker, and his sons whined that their trade brought them next to nothing in comparison with the farmers, but when Tolstoy offered to rent them eighty acres of his own land to work, on very favourable terms, they refused, suspecting their young master of trying to make a profit at their expense. There was no school in the village, and besides, nobody in it knew how to read. Negligence, ignorance, disease, sloth and cunning prevailed. They muddled along from day to day and harvest to harvest, and nothing was done to better the condition of anyone. Could one lone man budge this mountain of wretchedness? And yet, how was one to avoid getting involved with it? The serfs overran their lord's existence – he was as much theirs as they were his. If he did not go to see them in their village, they came to him in his handsome house.

Assembled before the steps [Tolstoy wrote] were a woman in bloodstained rags, screaming that her father-in-law had tried to kill her; two brothers who had been quarrelling over the division of their property for two years, glaring at each other with loathing; a grizzled, unshaven old house-servant with the shaking hands of a drunkard, whom his son, the gardener, had brought to the master to be scolded; a muzhik who had run his wife out of his house because she had not done a stroke of work all spring; and the wife in question, sick and sobbing, not uttering a word, sitting there on the grass in front of the steps, holding out her swollen leg wrapped in dirty rags.[1]

The young master swallowed his distaste, swelled out his chest and, calling upon the vast stores of his inexperience, scolded some and consoled others; then, with a feeling compounded of weariness, shame, helplessness and remorse, he went back to his room.[2]

However, although he deplored the wretched lives of his

serfs, Tolstoy did not condemn serfdom itself. 'The idea that the serfs should be liberated was quite unheard-of in our circle in the forties,' he wrote in his *Reminiscences.* 'The hereditary ownership of serfs seemed an indispensable fact of life.' After losing his illusions as to the opportuneness of the reforms he had dreamed of carrying out, he came to think it was better for the muzhiks to go on vegetating and the stewards fleecing them, and the estate to slumber on. 'My peasants are no better off, and it grows harder for me to bear every day,' said his hero Nekhlyudov in *A Landlord's Morning.* 'Ah, if only I had seen my projects crowned with success, or gratefully accepted. . . . But no: I see nothing but pointless routine, vice, mistrust, impotence. I am wasting the best years of my life.' And also, 'It is easier to find happiness for oneself than to give it to others.'

In the country, as in town, Tolstoy went on reading everything that came into his hands, and took notes on a wide variety of subjects. Ever precise, he drew up a list of his literary discoveries over the years, marking opposite each the degree of admiration it had aroused in him:

> *The Gospel According to Saint Matthew* (immense influence).
> Sterne's *Sentimental Voyage* (very great influence).
> Rousseau's *Confessions* (immense influence). *Émile* (immense influence).
> *La Nouvelle Héloïse* (very great influence).
> Pushkin's *Eugene Onegin* (very great influence).
> Schiller's *The Robbers* (very great influence).
> Gogol's *The Overcoat, Ivan Ivanovich, The Nevsky Prospect* (great influence).
> *Vii* (immense influence). *Dead Souls* (very great influence).
> Turgenev's *A Sportsman's Sketches* (very great influence).
> Druzhnin's *Pauline Saks* (very great influence).
> Grigorovich's *Aton Goremyka* (very great influence).

Dickens's *David Copperfield* (immense influence).
Lermontov's *A Hero of Our Times* (very great influence).
Prescott's *Conquest of Mexico* (great influence).

At least two works in this motley collection dealt with the muzhiks: *Anton Goremyka* and *A Sportsman's Sketches*. Tolstoy marvelled to see that in Grigorovich's latest book the muzhik was no longer regarded as 'a part of the landscape', but as a 'teacher of life', and that the writer spoke of this humble hero 'with love, respect and even a sort of trembling compassion'.[3] As for Turgenev's tales: Tolstoy was equally enchanted by the charm of their style and the liberality of their equalitarian ideas. He later said that *A Sportsman's Sketches, Anton Goremyka* and *Uncle Tom's Cabin* had been instrumental in abolishing slavery from the world.[4]

At the moment, however, a different form of slavery was bothering Tolstoy: that of the flesh. He raged against himself for being so susceptible to the diabolical allure of women. 'How difficult it is for a man,' he wrote in his diary on 14 June 1847, 'to cultivate the good in him when he is surrounded by nothing but evil influences.' While he was striving to get the upper hand of his spring fever – treacherously abetted by the warm weather, the twittering birds and the sight of the peasant girls working in the fields – little Dunyasha arrived at Yasnaya Polyana with her husband at her side.* For him, she had always been like a sister; the thought that she might also be a woman had never entered his head. And here she was, a young bride, back to spend a few nights under his roof. A room was prepared for the couple. Tolstoy could not refrain from imagining scenes of lascivious intimacy between her and her husband. 'Yesterday I was in an excellent frame of mind,' he wrote on 15 June, 'and would no doubt have remained so until even-

---

* Dunyasha Temyashov (Dunyechka), ward of Leo Tolstoy's father, had gone with the family to Kazan and married there.

ing, if the arrival of Dunyasha and her husband had not affected me so strongly that I had to forgo the satisfaction of being pleased with myself.'

The expressions 'I am pleased with myself' and 'I am not pleased with myself' recur often in his writing, and are probably code-words to cover up reprehensible practices. His splendid health and prodigious appetite for life demanded, or so he thought, these solitary 'purges'. Otherwise he would have succumbed to temptations yet more base. But no sooner had he divested himself in this manner of his obsession with women than the creatures reappeared, more shameless than ever, in his imagination, revenging themselves upon him for trying to do without them. He indignantly undertook to confound them with dialectics, posing as the champion of a sacred cause. The next day, 16 June, he was still unable to forget Dunyasha: 'Will a day ever come when I shall no longer be dependent upon external contingencies? In my opinion this would be a huge stride towards perfection. ... Now I shall set myself the following rule: regard the company of women as a necessary social evil and avoid them as much as possible. Who indeed is the cause of sensuality, indolence, frivolity and all sorts of other vices in us, if not women? Who causes us to lose our natural qualities of courage, resoluteness, reason and justice, etc, if not women?'

He felt better after writing down this peremptory excommunication. But then, a strange feeling of disenchantment stole over him, he no longer saw any point in continuing to record his daily impressions: without a sigh, he put the notebook away in a drawer along with some other papers, and was not to resume his diary until three years later.

Leo Tolstoy had planned to spend at least two years at Yasnaya Polyana with his dear Aunt Toinette, but after eighteen months, having lost faith in the muzhiks, he conceived a loathing for the country. He read, yawned, dreamed of the city, women, lights. Towards mid-October 1848, when the peasants had dug themselves into their isbas and a sleet-storm was lashing at the trees, the anchorite of Yasnaya Polyana decided to go to Moscow.

He stayed only a few weeks – long enough to cultivate a few connexions and suffer heavy losses at cards – and then, at the end of January 1849, he abruptly left for St Petersburg, where two of his friends, Ozerov and Fersen, were also going. At first he felt out of place in the foggy, damp European capital, divided by broad rectilinear avenues, where fake Greek palaces stood perishing of boredom beneath a polar sky. The passers-by in the street all seemed to be travelling along a wire that drew them unwillingly towards their work. Not one familiar face. Hardly any trees. Granite, marble, bronze. Surrounded by so much austerity, his love of study returned. He was even glad to be in a city in which everything spoke to him of order, labour, career. Always eager to give himself good reasons for his optimism, he wrote to his brother Sergey on 13 February 1849, saying that he intended to sit his remaining law examinations in Petersburg and then go into the government, as a fourteenth-class civil servant if need be: 'I know you won't believe I have changed, and you'll say, "That makes at least the twentieth time; no good will ever come of him, he's a dead loss." No; this time, the change is completely different; before, I said, "I shall change". This time I see I have changed and I say, "I have changed".'

He immediately confirmed these resolutions in a letter to Aunt Toinette.[5]

I like life in Petersburg. Here everyone has his job, everyone works and minds his own business and pays no attention to anybody else; even though the atmosphere is cold and selfish, it is essential for young people like us, who are inexperienced and lack *savoir faire*; it will teach me to be orderly and keep myself occupied, the two indispensable qualities in life, of which I am totally devoid. ... As for my plans, here they are: before I do anything else, I want to sit my examinations at the University of Petersburg and then enter some administrative department, here or somewhere else, however circumstances decide. ... Don't be surprised, dear Aunt, I have truly changed, I am not in one of those philosophical ecstasies you so often used to reproach me for at Yasnaya ...

Between 'rules of life' and life itself, what a chasm! To be sure, Tolstoy began to study, prepared his law examinations and even muddled through one or two, but then gave up the rest overnight.* Once more his passion for the legal science palled. Too many pleasures and too many worries were crowding his mind – the latter resulting, as is only proper, from the former. And at the head of the list, there were his gambling debts. He turned automatically to his brother Sergey, to whom he had declared two months previously that he was a changed man. On 1 May 1849 he confessed his relapse in a missive bearing at the top the terse comment: 'Read this letter alone.' He was probably afraid its receiver would alert Aunt Toinette. 'Sergey, you must be saying – I can hear you – that I am a good-for-nothing, and you are right,' he wrote. 'My God, what have I done? I came to Petersburg for no good reason, I've done nothing worthwhile here except spend masses of money, and I've gone into debt. It's so stupid, so unbearably stupid. You can't imagine how it infuriates me. First of all, there are the debts I *must* pay and without a moment's delay, for if I don't pay them soon I shall lose not only the money but my reputation to boot. For the love of heaven, do this: say nothing to the aunts, or to Andrey† and sell Vorotinka.‡ ... While I'm waiting for the money to come through, I must absolutely have 3,500 roubles right away.§ ... I know you will moan and groan, but what else can I do? You only make this kind of mistake once in a lifetime. My freedom and my philosophy are expensive and now I am having to pay! ...

* Afterwards he wrote, in *Education and Instruction*: 'I passed an examination at the University of St Petersburg without knowing a single thing, having begun to study for it, at most, one week in advance.'

† Andrey Ilich Sobolev, administrator of Leo Tolstoy's property at Yasnaya Polyana.

‡ A piece of Tolstoy's property comprising twenty-two peasants.

§ In the neighbourhood of $9,900.

There was nobody to give me a beating, that's what's the matter!'

Not for one moment did the would-be saviour of the muzhiks falter at the thought that in order to pay his gambling debts he had to sell a score of men, women and children along with his wood, land and livestock. He was merely acting according to the customs of the times. Anything, rather than be declared insolvent by his creditors, who had taken his word. Besides, he had not lost hope. No one scrambled back into the saddle more quickly than he, after a tumble. Yesterday he fancied himself a law graduate, senior civil servant, diplomat. ... Errors all! He would be a soldier, or more precisely a non-commissioned officer in the Horse Guards. The moment seemed propitious: Nicholas I, his nerves already on edge after the Revolution of 1848 in France, had decided to send an army to Hungary to put down Kossuth's proletarian uprising and seat the young emperor Franz-Josef more firmly on his throne. A fine opportunity to gain glory serving his country. Of course, he would be fighting people who claimed allegiance to republican doctrines – but those were foreign notions, French ideas, which need not trouble a Russian mind. Tolstoy admired Montesquieu and Rousseau, abominated oppression and desired the good of the poor, but the events of the Revolution of 1848 left him cold, whereas the promise held out by the campaign of 1849 tickled his warrior's bump. Indeed, it was not among his gambling-cronies that he would have been likely to find a professor of political science. His great friend of the moment was Konstantin Islenyev, a homeless rake who refused work of any kind, took life as it came and subsisted from day to day on money extorted from his father. The presence of this jolly debauchee prevented Tolstoy from making friends with people of higher moral cast. He was not over-amazed to learn that in the night of 22 April 1849 a group of young men suspected of conspiring against the government under the leadership of Petrashevsky, an official in the Ministry for Foreign Affairs, had been arrested and thrown into prison.* He was vaguely acquainted with two of the conspirators, Milyutin and Beklemishev. Also said to be among them was a certain Fyodor Mikhailovich Dostoyevsky, whose first novel, *Poor Folk*, had caused something of a stir in 1846. Tolstoy had never met the author, and could not have cared less whether he had any talent or was guilty or not. He was a long way, in those days, from art, literature or the principles of non-violence.

'I have high hopes for my military service,' he wrote to Sergey. 'It will accustom me to the practical side of life and I shall be forced to stay in until I receive a commission, whether I like it or not. If I am lucky, that is, if the Guards see any action, I could be promoted within two years.'

A few days later, a new about-face. Tolstoy had told his brother he would enter the Horse Guards, 'provided the war were in earnest'.⁶ But the war must not have been earnest enough, for he suddenly decided not to enlist. He no longer saw his salvation in Hungary and in uniform, but at Yasnaya Polyana, in work, thrift and thought. Besides, Sergey, alarmed at his brother's spending, agreed to help him only on condition that he go back to live on his estate. On 26 May 1849 Leo Tolstoy wrote to Aunt Toinette, once again in French:

'Forgive me, dear Aunt, I am a good-for-nothing wretch to make you unhappy on my account. I know I am the cause of your grief, and I have made up my mind to come back to you as soon as I can and never to leave you any more, except now and then for a few weeks.'

It was a somewhat crestfallen Tolstoy who left Petersburg early in June, after paying a few of his creditors and leaving sizeable debts behind him with Dussot's Restaurant, Sharmer the tailor and three or four overtrusting friends.

Aunt Toinette welcomed him with open arms. She knew all, forgave all. Gambling debts were traditional in great

---

* The prisoners were convicted and led out to a mock execution, after which they were sent to Siberia.

families. It would have been as abnormal for a young gentleman not to lose at cards as for him not to have a mistress.
Since Leo had no mistress, honour required him to lose at
cards. Even so, she gave a start when he began to quote
figures. Extreme in everything, her dear Leo! She frowned,
while her heart melted.

Unfortunately, Leo was not alone. He had brought back
from Petersburg a German pianist named Rudolf, a man he
had picked up in a cabaret, who was, he said, a genius.
Under this virtuoso's tutelage, he imagined that he, too,
could become a composer. In his enthusiasm he seriously
considered writing a treatise entitled *Foundations of Music
and Rules for Its Study*. In the meantime, he learned
Rudolf's works by heart: *Hexengalop* and *Cavalry Trots*.
The two melomaniacs were carried away by their harmonies
far into the night. But Rudolf was also carried away by
vodka. And as his fingers often left the keyboard to stray
among the conservatory of servant girls, he had to be sent
packing. Thereupon, Aunt Toinette remembered that she
had once been a good musician herself. To please her
nephew she took up the piano again, and, four-handed, they
played his favourite études and sonatas. Delicious moments.
A male presence at her side. A smell of tobacco in the
house. She transferred to the son her old mute worship of
the father. He became the second man in her life. Sometimes, in conversation, she would call him Nicholas, on
purpose, and with guilty pleasure. 'I was especially touched
by this,' Tolstoy wrote, 'for it showed me that my father's
image and my own had merged into one in her love for us.'
She was fifty-seven, her body had thickened and her hair
was turning grey, but her eyes still gave off the light, keen
glimmer of agate. Her nephew came to her room almost
every evening, sat down in a tapestried armchair, nibbled
a piece of candy or a date and helped her to lay out her
solitaire, watched over by a tall silver-sheathed saviour.
'Every time I see Aunt Toinette,' he wrote to his brother
Nicholas, 'I find more excellent qualities in her. The only

fault one can find with her is that she is too romantic; but that is because she has such a good heart and such a good mind, and she had to occupy her mind with something, so for want of anything better, she chose to build the whole world into one great romance.'[7]

And Aunt Toinette confessed, in her private diary and drafts of her letters, that her nephew's affection made her forget the 'cruel torment' that gnawed at her heart; he was the 'light of her life', she could not live without him. 'When you sat beside me on the divan,' she wrote, 'I looked at you with all my soul and all my senses, I was transformed into that look, I could not utter a word; my soul was so full of you that I forgot everything else.'[8] This love, more or less repressed, more or less disguised, did not prevent the old spinster from judging 'her Lyovochka' with clear eyes. She said he was 'a man for challenges' and that in order to use up his excess energy he should be 'writing novels'. Attached to him so intensely by the complex feelings of pseudo-mother and pseudo-mistress, she might well have dreaded the thought that another woman could come and take him away from her. But she was above such petty jealousy; on the contrary, it pained her to see her attractive nephew living so sedately. She yearned for an amoral, brilliant future for him in keeping with the fashion of the time. 'The good aunt with whom I lived, the purest creature alive,' Tolstoy wrote in *Confession*, 'was always telling me there was nothing she wanted so much as for me to have an affair with a married woman. "There is no better education for a young man than an affair with a woman of good breeding!" There was another blessing she desired for me: to be an aide-de-camp, preferably to the emperor; but the very summit of bliss would have been for me to marry a very rich girl, so that I might acquire many serfs.'

None of these projects appeared outrageous to the young man at the time, but neither did any of them tempt him. To be sure, he had given up his solitary pleasures, but when he sought the company of women now, he wanted them easy to take and easy to leave. His roving eye first fell upon one of Aunt Toinette's servants, Gasha,* who was a virgin, guileless and clean. She had eyes that were 'black as wet currants', a candid smile on velvet lips, a white apron over a round belly – her very walk disturbed him, the mere sound of her voice. He pursued her down the corridors, stole a few kisses from her and, one night, entreated her to open her door to him. The latch dropped back, he slipped through the crack and clasped in his arms a quaking body huddled inside a coarse linen nightshirt. His desire quenched, what disgust, what lassitude! 'What does all that mean?' he asked himself. 'Is what has happened to me wonderful or horrible?' And he concluded, 'Bah! it's the way of the world; everybody does it!'† Aunt Toinette soon discovered the liaison, duly flew into a rage against her maid – not her nephew – and dismissed the poor girl. 'I seduced her, she was sent away, and she perished,' Leo Tolstoy later told Biryukov, his biographer. And when, in *Resurrection*, he told the story of the young servant-girl who was deflowered by her benefactress's nephew, turned out of the house pregnant, and driven to prostitution, penury and theft, it was Gasha who was haunting his memory. Contrary to Tolstoy's assertions, however, Gasha's fate had nothing in common with that of the Katyusha Mazlova of the novel. After her 'fault', Gasha became a chambermaid to Marya Nikolayevna, Leo Tolstoy's sister, gained her confidence and raised her children.

Another house-servant next attracted the young master's attention and received the honour of his favours. Her name was Dunyasha and she was later to marry a steward of the Tolstoy family named Orekhov. After riding by their trysting-place at the age of sixty-nine, Tolstoy wrote in his diary, 'I remembered the nights I spent there, Dunyasha's beauty and youth (I did not have a real affair with her), her strong womanly body. Where is it? Long since, nothing but

* Her full name was Agatha Mikhailovna Trubetskaya.
† *Resurrection*, Book I, Chapter XVII.

bones.'[9] He was also to confess to a relationship with a serf-woman from the village. Did he, like Irtenyev in his short story *The Devil*, meet his mistress in the gamekeeper's cottage? Irtenyev behaved as he did because it was 'essential to his health and peace of mind'. The woman the gamekeeper had provided for him 'wore a white blouse and an embroidered skirt, had a red scarf on her head and was barefoot – fresh, sturdy, comely, smiling'. Thanks to her, he was able, the author states, to overcome 'the major drawback of country life: voluntary chastity'. But what Irtenyev believed to be only a passing fancy developed into an abiding passion. This was not the case with Leo Tolstoy who, while having a whirl with the girls in his house and village, kept enough of a cool head to work.

Every time he took up some new activity, he wanted to write a treatise on it. The treatise on music, *Foundations of Music and Rules for Its Study*, was followed by one in French, *On Gymnastics* – because he had resumed his morning limbering-up exercises – and another, *On Cards* – because he had lost so much money playing them. He might also have written a treatise on the habits and customs of the Bohemians, for he had been haunting the singers of the gypsy chorus at Tula for some time. The distance between Yasnaya Polyana and Tula was small and the road was paved. Officially, Tolstoy went to town now and then on business (he had signed up to work part-time for the Chancellery of the Assembly of Representatives of the Nobility, at Tula). But in fact, once he got there, he sped from elegant reception to low dive, from the young ladies to the girls. His passion for the gypsies was shared by his brother Sergey, who had fallen in love with a little singer, Marya Shishkin, a wasp-waisted lass of seventeen with intense black eyes and a throaty voice. She became his mistress. After paying a steep price for her to the leader of the chorus, he intended to take her to his estate at Pirogovo and break off all relations with any neighbours who dared to raise their eyebrows.

Leo Tolstoy was not in love with any particular gypsy; he

mixed them all up together in one impersonal desire and admiration. Their husky singing so moved him that the tears spilled out of his eyes every time he listened. 'Suddenly the chorus is still,' he wrote in *A Holy Night*. 'Then there is a chord, and then the same melody, over and over, in a gentle, tender, sonorous voice with extraordinary inflections and astonishing flourishes, and the voice grows steadily stronger and more vigorous until the melody is imperceptibly transmitted to the chorus, which takes it up in a group.' And the hero of *The Living Corpse* said about the gypsy songs, 'They're the steppe, they're the tenth century, not freedom, but independence. ... How is it man can attain that ecstasy and then can't make it last inside him? Ah, Masha, Masha, how you made my guts heave!'

On his way home from these nocturnal sprees his head whirled with the thrum of guitars, the smell of smoke, the silhouettes of the girls in their many-coloured dresses, the metallic taste of champagne, a bottomless melancholy, a desire to walk to the ends of the earth, to love – anybody, to die, to be born again, to have a drink of cold water and go back to the place he had just left. He wrote in his diary, 'No one who has known the gypsies can ever cease humming their songs over and over, in or out of tune, but always with pleasure, because they remain so sharp in his memory.'[10]

Back home, he sank gratefully into his quiet, peaceful humdrum existence and the gentle face of Aunt Toinette, waiting for him.

After the wicked life in Tula, with the neighbours, cards, gypsies, the hunting and idiotic futility, I returned home and went to her. ... According to the old custom, we kissed each other's hands: I, her pretty, lively hand; she, my dirty, sinful hand; we greeted each other in French, again according to the old custom; I would tease Natalya Petrovna [her servant] for a moment, and sit in my armchair. She knows everything I have done and is miserable because of it but will not say one word to me about it; always the same good-will, the same love. I sit in the armchair, I read, I think, I listen to her conversation with Natalya Petrovna. Some-

times they talk of the past, sometimes they play solitaire, sometimes they discuss omens, sometimes some remark amuses them,
and then the two little old ladies begin to laugh, especially my
aunt, the way children do – a charming laugh I can still hear
today.[11]

But all the time she was pretending to chat with Natalya
Petrovna, Aunt Toinette was watching her nephew out of
the corner of her eye. She was clever enough to guess that
he would soon be leaving her again. And one day, after
losing four thousand roubles* to his neighbour, the young
landowner Ogarev, he suddenly became panic-stricken.
Luckily, he won the money back, down to the last kopeck,
which enabled him to observe that he had a rare degree of
self-control, except when he was with the gypsies, or drunk.
'But I have sworn not to get drunk any more,' he wrote. In
any case, he would be better off away from Tula and the
gypsy singers. ... Moscow was the place where he could live
a life of virtue. He packed his bags on the spot. Left gasping by the suddenness of this decision, Aunt Toinette swallowed her tears, made the sign of the cross over the
traveller's head, ordered supplies for the trip and went out
on the steps to watch the carriage roll away down the broad
drive, its trees stripped by the autumn wind.

In Moscow, Tolstoy rented a small furnished apartment
in the Arbat district. His lodgings consisted of a drawing-
room, with armchairs and sofa upholstered in red rep, a
dining-room with a piano – a rented 'royalino' – in solitary
state, a study with the leather couch indispensable to all
Russian reveries, a bedroom, a dressing-room and an antechamber. For forty roubles a month, he hired a *pochevny*, a
sort of sledge in fashion that year. He even bought an expensive harness; his turnout was, in his own opinion, flaw-
lessly elegant. All this was necessary for the new project he
had adopted. For, as always, he intended to forge ahead.
Only he had changed his tack. As soon as he was settled, on
8 December 1850, he sat down to take stock in his diary: 'I

* Or $11,300.

have stopped building castles in the air and making plans beyond all human power to carry out. ... In the past, everything that existed in the ordinary sense seemed unworthy of me. Now, on the contrary, I will not acknowledge as good or true any conviction I cannot test in action and apply in practice. . .' With this as his point of departure, he drew up the following programme: '(1) Join a group of card players, to try my luck when I am in funds. (2) Get into the best society and, under certain conditions, marry. (3) Find a good position.'[12] And, to fill in the details of the role he meant to play, he set down some 'rules of society' for his personal use: 'Try to control the conversation at all times, speak in a loud voice, slowly and distinctly; always contrive to begin and end the discussion. Seek out the society of people more highly placed than I. In a conversation, do not shift from French to Russian or Russian to French. At dances, invite the most important ladies and do not be discouraged by a refusal. Be as cold as possible and let no feeling show. ... Do not stand for an impertinent remark but redeem it immediately by one twice as impertinent.' Thus the apostle of Yasnaya Polyana became a social climber. He was seen in every salon: calls on Governor General Zakrevsky, on the Gorchakovs, the Volkonskys, the Lvovs, the Stolypins, the Konivalskys, the Perfilyevs; work-outs at the riding academy, exchange of bows along the paths in Sokolniki Park, concerts, theatre, balls, dinners, gymnastics, and fencing in Poiré, the Frenchman's, famous fencing school. All the while Tolstoy was writing in his diary that this existence was vain and futile, he made no attempt to elude it. And, as at Tula, he returned to the gypsies. For variety, he would leave some stiff evening party full of marriageable young ladies, with cold buffet, rubber plants and musicians in tailcoats, to descend, with his habitual drinking companions – Islavin in the lead – upon the suburban cabarets where the beautiful Bohemians with gleaming teeth were performing – the terror of fiancées, wives and mothers. There they sang, drank champagne, broke glasses and spent money with the deli-

cious feeling that they were committing a fatal folly, poetic
and irreparable. After solemnly noting in his diary, on 24
December 1850 – Christmas Eve – 'in accordance with the
laws of religion, stay away from women,' he confessed two
days later: 'A bad day, went to the gypsies.' Again, on 28
December, 'to the gypsies'. And on 29 December, 'I am
living like a beast. . . . In the evening, drew up precepts, then
went to the gypsies.'

Seated on Leo Tolstoy's knees, Katya the gypsy hummed
his favourite song, 'Tell Me Why', and vowed between
verses that she had never loved another man. 'That evening
I believed her sly gypsy chatter with all my heart, I was in a
good mood and no "guest" came to disturb me,' he admitted
a few months later. His acquaintance with the gypsies gave
him a desire to write a story about them. What fun it must
be to tell a story, let your pen flow across the paper. . . .
After blackening a few pages, he changed his mind; he was
toying with an idea for a novel: Aunt Toinette's love life –
her sacrifices, defeat, resignation. . . . But did one have the
right to divulge the innermost secrets of the heart, just for
the pleasure of composing a work of art? He sorrowfully observed, 'Aunt Toinette's life would make a good book,' and
abandoned the idea. The best thing of all, he said to himself, was to seek material from his own life. And by good
fortune, he thought he had just fallen in love with Princess
Sherbatov. What a godsend for a writer! All he had to do
was tell the truth. The title would be *Story of Yesterday*. But
his social commitments prevented him from setting to work
at once. More gypsies, supper parties, balls – at one costume
ball, he turned up dressed as a cockchafer! [13] . . . At last, he
made up his mind. Progress was fitful, the characters would
not come to life, the style was heavy, cluttered with metaphor. But the author already knew how to suggest a mood
by a gesture or a look, and made skilful use of monologue.
'I told myself,' he noted, 'I shall just go ahead and describe
what I see. What is the best way to describe? Letters make
up words and words make sentences, but how to transcribe

feelings? Description is not enough.' Dissatisfied, it occurred to him that he would feel more at ease relating the circumstances that had made him what he was, rather than those of his present life. His childhood was still within reach; in the process of recounting it he would be stimulated by it, his writing would improve. He set to work with a will. Strict timetable. Iron discipline. Gymnastics and creation. Once again, the torrent drained away into the sand, and the manuscript of *Childhood* was abandoned after a few pages.

Never lacking an excuse, Tolstoy declared that it was the irregularity of his life alone that prevented him from writing. And, indeed, his gambling debts had mounted at an alarming rate since his arrival in Moscow. Naturally, he was sure he could win it all back in two or three lucky plays, provided he played systematically; he invented extravagant martingales, none of which, alas, worked; and he wrote down comminatory precepts in his diary: 'Play only with people richer than myself.' Or, 'Never play for less than twenty-five silver kopecks.'

While waiting to recoup his fortune at cards he spent every cent that came to him from the estate, pawned his watch, ordered extra fellings of timber, mortgaged a few acres and humbly inclined before Aunt Toinette's lamentations.

'Dear Aunt,' he wrote in French, 'everything you tell me of my passion for cards is perfectly true, and I often think the same. That is why I believe I shall play no more. I say "I believe," but I hope I can soon tell you "I know"; you see, it is very hard to let go of an idea one has had for a long time.'[14]

At one point, in urgent need of money, he, the Muscovite dandy, conceived the idea of becoming a postmaster. He would expand the postal service between Moscow and Tula. The application for a government licence was processed in record time. But a few weeks later he backed out of the undertaking, fearing he might lose his last shirt: oats were too expensive and his partner untrustworthy. Ashamed of his idleness, his 'nullity', he decided to begin a special column in his diary, to which he would consign his weaknesses, 'in the manner of Benjamin Franklin'. For one month, without missing a day, he set down, page after page, the most torrid self-accusations: 'vanity', 'boasting', 'conceit', 'sloth', 'apathy', 'affectedness', 'deceitfulness', 'instability', 'indecisiveness', 'waiting for miracles', 'tendency to copy others', 'cowardice', 'contrariness', 'excessive self-confidence', 'inclination to voluptuousness', 'passion for gambling'. ... How he revelled in reviling himself! Driven by the demon of analysis he split himself in two and became teacher and pupil at once. The teacher set a programme for the pupil ('Tomorrow, from 8 a.m. to 10 a.m., write; from 10 to noon, look for money and fence; from 6 p.m. until nightfall, write and receive no one ...') and scolded the pupil when he did not adhere to it. The pupil confessed his sins to the teacher ('I am not pleased with myself ... I behaved neither well nor badly. . . . Lack of perseverance. . . .') and promised to 'do better' next time. In fact, nothing fascinated Tolstoy as much as himself. He peered at his diary as though it were a mirror, experimenting with new faces and then grading himself on them. Other people interested him only in terms of his effect upon them. When he thought of the exalting struggle that lay ahead, before he would become morally irreproachable, he was almost happy to be nothing but an amalgam of vices, a kneaded lump of straw and mud.

As spring drew near, something like a breeze blew through his soul. He wrote to Aunt Toinette: 'With the rebirth of nature, one would like to feel reborn oneself; one regrets the past, the wasted time, one repents of one's weakness, and the future lies ahead like a shining light.'[15] He was eager to leave behind his haggard companions in pleasure, the green baize, the smoke, the gypsies and empty bottles, and plunge back into the calm countryside of Yasnaya Polyana, where the trees were budding. Easter with the family. This time, in addition to Aunt Toinette, he would see his brother Nicholas, artillery lieutenant in the

Army of the Caucasus, who had been given a six-months furlough.

Nicholas had arrived home on 22 December 1850, and Leo had gone to Pokrovskoye to see him at the home of their sister Marya, who was expecting a baby.* After four years, his meeting with his eldest brother had made such an impact upon him that he still thought of it with alternating affection and uneasiness. Nicholas, now twenty-seven, appeared to him in his officer's uniform as a man of experience, self-assured, poised, upright, modest and dignified. Oh, he still liked to laugh and drink, and he told stories as well as ever, but his whole being gave off an air of worldly wisdom and lassitude which commanded respect. He never argued, never condemned, he merely smiled to express his doubt or disapproval. Leo had expected to dazzle him with his elegant outfit from Sharmer's, his fine linen and tales of nights spent at the gaming tables, in aristocratic drawing-rooms and with the gypsies; but Nicholas had pursed his lips into a faintly mournful grimace and changed the subject. 'Either he is completely blind or else he doesn't like me,' Leo noted in his diary after their first meeting. 'Or else he is simply pretending not to notice and not to like me.'[16] This uncomfortable feeling had worn off during Nicholas's short trips to Moscow. But Leo needed to see him back at Yasnaya Polyana, in the atmosphere of their childhood, in order to regain his confidence in their friendship. Unconsciously, he was looking for advice, for a revelation, from his brother, as in the far-off days when they had played at being Ant Brothers together.

Borne up by this unacknowledged hope, he set off, on 2 April 1851, for his domain. Alas! Once the joy of greeting Aunt Toinette and his brothers and sister had worn off, he relapsed into boredom and self-disgust. 'April 5. Went to see Sergey (at Pirogovo). Lied, boasted and acted like a coward.' 'April 6. Did nothing. I lied and boasted a great deal. Fasted, but without thinking about it, absent-mindedly

* A son, Nicholas, was born to Marya Tolstoy on 1 January.

...' 'April 7. Lazy and soft. Tomorrow, Easter Sunday ...'
'April 8. Easter. Wrote a sermon; half-hearted, puny, afraid
to speak out.'

Since he had been at Yasnaya Polyana, his continence
had begun to prey upon him. There were so many serf-girls
in the house and village. Even when he avoided them he felt
attracted to them: the sway of a skirt, glow of a bare arm,
sweat-stain on a shirt clinging to a body. ... His periods of
concupiscence and asceticism always alternated in rapid succession. He was two men – a sybarite and a saint – sewed
up inside one skin, each loathing the other. After struggling to remain pure for three days, he gave in: 'April 18.
Could not hold out. I motioned to something pink which
looked very nice from a distance. I opened the back door.
She came in. Now I can't stand to see her any more; everything is vile and ugly; I hate her, because she drove me to
break my resolution. ... I bitterly repent of it. I have never
felt it so strongly as now.'

The day after his 'relapse', his brother Nicholas, sister
Marya and brother-in-law Valerian Tolstoy arrived at Yasnaya Polyana. It was a momentous occasion for Leo.
Nicholas had already tried several times to explain to his
younger brother that the dissolute life he was leading in
Moscow was a mistake and that none of the alternatives he
proposed for getting himself out of his troubles was worthy
of him. This time he repeated his arguments, more emphati-
cally. According to him, of the three solutions advocated
by Leo the first (gambling) was simply ridiculous, the second
(a position in the administration) would require him – since
he did not have a university degree – to complete a tedious
two-year period of preparation in the provinces, and the
third (a rich marriage) was distasteful in the present and
perilous for the future. Since Lyovochka didn't seem to
know what to do with his excess energy, why didn't he come
to the Caucasus? The country was magnificent: hunting,
long horse rides, fraternity of the bivouacs, skirmishes with
the rebel mountain dwellers. ... As this captivating scene

unfolded, Leo felt his enthusiasm rise. Why hadn't he thought of it before? To triumph over his bad habits, there was only one remedy: the Caucasus!

Aunt Toinette bravely accepted this new whim, hoping that Lyovochka would mend his ways under the influence of Nicholas. A small family council was held to discuss the best way of managing the young man's affairs during his absence. His brother-in-law Valerian volunteered to take care of the estate, applying the income, by priority, to the repayment of his debts. The traveller would simply have to tighten his belt a notch or two. He was already determined to do so. The harder it was, the better he would like it.

Until the last minute, Aunt Toinette kept expecting another about-face. Once before, he had taken it into his head to follow Valerian when he was leaving for Siberia on business, and instantly had gone racing after the tarantass like a madman; then, noticing that he had come off without his hat, he turned back to the house and, suddenly deflated, began thinking of something else. ... What if he forgot his hat again this time? But he forgot nothing. On 20 April 1851 the two brothers, one in civilian dress and the other in uniform, said their good-byes to the old lady, who tried not to cry as she blessed them, and jumped into the coach. Tragic barking resounded through the house until the horses moved off: Leo had locked up his dog Bulka to prevent him from following them. At the first relay, as he was climbing back into the tarantass, he saw a black ball rolling down the road – it was Bulka, without his brass collar. 'He came running like the wind and threw himself upon me, licked my hands, and then went to lie down in the shadow of the coach,' Tolstoy wrote. 'Afterwards I learned he had pushed out the windowpanes, jumped out and, following my scent, covered the twelve miles at a dead run in the suffocating heat.'[17] He could not bring himself to send the dog back, so he settled him on his knees and they pursued their journey with an additional passenger, who had heaving flanks, a lolling tongue and blissful eyes.

As Nicholas had a month in which to rejoin his regiment, the two brothers made a detour by way of Moscow, where they spent two days visiting friends, going to restaurants, looking in on the gypsies in Sokolniki Park and playing in the gambling houses. The late-period Leo felt nothing but contempt for this debased world in which early-period Leo had experienced such potent joys. The singing girls with their medallions on their foreheads might flash their black eyes at him, glittering from the candle flames, to their hearts' content: he was made of stone. Immensely pleased with himself, he wrote to Aunt Toinette: 'I went among the common people, in the gypsies' tents. You can easily imagine the struggle that I waged there with myself, for and against; but I emerged victorious – that is, having given nothing more than my blessing to the joyous descendants of the illustrious pharaohs.'[18]

He confessed, however, that he had not been able to keep away from cards; and a good thing it was, too, for he won four hundred roubles. 'I am afraid this may alarm you. You will think I am playing and am going to play again. Do not worry, this was just one exception I allowed myself.'

Before they left, the two brothers had their photograph taken together in Maser's studio. In the daguerreotype, which has been preserved, we see Leo Tolstoy seated, his hands crossed on the pommel of his stick, his neck shortened by a badly knotted tie, with stiff hair, staring eyes, a rough, peasant face, and the shadow of a moustache above his upper lip; Nicholas has a sickly, triangular face with a mild expression, a lock of hair across his forehead, his shoulders artificially broadened by epaulettes, and seven brass buttons down his hollow chest. In spite of his uniform, he is the less martial-looking of the two.

The departure from Moscow probably took place at dawn after a farewell 'stag' supper, noisy and hearty, like the one Tolstoy described in *The Cossacks*. The coach awaiting him was a common tarantass, made at Yasnaya Polyana. The box of this chariot rested on eight long, flexible wooden poles, intended to serve as shock-absorbers. The front and rear wheels were set far enough apart to allow some play in the poles. The volume of piled-up baggage determined the amount of space left to the passengers. The whole badly-balanced contraption creaked at the slightest bump. In case of breakdown, vehicles of this type were repaired with an axe: there was always wood to cut along the side of the road. They went through a poor, dingy part of the city which Tolstoy had never seen. 'It seemed to him that only people setting out on journeys ever went down these streets,' he wrote of his hero Olenin. And, further on, 'Olenin was a young man who had never completed his studies anywhere, had no job ... had run through half his fortune and, at twenty-four, had not yet chosen a career and had never done a thing. He was what was known as a "young gentleman" in the high society of Moscow. . . . Now his imagination was turned to the future, to the Caucasus. His dreams were coloured by visions of Amalat-Beks, Circassian women, mountains and gorges, terrifying torrents, and danger.'[19]

On their way, the two brothers stopped to spend a week in Kazan with their Aunt Pelagya Yushkov. Leo Tolstoy found a childhood friend in town, Zinaida Molostvov, whom he had thought he was in love with in his university days. Seeing her again, he was not disappointed. She was not pretty, but she was lively, mischievous, witty. Her shining eyes overwhelmed him. He danced with her, went walking with her shoulder-to-shoulder, but never spoke of love; he wanted to carry this tender, pure memory away with him on his trip, to muse over nostalgically, lulled by the lurching coach and jingling bells. A few days later he wrote in his diary, 'Do you remember, Zina, the little side-path in the Archbishop's Garden? I nearly said it then, and so did you! It was for me to speak first. But do you know why, I think, I didn't? I was so happy that I wanted nothing more. I was afraid to spoil my happiness, or rather ours. ... Those delicious moments will remain among the finest memories of my life.'

From Kazan the Tolstoy brothers went, still by tarantass, to Saratov, where they loaded the coach on to a flatboat, hired a pilot and two oarsmen and abandoned themselves and their baggage to the current. The trip from Saratov to Astrakhan took three weeks, during which Tolstoy was deeply affected by the horizontal placidity of the banks, the silence of floating, the changing intensity of the sky reflected in the water. The Volga was swollen by the spring thaws and had overflowed her banks. The mornings were chilly, the sun swam slowly up out of the fog. Now and then they passed a heavy barge towed by ragged, singing boatmen; or a steamboat, churning the water with its flashing paddle wheel and blowing grey smoke, soon dissipated by the wind, up to the sky. Here and there white sails glided by with seraphic ease, and then along came a forester's raft with a wooden cabin built on a platform of rough-hewn tree trunks. At twilight the nightingales all began to sing at once, and did not stop, even when men came near. The boat was tied up and they spent the night ashore, and at dawn the crew returned to their oars. Leo strolled back and forth on the deck, read, argued with his brother and grew to like him better. 'Nicholas finds me a very pleasant travelling companion, except for my cleanliness; it makes him angry, as he says, to see me change my shirt a dozen times a day,' he wrote to Aunt Toinette. 'I find him, too, a very pleasant travelling companion, if only he weren't so dirty.'[20]

At Astrakhan the tarantass was unloaded, patched together and harnessed, and they took to the road again. They had one hundred and sixty-four miles to cover across the steppe before reaching the Starogladkovskaya *stanitsa* where Nicholas's regiment was quartered.

PART II

—

A TIME OF VIOLENCE

[6]

The Caucasus

SINCE the beginning of the century the eyes of every young Russian who dreamed of mystery, adventure and deeds of glory had been turned to the Caucasus. Alexander I had annexed the kingdom of Georgia in 1801, but the savage tribes who lived high in the mountains were still fighting the regular army troops sent to occupy their territory. The tsar's forces had set up a cordon of military posts on the left bank of the Terek and the right bank of the Kuban from which they could make gradual inroads into the rebels' land; the posts were held by Cossacks, and were known as *stanitsas*. Expeditions went out from these *stanitsas* to raid the *aouls*, or Circassian villages; they destroyed the pasture land, kidnapped the livestock, took as many prisoners as possible, and dashed back to camp. The riposte was swift and certain. Often, the Russians were ambushed before they could get back inside their lines. Or, just as the *stanitsa* was dropping peacefully off to sleep, warriors agile as devils would spring up out of nowhere in the midst of the camp, slit the guards' throats, bear off the screaming women and set fire to the huts. In the course of this last-ditch war, which had been going on for the past fifty years, Cossacks and mountain-dwellers had gradually acquired a kind of bitter esteem for each other. The most dreaded of the Caucasian tribes were those of Daghestan and Chechenya. Their leader, Shamil, had managed to convince his men that they were engaged in a holy war against the Christian invader; for these fanatics, death was Allah's reward.

Although he knew the Caucasian poems of Pushkin and Lermontov by heart, Tolstoy was sure a revelation lay in store for him. When would he finally see those snowy peaks he had heard so much about? One evening the postilion

waved his whip at some greyish shapes that stood out
against a background of cloud. He was disappointed. But
upon awakening the following morning to the distant white
architecture in the limpid sky, he felt an almost religious
thrill of joy. They began to meet occasional Cossacks on
horseback; high up on the other side of the Terek, thin
plumes of smoke identified the enemy *aouls*. Tolstoy took it
all in, but he was not going to be tempted by any
postcard prettiness. To look closer, weigh one's words,
tell the exact truth, already seemed to him, at twenty-
two, to be the key to art, and perhaps to human relations as
well.

When, on 30 May 1851, he entered the Starogladkovskaya *stanitsa*, he was appalled: a tiny Cossack encampment at the bottom of a hollow, encircled by woods, copses
and thickets, with little houses on stilts, a watchtower, an
old cannon on a wooden gun-carriage, an alarm bell and
a few shops where sunflower seeds, gingerbread and lengths
of cloth were sold. That evening he wrote in his diary, 'How
on earth have I ended up here? I don't know. Why? I know
even less!'[1] And a little later, he wrote to Aunt Toinette (in
French): 'I was expecting the country to be very beautiful,
but it isn't at all. The *stanitsa* is on low ground, so there is no
view, and the quarters are inadequate, along with every
other amenity of life. As for the officers: they are, as you
can imagine, an ignorant lot, but very decent fellows otherwise and, above all, devoted to Nicholas.'

He had no time for further complaint. A week after he
arrived Nicholas was sent with a detachment to Fort Stary
Yurt, to protect the patients being treated at the hot springs
in the nearby village of Goryachevodsk, and thither Leo
Tolstoy followed his brother. This time, he met the real
Caucasus, the one he had dreamed about and begun to
doubt the existence of, down in the hollow at Starogladi-
kovskaya. Sheer rock, dizzying paths, steam-draped boiling
waterfalls. Three mills, one on top of the other, stood over
the main stream, whose water was so hot that it would cook

an egg in three minutes. The Tatar women did their laundry there, and squeezed the water out by jumping up and down. Seated on the bank with his pipe in his mouth, Tolstoy delighted in the scene. He could not resist describing it to Aunt Toinette, but he emphasized the purely artistic quality of his admiration: 'It is like an anthill in perpetual movement. Most of the women are handsome and well built. Despite their poverty, their oriental dress is attractive. The picturesque groups they form, coupled with the wild beauty of the place, make a truly splendid sight. I often spend hours admiring this scene.'[2]

Even in his tent at night, the charm of this life of freedom occupied his thoughts. His head filled with all the things he had seen, it seemed to him that his communion with nature brought him closer to God. Nevertheless, he refused to yield to grandiloquence. How to reconcile the loftiness of his feelings with simplicity of expression? The preoccupations of the artist mingled with the preoccupations of the Christian. He wrote in his diary, 'I don't know how other people think, but everything I have heard and read proves to me that they do not think as I do. They declare that the beauties of nature make them conscious of the immensity of God and the insignificance of man; lovers see the image of their beloved in the water; others say *the mountains seem to speak, the leaves say this and that, the trees are calling to us. . . .* How do such ideas take root in people's brains?'[3] The thoughts that came into his head, when he let himself be carried away by his imagination, were, in his opinion, either trivial or untrue. But when he tried to tell what he saw and felt in plain, everyday words, it seemed to him that there was indeed a mystery in the commonplace, and greatness in what was least. Could it be that in literature as in morality, simplicity was a paying proposition?

When everyone else in camp lay sleeping, he jotted down a few sketchy notes, which could presumably be of interest to no one.

The night is clear. A cool breeze passes through the tent and makes the candle flame waver. Far away, the *aoul* dogs are barking and the sentries are calling out to each other. The air is full of the fragrance of the oak- and plane-tree leaves used to thatch the tent. I sit on a drum in a little shed adjoining the tent. ... Everything in there is dark, except for one bar of light falling across the end of my brother's bed. But just in front of me, in full light, a pistol, sabres, a sword and a pair of underpants are hanging on a partition. Silence. A gust of wind. A gnat buzzes past my ear. Close by, a soldier coughs and sighs.[4]

He did not feel like sleeping, but the observation of scenic details was no longer enough. Out of the silent night, sleeping men, and flickering candle flame that lighted the dome of dried, plaited leaves, a feeling of happiness and sorrow arose and spread through him. Suddenly his childhood prayers rose to his lips.

I was not praying [he wrote], if prayer is taken to mean entreaty or a gush of gratitude. I was yearning for something higher, something perfect. But what? I could not say. And yet, I understood exactly what I wanted. I wanted to become one with the supreme Being. I begged him to forgive my errors. No; I was not begging, because I felt that if he had granted me this minute of ecstasy, that meant he had already forgiven me. ... All my fears vanished. Faith, Hope and Love merged into one indissoluble feeling inside me.

As always, ebb followed flow. Just when Tolstoy thought he was at the summit of mystical bliss, a more profane vision crept into his mind: 'I could not feel my own body. I was pure spirit. And then, the wretched carnal side took over again, and hardly an hour later I was listening to the voices of vice, ambition, vanity, life. I knew where these voices came from, I knew they were destroying my happiness; I struggled, I lost. I fell asleep dreaming of fame and women. But I am not to blame, it was stronger than I.'

These bursts of religion, inspired by the beauty of the land and ending in the arms of an imaginary woman, occurred frequently. Tolstoy also thought about death, and made an effort to treat all things with philosophical detachment, which did not prevent him from eagerly awaiting the arrival of a new saddle or despairing because his moustache rose higher on the left side than on the right. His position in camp was highly irregular. As the only civilian in a group of officers, he passed for an idle aristocrat, an irresponsible tourist. He did not like his brother's comrades, or his superiors. They were rough and ignorant, their only subjects of conversation were horses, women, promotions and deeds of heroism. Lieutenant-Colonel Alexeyev, commander of the battery, was a little fellow with reddish-brown hair, cheeks coarsened by sideburns and a piercing voice. He was a fervent Orthodox who preached temperance and invited his subordinates to dine with him 'informally'. There was also the young Buyemsky – almost a child, with a candid pink face – and Khilkovsky, captain of the Ural Cossacks – a typical 'old soldier, simple but noble, brave and good'[5] – and a certain Lieutenant Knoring, a tall man with a broad, soft face and high cheekbones, looking a good deal, Tolstoy wrote, like the kind of horse that is known as 'hammerhead'.[6] When he laughed, he looked 'simple-minded and slightly mad'. His manners were vulgar. He pummelled Nicholas and called him 'old snout!' Tolstoy gave him a very cold shoulder for a few days; then he became used to his laughter, his smell of bad tobacco and his fishwife's jokes.

Lieutenant-Colonel Alexeyev might forbid the serving of alcohol at his table, but the men made up for lost time in their tents. Sometimes Nicholas drank himself into a stupor. Leo exercised as much self-restraint as he could, and he also refrained from playing cards. 'Several times, when the officers have talked of cards in front of me, I have felt like showing them that I too know how to play; but I resisted. I hope I shall go on refusing, even if they drag me bodily to the table.' He wrote these words in his diary on the morning of 13 June, and that evening he owed 850 roubles* to

* Around $2,400.

Lieutenant Knoring. 'Two hundred roubles of my own, 150 borrowed from Nicholas; leaving 500.' How to pay? He would worry about that later – Knoring had generously taken an I O U for a date in the distant future (January 1852) – but for the moment (well-timed diversion!), the camp was busy preparing for an expedition against the mountain tribes. Eager to see some action, Tolstoy asked for and obtained permission from Prince Baryatinsky, commander of the left flank of the Caucasian Army, to take part in the operation as a volunteer.

In the second half of June the troops began to move: an infantry battalion, all available cavalry, nineteen cannon, supply wagons and ammunition. A long, dark snake bristling with bayonets crawled along a precipitous trail. The drums rolled in the distance. The soldiers sang. Tolstoy, riding near his brother, felt his heart pound with the excitement of the morning of a great ball. At every halt the soldiers stacked their arms and rushed to the stream to drink. Lieutenant-Colonel Alexeyev, sitting on a drum, invited his subordinates to share his meal. A few officers withdrew to the shade of a tree with vodka, glasses and cards. 'I was curious to hear the conversation of the soldiers and officers,' Tolstoy wrote in his autobiographical story *The Raid*: 'I watched their faces closely; in none of them did I see any trace of the vague fear I was feeling myself. Joking, laughter, gay banter, gambling and drink expressed a universal indifference to the approaching danger. It was as though it were impossible to imagine that some of these men would not be coming back by this same road – it was as though all of them had already left the world long ago.' A little later, when the detachment was slithering through a deep gorge, the enemy outposts opened fire. The hillsmen howled fiercely, but their shots were harmless at that distance. After fording the stream, the Russians regrouped in the forest and the general gave the order to attack. The firing became steady. Men fell. 'What a pretty sight!' said Prince Baryatinsky in French. And his aide-de-camp, anxious to please, outdid him – also in French – with: 'It's a real pleasure to make war in such beautiful country!'[7] The cannon joined in. The cavalry disappeared into the underbrush, raising a cloud of dust. Abandoned by its inhabitants, the enemy *aoul* was soon plundered. 'A roof collapses, an axe rings out against hard wood, a door bursts open; a heap of straw goes up in flame. ... A Cossack drags a sack of flour and a rug out of a hut; a grinning soldier carries off an iron jug and a towel; another, spreading his arms, tries to catch two hens that are cackling and struggling to get over a palisade; a third has found an enormous crock of milk, and he empties it and hurls it to the ground with a howl of laughter.'[8]

On the way home, the hillsmen duly attacked the column in the forest. The Russians countered and young Tolstoy, aglow with patriotism, noted the great superiority of Russian courage – silent and dignified – over the strained and ostentatious bravery of the French, as exemplified by the heroes of Waterloo. 'After that, how is one not to suffer, in his Russian heart, when he hears our young officers uttering tasteless French phrases and trying to imitate the so-called French gallantry which has become so woefully obsolete?'[9] he wrote. At last the shooting subsided, the column resumed its march and, once back in camp, Tolstoy learned to his intense delight that Prince Baryatinsky had been pleased at the 'young civilian's' composure under fire. He himself was not altogether satisfied, however. The razing of the *aoul* preyed on his mind, as did the three dead and thirty-six wounded in the expedition. 'It is so good to be alive,' he thought, 'nature is so beautiful, and men so evil; they do not know how to appreciate what they have!'[10]

At Fort Stary Yurt he returned to his book about his childhood, but he thought he would never have the patience to finish it. 'You have to sit down at an ink-stained table,' he wrote, 'take a sheet of grey paper, an inkwell, dirty your fingers, line up letters on the paper in a row; the letters make words, and the words make sentences. But is it possible to translate a feeling? To transmit one's own ideas about nature to someone else? Why are poetry and prose, joy and sorrow so closely related?'[11] His thoughts drifted back to Zinaida Molostvov, whom he had left in Kazan without daring to avow his love. Absurd regrets gnawed at him in his solitude. 'Is it possible that I shall never see her again?' he wrote. 'Is it possible that one day I shall hear she has married some Beketov or other? Or, still more dreadful, shall I see her again, wearing a bonnet and laughing, with her same wide-open eyes, gay and full of love? I have not given up my plan of going back and marrying her; I am not quite certain that she can make me happy, but I am in love with her. ... Otherwise, what is the meaning of the sweet memories that fill me? ... Why not write to her? But I only know her first name and not that of her father.* And all because of that, I may be depriving myself of a great happiness!'[12]

When his ardour cooled, he forgot all about his matrimonial plans and began seriously considering joining the army. But there again, he did not want to be too hasty. At the beginning of August his detachment returned to the Starogladkovskaya *stanitsa* and he took advantage of this momentary lull to revise his life principles once more:

On August 28 – my birthday – I shall be twenty-three years old. From that day forward I want to live according to the goal I have set myself. Tomorrow I shall think about all this at leisure; but, starting right now, I shall return to my diary, write down my schedule of activities, and make a table summarizing the faults I have to correct, according to Franklin's method. ... Beginning at sunrise I shall do my accounts and organize my papers and books and work in progress; then I shall collect my thoughts and begin to copy the first chapter of my book.[13] After lunch (I shall eat little), study of the Tatar language, drawing, marksmanship, gymnastics and reading.[14]

As he set down these directives in his diary for the twen-

* It was an absolutely elementary rule of courtesy in Russia that a person must be addressed by his own first name, followed by that of his father.

tieth time, Tolstoy was doubtless unaware that he had inherited his mania from his mother, whom he could not
remember: when she was young she, too, had been much
preoccupied by her words and deeds, and had written edifying maxims and attempted to transform her moral principles
into an exact science. But she, in so doing, was thinking of
the happiness of her loved ones, whereas Tolstoy, eternally
concerned with himself, was aiming only at his own
improvement.

Life at Starogladkovskaya was quiet, but not dull. It was
the psychology of the inhabitants, rather than the relatively ordinary countryside, that fascinated Leo Tolstoy.
Nothing in common with the resigned and cunning muzhiks of Yasnaya Polyana. The Cossacks had never been serfs,
and valued freedom and bravery above all else. They hated
the hillsman who killed their brother less than the simple
Russian soldier who was camping on their land to help them
defend their village. Their best weapons and finest horses
were bought or stolen from their enemies. Out of affection, they even aped the hillsmen's dress and willingly
spoke their language. 'And even so,' wrote Tolstoy, 'this
little Christian nation buried in a remote corner of the
world, surrounded by half-savage Moslem tribes and soldiers, considered itself to possess a high degree of civilization and did not acknowledge anyone as a real man who
was not also a Cossack.' [15] In all the *stanitsas* scattered along
the river, the men divided their time between turns on
guard duty, campaign service, fishing and hunting, thus
leaving the hardest domestic chores to the women – which
only increased their authority in the household. Although
the Cossack men pretended to treat their women like slaves,
oriental fashion, they actually respected and feared them.
The women wore the Circassian costume – Tatar shirt, short
stitched jacket, light, flat-heeled shoes – but they tied kerchiefs around their heads in the Russian manner. Their
homes were clean. Unmarried girls were allowed much freedom in their relations with men.

Leo Tolstoy lived with an old Cossack named Epishka
(Epiphany Sekhin), who had taken an immediate liking to
him. At ninety, Epishka was a hearty hulk of a man with a
bulging chest, Herculean shoulders and a wide beard as
white as a swan's plumage. Enchanted with this character,
Tolstoy transplanted him bodily into *The Cossacks*, under
the name of Uncle Eroshka:

He wore a ragged smock stuffed into his trousers, deerskin shoes
laced over the bands wrapped around his calves, and a stiff little
white fur bonnet. Slung across his back on one side were a
pheasant-decoy and a bag containing a pullet and a merlin for
luring hawks, and on the other, dangling from a strap, was a
wildcat he had killed; from his belt hung little pouches for
bullets, gunpowder and bread, a horse's tail to drive off the mosquitoes, a big dagger in a torn sheath stained with old blood,
and two dead pheasants.[16]

Tolstoy spent long evenings with his host, who waxed
loquacious in his cups. Elbows on the table, face brick-red,
eyes sparkling in a network of deep wrinkles, Epishka talked
on and on, and around him a complex aroma began to
thicken, 'strong, but not at all unpleasant, compounded of
chikhir,* vodka, gunpowder and congealed blood'.[17] He told
of his wild youth, his battles and hunts. He had never
worked with his hands. Nature had always provided for
him. He was a drunkard, a pillager, and an expert at catching horses in the hills, and he feared neither man nor beast:
'Look at me, I'm as poor as Job, I have no wife nor garden
nor children, nothing – just a gun, a sparrow hawk and
three dogs, but I have never complained of anything and I
never shall. I live in the forest, I look around me – everything I see is mine. I come home and I sing a song.'[18]
Sitting across from his young guest, who was asking himself
so many questions about good and evil, he also said, with a
roar of laughter that tore his white beard apart, 'God created
everything for the joy of man. There is no such thing as
sin anywhere. Do as the animals do. They live in the

*A primitive red wine.

Tatar's bullrushes and in ours. Their home is where they are. What God gives them, they eat!'[19] From there it was only a step to claiming that it was wrong to worry about seducing girls, and Epishka took it in his stride. He even offered to procure distraction for Tolstoy. And when the young man halfheartedly objected to such practices, he cried, 'Where's the sin in it? Is it a sin to look at a pretty girl? Have a good time with her? Is it a sin to love her? Is that how things are where you live? No, my friend, that's no sin, it's salvation! God created you, and he created the girls, too. So it is no sin to look at a pretty girl. She was created to be loved and to give pleasure!'[20]

How long did Tolstoy resist Epishka's counsel? Trying to subdue the demands of the flesh, he went out hunting with the old pander. Game was abundant – pheasant, bustard, snipe, teal, grey hare, fox, and even buffalo, deer and wolf. All went well as long as he was out in the blind, but once back in the *stanitsa* the young man's heart raced at the mere smell of the smoke from the fires of the village huts. He stared at the fair-skinned, black-eyed girls, imagined the outline of a panting breast beneath a blouse. Some of them came prowling around the soldiers' huts in the evening and sold themselves for a few coins; others wanted a little persuasion before they would let themselves be pushed down on to a bed of leaves, mouth open and eyes closed. In his diary, Tolstoy recorded the fluctuating temperature of his lust: 'Last night a Cossack girl came to see me. I hardly slept all night. ...'[21] 'That drunkard Epishka told me Salomonida looked like an easy mark. I would want to take her away and scrub her first. ...'[22] 'I absolutely must have a woman. Lechery gives me no peace. ...'[23] 'I have no perseverance or stability in anything. If I persevered in my passions for women I would have conquests and memories to look back on; if I persevered in my abstinence I could be proud of my self-control. Eschew wine and women. The pleasure one gets from them is so slight and uncertain and the remorse so great! ...'[24] 'No, that's all wrong! My desires are natural. I only find fault with them because I am in an unnatural position: unmarried at twenty-three! Nothing can help me, except will-power and my prayers to God to save me from temptation.'[25]

After a few days of heroic self-denial, he again asked Epishka to arrange a rendezvous for him. But these venal affairs, soon begun and sooner ended, could not satisfy him. He was longing for a real passion, exotic, romantic, with some native woman. And he found it, with the haughty Maryanka – who became the Maryanka of *The Cossacks*. 'She was not pretty, she was beautiful. Her features might have seemed almost masculine and coarse, had it not been for her tall, well-proportioned figure, her powerful chest and shoulders, and above all the expression, tender and severe at once, of her wide black eyes, ringed by dark shadows, beneath black brows. She radiated virginal strength and health.'[26] When he watched her at work, shovel in hand, shivers of desire ran through him. Hoping to approach her, he made friends with her father. He even contemplated marriage. After all, would it not be wiser to forsake the artificial allures of civilization and discover the true meaning of life with a woman whose mind had not been contaminated by the West? 'Perhaps it is nature I love in her, the expression of everything beautiful in nature,' said his *alter ego* Olenin in *The Cossacks*. 'Loving her, I feel myself an indivisible part of the good Lord's whole happy universe.' And, 'The instant I imagine those drawing-rooms, those women with their pomaded hair held up by artificial curls, those unnatural mouths, weak, camouflaged, deformed limbs, and that sophisticated babble that is mistakenly thought to be conversation, in the place of my little hut, my woods and my love, I am overcome with revulsion.' How far did Tolstoy go in his intimacy with the young Cossack girl? His diary does not tell. It is likely, after a few nocturnal walks, a few bashful kisses, a few vows exchanged, half in Russian and half in Tatar, that he realized it was all an invention on his part. 'Ah, if only I could become a Cossack,' sighed Olenin-alias-Tolstoy, 'steal horses, get drunk on *chikhir*, sing songs, kill people and, dead drunk, go climbing in at her window and spend the night without asking who or why I am – then it would be different, then she and I could understand each other, then I could be happy.'[27] In any event, he had got hold of a first-class subject for a novel! The mad passions of his characters would console him for his own exemplary conduct; there was nothing to equal therapy-by-writing. But he would think about the Cossacks later; first, he had to get on with his *Childhood*, a mixture of fiction and fact. To put himself in the mood, Tolstoy talked to his brother about their early years at Yasnaya Polyana and in Moscow. Although Nicholas had become an inveterate drinker, he was still an authority to his younger brother, even on literature. With Nicholas's help, he was sure of success. But he lacked patience. He was continually torn from his worktable by some welcome distraction. After Stary Yurt, he returned to cards with a vengeance. He had not finished paying Lieutenant Knoring when he suffered fresh losses; he was borrowing from his right hand to pay back his left, and he began waking up in the middle of the night to go over his accounts. Each time, he sat down to play in the hope that a lucky run would put him back on his feet. During one of these heartbreaking evenings, he befriended a young Chechenian, Sado, who lived in the Russian-controlled neighbouring *aoul* and often came to the camp to play with the officers.

'His father,' Tolstoy wrote to Aunt Toinette, 'is quite a rich man, but he has buried all his money and won't give his son a cent. To get money, the son goes over to steal horses and cattle from the enemy; sometimes he risks his life twenty times to steal something that isn't worth ten roubles; but he does it for glory, not because he covets the things he steals. The biggest thief is respected here, and called a *dzhigit*, or brave. Some days Sado has a thousand silver roubles on him, others not a kopeck.'[28]

As Sado did not know how to count, his opponents at cards fleeced him unmercifully. Tolstoy rebuked them heat-

edly and took the young man under his wing, in return for
which Sado, wild with gratitude, offered to be his *kunak*,
that is, his life-and-death friend. According to Caucasian
tradition, if your *kunak* asks you for your money, your horse,
your weapon or your wife, you cannot refuse him, just as he
must give you anything you fancy in his house. The two
young men exchanged gifts to seal this precious bond of
companionship. Sado gave Tolstoy a purse, a silver bridle, an
oriental sabre worth a hundred roubles and, a little later,
a horse. Tolstoy, less liberal, responded with an old gun,
bought for eight roubles long before, and a watch. The fact
was that his circumstances were at their most straitened during this period. The five-hundred-rouble I O U he had given
Lieutenant Knoring fell due in January 1852: the fateful
day was drawing near and he saw no possibility of meeting
his obligation. As a last resort, he tried to interest God in
his case. 'When I said my prayers this evening,' he wrote to
Aunt Toinette, 'I prayed to God very fervently to get me out
of this unpleasant situation. "But how can I get out of it?" I
thought as I went to bed. "Nothing can happen that will
enable me to pay this debt." I was already imagining all the
unpleasantness I would have to suffer on account of it: he
(Knoring) would lodge a complaint, my superiors would
demand an explanation, why don't I pay up, etc. "Help me,
Lord!" I said as I fell asleep.'[29]

And the miracle occurred. While Tolstoy was fretting,
alone and insolvent by the light of his candle, Sado was
playing cards with some officers at Stary Yurt and winning
back from Knoring the I O U signed by his *kunak*. The next
day he brought it to Nicholas Tolstoy, who was also at
Stary Yurt on a mission, and said to him, 'What do you
think of that? Will your brother be pleased that I did it?'
When he received Nicholas's letter announcing the good
news, Tolstoy was struck dumb with gratitude. He looked at
the torn I O U in the envelope and did not know whether to
thank God or Sado for this last-minute reprieve. 'Isn't it
astonishing to see one's wish granted the very next day?' he

wrote to Aunt Toinette. 'That is, the only astonishing thing is the existence of divine mercy for a being who has deserved it as little as I. And isn't Sado's devotion wonderful?' [30]

He instructed Aunt Toinette to buy a pistol, six bullets and a little music box for Sado in Tula, 'if it doesn't cost too much'. Singular concern for economy in a man just rescued from a truly serious predicament! When he received the presents, he found them so much to his liking that he could hardly bear to part with them. The music box in particular charmed him with its melancholy ritornello: 'I am sorry to send it to Sado. Nonsense. Off it goes!' [31]

It was making Tolstoy increasingly uncomfortable to be a civilian among soldiers – a little as though he were refusing to help his hosts with their housework. He did not fancy himself in the role of a parasite. Still less that of a cad. 'Prince Baryatinsky thinks very highly of you,' said his brother. 'I think you have made a good impression on him and he would like to have you as a recruit.' The promise of such lofty backing removed Tolstoy's last doubts. He wrote to Tula for the necessary papers to enlist and set off with his brother to Tiflis, where he could take the induction examination. He became ecstatic as they travelled along the Georgian military road through the Caucasus. Rock cliffs hung out over the roadway, the strangled Terek roared below at the bottom of the gorge, eagles sheared through the narrow strip of sky above their heads, there were glimpses of snowy peaks and clinging villages, the stone was cool, the native *arbas* creaked, everything spoke of freedom, endless space and wildness.

He arrived in Tiflis only to be told by General Brimmer that the papers from Tula were insufficient; to complete his file, he needed a certificate from the governor of the province stating that he was no longer a civil servant. Disappointed, he decided to wait for the document there and, letting his brother return to Starogladkovskaya alone, he rented a room in a modest house in the suburbs – the fav-

ourite haunt of the German colony,[32] among the vine-
yards and gardens on the left bank of the Kura.

South of the German settlement, on the same side of the
river, the native quarter spread along the mountainside:
steep narrow streets, houses with overhanging balconies, a
languid sibilant throng in which veiled Moslem women
brushed against Persians with scarlet-painted fingernails and
high hairdresses, Tatar mollahs in loose gowns and green or
white turbans, hillsmen from the conquered tribes wearing
Cherkesska belted at the waist. The hieratic camels' heads
swayed above the crowd. It was hot, even in November. The
air smelled of dirt, honey, incense and leather. On the right
bank of the Kura lay the Russian town, clean, neat and
administrative, exhaling the tedium of a provincial capital
beneath the sun. Occasionally Tolstoy would go to the
theatre or the Italian opera, but he immediately regretted
the few roubles he had spent on his ticket. His disposition
was sour for two reasons: he was short of money and he
was ill – which of the Cossack girls at the *stanitsa* had left
him this searing remembrance of a night of love? Furious,
he began a three-week course of treatment. 'My illness has
cost me dear enough,' he wrote to his brother Nicholas.
'Druggist: twenty roubles; twenty visits to the doctor; and
now cotton wadding and the cab every day are costing me
another one hundred and twenty. I am telling you all these
details so you will send me as much money as you can in a
hurry. ... The venereal infection has been cured, but the
after-effects of the mercury are painful beyond belief.[33] The
inside of my mouth and tongue are covered with sores.
Without exaggerating, I am now in my second week without eating or sleeping for a single full hour.' Five days later
he also described his condition to Aunt Toinette; but this
time, out of consideration for the old spinster, his pen transformed the venereal disease into 'a kind of high fever that
has kept me in bed for three weeks'.[34]

This period of forced inactivity was beneficial. Far from
his world of the present, he plunged voluptuously back into

the story of his childhood. 'Do you remember, dear Aunt,' he wrote to Aunt Toinette, 'a piece of advice you gave me long ago: to write novels? Well, I am taking your advice and literature has now become my occupation. I do not know whether what I write will ever appear publicly but it is something I very much enjoy doing, and have kept at it too long now to abandon it.'[35]

As his health improved, he began going out more often, met a few friends, played billiards – losing more than a thousand games to a master marksman[36] – and hunted with fervour:

The hunting here is magnificent, [he wrote to his brother Sergey on 23 December 1851]. Open country, little swamps full of grey hare, islets covered with bullrushes instead of trees, where the foxes are hiding. I have gone out nine times in all, at a distance of eight to ten miles from the Cossack village, with two dogs, one first-rate and the other worthless; I have bagged two foxes and sixty or so hares. When I come back here I shall have a go at deer-hunting on horseback. [And he added casually,] If you want to impress everyone with the latest news from the Caucasus, you can tell them that the most important person around after Shamil, one Hadji Murad – has just surrendered to the Russian government.[37] The boldest (a *dzhigit*) and bravest man in all Chechenya has committed an act of cowardice.

The official papers were long in coming and Tolstoy chafed at being forced to continue wearing civilian clothes – an overcoat from Sharmer and a ten-rouble top hat – when every fibre of his body had already been militarized. It was all he could do to keep from saluting when he saw a general pass. To humour his impatience, the commanding officer at the recruitment centre agreed to give him a provisional assignment that would become final upon receipt of the exeat from the governor of Tula. Tolstoy was attached to the 20th Artillery Brigade, 4th battery (his brother's). A mock examination, held on 3 January 1852, entitled him to the rank of cadet or *junker*. Donning his uniform, he felt curiously happy 'not to be free any more'. His erratic

behaviour and unstable nature may at last have been beginning to alarm even himself. The only salvation he could see
lay in discipline, imposed by superior officers, and in the
gift of his person to the army, to help annihilate 'the cunning pillagers and rebel Asiatics'.[38] On the way to Starogladkovskaya he stopped at the Mozdok post station, where
he was suddenly seized by doubt. Had he been right to
choose the military career? From the posthouse he wrote to
Aunt Toinette:

'A year ago I thought that entertainment and gadding
about were my only source of happiness; now, on the contrary, serenity, both physical and mental, is what I long
for.'[39] To be sure, he admitted that his unmotivated jaunt
to the Caucasus had probably been inspired by God and that
everything that happened to him there would accordingly
be for the good of his soul, but he still believed he would
return to Yasnaya Polyana one day to satisfy his true
destiny, as a peace-loving man with a full quota of family,
learning and virtue. Curious cadet, this, who longs to resign
from his post the moment he receives it, and immediately
begins expounding the joys of carpet-slippered retirement
to his aunt, in the following terms:

After an indefinite number of years, neither old nor young,
I am at Yasnaya – my affairs are in order, I have no worries or
problems; you are living at Yasnaya too. You have grown a little
older but you are still active and well. We live the life we lived
before, I work in the morning but we see each other almost all
day long: we have dinner, I read something amusing to you in
the evening, and then we talk. I tell you about my life in the
Caucasus and you tell me your memories – of my father and
mother – you tell me the 'terrible tales' we used to listen to with
frightened eyes and mouth agape. ... We will have no social
life – nobody will come to bother us or gossip to us. A beautiful
dream; but I let my dreams go farther than that. I am married
– my wife is a gentle, good, loving person, she loves you as I do.
We have children who call you 'Grandmaman'. You live in the
big house. The whole house is the way it was when Papa was
alive, and we begin the same life over again, only the parts are

changed; you play Grandmother's part, but you are even better than she; I play Papa's part, although I despair of ever being worthy of it; my wife plays the part of Maman and the children ours. Marya plays the two aunts, without their miseries. Even Gasha will take the part of Prascovya Isayevna. But one person will be missing, to play the part you did in our family. There will never be another soul as fine and loving as yours. You will have no successor. There will be three new characters who will make an occasional appearance on the scene – the brothers; and one in particular will often be with us: Nicholas. An elderly bachelor, bald, retired from the army, still as fine and noble as ever. I picture to myself how he will tell the children stories he will make up as he used to do, how the children will kiss his filthy hands (which deserve to be covered with kisses), how he will play with them, how my wife will cook his favourite dishes for him, how we will all talk over our memories together, how you will sit in your usual place and be happy listening to us, how you will call us, the old ones, Lyovochka and Nikolenka,* as always, and how you will scold us – I because I eat with my hands and he because he hasn't washed his. . . . All of this could happen, and hope is so sweet a thing. Here I am crying again. Why do I cry when I think of you? These are tears of happiness. I am happy to know how to love you.[40]

The persom writing these lines in the posthouse at Mozdok, with moist eyes and a heart aching with tenderness, was the same little boy who, when punished by Prosper de St Thomas, invented a heroic future to console himself for being locked up in the dark closet; the virgin student of Kazan, too timid to talk to the girls, living on prodigious fairytales of love with H E R, the ideal woman; the Moscow playboy going off to the Caucasus to massacre the hillsmen, seduce a Circassian slave and teach her to read French in *Notre-Dame de Paris*:[41] the same eternally galloping imagination, the serpentine embroidery of every thought, the need to embellish the future in order to compensate for the present. The fact that he was in the process of writing his childhood memories made him doubly vulnerable to nostalgia for the past. The more he thought of the scenery

*Diminutives of Leo and Nicholas.

and people that had witnessed his first years, the more sorely he needed to see them.

On 14 January 1852, however, what he saw was not Yasnaya Polyana, but the Starogladkovskaya *stanitsa* with its white houses on stilts, watchtower, shops, laughing girls and easy-going Cossacks. ... Alas! his brother Nicholas was already on the march. He set off to join him at once, and spent the entire month of February 1852 in marches, counter-marches, and skirmishes. 'I am indifferent to life: it has given me too little joy for me to love it; therefore I am not afraid of death,' he wrote in his diary on 5 February 1852. 'Nor am I afraid of pain. What I am afraid of is not being able to bear pain and death with dignity.' Nearly every day they traded fire with sharpshooters perched in the rocks or buried in the depths of the forest. On 17 February, in the capture of the Kozmy, Lyachi and Indy *aouls*, and on 18 February in the attack on the Chechenian positions on the banks of the Michik River, cadet Tolstoy bore himself with composure. An enemy ball tore off one wheel of the cannon he was serving; another killed a horse two feet away from him. As the enemy's aim was becoming increasingly accurate, Nicholas, who commanded the battery, ordered it to retreat and continue firing. The exhausted soldiers had to thread their way between detachments of hillsmen who picked them off as they went. 'The fear I experienced at that moment was the greatest I have ever known,' Tolstoy said years later, in 1900. 'At last we came to the Cossack camp. For supper, in the open, there was a roasted kid, the most succulent I have ever eaten. We all slept in the same cabin, eight men side by side. But the air was delicious ... like the kid!' [42] The next morning, thinking back over his behaviour, Tolstoy's judgement was severe. 'Danger opened my eyes,' he wrote in his diary on 28 February 1852. 'I wanted to believe that I was perfectly calm and in command of myself. But the engagements of the seventeenth and eighteenth did not confirm this.' Dissatisfied with himself, he was nevertheless furious to learn that his superiors, who wanted to nominate him for the St George Cross, had been forced to remove his name from the list for the idiotic reason that he was still not officially in the army. That confounded exeat that wouldn't come! What were they doing in their offices back home? He would complain to Aunt Toinette: 'I frankly confess that this one little cross is the only one of all the military honours I was vain enough to desire and this incident has infuriated me beyond words, especially as there is only one opportunity to receive it and now I've lost my chance.'[43]

Back at Starogladkovskaya, he began to neglect the army more and more. 'Marching and all this cannon practice are not much fun, especially because they upset the regularity of my life.'[44] His comrades found him haughty and distant. Often, instead of joining in their discussions, he ostentatiously read a book or stared off into space. He confided to his aunt that 'The education, feelings and attitudes of those I meet here are too different from mine for me to enjoy their company. Nicholas alone has the gift, despite the enormous differences between him and all these men, of amusing himself with them and being loved by all. I envy him this gift, but I know I cannot do the same.'[45] More than anything, Tolstoy suffered from having to follow the orders of the redhaired Alexeyev, whom he judged to be a pretentious, loudmouthed fool. The lieutenant-colonel set great store by his prerogatives, and vowed to bring the new cadet to heel. It was a tradition that the officers dined at their commanding officer's table. During meals, Tolstoy displayed a disrespectful degree of boredom, did not laugh at his host's jokes and left as soon as dessert was over, Alexeyev finally stopped inviting him. 'I no longer dine or have supper at Alexeyev's.' (Diary, 30 March 1852.) 'Alexeyev is such a bore that I shall never set foot in his place again.' (5 April 1852.) 'Received a rude and stupid note from Alexeyev in reference to my absence from drill. He is absolutely determined to prove that he can make trouble for me.' (8 April 1852.) 'Saw Alexeyev's conceited face at drill and was unable to keep back a smile.' (11 April 1852.) One day, however, dropping in at Alexeyev's, he was overcome with humiliation to see his brother sprawled out, dead drunk, by the table. 'It is a shame he does not realize how it pains me to see him drunk. ... The worst part of it for me is that people who are inferior to him judge him and pity him.' (31 March 1852.)

Once sobered up, however, this scrawny, balding brother with the teasing eye and dirty hands was the most delightful of companions. Leo read him everything he wrote. *Childhood*, his novel, was giving him trouble. He crossed out, wrote over, started again, and meditated on the difficult profession of author. 'My brother came,' he wrote in his diary on 27 March 1852. 'I read him what I had written at Tiflis. He thinks it is not as good as the rest and I think it is no good at all. ...' 'Definitely, I am convinced it is worthless. The style is too loose and there are too few ideas to make up for the shallowness of the rest.' (7 April.) 'It is an odd thing, but reading bad books helps me to detect my own faults more than good ones. Good books reduce me to despair'. (1 April 1852.)

The creative trials and tribulations of the beginner were intensified by the state of his health, which was far from good. Rheumatism, sore throat, toothache, enteritis, mysterious spells of weakness. ... After consulting a physician at Kizlyar and taking a cruise around the Caspian, he returned to Starogladkovskaya and applied for leave to undergo treatment in a neighbouring spa, preferably Pyatigorsk. Alexeyev, who did not bear grudges, gave him permission to go and even advanced him some money for the trip.

On 16 May, Tolstoy arrived, worn out, at Pyatigorsk, found lodgings outside the town in a house with a view of the snowy peak of Elbrus, and began treatment immediately. Rising at dawn, he took long sulphur baths, drank thermal water until it nauseated him, ate Turkish delight, slept in the afternoon and observed no improvement in his condition. The distractions offered by the little city, which was famous for its pure air, tidy little houses and magnifi-

cent setting, did not tempt him: walks along the boulevards
to the music of the orchestra, elegant chit-chat in the pastry
shops, theatrical performances, fashion competitions between officers on furlough and wealthy civilians, the
coquetry of ladies with too much time on their hands, intrigues, weddings, duels, picnics and cavalcades – to him it
all seemed a ridiculous parody of *'la vie parisienne'*.[46] Even
the advances of his pretty landlady left him unruffled. She
plays the flirt with me,' he wrote, 'she tends her flowers
under my window and hums songs, and all these thoughtful
little attentions interfere with my peace of mind. I thank
God for making me bashful; it saves me from sin.'[47] Had
his health been better, he would probably not have resisted
temptation. What an oddly made fellow he was: average
height (5ft 9in.), a stocky, solid body, sinews of steel, and
the nerves of a fainting female. When the least little thing
went wrong, he had a flush of fever or stomach cramps.
Even the escapades of his dog Bulka, who was a roving type,
threw him into exaggerated states of anxiety. One day when
he was afraid the animal had been shot by the police, his
nose began to bleed. He was so vexed because he could not
find a good copyist in Pyatigorsk that he developed a migraine. In the end, he turned over his rough drafts to his serf
Vanyushka, who copied them out as best he could. But
Vanyushka fell ill. New source of exasperation for the
young gentleman. No doubt about it: the whole world was
conspiring against him. Manfully making the best of it, he
cleaned his room himself, did the cooking and nursed his
servant devotedly. The only trouble was that by lolling in
bed and being served by his master the fellow was acquiring
a taste for laziness and saucy retorts. Once he was back on
his feet, he had to be threatened with the knout. But as Tolstoy had had Alyoshka, another of his servants,[48] flogged a
few weeks before, the warning bore fruit, and Vanyushka
went back to work. Thus, at the same time as he was congratulating himself on his growing love for the human race,
the young count was unable to forget either the distance

that separated him from his serfs or the best way of making them behave. On 29 June 1852 he enthusiastically noted in his diary, 'The man whose only goal is his own happiness is bad; he whose goal is the good opinion of others is weak; he whose goal is the happiness of others is good; he whose goal is God, is great! ...'

For the moment, he was not very sure which was his goal. One thing was sure: he was furiously working away at his novel. On 27 May 1852 he completed the third draft. And immediately started over again. 'Perhaps it will be like the labour of Penelope,' he wrote to Aunt Toinette on 30 May (in French), 'but that doesn't discourage me. I am not writing out of ambition, but because I like to; work gives me pleasure and a sense of purpose, and I am working.' The same day, he wrote in his diary, 'Do I have talent, in comparison with the new Russian writers? Assuredly not.' But, three days later (2 June), he qualified this categorical statement: 'I am not yet certain that I have no talent. I think what I lack is patience, skill, precision; nor do I have any grandeur of style, feeling or thought. On that last point, however, I will reserve my opinion.' While wearily and crossly revising the fourth draft of *Childhood* – 'in which there are sure to be spelling mistakes!' [49] – he began a story based on his military experience: *The Raid.*

He was putting the finishing touches to the last chapter of his novel when, on 1 July, he received a letter from his steward at Yasnaya Polyana, notifying him that Kopylev, the lumberman, was threatening to sue him in Moscow for defaulting in his payments. If this happened, the court might order the seizure of his property. 'I could lose Yasnaya Polyana,' he wrote in his diary that night, 'and in spite of all the philosophies in the world, that would be a dreadful blow for me. ... I ate dinner, wrote a little, badly, and did nothing useful at all. Tomorrow I shall finish *Childhood* and decide what to do with it. To bed at eleven-thirty.'

On the following days, he alerted his brother Sergey and begged him to deal with the matter of the outstanding payments,* read his manuscript over one last time, found it neither good nor bad, and decided, without much hope, to send it to a magazine. He could choose between *The Contemporary, Fatherland News* and *The Reading Library*. He opted for *The Contemporary*, which had been founded by Pushkin and was foremost among the monthly publications of the time. The famous poet Nekrasov was its director. On 3 July 1852 Leo Tolstoy wrote to him:

'Sir, the favour I am going to ask of you will demand so little of your time that I am sure you will not refuse me. Glance through this manuscript and, if it is not worth printing, send it back to me. Otherwise, tell me what you think of it, send me whatever amount you think it is worth and print it in your review. ... Actually, this is the first part of a novel that will cover four periods. The publication of the following parts will depend on the success of the first. I am eager to know your verdict. Either it will incite me to continue in my favourite occupation or it will oblige me to burn everything I have begun.'

The manuscript was entitled *Story of My Childhood* and both it and the letter bore the initials L.N. The reply, a postscript added, was to be sent in care of Count Nicholas Nikolayevich Tolstoy, Second Lieutenant of Artillery, for L.N., at the Starogladkovskaya *stanitsa*.

Once the package had gone, Tolstoy felt both relieved and enfeebled, happy and unhappy, and was tormented by one thought: how long did it take a very famous and very busy man to read a manuscript? To distract himself, he went for treatment to another spa, Zheleznovodsk. After sulphur water, iron water. He bathed in it, he drank it: no change. His toothache, acid stomach, rheumatism continued. Would he never get well? And when it wasn't his body that was sick, it was his soul. At Zheleznovodsk he wrote more of his short story *The Raid*, went for walks, cursed the rain and the army, and even wondered whether the time had not come for him to resign his commission. Deeper doubts also

* Which Sergey managed, without too much difficulty.

nagged at him: 'I have seen bodies die, so I suppose my body will die; but since nothing proves to me that my soul will die as well, I say it is immortal. ... The idea of eternity is a mental disease ...' [50] For the first time, he included the established order in his criticism, and thought of writing an explosive novel inspired by Plato's *Politics*: 'In my novel I shall show all the evils of the Russian government and, if I find this first experiment satisfactory, I shall devote the remainder of my life to working out a scheme for collaboration between an elected house of representatives of the aristocracy and the present monarchical government.' [51]

On 7 August, he was at Starogladkovskaya again, where he fell back into and was carried away by the tedium of routine: drill, cannon practice, idiotic scoldings by Alexeyev, petty drinking bouts, cards, hunting ('Shot five snipe. . . . Shot three pheasants. . . . Shot two partridge'), toothache, reading, women, boredom, work, writer's daydreams: 'It would justify a whole lifetime to write one good book.' [52] On 28 August 1852, his birthday, he made a melancholy note in his diary: 'I am twenty-four years old and I have still done nothing. I am sure it's not for nothing that I have been struggling with all my doubts and passions for the past eight years. But what am I destined for? Only time will tell. Shot three snipe.'

The following day, 29 August, the face of the world was transfigured: 'I received a letter from the editor, which has made me happy to the point of imbecility,' wrote Leo Tolstoy.[53]

He read Nekrasov's short, tense note ten times over:

I have read your manuscript (*Childhood*). Without knowing the sequel, I cannot make any final judgement, but it seems to me that the author has talent. In any case his ideas, and the simplicity and reality of his subject, form the unquestionable qualities of this work. If, as is to be expected, the sequel contains more animation and action, it will be a fine novel. Do send me the following sections. Your novel and your talent interest me. I advise you not to hide behind initials but immediately to begin publishing under your real name, unless you are to be only a bird of passage on the literary scene. I await your reply ...

When his first burst of joy had subsided, Tolstoy remarked to his annoyance that there was no mention of money among the words of praise. And his finances were in a very bad way. After considering the matter for a few days, he wrote to St Petersburg and asked for an explanation. His letter crossed a second one from Nekrasov, announcing that the novel was at the printer's. He must have written yet again, for he received a third letter from the director of the review: 'I have not spoken to you about money in my previous letters for this reason: it has long been the custom of our foremost reviews not to pay a beginner who is being presented to the public for the first time. ... In the future, you will receive the same amount as we pay our top writers of fiction (of whom there are very few), that is, fifty roubles per printed page. ... We are *obliged* to know the name of the author whose work we are printing, which is why you must give us positive information in this matter. If you desire, no one else need know. ...'

It was not until 31 October 1852 that Tolstoy received the issue of *The Contemporary* containing his story. After the thrill of seeing his prose printed in black on white, like a real author, he flew into a rage because Nekrasov had made a few cuts and even changed the title (*Childhood*, instead of *Story of My Childhood*). He expressed his displeasure in a letter which, after reading it over, he did not dare to send. The tone of the second, which he signed and sealed, was still surprisingly peremptory for a novice: 'I shall ask you to promise, Sir, with regard to my future writings – should you continue to wish to publish them in your review – that you will make absolutely no changes in the text.' [54]

When he began *Childhood*, Tolstoy intended to write about his play-fellows – Vladimir, Michael and Konstantin Islenyev – and their father, whom he had known in Moscow, but not about himself. The personality of the father, 'gallant, bold, self-confident, affable, libertine ... a connoisseur of everything that can procure comfort and pleasure,' was scrupulously transcribed by the author. The mother, on the other hand, was purely fictional. It was inevitable that in his efforts to describe the life of this family, Tolstoy should be tempted to incorporate his personal reminiscences. Little by little, his own memories crept into the outline he had drawn. 'The result,' he later wrote, 'was a deformed mixture of events drawn from the childhood of the Islenyevs and my own.' [55] To portray Volodya, the narrator's brother, he borrowed the features of his brother Sergey; the Lyubochka of the novel was copied from his sister Marya; Grandmother was taken over bodily into the book; Karl Ivanovich, the tutor, was none other than Fyodor Ivanovich Rössel, and St Jérôme was Prosper de St Thomas; Natalya Savishna's flesh-and-blood counterpart lived at Yasnaya Polyana under the name of Prascovya Isayevna; Prince Ivan Ivanovich was strongly reminiscent of Prince Gorchakov; Sonya Valakhin was a faithful image of Sonya Koloshin – the author's childhood sweetheart; the Ivin brothers had more than one point in common with the Musin-Pushkin brothers; as to the narrator himself, Nikolenka Irtenyev – his feelings about those close to him, about nature, animals and servants, were exactly those of Leo Tolstoy at the age of his first discoveries. Thus this first work, which he wanted to be as detached from himself as possible, was unconsciously nourished with all his affection for the warm years of his childhood. Fifty years later he wrote that the book, which he no longer liked, had been written under the influence of Sterne (*Sentimental Journey*) and Töpffer (*La Bibliothèque de mon oncle*). He might as well have added Rousseau, Dickens, Gogol and – why not? – Stendhal.

In fact, Tolstoy's originality was apparent in those very first pages. He instinctively refused to see people and things in terms of others before him. He looked at the world with the eyes of a man who has read nothing and learned nothing, who is discovering everything for himself. 'When I wrote *Childhood*,' he later told Bulgakov, 'I had the impression that nobody before me had ever felt or expressed the wonderful poetry of that age.' He applied this constant concern for sincerity and probity to technique as well as to thought. He was not writing to please, but to translate the different aspects of life as faithfully as he could. By divesting his language of threadbare metaphor, he sought the shortest road from the object to the heart. The grandiloquent comparisons of a Lamartine drove him wild with anger. What a heap of rubbish, all those tears that resembled pearls and eyes sparkling like diamonds! 'I never saw lips of coral,' he wrote in one draft of *Childhood*, 'but I have seen them the colour of brick; nor turquoise eyes, but I have seen them the colour of laundry blueing.' 'The French,' he also said, 'have a strange propensity for translating their impressions into tableaux. A face? "It is like the statue of. ..." Nature? "It reminds one of such-and-such a painting." A comely group? "One might say a setting from an opera or ballet." But a handsome face, or a scene in nature or a group of live people will always be more beautiful than any statue, panorama, painting or stage setting.'

Armed with these principles, Tolstoy vowed from the outset to use the right word every time, even if it was crude, trivial or unaesthetic; to put it down on the paper without fear of being repetitious, and never to sacrifice the truth for elegance or poetry. He had the same mistrust of traditional forms of construction. In his opinion one should not begin by describing the characters, and then setting the scene, and then opening the action; instead, one should familiarize the reader with the characters by little touches scattered about as the action progressed. In short, he intended to write simply and be read by simple people.

In his campaign of demystification, he was aided by a Dionysiac sensuousness. He strode through the world with his eyes wide open, ears pricked and nostrils flaring. The shuddering of the leaves, smell of ploughed earth, chill of a pane of glass under the hand, taste of a fruit melting on his tongue, barking of a dog in the country – all his perceptions coursed through his body in sharp waves, collided together and muddled his brain deliciously. He was perfectly attuned to the rhythm of nature, and it was no effort for him to imagine what beings very different from himself might feel. With equal truthfulness he could be lord, muzhik, woman, child, girl, horse and bird in turn. And he showed as much concern for the truth in his psychological notations as in his descriptions of the world: 'In the course of my life,' he wrote in one draft of *Childhood*, 'I have never met a man who was all bad, all pride, all good or all intelligence. In modesty I can always find a repressed urge towards pride, I see stupidity in the most intelligent book, intelligent things in the conversation of the greatest fool alive, etc.' At the age of twenty-three, he had already rejected one-sided characters, figures that were all shadow or all light. He decomposed the individual into an infinity of tiny spots, in the manner of the Impressionists. And out of the juxtaposition of this multitude of apparently disconnected lines, a unique character was born. After a dance, little Nikolenka looks at himself in a mirror – ugly, perspiring, his hair mussed, 'but the overall expression on my face was so gay, so good and healthy that I was pleased with myself.'[56] At his mother's death he was sad, to be sure, but a curious feeling of self-importance mingled with his sorrow: 'Sometimes it was the desire to show that I was more deeply afflicted than the others, sometimes concern for the effect I was producing. ...'[57] Seeing his father in a black redingote, pale, pensive and handsome during the funeral, he was angry with him 'for looking so dashing at such a moment'. It even seemed to him (in an early draft of *Childhood*) that his grief-stricken father was not insensitive to the bare white arm of a neighbour who had come to nurse Maman.

Even in *Childhood*, his art of suggesting a character's psychology in a few casually sketched physical traits was abundantly displayed. Tolstoy had only to describe a gesture or underline a detail of dress, and the hidden recesses of a soul were lighted up in some mysterious manner. His characters were surrounded by an aura that distinguished each from all the others, and yet its components remained indefinable. 'Who has not sensed these mysterious, tacit relationships caught in an imperceptible smile, a gesture, a look, between people who live constantly together: brothers, friends, husband and wife, master and servant, especially when they are not completely truthful with each other? How many desires, half-expressed thoughts and fears of being understood are revealed in a single chance glance, when their eyes meet, timid, unsure!'[58]

With its digressions, flashes of poetry, heavy load of memories, *Childhood* is at once a naïve and cynical book, quite singularly new by its very refusal of innovation, a triumph of heart over mind, sincerity over artifice, raw instinct over the literary culture of the 'connoisseurs'. Nekrasov had not been mistaken. On 21 October 1852 he wrote to Ivan Turgenev expressing his admiration; and the latter replied, after reading *Childhood* in *The Contemporary* (28 October), 'You're right. This is a sure gift. Write to him and encourage him to continue. Tell him, in case he may be interested, that I welcome, hail and applaud him.'

In his first flush of enthusiasm Ivan Turgenev also showed the book by this unknown author, who modestly signed himself L.N., to Tolstoy's sister Marya, who lived near him in the country. 'Imagine our surprise,' Marya told Leo later, 'as we gradually began to recognize ourselves in the characters of the story, and the description of our whole family. Who had written these lines? Who could be so familiar with the most intimate details of our lives? We were so far from thinking that our Leo could be the author of a book that we decided it had been written by Nicholas!'

The story made an instantaneous hit with the public, underscored by the praise of the critics. With the exception of *Pantheon*, which said that *Childhood* was an 'amusing and uninspired little tale', the press unanimously hailed a genius. 'It has been a long time since we have had occasion to read so inspired a story, one so nobly written, so profoundly steeped in love for the reality the author has sought to depict,' wrote Dudyshkin in *Fatherland Notes*. 'If this is L.N.'s first effort, Russian literature may congratulate itself upon the appearance of an admirable new talent.' In *The Muscovite*, Almazov asked, 'What is happening to Russian literature? One might almost believe it is beginning to revive at last.'

Tolstoy was out hunting, in November 1852, when he received the first reviews. He read them in a cabin by candlelight, and was staggered by a violent burst of joy. 'I am lying down in an isba on a plank bed,' he later said,[59] 'and my brother and Ogolin are beside me. I read and wallow in all this praise. I say to myself, "Nobody, not even they, knows that all these compliments are for me."' And he wrote in his diary on 25 November, 'I read a review of my book with unbelievable joy!' On the following day, 26 November, he added, 'I want to begin more stories about the Caucasus right away. I started today. I have too much self-respect to write anything bad, but I don't know whether I have it in me to write something good.' He was working on *The Raid*, the *Novel of a Russian Lord* (the basis for *A Landlord's Morning*), *Boyhood* (sequel to *Childhood*), and taking notes for other short stories. His need to tell stories was so great that he doubted whether he would be able to use up the ideas whirling about in his head in a lifetime.

However, a short while later, in the depths of Siberia, another young writer, Fyodor Mikhailovich Dostoyevsky (seven years older than Tolstoy), recently released from prison and drafted by force into the infantry, read *Childhood* and told his friend Maikov, 'I like Leo Tolstoy enormously, but in my opinion he won't write much of anything else (after all, I can be wrong!).'[60]

Tolstoy had been in the Caucasus for two years and the 'wild, free life' had lost all its appeal for him. He was bored by his *kunak* Sado and the old drunkard Epishka, he no longer even looked at Maryanka, whose beauty had stirred him so deeply before, and the pointless banter of his companions-at-arms only increased his desire for solitude.

In January 1853 another expedition went out against Shamil's Chechenians. The operation no longer had the spice of novelty for Tolstoy, so he saw only its futile and depressing sides: 'War,' he wrote in his diary on 6 January 1853, 'is so unjust and ugly that all who wage it must try to stifle the voice of conscience within themselves.' At Fort Groznaya, where the men were resting briefly before going into battle, there was heavy drinking and gambling: 'They all drink, especially my brother. How I hate it.[61] This evening Knoring came in drunk with Hesket. He brought along some port. I got drunk too. Some officers from Tenginsk happened along with some prostitutes. ...'[62] Altercation, insults, a barely avoided duel. ... At last the 20th Brigade went into action. Artillery fire was heavy near Kurinsk. The eight cannons of the 4th battery, under Lieutenant-Colonel Alexeyev, overpowered the enemy battery of Shamil. The hillsmen fell back. Only ten casualties were recorded on the Russian side. On 16 and 17 February there were fresh engagements, and a few *aouls* were destroyed. On those two days, in his own opinion, Leo Tolstoy bore himself 'well'. Praised by his superiors, he again hoped he might be given the St George Cross.

But on 7 March, the day before the decorations were distributed, he was placed under arrest because he had been playing chess with an officer and had forgotten his turn at guard duty. The next day, when the regiment fell in for parade to the roll of the snare drum, he was left behind, alone and furious, locked in a cabin. He hated Captain Olifer, who had reported him, and General Levin, who had struck him off the honours list. The only reason he wanted that St George Cross was 'to impress the people in Tula' when he came home from the war. On 10 March 1853 he wrote in his diary, 'It made me dreadfully sad not to receive the Cross.'

Sulking, he waited to return to Starogladkovskaya, where

he tendered his resignation to General Brimmer, commander of the artillery brigade. It was refused. Another source
of disappointment: his short story, *The Raid*, which he had
sent to *The Contemporary*, had just been printed, but was
heavily cut by the censor. 'I ask you,' wrote Nekrasov on 6
April 1853, 'not to be discouraged by these annoyances,
from which all our great authors suffer. Sincerely, your story
is very vivid and fine, even in its present form.' His sister
Marya and brother Sergey also wrote, congratulating him
on what they considered a success. And Aunt Toinette
exulted, in the tones of a requited sibyl: 'Didn't I urge you
to take a serious interest in literature? Didn't I predict that
you would be successful at this type of work, because you
have in you everything necessary to be a good writer: intelligence, imagination and noble feelings?'[63]

Although these words of praise did not quite take the
place of the St George Cross, they did incite Tolstoy to settle
down to work again. 'I am writing *Boyhood* with as much
pleasure as I did *Childhood*,' he wrote on 22 May. 'I hope it
will be as good!' And he was already working on the outline
for the third part, *Youth*. These studious activities did not
save him from an occasional resurgence of 'carnal desires'.
He treated these attacks as symptoms of a disease. An
alarming force would begin to stir in his belly. He would go
sniffing and prowling around a woman, waiting for a sign to
speak to her. 'Because of the girls I have not had and the
Cross they refused to give me, here I sit wasting the best
years of my life.'[64] Salomonida remained the most recep-
tive of the Cossack women: 'I still like her, even though she
has grown ugly.' With her, at least, he could relax. But with
new girls, shyness fuddled his brain. In his presence, one of
his companions told pretty Oxana that he loved her, and he
could not bear this public declaration. 'I fled, in a state of
utter confusion!'[65]

Another flight nearly cost him his life. On 13 June he left
with his *kunak* Sado to ride with a convoy going to Fort
Groznaya. The convoy was inching along, and the two

young men were foolhardy enough to set off ahead of the escort at a gallop. A few versts from Groznaya, they were attacked by a score of Chechenian horsemen, seven of whom set out in pursuit of them. They had traded horses a short time before: Tolstoy's Kabardian was an excellent trotter, but heavy at the gallop. Sado, who had given him his own swift mount, was thus at a handicap. However, at the risk of being caught, Tolstoy held back level with his friend rather than outdistance him. He knew he would be killed if he were captured; but the thought of escaping alone was incompatible with his code of honour. He waved his sabre aloft; Sado brandished his gun – which was not loaded – and behind them the pounding hoofs and bloodthirsty howls and whistles were drawing dangerously near. The alarm was given, some Cossacks rode out of Fort Groznaya, and the Chechenians turned tail and rode away.*

This heroic deed might conceivably have reconciled Tolstoy with himself. Far from it. The moment he was back at Starogladkovskaya, after succumbing to his habitual temptations of women and cards, he took up his pen to scourge himself: 'All week long my behaviour has been so dissolute that I feel leaden and bleak, as always when I am not pleased with myself.'[66] And, in his own words, he undertook a 'soul cleansing'. He liked to clean house this way, at intervals, throwing open the windows and giving all his evil thoughts a good sweep with a broom. Afterwards he could stroll contentedly through his renovated domain and contemplate the future with emboldened confidence. 'This cursed regiment has turned me completely aside from the path of goodness I had begun to follow and want to return to at all costs, for it is the best. ... The goal of my life, it is plain, is the good ... the good I owe my serfs and fellow countrymen; the former because I am their master and the latter because I have brains and talent.'[67]

He had just sold another thirty of those serfs he so cher-

* Three officers in the escort were gravely wounded that day in an engagement with the main body of the Chechens.

ished, 'of masculine sex,' along with 365 acres of land bordering the village of Yagodnaya. This transaction had brought him 5,700 roubles – enough to keep him afloat for a few months. But shortly thereafter, in a surge of liberality, he had freed one of his peasants, Alexander Mikhailov, twenty-three years old, who wanted to become a monk in the monastery of Trinity St Sergey. One deed cancelled out the other, he trusted, in the eyes of divine justice.*

When summer came he obtained permission to return to Pyatigorsk, where his sister Marya and brother-in-law Valerian were also taking the waters. At first Marya amused him, then she disappointed him : 'She plays the coquette too much.' His brother-in-law Valerian was 'an honest, sober fellow, but devoid of that delicate sense of honour I deem essential in all to whom I give my friendship.' Thereupon Nicholas Tolstoy arrived; more fortunate than his younger brother, his resignation had just been accepted. This much-beloved and admired brother, in spite of his dirtiness, laziness and his fondness for wine, suddenly appeared to Tolstoy in a new light. He found him empty, and remote. As remote as his brother-in-law and sister. Strangers. 'My family's indifference torments me,' he wrote on 17 July 1853. And, 'Why is it nobody loves me? I am neither stupid, nor ugly, nor perverse, nor a cad. I don't understand it!' Two days later he wrote to his brother Sergey :

I must confess I was expecting more pleasure from seeing Masha and Valerian again than I actually felt. Poor Masha goes to all the parties here and finds them very insignificant affairs indeed. In the first place, it is a sad thing that she should enjoy herself in such trivial company, and sadder still that all her time is taken up with such distractions, which she prefers to the company of the brother she has not seen for two years. ... I may be oversensitive, as usual, but during the two weeks I have spent with them (Marya, Valerian and Nicholas), I have not heard a

*The sale of the village of Yagodnaya was concluded by Valerian Tolstoy on 10 April 1853; Alexander Mikhailov, the serf, was freed on 6 June of the same year.

single word from any of them that was – I will not say affectionate (for I had all of that I wanted) – but from the heart, and
proved to me that they love me and that I have a place in their
lives.

All the while he was fulminating against this idle existence, he tagged along with his brother's and sister's 'bunch',
down the boulevard, around the hot springs, on picnics. A
certain Theodorina caught his eye for a few days: 'July 25.
Talked to Theodorina. ...' 'July 27. The pretty women on
the boulevard have too great an effect on me. ... Yesterday,
Theodorina, utterly delightful, told me about her life at
boarding school.' 'August 1–4. Theodorina is in love with
me. I am not bored. I take baths.' 'August 6. Theodorina is
very infatuated with me. I shall have to make up my mind
one way or another. I confess it is some consolation.' 'August
7. Brushed against Theodorina several times during the
evening: she excites me very much.' 'September 3. Theodorina is a silly goose; I am sorry for her.' 'September
14. Theodorina is snubbing me and I won't see her again.'

Mere trifles. Tolstoy's true source of worry lay elsewhere.
The approach of the New Year incited him to meditate
upon himself. With beetling brows, he re-entered his sententious phase. Once again, his diary filled up with trenchant
formulas: 'Keep away from wine and women.' 'The pleasure
is so negligible and the regret so profound!' 'Abandon yourself entirely to everything you undertake.' 'When under the
sway of a powerful emotion, hold back; but after reflection,
act with determination even if you're wrong.' 'Overcome
depression by work, not by distractions.' And, as before in
Moscow, he kept his 'Franklin' notebooks, recording all his
misbehaviour. A ruthless inquisitor, he smacked himself
across the fingers with a shiver of delight: 'Broke my oath
not to frequent drinkers ...' 'Got up too late ...' 'Lied ...'
'Made a foolish purchase ...' 'Wandered aimlessly ...'
'Could not make up my mind ...' 'Went to sleep after
lunch ...' 'Offended Epishka ...' 'Struck a cat ...' 'Insulted
Alyoshka ...' 'Lost my temper and beat Alyoshka ...'[68]

The publication of *Childhood* and *The Raid* having made him, in his own eyes, a genuine man of letters, he soon added no less peremptory 'Rules of Writing' to his 'Rules of Life': 'When you criticize your work, always put yourself in the position of the most limited reader, who is looking only for entertainment in a book.' 'The most interesting books are those in which the author pretends to hide his own opinion and yet remains faithful to it.' 'When rereading and revising, do not think about what should be added (no matter how admirable the thoughts that come to mind) ... but about how much can be taken away without distorting the overall meaning.' In his excitement he even criticized Pushkin, whose prose he found poor and thin, and concluded with a flourish, 'I know perfectly well that I have genius.'

This was the very reason why, no doubt, he felt so lonely! 'I must get used to the idea, once and for all, that I am an exceptional being,' he wrote on 3 November 1853, 'a person ahead of his time, or else I have an impossible, unsociable nature, always dissatisfied. ... For a long time I lied to myself, imagining I had friends, people who understood me. How wrong I was! I have not met one man who is morally as good as I am, who is attracted to the good on every occasion, as I am, or ready to sacrifice everything for his ideal, as I am. That is why I can find no company in which I am at ease.'

How was it, when writing those lines, that he was not tempted to skim through the pages of his diary? He might have observed that he had previously dragged himself through the mire with the same relish he was now deploying to exalt his virtues. But, accustomed as he was to switching from angel to beast, he would not have been surprised by this inconsistency: after all, it is necessary to touch bottom before one can spring back up to the surface. Now up, now down, Tolstoy was constitutionally incapable of following a middle course.

In any event, he had had all he could take of the Caucasus; and as though in response to his desire for action,

Nicholas I declared war on Turkey (20 October [1 November] 1853). Russian troops, led by Paskevich, had entered the Danube Principalities four months before. France and England were up in arms, blustering and protesting in support of the sultan. Since Tolstoy's resignation had been refused, he decided to ask for a transfer to Moldavia. But he had to be commissioned first. Aunt Pelagya Yushkov, alerted in Kazan, pulled her most influential strings; Tolstoy himself wrote to Prince Sergey Gorchakov, asking for a recommendation to Sergey's brother, Prince Michael Gorchakov, general in the Danube army under the supreme command of Field Marshal Paskevich. But the mail was slow, the clerks in the offices swamped by paper. On 26 November 1853, with his fate still undecided, Tolstoy complained to his brother Sergey:

'I am counting on a change in my way of life next year. The life I am leading here has become intolerable. Stupid officers, stupid conversations, stupid officers, stupid conversations, nothing else. ... Even though Nicholas, God knows why, took the hounds with him (Epishka and I call him an s.o.b. for doing it), I still go out hunting day after day, all alone from morning to night, with one pointer. It's my only pleasure – not even a pleasure, but a way of wearing myself out. You're exhausted, you're hungry, you reach the house, you fall asleep like a lump of lead, and there's one more day gone.'

A month later he confided in Aunt Toinette: 'No friends, no occupation, no interest in anything around me. I am watching the best years of my life go by, bringing nothing to me or anyone else, and because of my sensitivity this position, which might be tolerable to someone else, is becoming increasingly trying. The price I am paying for my wayward youth is a high one.'[69]

Tolstoy had not really wasted his time in the Caucasus, although he liked to say so. His suitcases were bulging with sheafs of manuscripts. In *Boyhood*, written in the first person like *Childhood*, he studied the awakening of a personality at grips with its first challenges. The *Novel of a Russian Lord* recounted the adventures of a young nobleman who, after trying to achieve his ideal of justice and brotherhood in the country, was discouraged by the apathy of his muzhiks, turned to the joys of family life and realized in the end that true happiness lay in sacrificing one's individual interests to the general interest.[70] *The Raid, A Wood-Felling, The Fugitive* were short stories inspired by his military experiences. In *Memoirs of a Billiard-Marker* he described his despairing state on the eve of his departure for the Caucasus, when he was fed up with himself and did not know where to seek salvation: 'I am enmeshed in slimy nets and I can neither free myself nor learn to bear them.' In *A Holy Night*, it was Moscow under the snow, a ball, young love.

Even these minor or unfinished works revealed the author's exceptional talent, his gift for true sight and true speech, the pitiless candour of his approach to the world. However, at this stage of his travels, he needed a change of scenery to provide him with a new source of inspiration; the writer, as much as the man, was looking forward to the Army of the Danube as a fund of fresh experience. On 12 January 1854 he learned that he would be allowed to take the officer's examination for the rank of ensign* (a mere formality) and was attached to the 12th Artillery Brigade, in Moldavia. Overjoyed, he decided to set off as soon as possible, making a little detour (nearly seven hundred miles) to say hello to his aunt and brothers at Yasnaya Polyana. Lieutenant-Colonel Alexeyev approved his application for a furlough and advanced him one hundred and twenty-five roubles for the trip.

For a week, Tolstoy celebrated his promotion drinking *dzhonka*.† On the day of his departure he had a *Te Deum* sung 'out of vanity', handed some small change to the poor,

---

*In the Russian army, an ensign (*praporshik*) is the lowest-ranking commissioned officer, coming before second lieutenant.

†A rum drink into which flaming lumps of sugar are plunged.

'out of ostentation', and, just as he was about to climb into the carriage, suddenly felt a sorrow beyond words instead of the relief he had been expecting. His companions-at-arms were all standing at the side of the road, and his *kunak* Sado, and Uncle Epishka, and Lieutenant-Colonel Alexeyev, the 'pretentious imbecile'. Looking at them he realized that he had unconsciously come to love the people he was about to leave, as well as the country. 'I explained this change in my attitude by the fact that in military service in the Caucasus, as in other intimate surroundings, a man does not learn how to choose the best people, but how to find the good qualities in uninteresting ones,' [71] he later wrote. As the horses moved forward, Lieutenant-Colonel Alexeyev swept the back of his hand roughly across his tears. Tolstoy turned his head away. Was he to lose them all forever? No; already he dimly sensed that the Cossacks and the Chechens, Maryanka and Sado and Epishka and all the others would soon come back to life in a book.

Two days later he wrote, with customary self-assurance: 'There is one fact I must remind myself of as often as possible: at thirty, Thackeray was just preparing to write his first book* and Alexandre Dumas writes two a week. Show nothing to anyone before publication. One hears more unfounded criticism than useful advice.' And, yielding to his penchant for observation he added without any transition: 'There is a particular type of young soldier who has backward-bending legs.'

---

* Thackeray actually began to write around the age of twenty, and was thirty-six when *Vanity Fair*, his first novel, was published.

Sevastopol

RUSSIA lay buried deep in snow. The relays followed each other, identical, with myopic windows peering out beneath big white roofs, stacks of frozen straw in the courtyards, shivering grooms scurrying around the horses, hulking, silent coachmen. On the sixth day of the trip, one hundred versts from Novocherkassk, Tolstoy's sledge was caught in a blizzard. Whirling funnels of snow sped across the bare fields, sky and earth became indistinguishable and the eardrums ached from the screaming wind. No more road, no more horizon; in a cloud of vapour, the horse's head swayed back and forth under the wooden arch, the runners sank deep into cottony nothingness and the cold became so intense that not even the vodka he downed could keep the passenger warm. After heading his team blindly in every direction, the driver admitted that he was lost. Night was coming on. What to do? Stop and wait? Freeze to death, in other words. The tormented horse stumbled on through the squalls until dawn. Tolstoy vowed to base a story on this adventure if he came out of it alive.[1] For a writer, even fear can be grist to the mill. Dawn paled in the sky at last, the wind dropped and the smoke of a village appeared in the distance. Back among men once again, Tolstoy wrote in his diary, 'To succeed in life one must be brave, resolute and keep a cool head'.

Nine more days on the road and, on 2 February 1854, in a landscape of steam, frost and lace, the two towers marking the entrance to Yasnaya Polyana rose up at the end of a white-rutted drive. There was the house, with its neo-classical pediment, its columns, snow-powdered on the side facing the wind, its large, limpid windows; there, on the threshold, was the smell of childhood (tart apples and beeswax); there was Aunt Toinette, tiny and wrinkled, her eyes full of tears and light, coming forward, holding out her arms, falling on to the chest of her 'Lyova Ryova'.* They wept, kissed, exclaiming how well the other was looking.

That very evening, Tolstoy told Aunt Toinette all about his adventures in the Caucasus. He may have bragged a bit, omitted to mention the size of his debts and inflated that of his expectations, but he did so less from conceit than from a desire to give some happiness to the woman who, for so many years, had lived only for her nephews. He felt that his youth and his literary success were a present he was giving her. He scolded her because she kept saying in her letters that she was too lonely and wanted to die. He said she had no right to complain, because there he stood before her, bubbling over with optimism and good health. This princely selfishness made her smile. Hand in hand they looked at each other and sighed with love. A well-matched couple, one all youth and fire, the other all weariness and resignation.

Yasnaya Polyana was magnificent in the snow: the frozen Voronka, white ice where the pond used to be, crystal-lined trees. Tolstoy made his landlord's rounds, visited the village elder, ordered a *Te Deum* sung at the church, checked over the new manager's accounts – he looked honest – went on to the farm at Grumond and concluded from his inspection that everything was in order but that he himself had aged. After spending a few days with his sister Marya at Pokrovskoye, playing the piano and tumbling about with his nephews, he wrote out a will in view of his impending departure for the army, and returned to Aunt Toinette. In the meantime, his three brothers, Nicholas, Sergey and Dmitry, had also arrived at Yasnaya Polyana. It was strange to see Nicholas in civilian clothes, a shapeless jacket and hands of doubtful cleanliness. Sergey, the family eccentric, was becoming more elegant, ironic and independent than ever. Dmitry was unrecognizable, with a

* 'Leo Cry-Baby.'

beard bristling around his puffy face, a dissatisfied expression and bleary eyes. He had begun to drink, like Nicholas, but even more than Nicholas. Aunt Toinette whispered that he was living the life of a profligate in Moscow. The four brothers decided, either because there were not enough beds to go round or out of sheer stoicism, to sleep together on the bare floor.[2]

Tolstoy was so intensely happy to be with his family again in the house he was born in that no ill tidings could affect him. On 13 February, he read Nekrasov's letter[3] advising him not to publish the *Memoirs of a Billiard-Marker* – 'content excellent, but form mediocre' – without turning a hair.

'Your previous work was too promising,' Nekrasov wrote, 'to follow it up with something so undistinguished.' He had to admit that the director of *The Contemporary* was right, forgot his story and went to Moscow with his brothers. There they visited their acquaintances, caroused and revelled, and had their photograph taken together. At the right of the row sat Leo Tolstoy, stiff and intent, mutton-chop whiskers framing his face, his uniform stretched tightly across his chest, epaulettes jutting out, and thumb stuck into his belt strap. He had just bought a complete outfit: 'Greatcoat 135 roubles, accessories 35, boots 10 ...' A run over to Pokrovskoye to say good-bye to Marya, Valerian, Sergey and Aunt Pelagya, a hop to Sherbatchevka, Dmitry's estate, where Aunt Toinette had hurried to kiss the traveller good-bye and give him her blessing, and it was time to go. The parting was heart-rending. Aunt Toinette cried. Looking at all those tearful faces, Tolstoy could at last tell himself that he was loved as he wished to be. Happy in his woe, he wrote in his diary, 'It was one of the brightest moments of my life.'

On 3 March 1854 he set off. From Kursk he travelled to the Rumanian frontier via Poltava, Balta and Kishinev. He began the two-thousand-verst trip by sledge; then, when the snow turned to mud, he changed to a most uncomfortable sort of cart, 'smaller and more ill-made than the ones we use for carting manure at home'.[4] The drivers spoke nothing but Moldavian. Despairing of making himself understood, Tolstoy was constantly under the impression that they were cheating him. He reached Bucharest on 12 March, worn out and furious at having spent two hundred roubles without being able to account for them.

Two nephews of the commanding officer, Prince Michael Gorchakov, welcomed the young ensign with all the courtesy he could wish for and, four days later, the general in person received him in his palace on his return from a tour of inspection at the front. Strapped into his new uniform, Tolstoy went expecting a formal interview. But Gorchakov treated him as one of the family. 'He embraced me, made me promise to dine with him every day and wants to put me on his staff, but this is not yet certain.'[5]

The ease with which an honourably-born young man could find a comfortable position was a typical feature of Russian life at the end of the last century. Every great family had some representative in good standing at court, to whom it appealed in matters of importance to intercede with the emperor. Letters of recommendation took the place of diplomas and everything worked out in the end thanks to an aide-de-camp uncle or a lady-in-waiting cousin, and, after sowing their wild oats, young men who lacked any other qualification found themselves occupying enviable posts in the army or administration. On the strength of Prince Michael Gorchakov's cordiality, Tolstoy felt that his military career, which had made a slow start in the Caucasus, would now forge swiftly ahead. Accepted by the staff officers as one of themselves he found them brilliant, noble and, in short, absolutely *comme il faut.*[6]

A strange thing, this return of his *comme il faut* obsession after a ten-year lapse. The raw artilleryman of the Caucasus was transformed overnight into a drawing-room officer. Sixty miles away on the opposite bank of the Danube, bloody battles were being fought before Silistra, which was besieged by the Russians, but in the staff city of Bucharest the social whirl was in full swing. Dinners at the prince's house, balls, evenings at the Italian opera and French theatre, elegant suppers to the music of a gypsy orchestra, spooning of sherbets in tearooms – the pleasures of life became keener as the threat of death drew near. Having received a little money from his brother-in-law Valerian, Tolstoy considered his position 'relatively agreeable'. Indeed, he was in so little hurry to change it that he was thoroughly vexed to be sent, just for the form, to spend a few days with a campaign battery at Oltenitsa. The officers he met there seemed coarse and vulgar to him. He took a great dislike to the commander and was overjoyed at the arrival, in the heat of an altercation between them, of a courier bringing notice of his appointment to the staff of a division general. The commander had no choice but to swallow his insults and Tolstoy withdrew, his vanity flattered and his sense of justice uneasy. 'The higher I rise in the opinion of others, the lower I sink in my own,' he wrote.[7]

As ordnance officer for General Serzhputovsky he carried orders to various parts of the military zone, after which his chief could find nothing more for him to do and sent him back behind the lines at Bucharest. He took advantage of his free time to finish correcting the proofs of *Boyhood* and send the manuscript to Nekrasov. 'I have not yet smelled Turkish gunpowder,' he wrote to Aunt Toinette, 'and I am sitting peacefully here in Bucharest, strolling about, playing music and eating ice creams.'[8] He forgot to add that he was also playing cards and losing steadily.

Suddenly, there was a great stir in the offices. General Serzhputovsky had decided to transfer his staff to Silistra, on the right bank of the Danube. Headquarters were set up on a hilltop in the elegant gardens of Mustapha Pasha, governor of the besieged town. A vast and detailed panorama spread out below: the blue Danube, broad and sparkling, dotted with islands, the town, fortresses, the network of trenches crazing the surface of the earth; and from afar, a mass of little worms could be seen swarming about inside these furrows: the Russian soldiers. Perched on a wagon with telescope in hand, Tolstoy admired the view, which he found 'poetic'. The roses in Mustapha Pasha's garden perfumed the air around him. To while away the time, he exchanged a few blasé comments with the other young ordnance officers who, like him, were spectators at the inoffensive and charming game of war. At that distance it required a great effort of imagination to believe that those little black specks marching towards those little grey specks were men, about to kill each other.

The firing quickened during the night, because the Turks wanted to prevent the Russians from completing their earthworks. The Cannon joined in. Spasmodic flashes, dull explosions, trembling earth – one evening Tolstoy counted one hundred explosions per minute. 'And yet,' he wrote to Aunt Toinette, 'none of this, up close, is anything like as frightening as it seems. ... With these thousands of cannon balls, thirty or so men on both sides were killed.'[9] The tranquil book-keeping of the strategist!

Sometimes he rode out to the trenches with an order. There the anonymous figures in the painting suddenly turned into creatures of flesh and blood, with their fatigue and fear, dirt, wounds. ... He inhaled one gasp of this horror and rode quickly back to his balcony seat, from which the view of the battlefield was so enjoyable. A mine exploding under an enemy redoubt was a lovely display of fireworks: 'This was a sight and emotion of the kind one never forgets!'[10]

At last, Prince Gorchakov decided to make the final assault. The entire staff went down to the trenches. Mingling with the group of ordnance officers and aides-de-camp, Tolstoy observed his chief. As usual, he saw in him a mixture of the sublime and the ridiculous – his eternal holy hatred of statues. Gorchakov seemed grotesque to him, 'with his tall figure, his hands behind his back, his cap shoved back and his spectacles and way of talking like a turkey-gobbler'.[11] But 'he is so taken up with the progress of operations as a whole that balls and bullets do not exist for him. He exposes himself to danger so simply that one would think he had no notion of it and is involuntarily more afraid for him than for oneself. ... He is a great man, that is, an able and honest man.'[12]

On the eve of the day set for the attack, five hundred Russian cannon bombarded the fortifications. The firing went on without pause all through the night of 8–9 June. The attack was set for three in the morning. 'There we all were,' Tolstoy later wrote, 'and, as always on the eve of a battle, we were all pretending not to think of the coming day more than any other day, and all of us, I am certain, felt something clutch at our hearts (and not a little clutch, but a big one) at the thought of the attack.... The time just before an engagement is always the worst, for it is only then that one has time to be afraid. ... The feeling (of fear) subsided as the hour approached and, around three, when we were all waiting for the cluster of rockets that was to give the signal for attack, I was in such a cheerful frame of mind that I should have been cruelly disappointed had someone come to tell me it was not to take place.'[13]

What he feared most happened. Just as dawn was beginning to break, an aide-de-camp brought General Gorchakov a message from Field Marshal Paskevich, ordering him to raise the siege. 'I can say without fear of being mistaken,' Tolstoy wrote in the same letter, 'that the news was received by all, soldiers, officers and generals, as a real misfortune, especially since we knew, from the spies who came over from Silistra, and with whom I very often had occasion to talk myself, that if this fort was taken – and nobody doubted it would be – Silistra could not hold out more than two or three days longer.'

What Tolstoy did not know, or refused to take into account, was that part of the Army of the East sent by England and France had already disembarked at Varna, and Austria was calling up a reserve of ninety-five thousand men at the Russians' backs and massing troops along the frontier. While he fretted and chafed, he admired Prince Gorchakov's equanimity in such trying circumstances. To have laid such careful plans for an engagement only to be deprived of their fruition at the last moment was, in his eyes, a kind of injustice. Only a very superior person could bear the blow without reeling. 'He (Gorchakov), who is always so moody, did not display one instant of ill humour; on the contrary, he was glad to be able to avoid the slaughter for which he would have had to accept responsibility,' he wrote.[14]

His esteem for his commanding officer increased during the retreat, which Gorchakov directed in person, 'refusing to leave before the last of the soldiers had gone'. Austria, with Prussia's support, had ordered Russia to evacuate the Danubian Principalities, and Tsar Nicholas I grudgingly complied, in order to avoid additional international complications. What looked like a simple operation on paper became in reality a chaotic and painful exodus. Thousands of Bulgarian peasants, who were afraid of being massacred by the Turks once the Russians had gone, came down from their villages with their wives, children and livestock and herded themselves into plaintive crowds around the few remaining bridges over the Danube. Traffic became so badly blocked that Prince Gorchakov, moved to tears, was forced to refuse a passage to the late arrivals. With his aides-de-camp around him, he received deputations of harrassed and bewildered refugees who did not understand Russian, explained as best he could why the army must have priority use of the road, invited them to follow the troops on foot, without wagons, and offered money from his own pay to the neediest. Inflamed by his example, Tolstoy wrote in his diary on 15 June, 'The siege of Silistra has been lifted. I have not yet been under fire but my position among my fellow officers and superiors is assured. My health is good and, as to the moral side, I am firmly resolved to devote my life to serving my fellow men. For the last time I tell myself, "If I have not done something for someone else within three days, I shall kill myself." '

Eight days later he was still alive, but his deeds of selflessness had been confined to playing cards and borrowing money: 'A humiliating position for anyone, but especially for me,' he wrote on 23 June 1854, in his diary. The following day he recorded this rather curious thought, for a lover of mankind, 'I spent the whole evening talking to Shubin* about our Russian slavery. It is true that slavery is an evil, but an extremely nice evil.'

Once again, he was in Bucharest with very little to do, reading, meditating, writing. His teeth were troubling him more and more, so he consented to an operation: on 30 June a fistula was removed, after he had been anaesthetized with chloroform. 'I behaved like a coward,' he sternly observed when he recovered consciousness. And on 7 July he sketched a mocking picture of himself in his diary:

What am I? One of the four sons of a retired lieutenant-colonel, orphaned at the age of seven and brought up by women and foreigners, who, having acquired neither social nor academic education, became independent at the age of seventeen; without any great fortune or any solid position in society, and above all, without principles; a man who has mismanaged his affairs to the last degree, wasted the best years of his life in futile and joyless agitation and finally expatriated himself to the Caucasus to escape from his creditors and, even more, from his habits; whence, on the strength of his father's former friendship with the commander, he contrived to get himself transferred to the Danube army; an ensign, twenty-six years old, practically penniless except for his pay (for the money he has from other sources must go to pay off his debts), without influential connections, without social poise, without any knowledge of any trade, without innate talent, but possessed of boundless pride. Yes, that is my social position. Now let us look at my personality.

I am ugly, awkward, untidy and socially uncouth. I am irritable and tiresome to others, immodest, intolerant and shy as a child. In other words, a boor. Whatever I know I have learned by

---

* A lieutenant, one of his friends.

myself – half-learned, in bits and snatches, without any structure or order – and it is precious little withal. I am excessive, vacillating, unstable, stupidly vain and aggressive, like all weaklings. I am not courageous. I am so lazy that idleness has become an ineradicable habit with me. ... I am honourable, that is, I love the path of virtue ... and when I depart from it I am unhappy and am glad to return to it. Yet there is one thing I love more than virtue: fame. I am so ambitious, and this craving in me has had so little satisfaction, that if I had to choose between fame and virtue, I am afraid I would very often opt for the former. ... Today I have to reproach myself for three violations of my rules of life: (1) forgot the piano; (2) did nothing about the report concerning my transfer; (3) ate borscht, in spite of my diarrhoea which keeps getting worse.

A week later he was no better satisfied with his deportment: 'I am very displeased with myself, *primo* because I spent the whole day removing the pimples all over my face and body, which are beginning to annoy me; *secundo*, because of my pointless outburst against Alyoshka at dinner.'

The war was still on, however, and at the end of the evacuation begun the previous month, the staff left Bucharest on 19 July 1854, en route for the Russian frontier. Throughout this dreary tramp, which was to last more than a month, Tolstoy unflaggingly pursued his self-interrogation. On bivouac, in his tent, in barns, he continued his written indictment of his errors with the same morbid delight he had felt in squeezing the pimples on his face. On 16 August he inaugurated a new moral therapy. Henceforth each daily note in his private journal would conclude with the same statement: 'The most important thing in life for me is to correct the following three vices: laziness, lack of character and bad temper.' He kept his word. Between 16 August and 21 October 1854 the sentence recurred more than twenty-five times. But the exorcism was without effect.

On 9 September, after traversing Focsani, Barlad, Jassy and Skulyany, the staff finally set up headquarters at Kishinev. As soon as Tolstoy had set foot on Russian soil, he tried to interest some friends in founding a periodical with him – the *Military Gazette* – intended to bolster the soldiers' morale. 'The *Gazette*,' he wrote to his brother Sergey, 'will publish less cut-and-dried and more accurate accounts of the battles than the other papers; reports of heroic deeds, biographies and obituaries of the bravest men, chosen chiefly from among the humble and unknown; war stories, soldiers' songs, simplified articles on artillery and military engineering.'[15]

Money was needed for this undertaking. What is money? The previous year, when he had been afraid he would not be able to cover his gambling debts, Tolstoy had instructed his brother-in-law Valerian, in Pyatigorsk at the time, to sell the big family house at Yasnaya Polyana, without the land. His ancestors would just have to do without the respect he owed to them. After all, a good many of them had been gamblers, too. They must be feeling sorry for him up there, maybe even approving him. In September 1854 the house was dismantled, board by board, loaded on to telegas and transported to the estate of the buyer, a neighbour named Gorokhov, to be reassembled there. All that remained at Yasnaya Polyana were the two pavilions which formerly flanked the mansion house. Nicholas wrote to his brother in November 1854, 'You already know, no doubt, that the house at Yasnaya Polyana has been sold, dismantled and carried away. I went there recently. Its absence surprised me less than I had expected. The overall appearance of Yasnaya Polyana has not suffered.'[16] In any event, Gorokhov had paid up – five thousand roubles.* To finance the *Military Gazette*, he need only dip into the till. Valerian received an order to remit fifteen hundred roubles to editor-in-chief Leo.

As for copy, there was no shortage of that. Tolstoy was confident that he could fill the paper single-handed. Without further ado he began writing short stories: 'How Russian Soldiers die' and 'Uncle Zhdanov and the Horseman

* About $14,100.

Chernov'. In the latter he told how the non-commissioned officers flogged the young recruits, to instil a respect for discipline in them: 'Zhdanov was not beaten to punish him for his faults, but because he was a soldier and soldiers must be beaten,' he wrote with passion. Then, remembering that the story was intended for an official military paper, it occurred to him that the censor would never let it pass and he abandoned it. He wrote an article to replace it, and the specimen issue was sent to the minister of war by Prince Gorchakov. But, Tolstoy himself confessed, even the article was 'not very orthodox'.* In fact, his knowledge of the tsar should have discouraged him from the attempt altogether. How could Nicholas I, for whom discipline reigned supreme, tolerate the presence in his army of a periodical with humanitarian pretensions? Too much solicitude softens the men in the ranks; what they gain in learning, they lose in obedience! Once again, Tolstoy had mistaken his fancies for fact: suddenly bitten by the teaching bug, he saw himself educating the soldiers and – why not? – their leaders, too.

The truth of the matter was that the latter did not seem quite equal to their task. News from the front was increasingly alarming. On a mission from Kishinev to Letichev Tolstoy learned that the French and English forces had disembarked near Sevastopol and the Russians had been defeated at the Alma. He was staggered. So long as the fighting remained on foreign soil, his interest in the war had been that of a dilettante, an artist. But now that the enemy had a foothold on the Russian earth, he felt directly concerned by his aggression. And yet at Kishinev the intrigues and entertainment and dancing went on as before, and Grand Dukes Nicholas and Michael† came to the ball and charmed the ladies. Tolstoy could not bear it. 'Now that I have every comfort, good accommodation, a piano, good food, regular occupations and a fine circle of friends, I have

* The specimen copy of the *Military Gazette* has never been found, and nothing is known of the 'not very orthodox' article by Leo Tolstoy.
† Sons of Nicholas I.

begun to dream of camp life again and envy the men out there,' he wrote to Aunt Toinette.[17] On a furlough, he visited Odessa and Nikolayev, where the port was blockaded by the English fleet. He saw some English and French prisoners and was surprised by their robust appearance. 'The air and manner of these men gives me, why I don't know, a sinking certainty that they are far superior to our soldiers,' he wrote in his diary.[18]

Back at Kishinev, he abruptly applied for a transfer to the Crimea. He had now been promoted to the rank of second lieutenant. This time he did not ask to be attached to a general staff, but left his fate in the hands of his superiors. He set out the reasons for his decision in a letter to his brother Sergey: 'I have requested a transfer to the Crimea, partly to see this war at first hand and partly to get away from Serzhputovsky's staff, who do not exactly thrill me; but mostly out of patriotism, a sentiment which, I confess, is gaining an increasingly strong hold on me.'[19]

There was a fourth, more personal reason: his comrade Komstadius, with whom he had planned to edit the gazette, had been killed at the battle of Inkerman. Tolstoy's reaction to this news was to conceive a sudden loathing for his behind-the-lines safety and comfort. 'More than anything else, it was his death that drove me to ask for a transfer to Sevastopol,' he wrote in his diary. 'In a sense, I felt ashamed to face him.'[20]

On 1 November his transfer came through and he set out. Upon reaching Odessa the following day, he learned the details of the stupid defeat at Inkerman, due entirely to General Dannenberg's lack of forethought. 'I saw old men shedding bitter tears and young ones who had vowed to kill Dannenberg,' he wrote the same day. 'The moral strength of the Russian people is great indeed!'

It was rumoured at Odessa that an assault on Sevastopol would begin on 9 November at dawn. Tolstoy was afraid he would arrive too late to display his bravery; he reached the city on the seventh – but the attack did not take place.

Assigned to the 3rd light battery of the 14th Artillery Brigade, he found to his annoyance that he was quartered in the city itself, far from the fortifications and outworks.

To defend Sevastopol against attack by sea, part of the Russian fleet had been sunk in the roads. The entire city had been encircled by bastions. The offensive had come from the south, and reinforcements and supplies from the interior were still arriving by the north. The fortified Malakov Hill defended passing convoys. 'There is no way to take Sevastopol,' Leo Tolstoy wrote on 11 November. 'And the enemy seems convinced of this as well.'

Inside the city reigned a strange mixture of 'camp life' and 'town life'. The streets were one huge bivouac. The quay was thronged with infantry in grey, sailors in black, women in multicoloured garb, *sbiten*-vendors* with their samovars. A general sitting stiffly in his *calèche* passed a convoy of hay-carts. Bloodstained soldiers lay on stretchers on the peristyle of a stately mansion. The shifting breeze alternately brought the smell of the sea or the stench of overcrowded hospitals. Now and then disdainful camels passed, hauling corpse-piled flat wagons. Cannon boomed in the distance. Suddenly a military march was heard. The crowd bared their heads and crossed themselves: an officer's funeral. Pink coffin, flags unfurled. For church, tsar and fatherland. In a nearby restaurant, other officers, still hale and hearty, commented on their comrade's death as they devoured 'cutlets and green peas' and drank 'the sour Crimean wine baptized Bordeaux'.

Closer to the fortifications, the town assumed a more tragic aspect. Houses in ruins, roadways transformed into pitted dumps, bombs half-buried in the mud, the smell of carrion and cannon powder. Stooping over, soldiers crept along the maze of trenches. At the back of a casemate non-commissioned officers played cards by candlelight; sailors picked lice off each other on an esplanade surrounded by gabions; near a cannon a lieutenant rolled a cigarette in

* *Sbiten* is a beverage made of honey.

yellow paper. Balls whistled. Bombs crashed. The sentinels called out, 'Ca-a-nnon!' or 'Mortar!' to give warning. 'When the shell has gone past,' Tolstoy wrote, 'you revive, and an inexpressible thrill of joy and relief surges through you.' [21]

On 15 November he left Sevastopol for a week-long trip through the forward defence lines. What he saw in the trenches and bastions there heightened his love of the Russian people. 'The heroism of the troops beggars description,' he wrote to his brother Sergey. 'There was far less in the time of the ancient Greeks! When passing the troops in review, Kornilov said not, "Hello there, my lads!" but "If it has to be death, my lads, are you willing to die?" And the soldiers cried out, "We'll die, Your Excellency! Hurrah!" And there was no play-acting, you could see on every face that it was true, and twenty-two thousand have already been as good as their word. One wounded soldier, nearly dead, told me how they took a French battery on the twenty-fourth of last month, without reinforcements! He was sobbing. A company of sailors nearly mutinied when relief was sent to the battery they had been serving for thirty days under fire. The soldiers tear the fuses out of the shells. The women bring water to the men in the bastions, and many have been killed or wounded. The priests go from one fort to another brandishing their crucifixes and reciting prayers under fire. In one brigade there were one hundred and sixty wounded who refused to leave the ranks. These are noble days! ... I have not had the good fortune to see action yet myself, but I thank God for allowing me to be with these people and live through this glorious time!' [22]

After paying this enthusiastic tribute to the brave defenders of Sevastopol, Tolstoy soon discovered a dreadful truth beneath the patriotic imagery. The Russian soldiers were armed with muskets, the French had rifles. As a result of the parade-ground training advocated by Nicholas I, the new recruits knew how to march in step, but not how to fight.

The sorry condition of the roads in the south slowed down troop transport. Supply methods had not changed since 1812.

During this trip [Tolstoy wrote in his diary on 23 November 1854] I became convinced that Russia must either fall or be transformed. Nothing works the way it should, we do not prevent the enemy from consolidating his position, although it could easily be done. And we ourselves stand there facing him with inferior forces, without retrenching, with no hope of reinforcements, commanded by generals like Gorchakov,* who have taken leave of their senses, their common sense and their initiative, and are relying on St Nicholas to send storms and foul weather to drive away the intruder. The Cossacks are ready to plunder, but not to fight; the hussars and uhlans prove their military prowess in drunken carouses and debauchery; the infantry is conspicuous only for its thievery and money-grubbing. A sorry state of affairs for the army and the country. I spent a couple of hours talking to some English and French casualties. Every soldier among them is proud of his position and has a sense of his value, he feels he is a positive asset to his army. He has good weapons and knows how to use them, he is young, he has ideas about politics and art and this gives him a feeling of dignity. On our side: senseless training, useless weapons, ill treatment, delay everywhere, ignorance and shocking hygiene and food stifle the last spark of pride in a man and even give him, by comparison, too high an opinion of the enemy.

Why couldn't he state his views – in milder terms, of course – in one of the early numbers of his gazette? Tolstoy scarcely had time to ask the question: at the beginning of December, he was informed that the tsar had refused permission to publish it, on the ground that there already was a periodical, *The Army and Navy Gazette*, specializing in military literature. It was plain to see that intellectual officers were not trusted by those on high.

Furious, Tolstoy wrote to Nekrasov on 19 December, offering the texts he had originally intended for his gazette to

---

* Prince Peter Gorchakov, brother of the commander of the army of the Danube.

The Contemporary. Nekrasov replied by return post: 'Send your soldiers' tales to us. Why bury them in some old veterans' review?' This proposal both delighted and embarrassed Tolstoy, for he now felt obliged to write the stories, after being so vociferously unhappy when their publication was refused. But he was not in the mood for work. A short time before he and his battery had been sent to the rear – to Esky-Ord, near Simferopol. The year was ending quietly for him. Quartered in a comfortable villa, he was reading, 'playing various pianos and hunting red deer and roe'.[23] His comrades were pleasant for the most part, but he was afraid that because of his stand-offish manners, 'they like me less than before'.[24] As for women: he was missing them keenly. He was seeing all the young ladies, of course, but these little provincial idylls never led to anything more substantial. 'In these conditions, I am afraid I shall become a boor, incapable of living the family life I love so dearly!'[25] he sighed.

In January 1855 he was transferred to the 3rd light battery of the 11th Artillery Brigade, stationed on high ground on the banks of the Belbek, seven miles from Sevastopol. His spirits sank the moment he arrived. Into what hole had he fallen? And among what animals? 'Philimonov, the commander of my battery, is the dirtiest creature imaginable,' he wrote in his diary on 23 January 1855. 'Odakhovsky, the senior officer, is a revolting yellow-livered Pole. The other officers have no personality and let themselves be influenced by their superiors.'

In his *Reminiscences*,[26] however, Odakhovsky was to write, 'The slightest remonstrance by a superior automatically provoked an insolent retort or sarcastic comment from Tolstoy.' Once again, Tolstoy's haughty demeanour set him apart from his fellows. The shortage of books, absence of people to talk to, the cold, discomfort, remoteness of danger – all of them helped to sour his temper. Now and then, to astound his companions, he would perform some physical feat such as lying on the ground on his back and holding a

175-pound man at arm's length. 'He left behind him in the brigade the memory of a good horseman, a high liver and a Hercules,'[27] wrote the young officer Krylov. As usual, his favourite pastime was cards. It so happened that the fifteen hundred roubles intended to finance the *Military Gazette* had just arrived. As the publication had been forbidden, the money was going begging. Tolstoy played *stos* non-stop for two days and two nights. At dawn on the third day he had lost his last kopeck: 'The result is plain,' he wrote in his diary on 28 January, 'I've lost the house at Yasnaya Polyana for good. ... I am so sick of myself that I would like to forget I even exist.' And by way of penitence he wrote to Nicholas, who was, of all his brothers, the one able to judge him most harshly: 'I have lost all the money – fifteen hundred roubles – that was sent to me. I beg you not to blame me or reproach me for it, either in your letters or behind my back: I am continually blaming myself for this enormous piece of stupidity, and shall not stop until I have made up for it by my work.'

Three days later he yielded to temptation again. 'February 2. Playing with Meshersky on credit, I lost one hundred and fifty roubles I didn't have.' 'February 6. Played again and lost two hundred silver roubles. I cannot promise to stop playing. I hope to win it back and am in danger of going in over my head. ... Will propose to play again with Odakhovsky tomorrow, for the last time.' 'February 12. Lost eighty more roubles. ... I want to try my luck at cards once more.' 'February 17. Lost another twenty roubles. *I shall not play again.*'

After adding up his losses and throwing in a little nest-egg for good measure, Tolstoy sent another appeal for help to Valerian:

As you must know from my letter to Nicholas, I have lost the fifteen hundred roubles you sent me. Worse yet, I have lost another 575 roubles on credit. I *must* have the money right away. Be kind enough to sell enough wheat to make up the amount I am lacking and send the money to me at Sevastopol.

... I am ashamed and it hurts me to write to you. I ask you not to show this letter to everyone. I have stopped playing.[28]

To give himself the illusion that he was serving his country even though he was far from the fighting, he began to write a *Plan for the Reform of the Army*. The moment was well-chosen, for Russia had just learned, to its secret relief, of the death of Nicholas I, on 18 February 1855. With the disappearance of this violent and narrow-minded potentate, the cause of so many police-state exactions, unjust exiles and unsuccessful wars, all who aspired to a little more freedom in the empire began to raise their heads. His successor, Alexander II, was said to favour more humane policies and, on the strength of this rumour, Tolstoy opened his study with a courageous declaration of principle:

My conscience and sense of justice forbid me to keep silent in the face of the evil being openly perpetrated before me, causing the deaths of millions and sapping our strength and undermining our country's honour.... We have no army, we have a horde of slaves cowed by discipline, ordered about by thieves and slave traders. This horde is not an army because it possesses neither any real loyalty to faith, tsar and fatherland – words that have been so much misused! – nor valour, nor military dignity. All it possesses are, on one hand, passive patience and repressed discontent, and on the other, cruelty, servitude and corruption.

He went on to denounce the corporal punishment inflicted upon the soldiers, calling attention to 'the large number of Russian officers killed by Russian bullets, or slightly wounded and abandoned to the enemy,' and complaining that the generals leading the army had been chosen 'not because they had any ability, but because the tsar liked them.' It remained to expound the remedies. But it is easier to destroy than to construct. After exhausting his bile in his critique, the author grew bored and abandoned the positive part of his treatise. After all, nobody would listen to him anyway.

Still, the desire to repair, to improve things, would not

leave him. Despite his gambling losses, his 'fits of lust' and his 'criminal sloth', he felt the soul of an innovator stirring in his breast. Having failed to reform the army, he turned to religion. One evening, between two hands of whist and *stos*, he had an illumination that left him breathless, flooded with ineffable happiness. On 4 March he wrote in his diary that he had just had a 'grandiose, stupendous' idea. 'I feel capable of devoting my life to it. It is the founding of a new religion, suited to the present state of mankind: the religion of Christ, but divested of faith and mysteries, a practical religion, not promising eternal bliss but providing bliss here on earth. I realize that this idea can only become a reality after several generations have worked consciously towards it. One generation will pass on the idea to the next, and one day, through fanaticism or reason, it will prevail.'

The whole of Tolstoy's future doctrine is summed up in these few lines scribbled in his notebook: refusal to submit to Church dogma, return to early Christianity based on the Gospels, simultaneous search for physical well-being and moral perfection. Unfortunately, on the next line of the same diary: 'March 6. Odakhovsky won another two hundred roubles from me, and so my situation has become critical.' The prophet awoke from his trance, cards in hand.

The time was undoubtedly not yet ripe for a full spiritual flowering. But a slow process of fermentation had begun, deep within this unquiet soul, a subterranean and painful preparation for apostolate. He had a fleeting desire to give Yasnaya Polyana to his brother-in-law outright, in order to free himself from domestic cares and liquidate his debts, and devote the rest of his life to literature – one more castle in the air, like so many others, which he promptly forgot the next day. However, in the state of perpetual mental upheaval in which he lived, one idea remained constant: write. This was the picket he always came back to, after running about in every direction like a maddened goat at the end of its tether. 'The military career is not for me,' he wrote on 11 March: 'the sooner I leave it to devote myself wholly to literature, the better it will be.'

Nekrasov was crying for *Youth* (sequel to *Childhood* and *Boyhood*) and the promised accounts of the siege of Sevastopol. Tolstoy worked on both of these very dissimilar works at once. First he was the rich man's son, the spoiled student, happy and naïve, facing the anguish of his first examinations, first loves and first metaphysical doubts, and then the anonymous soldier in the inferno of Sevastopol. He received all the encouragement he could wish from behind the lines. His sister wrote that Ivan Turgenev was full of admiration for him, Nekrasov filled every letter with high praise, and the *Memoirs of a Billiard-Marker*, which *The Contemporary* had finally brought out after a year of hesitation, was warmly received by all the critics.

'What gave me most pleasure,' Tolstoy wrote on 27 March, 'was to read the critics' notices: they speak of the *Memoirs of a Billiard-Marker* in very flattering terms. This sensation is both pleasant and useful, for by feeding my pride it drives me to action. ... Alas; for the last five days I have not written a single word of *Youth*, although I did begin *Sevastopol by Day and by Night*.' The more deeply he became involved in his work, the harder it was for him to bear the hardships of camp life. Obviously, he would be more comfortable writing in an office. Prince Gorchakov had replaced Admiral Prince Menshikov as commander of the army of the Danube, so he applied for a transfer back to the staff. Aunt Pelagya Yushkov was pressed into service, to speak to the general – who was a relative of hers – in support of his request. On 30 March, refusal: 'I did not get the transfer because, I am told, I am only a second lieutenant. Pity!'

His annoyance increased when, instead of appointing him aide-de-camp and settling him in some more comfortable quarters, his superiors ordered him and his battery to the 4th (or Flagstaff) Bastion, south of Sevastopol, in the most dangerous sector of all. An artist needs distance; it is impossible to write about war in the thick of the battle! He who had been complaining of 'inactivity' a few weeks before suddenly balked at the thought of being exposed to fire like some common little officer up from the ranks. He had caught a cold in the casemate, his nose was running, he was coughing, he had a fever, and it was all the fault of the command, who did not know how to use its resources. In a rage, he wrote on 11 April 1855, 'Fourth Bastion. . . . It makes me furious, especially now that I am ill, to think that nobody has imagined I might be good for something other than cannon fodder of the most useless kind.'

When his cold abated his spirits rose, and in fact he displayed great courage. The 4th Bastion was closest to the French lines – a hundred yards or less. 'Not a day went by,' wrote Captain Reimers, who commanded the bastion, 'without heavy bombardment – on holidays the French sent in the Turks to relieve them. There were periods during which we received an average of two thousand shells from a hundred cannon within a twenty-four-hour period.' Tolstoy was on quartermaster duty four days out of eight. Off duty, he rested in Sevastopol in a humble but clean dwelling overlooking the boulevard where the military band was playing. When he was on duty he slept in an armoured casemate. A fir post in the centre held up the ceiling. Tarpaulins were hung halfway up to catch falling rubble. It was furnished with a bed, a table littered with papers, a clock and an icon with its vigil light. Inside this clammy den, the thunder of the cannonade was incessant. A flickering glare came through the narrow window. The ground shook, the walls cracked, the bitter, peppery smell of powder hung in the air.

At first he was terrified, then he mastered his quaking limbs and, from extreme fright, passed to extreme bravery; he did not know that the secret of his genius lay in just this rare capacity to shift from cowardice to heroism, or that it was his very flaws and inconsistencies that would later enable him to embrace the attitudes of each of his characters in turn with equal sincerity, or that his diversity as a man would be the foundation for his universality as a writer.

Twenty-four hours after grumbling at being treated as 'cannon fodder', he wrote in his diary, 'My little soldiers are very nice, I feel quite gay with them.' (12 April.) And then: 'The continual allure of danger, and the interest with which I observe the soldiers around me, and the sailors, and the war itself, are so rewarding that I would be sorry to leave this place, especially as I should be glad to see the attack, if there is one.' (13 April.) The firing grew more intense; a mine exploded, hurling chunks of stone and human debris into the air; deafened and tormented by the cries of the wounded, Tolstoy prayed to God: 'Lord, I thank you for your unwavering protection. How worthless I should be if you abandoned me. ... Help me, not to gratify my own futile ambition, but to attain the great eternal aim of life, which I do not know but am aware of.'

In this atmosphere of fever, upheaval and death, writing was a tall order. But Tolstoy had never felt so inspired. He wrote down his impressions on the wing and drafted his accounts for *The Contemporary* inside the bastion. He must have been the first real 'war correspondent'. He did not disown Stendhal's influence: 'I am in his debt more than any other's,' he told Paul Boyer in 1901. 'I owe my knowledge of war to him. Reread his account of the battle of Waterloo in *The Charterhouse of Parma*. Who, until then, had described war in such terms, that is, the way it really is?' But in *The Charterhouse of Parma* the battle of Waterloo is seen through the eyes of Fabrizio alone, whereas in the *Sevastopol Sketches* Tolstoy enlarged upon the method and entered into the minds of all his protagonists in turn, giving their dissimilar versions of the same engagement. There was no artistic premeditation in this concept of 'coverage', moreover; as always, the author was obeying his instinct, saying what he had seen and not caring whether he pleased or offended. He showed the reeking operating room, the wounded soldiers slavering with pain, the surgeon's assistant tossing an amputated leg into the corner, the death of a mud-covered sailor with clenched jaws ('Farewell, brothers!'), the military bands playing in town for the ladies who were languishing for a flirtation and the officers back from the front, the bastion under enemy fire, the shell – approaching like a fiery pinpoint, growing larger, whistling over their heads – the mountains of corpses, the smoke, ruins, wasted blood, the grandeur and misery of the anonymous soldier.

Hundreds of bodies who, two hours before, were bursting with hopes and desires, great and small, now lay with fresh bloodstains on their rigid limbs in the dew-covered flowering valley dividing the bastion from the trenches and on the smooth slabs of the mortuary chapel at Sevastopol. Hundreds more, with curses and prayers on their cracking lips, crawled, writhed and groaned among the corpses in the flowering fields, or on stretchers, camp cots and the blood-soaked boards of the ambulance station; but, as on the previous days, the heat-lightning flickered about Mount Zapun; the trembling stars dimmed; a whitish mist rose on the dark, tossing sea; the pink dawn lit up the east; long purple clouds wafted away to the horizon, which turned a luminous blue again; and, as on the previous days, the powerful, glowing star emerged, promising joy, love and happiness to all the awakening world.

One man has a sinister foreboding: 'I shall surely be killed today, especially since it wasn't my turn to go and I volunteered'; another heaves a cowardly groan of relief when his replacement arrives; a third thinks greedily, as he sees a comrade in danger of death and remembers his ten-rouble debt to him, that it may cancel itself in a moment. Tolstoy himself, who had more than one creditor in the battery, might have experienced the same sensation in similar circumstances. At the pitch of nervous tension a man is brought to by the continual threat of annihilation, his mind is no longer the master of the images that visit it. At the end of *Sevastopol in May*, Tolstoy could proudly declare, 'The hero of my tale, whom I love with all the strength of my soul, the hero I have tried to reproduce in all his beauty, who always has been, is and always will be admirable, is the truth.'

In the night of 10–11 May Tolstoy witnessed a series of attacks and counter-attacks under heavy fire. Over a thousand dead and wounded on the Russian side, and as many among the French. The following night, second attack: in all, five hundred men out of commission. During the day of the twelfth, hostilities were suspended to pick up the dead. 'The morale is falling lower every day,' Tolstoy wrote, 'and there is more than one sign that people are beginning to feel the possibility of Sevastopol being taken.'[29] In the meantime he had received Aunt Pelagya Yushkov's letter of recommendation and forwarded it to the general. But another two weeks and more went by without news of his transfer. He imagined himself staying in the 4th Bastion until the end of the war. 'No doubt it is better so!' he wrote in melancholy.[30] On 15 May he learned that he had been transferred and put in command of a two-cannon mountain battery on the Belbek River, fourteen miles behind Sevastopol. According to a legend as attractive as it is unlikely, the new tsar, Alexander II, was so deeply moved by *Sevastopol in December*, of which he read the galleys, that he gave orders to remove its author from danger. Unfortunately, it is difficult to believe that between 30 April, when the manuscript was sent to Nekrasov, and 15 May, when Tolstoy's transfer came through, the text could have reached St Petersburg and been read, set up and submitted to the sovereign, and that his decision could have travelled from St Petersburg back to the Crimea. The truth was that Aunt Pelagya's letter, added to Tolstoy's application, had persuaded Prince Gorchakov to humour his young relative, whose literary renown was growing.

In his new quarters, far from the clamour of battle, Tolstoy made an earnest attempt, at first, to carry out his duties. He officiated in person at drill, supervised his unit's supplies and was outraged by the fraud he saw on every side. Most detachment leaders spent the mess money exactly as they pleased, appropriated the remainder for themselves and falsified their accounts. When, out of honesty, Tolstoy tried to show a credit balance in his books, he compromised all his fellow officers and earned a reprimand from General Krizhanovsky, commander of artillery: 'What on earth have you done, Count?' said the general. 'The State has organized things this way in your own interest. You have to have something to fall back on in case the battery accounts show a deficit! That is why every battery commander must have some funds on hand. You are making trouble for everyone.'

'I do not see why I must keep those funds with me,' Tolstoy replied. 'The money belongs to the State, not to me.'[31]

In the end, however, he abandoned this uncompromising position. 'It is easy to steal – so easy that it is impossible to avoid it!' he fumed.[32] He had sworn to be good to his 'dear little soldiers', but sometimes their stupidity drove him to distraction. Then he became Count Leo Tolstoy, who saw red and hit hard: 'Beat the men I was drilling. It's amazing how revolting and wretched I can be, how I can disgust myself!' And later, 'Laziness, lack of character, vanity ...; bragged to my officers ...; showed off to the battery leaders. . . . It is really absurd that, after beginning to draw up rules at fifteen, I should still be doing so at thirty,* without having adopted or applied a single one.' The most serious fault he had to hold against himself was still his love of gambling. In the tedium of his life in camp he became obsessed by the cards once again: to be sure of winning, he spent whole days practising, playing against himself, noting infallible combinations for *stos*: '(1) The ante will be one-sixteenth of the amount to be lost; (2) Raise or

---

*In fact, he was only twenty-seven and a half at the time.

lower the ante on the thirteenth card; erase score of first series up to chosen card . . . etc.'

Unfortunately, every win on paper corresponded to a loss in the field. And the old familiar words erupted between the columns of figures in the diary: 'Laziness . . . Stupidity . . . Despair . . . Lust . . .'

However, he kept on writing. The insults he fired at himself were answered by the compliments his readers addressed to him. The censor had passed *Sevastopol in December* without any major cuts and, as a result, the entire literate public had been in contact with the awful reality of war for the first time in Russian history. 'All of us who love Russian literature,' Panayev wrote to Tolstoy, 'are praying God to spare you!'[33] 'Tolstoy's article on Sevastopol is a wonder!' Turgenev wrote to Panayev. 'I cried when I read it, I shouted "hurrah!"'[34] And Pisemsky, the author, growled, 'This little officer will outstrip us all!' From the critics, response was the same as from the writers. The success of *Childhood* and *Boyhood* was surpassed. 'Nowhere does the author express his admiration, and yet we are compelled to admire; there is not one exclamation point in all his descriptions, and we are astonished at every turn' (*Fatherland Notes*). 'Sevastopol is the work of a master, rigorously pondered, rigorously executed, with vigour and concision . . .' (*The Muscovite*).

The emperor, profoundly impressed, ordered the account to be translated into French and published in the newspaper *Le Nord*,* and the young empress wept over this frank narrative of her people's tribulations. Her tears did much to enhance the fame of the person who was still signing himself L.N.T. On 30 June 1855 he wrote in his diary, 'It seems I really am beginning to be known in Petersburg!'

The second instalment, *Sevastopol in May*, awoke the censor's suspicions. After an initial pruning, when the text had already been set up, the chairman of the Censor Committee demanded to see it himself. Shocked at the author's

* French-language Russian newspaper printed in Brussels.

audacity, he deleted all the passages that seemed 'anti-patriotic' to him, and the editors of *The Contemporary* printed the mutilated version. Nekrasov wrote to the author, storming against the crimes of the censor, but adding, 'Your work will not be lost, of course. ... The truth, in the form in which you are introducing it into our literature, is something totally new. I know no author today who can compel the reader to love and sympathize as deeply with him as you can. ... Your debut is so auspicious that even the most conservative souls are forced to hold out very high hopes.' [35] And Tolstoy commented in his diary, 'It seems the blues* have grown suspicious of me on account of my articles. I only wish Russia always had writers as moral as I; nothing in the world could force me to turn meek and mild, or write for the mere pleasure of it, without any idea or purpose.' In the meantime he had been awarded the St Anne Cross, fourth degree, for courage under fire and, together with a few of his comrades, had written a satiric ditty called the 'Song of Sevastopol':

> The toppest brass
> Sat down to meet
> And pondered long;
> Topographers
> Lined paper black;
> But all forgot
> The deep ravine
> They had to cross!

The song was inspired by the disastrous engagement of 4 August 1855† – the battle of Chernaya – in which the Russians lost eight thousand men, three generals and sixty-nine officers. Tolstoy, who had not been directly involved in the conflict, wrote to Aunt Toinette that day: 'I am safe and sane; but my morale has never been lower.' [36]

* The military police.
† 16 August by the Gregorian calendar.

A few days later, on 27 August,* a heavy bombardment began in preparation for the French assault on Malakov Hill. Tolstoy was in Sevastopol when the Zouaves and Mac-Mahon's *voltigeurs* charged. The sun was blinding. A cool breeze shook the leaves in the trees along the boulevard and swept up the dust of the ruined houses. Necklaces in puffs of white smoke appeared all along the line of fortifications. The explosions shook the ground with dull violence. Then the cannon-fire subsided, and the dry rattle of rifle-fire was heard. Soldiers came pouring back into the streets helter-skelter. A white-faced officer cried out, 'The attack!' And suddenly Tolstoy saw a red, white and blue flag floating over Malakov. 'It made me cry to see the town in flames and the French flags over our bastions,' he wrote to Aunt Toinette. 'These last few days I have become increasingly obsessed by my desire to leave the army.' [37]

In the night of 27–8 August, the Russian troops began evacuating the southern part of town. The glow of fires rose above the bastions. An occasional explosion tore open the sky and illuminated swarms of flying stones. The makeshift bridge across which the soldiers were filing swayed and sagged at breaking point. At two in the afternoon of 28 August, Fort Paul was blown up, with five hundred seriously injured men inside. The French, stopped on the summits, did not press their advantage. Tossed about in the flood of retreating regiments, the soldiers, their faces exhausted and clothes tattered, were observed by Tolstoy and his throat tightened with compassion. 'When they stepped off the other end of the bridge,' he wrote, 'all the soldiers took off their caps and crossed themselves. But underneath this feeling there was another – a deep aching, compounded of remorse, shame and anger. Almost everyone, looking back from the north at Sevastopol abandoned, heaved a sigh of unspeakable bitterness and muttered threats at the enemy.' [38]

After the fall of the city, Tolstoy was instructed by General Kryzhanovsky to write an account of the final

*8 September by the Gregorian calendar.

engagements based on the reports of the bastion commanders. For an author whose aim was to be honest at all times, such a task, performed on command in the style of an official dispatch, was a refined form of torture. He later said, 'It was a peerless example of the naïve and inevitable military duplicity employed in composing descriptions of this type.'[39]

With the defences of Sevastopol overrun, Tolstoy's battery moved to Kremenchug (19 September), then to Foti-Sala (26 September), where the Russians exchanged a few shots with the French vanguard, and then withdrew to the north. 'Did not wash or undress and behaved like an ass,' he wrote on 1 October. In the ensuing days, his desire to leave the army sharpened. 'My career is Literature! Write! Write! Beginning tomorrow I shall work at it all my life, or abandon everything, rules, religion, proprieties and all!' (10 October.) And later, 'Insurmountable laziness. It is absolutely essential that I get out of this rut of army life, which is bad for me.' (27 October.)

A letter from Ivan Turgenev – the first – gave a powerful boost to his inclination. One of Tolstoy's stories – *A Wood-Felling* – which had been published in *The Contemporary* (still under the initials L.N.T.), was dedicated to Turgenev.

'Nothing in my literary career has ever flattered me as much,' Turgenev wrote. 'But I dislike to think of you where you are now. Although in a way I am glad you are having these new impressions and experiences, there is a limit to everything; we must not tempt fate, which is only too happy to thwart us at every turn. It would be wonderful if you could get yourself out of the Crimea. You have shown sufficient proof of your bravery, but the military life is not for you. ... Your weapon is the pen, not the sword. ...' Inviting his young colleague to call on him when he was on furlough, he added, 'It seems to me that we should get along well together, we could talk frankly, and our acquaintance would be profitable to both of us.'

At last, early in November, Tolstoy, who had requested a mission, was detached from his battery and sent to St Petersburg as a courier. On the eve of his departure he lost another 2,800 roubles at cards.*

* About $7,900.

[8]

Introduction to
Civilian Life

TOLSTOY reached St Petersburg on the morning of 19 November 1855. He left his bags at the hotel, changed his shirt, put on a dress uniform in place of his travelling uniform and rushed off to see Turgenev, who lived on Fontanka Quay near the Anichkov Bridge. All he knew of the man he was about to meet, ten years his senior, was that he was a great nobleman and a great writer. *A Sportsman's Sketches* had conquered the intellectual elite and given serfowners a bad conscience. After rereading the book, Tolstoy wrote in his diary, 'It is difficult to write, after him.'[1]

In 1850, Ivan Sergeyevich Turgenev – who lived most of his life abroad in the wake of Pauline Viardot, the singer,* with whom he was in love – had returned to Russia to be with his mother at her death and collect his share of the inheritance. Two years later Nicholas I condemned him to live on his estate (after a month in prison) on account of his obituary article on Gogol, in which the censor had detected liberal tendencies. He had recently been permitted to live in St Petersburg but could not leave the country, and was suffering from this long separation from the object of his passion in France. Worse yet, his illegitimate child 'Paulinette' (alias Pelagya), whom he had thirteen years before by a seamstress-serf of his mother's, had been adopted by the Viardots and was living with them, in Paris and on their country estate of Courtavenel, at Rozay-en-Brie.

A friend of George Sand, Mérimée, Musset, Chopin and Gounod, Ivan Turgenev had a mind which exuded the same

* Pauline Viardot's husband, who was twenty-one years older than she, was director of the Italian Opera in Paris.

European elegance as his person. When Tolstoy crossed the threshold of his library, he saw before him a giant, with a massive, mild and gentle face, candid blue eyes, neat side-whiskers, large soft hands and a certain lassitude in the droop of the shoulders. A Hercules with doe's eyes. The two men embraced enthusiastically. They were equally eager to become friends, and the honeymoon began immediately. Turgenev insisted that his young colleague come to stay with him, and Tolstoy accepted with alacrity. A bed was assigned to him. That evening, introduction to Nekrasov. They dined, played chess, talked literature. After his rough life in the army camp, these intellectual conversations went to Tolstoy's head like wine after a long fast. He was submerged by the flood of compliments, and realized that he was an object of exceptional interest to his fellow writers. And, feeling loved and admired, he wanted to admire and love in return. 'Turgenev is a wonderful man ...' 'Nekrasov is interesting, he has many good qualities ...,'[2] he wrote.

His circle of acquaintances widened in the ensuing days. Everyone who worked on *The Contemporary* wanted to meet the glorious young writer and hero of Sevastopol. He met Druzhnin, Tyutchev, Goncharov, Maykov, Ostrovsky, Grigorovich, Sologub, Pisemsky, Korsh, Dudyshkin, Panayev, Polonsky, Ogaryov, Zhemchuzhnikov, Annenkov, etc.* The civilians were instantly charmed by the soldier. His name cropped up often in their correspondence and private diaries. 'You cannot imagine what a delightful and exceptional man [Tolstoy] is, even though I have baptized him the Troglodyte because of his barbaric ardour and bull-headedness,' Turgenev wrote to Annenkov. 'My affection for him is curious, one might almost say paternal.'[3] 'Leo Nikolayevich Tolstoy has arrived,' Nekrasov wrote to Botkin. 'What a delightful person, what intelligence! A

---

* All writers, poets, journalists. The biographical notes at the end of this book give the essential facts about them and some of the other people who played a part in Tolstoy's life.

likable, energetic, unselfish young man, a real falcon! Perhaps an eagle! I liked him better than his writing, and God knows that's good enough! He is not handsome, but he has an extremely attractive face, at once forceful and gentle. His look is a caress. I liked him very much.'[4] 'He's a first-class chap,' wrote Druzhnin to Liventsev, 'and a true Russian officer, full of wonderful tales; but he hates empty words and his attitude towards events is sound, if not rose-coloured.'[5] And he wrote in his own diary, 'Tolstoy behaved like a troglodyte and a bashi-bazouk. He did not know, for example, what the Censor Committee was and what ministry it was attached to. He then informed us that he did not regard himself as a man of letters ...'

His colleagues found the neophyte's candour utterly enchanting. How was it possible to be so gifted and so little a man of letters? The first thing they had to do was to acquaint him with the ideological quarrel that was tearing the capital's elite asunder. In one camp were the 'Westerners', who considered Russia a backward country in comparison with the West and thought she should seek regeneration by following the example of Europe. In the other were the Slavophils, who denied all alleged intellectual superiority of Europe and held that the Russians were too unique and exceptional a people to find their salvation from any foreign source. The former drifted readily from a passion for European painting into an appreciation of the merits of democracy, and the latter from a reverence for the old Slavic traditions into adoration of the tsar, 'blessed of God'. Each side had its militants; wild-eyed informants told Tolstoy all their names. Between the two camps hung the bulk of the undecided moderates – liberal Slavophils or monarchist Westerners. On *The Contemporary*, staunch Westerners formed the majority. A few contributors, however, were already eyeing other less distinguished but more literary reviews. Rival editors were outbidding each other for the best writers. This whole little menagerie was seething with emulation, vanity and jealousy. In the middle of the aviary, with the preening and pecking going on all around him, stood Tolstoy, solidly planted on his two legs; he felt that he belonged to a different species. After the horrors of war, he wanted only one thing: a good time. Juggling ideas was all very well for the impotent or the satiated; what he needed was reality, succulent and immediate. His appetite for pleasure shocked Turgenev, who was highly refined and inclined to resignation in matters of the heart. Once or twice he accompanied his guest on his revels and returned home aghast. He could not understand how the author of *Sevastopol* could sink so low, drinking himself into a stupor, singing with the gypsies, frequenting brothels. To be sure, Tolstoy subsequently repented of his nights on the town, but the reproofs he heaped upon his own head always covered a disgusted and angry desire to begin again. 'Went to Pavlovsk,' he wrote in his diary.* 'Disgusting. Girls, silly music, girls, mechanical nightingale, girls, heat, cigarette smoke, girls, vodka, cheese, screams and shouts, girls, girls, girls! Everybody tries to look as though he is having a good time and likes the girls, but in vain.' And, proud of his uniform, it annoyed him to see 'drunken, nasty' civilians trying to carry on like 'true officers'. For, although he claimed to loathe the military profession, he felt nothing but contempt for the townsmen in their dress suits who had never spent a night on sentry duty or seen a comrade shot down at their side. An inferior race, with stuffed paunches and sensitive behinds, pen pushers, intriguers, clods. Those without money were as contemptible as those who had 'what it takes'. Turgenev belonged to the latter category. After being charmed by him, Tolstoy turned on him and criticized him with vindictive severity. What futility in this overripe man. His handsome clothes, his perfume, his honeyed ways with women, his anxiousness to please, his faith in the future of science, his refined dinners. He had paid a thousand roubles

* Pavlovsk, a pleasure spot seventeen miles outside St Petersburg. The entry in the diary is dated 14 May 1856.

for his serf cook and was eternally bragging about his talents. To show that he was different from all these high-minded, weak-muscled gentlemen, Tolstoy brushed his hair back from his forehead and wore his moustache in a droop, which, he fancied, gave his mouth a determined and for-bidding expression. And thus he appears, in a photograph taken on 15 February 1856, standing stiffly, his arms folded across his chest, in a group of amiable colleagues striking languid poses: Turgenev, Ostrovsky, Druzhnin, Grigorovich and Goncharov.

One morning the young poet Fet, a fervent admirer of Ivan Turgenev, came to call on him and was surprised to see a sword decorated with the ribbon of the Order of St Anne hanging in the hall.

'Whose sword is that?' he asked Zakhar, the servant.

The latter motioned the young man to lower his voice, pointed to a door down the hallway on the left and whispered:

'It belongs to Count Tolstoy. He is staying with us.'

Fet went into the study, where Turgenev was drinking tea 'Petersburg-fashion'. His movements were relaxed, his features calm and his expression affable, but he kept glanc-ing towards the door. 'During the hour I spent with him,' wrote Fet, 'we talked in undertones in order not to awake the count, who was sleeping in the next room. "It is like this all the time," said Turgenev with a smile. "He came here straight from his battery at Sevastopol, moved in with me and plunged into a headlong spree. Orgies, gypsies, cards all night long, and then he sleeps like a dead man until two in the afternoon. At first, I tried to restrain him, but now I've given up."'

As Turgenev was rather sweet on Marya Tolstoy, whom he had met the year before in the country, he hid his an-noyance at his guest's crude behaviour for some time. But the more he restrained himself, the more Tolstoy delighted in provoking him. Their quarrels, amusing at first, rapidly turned venomous. The moment other people were present,

they could not abide each other, and Tolstoy's need to contradict everyone else was becoming second nature to him.
It was as though, by systematic opposition, he might prove
his own existence to himself. He seemed to say, 'I think –
the opposite of everyone else – therefore I am!' On more
than one occasion Fet, in consternation, witnessed grotesque
scenes between the two men. Stung by Tolstoy's remark on
the lack of convictions among writers, Turgenev began
sputtering with rage and gesticulating wildly, while Tolstoy,
deadly calm, pinned him with the fire of his grey eyes and
dryly proceeded:

'I refuse to believe that your words express a true conviction. Here I stand, with a dagger in my hand or a sword,
and I say, "So long as I live no one shall enter this room!"
That is a conviction. But you all try to hide your real
thoughts from each other, and you call that a conviction!'

'Then why do you come here among us?' cried Turgenev
in a voice that squeaked with rage. 'This is not the place
for you! Go to Princess —'

'I don't need to ask you where to go!' retorted Tolstoy.
'And it isn't my presence here or anywhere else that is going
to change your empty chatter into real convictions.'[6]

Grigorovich, another contributor to *The Contemporary*,
gives an account of a scene in Nekrasov's apartment:

Turgenev shrieks and clutches at his throat and whispers with
his dying-gazelle eyes, 'I can't take any more! I've got bronchitis!' and begins striding up and down all three rooms. 'Bronchitis!' growls Tolstoy. 'Bronchitis is an imaginary disease!
Bronchitis is a metal!' Nekrasov, the master of the house, stands
there with his heart in his throat. He is just as frightened of
losing Turgenev as he is of losing Tolstoy, because both are
a precious boon to *The Contemporary*, and he tries to arbitrate.
We are all at our wit's end and don't know what to say. Tolstoy
is lying full-length on the sofa in the middle room, sulking.
Turgenev, the tails of his short coat spread wide, keeps marching back and forth with his hands in his pockets. Trying to ward
off catastrophe, I come up to the sofa and say, 'Tolstoy, dear
fellow, don't work yourself up so. You know Turgenev loves and

respects you!' 'I shall not permit him,' says Tolstoy with flaring nostrils, 'to go on eternally doing everything he can to provoke me. Look at him now, pacing up and down on purpose, wiggling his democratic thighs in front of me!' [7]

Knowing that Turgenev admired George Sand, Tolstoy once declared, during a dinner at Nekrasov's, that if her heroines had actually existed it would have been necessary, to set an example, 'to lash them to the hangman's cart and drag them through the streets of St Petersburg'. Turgenev began to protest and received a volley of such scathing sarcasm that he had not recovered three days later. 'I nearly quarrelled with Tolstoy,' he wrote to his friend Botkin. 'A lack of education will always show in some form or other. ... At a dinner at Nekrasov's he said such nasty and insulting things about G. Sand that I cannot repeat them. The argument grew very heated. In a word, he disgusted us all and showed himself in his worst light.'[8] Nor was George Sand the young officer's only pet aversion. He was not above attacking Herzen, the exiled revolutionary, whose review, *The Bell*, was smuggled over the frontier. And Shakespeare and Homer, whom he called 'phrase-makers'. But storm and sneer as he might, his friends on *The Contemporary* forgave all. And their very indulgence exasperated him.

Disenchanted with the Westerners, he decided to join the Slavophils: he went to see Milyutin and Kavelin, became friendly with Aksakov, Gorbunov and Kireyevsky, listened to them professing their faith in the superiority of the good old Russian traditions over the veneer of European culture, and quickly perceived that they were no better than their opponents. 'Their views are too narrow and unrealistic,' he wrote. 'By dint of arguing and preaching their aims have become considerably distorted, as always happens in a group of intellectuals.' He also disliked them for their attachment to the Orthodox religion, which he condemned for its 'monstrous perversion of the truth and historical inconsistency'. And lastly, he could not respect them because they were protected by the government, whilst the censor 'smothered' the Westerners.[9] Decidedly, he could not make up his mind which side to join. He agreed with nobody. Why was that? Very simple: both Westerners and Slavophils had one fault in common – they were bourgeois, the priests of a godless religion.

These men, my literary brothers, saw life in the following way, [he wrote, years later, in *Confession*]. Life in general, they said, was moving forward; this progress was due chiefly to the thinkers and, foremost among them, the artists and poets, in other words, to us. Our vocation is to edify mankind. This principle granted, these men should then have asked themselves one fundamental question: what are we, and what are we to teach? Instead of which, their method was to avoid the issue by affirming that one need not know anything in order to teach, since artists and poets teach unconsciously.

The relatively comfortable circumstances of these 'professional' writers, their cosmopolitan culture, their love of the pleasures of the table and their refined manners offended him as an insult to the majesty of the Idea. Forgetting that he himself was a hard drinker and inmate of certain houses of ill repute, he accused them of being 'amoral men, most of them wicked, with petty natures'. He who had never sacrificed a hair to defend a conviction attacked Turgenev, who had braved and borne exile for his obituary on Gogol. Applauded from his first word by every writer of his time, he denounced their 'literary conniving'.[10] For him, the only things worthy of respect in Russia were the aristocracy and the people; he was a member of the former, and was attracted to the latter. Through the veins of a noble coursed the entire history of the country, and through those of a muzhik, all the wisdom of the earth. Between these two *true* beings, a third had insinuated itself, a new and entirely artificial, useless and untrustworthy creature: the intellectual. The intellectual was not nourished on experience but on books. He claimed the right to instruct his fellows and he had never fought or ploughed a field. Most of the time, his pen produced nothing but falsehood.

'Lies!' The word was recurring increasingly often in Tolstoy's conversation and in his diary. He soon moved out of Turgenev's apartment: his host's feminine sensitivity, elegant dress, love of order and gourmet's pretensions gave Tolstoy an imperious desire to live in a shambles and feast on sour cabbage. But after moving into a dark ground-floor apartment in Officer's Street, he continued to harry his friend every time they met. Suddenly, in the midst of the most trivial conversation, Turgenev would feel himself transfixed by a gaze as keen as a scalpel, the look of a man determined that nobody was going to put anything over on him, and knew that Tolstoy was on the warpath again. A word, the flicker of an eyelid or quiver of a nostril had convinced him that his partner was not being sincere. 'Ivan Sergeyevich Turgenev told me,' wrote Garshin, 'that he had never experienced anything so disagreeable as that piercing look which, coupled with two or three venomous remarks, was enough to drive a man mad unless he had considerable self-control.' After scenes of this type, Turgenev, shattered and tearful, would complain to his friends. 'There is not one natural word or gesture in him,' he moaned faintly. 'He is forever posing, and I cannot understand this ridiculous affection for a wretched title of nobility in a man as intelligent as he is. ... You can boil a Russian officer in laundry soap for three days without dissolving that way they have of coming all lordling and cadet over you; no matter what varnish of education you try to paint on to an individual like that, the brute in him always shows through. ... And to think that all that vulgarity is aimed solely at gaining attention!'[11]

One day he was talking to Panayev in this vein and the latter remarked, 'You know, Turgenev, to listen to you ranting away like this, I would think you were jealous of him if I didn't know you so well.'

'Why should I be jealous of him? Why? Give me one reason!' cried Turgenev.

And he suddenly burst out laughing.

And Tolstoy, while furiously condemning the faults of this literary pontiff, could not bear to be out of his sight. If Turgenev went home in a huff, his young colleague would race after him, dogging his heels like a 'woman in love'.[12] The reconciliation was as necessary as the quarrel. Without a victim, what executioner would not die of boredom? The ups and downs of this friendship are recorded with meticulous detail in his diary. 'February 7 1856. Quarrelled with Turgenev.' 'February 13. Dinner at Turgenev's; we made up.' 'March 12. Quarrelled with Turgenev, this time for good, I think.' 'April 20. Went to see Turgenev and had a most amusing talk with him.' 'April 25. Pleasant visit to Turgenev. Must book him tomorrow for dinner.' 'May 5. Insulted everyone; Turgenev went home. ... I am depressed.' And when Turgenev, at the end of his tether, retreated to his country home at Spasskoye, the repentant troglodyte wrote to Aunt Toinette, 'Now he is gone, and I feel that I was beginning to care for him a great deal, even though we did nothing but argue. Without him, I am perishing of boredom.'[13]

He did not like St Petersburg, he did not feel at ease among his fellow writers, whatever their persuasion, and he was going out more from habit than desire. His ever-indulgent superiors had transferred him to the School of Pyrotechnics, where he did not even need to put in an appearance. All that remained of his military career was his uniform. He devoted every minute of his free time to literature. On 12 January 1856 the third Sevastopol sketch (*Sevastopol in August*) was published in *The Contemporary*. For the first time, the initials L.N.T. were replaced by the author's name in full, 'Count Leo Tolstoy'. An editor's note stated that *Childhood, Boyhood, Sevastopol in December* and other stories previously printed under the initials L.N.T. were by the same author. While working on *Youth*, he dashed off a few shorter tales: *Two Hussars, The Snow Storm, A Landlord's Morning*. And just to prove to himself that he belonged to no school or party, he gave some

of his manuscripts to the Westerners at *The Contemporary*
and some to Katkov's *Russian Herald*, a reactionary Slavophil periodical. Since he was not dependent on his writing
for a livelihood, he did not have to cater to public, critics
or colleagues; he could do as he pleased, break down doors,
bang his fist on the table, speak out loud and true. Diplomacy was not his cup of tea, and flattery still less. They
would have to take him as he was. And, true enough, the
very people who were exasperated by his conduct were subjugated by his art. There was never a false note in the praise
that hailed each new work. He despaired of finding an
enemy worthy of him.

At the beginning of January 1856 he was called to Orel,
where his brother Dmitry, who had been suffering from
tuberculosis for some time, lay dying. Leo Tolstoy had not
seen him for two years. In the sordid bedroom he found,
in place of the jolly Mitenka of his childhood, a white,
bloodless being, so gaunt that he was frightened by him.
'His enormous wrist was as though soldered to the bones
of his forearm. His face had been devoured by his eyes;
they were as beautiful, as serious as ever, but now their expression was inquisitorial. He coughed and spat incessantly,
and he did not want to die, did not want to believe he was
about to die.'[14] At his bedside were his sister Marya,
brother-in-law Valerian, Aunt Toinette and a girl with a
pockmarked face and red eyes, a kerchief tied around her
head. This was Masha, a prostitute, whom Dmitry had
bought from a brothel a few years before – the first woman
he had ever known.

In this brother, ravaged by suffering and debauchery, Tolstoy saw a distorted reflection of himself. There seemed to
be a propensity in the Tolstoy blood for swinging from
good to evil, humility to pride, lechery to virtue, with unusual facility; they were all more or less creatures of extremes, lost in a world of happy-medium. Only, in Leo
reason moderated instinct, whereas Dmitry followed his
impulses to the end, however absurd their consequences.

There was something magnificent in this blind impulsion, something noble in this defeat. Of old, his brothers had laughed at him and called him 'Noah' because of his exaggerated piety. For years, in Kazan, he had continued his studies, caring for the sick, visiting the prisons and fasting to the point of inanition. Shabbily dressed, unwashed, stooped-shouldered and diffident, his only pleasure was abstinence. After receiving his law degree, he had gone to St Petersburg and appeared, looking like a tramp, before Tanayev, secretary of state of the Second Division, requesting employment: 'Anything at all, so long as I can be useful.' Such an aspiration coming from a person of such unlikely appearance could only arouse the official's misgivings. Disappointed with the results of this overture, Dmitry had gone back to Sherbachevka and tried simultaneously to make a living from his estate and treat his serfs decently. His friends were pilgrims and monks and an ugly old hermit, short, bandy-legged and dark, who spoke in tones of deepest mystery and was known as Father Luke. No alcohol, no tobacco, total chastity. One day, however, the youngest Islenyev son had prevailed upon the ascetic to accompany him to Moscow. At twenty-six, the life of sin came to Dmitry as a revelation. He began to drink, smoke, play cards and frequent brothels. But, pure even in his depravity, he resolved to keep the prostitute who had initiated him into the pleasures of the flesh. Scandal and consternation in the family! Brothers, sister, aunts, all opposed him. On his way back from the Caucasus, Leo himself had gone to Sherbachevka and tried to persuade Dmitry to get rid of the girl; for, despite his shining theories of redemption through love, the future author of *Resurrection* really could not condone such a misalliance. After Leo's lecture, Dmitry sent Masha away; but his conscience compelled him to fetch her back again before long. Perhaps he was afraid to die alone; the couple roamed from place to place until the day, at Orel, when Dmitry could no longer get up. Masha was there beside him, plumping his pillows, brewing tisanes, holding the basin. He asked to see a miraculous icon, and she brought it. Hands clasped, he prayed to the holy image. Tolstoy readily persuaded himself that his brother was in good hands and he could depart with a clear conscience. 'I was particularly loathsome at that time,' he later wrote. 'I had come from St Petersburg, where I was very active in society, and I was bursting with conceit! I felt sorry for Mitya [Dmitry], but not very. I simply put in an appearance at Orel and left immediately.'[15] Three weeks later he was informed that his brother was dead; he was expecting it. One dry note in his diary: 'February 2, my brother is dead.' And, in a letter written the same day to Aunt Pelagya Yushkov, these few words: 'He died a good Christian. That is a great comfort to us all.'

He did not bother to go to the funeral. As before, when his father and grandmother had died, his grief was mixed with a feeling of selfish annoyance. Dmitry's death created problems for him. That very evening he had been invited to a reception in the home of a relative of his, a lady of whom he was very fond. He wrote to excuse himself, saying there had been a death in the family. Then, unable to stand it, he dressed and went to her home. She was surprised to see him and asked why he had come. 'What I wrote you this morning wasn't true,' he said. 'If I am here, that means there is no reason why I should not be here.' A few days later he told his Aunt Alexandra Tolstoy* that he had also gone to the theatre. 'I trust you enjoyed yourself!' was her icy comment. 'Not at all,' he answered. 'I came home in agony.' 'And so that is how you twist the truth, in spite of all your claims to sincerity!' she cried. He looked at her hard and said, weighing every word, 'I must test myself in everything, down to the last detail.'[16] Later, writing of Dmitry's sorry end, he said, 'I honestly believe that what bothered me most about his death was that it prevented me from attending a performance at Court to which I had been

---

* Alexandra Tolstoy's father was Count Andrey Andreyevich Tolstoy, brother of Leo Tolstoy's paternal grandfather.

invited.'[17] But no event in his life was lost to literature. The furnished room at Orel, its walls covered with evil-looking stains; Masha, the prostitute with the heart of gold; Dmitry, reduced to skin and bones, dying in a garret; the smell of medicine and sweat, the rattling, coughing, spitting, change of nightshirt, doctor's visit – he found a place for them all in his description of the death of Levin's brother in *Anna Karenina*.[18]

The Crimean War, from which Leo Tolstoy now felt so far removed, ended with the signing of the Treaty of Paris, and Russia heaved a sigh of relief. On 19 March 1856 Alexander II published a manifesto promising the country that a great effort would be made to improve the legal rights of all his subjects. That day, a memorable occasion for the nation, was also noteworthy for Leo Tolstoy, but for a different reason. Having chanced to read an unflattering opinion of himself in a letter which Longinov, a contributor to *The Contemporary*, had written to Nekrasov, he issued a formal challenge to his detractor. 'God knows what will come of it,' he wrote two days later, on 21 March, 'but I shall be firm and bold. On the whole, this incident has had a beneficial effect on me. I have made up my mind to go back to the village, get married as soon as possible and not write under my own name any more.' The last two of these three resolutions were promptly forgotten, and he meant to wait until after his duel before carrying out the first. But Longinov did not answer the challenge, friends interceded and Tolstoy subsided, with the thought that the puny pen pusher did not even deserve to be grazed by his bullet. A few days later he received a piece of news that was very flattering to his self-esteem and effaced the last traces of the bad feeling left by his abortive duel: on 26 March 1856 he was promoted to the rank of lieutenant, 'for bravery and resolute conduct displayed on August 4 at the battle of the Chernaya'. He immediately requested an eleven-month furlough, for 'treatment' abroad. But he had nothing that needed treating and so, instead of going abroad, he packed his bags for Yasnaya Polyana. The spring must be magnificent just now! And, on the way, he could make a little side trip to pass the time of day with Ivan Turgenev on his estate at Spasskoye. Something had been missing from his life ever since the soft, gentle giant – like a dummy to stick pins into – had been out of reach. He was still thinking about him as he read one of his short stories on the train that carried him to Moscow: *Diary of a Superfluous Man.* And he fiercely recorded his reactions on 17 May: 'Appallingly syrupy, cute, clever and playful.' The very image of its author. Really, he could hardly wait to see him!

Yet once he got to Moscow, he was so pleased to be there that he prolonged his stay. As he had sworn before he left never to set foot inside a cabaret or brothel again,[19] he had to fall back on trips to the parks and monuments. In the gardens of the Hermitage, where he was loitering one bored afternoon, he ran into Longinov, erstwhile refuser of his challenge. His anger boiled up again, he could not decide whether to speak to the coward or pretend not to notice him, and strolled ostentatiously along in front of him with murder in his eye. Longinov did not turn a hair, however, and Tolstoy went away disconcerted. Another day he went as far as the Troitsa Monastery, where Aunt Pelagya Yushkov was making her retreat. 'She's still the same,' he wrote in his diary on 19 May. 'Vain, full of petty and amiable sensitivity, kind-hearted.' The next day he went to the sacristy: 'You would think you were watching a Punch-and-Judy show: numbers of people kissing icons, and one prostrate old woman braying with joy.' But mockery, in him, quickly gave way to compassion. Upon analysing his state of mind, he found himself divided into four compartments: 'Love, the pangs of repentance (pleasant, however), the desire to marry, and a feeling for nature.'

It was in this poetic mood that he met Dyakov's sister Alexandra once again, at her brother's home. He had been in love with her long before and had not seen her for years; she was now married to Prince Andrey Obolensky. 'Yes,' he wrote, 'even today it pains me to think of the happiness that might have been mine and has fallen to the lot of a distinguished man, A. Obolensky.' (22 May 1856.) 'She listened to me twice, very attentively. No, I am not mistaken when I say she is the most charming woman I have ever met. The most highly refined artistic nature and at the same time the most moral.' (24 May.) To subdue his passion, which he knew to be hopeless, he went out to the Sparrow Hills one evening to drink milk, bathe by the Moskva and sleep in the garden, 'while the monks were getting drunk with the girls and dancing polkas in the orchard'.[20] The following day at the Dyakovs', he had a conversation with the fair Alexandra that troubled him considerably. 'She *suddenly* gave me her hand. Her eyes filled with tears. ... I was beside myself with joy. ... Even though the feeling is hopeless, I very much like inspiring it. . .' But after an exchange of reminiscences, some transparent allusions and a few soft squeezes of the hand, Alexandra announced that she would shortly have to follow her husband to St Petersburg, whereupon Tolstoy decided that there was nothing further to detain him in Moscow.

He was famished for the green countryside. On the eve of his departure for Yasnaya Polyana, he dined at Pokrovskoye-Streshnevo,* eight miles outside Moscow, at the home of his childhood friend Lyubov Behrs (née Islenyev), the very woman he had once pushed off the balcony. She received him *en famille*: as she had let her servants off to go to church, the meal was served by her three daughters, Lisa (twelve), Sonya (eleven) and Tatyana (ten). A playful spirit of rivalry animated the pink-cheeked girls, with their sparkling eyes and skirts belling out over starched petticoats. Their eyes devoured the famous author whose *Childhood* and *Boyhood* they had read, the hero telling Papa about the war, his lips scarcely moving beneath his thick

---

* Pokrovskoye-Streshnevo, the Behrs' property, should not be confused with Pokrovskoye, Valerian Tolstoy's estate in the government of Orel.

moustache. After the meal they asked him to sing the 'Song of Sevastopol'; he willingly complied. Then they went for a walk. They even played leap-frog. 'What sweet, gay little girls!' Tolstoy wrote in his diary, on 26 May 1856. He did not dream that six years later one of them – Sonya, the second daugher – would become his wife.

The desire to revisit the scenes of his childhood was not the only thing that brought Tolstoy back to Yasnaya Polyana. For some time he had been thinking about the emancipation of the serfs. The idea was in the air. In March of that year, at the assembly of marshals of the nobility in Moscow, Tsar Alexander II had said it was better to 'abolish serfdom from above, rather than wait for it to abolish itself from below'. Then he convened a Committee for Peasant Affairs and instructed it to prepare a draft reform. The committee, determined to stall for time, had referred the question to a commission of which General Rostovtsev was chairman. Westerners and Slavophils alike united in condemning the delay. On 22 April 1856 Tolstoy noted in his diary, 'My relations with the serfs are beginning to prey upon my mind.' Hearing talk of the impending reform, he flung caution to the winds. Why couldn't he do, alone and at once, what it would take the government years to accomplish, because of the slowness of administrative machinery? This desire assuredly showed great good-will on his part towards the peasants, but once again, there was a large share of pride mingled with the master's generosity. Rather than submit, like any other landowner, to a decision from the tsar, he wanted to lead the field, take the initiative, be the first to put social justice into practice. He began his campaign forthwith. He went to see Kavelin the historian, and Milyutin, a member of the imperial commission, and drew up his own draft reform, which he submitted to Their Excellencies Levshin and Bludov for approval. The replies were evasive. Tolstoy was incensed: 'Wherever one turns in Russia, one sees that everything is beginning to change

– but the men in charge of the changes are old and therefore incompetent.'[21] In the end, although he was not officially authorized to act, he was not exactly forbidden to do so either. That was enough for him.

It was not really his intention to cast away all his worldly goods for nothing, especially as there was a two-thousand-rouble mortgage on his property which had to be repaid before anything else. Hence, no rash donations, no evangelical abdication; rather, an equitable arrangement respecting the interests of both master and serfs. The wisest course would be to free the peasants and lease the land they had hitherto farmed for their master's sole profit; in exchange, the peasants would pay rent for thirty years, after which the land would belong to them outright.

His pockets stuffed with papers, Tolstoy hurried back to Yasnaya Polyana, feeling himself the bearer of a priceless gift. Before leaving he had written out the speech he would make to the peasants: 'God has planted in my soul the idea of setting you all free.' After this preamble, he would propose to discuss the plan 'with the old men, the wise'. 'If anything about it seems unfair or illegal to you,' he would say, 'tell me, and I shall make it right and change it.' In advance, he savoured the surprise and gratitude of the crowd, and in his heart a kind thought stirred for himself.

When he arrived at Yasnaya Polyana on 28 May 1856, he hardly took time to kiss Aunt Toinette, and immediately gave orders to assemble the muzhiks. While he was waiting to speak to them, he hastily jotted down in his diary, 'At Yasnaya, life is sad, pleasant, not at all in harmony with my state of mind. Besides, when I compare myself as I now am with my old memories of Yasnaya, I see how far I have progressed towards a liberal approach ... in a little while I shall hold a meeting and make a speech. What will come of it?'

He went to the village square with a bad case of actor's stage-fright, and instead of reading out the text he had prepared in St Petersburg, greeted the serfs massed in front of him with a resounding 'Hello!' Then, very simply, he explained his idea to them. A few hours later he came back to his diary, full of optimism: 'Everything is all right. The peasants are delighted to understand me; they see me as a bold, forward-looking man and they have confidence in me.' The next day, second meeting, and first hitch. Living in St Petersburg, far from the serfs, Tolstoy had gradually forgotten their faults. Now he saw them again, just as they were before – suspicious, obstinate, crafty and stupid. Instead of snatching at a proposal that was so advantageous to them, they hung back, smiled, scratched their heads and said 'Thank you' as though it was not their place to say it, asked for time to consider and went away dragging their feet. Hardly containing his anger, Tolstoy talked to them individually, explaining every clause in the contract, and then called them together again to subject them en masse to the fire of his eloquence. There were five of these conferences, during which the project became even more liberal, the purchase-period being reduced from thirty to twenty-four years. The peasants were still unconvinced. From the house-servants Tolstoy soon learned the reason for their reticence: it was rumoured in the villages that at the coronation festivities next August, the tsar was going to free all the serfs and give them the land for nothing. So by offering to lease them the land they already farmed, their master was trying to cheat them, to 'stuff them in the sack' as their own saying went. He was a fine fellow, their master, but canny. He knew the laws. He was just trying to take poor innocent folk for a ride. Outraged, Tolstoy determined to have one last heart-to-heart talk with the muzhiks. On 7 June after the meeting, he wrote, 'Their obstinacy put me in such a rage that I could hardly control myself.' Three days later, another talk, another failure. This time, there could be no doubt: 'They don't want their freedom.' Their lord was just as much their slave as they were his. 'Two strong men are chained together; each is hurt when the other moves, and there is not enough room for them both to work together.'[22] The master put his plans back in his pockets: 'We shall return to the question in the autumn,'[23] he said, without much conviction. And he vented his spleen on that portion of the Russian intellectuals for whom the muzhik was the repository of all ancestral wisdom. Let no one say another word to him about the innate goodness and profound intelligence of the people!

'I'll tell those Slavophils what I think of the grandeur and sacredness of the Mir assemblies,'* he wrote to Nekrasov on 12 June 1856. 'What nonsense! I shall show you the minutes of the meetings, I've taken notes.' It was no longer the peasants he was pitying now, but the landowners. For if someone did not put a stop to the outrageous pipe-dreams that were sweeping the villages, the serfs would rise up in arms against their masters one day and simply demand the land the tsar had supposedly promised to give them along with their freedom. It would be the beginning of a fearful peasant insurrection. The worst was to be expected from a people as bigoted and cruel as the Russians, and the innovators who were trying to give them what they wanted would be swept under by the wave. Tolstoy personally was not at all tempted by martyrdom. One evening, in a panic, he wrote to Bludov, a minister, warning him against the stupidity of the masses:

There are two extremely grave and dangerous matters I must bring to your attention: (1) the conviction that a general emancipation is going to take place during the coronation period is firmly rooted among the people, even in the most remote villages; (2) the question of who owns the land populated by the peasants is being decided in most cases in favour of the peasants, who would like to appropriate all of their lord's property. 'We belong to you, but the land belongs to us.' When, at one of my meetings, they told me to give them all the land and I answered that I would then have to go barefoot, they simply laughed at me. ... The government is responsible for this state of affairs, because it has evaded the chief question of the day. ... I confess

*Russian rural community.

I have never understood why it could not be established that the land belongs to the landlords, and the peasants be freed without giving them the land. ... Freeing them with the land is not, in my opinion, a solution. Who is to answer these questions that are essential to a solution of the overall problem, namely: how much land shall go to each, or what share of the estate; how is the landlord to receive compensation; over what period of time; who is to pay the compensation? ... Time is short. ... If the serfs are not free in six months, we are in for a holocaust. Everything is ripe for it. Only one criminal hand is needed to fan the flame of rebellion, and we will all be consumed in the blaze.[24]

Having foretold the catastrophe, Tolstoy felt doubly relieved: his conscience was at peace because he had offered his people their freedom, and he had squared himself with the authorities by reporting the dangerous mood of the populace. What did still annoy him was the silent triumph of Aunt Toinette. She had opposed his project from the start – as narrow-minded as the peasants, she was, but in a different way; clinging, like them, to the tradition of a paternal relationship between lord and subjects; believing that God had given them to the master like big children to be brought up, protected and occasionally punished. 'One hundred years of explaining would not make her see the injustice of serfdom,'[25] he wrote on his arrival. And a few days later, on 12 June, 'I am beginning to develop a silent hatred of my aunt, in spite of all her affection.'

He did not like Yasnaya Polyana as much as before. After being sold to pay his gambling debts, the old wooden house in which he was born had been dismantled by the buyer, his neighbour Gorokhov, and put up again twelve miles away, in the hamlet of Dolgoye.* Contrary to Nicholas, he found that its removal had disfigured the estate. A riot of tall weeds and bushes grew in place of the old foundations.

---

* Gorokhov's land was later bought by the neighbouring commune and the peasants demolished the house, already badly run-down, for firewood. On 6 December 1897 Leo Tolstoy wrote in his diary, 'Went to Dolgoye on the fourth. Was moved by the ruins of the house. A host of memories.'

Tolstoy now lived with his aunt in one of the two small stone buildings that used to stand on either side of the main house. Within their walls, devoid of memories, he felt out of place, as in the home of strangers. His brothers and sister were far away. To pass the time, he wrote *The Cossacks*, corrected *Youth*, read Pushkin and Gogol, swam in the Voronka, surreptitiously overpowered a peasant girl in the bushes ('Awful lust, amounting to physical illness'[26]) and, in the evenings, played solitaire and yawned.

Shortly after his arrival he went to see his sister at Pokrovskoye. Alas; he found her so unattractive that he wrote in his diary, 'Masha has bad breath, a serious drawback!'[27] At five o'clock the next morning he called for his horse and set off for Spasskoye, Turgenev's estate, some fourteen miles away. When he arrived two hours later, his heart pulsing with friendship, Turgenev was not at home. He explored the house while he waited: 'There, I could see the roots of the man; it enabled me to understand many things, and reconciled me with him.'[28] At last, Turgenev returned. Embracings, tears of joy. The grievances of both had been left behind in St Petersburg. 'Lunched, walked, had a very pleasant talk with him, took a nap....'

The next day Masha and Valerian joined the two writers. Turgenev was full of attentions for the young woman; he must not have noticed her bad breath! He thought her pretty, with her childish face and frank, open expression and her unaffected manner. He had even dedicated a short story to her: *Faust*. After all, that fool of a Valerian deserved no better than he got, since he had been neglecting his wife for some time. 'I like the relationship between Masha and Turgenev,' Tolstoy wrote. And he went back to Yasnaya Polyana, convinced that he had renewed a friendship with his colleague that would stand the strain of time.

When he saw him again a month later, he changed his mind. His animosity flared up without apparent reason, like a brushfire after long smouldering. 'He is a man of no consequence, cold and unpleasant. I feel sorry for him, but I

shall never be able to be his friend.' (5 July 1856.) 'His whole
life is an attempt to ape simplicity. I am decidedly repelled
by him.' (8 July 1856.) 'He refuses to do anything, on the
pretext that an artist is powerless. But no man can avoid the
material side of life – the muzhik for us, like the bank for
the English.' (Notebooks, 31 July 1856.)

In August of 1856 Turgenev left for France. The moment
he was out of sight Tolstoy began to miss him. There was a
mysterious bond between these two that strengthened with
absence, for Turgenev, settled into the Viardots' home at
Rozay-en-Brie, was also haunted by the thought of his loving tormentor. With melancholy benevolence he analysed
the other man, whose superiority seemed still more patent
from afar. To be sure, he did not underestimate his own
talent: he knew (he had heard it so often!) that his style
was the most elegant in all Russia; but since reading *Childhood, Boyhood* and the *Sevastopol Sketches*, he felt that
everything he wrote himself was artificial and false. His
books turned out to be works of art, those of the other man
were chunks of life. Was this the beginning of his decline?
Was that young boor with the glittering eyes going to rele-
gate him to oblivion? He felt it coming, it made him sad,
but he did not protest against the judgement of posterity.
Out of intellectual integrity, he felt he must confess himself
to Tolstoy.

You are the only man in the world with whom I have had
misunderstandings, [he wrote from France] and they arose precisely because, with you, I did not want to remain within the
limits of a simple friendship. I wanted to go further and deeper.
But I plunged ahead recklessly, collided with you and upset you
and then, seeing my error, drew back, too suddenly, perhaps.
And that is why a 'breach' grew up between us. Then, too, I am
much older than you. I have followed a different path. . . . Your
whole life is facing forward, mine is built on the past.* . . . You
are too solidly planted on your own feet to become a disciple of

* Ivan Turgenev was thirty-eight at the time, Tolstoy was twenty-
eight.

anything! I can assure you that I never thought you were malicious or dreamed you were capable of literary jealousy. I saw in you (forgive the expression!) a considerable amount of confusion, but never anything evil. And you are far too perceptive not to know that if either of us has anything to envy the other, you are surely not the one. In a word, we will never be friends in Rousseau's sense, but we will love each other and rejoice in each other's success and, after you have settled down and all that is surging around inside you has subsided a little, then, I am certain of it, we shall meet again as joyfully and openly as on the day I met you for the first time, in St Petersburg.[29]

He hoped his words would mollify his correspondent – but they only irritated him. By what right, thought Tolstoy, was this 'European' preaching to him? He might criticize and revile himself in front of a mirror, but he would not allow anyone else to make reflections on any aspect of his character. 'Received a letter from Turgenev yesterday, and it did not please me,' he wrote in his diary.[30]

A few days later, further explanations from Turgenev arrived in reply to a letter from Tolstoy: [31]

I know I care for the man in you (for the author, it goes without saying), but there are many things in you that rub me the wrong way and, in the end, I have found it more convenient to remain at a distance. ... From afar my heart is full of fraternal sympathy for you, even tenderness. ... Once you liked my work, and it might even have had some influence upon you before you found yourself. Now it is pointless for you to study me, all you will see is the difference in the way we work, the mistakes and hesitations. What you must study is mankind in general, and your own heart, and the truly great writers. As for me, I am only the exponent of a period of transition, meaningful only for individuals who are themselves in a state of transition.[32]

And, as though to warn Tolstoy against the temptation of dogmatism which was already threatening him, he wrote on another occasion:

'Would to God your horizon may broaden every day! The people who bind themselves to systems are those who are unable to encompass the whole truth and try to catch it by the tail; a system is like the tail of truth, but truth is like a lizard: it leaves its tail in your fingers and runs away, knowing full well that it will grow a new one in a twinkling.' [33]

After hanging back, Tolstoy finally let himself be swayed by Turgenev's solicitude. He also recovered his former fondness for Aunt Toinette, whom he had been hating for her retrograde attitide towards serfdom. 'Aunt Toinette is an amazing woman! Now there's a case of love that endureth all!' (Diary, 1 July 1856). Even Yasnaya Polyana seemed pleasant to him, now that he had temporarily given up the idea of freeing the muzhiks and no longer needed to try to argue with them. He read, wrote, hunted, savoured the beauties nature spread before him. What was missing from this idyllic tableau? A woman, to be sure! Solemnly and persistently, Tolstoy began to wonder whether the time had not come for him to marry.

Early in the summer, when his friend Dyakov came to Yasnaya Polyana, Tolstoy poured out his matrimonial projects to him. Since, at last hearing, Dyakov's own sister was the woman he claimed to be in love with, his friend was greatly surprised to learn that the object of his passion was no longer Alexandra Obolensky, but a certain Valerya Arsenyev. This young person, an orphan, lived with her sisters Olga and Genia on the estate of Sudakovo, five miles from Yasnaya Polyana. An aged aunt and a companion, Mlle Vergani – French, according to the rule – mounted guard over the three maidens. As a neighbour, Tolstoy had known them for years. But he had recently come down from Moscow in the company of Mlle Vergani, who had succeeded in quickening his interest in little Valerya. He had gone to Sudakovo several times, vaguely paid court to the twenty-year-old maiden whom everyone was desperate to marry off, and now could not decide whether to propose or bow out. When consulted on this point, Dyakov, whose chief aim was probably to divert Tolstoy's attention from his sister, said he must lose no time: 'He advised me to marry Valerya. When I listen to him, I too, believe it would be the best thing for me to do. Can it be money that is stopping me? No; simply lack of opportunity. Then he took me back to the turning for Sudakovo.' And Tolstoy, with a shove from 'the best friend in the world', set off down the path that led straight to matrimony, certain that he was striding towards happiness. But when he actually came face to face with the girl, his ardour cooled. He had never really looked at her before. She was chubby, colourless, and had porcelain eyes. 'A pity she has no bone, no fire,' he wrote that evening. 'A wet noodle. Sweet, though – her smile is sickly and submissive.'[34]

From that day forward, he saw Valerya more and more often, testing her as much as himself. Marriage was such an important matter, he thought, that you mustn't commit yourself until you were sure, and had added up the good and bad points of your chosen one. Two columns: debit, credit. Under the suitor's probing eye, the total changed after every encounter. A detail of dress or hair style was enough to bring the whole project to a halt. If she talked clothes to him, he fretted: 'She is frivolous! In her it would appear to be a lasting passion, rather than a passing fancy.'[35] If she wore a white gown, he went soft all over, as though her dress were a promise of angelic innocence: 'Valerya had on a white dress. Very nice. Spent one of the most pleasant days in my whole life. Do I love her seriously? Can she be steadfast in love?'[36] If she used a bad word, his esteem turned to resentment: 'Valerya is impossibly uneducated, ignorant, not to stay stupid. The verb "to prostitute", which she used, pained me, God knows why, and coming on top of my toothache, plunged me into gloom.'[37] If she chanced to appear bare-armed, he left off criticizing her soul and turned to her body: 'She was wearing a white sleeveless dress: her arms are not pretty. This upset me. I began to tease her so bitterly that she had to smile, but her tears showed through. ... I felt fine, but she was miserable. I am

conscious of that.'[38] If, the following day, she received
him in a dressing-gown, sitting at her writing-desk wearing
a languid expression, it was worse still: 'Valerya, decked
out in that revolting, supposedly alluring peignoir again, was
writing in an unlighted room.'[39] If she described the dresses
she was going to wear in August for the coronation festivities, to which her family had been invited, he suspected her,
oddly enough, of lacking a maternal instinct: 'She is all
frivolity about everything serious, and terrifyingly light-
headed. I am afraid she is one of those people who does not
even love children.'[40] If she paid less attention to her dress
and drew her hair back to let her ears show, he warmed up
again: 'For the first time, I found her without "her gowns",
as Sergey says. She is ten times better like that, and above
all, more natural. She has put her hair behind her ears, now
that she sees I like it that way. ... Spent a positively blissful
evening.'[41] Three days later his beatitude turned to acute
physical excitement. After beating his brains out to convince himself that Valerya was nice, he began to find
her attractive instead: 'Odd that Valerya should be beginning to appeal to me as a woman, whereas before it was just
as a woman that she repelled me. Well, not always. It depended on my mood. Yesterday I noticed her arms for the
first time, which used to disgust me.' Perhaps, it was simply
the fact that she was about to leave for Moscow that made
her desirable. She was looking forward so intensely to those
coronation festivities, the suppers, receptions, balls and fireworks, that he was jealous *a priori* of every man who would
come near her! Around him, the two families were conspiring to force the hook down his throat, with Vergani, the
tireless companion, leading the pack; she had sworn to
marry off the poor creature before the end of the year, as
she had just done for Olga.* She invented a thousand oppor-
tunities for the young people to meet, whispered advice into
the girl's ear, chose her gowns, urged her on or held her
back according to the mood of the man she was supposed

* Olga Arsenyev had just announced her engagement in Moscow.

to ensnare. Sometimes it was Tolstoy who went to Sudakovo, and sometimes Valerya, chaperoned by the Frenchwoman, who came on some pretext or other to Yasnaya Polyana. There were walks in the forest, impromptu picnics at the haying camp, reveries, tête-à-têtes on a moonlit balcony and four-handed sessions at the piano, while the older generation gathered around the samovar and laid plans for the future. When he was alone with Aunt Toinette, Tolstoy had to submit to her remonstrances. She could not understand why he was still waiting to become engaged. In her opinion Valerya was perfect in every respect. If he waited, he might lose her. Hadn't he had enough of living like a wild animal? Ah! God had given her a heavy cross to bear with her nephews: Dmitry had died in the arms of a prostitute, and the three others stubbornly refused to marry! ... Aunt Pelagya Yushkov, who was visiting Yasnaya Polyana just then, shared Aunt Toinette's pro-marriage attitude. Sergey, on the other hand – the eternal sceptic – warned his brother against the folly he was about to commit. 'Conversation about Valerya,' Leo Tolstoy wrote. 'Sergey's words were like a cold shower.'[42] He was increasingly intimidated by the idea of marriage, but he did not have the courage to break off. She was to leave for Moscow on 12 August. On the tenth he ran over to Sudakovo in an extremely positive frame of mind: 'Talked marriage with Valerya. She is intelligent and exceptionally sweet-tempered.' On the eleventh, 'A storm prevented me from going over to the Arsenyevs, although I badly wanted to go.' On the twelfth he hastened along the sodden paths towards the girl he was already thinking of as his fiancée. What a lot of luggage! Trunks full of dresses and hats. The young lady was almost pretty in her travelling suit. Touching farewells, promise of a speedy return, admonitions on either side. That evening, in his bedroom, Tolstoy wrote, 'She was more simple and sweeter than ever. I wish I knew whether or not I am in love with her.'

When she was present, Valerya got on his nerves; absent, she seemed irreplaceable. Even the 'pretty peasant girls' he met in the forest, over whom he occasionally 'lost his self-control', as he put it, could not take his mind off her. 'These past days I have been thinking more and more of my little Valerya,' he wrote on 16 August. And the following day, flaunting propriety, he turned out a half-tender, half-teasing letter: 'To my great surprise, I am bored without you! ... I console myself in your absence with the thought that you will come back a little older, for being youthful to the point of childishness is a fault, albeit charming. . . . Was Mortier* pleased with you? I can see your mournful smile, I can hear you say, "He cannot live without moralizing." How can I help it? I have got into a bad habit, that of teaching others what I don't know myself.'

He hoped for a quick reply, but Valerya would not give him that satisfaction and, on Mlle Vergani's advice, fired off a letter to Aunt Toinette that was brilliantly calculated to make him jealous. It contained an enthusiastic account of the coronation entertainment, her success with His Majesty's aides-de-camp, a military procession during which her dress had almost been torn in the crush. After reading this bulletin of Valerya's social success, Tolstoy gave free rein to his wrath:

'I try to restrain the mild hatred your note to my aunt has aroused in me,' he wrote her. 'Not even mild hatred, but rather sorrow and disappointment, for "Drive nature out the window and it comes in at the door ..." How cruel. Why did you write that? Don't you know how it exasperates me?' He went on to say that she must be 'ghastly' in her ceremonial gown, that the 'current' pattern she spoke of sounded calculated to make her look ugly, that most of the aides-de-camp sniffing about her skirts were 'cads or imbeciles'. He concluded with these vengeful words, 'I shall not come to Moscow, although I should like to, if only to lose my temper at the sight of you. Wishing you every sort of

---

*Louis-Henri-Stanislas Mortier de Fontaine (1816–83), French pianist and composer, who was living in Moscow at the time and with whom Valerya studied music.

vanity-flattering joy, accompanied by its usual bitter ending, I remain your most humble, but also most difficult, servant.'

As soon as he sent the letter, he regretted it. Perhaps he was going too far? He had a few erotic dreams in rapid succession – each scrupulously noted in his diary* – and, on 8 September, took up his pen once again, to apologize to Valerya:

'I am tormented by the thought that I wrote to you without your permission and in such an awkward, stupid, vulgar manner. Send me one word to tell me whether you are angry and in what way. ... Are you still having a good time? ... How is your music? Are you coming back, and if so, when?'

Thereupon, he fell ill. Congestion of the lungs, he was sure of it. Aunt Toinette called in several doctors. They bled him and applied leeches: ten in one day. Quaking with fever, he thought of his brother Dmitry's demise and wondered whether he, too, might not be consumptive. 'I feel as though I am going to die,' he wrote. Which did not prevent him from revising the manuscript of *Youth* in bed. He was completely recovered when the Misses Arsenyev returned to the fold, on 24 September. That very day Mlle Vergani came over to Yasnaya Polyana, alone, to reconnoitre – she wanted to inspect the suitor's state of mind after a month and a half of separation. To arouse the young man's jealousy, she described Valerya's life in Moscow as one long triumphal procession from drawing-room to drawing-room. The dose was too big, the patient rebelled.[43] 'After what she told me,' Tolstoy wrote, 'Valerya disgusts me.'

Nevertheless, he saddled his horse next day and galloped over to Sudakovo. Once again, face to face with the girl, his spirits fell. 'Valerya is nice,' he wrote on 25 September, 'but, alas! just plain dumb.' And the following day, 'Valerya came to see me. Nice, but narrow-minded and incredibly trivial.' Was this the end? No! Mlle Vergani had her

*Beginning on 3 September 1856.

weather eye open: in the nick of time, Valerya began to re-
fer to her tender sentiments for Mortier de Fontaine,
her piano teacher in Moscow. Tolstoy immediately revived: 'Curious, it annoyed me. I was embarrassed for her
and for myself, but also, for the first time, I experienced
something resembling an attachment for her.'[44] This new
lease on love was not long-lasting. Two days later, calm and
gloomy, he confided to his diary, 'I am not in love, but this
relationship has had a great effect on my life. Still, I have
not yet known love and, judging by what I feel now from
this foretaste, I think I must be capable of experiencing it
with great violence. Please God, not for Valerya. She is shallow and cold as ice, and has no principles.' A few days later,
on 8 October, there was a decided turn for the worse: 'I
cannot speak to Valerya except to criticize her. I feel absolutely nothing for her, it's only a habit. She is no more than
an unpleasant memory for me.'

The snow had come. An infinity of white, a desert of in-
comprehension, spread out between Yasnaya Polyana and
Sudakovo. Tolstoy argued with Aunt Toinette, set off into
the country on horseback, hunted rabbit, arrived unannounced at the Arsenyevs', where everyone nevertheless
behaved as though they were expecting him. On 19 October
he found Valerya particularly homely; 'Looked at Valerya
more calmly. She has put on a great deal of weight, I most
decidedly feel nothing at all for her now.' This did not prevent him from returning to Sudakovo on 23 October and
telling Mlle Vergani the tale, invented by him, of one
Khrapovitsky and a certain Dembitskaya, from which it
emerged that marriage was a serious affair and a passion for
clothes was incompatible with a sound approach to connu-
bial bliss. Of course, he was counting on the companion to
repeat this fable to the young lady, which she did that
same evening. In the meantime, he had agreed to spend the
night at Sudakovo, in a room prepared for him. 'Went to
sleep in their house, almost at peace, but far from in love.'
The next morning Valerya came to breakfast in a radiant

twitter. She was all innocence, docility, sobriety, tenderness in person. Subjugated, Tolstoy took her to the ball at Tula: 'Valerya was delightful, I am almost in love with her,' he wrote upon his return, on 24 October. And, on the twenty-fifth: 'Talked to her. Went very well. Was even on the point of snivelling.' Two more days passed and, in a burst of honesty, he showed her a page of his diary ending with the words, 'I love her.' She tore it out and ran away. That night he rebuked himself for his rashness. Now she would surely imagine the affair was in the bag. To find out, he rushed over to see her the next morning – catastrophe! She was wearing that triumphant, mysterious air of the young fiancée that he dreaded above all else. 'Her hair arranged in a ghastly fashion, decked out with a mantle in my honour. I suffered, I was miserable, the day went by in tedium, conversation languished. I have become, without making a move, a sort of fiancé.' [45] The more clearly he saw the role he had been cast in by the Arsenyevs and all their neighbours and acquaintances, the more he wanted to quit the game. But could he, after all those months of arduous courtship, without dishonouring the girl to whom the entire province had unofficially united him? The devil take their wagging tongues! The time had come for trial by fire. He would go away for a few weeks, after which he would make up his mind and be able to know what he was doing. When Valerya heard that he was preparing to go to Moscow, she burst into tears. A final ball at Tula brought them closer again: 'She was very sweet. Plaintive voice, wanting to compromise herself, or make some sacrifice for me.' But he held his ground. Against Aunt Toinette, against Mlle Vergani, against Valerya, against himself. His departure resembled flight more than anything else. Several times during the trip he asked himself, as he lurched along in an uncomfortable sledge, whether he ought not to turn around and go back.

The moment he reached Moscow he rushed to see his sister Marya and explain his behaviour. But she sided with

Valerya against him. Then, to atone for his remissness towards her, he wrote a long rambling and preachifying letter in which he confessed that there were two men in him: 'the stupid man', who loved her only for her physical charms, and 'the good man' who held her in too high esteem to be content with any commonplace form of love. There followed a dialogue between these two halves of Tolstoy – both equally long-winded. 'And yet you are happy when you are with her, you look at her, listen to her, talk to her,' said the stupid man. 'Then why deprive yourself of this happiness? And then, is it not odious on your part to respond to her pure and devoted affection with cold rationalizations?' The good man's reply: 'In the first place, you lie when you say I am happy with her; it is a pleasure for me to listen to her, of course, and look into her eyes; but that is not happiness. ... Besides, sometimes her company weighs on me. ... I am happy because of her, even when I am not with her. ... You love her for your happiness, and I love her for her own.'

And, mixing heaven up with his affairs as usual, he proclaimed with unruffled hypocrisy, 'I thank God for giving me the idea of going away. ... I believe He has guided me towards the best course for both of us. *You* may be forgiven for thinking like the stupid man. But in me, it would have been a shame and a sin. ... A great task lies before us: to understand each other and preserve our affection and respect for each other. For this, I am counting on our correspondence, we shall be able to talk things over calmly.'

He began his education of the girl who might one day be his wife by giving her some advice (the eternal mania of 'Rules of Life'), and urged her to follow it:

'Please go for a walk every day, no matter what the weather is like! This is recommended by every doctor. Put on your corset and stockings by yourself and, in general, try to make various improvements of this type. But these are trivialities. The main thing is that when you get into bed at night you should be able to tell yourself, "Today, firstly, I have performed a good deed for someone else; secondly, I have become a little better myself." Try, please, please, to plan your occupations a day in advance and give yourself an account of them every evening. You will see what serene but intense joy results from being able to tell oneself, every day, "Now I am better than yesterday." ... Farewell, dear young lady, the stupid man loves you, but stupidly, the good man is ready to love you with the strongest love there is, tender and eternal ...' [46]

On 7 November 1866, he was in St Petersburg. There, he moved into a small furnished apartment at the corner of Great Meshanskaya and Vozhnesensky Prospect and went immediately to see General Konstantinov, director of the School of Pyrotechnics. He had tendered his resignation from the army on 30 September and was surprised to have had no news of it for a month. His superior assured him that the matter was pursuing its normal course, although Grand Duke Michael Nikolayevich, having heard that Tolstoy was the author of the highly irreverent 'Song of Sevastopol', was very cross with him. Indignant at this 'base calumny' – in which there was a fair share of truth – Tolstoy went to staff headquarters to vindicate himself, and they pretended to believe him.

He was more deeply disturbed by another misunderstanding, also founded, no doubt, on gossip. Just before he left Moscow he learned from Prince Volkonsky that, according to a number of eye witnesses, little Valerya Arsenyev really had fallen in love with Mortier de Fontaine, the pianist, and was even writing to him. So much duplicity in a young person who gave every indication of wishing to become his wife outraged him, it was an insult to his honour. He was sorry he had sent her such a friendly letter the week before. However, instead of leaping at this opportunity to break with her, he toyed with the idea of bringing her to her knees first. Did he care more for her since he suspected her of being faithless? On 8 November, needled by jealousy, he wrote her a letter of savage recrimination:

I no longer respect you as I did before, I don't believe you. ... Is it my fault? Judge for yourself. You knew me for three months, you saw what kind of friendship I felt for you, only you weren't sure whether I was going to propose, and you fell in love with Mortier. ... Then you stopped seeing him, but you haven't stopped thinking about him or writing to him. You learned that I was about to ask for your hand in marriage, and then you fell in love with me. ... But which was the real emotion, and is it an emotion? Did you really love Mortier? How far did your relationship go? Did he kiss your hands? ... Yes, I am in love with you and that is why I am continually oscillating between my feelings for you: passionate love and hatred.

Having thus poured out his heart, he could not resist his desire for even more sympathy and, as a consummate man of letters, added, 'I am in poor health and my books are selling badly.'* When he read it over, however, this epistle struck him as being too violent. He pencilled 'unmailed' across the first page and immediately wrote another, in milder tones.

I am furious with you because I cannot help loving you. ... If you would please tell me about your relations with Mortier, and say definitely that your feeling for him was a beautiful one, that you miss him, even that you still love him, I would prefer it to the indifference and feigned scorn with which you speak of him. ... The main question is whether we can live together and love each other, and it is essential for that very reason to reveal everything bad in ourselves. ... I should suffer, I should suffer horribly if I were to lose your affection for me; but better to lose it right away than have to reproach myself for a deception that would end in your unhappiness.

Having worked well the following day, 9 November, he felt disposed to love anyone and forgive anything, and Valerya immediately reaped the benefit of this change of heart. With soul raised on high and pen dipped in honey, Tolstoy wrote:

* Refers to *Childhood, Boyhood* and *Tales of Army Life*, published in one volume in 1856.

This extraordinary feeling I have for you, which I have not experienced for any other person, takes the following form: the instant anything disagreeable happens to me, whether important or trivial – any failure, any dent in my vanity – I think of you and say, 'All this is trivial, since a certain young lady back there exists; so nothing bad can happen to me. ...' Ah, if only you might learn, through suffering, to believe that the only possible happiness – true, eternal, elevated – is achieved through these three things: work, self-denial and love. ... You see, I want to love you so badly that I am teaching you how to make me love you. Because my real feeling for you is not love, yet, but a passionate desire to love you with all my strength. ... One can live magnificently in this world, if one knows how to work and how to love, to work for the person one loves and to love one's work.

Could the little goose from Sudakovo grasp the true meaning of that last sentence? Perhaps, for Tolstoy vainly awaited her reply. In the night of 11–12 November he wrote again to explain his views on marriage, using the two allegorical figures, Khrapovitsky and Dembitskaya. Khrapovitsky – alias Leo Tolstoy – spurned high society because worldly agitation destroys even the most beautiful, the most noble and purest of thoughts, and yearned for a 'healthy and peaceful' family life. Dembitskaya – alias Valerya Arsenyev – was the exact opposite; for her, happiness 'was the ball, the bare shoulders, the carriages and diamonds, her acquaintanceship with the Gentlemen of the Bedchamber and the aides-de-camp'. According to Tolstoy, the solution for these two characters was to live seven months of the year in the country and five in St Petersburg. He was already estimating the household expenses; that should be reassurance enough for the young lady! And yet four more days went by without a sign from her. Vexed, Tolstoy resumed his habits of the previous winter. He went out in society, dined at Dussot's, exercised at the gymnasium and found no pleasure at all in the company of his fellow writers. 'Love and love alone can provide certain happiness,'[47] he declared. If only Valerya were a better correspondent! Did she really have nothing to say, or didn't she know how to hold a pen? At last, on 19 November, he received two letters from his beloved. He should have been in transports of joy – but no: what he had longed for so keenly now left him cold. His fever had dropped. 'Strangely enough, when I am taken up by my work, I am indifferent to Valerya,' he wrote the same day. And he sat down with a sigh to grind out his answer. No more talk of love in this letter. The tone was brotherly, protective and gay. If he were still attracted to her it was only, he said, because he thought she might be 'good' and he had always been subjugated by virtue. And his jealousy had so diminished that he positively entreated her to go out with other men so that she could analyse her reactions to them:[48] 'Go to the ball on Wednesday. It would be interesting for you to test yourself. Do it, my dove, and then tell me your honest impressions.'

Days passed, and Valerya's stock rose a few points as a result of the prolonged absence: 'Thought a great deal about her,' he wrote. 'Perhaps because I have not met any woman of late.'[49] In the interim, he received another 'very sweet' letter from her, to which he replied with patronizing affection.

'I feel that you love me and so you are beginning to adopt a more serious attitude towards life. . . . By the grace of God, my dove, love me, love the whole world, God's world, men, nature, poetry, all the wonderful things that exist, and cultivate your mind so that you can understand things worthy of love. ... If the overall destination of a woman is to be a wife, her particular destination is to be *mother*, not womb.'

Not content with instructing his dove as to the best way of ornamenting her mind, he threw in for good measure a few lessons on the best way of ornamenting her body:

Alas, you are mistaken to believe you have taste. Your little blue hat with the white flowers is pretty, but it would only be right for the wife of a great aristocrat, stepping out of her coach behind an English trotter. Your little hat looks absurd enough on a person of modest means, with only a simple *calèche*, and even more on a person living in the country, with nothing but a tarantass to drive. There is another kind of elegance, based on modesty, that shuns everything exaggerated and loud. It may be seen in the smallest details of dress – in slippers, for example, and collars and gloves. It also requires spotless nails and neatly dressed hair.

If, after this, Valerya did not turn into a model young lady, there was no hope for the future of correspondence courses. Upon coming to the end of his letter, he was seized with a sudden frenzy, he was overflowing with tenderness, his pen was quivering with it: 'Farewell, my turtledove, turtledove, thousand times turtledove, whether you're angry or not, I'll say it just the same!'

After this flare-up he subsided, colder and more empty than before; two letters from Valerya could not fan the flame to life again. 'She is deceiving herself, I see it plainly, and I don't like it.' (27 November 1856.) 'I think little about Valerya and not very favourably.' (29 November 1856.) Nothing had happened to alter his feelings, but it was as though he were purged of an hallucination, and ashamed to have let himself be carried away. Yet he still did not have the courage to burn his bridges. He explained to Valerya that he was 'terribly afraid' of meeting her, for the shock might be irreparable:

'In our letters we inflate each other with all sorts of tender declarations ... we show off our best side, we hide the bad features in ourselves. ... When you see me again, all of a sudden, with my looks, my faded smile, my turnip nose and my temperament (gloomy, fickle, an easy prey to boredom) – all the things you have already forgotten – they will all seem new to you, and will come as a painful surprise.' [50]

He prevaricated less with Aunt Toinette, a militant partisan of his marriage to the young lady:

'I should very much like to be able to tell you that I am in love, or simply that I love her, but it is not there. The only feeling I have for her is gratitude for her love for me, and the thought that, of all the girls I have known and know now, she would make the best wife for me.' [51]

But distributing these analyses right and left was not helping him to find an honourable way out. He himself was surprised at his cowardice. There he was, quaking and limp-handed like an apprentice executioner facing a too-tender victim. He did not dare bring down the axe on the neck of this over-plump, over-silly and ridiculously over-dressed provincial scatterbrain. Was he afraid of hurting her, or of being hurt himself? On 10 December he received a stinging letter from her, reproaching him for 'boring' her with his 'preaching'. She was making it easy for him! 'Received an offended letter from Valerya and, to my eternal shame, was glad of it,' he immediately wrote in his diary. After thinking for two days, he replied:

'We are too far apart. ... Love and marriage would have given us nothing but misery, whereas friendship, I am certain, is good for both of us. ... Then, too, I think I must not be made for family life, even though it is what I most admire in all the world. You know what a difficult person I am, suspicious and moody, and God only knows whether anything will ever happen to change me. ... Of all the women I have known you are the one I loved most and still love most, but it is not enough.' [52]

This time Valerya could not fail to understand. The break had come, clean and sharp as a scalpel's edge. After posting his letter, he felt both relieved and uncertain. That night he had a nightmare so bizarre that he described it in his diary: 'A brown woman lying on top of me; she was stretching forward, completely naked, whispering into my ear.' Was this Valerya's last assault?

As he had expected, his break with the girl aroused general indignation in the drawing-rooms of Tula. He was blamed by his aunt, his sister, all his friends in the province; the best way to avoid hearing all this nasty gossip was to flee abroad. He had been toying with the idea for some time. His resignation from the army had been accepted on 26 November. He ordered civilian clothes and applied for a passport to leave Russia. He scarcely recognized himself in civilian dress! Was it possible that this inglorious garb was to be his for the rest of his life? Now he was nothing but a writer, a mere artist! He spent New Year's Eve listening to Beethoven in the apartment of his friend Stolypin. On 1 January he talked until midnight with Olga Turgenev.* 'I never liked her so well before.' On 3 January, at a costume ball, he met a young woman wearing a mask: 'Sweet mouth. I pleaded with her a long time. She finally agreed, after much hesitation, to come home with me. Inside, she took off her mask. As like A.D. [Alexandra Dyakov] as two peas. But with coarser features.' Two days later, another noteworthy encounter: the violinist George Kizevetter, a drunkard, a 'gifted madman'. Touched by Tolstoy's interest in him, the musician told him the story of his downfall. Tolstoy immediately decided to write a story about him, to be entitled *A Lost Man*.† But he soon realized that he was not in the mood for writing. Was the atmosphere of St Petersburg bad for him, or was it remorse at having offended Valerya that nagged at him? She had tried to get him back by letter; he replied, to discourage her for good. What a leech! Quick! He had to get away. He went to Moscow first, and there he wrote to Aunt Toinette on 14 January 1857:

I have received my passport and have come to Moscow to spend a few days with Marya.‡ ... You will surely understand, dear Aunt, why I do not want to – and must not – come to Yasnaya Polyana just now, or rather to Sudakovo.§ I think I behaved very badly towards Valerya, but if I were to see her now I should behave still worse. As I have already written you, I feel less than indifferent towards her and cannot go on deceiving myself or her. And if I were weak enough to go back there, I should begin telling myself stories again. Do you remember, dear Aunt, how annoyed you were with me when I told

*No relation to Ivan Turgenev.   †Later called *Albert*.
‡His sister.   §The Arsenyev estate.

you I was going to St Petersburg as a test? Yet it is thanks to that idea that I have avoided bringing both of us to grief – for do not believe it is capriciousness or infidelity on my part: I have not been attracted by anyone else during these two months; I simply saw I was fooling myself, and not only never have had but never would have the least feeling of genuine love for Valerya.

As Yasnaya Polyana was only a few versts from Sudakovo, he thought it wiser not to kiss his aunt goodbye before embarking on his travels abroad. If he should happen to run into Valerya, what a scene there would be. The girl in tears, Mlle Vergani's scathing reproaches! Anything, rather than this mudbath of sentiment. His target now was Paris, where good old Turgenev was waiting for him. As though by design, two days before he was scheduled to leave he met a woman who captivated him: Baroness Elizabeth Ivanovna Mengden, six years his senior. At the mere sight of her, he regretted that his passport was in his pocket and his seat reserved in the coach. How beautiful she was, pure and full of mystery, the stranger standing at the roadside while the horses whirl you off into the distance. Thinking of her, he wrote in his diary: [53] 'Does the attraction lie in remaining just on the verge of love?'

On 29 January 1857 he boarded the stagecoach. Cold, snow and the monotonous jingle of the horses' bells. Packed with strangers into the coach like a sardine in a tin, he thought back over his experiences of the last few years. In human relations, nothing noteworthy: no revolutionary friendships, no revelations in love, neither progress towards virtue nor backsliding towards evil. In the field of literature, on the other hand, he couldn't complain. *The Snow Storm, Two Hussars, A Landlord's Morning* had been smashing successes; *Youth*, which had just come out in the first issue of *The Contemporary* for 1857, had already gleaned some words of praise. It seemed to Tolstoy, however, that the friends who had read the manuscript or proofs had been more reticent than on previous occasions. Druzhnin, for ex-

ample, whose opinion he highly valued, had written on
6 October 1856, 'None of our other writers could have
grasped and portrayed the agitated and disorderly time of
youth better than you.' But he found some chapters too
'long-drawn-out' and said the author must guard against his
propensity for analysis as against the plague: 'One occasionally feels that you are about to write: X's thighs showed
that he wanted to take a trip to India.' He also criticized
Tolstoy's style, heavy, almost 'ungrammatical', encumbered
by never-ending sentences. Like Druzhnin, Panayev also
begged the author to lighten his 'otherwise admirable' text.
On 5 December 1856 he wrote, 'Your phrases are too long
and obscure, the same words keep recurring.' * On this point
Tolstoy conceded that Druzhnin and Panayev were right,
he did not have Turgenev's diaphanous style. But his desire
to approach ever closer to the core of truth in beings and
things prevented him from caring about the elegance of
his language. He piled up his relative clauses one on top of
the other, twisted his syntax, peppered his sentences with increasingly specific epithets, in order to capture some subtle
nuance. Asking him to lighten his style was tantamount to
asking him to change his vision of the world, to change
himself. Then, too, even though he agreed with Druzhnin,
he could not cure himself of his 'mania' for sketching in a
character by beginning with some detail of physiognomy
and proceeding by induction from matter to soul, from data
to idea. In this connexion his notebooks for 1856 are filled
with curious observations. 'For me,' he wrote, 'the back is an
important mark of physiognomy, and especially the place
where the neck joins the back; no other part of the body so
clearly reveals lack of self-confidence and false sentiment.'
And also, 'A straight back is a sign of passionate temperament.' Or, 'The physiology of wrinkles can be very telling

*On 6 December 1856, Panayev wrote to Turgenev, in reference to
Youth, that 'He [Tolstoy] simply does not know how to write. His
sentences are all two yards long. The thought is admirable, its expression often thoroughly obscure . . .'

and accurate.'[54] In *Youth* he had put his theory to the test even more than in his previous work. 'Dubkov,' for example, 'had the sort of hands that often wear rings and belong to people who like to do things with their hands and love beautiful things.'[55] Again, 'Sofya Ivanovna had that singular, florid complexion one encounters in very stout old maids who are short and wear corsets.'[56]

In painting the third panel of his triptych he had, as in *Boyhood*, combined the story of his friends, the Islenyevs, with his own. In particular, the Islenyev father's second marriage with 'a young beauty', Sofya Zhdanov, had given him the idea for the episode of Nikolenka's father and 'la belle Flamande'. As for Prince Nekhlyudov, he was to become one of the author's favourite aliases. Aunt Toinette, Dmitry and many others had posed for some of his characters; but however great the charm of these half-real, half-fictional figures, the real hero of *Youth* was its narrator. His relentless digging down into his self, to eject admirable and ignoble features pell-mell and reveal the naked man, compelled even the most superficial reader to venture into his own lower depths.

Aksakov wrote, in *The Russian Tatler*, 'Here analysis assumes the form of a confession, a pitiless exposure of all the seething activity of the human soul. And yet this self-indictment is perfectly healthy and straightforward, there is no hesitation about it, it is tainted by no involuntary desire to excuse what goes on within. ... There is something sickly, weak, uncertain about Turgenev's analysis, whereas that of Count Tolstoy is sound and uncompromising.'

Tolstoy left before he had seen this notice, and that of Basistov in the *St Petersburg News*: 'To present the hero of *Youth* as typical of Russian youth is an insult to both society and youth.' For the time being, he was planning to continue the series, but his ideas were not yet ripe.* Besides, he was unable to concentrate on anything inside the stagecoach. His mind flitted from one thing to another. He sighed for

* This project was subsequently abandoned.

Mme Mengden ('She is delightful, a relationship with her might be most enjoyable') and was sorry he had behaved so badly to Valerya ('I should like to write to Mlle Vergani and tell her I am not the guilty party, if there is one'[57]). He would have been greatly surprised to learn that the girl he was berating himself for having compromised would soon be married to someone else; but it would probably have astonished him less to be told that, accustomed as he was to using the events of his own life as his raw materials, this romantic interlude would become, two years later, a novel.*

On 4 February Leo Tolstoy stepped out of the stagecoach, exhausted, at Warsaw, after covering 900 miles in five days, or 180 miles a day. The sun was rising in front of him, 'setting the houses alight with bright colours'. He immediately sent a telegram to Ivan Turgenev, announcing his arrival in Paris. Nekrasov was there, too – double cause for rejoicing. He continued his trip by rail, went through Berlin without stopping and set foot on French soil on 9 February 1857,† in the crush, smoke and racket of the Gare du Nord.

---

*Valerya Arsenyev married A. A. Talysin, future magistrate at Orlov; in *Family Happiness* Tolstoy described what would have happened had he carried out his first matrimonial plans.

†9 February, Old Style (Julian calendar), 21 February, New Style (Gregorian).

PART III

===

TRAVEL, ROMANCE
AND PEDAGOGY

[9]

Discovery of Europe

TOLSTOY first went to the Hotel Meurice, which was then located at 149, rue de Rivoli; the following day, he rented a furnished apartment in a *pension* at No. 206 on the same street. The rooms were sunny, but cold. No Russian double windows, none of those excellent tile stoves with serfs to bank up their fires; no samovar steaming around-the-clock. The pale sun of dying winter shone on the Tuileries. Birds chirped in the bare branches of the trees. The music of the French language was pleasing to the ear. Sitting down to the *table d'hôte*, the traveller found himself among a score of *pensionnaires* who immediately engaged him in a conversation 'studded with witticisms and word-play'.[1] He was sorry, however, that he had not brought a servant with him, and had so few friends in this big city. Turgenev and Nekrasov came to see him on the evening of his arrival. Both disappointed him. 'Turgenev is unbelievably touchy and soft,' he noted, and 'Nekrasov looks gloomy.'

Ivan Turgenev, who lived with his daughter Paulinette and her governess at No. 208, rue de Rivoli, two doors away, was very unhappy indeed, because Pauline Viardot was neglecting him for a newcomer, the painter Ary Scheffer. Nevertheless, he wanted to make a festive occasion of his meeting with the 'troglodyte' and, as the Carnival was in full swing, dragged Tolstoy, still worn out after his trip, to a costume ball at the Opéra. On the evening of 9 February (21)* 1857 Tolstoy scratched one word in his diary: 'Madness'. The next day, he wrote to his sister:

* Dates included in parentheses are based on the Gregorian calendar. These are the dates as used by Tolstoy and others when writing from Europe.

'The little Frenchmen are very droll and nice when they are out for fun, which assumes monumental proportions here. An ordinary Frenchman dresses himself up as a wild Indian, daubs paint all over his face and, bare-armed and bare-legged, alone in the middle of the room, begins to caper about and bob up and down and whinny for dear life. He is not drunk, he is a respectable married man with a family, he is simply full of *joie de vivre*.

On the streets, in the cafés and shops and buses, he found the same air of buoyancy, frivolity and elegance. Even the poor people here seemed glad to be alive. Bold stares sped back and forth between men and women in public. The pedlars hawked their wares so wittily that there was always a ring of loiterers standing around to listen. Everyone, from the livery-stable driver to the soft-drink pedlar, had his own saucy line of patter, as though there were no police. Although Napoleon III claimed to be an emperor, his French despotism had nothing in common with the Russian variety. True, a lot of people were said to have been imprisoned and exiled after the coup d'état of 2 December 1851, but that did not prevent Paris from exhaling an air of devil-may-care nonchalance that would have been inconceivable in Moscow or St Petersburg. The air was cleaner along the banks of the Seine, one felt like throwing out one's chest, making smart remarks, thumbing one's nose at the authorities and crowing like a rooster. 'There is not one numbskull of an officer running after the whores or hanging around the cafés who is untouched by this sense of social freedom, which is the chief attraction of life in Paris,' Tolstoy wrote to Kolbasin.[2] And to Botkin, the same day: 'I am still in Paris ... and cannot yet foresee the day when this city will have ceased to intrigue me, or the life I am leading here lose its appeal. I am a flagrant ignoramus, I have never felt it so powerfully as here. If only for that, I should be thankful to have come, especially as my ignorance is not, I can feel it, irreparable. I am delighting in the arts here.'[3]

As a dutiful tourist, he went often to the theatre and,

back in his *pension*, jotted down notes on the plays he had seen: *Les précieuses ridicules* and *L'Avare* 'Excellent'; *Les fausses confidences* – 'Deliciously elegant'; *Le malade imaginaire* – 'Admirably acted'; *Le Mariage de Figaro* – 'Very good'; Racine's *Plaideurs* – 'Foul'. Moreover, 'The theatre of Racine and his ilk is the poetic plague of Europe. Luckily we do not and never shall have anything like it.'[4] Offenbach, at the Bouffes-Parisiens, is 'pure French! Funny! A sense of comedy so jolly and sprightly that he can get away with anything.'[5] The concerts swept him off his feet. He declared that nobody could play Beethoven as the French could.[6]

Determined to see everything, he set himself a schedule that would have brought a less robust man to his knees at the end of a week. He raced through the Hôtel de Cluny, the Sainte-Chapelle, the Bourse ('A horror!'), the Louvre, where he could not decide which was most admirable, the Mona Lisa or Rembrandt's portraits; Fontainebleau, Versailles ('There I feel how little I know'), La Bibliothèque Nationale ('The place is packed full of people!'), the Père-Lachaise cemetery, the racetracks, the auction gallery. He saw the Comte de Falloux being admitted to the Académie, and was amazed at all those men of letters in brocaded gowns, listening to such boring speeches. He pushed on to Dijon to see the churches and museum. Then, back in Paris, he went to the Invalides. At the sight of Napoleon's tomb, he was seized with indignation. Paying no attention to the guide, who was mumbling his commentary as though they were in church, he felt his ancient patriotic resentment rise within him against the invader of Russia and profaner of Moscow, and his historical hatred was intensified by the memory of a more recent war in which the French had again won the upper hand. Less than two years after Sevastopol, he could not tolerate this homage paid to the military prowess of the enemy. How could a people who claimed to be peace-loving, freedom-loving and reason-loving dedicate this haughty sarcophagus in red porphyry to a man who had drenched all Europe in blood? 'This idealization of a malefactor is shameful!' he thought.[7] He scowled furiously at the names of the victories carved in the walls of the crypt, among which he saw – O horror of horrors! – the Moskva! He left in a rage, and the sight of two old disabled veterans sunning themselves in the courtyard merely fanned the flames of his wrath. That evening the man who had once sung hymns to the bravery of the Crimean troops – whatever their nationality – wrote of these cocked-hatted and medallioned derelicts, 'They are nothing but soldiers, animals trained to bite. They should be left to starve to death. As for their torn-off legs – serves them right!'[8] A few days before he had written, in tones of equal surliness, 'Read a speech by Napoleon with unspeakable loathing.' And, enlarging upon this statement: 'No one has understood better than the French that people will worship insolence – a good punch in the face. The trick is to act with conviction; then everyone will step aside and even feel he is in the wrong. That is what I realized, reading Napoleon's speech.'[9] In his address, delivered on 16 February 1857 for the opening of the legislative session, Napoleon III had said that his greatest desire was to serve mankind, justice and civilization everywhere. Impossible for Tolstoy to give credence to such assertions, coming from the nephew of Napoleon I.

But with what delight, on the other hand, he listened to the lectures of the great masters of the day at the Sorbonne and Collège de France: Saint-Marc Girardin, Lefèvre de Laboulaye, Baudrillart! To fill in the gaps in his education, he took English and Italian lessons with a tutor. He already spoke fluent French and might have become acquainted with some French families, but he made no effort to do so. Neither the publication of Poe's *Tales of the Grotesque* and *Arabesque* in Baudelaire's translation nor the stir over the trial of *Madame Bovary*, both of which occurred early in 1857, had the least effect on him; he had never even heard of these authors. The only representatives of French literature with whom he had any contact at all were the traveller Xavier Marmier, Louis Ulbach the novelist, and a singer, Pierre Dupont. Turgenev could have introduced him to authors of higher rank – Mérimée, Dumas. . . . 'Why bother?' said Tolstoy to himself. He had too little esteem for his Russian colleagues to seek out the company of their French counterparts. What he wanted to know about France he could learn just as well from the Russians living in Paris. They had returned en masse after the signing of the peace treaty. Their salons were open to all comers; Tolstoy went to call on the Lvovs, the Orlovs, the Trubetskoys, the Bludovs, the Sherbatovs, the Klyustins, etc. With one or another of them he went to the theatre, the circus, the *café chantant*, dined at Durand's or at the Maison Dorée, had supper at Musard's or went out 'slumming'. As he made his way home at night along the deserted streets, he was haunted by 'bad thoughts'. When a female silhouette sidled furtively up to him he shuddered with desire and then hurried on, fleeing, red-faced with shame, and, once back in his room, wrote by candlelight: 'A lively lady. Was paralysed with confusion ...' 'Accosted. Spoiled my evening. Had a struggle with my conscience and tortured myself ...' 'Nothing, hush! ...' 'A woman disturbed me. I followed her home, but then remained firm. Depravity is a dreadful thing. ...'[10]

Tawdry streetwalkers were not enough to quench his thirst for love; he required tender feelings as well. He paid court to Prince Lvov's niece. 'The princess is so charming that for the last twenty-four hours I have been under a spell, and it has made my life very pleasant,' he wrote on 21 February [5 March]. A month later: 'I like her very much, I think I'm a fool not to try to marry her. If she marries some excellent man and they are happy together, it could drive me to despair.' An empty threat, like so many others. He was stirred by the grace, sweetness and intelligence of this young lady of society, but he was equally stirred by the charms of Louise Fitz-James, a dancer at the Opéra who lived in the same *pension* as he. He recorded in his diary the impression that 'Mrs Fitz-James's calves' had made on him, noted that on one occasion Mrs Fitz-James, 'perspiring freely', had played 'la coquette' with him, and expressed amazement at her boldness when she said in public, 'One is never as wicked as one would like to be!' At the time, he burst out laughing with the others, but her remark left him pensive: no doubt about it, the Parisians were all in league with the devil!

As though to add to his agitation, he received a letter from Valerya, who had swallowed her pride and was returning to the attack, wanting to know the reasons for the 'change' that had driven him away from her. 'There was nothing one could properly call a change,' he replied. 'I always told you I was not certain of my feelings for you, and it always seemed to me that something was wrong. ... In St Petersburg, the simple fact of not seeing you any more proved to me that I had not been and never would be in love with you.' [11] He had previously written the same thing to Aunt Toinette: 'Although I admit it was wrong of me to behave in such a flighty way, and I might have acted very differently, I still believe I was perfectly honest. I have never ceased to say that I am not sure what it is I feel for the girl, but I know it is not love.' [12]

The truth appeared to be that women existed solely in order to incite men to bestiality and then to frustrate them. A perfect example of the evil a woman could do to a man was unwittingly furnished by Ivan Turgenev: abandoned by Pauline Viardot, he had become a shadow of his former self. A kidney ailment, which he patiently nursed, aggravated his feeling of physical inferiority to the dazzling and faithless soprano, and he was continually worrying over the education of his daughter Paulinette, a difficult and quarrelsome child. 'Turgenev is flailing and floundering about in his misfortunes,' [13] noted Tolstoy. And he wrote to Aunt Toinette: 'His unhappy love affair with Mme Viardot, and his daughter, keep him in a state that is very bad for him, and he is pitiful to behold. I would never have believed he could love so deeply.'[14]

But if he pitied Turgenev one day, he could not abide him the next. The curious inconstancy he had shown towards Valerya Arsenyev reappeared in his relations with the contemporary Russian writer he most admired. They saw each other every day, and utterly contradictory judgements rained down on the pages of his diary: 'Dinner with Turgenev ... He is quite simply vain and petty.' (17 February [1 March]) 'Spent three pleasant hours at Turgenev's.' (20 February [4 March]) 'Spent another pleasant evening with Turgenev and a bottle of wine by the fireside.' (21 February [5 March]) 'Turgenev doesn't believe anything, that's what's the matter with him. He does not love, he is in love with love.' (25 February [9 March]) 'At dinner I told him something he had never suspected; namely, that I consider him superior to me.' (26 February [10 March]) 'Turgenev is really tiresome! Alas! He has never loved anyone.' (1 [13] March) 'Dropped in on Turgenev. He is a cold and useless man, but intelligent, and his art is inoffensive.' (4 [16] March) 'Stopped by at Turgenev's. No; I really must keep away from him. I have paid enough tribute to his merits, tried every possible way of making friends with him; but it's no use.' (5 [17] March) 'Turgenev came to see me around five. He looked guilty. What to do? I respect him, I value him, I can even say I love him, but I feel absolutely no warmth for him; and the same is true for him.' (7 [19] March) 'Turgenev is old.' (9 [21] March) 'Stopped by Turgenev's; he no longer talks, he babbles. He has lost all faith in reason and in men – believes in nothing.' (25 March [6 April].)

Turgenev, meanwhile, was confessing that he could not, despite all his admiration for Tolstoy, remain on good terms with him: 'Tolstoy has changed considerably for the better, but the creaking and groaning of his internal upheavals have a very bad effect on a man like me, whose nerves are already overstrained.' (Letter to Annenkov, 16 [28] February 1857.) 'I cannot establish any lasting friend-

ship with Tolstoy, our views are too different.' (Letter to
Kolbasin, 8 [20] March 1857.) 'No; after all my attempts to
get along with Tolstoy, I have to give up. We are put together too differently. Whatever I like he doesn't and vice
versa. I cannot relax with him, and he is probably no more
at ease with me. He lacks serenity, and yet he also lacks the
turmoil of youth. As a result, I don't know how to take him.
But he will develop into a remarkable man, and I shall be
the first to applaud and admire him, from afar!' (Letter to
Annenkov, 9 [21] March 1857. ('Tolstoy is showing signs of
tolerance and calm. When this new wine has done ferment-
ing, it will be a beverage for the gods!' (Letter to Botkin,
23 March [4 April] 1857.)

In fact, Tolstoy was still a long way from 'calm' and 'tolerance', when Turgenev made this indulgent assessment of
his character. His brother Sergey had just come to Paris
with Prince Obolensky. They rode horseback in the Bois de
Boulogne, went to see a few friends and soon discovered that
they were bored in each other's company. Who could be
more total strangers than two brothers, united only by childhood memories? Sergey left Paris at the end of a week, and
Leo wondered whether he, too, should not be thinking of
moving on. He was tempted by Switzerland, Italy, England ...

He was still trying to decide what to do next when he
heard that on 26 March (6 April) 1857 a certain François
Richeux, sentenced to death for robbery and homicide,
would be publicly executed in Paris. Fascination won out
over revulsion. There are experiences one cannot pass up, if
one's profession is to wield the pen! Feeling somehow
guilty, as though he were going to the theatre, he got up
long before day, dressed in his chilly room, found a cab and
drove to the Place de la Roquette. A dense crowd stood
silently beneath the still-dark sky: many women, a few
children.* All the bars around the square were open. Here
and there a lantern lighted up an islet of faces, a bottle, a

* Journalists on the scene estimated the crowd at 12,000.

hand waving a hat. Above this milling conglomeration, the sharp vertical contour of the instrument of death. A low murmur greeted the arrival of the condemned man. People shoved and pushed to get a better view. Tolstoy must have found a good vantage point, for he did not miss a single detail of the ritual. When the cleaver dropped, he felt the blow in his own flesh.

Back in his room, his mind reeling with horror, he set down his first impressions in laconic terms: 'Got up feeling ill, before seven, went to see the execution. Chest and neck firm, white, healthy. Kissed the New Testament. Then, death. Senseless! Strong impression, and not useless. ... The guillotine kept me awake a long time, made me keep looking back over my shoulder.' Haunted by the vision of the decapitated body, he wrote to Botkin the same day: 'I witnessed many atrocities in the war and in the Caucasus, but I should have been less sickened to see a man torn to pieces before my eyes than I was by this perfected, elegant machine by means of which a strong, clean, healthy man was killed in an instant. In the first case there is no reasoning will, but a paroxysm of human passion; in the second, coolness to the point of refinement, homicide-with-comfort, nothing big. A cynical, insolent determination to do justice, obey the law of God – justice as proclaimed by lawyers, who made utterly contradictory allegations in the name of honour, religion and truth. ... And the awful crowd! A father was explaining to his daughter how this very painless and ingenious mechanism worked, etc. Human law – what a farce! The truth is that the State is a plot, designed not only to exploit but also to corrupt its citizens. For me, the laws laid down by politics are sordid lies. ... I shall never enter the service of any government anywhere.'

Twenty-five years later, in *Confession*,* he returned to the lugubrious events of that day: 'When I saw the head part from the body and each of them fall separately into a box with a thud, I understood – not in my mind, but with my

* *Confession* was written in 1882.

whole being – that no rational doctrine of progress could justify that act, and that if every man now living in the world and every man who had lived since the beginning of time were to maintain, in the name of some theory or other, that this execution was indispensable, I should still know that it was not indispensable, that it was wrong.'

After that, Tolstoy turned against the entire French nation. 'There is no poetry in this people,' he wrote, 'their only poetry is politics. ... On the whole, I like the French way of life and the French people, but I have yet to meet one man of real value, either in society or among the people.'[15] This comment may seem strange coming from a traveller who had spent six weeks in the country virtually without setting foot outside the Russian colony in the capital. Nevertheless, he was now determined to leave it. Switzerland – peace-loving, clean and virtuous – would purge him of the horrors of France. Was it the guillotine alone, as fervent Tolstoyans would have it, that drove him to pack his bags? They are forgetting that one week before – the eternal impulsive – he had already made plans to leave Paris with his brother Sergey;[16] that, on the day of the execution, he qualified his letter to Botkin as 'silly'; and that on the following day, his brooding over capital punishment did not prevent him from contemplating marriage with Princess Lvov. The truth was that the guillotine gave him a dramatic excuse for leaving, and until then, in his usual shilly-shallying way, he had been unable to make up his mind to go.

On 27 March (8 April), he went to say goodbye to Turgenev, and once again, face to face with his abhorred colleague, he could not restrain his tears. He loved no one as well as the person he had demolished the day before. 'After I had said good-bye to him and left, I began to cry, I don't know why,' he wrote that evening. 'I love him very much. He has made a different person of me, and is still doing so.'

He was bored on the train, which left from the Gare du Lyon. In those days, there was no direct line from Paris to Geneva: one had to go through Mâcon and Bourg to Ambérieu and then continue by stagecoach. Tolstoy was glad to leave the cramped, lurching compartment. Sitting next to the driver, he inhaled the fragrance of the sleeping countryside and looked up at the sky; his heart filled with ineffable contentment and well-being: 'At night, with the full moon shining on the seat, everything fainted away and became transformed into love and joy. For the first time in a very long while, I thanked God for being alive, and meant it.' [17]

The first thing he saw in his hotel room in Geneva was the New Testament, placed on his night table by the Bible Society. After the turpitude of Paris, it was like an invitation to return to the paths of righteousness. He read a few pages with delight and looked out of the window. Moonlight on the lake, and the light of Christ in the soul – Switzerland was a wonderful place! In the throes of an extraordinary joy, he wrote to Turgenev forthwith, advising him to flee Paris, too – that capital of iniquity: 'I lived for a month in Sodom; deep is the layer of mud in my soul, and the two whores, and the guillotine, and the idleness, and the mediocrity.' [18]

The only thing he was sorry to abandon on the banks of the Seine was Princess Lvov, whom Prince Orlov was also courting. 'Tell me frankly,' he added, 'whether a girl such as she might love me; I only mean by that, whether she would not find it repugnant or monstrous that I should want to marry her. Such an eventuality seems so impossible to me that even writing it makes me want to laugh.' To prevent Turgenev from joining him in his laughter, he did not mail this letter, the draft of which has been preserved, but sent another, more moderate version, in its place, which presumably contained no mention of marriage.* After reading this second missive Turgenev wrote to Annenkov: 'He's an odd fellow, I've never met his like, and I don't fully understand him. A mixture of poet, Calvinist, fanatic and aristocrat; he reminds one of Rousseau, only more honest –

* The second letter has not been preserved.

sternly moral and at the same time somehow unattractive.'
And to Kolbasin, 'Tolstoy has left, after deciding that he
loathed Sodom and Gomorrah, as he puts it. He has gone to
Geneva, has taken a room on the lake, and is happy, waiting
... to grow bored with the place.' [19]

In Switzerland as in Paris, Tolstoy saw almost no one
but Russians, and in particular, two relatives of his, aunts
twice removed: Elizabeth and Alexandra Tolstoy. Neither
had married, and they lived most of the year in St Petersburg at the Marya Palace where, since 1846, they had been
maids of honour to Grand Duchess Marya Nikolayevna,
daughter of Nicholas I and wife of Prince Maximilian of
Leuchtenberg. Tolstoy had seen them at the palace several
times during the previous winters, and had a warm recollection of his conversations with Alexandra, the younger of the
two – though she was not very young any more: forty! But
what lovely grey eyes she had, with such a serene and intelligent expression, and what an angelic smile, what a captivating contralto voice, what tact, what culture, what
sensitivity! She had a most gentle disposition, coupled with
the most discriminating judgement. Her whole life was
illuminated by religion. When Paris had suddenly turned
his stomach, Tolstoy thought of her at once as the person
most likely to understand him.

The day after he arrived in Geneva he went to see her in
her villa, 'Le Bocage', on the lakefront not far from town.
He adored making sudden appearances like this, dropping
in out of the blue. Savouring his aunt's surprise at his wild-
eyed and radiant expression, he cried as he came in the
door: 'I have come to you straight from Paris. That city has
made me so sick that I nearly lost my mind. The things I
saw there! First, in the lodginghouse I lived in there were
twenty-six couples, nineteen unmarried; I was horrified beyond belief. Then, to test myself, I went to see a criminal
being executed by the guillotine. After that, I could not
sleep, and I could not stay there any longer. Luckily, I happened to hear that you were in Geneva and I came rushing

headlong here to see you, certain that you would save me!'[20]

She listened to his confessions and comforted him, and he felt that here at last he might find peace of mind. She was too young for him to call her 'Aunt', so he decided to go to the opposite extreme and call her 'Grandmother' (*babushka*), as a joke, perhaps in a more or less conscious attempt to guard against her attraction for him. As they were related, their long talks together gave him the twofold pleasure of being admired by a woman and understood by a sister. A tender friendship grew up between them, to the delight of both. 'Wonderful Alexandra,' he wrote in his diary. 'A joy and a consolation! I have never met a woman yet who is worth her little finger.'[21] Towards the end of his life he was to say, 'Just as a ray of light sometimes filters beneath a door in a dark hallway, so the memory of Alexandra, when I look back over my long and sorrowful life, remains an eternally shining light.' And in her account of their relationship,[22] Alexandra wrote: 'Our pure and simple friendship was a triumphant disproof of the widely held but false opinion that a friendship between a man and a woman is impossible. Our relations remained on a very special plane and I can honestly say that we were chiefly concerned, each in his own way, with that which ennobles life.' But all the while she was disclaiming the least particle of impurity in her feelings towards her nephew, her portrait of him betrayed deep tenderness: 'He was simple, extremely modest, and so lively that his presence animated everyone around him. . . . He was not handsome, but his keen eyes, kind and highly expressive, made up for the favours nature had withheld.' And also: 'Like a mirror broken into fragments, every facet of him reflected a little of the brilliant light he had been given from above.'

Mutually entranced, aunt and nephew became inseparable: together, they took boat trips around the lake, explored the countryside, went on picnics, played the piano. Tolstoy could not decide whether it was the flower-laden springtime or the company of the serene and smiling spinster that kept him in his state of euphoria. 'It's terrible, how easily I fall for people,' he wrote in his diary. 'Ah, if only Alexandra were ten years younger.'[23] He was forgetting that if she had been, he would probably have deserted her for fear of getting involved in sentimental complications. With his imaginative, ardent and apprehensive nature, the inaccessible women were the ones he liked best. Knowing that no physical consummation could either crown or spoil his hopes, he found in her company that rare satisfaction of safety in excitement, fulfilment in abstinence. Alexandra's ten years too many were her most certain attribute.

After spending a few days in Geneva, where he performed his Easter devotions with his aunts in the Orthodox church, he and Alexandra went by boat to the little village of Clarens – the place Rousseau had chosen to write *La Nouvelle Héloïse*. To think that at the age of fifteen he had worn a medallion with Jean-Jacques' portrait on it around his neck, and now, today, here he was in the very place in which his idol had lived. 'I simply cannot tear myself away from this lake and its shores, and I spend most of my time contemplating it in ecstasy, going for walks or staring out of my window,' he wrote to Aunt Toinette on 18 May 1857. This wonderful spot, 'all leaves and flowers', was to hold him captive for the best part of three months. Alexandra went back to 'Le Bocage', her villa near Geneva, and he began a flirtatious correspondence with her. He continually needed to remind her of his existence, amuse and intrigue and worry her. Poetic letters, droll telegrams and tender *billets* flew back and forth across the lake. One moment he would dash off a few lines of doggerel:

> Toward Bocage my thoughts race.
> Incessantly myself I tell
> With babushka I would dwell
> Even in the Fireplace.*

---

* 'The Fireplace' was Tolstoy's jocular name for the court of the Grand Duchess, to whom Alexandra Tolstoy was maid of honour.

The next, complaining of a painful sty on his eye, he yearned for his aunt – his *babushka* – to come and nurse him, and talked baby-talk: 'And baba, and nana, and kaka, and tata, and zaza, and papa, and all the other vowels ...'

He made friends with a group of Russians at Clarens, one of whom was Michael Pushchin, brother of the famous Decembrist friend of Pushkin's. For his part in the uprising of 14 December 1825, Michael Pushchin had been demoted and sent to the Caucasus as a simple foot-soldier. 'A splendid and good man,' Tolstoy said of him. Which did not prevent him from calling him a braggart, later on in his diary. Similarly, on 10 (22) April the Mesherskys were 'fine people', and on 12 (24) April, 'low, embittered, thick-skulled conservatives, convinced that they are the sole possessors of every virtue,' and on 4 (16) May, 'likable characters' whose conservatism was 'engaging'. Mrs Karamzin, another holiday acquaintance, was initially labelled 'an excellent creature', before ending up as 'artificial, and very tiresome'.

While criticizing this little group of idle rich, Tolstoy willingly shared its distractions. With one or another of them he went driving or canoeing, drank tea in a country inn, or hiked, alpenstock in hand, on longer excursions. On 15 (27) May he set out on a trip lasting several days, with an eleven-year-old boy as his companion – Sasha, the son of his friends the Polivanovs. He took his diary and a supply of paper in his rucksack. Sasha strode manfully alongside; but, probably over-excited by the exhilarating air, he asked too many questions. 'The boy is a nuisance!' noted Tolstoy. They slept in inns and started out at dawn. Near Les Avants, they were made giddy by the perfume of the narcissus; at Château-d'Oex a miller ferried them across the stream; at Interlaken they feasted on rye and milk; at Grindelwald they were caught in a torrential rainstorm ('Sasha is lagging behind') and had to undress when they reached the chalet. 'Attractive waitress,' he observed. The next day, after ascending the glacier, he returned to the inn, ate his supper, was unable to get to sleep and, at midnight, went out on to the second-floor balcony to look at the black and white mountains in the moonlight. A servant went by; he teased her a little, then let her go. He thought he saw another one, beckoning to him from below, and hurried down. But she suddenly became uncooperative, and struggled and cried out, arousing the hotel. 'Everyone came running and glared at me,' Tolstoy wrote after beating a retreat to his room. 'I can hear them up here, the whole household is awake. They've been going on about it in loud voices for nearly half an hour.' [24] At Thun, he dined with Sasha and eighteen pastors; at Berne he thought of marrying – but whom? – near Fribourg he was appalled at the sight of 'filthy, ragged children, a huge crucifix at a crossroads outside a village, inscriptions on the house-fronts and a garish statuette of the Madonna above a well'. But he was awed by the majestic view from the Jaman Pass. 'I love nature,' he wrote, 'when it surrounds me on all sides, spreading out as far as I can see, when the same warm breeze that caresses me goes rolling off and is lost on the horizon; when the blades of grass I flattened as I sat down accumulate into the endless green of prairies, and the leaves whose shadows flicker across my face in the sighing wind become, afterwards, the far-off line of the forest; when I am not alone to rejoice, but millions of insects are buzzing and spinning around me and the coupled beetles go creeping along and the birds are singing everywhere.' [25]

Back in Clarens he put his papers in order, wrote up his travel notes, a few pages of a short story – *Albert* – and one or two chapters of *The Cossacks*, wrote letters, read a little Balzac, some Proudhon, Las Cases' *Memorial*, the New Testament, accidentally broke a mirror and 'had the weakness to read my fortune, with a dictionary'. The words that came out – 'sole, water, satarrh, tomb' – were unedifying. The future refused to disclose its secrets ahead of time.

The following day, 31 May (12 June) 1857, he set out on another long hike; his plan was to go as far as Turin, where

Druzhnin and Botkin were staying. At the end of a zigzag itinerary, his friends disappointed him – they had aged, and could not bear each other's company – but the Piedmont entranced him. A pause to cool off and take a quick shower, and he set out again – on muleback this time, to Gressoney, where the servingwoman at the inn was a giant, and there was a superb view of the Val d'Aosta; then a long, jolting journey by stagecoach: he met an idiot wearing a hat like Napoleon's; visited the Hospice of St Bernard – enormous, adrift in the fog – and was given a 'honey-sweet' welcome by the monks in the great hall with the fireplace; went down through mist and snow to Martigny and Évian – 'the town is suffused with something mauve-coloured'.

The change of scene, his fatigue and the keen air had given him an appetite for love. At almost every halting-place he noticed some woman: 'A pretty tobacconist ...' (8 [20] June) 'A plump, jolly waitress.' (10 [22] June) 'It's pleasant, but incomplete: no women.' (11 [23] June) 'A freckled beauty. I want a woman, terribly. And a pretty one ...' (15 [27] June.)

He returned to Clarens unappeased, spent a few days and then, unable to hold still, strapped on his pack and set off to Geneva, and from there to Berne. A railroad car packed full of 'angular Germans', 'effete French', who 'want to be on a spree wherever they go', 'stocky, blooming Swiss', a class of schoolboys and girls with their teacher, shouting and laughing. ... When the train stopped in the middle of some fields, Tolstoy leaned out the door to breathe in the drowsing landscape: 'A moist prairie, lighted by the moon, with the cries of the landrails and croaking of frogs; something I can't define draws me out there, farther, farther. And yet if I went, I should be drawn farther still. My response to the beauty of nature is not joy, but a sweet pain.' [26]

Berne, flag-bedecked for some shooting match, was a disappointment. He was particularly ill-disposed, having dreamed again that night that he had tuberculosis. The oppressive jollity of the crowd, the shooting, the carousing, the people clambering on top of the tables and, in the zoo – oh, shame! – 'one wretched Russian bear', terrified by the din – no, he could take no more of that! When the shadows began to lengthen, he followed 'a fat beauty' down the street, returned to his hotel exhausted and, as soon as he fell into bed, dreamed the tuberculosis nightmare once again.

When he awoke he decided to go to Lucerne, where his two 'aunt-grandmothers', his beloved *babushki*, were staying. He went to the best hotel in town, the Schweizerhof, which stood on the edge of the Lake of Lucerne and was patronized almost exclusively by the English. In his room, he opened the window and was transfixed: 'I was literally submerged by the beauty of that water, and deeply moved,' he wrote to Botkin. 'I suddenly needed to hold someone in my arms, someone I love deeply, to hug her with all my strength, crush her against my breast and share my great joy with her. … The lake is greenish and mauve, striped with moiré bands, dotted with rowboats …'[27]

The magnificent view was unfortunately spoiled by the Englishwomen, 'shiny and scrubbed, with long red faces and Swiss straw hats' and the Englishmen, 'wearing cardigans and carrying travelling-rugs over their arms'. Looking at forty or fifty of them seated at two long tables in the dining-room. Tolstoy felt as though he were watching a collection of automatons, masticating, drinking and thinking nothing. 'As the eight courses come and go, each applies himself to eating more fastidiously than the others, and all are completely dead,' he wrote, 'literally dead. … I have listened to more than five hundred conversations between the English, I have talked to them myself, but if I have ever heard a single living word from one of them … may I be struck down by lightning.'[28]

One evening he met a Tyrolean in the street, who was singing and accompanying himself on his guitar with such skill and gaiety that Tolstoy invited him to play under the windows of the hotel. The Tyrolean consented. At the first notes, a crowd gathered around him: cooks in white coats

and tall hats, footmen in livery, doormen and chambermaids. Ladies 'in long, wide gowns' and gentlemen 'in
detachable white collars' appeared on the Schweizerhof balconies. After three songs the performer, a squat, deformed
little man, held out his cap, but nobody threw any coins
into it. He mournfully mumbled, 'Thank you, ladies and
gentlemen,' and turned away, dragging his feet, while the
flunkeys' snickers rippled at his back. 'It hurt me,' wrote
Tolstoy. 'I felt bitterness and shame for the poor fellow,
for the crowd, for myself. As though they had been laughing at me, as though I, too, were guilty. ...'[29] He raced
after the singer, caught up with him and invited him to
drink with him in the hotel. Scandal! The patrons cringed
in horror from the unwashed mountebank that so-called
Russian count was bringing into the lobby. A waiter with a
poisonous smile preceded the two men, not into the main
lounge, but into a room furnished with wooden tables and
benches, which was reserved for the personnel. Women
were washing dishes in a corner.

'Do you want vin ordinaire?' asked a maître-d'hôtel.

'Moët champagne,' snapped Tolstoy.

The bottle arrived. At first the Tyrolean thought his rich
stranger was trying to get him drunk as a joke. Then, understanding that his gesture of friendship was sincere, he began to tell the story of his life. The servants gathered
around. A doorman sat down unceremoniously beside the
narrator and stared at him, sneering. Tolstoy turned white
with indignation.

'What are you smirking at?' he cried. 'Stand up!'

The doorman got up, grumbling. But Tolstoy could no
longer contain himself.

'Why have you put us here, me and this gentleman, instead of in the other room? Well? Doesn't everyone who
pays have the same rights? Your dirty republic!'

'The other room is closed,' answered the doorman.

'That's not true!'

Intimidated by his tone of authority, which only a true

master could command, a footman led the count and his singer into the main hall, which was in fact open. There, an Englishman and his wife were eating mutton chops. The man murmured 'Shocking!' and the woman stared, pinched her lips together and left the room, 'flouncing her silken gown'. Soon afterwards the embarrassed singer also left. Tolstoy ostentatiously shook hands with him outside the door. The doormen, valets and patrons were all staring rudely at him. They needed a little lesson in Russian charity. To cool himself off, Tolstoy went for a walk, alone, through the streets, with clenched fists and feverish brow. The cool, star-studded night made him forget human pettiness. He raised his eyes and let himself be swept away in a mystical ecstasy. Beauty always prompted him to question himself and God. 'A marvellous night,' he wrote in his diary. 'What is it I so ardently desire? I do not know. At any rate, it is not the blessings of this world. How can one fail to believe in the immortality of the soul, feeling such incommensurable grandeur in one's own? ... It is dark, holes in the sky, light. I could die! My God! My God! What am I? Where am I going? Where am I?'[30]

The incident of the Tyrolean singer had impressed him so unfavourably that he began to write a story about it three days later, in the form of a travel letter: *Lucerne*. 'Which is more civilized, which more of a barbarian: the lord who stamped away from the table in a huff at the sight of the singer's threadbare suit, who refused to pay him for his work with the millionth part of his fortune, and who now, after eating a hearty dinner, is sitting in a handsome, well-lighted room, calmly passing judgement on events in China and justifying the murders committed there; or the little singer who has been out on the road for twenty years, with two sous in his pocket, risking prison, doing no harm to anyone, roaming over hill and dale, cheering people with his songs, and has now gone off, humiliated, almost driven away, tired, hungry and ashamed, to sleep in some nameless place on a heap of rotting straw?'

After what had happened at the Schweizerhof, Tolstoy could no longer stand the sight of his over-comfortable room, the dining-hall full of the gleam of 'real white lace, false white collars, real or false white teeth, white faces and white hands,' the feigned courtesy of the staff and the haughty manners of the English, whom he would cheerfully have cut to bits 'in the Sevastopol trenches'. He moved into a modest family *pension,* where he rented two attic rooms above the caretaker's cottage. Outside his windows there were apple trees, high grass, the lake and the mountains. And, as an added attraction, the landlady's daughter, aged seventeen, in a white blouse, who bounded hither and yon 'like a young cat'.[31] Temporarily reconciled with Switzerland, he took a few short trips – to Lake Zug, Sarnen ('Here one re-enters the region of bald women with goitres and blond, self-satisfied cretins'), Stans ('Two young ladies from Stans made advances to me, one of them with a magnificent pair of eyes; I had a wicked thought, for which I immediately punished myself by a fit of bashfulness!'), Ried ('A feeble-minded woman with blond hair asked me if I had ever seen a woman like her and began to yodel and prance about'), the Rigi ('Depressing, senseless panorama'). He observed, upon his return, that the landlady's daughter was still prowling around him, but she was 'too regal' to be used for impure purposes; he went to see his 'aunt-grandmothers', was bored by them for a change, and made plans for a long tour, the high points of which would be the cities of the Rhine, The Hague, London, Paris, Rome, Naples, Constantinople and Odessa.

Upon reaching Zurich, however, on 8 (20) July, he changed his mind and veered off towards Schaffhausen, Friedrichshafen and Stuttgart. One evening he looked out of his train window and saw the moon on his right – a good omen! This favourable impression was heightened by an acquaintance he made on the train: a Frenchman, M. Ogier, who said he was a banker, wanted to become a member of the Assemblée and was on his way to Baden-

Baden, which was famous for its gambling tables. Tolstoy
followed him. On 12 (14) July he was hard at it. On 13 (25)
July he wrote in his diary, 'Roulette from morning to night.
Lost, but made it up towards the end of the day. At the
house, the Frenchman [Ogier] and a girl.' On 14 (26) July,
'Roulette until six in the evening. Lost everything.' 'Everything' was three thousand francs.* M. Ogier, the banker,
accompanied him to his lodgings and stayed in his room
until three in the morning, talking of love, poetry and
politics. 'Revolting,' noted Tolstoy. 'I would rather be a foul
stinking creature with a goitre and no nose, the lowest of the
idiots or the most hideous monster alive, than a moral abortion such as he.' But the next day he shamelessly confessed
that the 'moral abortion' had bailed him out of a tight spot:
'Borrowed two hundred roubles from the Frenchman and
lost them at once. He has gone.' What to do? Polonsky, the
poet, was also at Baden-Baden; Tolstoy put the touch on
him, but all he got was two hundred francs. Botkin, quickly
alerted by letter, proved more liberal. He sent money from
Lucerne. Tolstoy breathed again, bathed, went to the casino
and noted in his diary that evening, 16 (28) July: 'Lost
every cent, you pig!' For forty-eight hours, his pockets
empty, he fumed with frustration at being kept away from
the wheel: 'Surrounded by human offal. And the biggest
offal of all is me.' (18 [30] July.) At last, the next day, Turgenev, who had also been called to the rescue, descended
upon Baden-Baden like the Saviour. Bearded, tender and
melancholy, he was still shuffling along in the wake of
Pauline Viardot. The two friends greeted each other rapturously. Turgenev scolded his troglodyte and lent him
enough to tide him over.

A fresh fit of the fever swept over Tolstoy. Not a minute
to lose! He ran to the casino, his heart pounding wildly,
played one number after another and watched the croupier
rake away every stake, and staggered out of the room. Turgenev's features registered dismay when he heard the news.

* Approximately $1,650.

'Vanichka [32] is very kind,' wrote Tolstoy. 'I feel ashamed of myself in his presence.'

That day events took another turn for the worse: a letter came to the hotel, from Sergey, announcing that their sister Marya, whose husband's misconduct had become open knowledge, had left him for good. 'I do not intend to be the favourite sultana in his harem,' she said. She had taken her offspring and gone to live on her estate at Pokrovskoye. 'I nearly choked when I heard it,' said Tolstoy. He stood up for his sister, but winced at the thought of the scandal, the broken home, the children's divided affections. The combination of family problems and lack of funds determined him to go back to Russia. He took the train to Frankfort, where he rejoined the inestimable Alexandra ('A wonder! A delight! Never met such a woman.'), borrowed enough from her to continue his journey, reached Dresden ('Pleasant town'), where he encountered Raphael's *Sistine Madonna*, which enchanted him, and Princess Lvov, who disappointed him. In Paris he had wanted to marry her; in Dresden he had no use for her. She was too intelligent, 'in the Russian manner', and surrounded by too many 'young puppies'. And yet, he liked her. 'I was,' he wrote to Alexandra, 'in the right state of mind for falling in love, having lost at roulette, being dissatisfied with myself and having nothing to do. It is my theory that love answers a need to forget oneself and that is why, like sleep, it comes upon you more readily when you are displeased with yourself or unhappy. Princess Lvov is pretty, bright, honest and good company. I tried with all my might to fall in love with her; I saw her often, and ... nothing! Am I a monster? I am probably lacking something!' [33]

On 26 July (7 August) he went from Dresden to Berlin; on 27 July (8 August), he boarded a ship at Stettin; on 30 July (11 August), after four uneventful days at sea, he reached St Petersburg. He gambled again on the trip, and had to borrow a few roubles from Pushchin the moment he arrived. Temporarily solvent, he abandoned himself to the joy of seeing Nekrasov, Panayev and the other writers, and finding himself once more on native soil: 'Blue morning – with dew and birch trees – Russian morning. How good it is!' he wrote on 31 July 1857. But on 6 August, 'Russia revolts me!' And he went to Yasnaya Polyana.

[10]

A Few False Starts

PERHAPS all the while Tolstoy had been disparaging depraved France, soulless Switzerland and vulgar Germany, he had actually been letting himself be contaminated by their Western ways; for upon his return, after seven months abroad, certain injustices in his native land struck him more forcibly than before. It was as though his skin had grown thinner while he was away, or become infected with that sickly European sensitivity. 'Yasnaya Polyana is a miracle,' he wrote on the evening of his arrival (8 August 1857). 'It is sweet and sad to be here, but Russia definitely disgusts me. I am beginning to feel hemmed in by the crude and hypocritical atmosphere here. ... Beatings and floggings! ...' The next day, after a trip to Pirogovo: 'The wretchedness of the people and sufferings of the animals are atrocious.' Every day some new incident confirmed his feeling that things were going wrong around him and that everyone was powerless to stop them. In less than a week he saw a woman striking a servant with a stick in the street, a civil servant half-killing a seventy-year-old muzhik whose telega had caught on his coach, the village elder at Yasnaya Polyana thrashing a gardener and sending him barefoot across the limefields to watch the herds, a landlord at Ozerki entertaining himself by getting his peasants drunk, the district commissioner exacting a cart of hay in return for issuing a passport to one of the count's servants. ... 'In Petersburg and Moscow everybody is shouting about something,' he wrote to Alexandra Tolstoy, 'everybody is up in arms waiting for a miracle to happen, while out here in the country, patriarchal barbarism, theft and arbitrary rule go on as before. ... For a long time I had to fight against a feeling of aversion for my country; now I am beginning to accustom myself to all the horrors that make up the human condition. ... Fortunately, there is one salvation : morality, the world of the arts, poetry and human relations. There, nobody bothers me, policeman or town councillor. I am alone. Outside the wind howls, outside all is mud and cold; I am here, I play Beethoven and shed tears of tenderness; or I read the *Iliad*, or I create my own men and women and live with them, covering sheets of paper ...'[1]

Sometimes, of course, in a fit of temper, all this virtuousness went flying out the window and, 'relapsing into a deplorable habit', as he put it himself, he would strike one of his serfs or have him flogged by the country police. Afterwards, he sometimes begged the culprit's pardon and slipped him three roubles in compensation, which left the muzhik utterly bewildered, and the master unsatisfied as well.[2] They contemplated each other across a chasm. While waiting for the day when he would be able to impose happiness upon mankind, Tolstoy decided to reforest his estate. He bought two thousand fir trees, five thousand pines and two thousand larches, and supervised their planting.

This done, he set off with his sister Marya to spend the winter in Moscow, took a furnished apartment on Pyatnitskaya Street and plunged back into the literary world. His spirits were at a low ebb. 'I was not able to leap over contingencies as I had done in the past,' he wrote to Botkin on 21 October 1857, 'and I saw to my horror that the painful, senseless and dishonest reality I lived in, far from being an accident, a regrettable incident affecting only myself, was in fact the law of all life. ... Farewell, youth!' In this unhappy frame of mind, Moscow soon became hateful to him. At Aksakov's, he detected the stink of 'base literary intriguing'; the 'extremely man-of-letters' side of Fet's 'conceited and empty' personality disappointed him; his childhood playmate Lyubov Behrs was 'dreadful, balding and debilitated'; and when he looked in the mirror he could not recognize himself, either: 'Good God, how old I have become! Everything bores me, I don't feel anything, even about myself. ... I am prepared, within the limits of my powers, to bear this sad burden of existence.'[3]

A trip to St Petersburg only added to his dejection. Talking to Nekrasov and the other writers on *The Contemporary*, he managed to persuade himself that his popularity was on the wane. His latest works had been all very well, no doubt, but they disappointed the admirers of the *Sevastopol Sketches* and *Youth*, who were expecting another thunderclap of truth from him, while he was wasting his time and talent in trivia.

'At first Petersburg gave me a feeling of bitterness, then it disgusted me completely,' he wrote on 30 October 1857. 'People have already forgotten about me, or are beginning to, and that made me very sad at heart. But now I feel better, I know I have a lot to say and the ability to say it forcefully.'

In spite of this proudly penned declaration, he was not over-confident about the future. He soon realized that the literary fashion in Russia had changed. Since Alexander II's accession to the throne, the public, aroused by his promises of reform, were clamouring for books reflecting the social problems of the time. Panayev, the champion of 'art for art's sake', reported to Botkin on 28 June 1857 that 'According to my observations, borne out a millionfold by the facts, the Russian public is now demanding more serious reading matter. ... Yes, yes, my dear old Vasily Petrovich, the time has come when the most fragrant, the most nobly inspired work of art will go unnoticed if it does not deal with the problems of the day, the living, essential concerns of the present. Sad, but true.'

As though he had read the letter, Tolstoy himself wrote to Botkin, from Moscow, on 1 November 1857: 'I must tell you that as a result of the new trend in literature most of our old acquaintances, including yours truly, no longer know what they stand for and are going around looking as though they had been spat upon from head to foot. Nekrasov and Panayev do not even dream of writing their own things any more, and content themselves with handing over piles of money to Melnikov and Saltykov.* Saltykov, by the way, has explained to me that the golden age of *belles-lettres* is at an end (not only for Russia, but in general) and that nobody in Europe will ever read Homer or Goethe again. This is all tripe, of course, but it is enough to drive you out of your senses to hear the entire world suddenly proclaiming that the sky is black when you see it blue, and in the end you begin to wonder whether there is something the matter with your eyes.'

Tolstoy's anxiety about his future as a writer was so acute that he was expecting to see the day when, outdistanced by his young colleagues and unable to adapt to their form of social art, he would simply have to give up writing: 'Thank God I did not listen to Turgenev when he told me an author must be an author and nothing else,' he wrote in the same letter to Botkin. 'Literature must not become a crutch, as Walter Scott said. ... *Our* literature, that is, poetry, is a phenomenon outside the law, if not positively aberrant, and that is why it would be unjustifiable to base one's entire life on it.'

Turgenev, to whom Botkin showed this letter, wrote straight back to Tolstoy on 25 November (7 December), 1857: 'No matter how I cudgel my brains I cannot make out exactly what you are, if not an author. Philosopher? Founder of a new religion? Civil servant? Businessman? Do be kind enough to help me out of my predicament by informing me which of the alternatives I propose suits you best. I am joking, of course, but joking aside, I would like to see you sail out into the open at last, full speed ahead.' And Botkin himself, worried by Tolstoy's state, begged him to consider that it was natural, after such a cruel war and humiliating defeat, for the public to want books denouncing the flaws of Russian society: 'Is it possible,' he went on,

---

* Melnikov-Pechersky (1819–83), author-ethnographer; wrote *In the Forests*. Saltykov-Shchedrin (1826–89), novelist; wrote *The Golovlyov Family*.

'that you can lose your faith in poetry and want to abandon it because of this, when your heart is already inside the gates of the kingdom? I resent your being upset by the vulgar rant of common mortals who deny the powers of poetry and art because they are incapable of experiencing them.'[4]

It was poor psychology on the part of Botkin and Turgenev to imagine that Tolstoy honestly intended to put down his pen. His fury and despair were principally designed to alarm his friends, and subsided in direct proportion as their anxiety mounted. At the same time as he was threatening to abandon literature, he was also making plans to found a literary magazine whose aim would be to protest against the invasion of the rightful territory of Art by legislation and sociology. His friends in Moscow and St Petersburg eventually dissuaded him from this venture, but he still could not find himself. On the one hand, he was passionately interested in the emancipation of the serfs and aspired to serve the people by his writing; on the other, he claimed allegiance to pure aestheticism and lived in terror lest the new novel become a weapon of political propaganda.

The battle was raging all around him. People were rabidly in favour of emancipation, or dead against it. The selfishness of the propertied classes was clashing with the ideology of those who had nothing to lose.

Ninety per cent are against emancipation, and all for different reasons [Tolstoy wrote to Botkin]. Some are panicky and nervous and don't know whom to trust because they are rejected by people and government alike; others – the hypocrites – hate the very thought of emancipation but are in favour of the form; still others – the ambitious, the empire builders – are the nastiest of all, because they refuse to understand that they are citizens and as such have no more or fewer rights than their neighbours; and others – the majority – are simply bull-headed and cowed. They say: we do not want to discuss the matter and we shall not; let them do as they like, take everything away or leave us as we are. There are also a few English-type aristocrats, and there are the Westerners and the Slavophils. ... But there is no

one acting out of sheer goodness, anxious to win over and reconcile people to each other in a happier world. As for *belles-
lettres*, it has become plain that there is no place for them. But
don't imagine this will stop me from loving them: more than
ever.[5]

When Russia learned, from the edict of 20 November
1857 to the districts of Kovno, Vilna and Grodno, that Tsar
Alexander II approved the action of committees of aristocrats wishing to adopt measures preparatory to the emancipation of their serfs, the liberals' hopes soared again. 'I
congratulate you from the bottom of my heart on this
great event,' Kolbasin wrote to Turgenev. And Annenkov,
also to Turgenev: 'The day is approaching when we shall
be able to say as we die, "I believe that now at last I have
become a decent man."' And Turgenev to Tolstoy: 'The
event so long awaited is now at hand, and I am happy to
have lived to see it.'

On 28 December 1857 Tolstoy, who was still in Moscow,
went to a banquet held by Professor Kavelin to unite all
the literary factions in favour of the abolition of serfdom.
Instead of running to join in the fraternal accolade, the
Slavophils stayed home and sulked. Even so, there were one
hundred and eight persons present, and numerous speeches
were made. All those toadying words about enlightened
authority, selfless nobles and honest muzhiks filled Tolstoy
with insurmountable nausea. 'I am tired of conversation and
discussion and haranguing,' he said. 'What is useful to the
State is harmful to men.' For him, a man bitten by politics
was lost forever to the empire of pure thought. The artist
should concern himself with eternal problems, not those of
the moment. 'There cannot be art in politics, for politics,
whose goal is to prove, can only be partial.'[6] Nekrasov and
his group disagreed. Reading the text of *Albert*, which Tolstoy had submitted to him, the director of *The Contemporary* was exasperated by such 'reactionary' sentences as
'Beauty is the sole and incontestable good of this world.'
He wrote to the author at once to express his displeasure:

'I feel bound to tell you that your story is no good and must not be published. ... Not only has the theme been worked to death, but it is an unpopular one, and so difficult that it is virtually impossible to handle. ... Ah, write more simple stories.'[7]

Chilled by this admonition, Tolstoy returned to *Albert*, revised it, and noted grimly on 25 December 1857: 'I shall publish it.' He had previously formed an association, with Turgenev, Grigorovich and Ostrovsky, which gave *The Contemporary* exclusive rights to its members' writings. But lately he had begun to disapprove of the review's radical tendencies. Nekrasov's criticism of *Albert* tipped the scales, and he deserted to the art-for-art's-sake camp led by Druzhnin and Botkin. On 17 February 1858 he notified Nekrasov that he was repudiating the agreement which, he said, was 'invalid'. As a parting offering he proposed either *Three Deaths* or the revised version of *Albert*. Nekrasov unwillingly agreed to release his chief contributor and publish the latter story, which he still disliked. The critics were severe. The contemporary press claimed that 'the observations of a half-demented man' were not a fit pretext for a work of art, and that the 'unfinished psychological study' made 'no impression' on the reader.[8] Tolstoy went on working, in spite of this drubbing – as usual, on several stories at once: *Three Deaths*, which he was continually revising, *Family Happiness*, based on his relationship with Valerya Arsenyev, and *The Cossack*,* which he hoped to make into something as sweeping and luminous as an epic by Homer. 'The *Iliad* has forced me to revise my whole concept of the story,' he had written on his return to Russia.[9]

Living with him in Moscow were his sister – who, separated from her husband, had grown bitter and difficult, his brother Nicholas, his nephews and his dear Aunt Toinette; but family life was not enough for him. He wanted action. His first outlet for his excess energy was the gymnasium on

*He called the novel variously *The Caucasian Story*, *The Fugitive*, *The Cossack* and *The Cossacks*.

Dmitrovka Street. 'It was worth the trip,' wrote Fet, 'to see Tolstoy's fierce concentration, trying to leap over a vaulting-horse in his gymsuit.' A large portion of his time was also devoted to music: he arranged concerts and even drew up the regulations for a chamber music orchestra to be directed by his former rival for Valerya's affections, the French pianist Mortier de Fontaine; the project fell through for lack of funds. The lights of the theatres, drawing-rooms and ballrooms drew him out almost every evening. He dressed with particular care, tied his white cravat, put on his new coat from Sharmer, his beaver-collared overcoat and a top hat, took up a silver-pommelled stick and strode resolutely towards the door. 'He had an imposing bearing,' Mrs Sytin wrote in her memoirs, 'there was something attractive in his very ugliness. His eyes were full of vitality and energy. . . . He always spoke in a strong, clear voice and with great feeling, even on trivial subjects. At his arrival, everything suddenly sprang to life.' Did he realize how attractive he was? Far from it. As always, women fascinated and troubled him, he was enamoured of four or five at once and could not make up his mind to love any.

First, he suffered a relapse for Dyakov's sister – his childhood sweetheart, the charming Alexandra Obolensky; 'so lovely,' he wrote, 'dancing the lancers with her little head tilted to one side.' He was furious because she was married; he hung around her, making veiled allusions to his condition which she pretended not to understand. 'Beyond any doubt, this woman tempts me more than any other.' (6 November 1857.) 'She can do what she likes with me and I'm grateful to her. Some evenings I am passionately in love with her and come home full of joy or sorrow, I can't tell which.' (1 December 1857.) 'I love her and become idiotic in her presence.' (4 December 1857.) That day, however, he also noticed that Katerina Tyutchev, the poet's daughter, had been particularly sweet to him. On New Year's Eve: 'Miss Tyutchev is imperceptibly beginning to make an impression on me.' 1 January: 'Katerina is very sweet.' 7 January:

'Miss Tyutchev – nonsense!' 8 January: 'No, not nonsense! Little by little, this feeling is taking hold of me entirely.' 19 January: 'Miss Tyutchev is continually in my thoughts.' 20 January: 'I feel that all I want is her love, but I have no compassion for her.' 26 January: 'Went to see Miss Tyutchev, prepared to love her: she is cold, trivial, aristocratic. Nonsense!' 8 March: 'Went to see Miss Tyutchev: so-so.' 31 March: 'I decidedly do not like Miss Tyutchev.' A few months later he found her 'ugly and cold', but wondered whether he ought not 'marry her without love'.[10] While he was following the twists and turns of this unrewarding idyll, he continued to sigh after Princess Lvov, whom he had loved a great deal in Paris and rather less in Dresden. He was also keeping a close watch on Princess Sherbatov, of whom he wrote that it had been a long time since he had seen 'anything as fresh as she'.[11]

But all the while he was fluttering back and forth between the matrons and the maidens, his heart really belonged to a spinster: aunt-grandmother, *babushka* Alexandra Tolstoy. She was in Moscow for a few days. Leo called on her often, chatted with her, found her 'delicious', 'unique', even dreamed of marrying her, then sobered up in a flash and noted, with chilling cruelty: 'She has grown old and ceased to be a woman for me.'[12] This did not, however, prevent him from seeing her the next day with renewed pleasure. They even set out together for Klin, where they spent a few days with a relative of theirs, old Princess Volkonsky. After Alexandra had gone back to St Petersburg, the fire her presence had dampened was rekindled in a flash. On Easter Monday, 24 March 1858, he wrote to her:

Christ is risen, beloved friend and *babushka*. Although I did not take Communion ... I feel so light-hearted that I cannot refrain from sitting down for a chat with you. When all is chaos inside me, you make me feel ashamed of myself, even when you're not there. ... Where does it come from, that warmth of yours that gives happiness to others and lifts them up above themselves? How happy it must make you to be able to dispense joy to others so easily, so freely. ... When I look at myself, I see I am still the same: a daydreaming egotist, *incapable* of becoming anything else. Where is one to look for love of others and self-denial, when there is nothing inside oneself but love of self and indulgence? ... My ambition is to be corrected and converted by you my whole life long without ever becoming completely corrected or converted.

Rare clear-sightedness: he knew that after confessing his sins to his *babushka* Alexandra he would receive a scolding, that the scolding would thrill him as a proof of her love, that he would not mend his ways, and that the next time it would give him a double thrill to proclaim himself doubly guilty.

With the first harbinger of spring his gloom vanished, and he became an impetuous child again, tipsy with completely unmotivated high spirits. Turning his back on drawing-rooms, young maidens and writers alike, he could think of nothing but Yasnaya Polyana: he left on 9 April 1858, and less than a week later his confidante received this blast of victory full in the face:

Babushka! It's spring! It is so good to be alive on this earth, for all good people and even for such as I. Nature, the air, everything is drenched in hope, future, a wonderful future. ... When I think about it more soberly, I know perfectly well I am nothing but an old frozen potato, rotten, cooked and served up with a tasteless sauce full of lumps, but the springtime has such a powerful effect on me that I sometimes catch myself imagining I am a plant that has just opened and spread its leaves among all the other plants and is going to grow up simply, peacefully and joyfully on the good Lord's earth. When this happens, such a fermentation, purification and orchestration goes on inside me that anyone who has not experienced it himself could not imagine the sensation. Away with all the old worn-out things, all the conventions, the laziness and selfishness and vice and all the vague and mixed-up relationships and regrets and remorse, to the devil with them all. Make way for the wonderful plant that is filling out its buds and growing in the spring.

At Yasnaya Polyana it seemed to him, as it did every time he returned to the scenes of his childhood, that he laid his finger on the truth. The weather was chilly and damp, the sun feebly stroked at the patches of snow that cracked and melted between tufts of new grass. At the end of the avenue of lime trees there was a hole where the old house had been; but the larch saplings planted in the rubble the previous year were taking hold and flourishing. The furniture and family portraits had been removed to the stone pavilion which was now the master's dwelling. There, Prince Nicholas Sergeyevich Volkonsky – black eyebrows, powdered wig, lace jabot and red caftan; Count Peter Andreyevich Tolstoy – full-cheeked and bright-eyed beneath a mop of curly hair; Count Ilya Andreyevich, who was so extravagant and so plaintive; blind Prince Nicholas Ivanovich Gorchakov, with lowered eyelids, and all the others welcomed Leo Tolstoy from their tarnished gilt frames. In the study, the scion of this great family cast a sentimental glance around at the book-laden shelves, the plain table, old armchair, hunting trophies and pictures of friends and writers hanging on the walls. A pious hand had slipped a branch of silvery pussy-willow behind the icon on Palm Sunday. The recent holiday was still in evidence everywhere, along with the promise of fine weather to come. Even the muzhiks looked clean and happy, standing outside their thatched isbas. Tolstoy embraced a few of them on the day after his return, and observed that 'in the springtime their beards have a surprisingly sweet smell'. He drank birch sap, played with his sister's children, galloped over the countryside, ogled the girls and was tongue-tied afterward, inspected the sprouting buds, watched the snowdrops pushing through the ground and heard, with a solemn thrill, the first nightingale. The air warmed, a vegetal mist shrouded the rough carpentry of the trees, the ground was dotted with pink and yellow blossoms. In the evening Tolstoy lingered on the terrace listening to the noises of the country, or played chords on the piano to attract the nightingales. 'I stop playing, they stop singing, I start again, they start again. I spent nearly three hours at this pastime; the terrace is open to the warm night, the frogs are busy at their work and the night watchman at his. What a wonder!'[13]

One night this communion with nature suddenly brought him to his knees. Coming out of his ecstasy, he wrote in his diary: 'I prayed to God in my bedroom, in front of the Greek icon of the Virgin. The vigil lamp was burning. I went out on to the balcony. Black night, swarming with stars. Faint stars, bright stars, a maze of stars. Sparkle, dark shadows, silhouettes of dead trees. He is there. Kneel to Him, and be silent.'[14]

These surges of vague and intense piety recurred frequently, and he never tired of analysing his reactions to the divine enigma. He increasingly felt that the Church degraded and dishonoured God by trying to make him comprehensible to human minds. How could God be conceived of as a kind of general administrator, always ready to lend an ear to supplications from below? 'What sort of God is it that can be seen clearly enough to be prayed to, entered into relations with?' he wrote. 'If I even try to imagine him like that, he loses all his grandeur in my eyes. A God who can be prayed to and served is a proof of our spiritual weakness. He is God exactly because I cannot conceive his whole being. Besides, he is not a being; God is Law and Power.'[15] Since God was beyond the reach of reason, he must be grasped with the heart. It was not the mind that led to him, but the senses. The best way of approaching the Creator was to become one with nature. All atremble with this discovery, Tolstoy wrote impassioned letters to his *babushka* Alexandra, telling her about it. Extremely devout, she replied that she was very unhappy to see him turn away from the Orthodox faith. He was deeply hurt, and wrote back: 'Do not despair, *babushka*, I am filled with Christian sentiment to the highest degree; I have a true concept of Christianity, and I cherish it: it is in my feeling for truth and beauty.'[16] Or, 'I have looked in the Gospels and found

neither God, nor the Redeemer, nor the sacraments, nor
anything. ... To be sure, I love and respect religion and I
think that men cannot be either good or happy without it.
... But I have no religion myself and I do not believe in it.
For me, religion comes from life, not life from religion. You
scoff at my nature and nightingales. But in my religion,
nature is the intermediary.'[17] Yes, now he was certain: it
was by uniting with the animals and plants that he would
penetrate the great mystery, by descending the stages of
creation that he would mount towards heaven, by giving up
intelligence that he would receive the light. Admiration
was already a form of prayer. The Beautiful led to the Good.
The Good led to God. Alexandra's faith ended in the same
truth as that of her nephew; but Alexandra relied upon
Scripture for support, and he upon his love of the earth. And
wasn't that the very thing that was so wonderful, this diversity of routes and identity of goals? There were as many
ways to the Lord as there were beings. 'Every individual,'
he wrote, 'has his own unconscious way, felt only in the
depths of his soul.' He was not even disconcerted by the contradictions that filled him: 'How can they all live together
inside me? I do not know and could not explain it; but it
is certain that dog and cat sleep together in the same
hovel.'[18] As a matter of fact, this particular dog and cat
were singularly fond of a good spat. With these two animals
warring in his breast, how could Tolstoy be otherwise than
eternally preoccupied with his internal upheavals? Pagan in
every fibre of his body, he wanted to be Christian by
thought. A sybarite with pretensions to apostlehood. A billy-
goat pining for purity.

His short story *Three Deaths* was intended to illustrate
this pantheistic Christian faith. The 'worldly lady' in the
story was 'contemptible and pitiful' because although she believed in life after death she was afraid to die, and just when
her Christian faith should have stood her in good stead, she
received no comfort from it. The muzhik, on the contrary,
died contented precisely because he was not a Christian in

the eyes of the Church, because nature was his religion and it seemed natural to him, having lived out his time, to return to the earth which had nourished him. 'A brute, you say?' wrote Tolstoy to Alexandra. 'Where is the harm in that? A brute implies happiness and beauty, harmony with the whole universe, whereas in the life of the lady there was nothing but discord.' And lastly, the third death, that of the tree: it expired with dignity, in silence and beauty. 'In beauty because it did not prevaricate or protest, it felt neither fear nor regret.' [19] After explaining the story to his *babushka*, Tolstoy added: 'There is my idea; you assuredly do not agree with it, but it cannot be contested.' How he missed having her by his side, so that he could talk to her for hours, of religion, literature, friendship, perhaps of love. He filled his letters with protestations of affection which must have thrown the old maid of honour into palpitations, at the Marya Palace in St Petersburg, in her stiff ceremonial gown with a diamond monogram on the shoulder. He told her she was his 'Madonna', he begged her to come to the country (knowing she would not), he urged her to write to him in French if that was more comfortable for her: 'A woman's thoughts are more easily comprehensible to me expressed in French.' [20]

Then, after sealing his letter, he would wander pensively into Aunt Toinette's room, sit down in the battered tapestry armchair, exchange a few words with the wrinkled little old lady who took the place of a mother for him, watch her begin to nod over her sewing basket, turn the pages of a book, read, daydream. ... Suddenly she would raise her head and mumble a few trivial words: 'Sergey went to Pirogovo a few days ago. ... I think Nicholas is going to stay on in Moscow with Mashenka. ...' Or she would ask him how the telegraph worked and, after listening to her nephew's explanation, comment: 'That's odd. I watched it for a whole half-hour and I didn't see a single letter going along the wire.' [21]

Tolstoy appreciated these soporific family evenings all the

more because he was exhausted by the end of the day. To preserve the excellent physical condition he had worked so hard to achieve in Moscow, he had a bar fixed to the wall of his study in front of the window and worked out on it every morning, to the mystification of the passing muzhiks. 'I come to the master for orders,' the steward said, 'and I find him hanging upside down by one leg on a bar. There he hangs, swinging back and forth with his head down. His hair is all on end and goes flying to and fro, and his face is purple. ... I don't know whether to listen to his orders or watch him perform.'[22] How was one to pay any heed to the exhortations of a country gentleman who behaved like a circus acrobat? And what a frightful spectacle for the maids! One girl told Marya Tolstoy, who wanted to send her to work at her brother's house, 'I won't go there, Madame. He runs about the place stark naked, turning somersaults.'[23]

The master progressed from bar to plough. He wanted to share in the work of the muzhiks, in order to understand them better. One in particular, Yufan, impressed him enormously by his strength and skill. The ever-ironic Nicholas Tolstoy told Fet that 'Leo was enchanted with the way Yufan spreads his arms when he ploughs. And lo and behold, Yufan has now become a symbol of peasant vitality to him. ... Following his example, he spreads his elbows apart, seizes the plough ... and Yufanizes.'[24] Tolstoy liked scything best of all – the rhythmic strokes, the mind a blank and sweat pouring down, taking care to remain on a line with the rest of the men. He often shared their meal, sitting on the ground in the shade of a copse. One day on a visit to Yasnaya Polyana Turgenev saw him carrying bales of straw on his back and concluded that he was 'lost to literature'. Tolstoy himself wrote in his diary, 'I am not writing, or reading, or thinking. I am completely absorbed in the farm. The peasants hem and haw and dig in their heels. Those from Grumond look gloomy, but are silent.'[25]

Once again he realized how incompetent he was when it

came to running a farm or managing the muzhiks. Haying with them was a joy, arguing a torment. There were times when he hated them: 'I am afraid of myself. I am beginning to feel a desire for revenge, which is something I have never known before.'[26]

However, on 1 September 1858 he attended an assembly of the nobility of the entire province held to elect representatives to the provincial committee at Tula, and, with one hundred and four other gentry, signed a request for the abolition of serfdom, whereby every peasant was to receive a piece of land and every owner a fair sum in payment. Most of the landowners in his district refused to endorse the project: liberals and conservatives showed equal selfishness where their own interests were concerned. 'The Cherkasky gang are no less a bunch of low-down scum than their opponents,' he wrote on 4 September when the deliberations were over. He returned to Yasnaya Polyana with the feeling that the grand idea of emancipation would never overcome the resistance of the local aristocracy. His neighbours accused him of 'going over to the peasants'. That was too much: for the time being, he confined his treason to having an affair with one of their women. She was married, her name was Axinya Bazykin, she was twenty-three years old and lived in a hamlet seven miles from the master's house. He saw her often, and her husband, an understanding type, did not take umbrage. 'In love all day long. ... Saw her for a short while. ... She is very nice. . . I am in love as I have never been before. ... Thought of nothing else. ...'[27] These sentences in his diary punctuate the phases of a healthy, straightforward and undramatic passion. He saw few people other than those at home, and had no desire to go out. After visiting Turgenev at Spasskoye he noted, 'Ivan Turgenev is impossibly difficult. ... He is behaving badly towards Marya. The pig!'[28] The truth was that Turgenev's feelings for Marya Tolstoy had cooled; he now thought her ugly, ageing and dull, but he continued to court her, just to pass the time, with mincing gallantry, vocal tremolo and poetic glances. Irritated by this play-acting, which was keeping the poor girl on tenterhooks, Tolstoy seized every pretext for quarrelling with his colleague. And, 'I'm through with Tolstoy,' the latter wrote to Botkin. 'He has ceased to exist for me. May God grant him every blessing, to him and his talent, but I who was first to say "Hail" to him now have an irresistible desire to tell him "Farewell". We are from opposite poles. If I eat soup and like it, I know by that very fact and beyond the shadow of a doubt that Tolstoy will not like it, and vice versa.' [29]

The widening gap between Tolstoy and Turgenev coincided with the former's growing affection for Fet. It was Fet who arranged for Tolstoy and his brother Nicholas to be invited to a bear hunt in December 1858, on the estate of a friend of his who lived near Volochek in the government of Tver. The first day (21 December), all went well. But the next day Tolstoy, who had neglected to trample down the snow in order to have room to move about in, suddenly saw the she-bear, maddened by gunfire, charging towards him down the narrow path. The huge shape, dark, soft and powerful, came straight at him. He took aim and fired, missed and fired again when the animal was almost on top of him. The bullet went into her mouth, she gave a roar of pain and threw herself full tilt upon him. He saw the open jaws dripping foam, and beyond, 'a bit of brilliant blue sky between purple clouds piled on top of each other'. He instinctively lowered his head and flung his arm over his eyes. The bear tore at his face. He thought the end had come. But a beater came running up with a stick in his hand, shouting, 'Where are you going? Where are you going?' and the frightened bear released him and ran off into the forest. Tolstoy looked at the blood-spattered snow and put a hand to his burning face. His left cheek was torn below the eye and a strip of flesh had been gouged from his forehead.* He bore the scars for the rest of his life. That

* Tolstoy based his essay *Desire Is the Worst Slavery of All* on this episode.

evening's entry in his diary reads simply, 'Went bear hunting. The twenty-first I killed one; the twenty-second, the animal took a piece out of me. Spent a lot of money.' Two weeks later he went out hunting again; this time they killed four fine specimens, including the bear that had attacked him. He received her carcass as a trophy and had it made into a rug for his study.

He returned to Moscow and *Family Happiness*, which had been a struggle to write from the start; after all, it was tempting fate to describe the creation and subsequent disintegration of a couple at a time when social problems were all the readers cared about. He was elected to Moscow University's Society of Friends of Russian Literature at the same time as Turgenev, and decided to defend the theory of 'art for art's sake' in his address to his colleagues. He was admitted to the Society on 4 February 1859 and, rising to speak with a spark of defiance in his eyes, denounced the increasing tendency of the public to regard literature solely as a means of 'arousing civic spirit in contemporary society'. Some people went so far as to pretend that Pushkin would soon be forgotten and 'pure art' was an impossibility. Before an audience stony with disapproval, he forcefully concluded: 'However important a political literature may be, a literature that reflects the passing problems of society, and however necessary to national progress, there is still another type of literature that reflects the eternal necessities of all mankind, the dearest and deepest imaginings of a whole race, a literature that is accessible to all and to every age, one without which no people has been able to grow powerful and fertile.'

Khomyakov, the president, replied that it was a man's duty to condemn the vices of society and that because of his exceptional sensitivity the writer unconsciously became a public prosecutor of his time, even if he hoped to be only a pure artist. 'Yes,' he said, turning to Tolstoy, 'you, too, will be a prosecutor, whether you like it or not. Follow, by the grace of God, the wonderful path you have chosen ... but do not forget that in literature the transient, the momentary, are heightened by becoming part of the artistic and eternal, and that in the end all the individual human voices blend to form one harmonious whole.'

Tolstoy certainly did not dream then that one day he would be repeating the words of this Slavophil theorist almost verbatim, becoming the opponent of pure art after being its most ardent champion.

As soon as he had finished *Family Happiness*, he became more strongly convinced than ever of its worthlessness. However, at Botkin's insistence he sold it to Katkov's *Russian Herald*. On 3 May 1859 he was at Yasnaya Polyana when the proofs arrived: 'What shameful offal! What a blotch!' he wrote to Botkin. 'You have made a fool, an utter fool of me by advising me to publish it. ... Now I'm done for as a writer and as a man. ... If you have any compassion for my suffering and if you want to be my friend, do persuade Katkov not to print the second part and let me return the money to him. ... I have kept my part of the bargain and corrected the proofs, with a revulsion which I find it hard to describe. Not one living word in the lot. And the hideousness of the language – stemming from the hideousness of the thought – is unimaginable. ... I was so right to want to publish it under a pseudonym. ... The last chapters have not been and must not be sent to me. It is agony to see the book, read it, remember it. ...'

Botkin, who had found a 'chill glitter' about *Family Happiness* when he first read the novel, and had said it moved 'neither mind nor heart', went over the proofs with a critical eye and replied, on 15 May 1859:

'To my amazement, the result was entirely different from what I had expected. Not only did I like the second part, but I find it beautiful in all respects. In the first place, it has dramatic appeal; in the second, it is an excellent psychological study; the descriptions of nature are most life-like; and in short, the whole thing is admirable, profoundly talented and meaningful.' By and large, the critics were of the same opinion. *Northern Flowers* hailed it as a 'poetic idyll', the *St Petersburg News* set the book on a level with *Childhood*, *Native Son* declared that the characters' psychology was portrayed with 'prodigious accuracy' and that the author was established as an exceptional 'connoisseur of the human heart'.

Tolstoy had in fact put a good deal of both himself and Valerya Arsenyev into the book. Sergey Mikhailovich, the hero, was also older than his fiancée, his estate was a mirror-image of Yasnaya Polyana, his looks and his views on life were those of the author: 'He had a simple, open, honest expression, coarse features, alert, intelligent, gentle eyes, a childlike smile,' we read in *Family Happiness*. And also: 'Everything he felt was reflected immediately and intensely in his face. …' 'He spoke with fervour, warmth and simplicity. …' 'He had occasional bursts of wild enthusiasm. …' 'His handshake was vigorous and frank, almost painful.' Every notation accentuates the likeness of the portrait. It was the painter himself, standing in front of a mirror drawing his own picture, line for line. The description of Masha, the heroine, was equally true-to-life: like Valerya Arsenyev, she was attracted to the glitter of high society, whereas Sergey Mikhailovich abhorred 'the dirt and idleness of this imbecilic class'. Disillusioned with marriage after years of being misunderstood, the young wife finally transfers her former affection for her husband to her children. Tolstoy was not able either to dominate or to say anything really new about the relatively trite theme of the transmutation of conjugal love into maternal love, and the story, a novella rather than a novel, was uneven, clumsily constructed and lacking in originality. But it was permeated by a remarkable feeling for nature: the reapers staggering under the sun, the monotonous movement of the telegas through the yellow dust, the smell of gardens at the approach of autumn, the red ashberries among leaves blackened by the first frost, the little church through which the priest's voice resounded 'as though there were no one else alive in the whole world', the winter sky, glowing with 'the ringed moon of the season of the frosts' – all these descriptions illuminate the inferior pages and save them from mediocrity.

Despite the book's success, Tolstoy continued to be dissatisfied with it and returned to his *Cossacks*, begun six years before. Would he have enough determination to see them through to the end? He no longer believed he could. He was suddenly filled with a mighty loathing for himself and the world. A series of disenchanted notes filled the pages of his diary. At one point, he considered Octave Feuillet a better writer than himself: 'Read Feuillet. Terrific talent. I am depressed when I think of myself. This year nothing can awaken any response in me. Not even sorrow. My one impulse is to work and forget, but forget what? There's nothing to forget.' (9 May 1859.) 'I am not pleased with myself. I am simply drifting.' (28 May 1859.) His nerves were on edge, he often lost his temper. There were quarrels with his sister and the neighbours, outbursts against the muzhiks. 'I am being ground in the mill of domestic problems again, with all their stinking weight.' (14–16 October.) How ridiculous to waste his time inventing stories, when life was surging about him on all sides, dragging him into the current. Writing stories was a game for children, not a fit occupation for a man. Man had been created to work with his hands, help his neighbour, and teach the young. Down with pure art, and social art, too! He wrote to Fet in a moment of anger, solemnly forswearing literature: 'I shall write no more fiction. It is shameful, when you come to think of it. People are weeping, dying, marrying, and I should sit down and write books telling "how she loved him"? It's shameful!'[30]

And to Druzhnin, who had asked for a story for his review *The Reading Library*:

I'm not much use as a writer any more. I have written nothing since *Family Happiness* and I don't think I shall ever write again. At least, I am presumptuous enough to believe that. ... Now that I have become mature, life is too short for me to

fritter it away making up books like the ones I write, which are
a source of embarrassment to me afterwards. . . . If at least there
were some subject that was really nagging at me, demanding to
take shape, impelling me to be bold, proud and strong. Then,
yes! But really, to write novels that are charming and entertaining to read, at thirty-one years of age! I gasp at the
thought.[31]

Tolstoy put the education of the people at the top of his
list of occupations that were worthy of a man. He had
already opened one school at Yasnaya Polyana in 1848, but
had been forced to close it when he went to the Caucasus.
He decided to try again. However, by educating these primitive beings, would he not arouse desires in them that could
not be satisfied afterwards? Would he not be condemning
them to lives of frustration, by trying to force his form of
happiness upon them? The master was apprehensive, but
his serfs were even more so, although for different reasons.
As always, they thought only of what he could be trying
to gain for himself from his scheme. Perhaps he wanted to
turn their sons into foot-soldiers so he could send them to
the army and be paid by the tsar. Long palavers were required to allay their fears. At last Tolstoy managed to
collect twenty-two children, whom he led into a converted
bedroom on the third floor of the house and, scarcely containing his joy and pride, began to chalk the letters of the
Russian alphabet on a blackboard.

Of course, there were recurrences of the parental misgivings. One muzhik did not want his son to continue at the
school because no floggings were administered there and he
would lose the habit of being beaten. Another was persuaded that the master was withholding something from his
pay for his son's lessons. Forced to control his anger, Tolstoy told himself that his peasants' thickheadedness was
providing him with an opportunity to learn evangelical forbearance. His educational system was founded on total freedom – of the teacher in relation to pupils, and the pupils in
relation to their teacher. Only those came who wanted to

learn. If they did not feel like working, nobody forced them. The teacher's moral authority should be enough to keep the class under control. No lessons to be memorized at home, no written work to prepare, no surprise quizzes to dread. 'The pupil brings nothing to the classroom but himself, his rational mind and his certainty that school will be as much fun today as it was yesterday.'[32] In this schoolboy's paradise Tolstoy taught spelling, arithmetic, religious history, history and geography, all mixed up together. The children listened distractedly, retained an occasional word; but their faces were becoming more alert every day. The enrolment rose from twenty-two to fifty, whereupon Tolstoy decided to publish an educational periodical. 'I am working at something that comes as naturally to me as breathing and, I confess with culpable pride, enables me to look down on what the rest of you are doing,'[33] he wrote to Chicherin. And to Borisov: 'I am swamped with work, and fine work it is. A far cry from writing novels!'[34] His friends hid their smiles and shrugged their shoulders: their Leo had clearly gone off his head! The eternal about-face, another new craze, words thrown to the winds. 'Leo Tolstoy is continuing his nonsense,' Turgenev wrote to Fet. 'It must be in his blood. When will he turn his final somersault and land on his feet at last?'[35]

During the warm weather, all the pupils at Yasnaya Polyana had to work in the fields and the master shut down the school. Besides, he did not have a free moment himself. He rose at four in the morning to help his muzhiks with the heaviest chores: 'After sweating blood and tears, everything seemed beautiful to me, I began to love mankind,'[36] he wrote. Then, broken with fatigue, radiant, ravenous, he went off to meet his serf-mistress Axinya Bazykin. As time passed, he had grown so fond of her full white peasant flesh that he could no longer do without it. 'I am afraid when I see how attached to her I am,' he wrote in his diary. 'The feeling is no longer bestial, but that of a husband for his wife.' What to do? He did not want their liaison to become official, and yet he did not have the courage to break it off. The best solution, he thought, would be to go away for a while. Conveniently, his brother Nicholas, who was suffering from tuberculosis, was planning a trip to Soden, a little German town whose waters were said to be very effective in pulmonary cases. Sergey and the patient set out together in the last days of May, and in spite of the summer work which should have kept the master at Yasnaya Polyana, Leo decided to follow them. Too bad for Axinya, school and harvest! This time, he would travel *en famille*; he took his sister Marya, who was ill herself, and her three children, Nikolenka, Varya and Lisa.

On 2 July 1860 they sailed from St Petersburg on the *Prussian Eagle*, a paddle-steamer bound for Stettin. Tolstoy was seasick. Since Dmitry's death he had been haunted by the fear of tuberculosis. When he stepped ashore at Stettin after a very rough two-day crossing, his mind was full of dire forebodings and his jaw was swollen with toothache.

[11]

Second Trip Abroad

FROM Stettin Leo and Marya Tolstoy and her children went directly to Berlin to consult a lung specialist, Professor Traube. He reassured everyone: there was not the slightest trace of tuberculosis in the lungs of the distinguished foreigners who had come to him for auscultation. However, to give weight to his reputation, perhaps, and to justify his fees, he advised Marya to take the waters at Soden, recommended sea baths for Varya, who was delicate, and treatment at Kissingen for Leo's dental neuralgia. On the orders of this leading light of medicine, the family separated. Leo stayed on in Berlin. When he thought of poor Nicholas coughing out his lungs at Soden, he told himself that he ought really to be there by the side of his dearly beloved elder brother. But the memory of his last interview with Dmitry was so chilling that, without admitting it to himself, he was afraid of another ordeal of the sort. With the unconscious selfishness of the healthy, he invented a thousand reasons for putting off a meeting which could give him nothing but grief. And to begin with, was it not his duty as an educator to acquaint himself with foreign teaching methods? He visited museums, went to the University to hear Droysen the historian and Du Bois-Reymond the physiologist; he toured the famous Moabit Prison, where the American practice of solitary confinement had been introduced, with Fraenkel, the student, as his guide, and he attended evening classes for workingmen. There, the students – all adults – asked whatever questions they liked by means of a question box, and classes took the form of an informal dialogue. In the children's classes, on the other hand, rigid discipline prevailed, at which the traveller was incensed. Leipzig, Dresden – everywhere he found the same teaching by rote, the same brutal punishment. 'Summer in school is awful,' he wrote. 'Prayer for the king, cuff on the head, everything by heart, children terrorized and be-numbed.'[1]

He had great admiration for the German novelist Berthold Auerbach, author of *Schwarzwälder Dorfgeschichten* (Scenes of Village Life in the Black Forest), who, judging from his books, shared Tolstoy's ideas about education. One morning Auerbach saw a short, stocky, bearded stranger, with little steely eyes beneath thick, bushy brows, enter his drawing-room, bow and say, 'I am Eugene Baumann!' – the name of one of Auerbach's characters. The author froze, thinking that this determined-looking individual was intending to sue him for defamation. But a smile flitted across his guest's thick lips and he added, 'I am Eugene Baumann by nature, not by name.' And he introduced himself: Count Leo Tolstoy, author and schoolteacher. Relieved, Auerbach invited the Russian to sit down. They understood each other from the first word. 'All methods are sterile,' said Auerbach. 'Anybody can be a great teacher. It's the children who create the best teaching methods, together with their teacher.'[2] Tolstoy scarcely had time to nod his head.

At Kissingen, where he went next for his teeth, he met Julius Froebel, nephew of the originator of the kindergarten and himself the author of *The System of Social Politics*. His impression of the German pedagogue was of a 'liberal-aristocrat' and a 'chatterbox', utterly 'emptied' by politics. He even went so far as to call him, disdainfully, 'nothing but a Jew'. Further, Froebel was unwilling to admit that all constraint in the education of the people was harmful and that education in Russia would ultimately progress faster because Russian children were still unspoiled, whereas the German children had been contaminated by retrograde methods. Despite these areas of disagreement between the two, Froebel introduced Tolstoy to the European systems of education and advised him what to read, recommending the economist Wilhelm Riehl's *Kulturgeschichte* in particular.

Now and then, for a change of scenery, Tolstoy went off on trips into Thuringia or the Harz Mountains. He went to Wartburg and saw the room in which Luther began his translation of the Bible, but it did not occur to him to go to Soden, only a short distance from Kissingen, where Nicholas was quietly dying. The sick man was saddened by Leo's delay: '*Uncle Leo* lingers on at Kissingen, five hours from Soden, but he does not come to Soden, and so I have not seen him,' he wrote to Fet on 20 July (1 August), 1860.

What was going on in Tolstoy's mind? Nothing very specific; he put off the painful duty of seeing his brother from one day to the next, he was playing for time, holding his anguish at bay, out of cowardice, because it was easier. But it suddenly became impossible for him to feign ignorance any longer: his other brother, Sergey, stopped at Kissingen on his way back to Russia. He had lost all his money at roulette and had to return to Pirogovo, where Marya Shishkin – the gypsy with whom he had now been living for some ten years – was waiting for him. According to Sergey, their brother's condition had deteriorated considerably. The news affected Tolstoy, but not enough to drag him out of his apathy. He remained at Kissingen, sighing over his elder brother's fate and ruminating a scheme for the abolition of roulette.

On 28 July (9 August) 1860 Sergey left for Russia and Nicholas arrived in Kissingen in person, exhausted by a five-hour train trip under a leaden sky. He could not bear his younger brother's silence any longer. Since Leo refused to come to him, it was he, summoning his last remaining strength, who went to Leo.

Although he had long since left the army, Nicholas was still wearing a faded artillery tunic. His hands were large, dirty and diaphanous. Great intelligent eyes burned with fever in his hollow scarlet-cheeked mask. He breathed as little as possible, for fear of starting a coughing fit. Alcohol and tuberculosis had consumed his body, but the same sadly ironic smile twisted his lips when he looked at his brother. He admired Leo's talent as a writer and teased him about his wordly escapades, flings with the peasant girls, turnabout moods and bouts of breast-beating, which were often nothing but disguised bursts of self-love. 'The attitude of humility that Leo Tolstoy cultivated in theory,' Turgenev said, 'was actually applied by his brother Nicholas. He always lived in some impossible slum in a remote part of town, and was ready to share whatever he had with the poor.'

Stricken with remorse at the sight of the condemned man, Tolstoy swore not to leave his side again. He wrote in his diary on 31 July (12 August): 'Nicholas is in a dreadful state. Extremely intelligent, clear-headed. At the same time, has a will to live but no vital energy.' But the next day he let Nicholas go back alone to Soden. His selfishness had triumphed over his conscience. And by staying where he was, he spared his sensitive soul. Besides, he had no talent for nursing: 'Nicholas has left. I don't know what to do. Marya is also unwell. I am being no use to anyone.' (1 [13] August 1860.) He complained of his uselessness for another two weeks, but it never occurred to him that by going to Soden he would be making himself useful. He continued to see Froebel, became more and more fascinated with the subject of education, wrote to Aunt Toinette for news of the Yasnaya Polyana school, which had just been reopened by a teacher [3] he had hired before he left. ... Suddenly, he wanted to be back among his muzhiks, wearing the same dress as they, instead of wasting his time abroad. In the night of 10–11 (22–23) August he had a nightmare that left him perplexed: 'Dreamed that I was dressed as a peasant and my mother did not recognize me,' [4] he wrote. Did this mean that 'going over to the people' was just a hollow pretence and his mother, whom he adored but had never known, was rejecting him from on high? His most noble thoughts were soured by a sneaking sense of self-deception, and he had caught cold, which made him even gloomier. 'All day long I was obsessed by fear for my lungs.'[5] He saw a doctor, who told him he was suffering from a 'vaso-motor' disturbance. This diagnosis abruptly tipped the scales: he took the train for Soden, to undergo treatment himself.

The welcome he received from Nicholas, so cheerful and confident in spite of his extreme feebleness, stirred him to the core, but he found his sister Marya 'boring and bored'. He felt better and quite forgot about his own treatment. Besides, the weather was turning bad, it rained all the time, a damp chill was creeping into the rooms. At Soden, and then at Frankfort, the doctors advised Nicholas to try the South of France. Leo, Marya and her three children accompanied him, and they all arrived together at Hyères, on 24 August (6 September), 1860. The two men stayed in town, at Mme Sénéquier's *pension* on the rue du Midi, and Marya and her children rented a villa a few miles away.

The long train and coach trip had worn Nicholas out. He smiled up at the blue sky and sun and felt his strength ebbing away. When he had a coughing fit, which was usually in the morning when he awoke, he was ashamed to be seen spitting blood into the basin and refused to have anyone in the room. Although the slightest effort exhausted him, he dressed and undressed himself out of discipline, and to keep up his dignity. But one day, in his toilet, he had to call his brother because he was too weak to straighten his clothes by himself. 'Help me,' he murmured. And afterwards said, 'Thanks, friend.' These words moved Tolstoy far more than a searing lament or an avowal of love. 'Friend. ... Do you realize what that meant, between us?'[6] he wrote to Sergey.

Nicholas no longer doubted that his end was at hand, and accepted defeat with equanimity. Seated by his bed, Tolstoy looked at the bloodless face, listened to the shallow breathing and thought back to their children's games at Yasnaya Polyana, the drinking bouts with the officers, the hunts with Uncle Epishka in the Caucasian forest and the green stick bearing the secret of happiness that Nicholas said was buried in the forest of Zakaz. Was it possible that this cherished vessel of memory, this lively intelligence, this warmth of thought were about to dissolve forever? What was the point of living, what was the point of work, if everything must end in this horrible slithering towards an abyss? On 20 September (2 October), 1860 Tolstoy saw that his brother would not live through the day. Marya had just gone back to her villa outside Hyères. Nicholas sank into unconsciousness. Then his eyes opened wide, his face winced in terror, he blurted out, 'What is it?' and died.

Eight years earlier Tolstoy had written to Aunt Toinette from the Caucasus: 'As God is my witness, the two greatest misfortunes that could befall me would be your death or that of Nicholas, the two people I love more than myself.'[7]

For once he had not been wrong in his predictions. He was literally *astonished* by an event he refused to understand. Death as he had seen it on the battlefield was brutal, heroic, awful, but the very strangeness of the sight distorted its meaning. Besides, one was quaking so hard with fear for one's own skin that one had no time to ponder over metaphysical problems. But here in Mme Sénéquier's pleasant family *pension*, death was not a sudden blow, but a long, slow wearing-down, an ineluctable advance of being towards nothingness, the most abominable destruction in the most intimate and commonplace setting, between basin and bedpan.

Terrible though it is, [Leo wrote to his brother Sergey] I am glad it all happened before my eyes and affected me as it should have done. It is not like the death of Mitenka [Dmitry], which I learned of at a time when my mind was completely taken up with other things. ... I was bound to Mitenka by childhood memories and a feeling of kinship, but that was all. But he [Nicholas] was, for you and for me, the man we loved and respected more than anything in the world. You know the selfish thought that was in our minds towards the end: the sooner the better – now, it is terrible to write that and remember that one could think it. ... He died without suffering, visibly at least. The next day I went down to his room. I was afraid to uncover his face. I thought it must be even more anguished and frightening than during his illness, but you cannot imagine how attractive it was, how good, cheerful and calm.[8]

During the burial at the cemetery at Hyères, Tolstoy thought of writing 'a practical Gospel, a materialist life of Christ'.[9] But it was not, he convinced, literary vanity that inspired this project. He was no longer interested in art. After the ordeal he had just been through, his sole aim was to tear off the absurd masks that religions had plastered on to the face of God, one on top of the other, down through the centuries:

When one really comes to think that death is the end of everything, then there is nothing worse than being alive. Why care, why work, since there is nothing left of what was Nicholas Nikolayevich? Strange idea of a joke! Be useful, virtuous, happy, people tell each other; but we and our usefulness, our virtue, our happiness, it all boils down to this simple truth which I have understood after thirty-two years of life: the situation in which we are placed is atrocious. ... No doubt, so long as one has the desire to discover the truth and say it, one goes on trying to discover it and say it. That is all that remains of my idea of morality. That is the only thing I shall do, only not in your form of art. Art is a lie, and already I am no longer able to love a beautiful lie.[10]

'It is almost a month since Nikolenka [Nicholas] died. This event has detached me terribly from life. Again the same question: why? I am no longer very far myself from the crossing-over. Over where? Nowhere. I try to write, I force myself, and I can't do it, for the simple reason that I cannot attach enough importance to work to muster up the strength and patience it demands. ... Nikolenka's death has hit me harder than anything I have ever experienced.'

But man is so made that the consciousness of the nothingness lying in wait for him paradoxically spurs him on to build. With his prodigious powers of recuperation, Tolstoy drew a strength from his grief that happiness could not have given him. 'Read my fortune in the cards,' he wrote on 16 (28) October 1860. 'Shilly-shallying, idleness, depression, thoughts of death. Must get out of this. Only one way: make myself work. It is already one o'clock in the afternoon and I have not yet done a thing. Finish the first chapter before dinner, then write letters.' And a little later, 'For the last three days I have been invaded by a host of images and ideas, such as I have not had for ten years.' [11]

After casting away art ('Art is a lie, and already I am no longer able to love a beautiful lie'), he turned and clung to it as though it were the most precious thing in the world. He even began a new novel, *The Decembrists*, the opening pages of which described the homecoming of one of the heroes of Russian liberalism after being exiled by Nicholas I for his part in the uprising of 14 December 1825.* In his portrait of Russian society as seen through the eyes of this ghost from the Siberian prison camps, he abandoned himself, in spite of his mourning, to a mordant irony and grim gaiety in which the joy of creation could be detected. He might have left Hyères and broken away from the sad memories there, but he preferred to stay until the end of the year, and moved into the villa 'Touche' with his sister. The little provincial town was full of tuberculosis patients. 'Wherever one goes,' wrote Marya Tolstoy, 'there are the sick, and what sick! A congress of dying comsumptives! Every minute one goes by in a chair, or held up by the arms by someone on either side, or dragging along alone with a cane; all their faces are livid, exhausted and dismal. In a word, this is an outdoor hospital. Hardly anyone has only a mild case; only those for whom all hope has been abandoned come here!' [12] And Tolstoy himself confessed to his *babushka* Alexandra that since his brother's death he could not look at the Hyères invalids without feeling that they were all 'part of the family', that they all 'had

* Tolstoy abandoned this novel after a few chapters.

some power over him'.[13] When he was too downhearted, his nephews helped him to combat his despair. Their candid eyes, laughter and questions revived his taste for life. With them and a little nine-year-old neighbour, Sergey Plaxin, who 'had a weak chest', he went for long walks up the Montagne Sainte, or over to the castle of the Trou des Fées (Fairies' Hole) or to Porquerolles to watch the men working in the salt flats. He told them fairy tales as they went; the story of the golden horse, the story of the giant tree from the top of which one could see all the cities and seas of the world. When Sergey Plaxin was tired, he lifted him on to his shoulders, and the little boy might pretend he was at the top of the magic oak. Back at the house, Tolstoy organized games: he hung a rig between the doors and did gymnastics with the children, or gathered them around him and asked them to write a composition on the theme, 'What distinguishes Russia from all other countries?' For one, the most striking thing about Russia was the blinis they ate during Lent and the painted eggs at Easter; for another, it was all the snow that fell there; for another, it was troikas.[14] Tolstoy was delighted with their replies. He felt his professorial calling stirring again.

To complete his documentation on the subject dear to his heart, he went to Marseilles one day and visited eight State schools. As in Germany, he found an atmosphere of stifling discipline in the classrooms. The children's talent for duplicity was cultivated by over-harsh treatment, and their memories were developed at the expense of their intelligence by forcing them to learn their lessons by heart. They gave the visitor the right answers as long as he asked his questions on the history of France in the order they occurred in the textbook, but when he began to skip from one chapter to another they told him that Henri IV had been slain by Julius Caesar. The orphanage he visited next was, to his mind, a prison for little children. 'At the sound of the whistle,' he wrote, 'four-year-olds revolve around their benches like soldiers, raising and crossing their arms on command, and in strange, quavering voices, sing hymns to God and their benefactors.'

And yet, in the streets, the personalities of the most ordinary people, their conversation and repartee, proved that they had all the wit they needed. 'The French are nearly all the things they believe they are: ingenious, intelligent, sociable, open-minded and, it is true, civilized. Look at a thirty-year-old town labourer: he can write a letter with fewer mistakes than the children in school can, sometimes without any at all; he has some notion of politics, history and modern geography. … Where has he learned it all?'[15] The answer, for Tolstoy, was simple: the Frenchman did not get his education at school – where the instruction was preposterous – but in his life, reading the newspapers and novels (among others, those of Alexandre Dumas), going to museums and theatres and the cafés, and to the *ginguettes* (country inns where people went to dance). He estimated that twenty-five thousand souls passed daily through each of the two huge *cafés-concerts* of Marseilles, where one could drink for ten sous. That made fifty thousand a day, watching comic sketches, listening to poems and songs. … There were two hundred and fifty thousand people in the city and so one-fifth of the entire population, according to Tolstoy, could be said to be informed every day 'as the Greeks and Romans were in their amphitheatres'. He called this 'spontaneous education', the kind that would 'put compulsory schooling out of business'. True, he could hardly open a *café-concert* at Yasnaya Polyana, but there, as here, education must be a joyful pursuit. On 13 (25) October he wrote in his diary: 'School is not at school, but in the newspapers and cafés.'

Towards mid-December, feeling that his pedagogical research was still incomplete, he went to Italy: Florence, Livorno, Naples, Pompeii – where he came unawares upon 'an image of Antiquity' – and Rome, where he was overwhelmed by the beauty of the ruins and the treasures in the museums; but what he was really in search of as he jour-

neyed from one town to another was man, not works of art.
One day at the top of the Pincio, the hill with the finest
view of the city, he heard a little boy crying for a toy. Suddenly the Villa Medici, the gardens and far-off ruins vanished. The only thing that existed and mattered in the
world was the unknown child with the shrill voice. Thirty-
eight years later, thinking back to Rome, it was not the celebrated monuments that came into his mind, but a dirty,
tear-stained little face with eyes as black as olives and a
screaming mouth: *'date mi un balocco!'*[16]

In less than two months he had exhausted Italy's stores of
tourist and academic attractions and returned to Hyères. At
the beginning of February 1861 he went to Paris, which
had left such an unpleasant taste in his mouth because of its
women of easy virtue and its guillotine. In the capital he
met Turgenev again, and was delighted with him, bought
quantities of books on education, visited more schools and
entertained himself by observing the French people in public buses. All the passengers seemed copied out of a book
by Paul de Kock! On 17 February (1 March) he wrote to his
brother that the reason he was prolonging his long trip
abroad was 'so that nobody in Russia could tell [him] anything about what was being done abroad in the field of education'. That day he left for London and arrived, once
again, with a toothache.

The moment the pain subsided, he dressed himself up as a
dandy – top hat and palmerston* – and went out to mix
with the people, in order to learn and criticize. The foggy,
smoky town, with yellow gaslamps glowing here and there,
impressed him by its orderliness, discipline and tedium. Not
one curious glance in the street, not one over-hasty movement, not a cry, not a smile. Nothing but measured, sober
citizens hiding their souls and going about their business
with no concern for that of others. Although London instilled in him 'a loathing for modern civilization', he was
fascinated by the cockfights and boxing matches, by a sit-

* A long coat fashionable in 1860.

ting in the House of Commons during which Lord Palmerston spoke for three solid hours, and by a lecture on education given by Dickens. The memory of Dickens also pursued him as he toured the English schools – no more alluring than those of Paris, Rome, Geneva and Berlin. But with what joy and pride, on the other hand, he went to call on Herzen, the revolutionary, who was living in a comfortable little cottage with his daughter Natalya. The fiery editorialist of *The Bell* had had a hard time recovering from the series of misfortunes that had befallen him in recent years. His mother and his son had perished in the shipwreck of the Marseilles–Nice mailboat off the Hyères Islands; his wife had died in childbirth, after being unfaithful to him. However, instead of the monument of woe he was preparing to greet, it was a paunchy, bearded, jovial little man who came into the room. Herzen's eyes were alight with intelligence. He exuded a kind of electricity. They complimented one another, talked of Russia, freedom, the Decembrists, popular education, the peasant problem – and literature, too. ... On 23 February (7 March) 1861 Herzen wrote to Turgenev: 'I am seeing a lot of Tolstoy. We have already quarrelled. He is stubborn and talks nonsense, but is naïve and a good man.' And, five days later, 'Count Tolstoy often oversteps the limits. His brain does not take time to digest the impressions it absorbs.'

On 5 (17) March Tolstoy read in the newspapers of the publication in Russia of the imperial manifesto of 18 February (3 March) 1861 abolishing serfdom. He was deeply moved, no doubt, but did not have time to share his impressions with Herzen, for he was leaving that day for Belgium. How had the muzhiks of Yasnaya Polyana reacted to the news? Had someone managed to explain the terms of the proclamation to them? Would there not be some hardheads among the people who would demand their freedom immediately and without payment? Tolstoy should have hurried home, to spare his beloved muzhiks any doubts or fears; yet once he reached Brussels, he showed no inclination to leave. After all, the abolition of serfdom did not concern him. Ah, if the government had only let him free his muzhiks first, with what zeal he would have rushed home to urge other landowners to follow his example! But as he had not been the instigator of the movement, his desire for social justice was frustrated. A man of his temperament could not be expected to display the same ardour in obedience as in apostlehood. He was made to storm the citadel alone, not to follow in the anonymous flood of foot-soldiers. Since the manifesto, published in every newspaper and posted on every church door, had become the law of the land, he would conform to it, certainly, but he was not going to break his neck over it.

However, the news that reached him from Russia was not reassuring; the manifesto was written in a complicated and pompous style, and the people had not understood it. It stated that for a period of two years the serfs – whether attached to the master's land (*krepostnye*) or to his person (*dvorovye*) – would be required to obey their owner as before, but the owner would not have the right to sell them, transfer them to another estate or dispose of their children in any way. During the period of transition they would be required to pay a tithe of thirty roubles per man and ten roubles per woman, and in 1863 they would be released from all obligations to their former master. The *dvorovye*, who were not attached to the land, might seek employment wherever they liked but would receive no land. The *krepostnye* would have the use of their enclosure (pen, croft, etc.) and a measure of arable land, to be calculated according to detailed scales varying with local conditions. This land would be ceded to the muzhiks in return for two kinds of payment to the owner: the *obrok* (payment in money, ranging from eight to twelve roubles per person per year) and the *barshina* (payment in labour, equal to forty days a year for men and thirty for women). The implementation of these measures was to be supervised by 'arbiters of the peace', appointed among the nobility in each district of each government. If the muzhiks wished to purchase the land they worked, the State would lend them the necessary amount to pay off their former master, and they would repay the loan over a period of forty-nine years, by annual instalments representing six per cent of the *obrok*, amortization and interest included. From these liberal and complicated provisions the muzhiks retained only three things: the land was not to be theirs at once, they were not to be free for two years, and if a dispute arose between them and their master, it was to be settled by the gentry.

From Yasnaya Polyana Sergey wrote to Tolstoy on 12 March 1861: 'These are fascinating days. The emancipation manifesto was read out to the people, who did not pay close attention, and it seems to me that they are all rather dissatisfied. The main thing is that they don't understand a word of the document and appear not to care. I offered to explain it all to the peasants at Yasnaya Polyana while I was there, but nobody seemed to want me to do so.'

Thus informed, Tolstoy wrote to Herzen:

'Have you read the exact terms of emancipation? To my mind it is utterly futile verbiage. I have received two letters from Russia telling me that the muzhiks are all dissatisfied. Before, they could hope that everything would turn out all right; now they know for certain that everything will be all wrong, at least for the next two years, and after that there will be more delays, and the whole thing is the work of the masters.' [17]

But although he was justifiably anxious about the future, he still made no change in his plans for the present. He had come to Brussels with two letters of introduction from Herzen – one to Joachim Lelewel, the Polish revolutionary historian who had been forced to flee the country after Nicholas I had quelled the insurrection of 1830, and the other to Proudhon. Knowing that the Russian police kept paid emissaries abroad, it required a certain amount of daring for Tolstoy to call on these illustrious political refugees.

He found Lelewel in a dust-carpeted attic cluttered with

books, talked to him of the legitimate aspirations of martyred Poland and withdrew full of respect for the withered, forgotten, poverty-stricken old man who had preserved his faith in liberty intact despite the passing years. Proudhon received him next, in his little apartment at Ixelles. He was just completing a philosophical work on armed conflict between nations: *War and Peace*; Tolstoy was struck by the title, and it remained engraved in his memory. The French publicist, very curious to learn what was going on elsewhere, questioned his guest about the state of opinion in Russia. Tolstoy did not dare to tell this stranger what he really thought of the recent emancipation measures and the deplorable conditions of public education. Patriotic first and foremost, he stressed the fact that the serfs were not being freed empty-handed and that all cultivated Russians knew that the education of the people was essential to the construction of a strong state.

'If that is true,' cried Proudhon, 'the future belongs to you Russians.' [18]

Tolstoy's pride thrilled to this prophecy. His host, with the air of a rough-hewn peasant, shaggy beard and spectacles, struck him as a man of consequence who had 'the courage of his convictions'. Proudhon, in turn, wrote to Gustave Chaudey after this visit: 'Russia is jubilant. The tsar proclaimed his emancipation degree in agreement with the boyars and after consulting all concerned. The pride of these ex-nobles must be seen to be believed. A highly educated man, Mr Tolstoy, with whom I have been talking the past few days, said to me, "That is what is called a real emancipation. We are not sending our serfs away empty-handed, we are giving them property along with their freedom."' [19]

Tolstoy found life in Brussels 'calm and home-like' after London; this sense of comfort and familiarity was due chiefly to the fact that he was a daily guest in the home of Prince Dondukov-Korsakov, vice-president of the Academy of Science. 'An old man, an old woman, two daughters ill and another aged fifteen; as you can see, there is no material for matrimony here,' he wrote to his brother Sergey on 12 (24) March 1861. 'Besides, I don't have much hope left on that score, because my last remaining teeth are crumbling to bits. But my spirits are high!'

Finding no prospect of a fiancée in the Dondukov-Korsakov family, he remembered that one of their nieces, Katerina Alexandrovna, who lived with her aunt, Princess Golitsin, in Hyères, had charmed him by her grace and distinction. True, he had not given a thought to her during the three and a half months since he last saw her; but should that stop him from contemplating marriage? The fever had seized him again: a wife – any wife – but quick, quick, a family, children! Without further ado he wrote to his sister Marya, who was still at Hyères, informing her of his project. Her reply was judicious:

'If it were to work out, wouldn't you suddenly begin asking yourself, "Why did I do it?" Wouldn't you, one fine morning, quietly begin to hate your wife, thinking, "If only I hadn't married ... ?' That is what I fear. If you have really made up your mind to let yourself be harnessed, then you certainly could not find a better girl. She could be happy with you and you could be happy with her. But can you be happy at all, as a married man? That is the question.'

Indignant cry of protest from Leo: how could Marya believe he was not certain of his mind? He loved Katerina with all his soul. It had simply taken him a while to realize it. Convinced by his protestations, Marya then advised her brother to propose without further delay: 'If you begin to think about it,' she wrote, 'all is lost. ... Put everything else out of your mind and come to Hyères.'

All Tolstoy required was to be told to put everything else out of his mind: he promptly put anything else into it. Just as the jaws of the trap were about to snap shut on him, he jumped back. Tie himself down for life to some young person whom he knew nothing about, who might be an utter nuisance? Never! He wrote an apology to his sister, another to Katerina Alexandrovna's aunt, and thought no more of all the little Tolstoys who might have issued from this union.*

Restored to bachelorhood, he redoubled his intellectual activities. During the three weeks he spent in Brussels, he continued his tour of schools, wrote an article on education, ordered banks of large type to use in children's primers and began to write his story *Polikushka*, based on an incident in Russian peasant life told to him by one of Prince Dondukov-Korsakov's sons. It was strange to be writing about the serfs when their independence had just been proclaimed. Overnight, the everyday, ordinary present had become history. One had to write about them in the past tense. Really, it was time he went back to Russia to see the faces of these new free men.

On 27 March (8 April), he started out. But instead of going straight through Germany he stopped at Eisenach, Weimar and Jena, doubled back to Weimar where he was presented to the grand duke, 'surrounded by idiotic court ladies', and received permission to visit Goethe's home, still closed to the public. In every town and hamlet he rushed to tour the schools and kindergartens. He would often walk into classrooms unannounced, with the high-handed manners of the boyar. Once he appropriated all the notebooks of the pupils of the German schoolteacher Julius Stoetzer, for his personal documentation. When their master respectfully pointed out that their parents, most of whom were poor, might not be overjoyed to have to buy new notebooks, he rushed away, bought out a stationer's shop and came back with his arms full of fresh white sheets of paper on which the pupils recopied their lessons for him. Then he identified himself with a flourish: 'I am Count Tolstoy of Russia,' collected the papers and handed them to a servant who stood wating in the courtyard.

At Jena he met a long-necked student named Keller, who

* Marya Tolstoy's still unpublished letters are preserved in the Tolstoy Museum.

had just finished his studies in the Department of Science and, in a surge of comradeship, took him on as instructor for the Yasnaya Polyana school at a salary of two hundred roubles a year, travelling expenses paid. 'I think I have made a lucky find in Keller,' he wrote in his diary.[20] But he had misgivings two days later when he met the young man's mother: 'When I first saw the lady I realized that by taking her son away with me, I had become responsible for him.'[21] Well, come what may! He sent Keller on ahead and went back to Dresden. Passing through Berlin he rejoiced to see Auerbach again ('the most admirable man alive') and met Professor Diesterweg ('unbending, heartless pedagogue, who imagines he can guide and cultivate children's minds with rules and precepts').[22] He was told at the hotel that 'young Keller', who had passed through a few days before, had been drinking Rhine wine at his expense. This annoyed him 'because of the exchange', and also because he was afraid he had misplaced his confidence.

At last he strapped his bags shut, piled his latest acquisitions – more books – into crates, and, as St Petersburg could not be reached by water at that time of year, decided to go home by rail, via Warsaw. Crossing the frontier on 12 (24) April 1861, he noted, 'Frontier. Health good. Am happy. Scenes of Russia go by unnoticed.' Sitting 'among Jews' in an ice-cold railway car, his head lulled by the rocking train, he dreamed of opening schools, publishing an educational review and, having failed to be the first liberator of the serfs, becoming at least their first instructor.

[12]

'Arbiter of the Peace'
and Schoolmaster

RUSSIA, for Tolstoy, was neither St Petersburg nor Moscow, but Yasnaya Polyana. Nevertheless, he took advantage of his presence in the two cities to see Druzhnin, who was also suffering from tuberculosis, Nekrasov, Katkov, his *babushka* Alexandra and one or two of the young ladies he had thought he might be in love with. This time Katerina Tyutchev seemed 'a ravishing girl, but too much of a hothouse plant, too well schooled in every refinement, too nonchalant', to share his life and work. 'She is accustomed to concocting moral bonbons, and I deal in earth and manure.'[1] Lisa, the eldest Behrs daughter (aged nineteen), on the other hand, quite appealed to him, although he did not dare 'to think of taking her for my wife'.[2]

He carried this vague regret away with him to the country; but for the present, his find was more taken up with friendship than with love. As soon as he put into port at Yasnaya Polyana, he received a letter from Turgenev, also home from abroad, inviting him to Spasskoye, 'while the nightingales are still singing and the spring smiling down'. From there they might go to Stepanovka, the nearby residence of their friend Fet. 'Excellent programme!' opined Tolstoy, who was ravenous for some literary conversation.

On 24 May 1861 he was at Spasskoye. After dinner, Turgenev settled him in the drawing-room on his famous couch, nicknamed the *samoson*[3] ('on which one goes to sleep automatically'), set out cigarettes and cool drinks for him and placed in his hands the manuscript of the novel he had just finished: *Fathers and Sons*. Was it travel fatigue, digestion after a heavy meal or the dullness of overpolished prose?

Whatever the cause, after skimming a few pages, Tolstoy's eyes refused to focus and he drifted off to sleep. 'I awoke with a most peculiar sensation,' he later said, 'and saw Turgenev's back retreating into the distance.'[4] His young colleague's lack of interest in his work rankled, but Turgenev did not let it show. Tolstoy, on the other hand, felt guilty at being caught in the act of inattentiveness and fumed because he could not justify himself by saying frankly that he did not like *Fathers and Sons*. No explanations were given. The book remained on the table by the *samoson*. And the next day the two men left for Stepanovka, fifty miles away, as though nothing had happened.

Fet and his wife Marya Petrovna gave them such a cordial welcome that their malaise rapidly vanished. The following morning, 27 May, they sat down with their hosts in the dining-room, around the samovar. Knowing that Turgenev attached great importance to the education of his illegitimate daughter Paulinette, Marya Petrovna asked him whether he was satisfied with his English governess, Miss Hinnis, who was looking after the girl in Paris. Turgenev immediately became defensive. He suspected his friends of criticizing him behind his back for allowing Paulinette to be brought up in the Viardot home, with the result that she knew hardly a word of Russian and, so to speak, had neither family nor country. He boasted that the governess was 'a real pearl' and employed British methods at all times. As an example, he told how, at Miss Hinnis's demand, he had been required to fix the amount Paulinette might spend every month 'for her poor'.

'Now,' he added, 'the governess insists that my daughter go in person to collect the clothes of the needy, mend them herself and take them back to their homes.'

'And you think that is a good thing?' asked Tolstoy, his thick brows beetling over a piercing glare.

'Of course! That way the benefactress is put into direct contact with real poverty.'

'Well! What I think,' growled Tolstoy, 'is that a little girl sitting in a fancy dress with dirty, foul-smelling rags on her knees is putting on a hypocritical, theatrical farce!'

Turgenev turned pale. His nostrils flared. His beard shook. 'I will ask you not to speak like that!' he cried.

'Why shouldn't I say what I think?' answered Tolstoy.

'So you think I am bringing up my daughter badly?'

'I am saying what I think without any personal allusions.'

Fet tried to intervene, but it was too late. Tolstoy sat stonily in his chair, petrified with anger. Then Turgenev clutched his head in his hands, rose from the table and rushed into the next room. A moment later he came back and said to Marya Petrovna:

'I beg you to forgive this scandalous behaviour, which I deeply regret.'[5]

He muttered a few words of apology to Tolstoy, and returned to Spasskoye. Before fifteen minutes had elapsed Tolstoy had also taken leave of his hosts and gone. He intended to head for Nikolskoye, an estate he had inherited from his brother Nicholas. But on the way his rage, far from diminishing, swelled to the proportions of an obsession. He could not go on living, soiled from head to foot by this affront. Upon reaching the first stopping-place, Novosyelky, which belonged to I. P. Borisov, a friend of his, he wrote a challenge to Turgenev and dispatched a servant to deliver it at a headlong gallop; in it, he demanded an apology that he could 'show to Fet and his wife', or else Turgenev must come in person to give him satisfaction at Bogoslovo, the next relay, where he would wait for him. To this peremptory epistle Turgenev, who had recovered his self-possession, replied.

I can but repeat what I felt it my duty to say at the Fets': carried away by an involuntary animosity which this is not the time to explain, I offended you, without the slightest provocation on your part, and I apologized to you for doing so. I am ready to repeat my apology in writing and I again ask your forgiveness. What happened this morning proves beyond all doubt that any attempt to reconcile two such conflicting personalities as yours and mine is doomed to fail. I perform this duty all the more willingly because this letter will probably be the conclusion of our relationship. I hope with all my heart that it will give you satisfaction and declare in advance that you have my consent to do whatever you wish with it.

These lines might have appeased their addressee had they reached him, but Turgenev sent the note to I. P. Borisov at Novosyelky, thinking Tolstoy was still there, instead of to Bogoslovo, where he was awaiting the reply at the post-house. The hours passed, and no messenger came, and Tolstoy's anger continued to mount. He wrote a second letter demanding a duel then and there; not one of those parodies of a duel with 'two authors bringing along a third' to fire at each other from a safe distance, taking good care to miss, and then falling into each other's arms and 'ending the evening drinking champagne'. No, no – a real fight, alone, face to face, with no seconds; a fight to the finish. He wanted blood, Turgenev's blood! He chose the place for their final meeting (on the edge of the forest of Bogoslovo), asked his offender to be there the next morning, with pistols, and sent to Nikolskoye for his own. He did not sleep all that night. At dawn a messenger arrived bringing Turgenev's answer to his first letter, and then another, gasping for breath, with a reply to the second. Turgenev accepted the challenge:

I shall say, in all sincerity, that I would willingly stand up to your pistol-fire if I could thereby erase my ludicrous words. It is so contrary to the habits of a lifetime for me to have spoken as I did that I can only attribute it to the irritation caused by the excessively intense and perpetual clash of our opinions on every subject. That is why, in parting from you forever – events like this cannot be forgotten – I believe it my duty to say once again that you are in the right in this affair, and I in the wrong. I add that the question is not for me to show courage or lack of it, but to acknowledge your right to call me on to the field, presumably in accordance with the generally accepted rules of duelling (that is, with seconds) and also your right to pardon me. You have made the choice that suited you, I submit to your decision.

Tolstoy crowed with victory. He wrote back: 'You are afraid of me, I despise you and want no more to do with you.'[6] Then he sent Turgenev's two letters to Fet, with a caustic commentary. Fet tried to reconcile the adversaries, but encountered a snarling refusal on either side.

As the weeks went by, however, Tolstoy came to regret his hot-headedness. Although he continued to resent Turgenev's insulting remarks at the Fets', he admitted that he had wittingly provoked him by contradicting him on a point as delicate as his daughter's education. 'With Turgenev, full-scale and final blow-up,' he announced in his diary on 25 June. 'He is a thorough-going scoundrel. But I think that as time goes by I shall be unable to keep myself from forgiving him.' On 23 September he could hold out no longer, and wrote: 'I have offended you, forgive me; it is unbearable to have you as my enemy.'[7]

But it was ordained that luck would always be against this pair in their epistolary relations. Turgenev had gone back to Paris, and Tolstoy, not sure of his address, asked Davidov, a Petersburg bookseller, to forward the letter. But Davidov, although continually in touch with Turgenev on business matters, forgot the letter, which lay in a drawer for months. In the meantime Turgenev heard from Kolbasin, a mutual friend and lover of gossip, that Tolstoy was spreading offensive remarks about him and giving out a false account of their quarrel, with supporting documents. Without questioning for one moment the accuracy of this information, he wrote to the person he regarded as his mortal enemy:

'I have learned that you are showing a copy of your letter around Moscow, the one in which you call me a coward because I supposedly refused to fight you, etc. After all I have done to make amends for those words that escaped from my mouth, I regard your conduct as offensive and disloyal and I warn you that I shall not let it pass. When I return to Russia next spring, I shall demand satisfaction.'[8]

Even though Tolstoy realized that his letter of apology of 23 September must not have reached its destination, the challenge came as a blow. Instead of becoming angry, however, as he might justifiably have done, he yielded to a wave of Christian charity. Perhaps, that day, he had made some new 'rules of life'. Or perhaps he wanted to use the incident as a springboard to saintliness. Or perhaps, contemptuous of Turgenev for his concern with the opinion of others, he wanted to prove that when one's name was Leo Tolstoy, public opinion did not exist. At all events, the man who had previously been roaring for a duel without seconds and blood on the grass, now dipped his pen in milder ink:

'Sir, you have called my letter and my conduct disloyal; you have also said that you would punch me in the head. And I offer you an apology, admit my guilt and refuse your challenge to a duel.'

Oh, the morbid joy of turning the left cheek after being struck on the right! One knew nothing of the soul's strivings after virtue until one had known that. Now it was the other fellow who must be feeling like a fool, storming around in a vacuum.

Having obtained satisfaction, Turgenev wrote to Fet, asking him to inform Tolstoy that he, too, was giving up any thought of a duel, but still had not received the letter of apology from Davidov. 'From this day forward, *de profundis* on the whole business!'[9] he concluded. Fet thought it would be diplomatic to inform Tolstoy of the terms of this conciliatory letter – rue the day! Tolstoy's angelic disposition vanished as quickly as it had come, and after his burst of indulgence, he reverted to his former humour, violent, stormy, demanding. He was not going to allow that high-caste fop with the greying beard and effeminate nerves to pass judgement on him in letters to mutual friends. And everybody who corresponded with him should get the same treatment. Traitors all, phrase-makers, mere products of civilization! ... In a frenzy of exasperation, he wrote to Fet:

'Turgenev is a *scoundrel who deserves to be thrashed*; I beg you to transmit that to him, as faithfully as you transmit his charming comments to me, despite the fact that I have asked you never to speak of him again. ... I also beg you not to write to me any more, for I shall not open your letters any more than Turgenev's.'

On 7 January 1862, Turgenev read the famous letter of apology which Davidov the bookseller had so long neglected to forward. He wrote to Fet forthwith:

Today, at last, I received the letter Tolstoy sent in September via Davidov the bookseller (admirable punctuality of our Russian businessmen!), in which he states that he had insulted me intentionally and apologizes, etc. And almost at the same moment, owing to certain gossip I think I told you about, I challenged him to a duel. All one can conclude from this is that the conjunction of our constellations in the heavens is decidedly unfavourable and it is therefore preferable – as he suggests, moreover – that we do not meet again. But you can write to him, or tell him if you see him, that I, at least (sincerely, and with no hidden meaning), am very fond of him, respect him and follow his progress with keen interest, *from afar*, whereas at close range, the results are exactly the opposite. What can we do? We must act as though we lived on different planets or in different centuries.

For seventeen years the two men neither met nor corresponded. Tolstoy's falling-out with Fet, on the other hand, lasted only a few days. In January 1862, Tolstoy saw the poet in a Moscow theatre, walked up to him, looked him in the eye, held out his hand and said, 'No; I do not want to be angry with you.'

When he thought back to this incident it seemed to him like a bad dream he had been living through, with grotesque after-effects in his waking life. One moment it was he who was demanding an apology and, after receiving it, was sorry he had demanded it; and the next it was Turgenev who, after admitting he was in the wrong, considered himself insulted and insisted upon satisfaction gun in hand. As in a circus act, they leaped on and off of their high horses, one in front of the other, in counterpoint. Letters crossed in the mail; clumsy friends botched everything up; the devil take all men-of-letters! The muzhiks were the only people one could live with!

It was for them and no one else that he had come home. Throughout his row with Turgenev, moreover, he had never ceased thinking of them. The emancipation proclamation had not changed them. The same rags, the same coarse faces, the same suspicious eyes, the same subservient bowing and scraping. Upon reaching Yasnaya Polyana at the beginning of May 1861, the master had called them together to explain, in his own way, the provisions of the manifesto of 19 February 1861. Determined to be more liberal than anyone else, he allowed them the maximum under the administrative regulations for his region – 3 *desyatins* (just over 8 acres) of land per person. This left him 628·6 *desyatins* (just under 1700 acres) at Yasnaya Polyana and 48·15 *desyatins* (130 acres) in the village of Gretsovka. But were the peasants grateful to him for giving them so much land, and all in single plots? Probably not. For them the land they cultivated had become their property generations ago, bought by their labour. The master was making them a present of what already belonged to them. At most, they conceded that he was not robbing them, like some of the other gentry in the district.

Tolstoy was still in Brussels when the governor of Tula appointed him 'arbiter of the peace' to settle disputes between landowners and peasants in the fourth precinct of the district of Krapivna. This decision raised a storm of protest among the local aristocracy, for whom the author was a dangerous liberal who would support the serfs against the landowners. Under the pressure of the opposition, V. P. Minin, marshal of nobility of the province, had even written to Valuyev, the minister of the interior, asking him to have the appointment revoked. But Lieutenant-General Daragan, the governor of Tula, had spoken to the minister in Tolstoy's defence, calling him 'a highly educated man, entirely committed to the task at hand ... and much respected'. Despite the opposition of his peers, the new arbiter of the peace remained in office.

It required great courage and perseverance on his part to perform his duties in the climate of hatred that surrounded him. He took every case seriously, as a matter of principle. Naturally inclined to favour the underdog, he did not want to be unfair to the landowners, whose position might become perilous after the emancipation. In sharing out the land, owners who wanted to salvage their privileges tried to foist off the poorest plots on to the muzhiks or extort illegal payment from them. The muzhiks, on the other hand, were convinced that they should have everything, complained of the arbiter's rulings and said he was not defending their interests energetically enough. Whatever decision his sense of equity led him to adopt, Tolstoy was sure to cause dissatisfaction on both sides. Mrs Artukhov, a local landowner, had lodged a complaint against her manservant Mark, who wanted to leave her on the grounds that he was now a free man. 'The arbiter of the peace Count L. Tolstoy' ruled as follows: 'By my order, Mark shall leave immediately, with his wife, and go wherever he pleases. As for you, I have the honour to ask you (1) to pay him three and one half months' wages for the period since the publication of the Emancipation Act, during which he has been illegally detained by you; (2) to pay him damages for the beating still more illegally inflicted upon his wife.' Furious at being treated like a common criminal, Mrs Artukhov appealed to the Assembly of Arbiters of the Peace, which was composed of aristocrats opposed to Tolstoy, who unhesitatingly reversed his decision. But the chancellory of lands, which was the court of last resort, confirmed the original ruling; Mark and his wife received damages and were allowed to go.

Shortly after, Tolstoy had a struggle to prevent the landowner Mikhailovsky from exacting excessive compensation from some peasants whose horses had destroyed his crops. He unmasked another land-owner, Kostomarov, who was trying to keep his land from the peasants by alleging that they were house-servants and not farmers. He attempted to defend a group of unfortunate peasants whose isbas had burned down and who were without money to rebuild them. He investigated every difficult case in person, negotiated with the villagers and the lord, urged both parties to accept the new situation without vain regrets and useless hopes. One day a delegation of muzhiks came to him and explained that their master had treated them unfairly by giving them a field instead of the pastureland they coveted. Tolstoy calmly examined the shares of the allocation and concluded:

'I am very sorry I cannot give you satisfaction, but were I to do so, it would be unfair to your landlord.'

The peasants looked at each other and scratched their heads. Then they began to whine:

"Do something, little father. ... Have pity on us. ... If you wanted to, you could fix it. ...'

Tolstoy turned away to hide his exasperation, and said to the steward standing near him:

'It would be easier to be Amphion and move mountains and forests like Amphion than to make a peasant see reason!' [10]

However, the landowners determined to have their revenge upon the man they regarded as a traitor to their cause. Not a day went by without some complaint against the arbiter of the peace of the fourth precinct of the district of Krapivna being lodged with the marshal of the nobility, the governor, the minister of the interior or the chancellory of lands. 'My activites as arbiter of the peace have furnished little useful material,' Tolstoy wrote on 25 June 1861. 'They have secured me the undying hatred of *all* the landowners and ruined my health.' And he wrote to Botkin a few months later, 'Quite unexpectedly, I have become an arbiter of the peace. And although I have been conscientious and unbiased at all times in the discharge of my duties, I have incurred the fell fury of all the nobility against me. They would like to flog me or drag me before the judge, and can do neither.'[11]

If only he didn't have to be a bureaucrat, too! But every new case raised a tempest of paper. He was submerged by reports, memoranda, lists, replies to questionnaires. In February 1862, after ten months in office, he asked the Chancellory of Lands to investigate the complaints against him. Then, on 30 April of that year, he submitted his resignation, for reasons of health. It was accepted by a senate decree dated 26 May, and the local landowners heaved a sigh of relief. But their trials were not yet over. Although Tolstoy was no longer directly concerned in their litigations, his attitude towards the muzhiks, which was held up as an example, prolonged his nuisance value. Even his pedagogical activities were suspect – he was probably training a generation of malcontents in that school of his at Yasnaya Polyana!

The school, which he had re-opened with a few young teachers selected and paid by himself, was now located in a small, two-storey building next to their own house; two rooms for classes, two for the teachers, and one used as a study. A bell and bell-rope hung under the porch roof. Gymnastic apparatus had been installed in the downstairs vestibule; in the upstairs hall, there was a carpenter's bench. A schedule – purely symbolic, since the motto of the establishment was 'Do as you like!' – was posted on the wall.

At eight in the morning a child rang the bell. Half an hour later, 'through fog, rain, or the slanting rays of the autumn sun', the black silhouettes of little muzhiks appeared by twos and threes, swinging their empty arms. As in the previous years, they brought no books or notebooks with them – nothing at all, save the desire to learn. The classrooms were painted pink and blue. In one, mineral samples, butterflies, dried plants and physics apparatus lined the shelves. But no books. Why books? The pupils came to the classroom as though it were home; they sat where they liked, on the floor, on the window-ledge, on a chair or the corner of a table, they listened or did not listen to what the teacher was saying, drew near when he said something that interested them, left the room when work or play called them elsewhere – but were silenced by their fellow pupils at the slightest sound. Self-imposed discipline. The lessons – if these casual chats between an adult and some children could be called that – went on from eight-thirty to noon and from three to six in the afternoon, and covered every conceivable subject from grammar to carpentry, by way of religious history, singing, geography, gymnastics, drawing and composition. Those who lived too far away to go home at night slept in the school. In the summer they sat around their teacher outdoors in the grass. Once a week they all went to study plants in the forest.

As a disciple of Jean-Jacques Rousseau, Tolstoy wanted to believe that human nature was basically good, that all evil was a product of civilization and that the teacher must not smother the child under the weight of learning, but must help him, little by little, to shape his own personality. He was even tempted to believe that the stonier the ground, the more chance there was of a rich harvest. Thus Russia, being backward, would inevitably produce more geniuses in the years to come than more advanced countries. There might well be a Lomonosov, Pushkin or Tolstoy among the schoolboys at Yasnaya Polyana, asking only to be brought to life. One must take heed, when planting seeds in these virgin minds – meditate upon the teachings of Montaigne, who said that the main goals in education were 'equality and freedom'. At all times, start at the opposite pole from the German, French and English methods. Innovate, Russianize! ...

However hard Tolstoy tried to keep him down, the man of letters kept pushing through the pedagogue. In his inspirational form of teaching, with no curriculum, no punishment and no rewards, he tried to put himself on the level of his young audience, marvelled at their every word and solemnly noted, 'Should the muzhiks' children learn to write

from us, or should we learn to write from them?' He proposed that the group improvise a tale on the theme of a
Russian proverb: 'He feeds a man with a spoon and then
pokes the handle in his eyes.' The children stared at him
blankly. 'Suppose,' he explained, 'a peasant gives shelter to a
pauper and then tries to hold his good deed over the other
man's head. He will have fed him with a spoon and poked
the handle in his eyes.' Then, to show them how a story was
told, he wrote out the beginning himself. The children
leaned over his shoulder and began to dictate: 'No, not like
that! ...' 'Make him just an ordinary soldier! ...' 'It would
be better if he stole them! ...' 'There has to be a wicked
woman in it! ...' The two most gifted boys were Syomka
and Fyodka. Taking down their dictation, Tolstoy felt that
he was drinking from a well of truth. This exalting collaboration continued from seven until eleven o'clock in the
evening. The children spent the night in Tolstoy's study.
Fyodka, overexcited, his eyes feverish and his hands trembling, could not go to sleep. 'I cannot describe the emotion,
the joy and fear I felt that evening,' wrote Tolstoy. 'I saw a
new world of delight and suffering rising up before him
[Fyodka]: the world of art. It seemed to me I had witnessed
what no one has the right to see: the opening of the mysterious flower of poetry. ... I felt such joy because, all of a
sudden, by sheer chance, I saw unveiled before my eyes that
philosopher's stone I had been seeking in vain for two
years: the art of learning to express one's thoughts. I felt
fear because that art created new demands, a flood of desires
foreign to the world in which, I believed at first, the pupils
lived.'[12]

To interest them in the history of their country he told
them his version of the campaign of 1812. The boys' patriotism awoke immediately. They interrupted him with
vengeful exclamations: 'Alexander'll show that Napoleon!'
'Not so hot, Kutuzov; what's he waiting for?' The burning
of Moscow was unanimously approved, there was applause at
the retreat of the Grande Armée. It was all Tolstoy could

do to wrest a crumb of compassion from his audience for
'the frozen French'. He probably did not insist upon it,
moreover. That evening the German teacher Keller, who
had been listening, reproached him for his chauvinism.
Tolstoy conceded that he had taken a few liberties with
historical truth in order to capture his pupils' attention; but
after all, it was no crime to heighten the colours a little,
sound the trumpets and the drums. ... He was better inspired when, on walks in the country, he described the customs of the Caucasians and Cossacks, their merciless com-
bats, Shamil's exploits and the wiles of Hadji Murad.
Fyodka gripped two fingers of Tolstoy's hand inside his own
and stammered, tripping over his feet, his eyes fixed on his
teacher, 'Again! There! That's the way!' Occasionally, an
argument broke out.

'What good is singing or painting?'

'What good is a tree if you don't cut it down?'

Leo Tolstoy explained, like God the Father, that the good
of a tree consisted first of all in its beauty. Another question
suddenly dropped into the group like a brick into a pond:

'What good are the classes of society?'

The children pondered together and, after a moment,
Tolstoy delightedly recorded the following reply:

'Peasants till the soil, house-servants serve their masters,
merchants do business, soldiers do their service, copper-
smiths make samovars, priests say mass, and gentlemen do
nothing!'

Enchanted by the quick wits of his young disciples, Tolstoy tried to interest them in Russian literature. He read
Pushkin and Gogol to them. Alas, the simple, harmonious
verse and rich prose left them cold. Their master should
have concluded that they were not ready to savour their
country's great authors. But he instinctively wanted the
people to be right and the upper classes wrong. If anyone
was wrong, it could not be the peasant who was pure by
definition; still less a peasant's child, purest of the pure. 'Perhaps they do not understand and do not want to understand

our literary language,' he wrote, 'simply because our literary language is not suited to them and they are in the process of inventing their own literature.'[13]

Once he had formulated this idea, he could not get it out of his head. It suddenly became clear to him that literature, music, painting and sculpture were nothing but an amalgam of errors, false notes and dandified sophistication, because they had not been demanded and endorsed by the masses. With iconoclastic zeal he set out to revile the works he had adored, solely and simply because Fyodka and Syomka were unable to appreciate them. Instead of elevating the muzhiks to the level of art, he decided that art must immediately be brought down to them. What was the good of Shakespeare, Racine, Goethe, Rembrandt and Mozart if they bored the village idiot? 'I became convinced,' he wrote, 'that a poem such as "I remember the Marvellous Moment,"[14] or a piece of music such as Beethoven's Ninth Symphony, is less worthy of admiration than Vanka's song or the lament of the Volga boatmen, and that we do not like Pushkin and Beethoven because they are expressions of absolute beauty but because they flatter our hideously overstimulated sensitivities and our weakness ...' And further on: 'Why are the beauty of the sun, the beauty of a human face, the beauty of a folk song, the beauty of an act of love or self-denial intelligible to all, without any special training?'[15] Tolstoy saw a blinding proof that art, as defended by the aesthetes, was nonsense, in the following arithmetical observation: 'We are thousands and they are millions.'[16] The artist must obey the law of the greatest number. Write what *they* want. And not write at all, if they do not want anything. After all, one could live perfectly well without writing. The people, whose very dirt was sacred, were sufficient unto themselves. They needed no one to satisfy their aspirations for work, pleasure, thought and creativity. Then what was the good of the Yasnaya Polyana school? Ah, but wait a minute! He was not committing the sacrilege of teaching the children. They were simply being encouraged, with all due caution, to become aware of themselves. Future peasants were being taught the poetic significance of the peasantry. Tolstoy himself sometimes dreamed of abandoning his house and building himself an isba, of tilling the soil and marrying a village girl. 'To marry a woman of society,' he told his staff of teachers, 'is to swallow all the poison of civilization.'[17] His pupils, to whom he also announced his plan, took him quite seriously and began to look for a suitable fiancée among the girls of Yasnaya Polyana.[18] Smiling tenderly, he made no effort to stop them; after all, he had already wanted to marry a Cossack maid, for love of the simple life.

On Shrove Tuesday 1862, blinis were served to all the children, followed by bonbons; for Easter they received lengths of brightly coloured cotton cloth, pencils, harmonicas and hats. Encouraged by his success, he opened more schools in the neighbouring villages. Soon there were fourteen of them in the Krapivna district, which had a population of ten thousand. New teachers had to be recruited to guide all these souls: most of them were famished students who flocked in from Moscow with their heads full of revolutionary ideas. But Tolstoy was immovably opposed to politics. He wanted to reveal the people to themselves, not Herzen or Proudhon to the people. In a few hours of conversation he converted the new arrivals to his theory of spontaneous learning. After listening to him, they went off and burned the subversive tracts they had brought along.[19] 'Civilization', he told them, 'perverts healthy minds. And even though we are all products of civilization, we must not contaminate the common people with this poison; instead, we must purge ourselves through contact with them.'[20]

To do this, each young man moved into a village in the heart of a rural community. The school was an isba, with benches, a table and a board hut in which the teacher slept. Wages: fifty kopecks a month per pupil. General rule: love of children and hatred of constraint. Additional obligation: keep a diary. Tolstoy demanded that every teacher confess his faults, from time to time, in writing; he considered it an excellent exercise for the soul. After all, he had been practising it all his life. Without much success, he did admit. But the habit had stayed with him. Setting the example, he wrote: 'Became confused ...' 'I am the worst of all – I lose my temper! ...' 'Have tried to discover the rule for progress and could not.'

Every Saturday he convened a meeting of the teachers at Yasnaya Polyana and discussed their experiments and results with them in such a relaxed manner that they were all perfectly at ease with him, and some felt something akin to veneration for him. They were subjugated by the forcefulness of his look and the heat of his voice. 'The school is my whole life, my convent, my church,' he said. Impossible to remain indifferent to this devil of a man! You arrived intending to pick up a few roubles without straining yourself and you found yourself ensnared in the devotional rule of a priesthood. The little peasants pried your affection, your strength, your very life out of you, merely by interrogating you with their candid eyes. When Tolstoy went to Moscow for a few days, Serdobolsky, a student, wrote to him:

You may rest assured that your cause has now become ours. ... We are all impatient for you to come back. Without you, it isn't the same. It seems to me that our common task cannot go on without you to lead it, it needs the fire of your dedication. ... I do not know whether all the teachers love their work now, but I am convinced they all will come to love it as I do if they are capable of appreciating the poetry and enthusiasm that emanate from you when you are engaged in it. Therefore, do not deprive us of your presence for too long.

Forty years later, remembering his stay at Yasnaya Polyana, Markov, another of the teachers, wrote: 'I have never met a man capable of firing another mind to such white heat. In the course of my spiritual relationship with him I felt as though electric sparks were striking into the depths of my soul and setting in motion all kinds of thoughts and plans and decisions.'

To gain a wider audience for his ideas Tolstoy founded a monthly review, *Yasnaya Polyana*, whose publication was authorized by the censor beginning in January 1862. The epigraph of this periodical was Goethe's aphorism: *Glaubst zu schieben und wirst geschoben* (You think you're leading and it's you being led).* Tolstoy filled the twelve issues of its existence, defrayed by him, with articles on his theory of education, accounts of the activities of the schools, and reading matter for children. The first number proclaimed the following noble principle: 'In order to determine what is good and what is not, he who is being taught must have full power to express his dissatisfaction or, at least, to avoid lessons that do not satisfy him. Let it be established that there is only one criterion in teaching: freedom!'

Having dropped his bomb, he waited for the explosion. ... There was none. A few Slavophil newspapers praised the new educationist for his confidence in the Russian people, a few liberal papers criticized him for allowing illiterates to choose their form of education; but on the whole, this woolly and inconsistent theory did not stir the public. But in official circles, important persons were pointing out the dangers of propaganda such as this. On 3 October 1862 Valuyev, the minister of the interior, wrote to his colleague Golovin, the minister of education:

A close perusal of the educational review *Yasnaya Polyana*, published by Count Tolstoy, inclines me to think that by advocating new teaching methods and principles for the organization of schools for the common people, this periodical is spreading ideas which are not only false but dangerously biased. ... The continued publication of the periodical would seem undesirable, especially as its author, who has remarkable and persuasive literary powers, is above all suspicion of criminal intention or dishonesty. What is harmful is the inaccuracy and eccentricity of his views which, set forth with exceptional eloquence, may be convincing to inexperienced teachers and may thus orient education in the wrong direction.

* Spoken by Mephistopheles in *Faust*.

Upon receiving this letter the minister of education instructed one of his minions to look into Tolstoy's activities. A few days later he found a detailed and on the whole favourable report on his desk: 'To establish a simple, easy and independent relationship between master and pupil; cultivate mutual affection and trust; free lessons from constraint and learning by rote; transform the school into a kind of family in which the teacher acts as parent: what could be better, more desirable and more profitable for all?' However, the anonymous author of this study criticized Tolstoy for dispensing the children from all work – work being 'our whole life' – for relying upon their unformed taste as a criterion of quality in literature, and for flatly stating that Pushkin and Beethoven, for example, were inferior to ballads and old folk tunes.

After reading the report the minister of education transmitted it to the minister of the interior with the following comment: 'I am bound to say that Count Tolstoy's educational activities command our respect and that it is the duty of the ministry of education to help and encourage him, although it does not share all of his ideas – which, moreover, he will undoubtedly abandon after more thorough investigation.'

But he did not know Tolstoy – although he soon stopped publishing the review and lost all interest in the school, his views on education never changed. In every field, he was determined to oppose administrative coercion. But oddly enough, although he clamoured for liberal reforms, he did not stop to think that it was thanks to the existence of aristocratic prerogatives in Russia that he was able to carry out his educational experiments, and that if education were exclusively State-run, it would be impossible for him to teach the children of Yasnaya Polyana according to his own theories.

He was in Moscow when the first issue of the review came off the press. But it was not to complete his educational archives that he had gone there: the emulator of Rousseau,

friend of the poor and spurner of civilization had suddenly
felt a need to divert himself, to inhale the foul breath of
the city. Besides, there were a few decent souls even among
the pharisees. On 13 January 1862 an unknown lady wearing a veil had come to his hotel and offered him a thousand
roubles * for the relief of the poor. Moved to tears, he
thanked the donatress and sent the money to Yasnaya Polyana to be distributed among the needy peasants – and a
good thing it was, too, for a few days later he succumbed to
his old weakness for gambling and lost exactly the same
amount, to a penny, trying his luck at Chinese billiards with
a passing officer. What would he have done had the veiled
lady's thousand roubles been in his pocket at that moment?
Better not think about it! His creditor gave him two days,
on his word of honour, to pay his debt. Tolstoy went to
Katkov, director of the *Russian Herald*, and offered him the
rights to his forthcoming but still unfinished novel, *The
Cossacks*, for one thousand roubles. He had been fussing
over the manuscipt for ten years, adding three lines here
and cutting a chapter there. Cross his heart, it was a good
story. It could be bought with complete confidence. The
author undertook to deliver the corrected text towards the
end of the year. Katkov accepted, the sum was paid over to
the creditor, and Tolstoy wrote to his friend Botkin : 'When
all is said and done, this solution suits me down to the
ground, for the novel, of which I've written over half, would
otherwise have been left to rot and finally been used to stuff
the cracks in the windows.'

When Tolstoy told this tale to his friends the Behrs, the
doctor's three daughters (Lisa, nineteen; Sonya, eighteen;
Tatyana, sixteen) protested that it was madness, that the
editor had certainly taken advantage of him. They flounced
up and down the room and tears of indignation shone in
their eyes. The oldest was quite pretty, serious, passionately
interested in intellectual questions. Tolstoy had wondered
several times whether it would not be sensible of him to

* Or $2,830.

marry her. It seemed to him that she took special pains with her dress when he was coming to call. As for the parents, they were already regarding him with worried benevolence, as though they sensed a potential 'fiancé' in him. Once again, when the idea of marriage assumed concrete form before his eyes, he shied away: just then his nerves were more ragged than usual, his health was poor, his labours as teacher and arbiter of the peace had taxed him heavily, the air of Moscow was bad for him. He took an awkward leave of the Behrs family and fled to Yasnaya Polyana.

He was relying on the country, the school and the children to restore his love of life, but in the spring his health grew worse, he started to cough blood. The spectres of his two dead brothers began to haunt him. Tuberculosis! He went to Moscow to consult Dr Behrs, either because he had confidence in him or, possibly, because he wanted to remove all doubt as to his desirability as a son-in-law. After examining him, Dr Behrs agreed that his lungs were weak and advised him to go to Samara for a *kumys* treatment. *Kumys* – fermented and mildly carbonated mare's milk – was highly esteemed in Russia as a tonic. It was made by the Bashkir nomads. Those who went to take the cure lived on the steppe like the nomads, in felt tents or caravans. The idea of a change of scenery delighted Tolstoy: 'I shall read no more newspapers, receive no more letters, forget what a book looks like, wallow on my back in the sun, drink *kumys*, gorge myself on mutton until I turn into a sheep myself, and then I'll be cured!'[21] he told his intimates.

On 19 May he left Moscow by rail with his manservant Alexis and two of his pupils who had suspicious-sounding coughs. At Tver they boarded a ship and steamed down the Volga: it was the same trip Tolstoy had made ten years before, with poor Nicholas. Seeing the broad river again, its banks of green mist soaked by the spring floods, he should have felt old at the memory of his first trip. But the air was so bracing, the sun played on the wavelets, at night the stars

shone pensively above the water, at every stop a crowd of
passengers – dusty-faced pilgrims, bearded monks, muzhiks,
Tatars – surged up the gangplank, and it was all so animated, variegated, so 'Russian', that he was unconsciously
filled with joy. After a short stop at Kazan – to kiss old
Uncle Yushkov – the travellers resumed their voyage in that
state of contemplative serenity procured by detachment
from the land.

On 27 May they disembarked at Samara and set off again
by tarantass for Karalyk, over eighty-five miles across the
steppe – an undulating prairie, crossed by little streams,
punctuated by ponds, bristling with rocks and bushes. At
last, Tolstoy was back in the wilds he so loved. He adopted
the customs of the Bashkirs, moved into a round felt tent,
ate mutton and dried horsemeat, steeped himself in *kumys*
and 'brick tea'. * With the old Bashkirs, he talked of times
gone by, of different faiths, God, Christ and Mohammed;
and with the young ones, he ran and leaped and wrestled.
He was so strong that only one of the nomads could match
him. The days and weeks sped past. His spirits high and his
mind at peace, he sadly thought that he would soon have to
return to civilization. But had he known what was going on
at home during his absence, he would have left by the first
dogcart.

On 6 July at dawn, while he lay sleeping in his tent on
the banks of the Karalyk, three swift troikas, their bells
jangling for all they were worth, swirled up to the door of
Yasnaya Polyana. The gaping peasants watched as a few
grim-visaged officers climbed out of the coaches: Durnovo,
colonel of the constabulary, who appeared to be directing
operations; the chief of police of the Krapivna district, the
chief of the rural police, constables. ... Hearing the racket,
old Aunt Toinette and Marya Tolstoy, who was visiting at
her brother's house, rushed into the hall, half-awake and
half-dressed, and stopped short in amazement in front of

* A primitive form of tea compressed into bricks and broken apart
before boiling.

the body of armed men. Colonel Durnovo curtly announced that he had come to search the house, 'on orders from my superiors'. The two women were thrust protesting back into their rooms. Police encircled the house and the search began. Cupboards, dressers, tables, chests, everything was turned upside-down. They had a wonderful time in the study, leafing through Tolstoy's manuscripts, reading his private diary and letters out loud, noting down the names of his correspondents, tapping the walls and floors in search of a secret hiding-place, breaking locks and ripping open the curtain linings. They pried up the flagstones in the stables. They also dragged the ponds, but netted only carp and cray-fish, instead of the diabolical instruments they were un-doubtedly hoping to find. Furious to end their search empty-handed, they rushed around the schools, seized the books and the pupils' notebooks and arrested the nine students who were teaching the young muzhiks in the master's ab-sence. Suddenly they fetched up short in front of a camera – almost an unknown object in Russia at that time.

'What's being photographed around here?' asked the offi-cer in charge of the detachment.

'Herzen himself,' a student retorted.

His witticism nearly cost him his freedom. Fortunately, everyone's papers were in order. They would not be de-tained. But just in case, a constable added the names of those present to his list of suspects. Meanwhile, Aunt Toin-ette and Marya Tolstoy had managed to lay their hands on a few forbidden books and some letters from Herzen; Peter-son, one of the teachers, was instructed to hide them in a safe place. The police were already on their way back to Yasnaya Polyana, where they demanded food and drink and ordered their horses to be looked after.

They camped in the house for two days, treating everyone as a suspect, coming into rooms without knocking, pawing over the library books and linen and accounts, prying into the family secrets, peering into wastepaper baskets, under the lid of the piano and behind the toilet, talking in loud voices, guffawing and slamming doors. From Yasnaya Polyana they moved on to Nikolskoye, where all they found for their pains were the private diaries of the deceased Nicholas. Slim pickings after forty-eight hours of searching.

Colonel Durnovo was not happy. This whole business had been embarked upon too lightly. The police had been watching Tolstoy for a long time; although his activities were not actually illegal, his fondness for the muzhiks was overconspicuous and he proclaimed his love of freedom altogether too loudly. Many landowners, vexed by his hostility towards them during his term as arbiter of the peace, had vowed his downfall. It was undoubtedly one of them who had written to Voykov, colonel of the Moscow police, accusing Tolstoy of harbouring at Yasnaya Polyana a student known to have circulated anti-government tracts. Shipov, a police stool-pigeon who was sent to have a look around a short time later, had certified that Tolstoy was paying 'a score of students', all liberals, out of his own pocket, that he had ordered and received printing equipment, and that they were preparing to send out a subversive manifesto in August, for the thousandth anniversary of the founding of Russia. 'There are secret doors in his house,' wrote the spy, 'and hidden staircases, and at night the residence is guarded by a large number of sentinels.' Of course, Shipov himself had just been arrested for 'indiscretion and drunkenness' at the time he was making these remarkable allegations, but the authorities could not be certain there was no truth in what he said. Prince Dolgorukov, national chief of constabulary, consulted Alexander II and then instructed Colonel Durnovo to lead the investigation in person. At all costs, they must locate that secret printing equipment, those lithographic stones and those stacks of proclamations.

When Colonel Durnovo had been convinced of his error, he apologized to Aunt Toinette and assured her that she could relax, but advised her to see that her nephew stayed well away from politics, for they had their eye on him. Besides, they might need to come back in a little while. ...

The peasants and house-servants were terrified by this invasion of blue uniforms on their master's estate, and wondered what dreadful crime he had committed. Over night, he had ceased to be infallible. Ought they to go on sending their children to a school of which the tsar disapproved?

Unconcerned by the crisis he had just provoked, Colonel Durnovo wrote to Prince Dolgorukov, on 14 July 1862.

A search of Count Tolstoy's house revealed it to be very modestly furnished, containing no secret doors, hidden staircases, or lithographic stones or telegraph. ... I found no compromising papers, either at Yasnaya Polyana or at Nikolskoye. ... Count Tolstoy is very haughty with his neighbours and has made enemies of the local landowners by systematically defending the muzhiks during his term as arbiter of the peace. ... His relations with the peasants are remarkably simple and he is on very friendly terms with the children at the school.

Upon reaching Moscow on 20 July 1862, in the best of spirits after his *kumys* treatment, Tolstoy learned of the search: his manuscripts, letters, his private diary subjected to the lewd prying of a bunch of cops! His hearth profaned, his integrity challenged before every peasant on his estate – he was not going to stand for that! Filled with a truly lordly wrath, he wrote to his aunt, *babushka* Alexandra Tolstoy, who represented the court in his eyes:

A nice lot, your pals! All those Patapovs and Dolgorukovs and Arakcheyevs – they are your pals, aren't they? ... One of your friends, some stinking colonel, has read the letters and private diaries I intended to leave at my death to the person dearest to me in the world. ... It was my good fortune, and that of your friend, that I was not home at the time – I would have killed him! ... If only there were some way to avoid these brigands, who wash their cheeks and hands with perfumed soap and smile so benevolently. If I am to live much longer, I shall have to shut myself away in a monastery, not to pray to God – a waste of time, in my view – but in order not to see any more of the moral ignominy of these people swollen with conceit and this society with its epaulettes and crinolines. How can you, a decent human being, go on living in St Petersburg? ... Do you have cataracts, is that why you don't see?

On 31 July 1863 he arrived at Yasnaya Polyana and heard all the details from Aunt Toinette. He let his rage accumulate for a week. When it had reached boiling point, he wrote a second letter to Alexandra Tolstoy:

I will not and cannot let the matter rest. Everything that was a source of joy and satisfaction to me has been ruined. Already the peasants have ceased to regard me as an honest man – a reputation it took me years to acquire – and are treating me as a criminal, an arsonist or counterfeiter who had to finangle his way out of a tight spot. ... 'Aha, old boy, they've caught you!' they think. 'That's enough of your speeches about honesty and justice. You almost got sent up yourself.' ... And the landowners, I need hardly add, are chortling with glee. After consulting Perovsky, or Alexis Tolstoy or whomever you will, write to me, I beg you, as soon as you can. Tell me how to draft my letter and through whom I should send it to the tsar. I have only one choice: either I must obtain reparation, as public as the offence (it's already too late to patch up the matter quietly), or else leave the country, which I am firmly resolved to do. I shall not join Herzen. He has his life and I have mine. I shall not hide, and I shall make it known to all that I am selling my property in order to leave Russia, where nobody can be sure one minute that he will not be thrown into irons and flogged the next, along with his sister and wife and mother.

He concluded with a vague threat of suicide or murder, well calculated to terrify the old spinster:

'There are loaded pistols in my room. I am waiting until the matter is decided one way or another.' [22]

The insinuation that she was no better than the infamous brutes of the tsar's police force simply because she was a maid of honour at court pierced Alexandra Tolstoy to the quick, but she mastered her hurt feelings and wrote a tender and dignified reply to her impossible nephew:

'Your first letter caused me grief enough, my dear Leo, but the one I received yesterday made me weep bitter tears.

... My blood boils when I think of them prying and snooping about in your sanctuary.'[23]

She promised to take steps to see that he received satisfaction and assured him that the emperor, and even the chief of police, had no knowledge of the methods employed by 'their deputies'. There were, she said, too many plots, too much 'democratic ferment' in Russia, the police no longer knew where to turn. 'Hence these investigations on all sides, and these – grant me the adjective – involuntary injustices, which often fall upon the heads of innocent and honest people.' The number of suspects was mounting all the time, so it was no dishonour to be accused of harbouring evil thoughts against the authorities. The chief thing was to have a clear conscience and subdue one's wounded vanity. 'In the name of all you hold most holy, I beg you not to do anything rash. ... It is a strange thing that we do not hesitate to commit a thousand iniquities and injustices against the Lord, but the first one to strike our person appears monstrous and intolerable.' How could her nephew write that although he did not want to compromise her, he hoped she would rise above such petty considerations and give him the support of her friendship? 'It has never occurred to me to fear being compromised by your letters, and I am amazed that you could even think such a thing. I am what I am – openly – and I shall never even understand what you mean by "petty considerations". ... I bless you from afar, with a mother's tenderness. May God inspire your steps.'

But it was the Behrs family, not God, who inspired Tolstoy's next steps. He had returned to Moscow where, facing the three daughters who implored him to be reasonable, his anger melted away. On 22 August 1862 he wrote a very deferential letter to the emperor, asking that the names of his accusers be revealed and that His Majesty kindly make amends for the injury done to him. Count Sheremetyev, an aide-de-camp, transmitted the request to the tsar, who was in Moscow for the autumn manoeuvres.

While awaiting the results of his appeal, Tolstoy felt, in

his own words, like a man 'whose feet have been stepped on,
who is absolutely determined to find out whether it was
done on purpose; if so he demands reparation for the injustice, if not, simply that somebody say, "Excuse me" to
him.'[24] Alexandra Tolstoy pulled every string she had, the
tsar deigned to recall that he had once been given a liberal
education, and on his order Prince Dolgorukov, the chief of
police, asked Daragan, the governor of Tula, to assure Count
Tolstoy that despite the subversive writings found in the
possession of some of the students living under his wing,
charges would not be preferred and he would suffer no further inconvenience. Coming from the emperor, such conciliatory terms were tantamount to an apology. Tolstoy
accepted it. For some time his mind had been occupied
elsewhere, and on 7 September 1862, in a burst of heedless
cruelty, he wrote to his aunt Alexandra, who had gone to so
much trouble to see that he got his 'public reparation', the
words that could cause her the sharpest and most unavow-
able pain of all: 'And a third catastrophe – or blessing,
judge for yourself – has just befallen me: I, aged, toothless
fool that I am, have fallen in love.'

PART IV

======

SONYA

[13]

Betrothal

WITH the Behrs family, Tolstoy had the double sensation of reliving his past and committing his future. Mrs Behrs, née Lyubov Alexandrovna Islavin, belonged to the past: only three years older than he, she had been his childhood sweetheart, the very girl he had injured by pushing her off the balcony in a fit of jealousy; and the daughters of the house belonged to the future. Lyubov Alexandrovna's father was Alexander Mikhailovich Islenyev, libertine and irrepressible gambler, who had been Leo's fellow-roisterer on more than one occasion and who appeared, under the name of Irtenyev, in *Childhood*. Alexander Islenyev had had a checkered domestic career: his secret marriage to Sofya Petrovna Zavadovsky, who was separated from her first husband, Count Kozlovsky, had been extremely fruitful – but the count had had the marriage annulled, and the six children born of it, among whom was little Lyubov, were technically illegitimate. Officially, they were not even called Islenyev, but Islavin. After their mother died, their father observed a respectable period of mourning and then married a famous beauty of the day, Sofya Alexandrovna Zhdanov,[1] by whom he had three more daughters. This addition to his family and responsibilities had not deterred him from gambling away what remained of his immense fortune. Nine-tenths bankrupt, but still waggish and vivacious, he retired to the estate of his second wife, at Ivitsi in the district of Odoyev, thirty-five miles from Yasnaya Polyana.

At the age of sixteen his daughter Lyubov Alexandrovna married a young doctor of German extraction, Andrey Estafievich Behrs (or Bers), with whom she had fallen in love while he was treating her for 'brain fever'. The practitioner was eighteen years older than his patient, and the family also disapproved of his German ancestry – a forbear of his had been one of the four officers whom the King of Prussia sent to Tsarina Elizabeth to act as military experts. But that had been long ago and, with the passing of generations, only a fraction of the blood in the doctor's veins was German. As for the difference in age, it did not prevent him from siring thirteen children, eight of whom survived: five boys and three girls.

A family man with a sense of duty and a love of scholarship, Dr Behrs was the physician of the administrative staff of the Imperial Palace in Moscow, and lived in a cramped, sunless apartment in the Kremlin. The rooms all opened into one another, the office was so tiny that a patient could hardly be squeezed into it, and the children slept on sofas with sagging springs. But no caller could remain insensitive to the gaiety and high spirits of the inmates, dominated by the shrill laughter of children. Students and cadets, attracted by the three daughters – aged twenty, eighteen and sixteen in 1862 – flocked to the Behrs', where the door was always open and the table always set, according to the old custom of Russian hospitality. Here, as in all the better homes of Moscow, a large company of servants, underpaid and underemployed, loitered about in the hall, ate the leftovers from the meals and slept in the doorways and closets. The chairs and tables were stout and massive and upholstered casually, indifferently; their purpose was functional, not decorative. Poor relations or strays, blown in by the wind like seeds, took root between a screen and a leather sofa and stayed for years, or for life. In those days, Moscow was still a patriarchal, unsophisticated city in which formal invitations might be issued to a supper or a ball, but the old custom of 'tapers' was still in use for all other occasions. Those wishing to receive callers set lighted candles in a window looking out on the street, and any acquaintances happening to pass that way knew from the signal that they would be welcome, and rang the bell. When a couple was bored with their own company, they sent out a servant to see if there weren't any 'tapers' in the neighbouring windows, and when the servant returned and recited a list of names, all that remained was to choose with whom they would spend the rest of the evening. The streets were muddy, with a lantern flickering here and there. Water was brought to the door in perspiring barrels on carts. As a measure of economy, tallow candles were used for light in the Behrs household; tallow was also used as a remedy, in pomades or poultices, for coughs and colds. But the girls melted real wax in secret, to tell their fortunes in the strange shapes formed by the drops as they congealed.

With the first warm days, the family moved to their country house at Pokrovskoye-Streshnevo, only eight miles from town – near enough for the faithful swains to continue paying their calls. Starry nights, singing nightingales, fragrance of hay and flowering lilacs – everything was ideal for setting hearts on fire. Each of the three girls – Lisa, Sonya and Tanya, entertained her own private fantasies and held those of the other two in utter contempt. When the young men came they played four-handed piano, danced, rehearsed plays and exchanged languorous glances; afterwards, the overexcited young ladies tossed and turned in their beds for hours before falling asleep.

The most animated gatherings took place on Saturday evenings in the winter in Moscow. The drawing-room was lighted, the samovar steamed amidst cream 'cutlets' and heavy dough cakes. At eight o'clock, the cadets and students who were friends of the family came trooping in, their noses scarlet and their coats covered with frost. The girls, with their hair dressed for the occasion, came towards them with a swirl of wide skirts, but their governess stopped them with a cry: 'They're all cold! Don't go near them yet!'

Their mother brought her daughters up strictly and kept a close watch over them, but according to Fet all three possessed 'that particular form of appeal the French call *du chien*' (a rather knowing allure). The eldest, Lisa, had lovely, regular features and pretended to be as aloof as a statue, accepting admiration without ever provoking it; she was interested in literature and philosophy and smiled condescendingly when her sisters teased her, calling her 'the scholar'. At the other extreme was Tanya, the youngest, all bright mischief and emotion. One moment she would be sighing over the novel she was reading in hiding, and the next she would be giggling in front of her mirror at some new grimace she had invented. Two jet eyes, glittering with mettle and wit, flashed in her narrow face with its full lips and big nose. One day she wanted to be a dancer, the next a singer, the next a mother. She had a pleasant contralto voice and, with clownish deference, Tolstoy nicknamed her 'Mme Viardot'. Sonya, more pliant than Lisa, less mercurial than Tanya, boasted a graceful carriage, lovely complexion, dark hair, a smile of dazzling whiteness and large, dark, somewhat myopic eyes whose attentive and wondering expression was as disturbing as a confession. She was withdrawn, wilful and melancholy and seemed, as Tanya wrote in her memoirs, 'to be suspicious of happiness, never really able to grasp or enjoy it fully'. She read a great deal, cultivated herself, wrote stories, painted in watercolour, played the piano and had chosen the education of children as her life work. At seventeen she had received her teacher's certificate: the student who helped her to study for her examination had also tried to convert her to atheist materialism, but she speedily recovered her faith. Like her sisters, all her hopes were centred on love and marriage.

The young horse guardsman Mitrofan Polivanov, a friend of her brother's, was already courting her assiduously. Would she become Mrs Polivanov and end her days as the wife of a general? The idea did not horrify her, but neither did it thrill her. Her older sister Lisa would have a more exotic fate should she, as was likely, marry Count Leo Tolstoy. He was coming to the house more and more often, but could not make up his mind to propose. And to tell the truth, Lisa was so cool and haughty that she was not making it any easier for him. Sonya thought to herself that in her sister's place she would have spared no effort to elicit his impassioned avowals. She was awed by Tolstoy's talent, his fame, his legend. She remembered that in 1854, when she was ten,* he had come to call on her parents at their apartment in the Kremlin. He was in uniform then, about to join the Army of the Danube. After he left she had tied a ribbon around the low mahogany chair, upholstered in cerise, on which he had sat. She learned whole passages of his works by heart and had copied out a few lines of *Childhood* which she kept as a talisman inside her schoolgirl shirtwaist. He had reappeared in 1856, still in uniform, full of war stories and plans for novels. Now he had left the army, but seemed no happier than before. He wrote less, travelled, gave all his time to his village schools. True, he was not handsome. Average height, stocky, bony and brawny, his face overgrown by a bushy chestnut beard, thick lips planted in the midst of all that hair, a crooked nose and iron-grey eyes with a piercing glint. A muzhik, with calloused hands and a mystic's stare. His body was used to the unconstraint of country life, and was uncomfortable in the elegant attire he wore in Moscow. He looked as though he were in disguise and hating it. Thirty-four years old – an old man! And to top it off he had lost nearly all his teeth. The girls must have discussed this detail among themselves, ruefully. But Lisa was not going to marry a man for his teeth. For her, marriage meant founding a home, making a distinguished entrance into the world: Countess Leo Tolstoy. ... Her sisters, who did not like her very much, teased her because when the count was there her expression changed, she warbled and cooed and, they said, played the 'sweet almond'. Sonya sometimes felt that she would know better than Lisa how to make a great author happy. To whom could she turn in her dilemma? No one would understand. Before going to bed, she spent ages in prayer before the icon. Little

* Sofya Andreyevna Behrs was born on 22 August 1844.

Tanya surveyed her out of the corner of her eye, and one evening, when the two had just gotten into bed and blown out the candle, asked in a low voice:

'Sonya, do you love the count?'

'I don't know,' she answered.

Then, after a pause, she sighed:

'Oh, Tanya, two of his brothers died of consumption.'

'What of it?' said Tanya. 'His complexion is not at all like theirs. Believe me, Papa knows better than anyone else.' [2]

Sonya lay awake a long time. In the ensuing days she wrote a story to ease her aching heart. The heroine was Helen, a charming girl with black eyes and a passionate temperament; she had two sisters: Zinaida, the elder, who was fair and distant, and Natasha, the younger, who was petite, spritely and sweet-natured. Although a young man of twenty-three (alias Mitrofan Polivanov) was courting Helen, she had eyes only for a friend of the family, a middle-aged man of unprepossessing appearance named Dublitsky. Dublitsky, who was about to become engaged to the fair-haired and disagreeable Zinaida, was being increasingly drawn to the dark-haired and charming Helen. Torn between love and duty, the girl planned to enter a convent. ... She read this transparent tale to her younger sister, who thought it splendid, but she did not dare to show it to 'the count'.

July was almost over when Tolstoy, dreadfully upset by the police search in his house, next saw the Behrs, in Moscow. Pale and tense, his eyes flashing lightning, he talked of leaving the country if the government did not make amends to him. Seated at the end of the table, Sonya never took her eyes from him, and silently prayed that he would stay in Russia. He returned to Yasnaya Polyana, and a few days later Lyubov Alexandrovna Behrs was suddenly inspired to visit her old father at Ivitsi and take her three daughters and her son Volodya with her. Now, Ivitsi was not far from Yasnaya Polyana, where Leo's sister Marya, an intimate childhood friend of Lyubov Alexandrovna's, was staying. By all means, Mrs Behrs would call on her old friend. Indeed she was looking forward to the meeting; also, by bearding the lion in his den, she hoped to force his hand, overpower him and compel him, after so many months of indecision, to propose to Lisa. Her thoughts full of this subtle maternal stratagem, she persuaded her husband that the trip was absolutely essential and ordered new gowns for the girls. A coach for six was hired from Annenkov the coachmaker, baggage was piled on to the roof until the springs groaned, and, leaving the anxious doctor waving his handkerchief behind them, they drove away in a cloud of dust.

After spending a day in Tula, the travellers set out in the direction of Yasnaya Polyana, quivering with anticipation. The cornfields rolling away to the horizon, the forest of Zasyeka, crowded and dim, the bright village of Yasnaya Polyana with its thatched huts, village pump and little church – Sonya loved it all, and saw the owner's reflection in everything: the bearded count with the shining eyes. Evening was coming on as the coach passed between the two whitewashed brick towers at the entrance to the grounds. Leaning out over the door, the girls watched as two rows of birches followed by lime trees, lilacs, tousled bushes and a meadow of tall grass strewn with buttercups rolled by in a joggling phantasmagoria. Here the vegetation seemed to explode in riotous rejoicing. In the midst of a tangle of green stood the white house with its Greek pediment and covered veranda. The carpenter had cut out a series of figurines in the wooden railings – a rooster, a horse, a woman with outstretched arms. Heavy linen curtains hung at the windows.

Lyubov Alexandrovna had announced her arrival, but not the exact day. At the sound of the harness bells the house, drowsing in the dusk, awoke with a start. While the servants were bustling about with the baggage, Mrs Behrs fell into the arms of her girlhood chum, Marya Tolstoy. Then old Aunt Toinette hobbled out and welcomed the travellers in

French. Behind her stood her companion and attendant, the faithful Natalya Petrovna, in a pelerine and white piqué bonnet. The girls curtsied. Everyone talked at once:

'Sonya looks just like you. . . . Tanya is very like her grandmother . . .'

At that point Leo Tolstoy appeared, so gay that Sonya thought he looked positively young.

After a tour of the orchard, where the wide-eyed young urbanites picked raspberries, their mother sent them to unpack in the vaulted ground-floor room that was to be their dormitory. Plain wooden cots lined the walls. The extremely hard mattresses were covered with blue and white striped ticking. The stout birch table had been made by the village carpenter. Iron hooks protruded overhead, from which harnesses, saddles and hams had hung in Prince Volkonsky's day. Dunyasha, the chambermaid, 'rather imposing and not too ugly', made up the beds on the couches. But there were only three cots and, with Volodya, there were four children. Tolstoy solved the problem by proposing to add a footstool at the end of a deep armchair. This arrangement amused Sonya, who gaily said:

'I want to sleep in the armchair.'

'And I shall make your bed,' said Tolstoy, in a tone that allowed no argument.

He awkwardly unfolded and spread the sheet. Sonya helped him, laughing to hide her confusion. 'It did seem a little embarrassing,' she wrote later,[3] 'to be making a bed with Leo Nikolayevich, but it was very nice and delightfully intimate.'

When she and Tolstoy had finished arranging her bed, she went back up to the drawing-room where her sister Lisa gave her a cold, questioning look. Her emotions in a whirl, she went out to sit on the veranda. There, staring into the night, she floated off into an insane and happy fantasy. 'Was it the effect of the country air, nature, space? Was it a premonition of what would happen six weeks later, when I returned to this house as its mistress? Or was it simply my

farewell to my girlhood and my freedom? ... I do not know.
... I felt solemn, and happy, and something I had never
known before, something infinite.'[4]

Tolstoy came to call her in to dinner, but she would not
go:

'I'm not hungry. It is so lovely out here.'

Reluctantly, he left her. Behind her back she heard voices
and laughter and the clink of china. Lisa must be trying to
regain her lost ground. A board creaked under a footfall.
Sonya turned around. It was Tolstoy, abandoning his guests
at the table, coming back to her. They exchanged a few
words, softly, in the darkness. Suddenly he whispered:

'How simple and clear you are.'

And so she was, but what unconfessed scheming, what
unconscious hopes lay behind that candour! She lowered
her eyes, for fear of being discovered. It was late. Lyubov
Alexandrovna sent the girls to bed. Sonya went down to the
vaulted hall, cherishing, deep in her heart, the words Tolstoy
had spoken to her on the terrace. She repeated them over to
herself as she curled up in her nightgown between the arms
of the uncomfortable armchair. Sleep would not come. She
listened to her sisters' breathing, tossed and turned and
smiled in rapture at the thought that it was the 'count's'
big hands that had made her bed.

She awoke at dawn, radiant. The sun was shining in a
cloudless sky. The air was exhilarating. 'I wanted to run
everywhere, look at everything, talk to everybody,'[5] she
later wrote. Just the thing: Tolstoy had planned a picnic in
the forest of Zasyeka. Baraban, a chestnut, and Strelka were
harnessed to a sort of primitive charabanc that could carry
twelve people seated back to back. Sonya admired the grey
Byelogubka, wearing an old side-saddle, and Tolstoy asked
whether she would like to ride him. She had on her pretty
yellow dress with the black velvet buttons and belt.

'How can I? I didn't bring a riding habit,' she frowned.

'Never mind that,' he laughed. 'We're not in society here.
There's nobody to see you but the trees.'

And while Lisa stood by biting her lips, he helped Sonya up on to Byelogubka's back. She wrapped her yellow skirt tightly around her legs to cover them down to the ankle, arched her back and strove to appear elegant. He straddled a magnificent white stallion and they cantered off side by side under the low branches. The wagon followed with the rest of the group in a medley of hats and parasols, jolting with every turn of the wheels. Neighbours and friends had joined the outing. The entire company gathered in a clearing with a haycock in the centre. Lyubov Alexandrovna Behrs and Marya Tolstoy spread out the cloth on the grass and set the places, opened hampers and lighted the samovar. After tea, Tolstoy led his guests in games, climbing up the haystack and sliding down again. In the midst of the shouting and laughter Sonya – her yellow dress all crumpled and her hair full of straw – was in heaven, but Lisa was beginning to glower. Towards evening the whole party sat on top of the haystack and sang in chorus: 'The brook flows over the pebbles ...'

The next day the Behrs family went on to Ivitsi. Sonya left with a heavy heart, but was soon cheered by the sight of her grandfather Islenyev. He was so comical; a little, close-shaven, bald old man with a black skullcap, an aquiline nose and mischievous eyes glinting between wrinkled lids. Pinching the girls' cheeks between thumb and forefinger, he called them 'the young ladies from Moscow', questioned them about their love affairs and uttered antiquated gallantries that brought a scowl to the face of his second wife, Sofya Alexandrovna – the erstwhile beauty with the bewitching black eyes, who had become a gaunt, toothless crone who smoked a pipe from dawn to dark, which distended her lips and muddied her skin. To make certain that his young guests would not be bored in his home, the old man had planned a series of outings and dances for them, to which all the local young bloods were invited. But Sonya was not to be jarred from her dream world by the chatter of such provincials. Two days after their arrival at Ivitsi, she was in her bedroom with Lisa when little Tanya opened the door, eyes bulging and cheeks on fire, and cried out:

'The count! ... The count has come to see us!'

'It's not true!' exclaimed Lisa, blushing.

'Is he alone or with his sister?' asked Sonya faintly.

'Alone! On horseback,' Tanya answered. 'Hurry!'

They clattered down the stairs and stopped outside the door, paralysed, in front of Leo Tolstoy, who was heavily dismounting from his white horse. He was covered with dust, his forehead shone with sweat and his eyes showed shy delight. Sonya did not dare hope he had travelled the thirty-five miles between Yasnaya Polyana and Ivitsi just for the pleasure of seeing her again. The entire household had already assembled to congratulate him. Grandfather clapped him on the shoulder and asked:

'How long did it take you?'

'A little over three hours,' Tolstoy answered. 'I didn't hurry. It was very hot.'

Suddenly, at that instant, Sonya wanted to love him, and just as suddenly she was afraid of becoming attached to him. She thought of Lisa, whom she was betraying, and of the young and amiable horse guardsman Mitrofan Polivanov who would one day ask for her hand, and she felt guilty, but she could not think of anything particular that she had done wrong. In the evening, after a walk, all the young people in the neighbourhood – officers from the near-by garrison, country squires, students on vacation – gathered in the big drawing-room at Ivitsi. Parlour games were followed by dancing. Volunteer muscians took turns at the piano, pounding the keys and pumping at the pedals. Sonya wore a thin white woollen dress with a lilac-covered rosette on one shoulder, from which trailed down long ribbons known as *Suivez-moi jeune homme* (Follow me, young man).

'How elegant you are, here,' said Tolstoy.

'Aren't you dancing?' she asked.

'No. What's the use? I'm too old.'

She demurred. After supper the guests began to leave. But someone wanted Tanya to sing a *romance*. She was not in the mood, so she hid under the piano to avoid being forced to perform, and was forgotten there. And thus she became an involuntary witness to a strange scene. The house had grown quiet again, when Tolstoy and Sonya came into the room. Both very intent, they sat down by a card table that had been left open.

'And so you'll be leaving again tomorrow?' said Sonya. 'Why so soon? What a pity.'

'My sister Marya is all alone and will soon be going abroad.'

'Will you go with her?'

'No. I should have liked to go, but now I can't.'

Unaware of her younger sister's presence in the room, Sonya never took her eyes from the doleful and supplicating face of the man leaning towards her. As the silence began to lengthen, she murmured:

'We had better be getting back to the dining-room. Otherwise they'll begin looking for us.'

'No,' he said. 'Wait a moment. It's so nice here.'

And, taking up a piece of chalk, he wrote something on the baize.

'Sofya Andreyevna,' he resumed, 'can you decipher what I have written there? I put only the first letter of every word . . .'

'I can,' she confidently said.

He went on writing. 'I watched his big reddish hand,' she later wrote, 'and felt my entire soul, all my energy and attention, focused on that piece of chalk and the hand guiding it.' She read: 'y.y.a.y.t.f.h.r.m.c.o.m.a.a.t.i.o.h.f.m.' She felt suddenly inspired. The blood hammered in her temples. No mystery could resist her love. With only occasional prompting from Tolstoy, she read, 'Your youth and your thirst for happiness remind me cruelly of my age and the impossibility of happiness for me.'

Amazed at her intuitiveness, he said:

'Then do this too.'

And he wrote: 'y.f.i.m.a.m.a.y.s.L.H.m.t.d.m.y.a.T.' She translated:

'Your family is mistaken about me and your sister Lisa. Help me to defend myself, you and Tanya.'

It was not a proposal. Nor even a declaration of love. But Sonya was too clever not to realize that this correspondence in code assumed a communion of minds between her and her partner that meant more than any protestation. Cutting through her exaltation, she heard her mother's voice crossly ordering her to bed. Before lying down she lighted a candle, sat on the floor and propped her notebook on a chair, and copied into her diary the words Tolstoy had initialled in chalk on the card table cover. Coming out of her hiding place, Tanya joined her a few moments later and confessed that she had heard and seen all, and was afraid there would be trouble ahead. Sonya was too happy to worry.

Tolstoy returned to Yasnaya Polyana the next day, but not before he had extracted a promise from the Behrs family to call again on their way back to Moscow. Behind him, he left a girl of eighteen quivering with hope, a girl of twenty smarting with jealousy, and a girl of sixteen moping because she was only a confidante. One day Lisa took Tanya aside and told her, with tears in her eyes: 'Sonya is trying to take Leo Nikolayevich away from me! ... The way she dresses and looks at him and goes off alone with him, it's as clear as day.' Tanya tried to comfort her – in vain. The atmosphere was strained, as the young ladies prepared for the return trip.[6]

As agreed, they spent a night at Yasnaya Polyana. Marya Tolstoy had decided to take advantage of their coach as far as Moscow, before continuing abroad. Her departure saddened Aunt Toinette and the entire household. Leo was glum. At dawn, Annenkov's big coach rolled up to the door and the farewells began. Suddenly, Tolstoy, dressed in his travelling clothes, strode into the circle of weeping women, who were embracing each other and crossing themselves. His valet Alexis followed him with a suitcase.

'I am going to Moscow with you,' he announced. 'How could I stay on at Yasnaya now? It would seem so dull and empty.'

Suffused with joy, Sonya struggled to keep her face under control as her mother watched her intently.

There was room for four inside the coach and two outside, behind the box. It was decided that Tolstoy would take one of the two outside places and Lisa and Sonya would take turns sitting beside him. The post horses trotted smartly along. Now and then the coachman blew his horn. The hours Sonya spent inside, with her mother and Tanya and her little brother Volodya and Marya Tolstoy, seemed endless. She envied Lisa out there in the open air, conversing freely with the writer. To while away the time, the travellers nibbled at bonbons and fruit, but Sonya refused all such treats. Leaning out, she counted the striped mile-posts. At last, the relay! Her turn to mount beside Tolstoy. Evening was coming on. It grew cold. Nestled against her big friend's shoulder, she listened to his tales of the Caucasus, Sevastopol, the war, the savage Circassians, the French, the English, the Germans. ... He had seen so many countries, known so many people, gone through so much! She felt very ignorant and vulnerable next to him. Light-headed with fatigue, she closed her eyes and dropped off, awoke at a sudden jolt and thrilled to find the warmth of a male body next to her, and the sound of a deep, gentle voice mixed with the jingling bells. They drove on like that all night. Inside, the family slept. Except for Lisa, perhaps, awaiting her turn ...

At the last relay before Moscow, when it was again Sonya's turn to sit beside Tolstoy, Lisa asked her to give up her turn on the pretext that it was too stuffy inside and she could not breathe. Sonya was enraged at this manoeuvre, but at her mother's command, she climbed inside.

'Sofya Andreyevna,' Tolstoy cried out, 'it's your turn to sit behind.'

'I know,' she said reluctantly, 'but I'm cold.'

Lisa was already settled triumphantly on the empty outside seat. Tolstoy stood a moment, hesitating, in the posthouse courtyard; then, without a word, he climbed up beside the driver and Annenkov's coach rolled away with the girl sitting behind, alone and humiliated, offering her tears to the wind.

Tolstoy and Marya left them in Moscow and the Behrs went on to their country house at Pokrovskoye-Streshnevo, where the doctor was waiting for them. Fresh quarrels broke out between the two sisters, so violent that their parents could no longer pretend not to understand. The doctor, who was a man of principle, held that if a proposal were forthcoming Sonya, as the younger sister, should decline in favour of Lisa. Lyubov Alexandrovna, who was a woman of common sense, would have preferred to give priority to her children's hearts. Tanya felt sorry for the stiff and haughty Lisa, but sided openly with Sonya. Even the brothers became involved in these feminine complications. However, by tacit agreement, no one presumed to ask 'the count' point-blank what his intentions were. He was too important a person, too intimidating. He must be allowed to reach his decision in his own good time, without being hurried in any way.

After Marya left for Europe, Tolstoy rented an apartment from a German bootmaker in Moscow, but he could not feel comfortable in it. He was obsessed by Sonya. One thing was certain: she, and not Lisa, was now his favourite among the three Behrs daughters. But should he propose to her, in spite of the difference in their ages? Would it not be better for a man like him to preserve his independence at all costs? He had never regretted breaking off with Valerya. But on the other hand, he had never felt for her what he felt for Sonya. If he disappeared from the scene and she were to marry someone else, he would regret it his

whole life long. What to do? He was exhausted by his own
indecisions. He read his fortune in the cards, looked for
good and evil marriage omens, and hiked almost daily the
eight miles to Pokrovskoye-Streshnevo. He would reach the
house at twilight, covered with dust, his throat dry and his
heart thumping. The girls' bright-coloured dresses, high
voices and the charming nonsense they chattered rewarded
him for his long walk. 'When I am empress, I shall issue
my commands and orders – like this!' Sonya said one
evening, sitting in an unharnessed cabriolet in the courtyard. Tolstoy seized the shafts, set the heavy vehicle in
motion with one heave of his back, and trotted off,
crying:

'And this is how I shall take my empress for a drive!'

'No, no! It's too heavy! Stop!' implored Sonya, clasping
her hands.

But she was delighted. 'This incident shows how strong
and healthy he was,' she wrote in her memoirs. Of course,
the count must stay to supper; a bed was prepared for him.
Ah, those dangerous folds of comfort in which the parents
of a marriageable daughter can swathe an undecided
bachelor! At Pokrovskoye-Streshnevo nature itself conspired to concentrate the suitor's mind on thoughts of
romance. The nights were so beautiful, the moon shone in
the nearby pond, the grass in the meadow shivered as
though covered with silver powder, the earth, which had
drunk in the heat of the sun all day, exhaled its perfumes
in the lengthening shadows. Sitting under the arbour with
the girls, Tolstoy talked of this and that, forgot his worries
and strove to make himself agreeable. A rival had appeared
on the scene of late, a certain Popov, professor of Russian
history at the University of Moscow, who kept looking
intently at Sonya and then turning away and heaving
sighs. But he proved no more dangerous than the horse
guardsman Mitrofan Polivanov, whom the girls were expecting any week. Twenty times Tolstoy's declaration was on his
lips, and twenty times he bit it back. When the feeling be-

came too strong for him, he would lean on the wooden railing of the balcony and murmur, 'Nights of madness!'

Consumed with anxiety, he returned to his diary. 'Slept at the Behrs',' he wrote on 23 August 1862. 'A child! Or certainly looks like one. And yet, what utter confusion. Oh, if only I could put myself in a clear and honourable position. ... I'm afraid of myself: what if it is only the desire for love again, and not love itself? I try to see only her weaknesses, but it doesn't seem to make any difference. A child! Or certainly looks like one.'

Three days later he asked the child whether she kept a diary. Her answer was evasive, but she admitted that she had written a story. He insisted upon seeing it. What went on in her mind in that moment? She knew Tolstoy might be offended by the unattractive personality she had given Dublitsky in her autobiographical tale. But hurt feelings or even an open conflict would be better than this stagnation in her love life. Since they were both too shy to speak out, and since he had made one confession to her with the initials chalked on the table cover, why shouldn't she do as much through her thinly disguised characters? Burning with embarrassment, she handed him her notebook, staking everything on one throw of the dice.

He took the story home with him to Moscow and raced through it, and it was as though he suddenly saw his own face in the mirror, after forgetting how ugly and eroded it had become. Wounded vanity was his first reaction. Then he reflected that even though the heroine found Dublitsky ugly, old and moody, she was none the less in love with him. This observation only half-consoled him. 'She gave me her story to read,' he wrote on 26 August. 'How furiously she insisted upon truth and simplicity. Anything unclear torments her. I read it all without a twinge, without a glimmer of jealousy or envy. Even so, expressions like "unattractive outward appearance" and "inconsistent in his opinions" hit me hard.' So hard that two days later, 28 August – his birthday – he concluded that he was 'too great' for the common path of matrimony. Wounded in masculine pride, he sought refuge in his author's pride: 'I am thirty-four years old. ... Got up with my ususal feeling of depression. ... Ugly mug. Give up any thought of marriage. Your vocation is elsewhere, that is why much has been given to you.'

But work could no longer content him. Little Sonya had played the right card when she showed him her story. Now, every wriggle he gave to shake the hook loose only drove it deeper into his flesh. He went back to Pokrovskoye-Streshnevo, saw her again, hesitated, hoped, filled his diary with conflicting entries: 'It is no longer love as before, or jealousy or even regret, but something similar I cannot name, very sweet; something like a bit of hope (that must not be). Pig! A little regret and sorrow too. Delicious night. Good, comfortable feeling. ... I was confused. She too.' (29 August.) 'I am not jealous of Popov when he is with Sonya, I cannot believe she doesn't prefer me. I think the time has come, but it is night now. Her voice, too, is sad, peaceful. We took a walk. In the arbour. Back at the house, supper – her eyes. What a night! Dolt, this is not for you; yet you're in love, like with Sonya Koloshin or Alexandra Obolensky – but no more than that. Spent the night there, could not sleep, her again! "Have you never loved, then?" she says, and I want to laugh, I am suddenly wildly gay.' (30 August.) 'Never have I imagined my future with a woman as clearly, as joyfully and calmly. ... Memento: Dublitsky, loathsome creature!' (3 September.) 'Did not sleep all night, so clear was the picture I was painting of my happiness. In the evening we talked of love. From bad to worse.' (5 September.) 'Dublitsky, don't go poking your nose into youth and poetry and beauty and love. There are cadets for that, old man. ... The monastery – work, there's your vocation, and from that summit you can look calmly and contentedly down upon the love and happiness of others. I have lived in that monastery and shall go back to it.' (7 September.) After writing that sentence Tolstoy had a second thought and noted above it: 'My diary is not truthful. Underneath, I am thinking that she will be here beside me one day, reading, and ... and this is for her.'

The next day the Behrs moved back to their apartment in the Kremlin, and Tolstoy rang at their door once again: 'Sonya opened. ... She looks thinner. There is nothing in her of what I have always seen in the others: neither false soulfulness nor the conventional tricks of allure. I am irresistibly drawn to her.' (8 September.) 'She blushed, she was deeply disturbed: "O Dublitsky, do not dream! ..." I cannot, *I cannot* tear myself away from Moscow. ... Sleep impossible until three in the morning. Dreamed, and worked myself into a state like a kid of sixteen.' (9 September.)

That night he resolved to abandon all hope of the joy he deemed impossible, and wrote a long letter of explanation to Sonya, telling her that her parents were wrong to believe that he was in love with the fair Lisa, but that he was not wrong to identify himself with the horrible Dublitsky:

'When I read your story I recognized myself in Dublitsky and that unfortunately reminded me of what I really am and all too often forget: 'Uncle Leo, an old, exceedingly unsightly devil who needs to work, alone and unremittingly, at what God has given him to do, and not to think of any other felicity than that afforded by the knowledge of work well done. ... I am gloomy when I look at you, because your youth reminds me too vividly of my age and the impossibility of happiness for me. ... I am Dublitsky, but to marry simply because one must have a wife is something I cannot do. I demand something terrible, impossible, of marriage. ... I demand to be loved as I love. ... I shall not come to see you any more.'

What a relief to have written that letter! Such a relief that he popped it into a drawer and promptly forgot all about it.* On 10 September he awoke with cramped muscles

*He gave the letter, dated 9 September 1862, to Sofya Andreyevna after their marriage.

but renewed optimism. His resolution not to see Sonya again vanished with the day. He hardly took time to dress before rushing over to her home: 'To the Kremlin. She wasn't in. ... Then she arrived, severe, serious. I left, discouraged again, and more in love than ever. *Underneath everything else*, hope lives on. I must, I absolutely must free myself. I am beginning to hate Lisa, and pity her at the same time. Lord, help me, tell me what to do! Another cruel, sleepless night coming, I can feel it; I who scoffed at lovers' agonies! I shall perish by the sword I have wielded! How many times I have planned to tell her, or Tanya, but in vain. ... Help me, Lord, teach me what to do. Holy Virgin, help me!' (10 September.)

He was frightened by the fullness of his love as by a disease. The sole activity of which his mind was capable was obsessive thought about this soft-skinned little girl. The older and uglier he felt himself, the more desirable she seemed. On 11 September he forced himself to stay at home and spent the day in prayer. On the twelfth he called on the Behrs and arrived in the midst of a party of friends, whose chatter made him dizzy. Sonya was inaccessible among all those trivial, fluttering people. He wanted to pick her up bodily and carry her away, bear her off to the country. ... 'I am in love as I did not believe it possible to be,' he wrote that evening. 'I am insane, I shall put a bullet through my head if this goes on much longer. There was a party at their place. She is delightful in every respect. And I am the repugnant old Dublitsky. I should have taken my precautions sooner. Now I cannot stop. Dublitsky, so be it; but transfigured by love. Yes, I'll go tomorrow morning. There have been propitious moments, and I have not taken advantage of them. I was afraid, when I should simply have told her. I feel like going back now and saying it in front of everybody. Lord, help me!'

On 13 September, having broken his promise to himself again, he renewed it: 'Tomorrow I shall go and speak out, or else I shall kill myself.' On second thought, he crossed out the last part of the sentence. He would not kill himself. Nor would he speak out. He would present his proposal in writing. After all, it was easier that way. What despair if she were to refuse! What dread if she were to accept! Not a sound in the house; a candle burned on the table. He let his pen slide across the paper. When he had finished, he wrote in his diary: 'Four in the morning. I have written her a letter which I shall give to her tomorrow, that is, today, the fourteenth. God, I am afraid I shall die! Such happiness seems impossible. Help me, my God!' Then he closed his notebook, picked up the letter and calmly read it over:

Sofya Andreyevna, the situation has become intolerable to me. Every day for three weeks I have sworn to myself: today I shall speak; and every day I leave you with the same anguish, the same regret, the same terror, the same joy in my heart. ... I am bringing this letter with me, to give you in case I lack the opportunity, or the courage, to speak. ... Tell me, tell me truthfully, do you want to be my wife? But do not answer yes unless you can do so fearlessly, from the bottom of your heart. If you cannot, if you have the shadow of a doubt, then it is better to answer no. For the love of God, be certain! If you say no, it will be awful for me, but I am expecting it and shall find strength to bear it. For if I were your husband and were not loved as much as I love, it would be more awful still.

He did not give his letter to Sonya on either the fourteenth or the fifteenth of September. But on the fifteenth, he whispered to her that he had something important to tell her. She looked up at him with her great dark astonished eyes. Did she really not understand, or was she pretending not to understand? He felt the letter in his pocket, did not say another word, and beat a retreat.

When he returned to the Kremlin after dinner the following day, 16 September, he found Sonya at the piano playing '*Il baccio*', an Italian waltz. She was so nervous that her fingers caught on the keys. To hide her confusion, she asked her sister Tanya to sing. After a bit, as she was getting the notes all wrong, Tolstoy took her place at the piano. He vowed that if Tanya sang the last note well, which was very high, he would give Sonya the letter. If not, he would conclude that God counselled him to wait. The end of the song drew near. The note welled out of the girl's throat, pure, crystalline, imperative. Tolstoy felt as though he had received a blow on the head, and put his hand to his pocket. Tanya went to make tea. As though diving off the top of a tower, he murmured:

'I wanted to speak to you but I was not able to. Here is the letter I have been carrying with me for several days. Read it. I shall wait for your reply here.'

Sonya snatched the letter, pounded along the hall and shut herself into the room she shared with her two sisters. Her heart was beating so hard that she scarcely understood what she read. Just as she reached the sentence: 'Do you want to be my wife?' someone knocked at the door. It was Lisa.

'Sonya!' she cried out. 'Open the door! Open the door immediately! I must speak to you!'

Sonya opened the door a crack.

'What has the count written to you?' Lisa said in a choked voice. 'Tell me! Tell me! . . .'

'He has proposed to me,' answered Sonya in French.

Lisa's eyes grew wider, the tears spilled over and her mouth twisted into a sob:

'Refuse! Refuse right away!'

Sonya, petrified with joy, said nothing; alerted by Tanya, her mother came running. She scolded Lisa, ordered her to take hold of herself and show a little dignity, and pushed Sonya forward by the shoulders, saying:

'Go give him your reply.'

Borne on a gust of wind, she flew into the room where Tolstoy was waiting, pale, backed up against the wall. He took her hands in his and said weakly:

'Well?'

'Yes, of course!' she burst out.

At her words, fear and joy surged through him so violently that he felt faint. Two minutes later the whole household had heard the news and he had to submit to the avalanche of congratulations. But Lisa stayed away, weeping in her room, and Dr Behrs sent word that he was not feeling well and also failed to appear. He thought it highly improper of Tolstoy to choose his second daughter, when he had intended him to marry the eldest.

After the fiancé's departure, Mrs Behrs set out to win over her husband. She pointed out that with their large family and slender resources they had no right to reject a rich, talented and noble suitor on a mere point of order, that they would gain nothing by trying to oppose true love and that, furthermore, the important thing was not principle but Sonya's happiness. Mastering her resentment, Lisa joined her mother in pleading the cause of the future couple. Together, they won the doctor over; he blessed Sonya with the family icon and everybody cried.

Meanwhile, back in his apartment, Tolstoy, worn out by emotion and incapable of articulating his thoughts, wrote down these few words in his diary: 'I told her. She: "Yes." Like a wounded bird. No point in writing. Impossible to forget or to relate.'

The next day, 17 September, Mrs Behrs was entertaining in honour of her nameday. Her two eldest daughters, Lisa and Sonya, were dressed alike, according to custom. Lilac and white woollen dresses with round necklines and rosettes of lilac ribbons at waist and shoulder. Both were pale, there were shadows under their eyes and beneath their piled-up hair their faces were drawn. The table groaned under the weight of the victuals and all the vases were full of flowers. At two in the afternoon the room began to fill. Every time a guest came up to wish Lyubov Alexandrovna many happy returns, she smiled graciously and said, 'You may also congratulate us upon our daughter's engagement.' Before she had time to say which daughter, the new arrival was bearing down on Lisa, who blushed, forced a social half-smile and

indicated Sonya, who blushed in turn. And to make matters
worse, a magnificent horse guardsman suddenly strode into
the midst of the crowd: Mitrofan Polivanov, coming to pay
his respects to the mistress of the house and give his regards
to the young woman whom he already regarded as a sort
of fiancée. Sonya drew herself up stiffly to hide her discomfort. Her brother Sasha took the young man aside. After a
whispered explanation, Mitrofan Polivanov came up to
Sonya and muttered between clenched teeth:

'I knew you would betray me. I could feel it coming ...'

Tolstoy anxiously observed this uniformed fop whispering
to the girl who was soon to bear his name. Lisa stood a little
way off, her head high and her lips pinched together.
'Fiancé, gifts, champagne,' wrote Tolstoy that evening. 'Lisa
pitiful and difficult. She ought to detest me, she embraces
me.'

It remained to set the date. Like most people who can
never make up their minds, once he had reached his decision Tolstoy could not bear a moment's delay. Leaving
Sonya's parents flabbergasted, he demanded that the service take place on 23 Spetember 1862, one week after the
engagement had been announced. Lyubov Alexandrovna
objected that the trousseau had to be prepared.

'Why?' he said. 'She is perfectly well dressed the way she
is! What more does she need?'

With a sigh, Mrs Behrs acquiesced. Having got his
way on this point, Tolstoy then asked his fiancée whether
she wanted to take a honeymoon trip abroad or go immediately to Yasnaya Polyana. She opted for Yasnaya
Polyana, in order 'to begin real life right away, family life'.
He was grateful to her for this. Of course, they would not
be alone in the big house, Aunt Toinette was part of the
furniture. But Sonya already dearly loved the old spinster
and was sure to find an ally in her. Only six days left! The
girl was suddenly caught up in a whirlwind of calls, letters,
seamstresses, shopping, invitation lists. ... Tolstoy disapproved of all this futile agitation, motivated by coquetry.

Souls, not dresses, were what counted in marriage. It was wrong to try to appear more handsome than one really was, to the person in whom one had placed one's faith; on the contrary one must stand before him naked. Naked in all one's ugliness. If love could survive this trial by truth, then a family could be born. If not, better to separate, each to his own.

It was in this spirit of sincerity that he decided to give his fiancée his private diaries to read. She had thought to portray him, in her Dublitsky of the unprepossessing outward appearance? He would show her that Dublitsky's interior was even more spine-chilling. His wild ambitions, his absurd rules of life, his intellectual acrobatics, his somersaults, his toothache, his rages, his diarrhoeas, his erotic dreams, his false engagement to Valerya, his real affairs with the peasant women, she would know it all. In his wedding basket he would deposit this bundle of dirty linen; if she did not turn up her nose at the smell, then she could understand anything. He revelled in debasing himself thus, in the true Russian manner, in the eyes of the person whose respect was most essential to him. A few days before, he had held her in his arms for the first time, there between the wall and the piano, and she had given him a clumsy kiss. He had been so excited by this that he wrote, when he came home, 'Apparition of Satan. Jealousy of her past. Doubted her love and thought she was deceiving herself about her own feelings.'[7] Let her read that, too! He was as tense as though he were staking his entire fortune on a single card.

Sonya accepted the notebooks with misgivings, and spent a whole night reading them. As she turned the pages, the image of her future husband became steadily blacker. Revelations that an experienced woman of the world might have found it hard to pardon horrified the eighteen-year-old girl raised by her mother in total ignorance of the 'nasty side' of life. She did not understand how a man who spoke so wonderfully of virtue, sacrifice and courage could be a weak-

ling and profligate at the same time. And all those sudden
about-faces, in politics, art, love! What avid fascination
with everything relating to his own person! If he were so
concerned with himself, would it ever occur to him to pay
any attention to her? If he laid down such stern principles
for himself, would he not demand a degree of moral perfection of her that was beyond her reach? If he changed
his mind so rapidly, would he not tire of her the morning
after the wedding? The most contradictory nature in the
world, a two-faced Janus, one side of light and the other of
darkness. Terrible sentences leaped to her eyes: 'Regard
the company of woman as a necessary social evil and avoid
them as much as possible. Who indeed is the cause of
sensuality, indolence, frivolity and all sorts of other vices
in us, if not women? ...' 'Felt voluptuous desires ...' 'Went
home with a girl ...' The abbreviated style of the diary
accentuated the air of cynicism it exuded. Sonya began to
cry. 'How stricken I was by those pages he insisted, in his
excessive honesty, that I read before we were married!' she
later wrote. 'Wasted honesty! I shed many tears over that
look into his past.'

By dawn, she had grown calm again. Red-eyed and with
feverish cheeks, she greeted her fiancé, who had come to find
out her reaction, with a smile. He seemed tired and nervous.
She reassured him, forgave him, handed back his notebooks.
But she knew at heart that something irreparable had happened to her. She had been marked for life by that desecra-
tion.

The wedding was to take place on 23 September 1862, at
eight in the evening in the imperial Church of the Nativity
of the Virgin in the Kremlin. Halfway through the morning, when the entire household was topsy-turvy, Tolstoy arrived unexpectedly and burst into the girls' room. Custom
forbade a fiancé to call on his betrothed on the wedding
day. At the sight of him, Sonya's heart gave a leap. What
new bombshell was he going to drop? White and haggard,
his eyes staring fixedly ahead of him, he sat down next to

her on a trunk already strapped and asked her whether she
was absolutely sure she loved him, whether she did not
regret Mitrofan Polivanov or some other suitor, whether
she did not want to take back her promise. He personally
didn't care a hoot about what people said; a good break was
better than a bad marriage! She thought he was looking
for some pretext to back out, and burst into tears. While
he was trying to console her, Mrs Behrs swept into the
room, borne aloft by maternal indignation as a ship on an
ocean swell.

'You've chosen a fine time to come and worry her to
death!' she cried. 'The wedding is today – there's quite
enough to do already. And then all that distance to travel
– and there she sits in tears.'

The chastened fiancé apologized profusely and slunk
away. At six o'clock Sonya, utterly limp, began to dress.
Her sisters and girlfriends arranged her hair and placed on
her head a long tulle veil and a crown of flowers. Her dress,
also of tulle, bared her neck and shoulders in the fashion
of the time. 'The light, transparent material surrounded me
like a cloud,' she wrote.[8] But she was worried because her
shoulders were too thin.

According to the Orthodox ceremony, the fiancé reached
the church first; as soon as he got there, he sent his best
man to inform the bride that she could start. Sonya had
long been ready and was standing stiffly in her haze of
gown, biting her nails in the midst of her family. Thirty
minutes went by, an hour, an hour and a quarter, still no
messenger! A chilling thought crossed her mind: he had
decamped! She remembered all he had said that morning,
and her doubt became a certainty. Half-dead with shame,
she did not dare to look at her parents, who obviously
shared her apprehensions. At last Tolstoy's manservant
Alexis appeared, instead of the groomsman, in a terrible
state of agitation. When packing his master's things he had
forgotten to leave out a clean shirt. It was Sunday, the shops
were closed and all the future couple's belongings were al-

ready waiting at the Behrs'. The trunks had to be opened and searched. Finding the precious shirt at last, Alexis set off at a run.

Another long moment went by before the best man appeared, radiant, to announce that Count Leo Tolstoy, fully dressed, was waiting for his fiancée on the steps of the church. This was the signal for the farewells, exhortations and tears to begin:

'What will become of us without our little countess?' moaned the old nanny.

'I shall die of sorrow without you!' said Tanya.

Dr Behrs, who was ill, stayed behind in his office, so Mrs Behrs blessed her daughter with the icon of St Sofya the Martyr. Then Sonya, leaving her parents at home as was the custom, climbed into the coach and set off alone for the Church of the Nativity of the Virgin, a stone's-throw away. She cried all the way. Through a veil of tears she saw the winter garden, Tolstoy standing in formal black and stiff white shirtfront, the illuminated nave, a crowd of strangers whispering as she passed. ... The service was celebrated by two priests in heavy gold- and silver-embroidered dalmatics. The court choirs sang hymns of hope. Behind the couple, the groomsmen took turns holding the wedding crown. One of them, decked out in the handsome uniform of the horse guards, was none other than Mitrofan Polivanov, the rejected suitor. Majestic in his restrained suffering, he had accepted this final sacrifice for love of Sonya. She, however, was so exhausted that she began to grow numb. 'It seemed to me,' she wrote, 'that some event was taking place as fatal and inevitable as an act of God and that there was no longer any need to think.'[9]

After the ceremony, intimate friends gathered in the Behrs' apartment to wish the young couple long life and happiness. More champagne and bonbons. The time to change from her tulle gown into a dark blue woollen travelling costume, and Sonya announced that she was ready to leave. Tolstoy's brother Sergey had come to Moscow to pay

his respects to his future sister-in-law and then gone to
Yasnaya Polyana, the day before the wedding, to help Aunt
Toinette with the preparations for the newlyweds' arrival.
The Behrs' old chambermaid Varvara, nicknamed 'the
Oyster', was to accompany her little mistress to the country.
She would be all that was left to Sonya of her girlhood.

At the moment of departure, the drawing-room resounded
with tragic lamentations. The entire family was sobbing.
One might think the young bride was being led off to the
torture chamber. In the midst of this concert of wailing
Tolstoy stood silent and restless. When Lisa came up to kiss
her sister, Sonya looked long and hard at her. Tears swam
in the eyes of the girl who had been left behind. After the
Russian custom, everyone sat for a minute of silence, commending the travellers to God. After this unspoken prayer,
they all stood up again and the well-wishing, exhortations,
benedictions and signs of the cross resumed louder than
before.

Outside in the night, an immense *dormeuse* stood waiting, harnessed to a team of six post horses and driven by a
coachman and postilion. It was raining. The lanterns' light
gleamed in the puddles. The black trunks, strapped and
roped, were loaded on to the roof. As Tolstoy kept looking
impatiently at his watch, Sonya tore herself from her
mother's embrace and climbed into the coach without looking back. A loud cry pierced his ears. Mrs Behrs was still
calling her daughter! Quick! Tolstoy sat down beside his
wife and slammed the door. Alexis, the valet, and the servant Varvara, the Oyster, clambered up on to the outside
seats. The heavy vehicle lumbered off in the rain.*

Inside the dark, narrow, roughly jolting box Sonya continued to cry. She heard the rain drumming on the roof,
the horses' hoofs splashing through puddles, the bitter wind
blowing under the door; now and then, the livid glow of a
lantern shone through the deluge around her; everything

* Tolstoy used all the incidents of his engagement and wedding in
Anna Karenina.

seemed sodden, deathly cold, weird and frightening. Separated from her family for the first time in her life, her flesh crawled in terror of this bearded old man beside her, who had now acquired dreadful powers over her of which she knew absolutely nothing. It was not for nothing that she had called him Dublitsky in her story: Dublitsky, the double man, capable of the best and the worst. As she sighed and turned away, he remarked that she must not love him very much, since it made her so miserable to leave her family. She could not reply, and so he turned away too.

However, at the relay at Biryulevo he tried to dispel their malaise and became tender and even gay. In honour of this young couple with the distinguished name who had driven up in the brand-new *dormeuse*, the innkeeper offered to open the tsar's chambers for them: a vast, gloomy apartment full of furniture upholstered in red rep. In this garish and pompous setting, Sonya's discomfort increased. Cowering in a corner of the sofa, she remained silent, 'like a person condemned to death'. A woman brought in the samovar.

'Well,' said Tolstoy, 'wouldn't you like to do the honours; how about serving tea? ...'

Sonya obeyed. Her movements were awkward. She didn't dare to use the familiar form of address to her husband, or even call him by his first name. Her flesh frozen, her mind in chaos, she was waiting for the moment when he would pounce upon her, throw her down on the bed and perform that hideous act, that pleasure he talked about so much in his diary. It was still raining. Coaches stopped in the post-house courtyard. Doors slammed, horses whinnied, grooms cursed. That was the night Tolstoy first possessed his young and terrified wife. Brutal and disillusioning combat between an experienced man and a virgin struggling to defend herself, weeping and imploring and then dropping back inert. The act over, he noted, for the record: 'She knows all. Simple. Biryulevo. Her terror. Something morbid.'

In the evening of 24 September the *dormeuse* drawn by

six muddy horses pulled up at the door of Yasnaya Polyana. Aunt Toinette, clutching the sacred image of the Annunciation to her bosom, came forward in the hall to welcome the new mistress. Sergey, Leo's brother, stood beside her holding the bread and salt of hospitality on a tray. Sonya bowed to the ground, made the sign of the cross, kissed the icon and embraced the old woman. Tolstoy followed suit. Then, arm in arm, they entered, as though a cathedral, the waiting house.

The next day Tolstoy wrote in his diary, 'Immense happiness. ... It is impossible that all this should end except with life itself.'

[14]

A Terrifying Happiness

SONYA was so young; he could not get over it. He watched her 'playing grown-up' and continually wanted to carry her off to their room and smother her with kisses. 'I lived for thirty-four years without knowing it was possible to love so much and be so happy,' he wrote on 28 September 1862, to his beloved Alexandra Tolstoy. 'I keep feeling as though I had stolen some undeserved, illegal happiness that was not meant for me.' He was even delighted by his first quarrel with his wife. After weeping as he consoled her in his arms, he went to write in his diary, 'She is exquisite, I love her more than ever.' Later, seeing her writing to her sister Tanya, he leaned over her shoulder and added a postscript: 'My dear Tanya, pity me, I have a stupid wife.' Sonya then added: 'He's the stupid one, Tanya!' Whereupon he continued: 'You must be deeply chagrined to learn that we are both stupid, but there is a good side to everything: we are very happy in our stupidity and would not wish to be otherwise.' 'But I *would* like him to be a little more intelligent,' concluded Sonya.

And they burst out laughing, delighted by this tomfoolery that showed the depth of their love. Yet Sonya was nothing less than a child-woman. She soon made up her mind that the house was going to be run her way. She did not like some of her husband's habits. For instance, he preferred to sleep like the muzhiks, rolled up in a blanket with his head on a leather cushion. She insisted that he sleep between sheets and use a pillow, like city folk. And the servants, who had been sleeping on the ground, in the corridors or hall or wherever they liked before she came, were each instructed to repair to a designated place for the night. How was one to teach obedience to this ignorant, immovable and slovenly horde? There was the cook: Nicholas Mikhailovich, the one who had played the flute in Prince Volkonsky's serf-orchestra.* When asked why he had traded his flute for a cookstove he sullenly replied, 'Because I lost my mouthpiece.' Often, he was too drunk to prepare the meal, and his feeble-minded helper Alyosha Gorshok took his place at the stove. Another remarkable character was Agatha Mikhailovna, the housekeeper, who was forever knitting a stocking as she walked and was so fond of animals that she could not swallow one bite of meat or step on a cockroach, and she gave milk to the mice and flies to the spiders. One of her duties was to bring up the innumerable litters of Tolstoy puppies, which she kept in her own revoltingly filthy room; she covered them with her own clothes to keep them warm and, if one was sick, lighted a candle for it before the icon of St Nicholas. Then there were Dunyasha, the buxom chambermaid, Alexis the valet, the laundress and her daughters, Vasily Ermilin the village elder, the red-headed coachman Indyushkin and all manner of assistants, apprentices, errand boys, sewing-women and charwomen, whose faces and names were hard to remember. Mild old Aunt Toinette had given them free rein for years; Sonya took them in hand with stern authority. Her furious pulls on the bell-rope roused them from their apathy. She scolded Dunyasha, Alyosha Gorshok and even Agatha Mikhailovna. Tolstoy was startled by the loud voices that penetrated the walls of his study, but he did not yet begin to worry. He could not imagine that his wife – so young! – might be difficult or hard to live with. Yet he did see that Aunt Toinette, dispossessed of her prerogatives as mistress of the house, was withering and fading away at the side of her inseparable companion Natalya Petrovna. The woman who had brought him up from infancy, known and pardoned all his youthful follies, jealously guarded his privacy when he grew up, was now withdrawing into the shadows,

* Like old Tikhon, who had been a footman in the time of Tolstoy's father.

feeling that her work was done. 'Aunt's face has suddenly begun to age, to my sorrow,' he wrote in his diary.[1]

Although Aunt Toinette had shrivelled away almost to nothing, the mere fact of her presence maintained an odour of debility and decrepitude about the house. Coming from her big, boisterous, jolly family, Sonya soon began to suffer from the tedium of life at Yasnaya Polyana. When the joy of discovery had worn off, she suddenly found herself very much alone. Her husband, preoccupied with the management of his estate, spent much of his time away in the country. The moment he was out of sight, she fell into a state of torpor. She took up her diary again; perhaps Tolstoy even encouraged her to do so. Naturally, she only felt like writing in moments of melancholy, so her recital spins out like an unfinished tapestry, from which the light threads are missing that would give relief to the pattern. 'This solitude weighs upon me terribly,' she wrote. 'There was so much animation at home and here, when Leo is gone, everything is so colourless. He has almost always lived alone and does not understand what I feel. ... There is never a joyful shout in this house. It is as though everyone were dead. ...' 'I feel guilty towards Aunt. I should have more consideration for her, if only because she cared for my husband when he was little and will care for my own children later. ...' 'I do not think I love Aunt, and that disturbs me. I am irritated by her age rather than touched by it. ...' 'Aunt is sweet and good-tempered, but I find it hard to be around her: she is old. ...'[2]

Sensing her difficulties, Aunt Toinette looked on in silence and pitied her. One evening when Tolstoy was away she came up to the young woman, took her hand and kissed it. 'Why?' wrote Sonya. 'I believe she has a kind heart, and it pains her to see me alone.'

To combat this stultifying atmosphere, Sonya threw herself into her work. With a bunch of heavy keys dangling from her belt, she sped from basement to attic, toured the farmyard, kept an eye on the milch-cows' yield, presided over the cucumber-pickling and kept the account books. And Tolstoy, after dismissing his stewards, decided he would manage the eighteen hundred acres that were left to him alone. Always eager to try any new-fangled agricultural gadget, he launched out into bee-keeping, setting up his hives over by the Zasyeka forest, planted apple trees in his orchard, tried growing cabbage on an industrial scale, built a distillery, had a go at sheep-farming, and imported some Japanese pigs he had seen at Shatilov the stockbreeder's. When the first consignment arrived, he exclaimed, 'What snouts! What an exotic breed!' and entrusted the precious specimens to the care of an old drunkard, one of his protégés whom he naïvely hoped to reform through work. But the swineherd did not appreciate the great favour that had been bestowed upon him, it offended him to be asked to take care of pigs, and he took his revenge by letting them starve to death. Tolstoy attributed their demise to an epidemic, and turned to new fields of exploration. 'My sole preoccupations are money and commonplace, pedestrian comfort,' he confessed.[3] And Sonya echoed, 'Can it be that he cares for nothing but money, managing the estate and running the distillery? When he is not eating, sleeping or being silent, he is loping about on business, running, running, always alone.'[4]

Fet, the poet, called at Yasnaya Polyana one day and found the master of the domain directing a team of men who were seining the pond for carp. Completely absorbed in the delicate business of placing the nets, Tolstoy greeted his guest distractedly and called to his wife, who came running dressed all in white, with her heavy keys jangling at her waist. To gain time, she leaped over a hedge.

'What are you doing, countess?' cried Fet. 'You must be careful!'

'It's nothing, I'm used to it,' she answered.

And when Tolstoy ordered a sack brought from the storehouse, she detached a key from her ring and gave it to a boy who sped away like an arrow:

'There!' said Tolstoy. 'You see our method at work: keep the keys on one's person and send the youngsters to do the work.'

The youngsters were particularly easy to come by, since the village schools had been closed. On 1 October 1862, immediately after his return to Yasnaya Polyana, he wrote: 'Have said good-bye to the students and the common people.' And a fortnight later: 'Decided to give up the review; the schools too.' Surprising decision from a man who, a short time before, had been claiming that the education of the peasants was the supreme goal of his life. Once again, without the slightest hesitation, he took a stand directly opposed to his previous position. His passion for teaching was followed by utter indifference to education in any form. He allowed his associates to continue for a few weeks, but without any supervision or counsel, and then he dismissed them. 'The students are going away,' he wrote on 29 December 1862. 'And I feel sorry for them.' They had all scented the danger, moreover, when they saw Tolstoy arriving with his child-bride dressed in city clothes. They could not understand how he had married an upper-class girl after declaring that 'to marry a woman of society is to swallow the whole poison of civilization'. Sonya immediately felt their animosity, and was on her guard. To her the school, the muzhiks, the long-haired students with their equalitarian theories were just so many sworn enemies of her love. Since her husband was attracted to them, she must fight them. With remarkable intuition she wrote in her diary, two months after her marriage: 'He makes me sick, with his 'people'! I feel he is going to have to choose between the family, which I personify, and those people he loves so passionately. It's selfish of me? Well, too bad. I live for him and by him and I want it to be the same for him. If I am not interesting to him, if I'm only a plaything, not a *human being*, then I neither can nor will go on living like this.' To force him to choose between her and his muzhiks, she ran away and hid in the garden. 'One feels so free outdoors!

... He has come out, he's looking for me, he is worried.' After winning the battle of the students' dismissal, she began to be alarmed by the ease of her victory. Would he remain faithful to her, if he could so readily abjure what he had once worshipped? 'He loves me just as he has loved the school, nature, the people, perhaps literature as well, one after the other. Then the craze passes and he becomes enamoured of something else.'[5]

To justify this latest switch in his own eyes, Tolstoy now affirmed that his interest in popular education had been nothing but 'an exaggerated impulse of youth, no more nor less than exhibitionism' and that he could not continue it now that he had 'come of age'. He added: 'She has done it all. She does not know, she does not understand that she has changed me far more than I have changed her.'

After disposing of the schools, Sonya's next move was to sweep out the sentimental cobwebs that clung to her husband. She had read his diary, she knew about his past, and she did not like to inhale the reminders of it that eddied around her. To begin with, she could not abide Leo's tender affection for his dear aunt, his little grandmother, his *babushka* Alexandra Tolstoy. The more he praised the noble soul, sensitivity, piety, intelligence and culture of the old maid of honour, the more he annoyed his wife, who felt inferior to this paragon of all the virtues. 'She does not want to write to the aunts at court,' he sorrowfully noted on 1 October 1862. And he added, marvelling at her perceptiveness, 'She senses everything.' Four days of persuasion were required to induce the bride to produce her letter of convention, written in French:

'Leo has spoken to me about you so often that I have already grown to love you and I treasure your affection for my husband ...'

The sentences followed each other with artificial elegance. Her heart was clearly not in it. She signed: 'Countess Sofya Tolstoy.' Upon reading over this classroom theme, Tolstoy felt how cold it was and added a postscript in his own hand, by way of apology:

I am not at all happy with the letter Sonya has written to you, my dear friend Alexandra, and I know your personal relationship will be a very different matter. ... You understand that I cannot tell you the truth about her now, for fear of being carried away and lending fuel to the sceptics' fire. I can only say that her most striking feature is that of a 'man of integrity' – I mean what I say: both 'integrity' and 'man'. ... What a dreadful responsibility it is to live with another person! ... She is reading what I write to you and understands nothing – refuses to understand (Besides, she doesn't need to understand!) that state we men reach after wrestling with a long, laborious and painful series of doubts and sufferings ...

Whereupon Sonya interrupted, and wrote:

'I cannot let that pass, dear Aunt. He is wrong, I understand everything, absolutely everything that has to do with him, and his letter is gloomy because he has a headache and is in a bad mood.'

At the bottom of the page Tolstoy merely commented, 'There, you see!' And the missive went off as it was, bittersweet, evasive, odd. Reading it, Alexandra understood that the bride had determined to clear the air around her husband, and did not need to be told twice. She wrote an amiable, formal letter in reply and signed it, 'Your old Aunt.'

Reassured on that score, Sonya conceded a few months later that Alexandra was a remarkable person. 'I would not mind if they continued to correspond,' she wrote, 'but I should hate Alexandra to think that Leo's wife had nothing more to recommend her than an easy-going nature, barely competent to be a children's nursemaid. No matter how jealous I am of Leo, jealous of his heart, I know Alexandra cannot be rubbed out of his life. Besides, she must not be removed from it. She has played a pretty part, one I am incapable of playing. ... I should so like to know her better! Would she find me worthy of him? ... Since reading Leo's letters to her, I have been thinking about her constantly. I might even like her ...'[7]

Tolstoy's letters to Alexandra, of which he kept the drafts, were not the only ones Sonya read. In his effort to be completely honest, he let her explore all his correspondence to her heart's content. She bore his name, she shared his bed, and so she was entitled to know everything about him. Thus she renewed her acquaintance with Valerya Arsenyev, of whom she had already had a glimpse in her fiancé's diary. She immediately saw that this was not a dangerous rival. 'Pretty but insignificant,' she noted. And she applauded Tolstoy's moral exhortations to the girl: 'I recognize him in every line. The same principle, the same striving after the good. ... Reading those letters I felt no jealousy at all, as though Valerya were not some other woman he may have cared for, but myself. ... It was not Valerya he loved, but love and goodness.'[8] Her indulgence towards this harmless spectre of the past vanished, however, when it encountered Axinya, the peasant who had been Tolstoy's mistress for three years before his marriage. An illegitimate child, Timothy, had been born during their affair, and it was the general opinion that he greatly resembled Tolstoy. The mother and her boy lived in a hamlet close to the main house. Every time Sonya passed them, she felt a fresh surge of protest and depression. How had her husband been able to find pleasure in caressing that blowsy and probably unclean female? Was the animal instinct in men so powerful that anybody would do to satisfy them? To think that Leo had written about the creature in his diary! And in flattering terms, too! 'She is very fine. ... I am in love as I have never been before. ... The feeling is no longer bestial, but that of a husband for his wife.'[9] Countess Tolstoy, stepping into the shoes of a village trollop! One day Sonya recognized Axinya among the women scouring the floor in the house. Choking with rage, she drowned Tolstoy in reproaches, and wrote that evening, with trembling hand: 'I believe I shall kill myself one day out of jealousy. "In love as

I have never been before!" And with whom? A fat peasant, a vulgar woman with white skin. It's ghastly! The sight of the sword and gun comforted me. Just one shot, it's so easy! As long as I have no children! ... And to think the woman is there, a few steps away from us! I am quite simply losing my mind. I shall go for a drive. Maybe I shall meet her. How he loved her! If only I could burn his diary and his past with it.'[10]

Axinya and her child pursued Sonya even in her nightmares. One night she dreamed she was having an argument with the insolent woman, who had put on 'a black silk dress' to provoke her. A murderous wave swept over her brain. In her dream she indulged the lust for vengeance which she knew she could not satisfy awake. The scene was so horrible that when she awoke the next morning, she recorded it in her diary in all its gory detail. 'Suddenly I was in such a rage that I seized her child and tore it limb from limb,' she wrote. 'I tore off its legs, its arms, its head. I was in a frenzy of anger. And at that moment, Lyovochka arrived.[11] I told him they were going to deport me to Siberia, but he picked up the scattered limbs and comforted me, telling me it was only a doll. I looked, and lo and behold, instead of a body I saw nothing but a few strips of deerskin and lumps of cotton wadding. I was very cross.'[12] Sonya wrote of her hatred of Axinya several times in her diary: 'It upsets me dreadfully whenever I think of her.'[13] 'That disgusting woman again. How does she dare to keep turning up in front of me all the time?'[14] Then, obsessed by jealousy, she persuaded herself that her husband could not look at a peasant without sleeping with her. To test him, she disguised herself as a common woman, tied a scarf down over her eyes, and ran after him on the road. She was certain he would take her for someone else and motion her to follow him into the bushes. But she could not find which way he had gone and came home worn out and embarrassed by her get-up.

Besides, she did not need a flesh-and-blood rival to arouse her jealousy. She had only to read Tolstoy's books for her wifely dignity to feel offended by the sensuality of some of his descriptions. The words of love, the kisses exchanged by his characters made her flush with shame as though Lyovochka had put on an obscene exhibition of himself in front of a crowd. She was tormented by the thought that the sexual joy he attributed to one or another of his heroes was merely an echo of the pleasure he had himself known with someone else. 'I read the beginning of his book,' she wrote on 16 December 1862.[15] 'Every time he speaks of love or women I have such an awful feeling, such loathing, that I could burn the whole thing. I want nothing to remind me of his past! And I would not even spare his writing, for jealousy has made me terribly selfish.' And she ended her confession with this chilling sentence: 'If I could kill him and create another new person exactly like him, I should do it with pleasure.'

And yet, by a strange inconsistency in her nature, the intensity of her jealousy of the other women in her husband's life was equalled only by her indifference to his passion for herself. She was flattered to see that she aroused such powerful desire in him. But when he took her in his arms, she turned to stone. Passive and attentive, she followed the signs of amorous disarray on his panting countenance with a mixture of curiosity and terror. At the end of the struggle, she felt bruised and soiled; he was happy. 'When he embraces me,' she wrote, 'I think that I am not the first woman he has crushed to him in the same way. ... It is bitter and painful to think that my husband is like the rest of the world. ...' (8 October 1862.) 'All this commerce of the flesh is repellent.' (9 October 1862.) 'The physical side of love plays a very big role for him, and none at all for me.' (29 April 1863.) At first, though shocked by his ardent virility, she kept her revulsion to herself. A shrewd feminine instinct warned her that by showing a semblance of pleasure she might increase her hold over Lyovochka. The inconvenience of being mauled about now and then was a small price to pay for the satisfaction of dominating a man.

He, however, was not unduly worried by his wife's bashfulness. On the contrary, everything that was young and virginal about her excited him. The master subduer of farmgirls was presumably having his first taste of the delights of profaning more refined flesh. His confidences to his diary were becoming a hymn to wedded bliss:

I love her when, at night or early in the morning, I wake up and find her looking tenderly at me. Nobody – and I less than anyone else – can prevent her now from loving me in her own way, the way she wants to. I love her when she is sitting close to me and we are both feeling that we love each other with all our strength. She says, 'Lyovochka,' and adds, after a pause, 'Why are stovepipes set on straight?' Or, 'Why do horses have such a hard life?' etc. I love her when, after we have been silent together for a long time, I finally say, 'Well, Sonya, what shall we do now?' And she laughs. I love her when she is angry with me and suddenly widens her eyes and tries to look mean and nasty and snarls, 'Leave me alone! You're bothering me!' And the next minute she is smiling shyly at me. ... I love her when, a little girl in a yellow dress, she shoves her chin forward and sticks out her tongue at me. I love to see her head thrown back, her face solemn and frightened, her passionate child's face. I love her when ...[16]

Sometimes his exultation was so intense that he became worried, as though God had given him a gift by mistake and were about to snatch it away from him: 'Just lately, we felt that there was something terrifying in our happiness. ... We started to pray.' (1 March 1863.) And a little later: 'I love her more and more. Today, after seven months, a feeling of humility that I had not had for a long time came over me in her presence. She is ineffably pure, and good, and virginal in my eyes. At those times I feel that I do not possess her, even though she gives all of herself to me. I do not possess her because I dare not, I do not feel worthy. I am anxious; that is why my happiness is not complete. Something keeps tormenting me: I am jealous of the man who could be entirely worthy of her. I am not.' (24 March 1863.) Sonya's youth and grace made him over-sensitive. She was afraid she would lose him because of his excessive sexual demands, but he was afraid he would lose her because of her predilection for flirting. One day he had been alarmed because she was paying too much attention to young Erlenwein, one of the student teachers at Yasnaya Polyana. Another time a young man named Pisarev came out from Moscow to spend some time with them; Leo found him over-assiduous in his attentions to Sonya and suddenly announced, without any explanation, that his carriage was at the door to take him back to the city.

The fact was that Tolstoy, who claimed to be so broad-minded, was extremely old-fashioned when it came to women. A champion of freedom outside the home, he applied the principles of tyranny under his roof. According to him, a wife should abandon all interest in her appearance, turn her back on the 'futilities of society' and devote herself to running the household, educating her children and distracting her husband. The very qualities that had attracted him to Sonya unwed – her gaiety, spontaneity, elegance, eagerness to amuse herself and please others – now seemed incompatible with the position she had acquired at Yasnaya Polyana. If she changed her dress or did her hair differently, he accused her of frivolity. This made her rebellious; she felt like 'flirting with someone', 'losing my temper with a chair', 'going to a ball', or 'kicking up my heels, instead of going upstairs to bed'. 'I am surrounded by decrepitude. Everyone I see is old. I try to restrain every sign of youth because it seems so out of place in this staid and sedate atmosphere. ... Lyovochka's only occupation in life is to tell me "That's enough!"'[17] At such moments she was sorry she had left Moscow. 'Dearest Maman, dearest Tanya, how sweet they were! Why did I abandon them? I made poor Lisa suffer horribly and now I feel guilty when I remember.'[18] She called her husband a 'kill-joy', she complained that she was growing 'numb', she wrote: 'I have a wild desire to escape from his influence, which I sometimes

find oppressive, and not to care about him any more.'[19]
And yet, as soon as he left to inspect the farm or attend to
some business in Tula, she was lost. A thousand wild ideas
tormented her: he no longer loved her, perhaps he was being unfaithful to her, she was not worthy of him, he was not
worthy of her. ... But he came back. Ecstasy: 'He still loves
me! His expression is so gentle, so humble, the eyes of a
saint!' She had hardly finished purring over him, though,
when she began moaning over her fate again. Her lightning
changes of mood were enough to astonish Tolstoy, himself
a sufficiently unstable character. To balance the impetuous
side of his own nature, he thought, a forbearing and even-
tempered partner was what he needed. And here he was with
a wife who delighted in analysing herself, discussing herself,
pitying herself, switching from anxiety to effervescence, love
to loathing, tears to laughter with hair-raising speed, provoking thunderstorms in order to bask in the ensuing lull.
Sometimes she wanted to be 'more permeable to her husband's influence', and sometimes she was afraid she no
longer saw anything 'except through his eyes', which put
her in 'a position of inferiority'; sometimes she insisted how
happy she was to live in the shadow of a great man, and
sometimes she exclaimed, 'I have a senseless and involuntary desire to test my power over him; that is, I want to
make him obey me'; sometimes she found him too cold, and
at others too forward; sometimes he seemed 'old', 'odious',
'boring', 'selfish', and at others she confessed, 'There are
moments – and they are not rare – when I am sick with love
of him. ... It hurts me to look at him or hear him or be near
him, as it must hurt a devil to be near a saint.'[20]

The rhythm of their periods of love, suspicion and resentment was unfortunately syncopated, which gave rise to tem-
pestuous outbursts. What complicated their relations was that
each had given the other permission to read his diary, and
thus their private confessions unconsciously turned into arguments of prosecution or defence. All too often, they set
down on paper what they had not dared to say out loud.

Then, with their own conscience at rest, they awaited results
with morbid curiosity. 'Lyovochka has said nothing and has
not made the slightest allusion to my diary. Has he read it?
I don't know. What I wrote is vile and I don't like to read it
over.'²¹ The result of this practice was that the couple lived
on two levels, one of speech and the other of writing. Decisions won by one of them in the lower court were appealed
by the other in the upper. They could hardly have striven
more mightily to bare their naked souls if their chief object
had been to become thoroughly disgusted with each other.
The miracle is that their marriage stood the strain of this
continual rivalry to see which could be most truthful.

As Sonya complained of being lonely Tolstoy agreed,
after three months of marriage, to go to Moscow with her.
She was very eager to see her family again, but to avoid tension with Lisa it was decided that the young couple would
not stay at the Behrs', but at the Hotel Chevrier on Gazet-
naya Street behind the University. The moment Sonya arrived, on 23 December 1862, her enthusiasm collapsed. Oh,
she was glad to see her parents and brothers again, and her
mischievous Tanya whom Tolstoy cheerily addressed in the
familiar form, and even Lisa, who showed nothing of her
chagrin; but she no longer felt at home among these people
who had previously been her whole world. Her hopes and
cares were elsewhere. Back in her childhood circle, she
had the impression that she was wasting time. 'Maman is
right, I have grown dull,' she wistfully wrote. 'I miss my
former liveliness.' Parties and society no longer interested
her. She often let Tolstoy go off by himself to visit his
friends, and waited for him in their hotel room, dreaming
of Yasnaya Polyana in the snow. 'Let us hurry back to Yasnaya Polyana, where Lyovochka lives more with me and for
me, and where I am alone with Auntie and him,' she wrote.
'I adore that life and would not change it for any other.'²²
And Moscow was a disappointment to him, too. Everything
irritated him. He was jealous because Sonya had seen handsome Mitrofan Polivanov again, who had almost been her

fiancé. Of course, after his tantrum, he begged her to forgive him. 'We patched things up as best we could,' he wrote. 'I am always annoyed with myself on such occasions, mostly because of the kisses, which are just false plaster. ... After dinner the plaster cracked. Tears, fits of nerves. The best proof that I love her is that I was not angry. It is hard for me to stay home with her alone. I see that she is unhappy, but I am still more unhappy myself and can say nothing to help her; besides, there is nothing to say.'[23] But if he came home late, it was her turn to attack: 'It will soon be three o'clock and he is still not back. Why did he promise? Is it fair for him to be so unpunctual?'[24] And: 'Lyovochka has seen fit to impress upon me that he cannot be content with family life, he needs other distractions.'[25] And as she was writing this in her diary, he tiptoed into the room, took the pen out of her fingers and added in his own hand, 'I need nothing and no one, except you.' That was enough to keep her smiling for the rest of the evening, but the next day her doubts and fits of temper and anxiety returned. She did have some excuse: for the last few weeks she had known she was pregnant. A feeling of mingled pride and fear took root in her heart.

On 8 February 1863 she set out with her husband for Yasnaya Polyana and the unvarying routine of country life, poorly lighted, half-heated rooms, slovenly servants, whining Aunt Toinette, and the blank, interminable hours spent waiting for Lyovochka, who was out looking after the estate or beating the forest, gun in hand. In Moscow the writer's friends had reproached him for neglecting his writing. After some hesitation, he finished *Polikushka*, which he had started in Brussels, and began the tale of a horse – a piebald gelding named Kholstomer (Strider). The idea for the story had been given to him by his friend Alexander Stakhovich, whose brother Michael owned a stud farm and used to listen to the tales of a doting groom. This long story proved so difficult to write that the author abandoned it and did not finish it until twenty-two years later.[26] The final version bore the stamp of Tolstoy's subsequent spiritual development: at first the author had only wanted to pierce the secrets of the soul of an animal; but afterwards, when he returned to the piebald gelding who tells the story of his life, he sought and achieved a brilliant analysis of the problem of the interdependence of all beings, the master's rights over the slave, the injustice implicit in any form of ownership, and the ultimate imperatives of every individual. The piebald cannot grasp the fact that he is regarded as a piece of property: 'The words "my horse", spoken in relation to me, a living horse, seem as strange as it would be to say "my earth", "my air", "my water". ... Men have agreed among themselves that a single object can be called "mine" by one person only. And, under the rules of this game, he who can say "mine" of the largest number of objects is counted the most fortunate.' But for the horse, as for Tolstoy, every creature of God belongs to God alone. Suffering from his menial position, his ugliness, age and frustrated ambition, Kholstomer nevertheless leads an exemplary existence in comparison with his master. Even the poor old nag's death serves some purpose – a she-wolf and her cubs eat his carcass – while the man, after spending his life in total idleness, continues to be a general nuisance even as he breathes his last: a grotesque, debauched, fatuous figure who will be dressed up in a fine uniform and put into a wooden box, then in a coffin of lead, and a great deal of money will be spent on a mass in his memory. 'Neither his skin nor his flesh nor his bones could be used for anything,' wrote Tolstoy with tragic savagery.

Having given up the idea of publishing the first version of *Kholstomer*, he turned his energies to correcting the proofs of *The Cossacks*, the first part of which he had promised to deliver to Katkov.* 'Abysmally weak,' he noted. 'But it will please the public for that very reason.' His mind was whirling with projects, but none succeeded in capturing his fancy entirely. He toyed with the idea of describing the fate

* This 'first part' was the only part Tolstoy wrote.

of a young pro-Western professor vitiated by his false culture; or a husband with high ideals of marriage, whose wife could not resist the appeal of 'waltzes and tinsel and the poesy of the passing moment'. Then, just to amuse himself, he dashed off two little plays, *The Nihilist* and *The Infected Family*. The first was produced in the family circle at Yasnaya Polyana, and all the parts were played by women. The audience howled with laughter at Marya Tolstoy, dressed up as an old bigot, contorting her features and making signs of the cross while the hero spewed revolutionary slogans. She invented lines and added them to her part, to the author's delight. He hoped his second play, *The Infected Family* – a rather heavy satire on nihilism and feminism – might be produced by the Moscow Little Theatre, but the managers turned it down the following year.*

At Yasnaya Polyana, the first warm days brought a flock of visitors: charming Tanya Behrs, old friend Dyakov, Fet the poet and his wife Marya Petrovna, Samarin, Bibikov, Sergey Tolstoy on a neighbourly call from Pirogovo. ... Improvised theatricals, musical evenings, picnics, charades, readings ... In spite of all the movement and laughter in the house, Sonya was bored, with her heavy stomach, drawn face and frayed temper. She cursed her pregnancy for preventing her from going to look at the bees or walk in the forest with Lyovochka. 'Lyova resents my weakness, as though it were my fault that I am pregnant,' she wrote in her diary. Or, 'My condition is intolerable to me, both physically and emotionally. ... And I have ceased to exist for Lyova. ... I can give him no joy, since I am pregnant.'[27] She thought of him crouching in front of a hive with the net over his head, or striding down a path, or bantering with a peasant woman leaning over a fence, and every moment he spent away from her seemed torn out of her own life. Even the thought of the child she was carrying

* Ostrovsky, the dramatist, to whom Tolstoy read the play in 1864, wrote to Nekrasov: 'It is such a piece of filth that my ears blenched during the reading!'

could not reconcile her to her fate. A lot of good it would do her to become a mother if she were to lose her husband as a result! Sometimes, wild with frustration, she wanted to get rid of her encumbrance: 'Yesterday I ran through the garden, thinking I would surely have a miscarriage,' she wrote. And concluded with cold regret: 'But nature is as strong as steel.'[28]

Although he sympathized with her, Tolstoy found her tears, her persecuted smiles and senseless chatter hard to bear. It seemed to him that it was somehow her fault if he could not settle down to write. When he could take no more, he fled to nature to be alone with his problems. He anxiously questioned himself: he had never had any friend or confidant other than himself, and now he was suddenly supposed to share everything, his thoughts, his freedom, his life, with the being least calculated to understand him: a woman. Even though he tried to put Sonya temporarily out of his mind, he could not forget that she would reproach him for bolting out of the house with his dogs, would be waiting for him, weeping, with her forehead pressed against the windowpane, and that he would feel guilty afterwards. Was he going to disintegrate completely – mind, will, talent – in this paralysing conjugal atmosphere? 'Where is it – my old self,' he wrote on 18 June 1863, 'the self I loved and knew, who still springs to the surface sometimes and pleases and frightens me? I have become petty and insignificant. And, what is worse, it has happened since my marriage to a woman I love. Nearly every word in this notebook is prevarication and hypocrisy. The thought that she is still here now, reading over my shoulder, stifles and perverts my sincerity. ... I must add words for her because she will read them. For her I write not what is not true, but things I would not write for myself alone. ... It is appalling, dreadful, insane, to allow one's happiness to depend upon purely material things: a wife, children, health, wealth ...'

When Sonya read these lines, intended for her eyes, they probably sent her into a fresh paroxysm of despair. Why

suffer all these months of fatigue and nausea, missing all the
fun of life, if Lyovochka did not even want the child she
was preparing to bring into the world? On 27 June, in the
dead of night, the first pains came. Tolstoy ran to fetch the
midwife from Tula. When he returned, Sonya was pacing
up and down in her bedroom, 'in a peignoir open over her
lace-inset gown, her black hair in disorder, her face afire,
her dark eyes shining with extraordinary intensity'. How
beautiful she was, with her expression of suffering, shy reserve and majesty! He helped her to stretch out on the
leather couch on which he himself had been born. Touching her half-naked body gave him a feeling completely
unlike any he had ever known in other circumstances: not
desire, but compassion, and incisive attention to every detail,
the curiosity of a professional writer eager to learn something new. But when the pains began to come more quickly,
he lost his self-possession. He could not recognize Sonya in
this 'screaming and writhing' female. She pressed his hand
weakly between contractions. The midwife, the Polish doctor sitting in the corner smoking cigarettes, the candles
burning in their sockets, the smell of vinegar and eau-de-
Cologne, the twisted sheets, rags, basins, it was all part of
a nightmare. Suddenly there was a terrible heaving and
thrashing around the leather couch. The midwife and doctor were bending over a slaughter. A sharp cry cut through
the jerking gasps of the mother. The doctor said, 'It's a
boy!' Tolstoy saw a tiny creature, 'strange and reddish',
with a big soft head. Remembering the scene, he wrote in
Anna Karenina, 'Levin had to make an enormous effort to
believe that his wife was still alive, that she was all right,
that this wailing baby was his son. . . . Why this child? Who
was he? Where did he come from? He had great difficulty
in accepting the idea. It took him a long time to get used to
it.'

When Tanya Behrs was allowed into the room, she saw
Tolstoy 'white-faced and red-eyed with weeping', and Sonya
'appeared tired, but happy and proud'. [29] Champagne was

drunk. They decided to call the child Sergey, after his uncle. Receiving his family's congratulations, Tolstoy was surprised to find that he felt neither joy nor pride but a sort of apprehension, as though from that day on there were 'another area of vulnerability' in his life. Wouldn't this added source of care drive him still farther away from himself and his work? The only good thing about the birth, he thought, was that Sonya, filled with the new joy of motherhood, would become even-tempered and cheerful once more. He was prepared to worship her, if only she would behave like a proper wife again.

It was he, however, who started their first quarrel. As befits a true disciple of Rousseau, he believed that all mothers should nurse their babies. Sonya herself agreed, although paid wetnurses were more the custom in her circle. But from the beginning, she suffered excruciating pain. Her breasts were soon fissured and the doctors ordered her to stop. Tolstoy protested vehemently, in the name of nature, against 'official pretexts' that allowed a young mother to shirk her obligations; he asserted that his wife was spoiled and soft, her mind perverted by civilization, and he demanded that she fulfill her role as giver-of-life to the bitter end. When Sonya, exhausted, engaged a nurse, he refused to enter the nursery because he could not bear to see the heir to his name suspended from the breast of a strange woman. Why must a common girl be able to perform what Countess Tolstoy considered beyond her strength?

Exasperated by his son-in-law's irrational obstinacy, Dr Behrs wrote to the couple:

I see you have both lost your wits. . . . Be reasonable, dear Sonya, calm yourself, don't make a mountain out of a molehill. . . . As for you, dear Leo Nikolayevich, rest assured that you will never be transformed into a real muzhik, any more than your wife will be able to endure what a Pelagya can endure. . . . And you, Tanya, do not let your mad sister out of your sight for one moment, scold her as often as possible for her crazy notions that are enough to try the patience of the Lord, and pitch the first

object that comes to hand straight at Leo's head, to knock some
sense into it. He is a great master at speechifying and literature,
but life is another matter. Let him write a story about a husband who tortures his sick wife by forcing her to nurse her baby.
He will be stoned by every woman alive.

Neither Dr Behrs' letter nor Sonya's tears nor the gentle
remonstrances of Tanya made any dent in Tolstoy's dogged
disapproval. He could not look at his wife without finding
fault with her. In his diary – which she read – he sarcastically called her 'the countess':

I arrive in the morning, full of joy and gladness, and I find
the countess in a tantrum while Dunyasha, the chambermaid, is
combing her hair; seeing her thus I mistake her for Mashenka *
on one of her bad days, everything collapses, and I stand there
as though I had been scalded. I am afraid of everything and I
see that there can be no happiness or poetry for me except when
I am alone. I am kissed tenderly, out of habit, but then the
quarrels resume immediately, with Dunyasha, Auntie, Tanya, me.
... One o'clock in the morning already, and I can't sleep at all,
much less in her room with her, when I have such a weight on
my heart; she will begin to whine and moan as soon as she
knows there is someone to listen; just now she is snoring peacefully away. She will wake up absolutely convinced that I am
wrong and she is the most unfortunate woman alive. ... And
the worst of it is that I must hold my tongue and sulk, however
much I execrate and despise such a situation.[30]

And, pen in hand, Sonya exhaled her despair:
'It is monstrous not to nurse one's child! Well, who says it
isn't? But what can I do in the face of a physical impossibility? ... He would banish me from the earth because I am
suffering and not doing my duty, and I cannot bear him because he is not suffering and he is writing. ... How can one
love a fly that will not stop tormenting one? ... I shall
take care of my son and do everything I can, but not for
Lyova, certainly, because he deserves to get evil in return for
evil.'

* Marya, Tolstoy's sister.

After letting off steam, she melted, and ended: 'It's starting to rain. I am afraid he will catch cold. My irritation has vanished. I love him. God protect him.' [31] Sincere statement or subtle manoeuvre? As soon as he had read these lines Tolstoy, deeply touched, wanted to retract what he had written and added, below her entry: 'Sonya, forgive me ... I was cruel and crude. And to whom? To the person who has given me the greatest joy in my life and the only one who loves me. ... Sonya, my darling, I am guilty, but I am wretched too. There is an excellent man in me, but sometimes he is asleep. Love him, Sonya, and do not criticize him.' A fresh quarrel broke out immediately afterwards, he snatched up the notebook and furiously crossed out what he had just written. And at the bottom of the desecrated page Sonya, the tears welling in her eyes, added: 'I had deserved those few lines of tenderness and repentance, but in a moment of anger he took them away from me before I had even read them.'

Nursing his resentment, Tolstoy sought a pretext – any pretext – for getting away from the house. An insurrection had broken out in Poland and he already had visions of himself taking up arms to put down the rebels whom France, England and Austria had the effrontery to support. 'What do you think of the Polish business?' he wrote to Fet. 'It looks bad, doesn't it? Maybe you and Borisov and I shall have to take down our swords from their rusty nails.' [32] It little mattered to the future anti-autocrat that Marion Langiewicz's rebels were idealists ready to die for independence. As a loyal subject of the tsar, he put his faith in the wisdom of the government. The fact was that he wanted to enlist less to exterminate the Poles than to get away from his wife. He later made Prince Andrey say, in *War and Peace*, 'I am going to the war because the life I am leading here does not suit me.' [33] And elsewhere, 'Marry as late as possible, when you're no good for anything else. Or else everything good and noble in you will be lost. You will be submerged by triviality. ... If, now, you expect anything from the future, then you will feel at every step that all is finished, that for you it's all over.' [34]

Keeping these thoughts to himself, he set out to convince Sonya that he should go. But – whether out of utter absent-mindedness or archfiendish cruelty – he selected the eve of their first wedding anniversary to inform her of his designs. Stupefied, she burst into dire imprecations, first to him and then to her diary:

> To war. What is this latest whim? Irresponsibility? No, not that, sheer instability! ... Everything in him is whim and passing fancy! Today he gets married, the idea appeals to him, he has children. Tomorrow he has a hankering to go off to war and he abandons us. All I can do is hope the child will die, for I shall not live after Lyova. I do not believe in such enthusiasm and love of the fatherland in a man of thirty-five. As though children weren't the fatherland, as though they weren't Russian too! He is ready to neglect them because he thinks it's fun to go galloping about on a horse and admire the war and hear the shells whistling past.[35]

The mere act of imagining that he would soon be engaged in battle was enough to bring Tolstoy back to earth. Having thrown Sonya, Aunt Toinette and all his friends into a dither, he felt better. Besides, there wasn't going to be any war. While the Western powers were still planning their campaign, the uprising had been quelled. They were already hanging the instigators. Reassured, the future apostle of universal peace contemplated his married life and concluded that it was not so bad as he had thought: 'It is over,' he wrote on 6 October 1863. 'There was nothing true in it. I am happy with her; but I am dreadfully unhappy with myself. ... My choice has been made for a long time: letters, art, education and family.'

Contrary to his affirmations, Tolstoy was not giving education a thought, having closed the schools and let most of the teachers go. And as for his family, he hoped he would not be required to do much about it, and Sonya would supervise the household. But art and literature were calling him once again.

The publication of *The Cossacks*, early in the year, had revived his desire to write. He had filled the book with all his memories of his years in the Caucasus. Like the author, its hero, Olenin, was a disoriented young nobleman who found a renewed taste for life among more simple people. Like the author, he fell in love with a Cossack girl, deeply enough to contemplate marriage. Like the author, he was surrounded by rustic and picturesque companions: Eroshka the hunter, Lukas the *dzhigit*. ... Like the author he left, sore and disappointed, having failed to integrate himself into the primitive life whose charms had so long held him in sway. The character of the young man who leaves the city to discover the joys of a profound union with nature after the artificiality of civilization does, it is true, bear some resemblance to Aleko in Pushkin's *Gypsies* or Pechorin in Lermontov's *A Hero of Our Time*. But despite their attempt at sobriety, both those authors' works are still draped in romanticism. Their Caucasus was wreathed in operatic mists, whereas Tolstoy stuck to the truth. His description of life in a *stanitsa* was a valid ethnological document. The slightest detail, whether referring to the Cossacks' morals, dress, weapons, hunting or fishing customs, or their songs or the behaviour of their girls and women, was drawn from life and striking in its accuracy. And the large proportion of description did not detract from the swift-moving action of the story. One felt the narrator's youth, his appetite for life, the remarkable vivacity of his eye and breath. The manuscript had been fussed over for ten years, started twenty times, successively entitled *Caucasian Novel*, *The Fugitive*, *The Fugitive Cossack*, *The Demoted*, *The Terek Line* and *The Cordon;* amputated of a final romantic passage in which Lukas was seen fleeing to the mountains and Olenin wedding Maryanka; by what miracle did the finished product acquire that air of a quickly written, smooth and flawless book?

Contemporary reaction was reticent, at first. Alexandra
Tolstoy wrote to her nephew: 'My friends, Boris and others,
were enchanted; others criticized *The Cossacks* for a certain
crudeness which, they say, inhibits the aesthetic response. ... I personally said to myself, with a small sigh,
that what is lacking in your scenes is the sun, for all that
is light in them comes from yourself. While one is reading,
the book is satisfying, a very accurate and truthful photograph, but when one has finished, one is left thirsting for
something bigger, on a more elevated level. It is as though
your universe were nailed to the floor, as someone said. Well,
that may come one day.'

Some of the critics, too, were rather starchy. In *The
Times*, Polonsky praised the author for capturing 'the very
breath of the Caucasus' in his story, but thought the hero,
Olenin, only a 'pale copy of the characters of Pushkin's
day', and said that several episodes, such as Abrek's death at
the hands of Lukas or the repurchase of the corpse or the
skirmish between Cossacks and mountaineers, were 'stories
within a story'. Golovachev, in *The Contemporary*, thought
Tolstoy was a 'good storyteller, not lacking in skill', but a
superficial observer and no thinker at all. In *Fatherland
Notes*, Mrs Salias de Tournemir expressed her indignation
at Tolstoy for daring to 'romanticize drunkenness, piracy,
theft and blood-lust' and allowing Olenin – 'the representative of civilized society' – to be 'debased, degraded, defeated ...'

In the *St Petersburg News*, on the other hand, Annenkov
declared Tolstoy's work 'a capital achievement in Russian
literature, able to sustain comparison with the greatest
novels of the last decade', and said that 'a score of ethnographical articles could not give a more complete, exact and
colourful picture of this part of our land'.

In the meantime, Ivan Turgenev was writing to Fet from
Paris: 'I have read *The Cossacks* and was carried away. ...
The character of Olenin is the only thing that detracts from
the overall impression, which is magnificent. To mark the

contrast between civilization and primitive, unspoiled nature, there was no necessity to trot out this individual who is incessantly preoccupied with himself, boring and un-healthy.'

Fet himself was in raptures: 'How many times I men-tally hugged you as I read *The Cossacks* and how many times I laughed at your derogatory remarks about the book,' he wrote to Tolstoy. 'You may write other books that are very fine, but *The Cossacks* is a sort of masterpiece. After *The Cossacks* it is impossible to read a book on the life of the people without bursting out laughing. The ineffable superiority of talent!'

Although he claimed to be impervious to the opinions of others, such high praise encouraged Tolstoy to show what he could do in a larger work. For some months his thoughts had been occupied by a subject that was not yet clearly de-fined. On 17 October 1863 he wrote to Alexandra Tolstoy, 'I have never felt my mental and even moral powers so free and ready for work. And the work is there in front of me: all this autumn I have been completely taken up with a novel about the years 1810 to 1820.'

The Great Labour

At first, Sonya was sceptical: Leo changed his mind too often for her to believe he would continue the big historical novel he was working on. 'Story about 1812,' she wrote on 28 October 1863. 'He is very involved with it. But without enjoyment.' And three weeks later: 'He is writing about Countess So-and-So, who has been talking to Princess Whosit. Insignificant.' But soon afterwards, seeing him persevere, she instinctively realized that her role was beginning. She was filled with reverence for her husband's talent, and did not, of course, try to exert a direct influence on the book. She did express her opinion on the pages he gave her to copy. He listened to her suggestions, as he did to Tanya's and those of his friends and critics, and, most of the time, paid no attention to them. But although Sonya may have contributed nothing to the novel, she contributed a great deal to the novelist. In the past, he had always thrown himself headlong into all kinds of different activities, skipping from one to another as the mood took him, blowing hot and cold for religion, gymnastics, high society, soldiering, agriculture, art for art's sake, sociology, pedagogy – writing several books at once, dropping the admirable *Cossacks* to dash off a mediocre play. And in spite of his success in the literary world, he liked to think of himself as an amateur. Whatever the object he coveted, his passion did not seem able to outlast the possession of it. 'Inconstancy, hesitation, laziness, those are my enemies,' he wrote on the eve of his great decision. And suddenly, this prodigious dilettante plunged into a project that held him fast for six full years. If he was able to muster the determination and patience to undertake such a task, the reason, beyond any doubt, was that Sonya had succeeded in creating the atmosphere of peace and quiet that was necessary for the work to mature in him. Had she not kept such jealous guard over his peace of mind and body, he might have abandoned *War and Peace* by the wayside. After all, he was not forced to write by material necessity. Unlike Dostoyevsky, he did not live on the income from his books; no publisher was hounding him for his copy at fixed deadlines. Being without constraint made it all the more difficult for him to resist the temptations that drew him away from his work.

One by one, ruthlessly, Sonya eliminated them. To relieve her husband of the burden of domestic affairs, she took over the management of the estate; she did not want him to clutter up his mind with money matters, so she also appropriated the household accounts; and she took on the education of their offspring single-handedly. No one, children, parents, friends or servants, must disturb the master when he was in the study he had arranged for himself on the ground floor. With the schools shut down, the teachers dismissed, the ledgers never out of sight and a bunch of keys at her waist, Sonya found herself, at twenty, responsible for everything that affected, directly or indirectly, the daily life of Leo Tolstoy. She was the buffer state between him and the outside world. When he raised his eyes from his manuscript, she was what he saw. Everything he knew of the world came to him through her. Dedicating herself body and soul to her role of warden, she was satisfying a twofold desire: to help her husband in the immense task he had undertaken, and to put him completely in her power, to bury him, far from foreign eyes, deep in the family thicket. More or less consciously, she relieved her jealousy by serving the cause of Literature.

The total understanding that the couple had been unable to achieve by themselves, even after repeated explanations, both written and oral, was created for them by fictional characters. Absorbed in the fate of his heroes, Tolstoy became less concerned with himself. By distributing his contradictory emotions among a cast of imaginary characters, he forged his own unity and thereby his balance. Significantly, as soon as he began work on the book, towards the end of 1863, the entries in his diary became shorter and less frequent. He no longer had either the time or the inclination to analyse himself. Imaginary joys and sufferings occupied all his thoughts. In 1865, he closed the notebook in which he had made a habit of relating his life and did not reopen it for more than thirteen years.* But before doing so, he recorded this statement: 'My relationship with Sonya has grown stronger and steadier. We love each other, that is, we are more precious to each other than any other human being and we face each other with equanimity. We have no secrets and no shame.'[1] And later, 'Not one person in a million, I dare say, is as happy as we are together.'[2] And she wrote, 'Are there any couples more united and happier than we? Sometimes, when I am alone in my room, I begin to laugh and cross myself.'[3]

True, they still quarrelled frequently. Then Tolstoy would bluster, 'You are in a bad temper. Go write your diary.' And she told herself he was nursing 'a secret hatred' of her; she accused him of being 'too old', or 'too demanding'; she swore she was going to be more than the 'Nanny' to a great man. But after the storm, how gratefully she fell into his arms! 'Lyovochka came back, and everything seemed light and easy to me. He smelled of fresh air and he himself was like a breath of fresh air.'

Her greatest source of pleasure, however, was not her husband's embraces (she was never a passionate lover), but the manuscript he gave her to copy. And what a labour of Hercules it was, to decipher this sorcerer's spellbook covered with lines furiously scratched out, corrections colliding with each other, sibylline balloons floating in the margins, prickly afterthoughts sprawled all over the page. Often the author himself could not make out what he had written. But

* An entry in the diary for 1878 dated 17 April, reads: 'After thirteen years I want to take up my diary again.' He had made a few notes in 1873.

Sonya, who was endowed with a remarkable sixth sense, deciphered the amputated words and finished off the half-sentences just as, once before, she had deciphered Tolstoy's thoughts from the initials he chalked on the green card-table cover. In the evening, after the child had been put to bed and the servants had gone up to their garrets and silence settled over the house, she sat down at her table in the round glow of a candle and made a clean copy of the drafts. Her beautiful curling script flowed across the page for hours. It was not uncommon for Tolstoy to hand the same sheets back to her the next day, disfigured by a swarm of microscopic corrections. Sometimes she had to use a magnifying glass to make them out. According to her son Ilya, she recopied most of *War and Peace* seven times. Fingers clutching the pen, shoulders tensed and eyes smarting, she never felt her fatigue. She was possessed by a poetic exaltation, as though she had established telepathic contact with another world. 'As I transcribe the work,' she wrote, 'a swarm of impressions pass through my mind. Nothing affects me as strongly as his ideas and his talent. This has only been true for a short time. Have I changed, or is the book really very good? I don't know which. I write quickly enough to keep pace with the action and not lose interest, and slowly enough to think over, feel, weigh and judge every one of Lyovochka's ideas.'[4] Tears came to her eyes, and she sighed, simultaneously stirred by the characters' sufferings and the author's genius.

He, however, was going through the throes of a difficult creation. Slowly, by fits and starts, the plan of the work took form in his mind as he went along. Even the title, *War and Peace* – borrowed from Proudhon – did not come until late. His original idea had been to write a book on the 1825 uprising whose leaders were exiled to Siberia by Nicholas I and not allowed to return until 1856, when they were pardoned by the new tsar, Alexander II. He had written three large sections of the book. What attracted him about the Decembrists was that nearly all of these pioneer Russian revolutionaries were officers of the Guards, noblemen, confirmed idealists. He felt related to them by his military experience and his love of high ideals. However, when he began to look more closely into their history, he discovered that most of them had taken part in the campaigns against Napoleon and their liberalism had been acquired during their stay in France with the occupation forces. To understand their revolution completely, therefore, he had to go back to 1812–14. 'A period whose scent and sound are still perceptible to us,' he said, 'but remote enough for us to contemplate it unemotionally.' However, this so-called 'patriotic' war that had been so glorious for Russia only took on full meaning in relation to the previous disaster of 1805. 'I hesitated to describe our triumph over Bonaparte's France without first describing our defeat and humiliation. If the final victory was due not to chance but to the spirit of the Russian army and people, then that spirit ought to stand out even more sharply, I thought, in moments of misfortune and defeat.' Expanding this theme, he became fascinated by the horizons that opened before him. The Decembrists were forgotten. The work, as he came to conceive it, would stop with 'the first forewarning of the movement that led up to the events of 14 December 1825'. It would be a confrontation between the great events of history and family life in the upper ranges of society. He said, in a preface that was never published, 'The lives of civil servants, tradespeople, seminarians and muzhiks do not concern me and are scarcely comprehensible to me' – a view he was subsequently to modify. But from the start he was certain of one thing: real people – Napoleon, Alexander, Kutuzov, Bagration, Speransky, Murat – would mingle with the fictional ones.

What a rich and variegated period! How did it happen that no Russian writer had exploited it? There were enough eyewitnesses left for the author to question them directly. He himself, as a child, had heard episodes related by his family, friends and old servants that he would transpose in his book. Besides, customs had hardly changed in sixty years. Wherever his heroes went, Tolstoy was sure to feel at home. He had known military life in the Caucasus and Sevastopol, the Moscow aristocracy, the life of the landed gentry at Yasnaya Polyana. And there was no shortage of models for his characters. His paternal grandfather, the weak-willed and erratic Ilya Andreyevich Tolstoy, became Ilya Andreyevich Rostov in the novel. Nicholas Ilich Tolstoy – Leo's father, who had married a fortune and retired to the country – lent his personality to Nicholas Rostov. To portray Natasha Rostov, the writer borrowed some features from his wife and others from his sister-in-law. 'I took Sonya,' he said, 'ground her up in a mortar with Tanya, and out came Natasha.' (Actually, Tanya posed almost exclusively for Natasha as a girl and Sonya for Natasha married.) Old Prince Nicholas Bolkonsky, living as a tyrant on his estate, was a faithful copy of Nicholas Volkonsky, the author's maternal grandfather. The imaginary estate of Lysya Gory could easily be mistaken for Yasnaya Polyana. Marya Bolkonsky, a pure, pious and secretive girl who worshipped and feared her father, was Leo's mother, Marya Volkonsky, whom he had never known but blindly idealized. The French companion, Mlle Bourienne, was a fictional replica of Mlle Hénissienne; Dolokhov was a mixture of the partisan Dorokhov, his son Reuben, a distant relative of the author's called Tolstoy the American, and the partisan Rigner; Vasily Denisov owed much to Denis Davydov; Prince Andrey Bolkonsky and Pierre Bezukhov alone had no close counterpart in reality.

Tolstoy spent the entire winter of 1863–4 familiarizing himself with the period he wanted to recreate in his book. His father-in-law sent him original source material from Moscow. He himself bought up, pell-mell, an assortment of books on the Napoleonic wars: Mikhailovsky-Danilevsky, Bodganovich, Zhikharev, Glinka, Davidov Liprandi, Korf, the *Documents historiques sur le séjour des Français à Moscou, en 1812*, the *Souvenirs de campagne d'un artilleur*, the *Correspondance diplomatique* of Joseph de Maistre, Marmont's *Memoirs*, Thiers' *Histoire du Consulat et de l'Empire*, etc. 'You can't imagine the difficulties of this preparatory work, ploughing the field I shall have to sow,' he wrote to Fet towards the end of 1864. 'Studying, thinking over everything that might happen to the future heroes of a very big book, devising millions of schemes of all varieties and selecting the millionth part of them, it's terribly hard work.'

At first, the book was to be called *The Year 1805*. The first chapters had already been written when, on 26 September 1864, Tolstoy was out hunting for hare in the country near Telyatinki and was thrown from his horse going over a ravine. He hit the ground so hard that he lost consciousness. When he came to his senses, a thought hit him like a thunderbolt: 'I am a writer!' And joy welled through his mind, while he felt a searing pain in his shoulder. He realized that he had dislocated his right arm. But it seemed to him that the accident had occurred in some far-distant past and he had been asleep for years without knowing what was happening. His horse had run away. With a superhuman effort, he clambered to his feet and, holding his right arm, dragged himself to the road, over half a mile away. There, at the end of his strength, he lay down on the bank. Some muzhiks going by in a telega found him and carried him to an isba. He did not want to go straight home, in order to spare Sonya, who was pregnant. When the news was diplomatically broken to her, she came running in alarm to fetch her Lyovochka home, pale and moaning. The country doctor she sent for proved utterly incompetent; eight times, he tried and failed to put the arm back in place, but he was so clumsy that he only made the pain worse. A doctor from Tula came to the rescue the next day. Tolstoy was chloroformed and two sturdy peasants realigned the bones according to the physician's instructions. When the operation was over, the doctor pronounced it a success. His patient did not agree; at the end of the prescribed six weeks of rest, he fired a gun to test his arm and the recoil sent a blinding pain through his shoulder. Concluding that it was not properly healed, Tolstoy consulted his father-in-law. Dr Behrs ordered him to come to Moscow without delay. Unfortunately, Sonya had just given birth to a daughter [5] and was still too weak to travel.

He stayed with the Behrs in the Kremlin. The doctor convened a group of colleagues: some advised baths, others special exercises, still others favoured surgery. Worried by the doctors' inability to agree among themselves, Tolstoy did not know what to do. On 27 November 1864, he let himself be dragged to a performance of Rossini's *Moses* at the Great Moscow Theatre. Suddenly, the lively, colourful music, the rising swell of the singing and graceful turns and swoops of the dancers so filled him with light-heartedness and the desire to live that he enthusiastically opted for the most radical alternative. The next day Mrs Behrs' bedroom was scoured and prepared for use as an operating theatre. Two surgeons, Popov and Haak, supervised the preparations. Tolstoy was very calm. It required a massive dose of chloroform to put him to sleep. Just as he was about to lose consciousness, he sat bolt upright and bellowed:

'My friends! We cannot go on living like this! ... I think ... I have decided ...'

He fell back and did not utter another word. Was this his old 'Rules of Life' coming back into his consciousness? Two male nurses wrenched apart the badly knit joints in his arm. Then the surgeons replaced the disconnected bones and enclosed the arm in a sort of cast. Tanya was present throughout the operation and could not take her eyes off the colourless face from which all life seemed to have fled. She and her mother sat up all night with Tolstoy. He was racked by nausea from the chloroform. The next day he felt better and wanted to write. As he could not use his right hand, he asked Tanya to be his secretary. After this enforced interruption, his creative drive was so strong that he could have dictated non-stop for days on end. The girl could hardly keep up with him. He was not even aware of her presence. With his arm in a sling, he paced up and down the room like one possessed. His eyes stared through the walls. Sometimes he spoke slowly, sometimes in a staccato rush, unable to articulate the flood of words in his mouth. Suddenly he would stop, furious:

'No, that's no good! ... It won't do! ... Scrap all that!'

Tanya crossed out everything she had written and, frozen with awe, waited. 'I felt,' she later said, 'as though I were prying, as though I had become an involuntary eyewitness to the events in that inner world he hid from us all.' Then he would emerge from his trance and see his sister-in-law's exhausted face, be pricked by an overdue pang of conscience and say:

'That's enough for today. I've worn you out. Go skating.'

But sometimes he was not in the mood, and dictated without feeling. 'And,' he would say, 'without feeling one cannot write anything decent.' In addition to his dictation, he took advantage of his stay in Moscow to continue his search for source material, pawing through bookshops, borrowing books from Professors Eshevsky and Popov, hounding the Rumyantsev Museum library, obtaining, by special favour, important documents from the palace archives, questioning old people on their reminiscences of 1812. The wealth of material both delighted and alarmed him. He was afraid of drowning under the ocean of detail. He was continually forced to tear himself away from historical data and return to his characters. 'Napoleon, Alexander, Kutuzov and Talleyrand are not the heroes of my book,' he said. 'I shall write the story of people living in the most privileged circumstances, with no fear of poverty or constraint, free people, people who have none of the flaws that are necessary to make a mark on history.'

One evening he read the opening chapters at the Perfilyevs' house. The drawing-room in which his audience had assembled was plunged into darkness. On a little table stood lighted candles and a pitcher of water with a glass. Tolstoy began haltingly, then gained confidence, straightened up, began to change voices for different characters. With his rusty beard, harsh, wrinkled face and eyes of steel, he was in turn a young girl, an old man, a Russian officer, a foreign diplomat, a servant in a great family. The faces around him were stretched towards him, wearing expressions of intense curiosity. But was it his story that had captivated the Perfilyevs' guests, or simply their effort to identify their friends in his characters? Tanya wrote to Polivanov:

The opening scene is so delightful. I identified so many of our group. ... People said the Rostovs were living persons. For me, in any case, they seem terribly close. Boris is much like you, in his external appearance and manners. Vera is Lisa to a T: her solemn ways, her behaviour with us. ... Countess Rostov is Maman, especially in her attitude towards me. At Natasha's entrance, Varenka winked at me, but I don't think anyone saw her. But wait a bit, now you'll laugh: my great doll Mimi has stolen the honours of the book. Do you remember how we married you to her, and I insisted that you kiss her and you didn't want to, and you hung her on the door and I complained to Maman? ... Yes, you will recognize many things in this book; don't throw away my letter until you've read it. Pierre is the one the others liked least, but I liked him better than anyone else in the book. I am very fond of his type of person. The little princess was the ladies' favourite, but they couldn't decide who was Lyova's model for her. There was an intermission and everybody had tea. They were all, I think, delighted by the reading. Among the ladies all one heard were guesses as to whom Lyovochka had been describing, and one name after another was mentioned. All of a sudden Varenka said right out loud, 'Maman, I know – Marya Dmitrievna Akhrosimova is you! She's exactly like you.' 'I don't think so, Varenka; I'm not interesting enough to put into a book,' answered Natasya Sergeyevna (Perfilyev). Lyovochka began to laugh and said nothing. Papa was in seventh heaven because of his son-in-law's success. It made me happy just to look at him. What a pity Sonya couldn't be there.[6]

After completing the first part of *The Year 1805*, Tolstoy negotiated with Katkov for the publication of the novel in the *Russian Herald*, at three hundred roubles per printed sixteen-page sheet. On 27 November 1864 the publisher's secretary came to collect the manuscript. After he had gone, Tolstoy felt bereft, anxious, despoiled. As long as the pages were in his possession, he could go back and change them again. Now they were out of his power, they had become a piece of merchandise. His wife wrote, 'I used to scold you for making too many corrections, but now I am sad because you have sold your work.'

It was the first time the couple had been separated for so long. Their respective grievances faded with distance. Each idealized his love to the point of frenzy, as the other was not there to disappoint him. True, their almost daily letters were cluttered with trivial reminders and discussions of nursing bottles, diapers and diarrhoea, but this dreary domestic fare was perpetually transfigured by love. 'Without you, I am nothing,' wrote Sonya. 'With you, I feel like a queen.' He answered, 'The bell rang during dinner. It was the newspapers. Tanya ran to the door. The bell rang a second time. It was your letter. They all asked me to let them read it, but I did not want to give it to them. ... And they did not understand. It affected me like a piece of good music: made me feel both happy and sad, pleasant and wanting to cry.' On 2 December 1864, four days after the operation, he dictated a letter for his wife to Tanya, and painfully added in his own hand, 'Good-bye, my darling, my dove. I can't dictate everything. I love you very much, with every kind of love. And the more I love you, the more frightened I am.'

'Your letter has just come, my dear Leo,' she replied on 5 December. 'What joy to read the scribble you added with your own sick hand! Every kind of love you say? And I can't tell any more what kind of love I love you with!'

And two days later, 'I went into your study and everything came back to me: how you dressed, over by the cupboard that contains your hunting clothes; how excited Dora was [the dog], bounding around you; how you wrote, sitting at your desk, when I peeped fearfully through a crack in the door to see whether I was disturbing you. And then, feeling how intimidated I was, you would say, "Come in!", which was what I wanted.'

He finally left Moscow on 12 December, restored to health, his spirits high, ardently eager to see Sonya again and resume the patriarchal life at Yasnaya Polyana that was so beneficial to his work. Guests were usually rare in winter, because of the snow-blocked roads; but on Twelfth Night that year (6 January 1865), Tolstoy organized a costume ball. The house, decorated with paper flowers and hung with green cloth, was transformed. Neighbours and relatives and friends, the Bibikovs and the Dyakovs, drove up in sledges. Sergey brought his illegitimate children* and trunks stuffed full of material for costumes. The house-servants also took part, of course. Dunyasha, the chambermaid, was dressed as an old army major and sat astride a charger formed by two muzhiks under a piece of brown cloth; the cook was dressed as a nursemaid, the coachman's wife as a lord, and the children as Algerians, Harlequins, Pierrots, shepherdesses and pages. Peasant musicians played the violin and the *bandura*.† They drew lots for the king's crown and ate the cake, and then there were fireworks, fights with bags full of water, and Bengal lights. Suffocated by the smoke, a few guests withdrew to vomit in the corners. But those with more solid stomachs sang and danced on until dawn. Tolstoy was as frantic as the youngest of his guests. Echoes of the party were to appear in the book he was writing.‡ He was so fashioned that sooner or later his whole life had to go into his work. A few days after this colourful party, he jokingly wrote to his friend Fet, 'I am glad you love my wife, although I love her less than my book. Of course, as you know, that is my wife. Someone is coming! Who? My wife!'⁷

* Those he had had by Marya Shishkin.
† A type of round guitar.
‡ See, in *War and Peace*, the description of the ball at the Rostovs', in Book VII, Chapters IX to XI.

Formerly indifferent to the opinion of others, he suddenly became very anxious to know what his friends thought of *The Year 1805*. 'I set great store by your opinion,' he wrote to Fet in the same letter, 'and by that of a man I love less and less as I grow up: Turgenev. I regard the books I have published thus far as mere exercises in penmanship.'

Publication of the first part of the book (Chapters I to XXVIII) began in February 1865, and at first even the most indulgent readers were disappointed by the slowness with which the story moved, the plethora of detail, the author's digressions and excessive use of conversation in French. His friend Botkin could scarcely hide his disappointment: 'This is only a preface, the background of the picture to come,' he said. Borisov told Turgenev, 'I think Fet was not very impressed by it.' And Turgenev, whose verdict Tolstoy was so impatiently awaiting, told Borisov in reply, 'The thing is positively bad, boring and a failure. ... All those little details so cleverly noted and presented in baroque style, those psychological remarks which the author digs out of his heroes' armpits and other dark places in the name of verisimilitude – all that is paltry and trivial, against the broad historical background of a novel. ... One feels so strongly the writer's lack of imagination and naïveté! ... And who are these young ladies? Some kind of affected Cinderellas ...' [8]

Although he had yet to learn the public's reaction to the opening chapters of his book, Tolstoy guessed by a thousand indefinable signs that he had not been understood. But he had gone too far out into midstream to lose heart now. Sometimes the world of his characters seemed closer to him than the one he inhabited with Sonya. He discussed them with his wife as though they were flesh-and-blood people. 'I write, I cross out,' he wrote on 7 March 1865. 'It is all clear in my head. But the immensity of the task ahead is frightening.' Knowing how unstable he was, he vowed to make himself work every day, whatever the results. Simply, as he said, 'in order to keep in the habit'. His friend Dyakov came to Yasnaya Polyana to see him on 11 March. Tolstoy was looking forward to his visit, but that evening he wrote with annoyance, 'Dyakov was here. One day wasted.'

With Sonya, on the other hand, he was more comfortable than before. Their meeting, after the long separation, had been very sweet. Even the children, in whom he had previously shown no interest, began to delight him. 'I am beginning to be very fond of him,' he wrote of his son Sergey. 'This is a new feeling for me.' His new passion for his family coincided with the more intimate scenes of his book. Was it because he loved this atmosphere of calm and quiet that he described it so well in his book, or was it because some of his characters had found that kind of happiness in the book that, by mimicry, he sought it for himself in his life? At his present stage of spiritual maturity, he felt a need to lighten his palette, to paint simple figures of noble dimensions, as 'unoriginal' as possible, but capable of affecting the reader by the warmth that flowed from them.

Towards Easter, his zeal for work began to flag. Every year when spring came, he felt the call of rebirth and laid down his pen to return to the land. He sorted camellia and azalea seeds, made improvements in the farmyard, planted birch trees, fished for pike, hunted hare and snipe. 'Only the hunter and landowner have any real feeling for the beauty of nature,'[9] he was wont to say. For some time, although he claimed to be fully contented by his relationship with his wife, he had been missing his sister-in-law, the fantastical, mischievous Tanya. In February he had written her a singular epistle, confessing that he was as enthusiastic 'as a boy of fifteen', that he felt 'surges of emotion' on any and every occasion, that he missed her and that she must not show his letter to anyone, 'or people will think I am out of my mind'.

She arrived with the first rays of sun, to spend the entire spring and summer with her sister; Marya Tolstoy and her children also moved to Yasnaya Polyana.* Other guests appeared, turning up for a few days or staying for weeks: Sergey, Prince Gorchakov's daughters, the author Sologub and his two boys, Prince Lvov, Dyakov, Bibikov. ... Tolstoy was still working, but intermittently. Sometimes his family saw him emerge from his study wearing a far-off expression, absent-minded and happy – it was hard for him to get his bearings in real life after spending hours in the company of his heroes. 'Leo was always tense,' Tanya later wrote, 'he had a "high spirit" as the English say, bold and gay and full of energy.' When he was pleased with himself his eyes gleamed, he rubbed his hands together and said, with a grimace of gleeful ferocity, that he had left 'a piece of his life in the inkwell'. In the evenings, to relax, he played solitaire with Aunt Toinette and attached great importance to the outcome; if he won, that meant the next part of the book would go well. He often read aloud what he had written during the day. His voice was warm and winning; as soon as he spoke his listeners were under a spell; Sonya had to steel herself afterwards to venture a criticism: the story dragged here, too much repetition there, that passage was too raw for her taste. ... She did not care much for the military scenes and was not afraid to say so. But he seldom took any notice. His confidence in his craft was growing. His concept of literature was becoming clearer. According to him, the 'novelist's poetry' lay 'first, in the interest created by juxtaposed events; second, in the portrayal of customs and manners against a background of historical fact; third, in the beauty and vividness of situations; fourth, in the characters of the people.'[10] Now a thousand leagues away from the theories of ideological art he later claimed to champion, he wrote to his young colleague Boborykin, in July 1865, 'The aims of art are incommensurable (as the mathematicians say) with the aims of socialism. An artist's

* Valerian, Marya Tolstoy's husband, had died on 6 January 1865, and his widow was living in a 'free union' with Viscount Hector de Kleen, a Swede.

mission must not be to produce an irrefutable solution to a problem, but to compel us to love life in all its countless and inexhaustible manifestations. If I were told I might write a book in which I should demonstrate beyond any doubt the correctness of my opinions on every social problem, I should not waste two hours at it; but if I were told that what I wrote would be read twenty years from now by people who are children today, and that they would weep and laugh over my book and love life more because of it, then I should devote all my life and strength to such a work.'

His reading during that period confirmed his views. He admired Victor Hugo's *Les Misérables*, an epic, sweeping, rushing novel in which imaginary people also came face to face with real ones. Nor was he insensitive to the intelligence and sobriety of Mérimée's *Chronique du règne de Charles IX*, although he considered its author 'devoid of talent'. But he hated *Consuelo*, 'a heap of rubbish, crammed full of scientific, philosophical, artistic and moral phrases, a pastry made of sour dough and rancid butter, stuffed with truffles, sturgeon and pineapple'.[11] His dream was to make *1805* as broad in scope, as serene and profoundly graceful as the *Iliad* and *Odyssey*. 'I am transported by joy at the thought that I can create a great work,' he wrote.

This feeling of plenitude was deflated, however, when he emerged from his study – a cool, vaulted room that had been used as a storeroom in Prince Volkonsky's day – and saw the wretchedness of the peasants. That year (1865) there was a terrible drought in the land. Nothing would grow in the rock-hard, glaze-cracked fields. The livestock were gaunt, the anxious muzhiks had little to eat and were praying for rain. 'We have pink radishes on the table, beautiful yellow butter, plump golden bread on a white tablecloth,' wrote Tolstoy to his friend Fet. 'Our ladies in their muslin gowns are so happy, sitting among the green plants in the garden, because it is hot and they are in the shadow. But beyond, the evil devil famine is already hard at work, covering the fields with weeds, crazing the arid soil, tearing the soles of the peasants' calloused feet and splitting the animals' hoofs, and will so shake and agitate us all that we, too, under the shade of our lime trees, with our muslin gowns and our lumps of butter on our flowered plates, will get what's coming to us.' [12]

As summer drew near, he began to fear an uprising. Under the merciless sky, he imagined the poor coming to demand justice from the rich, the panic-stricken ladies hiding behind drawn shutters, the doling-out of surplus food under the threat of scythes and pitchforks. Although he loved the muzhiks, he could not forget that he was a lord. Their friend, to be sure, but not their equal. Haunted by such grim forebodings, he told his father-in-law what was in his mind, and received an immediate answer: 'God preserve us from such a catastrophe as that! It would be more dreadful than the Pugachev uprising. But I think everything will turn out all right, there will be nothing but minor, local expressions of discontent and a few cases of suffering from famine, which will take the form of an unjustified resentment of the nobility.' [13]

As Yasnaya Polyana was not bloodied by revolution in the ensuing weeks, Tolstoy grew calm again and began to consider the question from a theoretical point of view. In the night of 12–13 August 1865 he had an illumination, and upon waking, he wrote in his notebook:

'The formula *Property equals theft* will remain true longer than the English constitution, as long as there are men. It is an *absolute* truth, but there are relative, accessory truths arising from it. The first of these concerns the attitude of the Russian people towards property. They deny the most tangible form of property, that which is least dependent upon work, that which creates most obstacles to the acquisition of property by others – namely, land. ... This is not fancy, it is fact, borne out in the Cossack communities. It is understood equally well by the Russian scholar and the muzhik who says, "Enlist us in the Cossacks, but let the land be free." There is a future for such an idea. The Russian revolution can be built upon nothing else. The Russian revolution will not be directed against the tsar and despotism, but against the ownership of land.'

Three days before, on 10 August 1865 to be exact, this enemy of land ownership had purchased seventy-five acres from his neighbour Bibikov, in the village of Telyatinki, for the very attractive price of 280 roubles.* His pleasure was as intense, one may suppose, when he was dreaming of a socialist republic in which meadows, fields and woods would belong to all, as it was when he was riding over the property of which he had just become sole owner. To add to one's worldly goods while sighing after holy equality – wasn't that the essence of modern man? The main thing was to feel guilty now and then. After his profession of faith on the abolition of property, Tolstoy set down the following sentence, undated: 'Every man lies twenty times daily.'

When he tired of manipulating serious thoughts, he looked at his wife and children and sister-in-law and felt rejuvenated. With her sparkling eyes, black curly hair, large expressive mouth and slender waist, Tanya was the life of the family. A funny word or an affectionate glance from her could calm her sister's tantrum or bring to her brother-in-law's lips one of those broad smiles that suddenly made him so attractive. In the evening she sang, accompanied by him at the piano. Their mutual friend Fet, moved by the purity of her voice, dedicated a poem to her: 'You Sang Until Dawn.'

Tolstoy often took Tanya riding with him in the forest, while Sonya moped at home. At the side of the nineteen-year-old girl, he savoured the coolness of a mountain spring; but all the time he was basking in the ambiguous pleasure of her company, the novelist in him was not forgotten. During their halts under the shade of the big trees, he questioned his sister-in-law about her adolescent loves. Flattered by his interest, she told him of her first crushes, her wild schemes, her passion for her cousin Alexander Kuzminsky,

* Or $790.

followed by a more intense attachment to a bold and
glamorous hothead named Anatol Shostak. He listened, his
mind vibrant. Unwittingly, Tanya was injecting life into
the veins of Natasha Rostov, and in the novel Anatol Shostak became Anatol Kuragin, the man who wanted to elope
with Natasha.*

At Yasnaya Polyana, however, the forsaken spouse took
umbrage at these long rambles by her husband and sister.
'I am angry with Tanya, she is taking up too much space in
Lyovochka's life,' she wrote as early as 3 May 1865. 'They
are inseparable. Going to Nikolskoye, hunting, on horseback
or on foot, always together. Yesterday, for the first time, I
felt jealous of Tanya and today I am suffering because of
her. I let her take my horse, which I think was very good of
me. ... And they have gone off hunting in the forest,
alone.... God knows what is going through my head ...'

The only thought that could allay her suspicions was that
although Tanya admired Lyovochka, she was really in love
with his brother Sergey. True, she was only nineteen and
Sergey thirty-nine, but he was not unattractive, with his
world-weary air, blue eyes and casual elegance. He was said
to have 'lived' a great deal. Looking into the distance, he
would sigh, 'The only good things in life are the song of the
nightingale, love, moonlight and music.' Tanya found him
extremely attractive. Their idyll had gone on for two years
and, despite the difference in their ages, the Behrs were not
opposed to the idea that their youngest daughter should also
marry a Tolstoy. Sonya, at any rate, was wildly in favour of
the scheme. Was Tanya's happiness uppermost in her
thoughts, or was it her own peace of mind? She decided that
the marriage must be consummated before the end of the
summer. Under pressure from her, the couple let themselves
be convinced. 'The fate of Tanya and Sergey was decided the
day before yesterday,' she wrote on 9 June 1865. 'They will
marry! What a pleasure to see them, to see their happiness,

---

* Tolstoy often let the characters in his books keep the first names
of their real-life models, changing only their family names.

I can enjoy it more than I did my own. They are out walking in the garden. . . . The wedding will take place in four or five weeks . . .' After a month of negotiation, kissing, daydreaming on the balcony and planning for the future, *coup de théâtre*! Sonya, foaming with rage, flung herself upon her diary, her pen scorching the paper: '12 July 1865. It's all off. Sergey has let Tanya down and behaved like the lowest of cowards. . . . I shall do everything in my power to get even with him!'

She ought, however, to have known what was coming. For years Sergey had been living at Pirogovo with Marya Shishkin, the gypsy, and had several children by her.* This disreputable liaison did not count in Sonya's eyes, and she was convinced that her brother-in-law, being a man of honour, would find some way of disposing of the wretched woman before the wedding. But Sergey – the fool! – had a last-minute attack of conscience. When he was with Tanya, nothing was too great a sacrifice for her, but when he went back to Pirogovo, he did not have the heart to evict his companion of such long standing, a gentle, humble and defenceless woman. He entrusted Leo with the task of explaining his compunctions to the young lady. Listening to her brother-in-law's halting speech, Tanya was so ashamed and miserable that she wanted to die. That evening, out of pity for Marya Shishkin and her children, she wrote to her fiancé to release him from his troth. He replied, 'You gave a beggar a million, and now you take it back.' But in the end he resigned himself. When announcing the break to his wife's parents, Tolstoy paid emphatic tribute to the noble soul of his little sister-in-law: 'Before, admiring her gaiety, I already sensed the quality of her soul. Now she has proved it with this act, so fine and generous that tears come to my eyes when I think of it. He is certainly guilty, utterly unpardonable. . . . I would feel better if he were a stranger and

---

* Three daughters, already grown up in 1865, and a son, who died of tuberculosis on 16 March of that year. 'Sergey's son is dead,' wrote Sonya that day. 'I cried all morning long. It made me so sad.'

not my own brother. ... She has suffered atrociously, but she can tell herself – and that is the greatest consolation in life – that she has behaved nobly.'

Pale, disconsolate and red-eyed, Tanya stared through many sleepless nights, dragged from room to room, refused to eat and confided in no one. To distract her, Leo and Sonya took her with them to their property at Nikolskoye, then to Marya Tolstoy's home at Pokrovskoye. Wherever she went, she thought of Sergey. 'There are three doctors nursing me here,' she wrote, 'but pills and drops will not cure me. God! Why can't anyone understand that? Leo is the only one who understands.'

And Tolstoy did lavish such solicitude upon her that she slowly began to recover, and her laughter and lovely contralto voice filled the house again. Sometimes she said she could not go on living with her sister, she must return to her parents in Moscow. Tolstoy blustered: 'What nonsense! Surely you don't suppose you are not paying for your keep? Why, you are posing for your portrait, my dear. I am putting down everything I know about you, black on white.' While commiserating with his sister-in-law's sorrow, the author in him was also busily digesting it. He could only thank God for having staged this sentimental drama before his eyes.

To the extent that he was preoccupied by his characters, he forgot his own worries. But he did not lose interest in himself altogether: physical considerations took the place of moral ones, that was all. In his diary reports of his basest bodily functions now took precedence over accounts of his most lofty processes of thought. While, with masterly clairvoyance, he was describing the war of 1805 through the eyes of Prince Andrey, Captain Denisov and cadet Nicholas Rostov, the pages of his intimate notebook bore witness to his acid stomach and flatulence. 'The humming in my ears has stopped, I feel better, but I am still belching and my tongue is coated, especially in the morning.' (30 October.) 'Same rigorous hygiene, slept well, did not urinate or defecate, tongue still white and headache.' (31 October.) 'Dry mouth, tongue coated. . . . Good stool in the evening. (November 2.) 'Supper brought on pleasant slumber, gas and slight humming in the ears.' (3 November.)

The holidays were dreary. Tanya had gone back to her parents in Moscow. After long months of work Tolstoy, too, felt a desire to dip into life in the capital again, in order to refresh his 'memory of society', which he needed to continue his book. 'I must be able to judge people accurately, since I am trying to describe them,' he wrote in a letter to Alexandra Tolstoy.[14]

At the end of January 1866 he left for Moscow with his wife, who was pregnant again, and their two children. They rented a six-room furnished apartment, on the 'right floor', on Dmitrovka Street. The rent was one hundred and fifty roubles a month, 'heat, samovar, water, dishes, everything included!' Sonya, suddenly anamoured of music, attended numerous concerts, and Tolstoy corrected proofs, saw friends and worked out at the gymnasium. He read a few more unpublished chapters of his book at the Perfilyevs' house and commissioned Bashilov, the painter, to illustrate a bound edition of *The Year 1805*. Then, Bashilov having revived his interest in the fine arts, he decided to attend classes in sculpture. After modelling a horse in clay he became discouraged and stopped. His heart wasn't in it. He was worried about his wife: even pregnant, she could be attractive. In Moscow they had met Sonya's former suitor, Mitrofan Polivanov. She had been clumsily kittenish with him, and he had been exceedingly impertinent with her. Stung by jealousy, Tolstoy heatedly berated his wife. 'Lyova is too severe and harsh in his judgement of me,' she wrote. 'Even so, I am glad of it; it proves he cares for me.'[15]

When they returned to Yasnaya Polyana the tables were suddenly turned, and it was she who complained of being forsaken and made to appear ridiculous. She had just given birth [at the end of May 1861] to her third child, a boy called Ilya, and was nursing him herself, despite the pain she suffered at every feeding. For reasons of convenience, she and her husband were sleeping apart for the first time. Wrapped up in his book, he had less and less time to devote to the estate. Besides, he had been forced to concede that the direct management system he had advocated was a failure, so he hired a new steward. And as luck would have it, the steward had a wife. And the wife was pretty. Worse yet, she was an intellectual, she read, she had ideas about things! A real nihilist! And Lyovochka, the idiot, spent hours talking to her! And, of course, the little schemer was bubbling over with conceit! 'It is wrong of him to show so much interest in talking to Marya Ivanovna,' Sonya wrote on 19 July 1866, in her diary. 'One in the morning soon and still I cannot get to sleep. I have dire premonitions. This nihilist, our steward's wife, is going to become the bane of my existence.' And on 22 July, 'Why has he gone over there, and in the rain, to boot? He is attracted by the woman, that's plain. It's driving me out of my mind. I wish her every possible evil, which does not keep me from being as sweet as honey to her. If only her husband would quickly turn out to be incompetent, then they would both go away ...' A fortnight later her jealousy subsided and she herself admitted that it was 'almost unfounded'.

It would indeed have been petty of her to harbour suspicions of her husband just then, for he had his hands full with a far more serious matter. Early in July 1866 two officers, Lieutenants Kolokoltsov and Stasulevich, had come to call on him in a state of great agitation; they were friends of the Behrs family and were serving in the 65th Moscow Infantry Regiment, which was on manoeuvres in the vicinity of Yasnaya Polyana, and they had come to tell him about Quartermaster Sergeant Shabunin, who was accused of having struck his captain. According to Stasulevich, Shabunin was a drunkard, rather weak in the head, and was convinced that he was persecuted by his commanding officer, who not only had him regularly put into prison for intemperance or misconduct, but also compelled him to copy documents over and over again, on the pretext that his writing was illegible or his lines crooked. It was because his sarcastic, frigid superior made him feel continually at fault that the poor wretch had resorted to violence. The case was serious, for under the Russian military code his offence was punishable by death. The two lieutenants had been appointed to sit on the court-martial with Colonel Yunosha, commander of the regiment, and they wanted Tolstoy to defend the accused. Tempted by the challenge, he accepted.

The next day he went to the village of Ozerki and obtained permission to interview Shabunin in the isba in which he was being detained. He found a stocky redhead who answered 'Quite so, quite so!' to every question, glassy-eyed, his little finger pressed against his trouser-seam. Nevertheless, this imbecile was a human being and, as such, worth no less than Colonel Yunosha himself in the eyes of God. Could one man be deprived of his life as punishment for striking another? There was a shocking disproportion between the crime and the punishment. Tolstoy spent the night preparing his brief on the basis of the meagre information he had been able to glean. He tactfully agreed that it was necessary to set an exemplary punishment for crimes such as that committed by Shabunin, but he asked the judges to note that the accused was covered by the provisions of Articles 109 and 116, whereby the penalty might be reduced if the criminal was not of sound mind. He argued that not only was the accused mentally retarded, but also, under the influence of alcohol, his condition bordered on insanity. Did one have the right to sentence a madman to death? At the close of his speech Tolstoy declared, 'The court must let itself be guided by the spirit of our entire legislation, which ever weights the scales of justice on the side of clemency.'

The court-martial sat on 16 July, in a nobleman's home in the village of Yasenki. A government-appointed judge made a special trip from Moscow. Tolstoy was intimidated, and read out his speech without conviction. At one point the tears came to his eyes. The quartermaster sergeant listened, gaping, to all these big words being used about his small self. The judges withdrew to deliberate. Tolstoy was certain his speech would move them to indulgence, especially as he thought he could count on the support of Stasulevich and Kilokoltsov, the assistants. But when they began to deliberate, Stasulevich alone favoured partial irresponsibility. Colonel Yunosha held out for the unqualified application of Article 604, i.e., the death penalty. Shaken by his intransigence, Kolokoltsov weakened, even though he had been the one to ask Tolstoy to defend Shabunin, and voted with his superior for fear of displeasing him. This shift settled the issue. 'He was,' said Tolstoy, 'a good lad, light-hearted and completely absorbed at that time by his Cossack horse, on which he loved to caracole.' Shabunin was sentenced to go before the firing squad.

Tolstoy immediately decided to appeal for an imperial reprieve. As always, when anyone in high places was involved, he called on his *babushka* Alexandra. The old maid of honour took her nephew's request to Milyutin, the minister of war. But in his haste, Tolstoy had neglected to mention Shabunin's regiment. Using this as a pretext, Milyutin replied that he could not submit an incomplete appeal to his emperor. Informed of this development, Tolstoy rushed to Tula and telegraphed the information: too late. The time limit for lodging an appeal had expired.

Shabunin was executed on 9 August 1866 in front of a mass of peasants from the neighbouring villages. Throughout his imprisonment they had brought eggs and cakes to his cell. They crossed themselves when he was led out, pale and calm; they obscurely sensed that the man's punishment was out of proportion to his crime, and the Russians have always sympathized with the victims of official justice. Shabunin kissed the cross held out by the priest and let them cover his eyes and tie him to the post. Twelve soldiers raised their guns and took aim. The drums rolled.

When the salvo rang out, the peasants fell to their knees and began to pray. According to the military custom of the day, the regiment, led by its band, paraded past the trench. Later, when the quartermaster sergeant's tomb had become a landmark for pilgrims, the authorities had it levelled and posted guards to prevent people from gathering at the scene of the execution.

Tolstoy felt doubly guilty for this death: first, because he had failed to sway the judges, and then, because he had made an unpardonable oversight in his appeal. Forty-two years later he said his plea to the court had been 'stupid and shameful'; he should have spoken out, affirmed that capital punishment was a revolting practice, 'contrary to human nature', and challenged the right of uniformed magistrates to dispose of the life of one of their fellows; he should have asked Alexander II, not to pardon the unfortunate man, for that was beyond the power of any human, but to pray for his own soul, 'in order to extricate himself from his dreadful position as accomplice to every crime committed in the name of the law'.[16]

It is not likely that this approach would have prevailed over either judges or tsar and, far from furthering Shabunin's cause, it would probably have destroyed his last chance of survival. But that way, at least, Tolstoy's conscience would have been clear. As he grew older, his theories' tangible results mattered less to him than the moral satisfaction they offered.

In 1866, he had not yet realized the role he was to play in the world, and he was thoroughly demoralized by this setback. After condemning the French and their guillotine, he could now condemn the Russians and their firing squad. Corruption, hence, was not a question of nationality, but of the period he lived in. To cast it off, one must cast off 'civilization'.

After such a cruel bout with reality, Tolstoy returned to his fictional visions with a sigh of relief. The engaging characters of *1805* soon hid Shabunin's bloody corpse from view. And as an encouragement to turn his mind to other matters, Bashilov, the painter, submitted his first drawings. The author experienced a childish delight when he saw his heroes' portraits: as though they were real people. He knew them so well that he began writing to the artist to suggest that he retouch this feature or that in order to obtain 'a better likeness'. He could not have been more precise in his suggestions had he been writing about his own family: 'Can't Helene be given more bust (beauty of form is her main characteristic)? ... Pierre's face is very well done, but his forehead should be made more thoughtful by adding a furrow, or two bulges above the eyebrows. ... Prince Andrey is too tall and his attitude should be more casual, scornful, gracefully negligent. ... Princess Bolkonsky is remarkably successful. ... Hippolyte's portrait is perfect, but it would be better to lift his upper lip slightly and cross his legs higher up – in short, to make him more ridiculous, more of a caricature.'[17] Later, he asked Bashilov to retouch Natasha: 'In the kissing scene, could she not be made to look more like Tanya Behrs?'[18]

Another confirmation of the relationship between Natasha and his sister-in-law. Her broken heart had mended, and she was in the best of spirits on 17 September 1866, Sonya's nameday.* Dinner was served on a new terrace. The cloth was heaped high with flowers, and Venetian lanterns glowed among the leaves. Suddenly the sounds of a joyful march were heard: *La Muette de Portici*.† Sonya turned in astonishment to look at her husband, who was chuckling into his beard. At the end of the drive, a military band appeared in full-dress uniform. As a surprise for his wife, Tolstoy had asked Colonel Yunosha to lend him his band – the same colonel who, hardly two months before, had sentenced Quartermaster Sergeant Shabunin to

* 17 September, according to the Orthodox calendar, is the day of the Blessed Martyrs Vera, Nadezhda, Lyubov (Faith, Hope, Charity) and their mother, Sofya.

† An opera by Auber.

death. Decidedly, this barrister–writer was without malice towards the judge who had refused to listen to him. Ah well, feelings are one thing and social life another: Colonel Yunosha in person opened the ball. His two assistants, Stasulevich and Kolokoltsov, were also there, so the entire military tribunal found itself dancing in the home of counsel for the defence. The musicians who had marched in front of Shabunin's body now played dances for the young ladies dressed in white muslin, whose eyes were devouring all the cocky young officers. 'I can see Lyova's animated and charming face; he had taken such pains to give us a good time and was being so successful at it,' wrote Sonya. 'To my utter surprise, unfrivolous as I am, I enjoyed the dancing immensely.' Tolstoy, flushed and hilarious, was the wildest of them all. He whirled his wife around in his arms, and his sister-in-law and a few of the guests. For the sixth figure in the quadrille the band broke into the *kamarinskaya*, a folk-dance.

'Get out there!' cried Tolstoy to Kolokoltsov. 'How can you stand still to a rhythm like that?'

Kolokoltsov circled around and stopped in front of Tanya. After a moment's hesitation she set off, one fist on her hip and the other hand swinging loosely back and forth in the manner of the Russian peasants. Someone tossed her a handkerchief, which she caught in mid-air. Tolstoy delightedly watched his sister-in-law and noted her every gesture with the deliberate intention of using her in his book. And so Natasha Rostov did a country dance, too, in *War and Peace*. 'Where, when, how, simply through the air she breathed, had this little princess, brought up by an *emigrée* Frenchwoman, imbibed so much of the national spirit that should have been obliterated long ago by the *pas de châle*?' [19]

Unfortunately, soon after this most successful party, Tanya fell ill with a dry, racking cough. 'Be still! Be still!' begged Tolstoy, watching her with tense affection. He had fresh visions of consumption. Once before, when she had been in a wildly gay mood, he had said to her, 'Tanya, do you know you will die one day?' And she had cried back, 'Die? Me? Never!' He could still hear her words as he watched her now, breathing in spasms with her hand over her mouth. He decided to take her back to Moscow and, at the same time, complete his documentation in the libraries there. On 10 November 1866 Sonya, who was obliged to stay behind and nurse her latest baby, blessed her husband and sister as they set out. Tolstoy insisted that Tanya hold an 'inhaling mask' in front of her face to protect her lungs from the cold air as they rode through the rain in a post-chaise.

In Moscow the doctors called in for consultation by Dr Behrs agreed that her lungs were weak and advised her to give up vocal exercise, diet and go abroad for a rest in the sun, after which she would soon be well again. Reassured, Tolstoy returned to his labours as ferreting historian.

For once in her life, Sonya was not jealous at the thought of his being far away with Tanya. She missed him, the nights were long, and she thought back to the evening of 17 September when he had danced with her and looked lovingly at her. 'The house is so sad and empty when he is away,' she wrote on 12 November. 'A meeting of minds closer than ours seems impossible to me. We are terribly happy in our relations with each other, with our children and with life.' He had left her a mountain of sheets to transcribe and she settled eagerly down to work. Mailing the copy off to him, she wrote, 'Now I feel that it is your child and consequently my child and, as I send off this package of paper to Moscow, I feel I am abandoning a baby to the elements; I'm afraid something may happen to it. I like what you are writing very much. I do not think I shall care as much for any other book of yours as this one.' [20]

From Moscow he kept her informed of his progress. He was living with his in-laws in the Kremlin, and every morning he went to the library of the Rumyantsev Museum, where he dug into manuscripts on freemasonry – which had been outlawed in Russia after the Decembrists' aborted coup d'état in 1825 – and became fascinated by them. His hero, Pierre Bezukhov, would be a freemason. But how they depressed him, all those yellow pages attesting to a puerile aspiration to virtue! 'The sad thing about these Masons,' he wrote to Sonya, 'is that they were all imbeciles.'[21] He wanted to know every detail of his characters' daily lives. To get a clearer picture of the world they lived in, he thought of buying a complete set of the *Moscow News*, which was already in existence in 1812, and advertised for it in the newspapers, offering two thousand roubles.

On 18 November 1866 he was back at Yasnaya Polyana, where he began to write again and did not stop all winter. He was so excited by the furious intensity with which he was working that his eyes would suddenly fill with tears. Sonya shared his emotion and she, too, wept when he read aloud the chapters he had just finished. He complained, increasingly often, of violent headaches. 'For the past two weeks my brain has been congested and I have such a strange pain that I fear an attack,' he wrote to his brother in February 1867.

Irritable, tired and overwrought, he welcomed his sister-in-law with open arms when she returned to Yasnaya Polyana after a restorative trip to Baden-Baden and Paris. But gloom redescended upon him soon afterwards: his friend Dmitry Dyakov had just lost his wife, and Elizabeth Andreyevna Tolstoy, Alexandra's sister, also died that year. Tolstoy was obsessed by these deaths, he was afraid for himself and those around him; he wrote to his *babushka*: 'There are times when one forgets it, *it*, death, and then there are others, like this year, when one keeps very quiet around those one loves, for fear of losing them, and watches in terror as *it* strikes here and there, cruel and blind, sometimes those who are best and the ones you need most.'[22]

Sonya thought she was pregnant again. She had engaged an English nurse, Hannah Tracey, a clean, energetic, cultivated woman, with whom Tolstoy himself could find no fault. The children were growing up, handsome and healthy. And yet, at the slightest pretext he became giddy with dread. One day in May, when Sonya was sitting on the floor of her room sorting and arranging the drawers of a chest, he came in, looked at his wife and suddenly, without reason or warning, felt a wave of rage sweep over him.

'Why are you sitting there on the floor?' he shouted. 'Get up!'

'Right away! I must just finish putting these away.'

'You are to get up at once!'

He went out and slammed the door. Stupefied, Sonya wondered whether she had unwittingly done something to offend him or whether he was angry because she was working in her condition. She went to his study and gently asked:

'Lyovochka, what's the matter?'

He exploded:

'Go away! Go away!'

As she began to draw nearer, he hurled a tray holding a coffeepot and cup to the floor, tore a thermometer off its hook and smashed it against the wall. Tanya, who was in the next room, came running when she heard the noise. Sonya had already left the room. Tolstoy was standing there, his arms hanging down limply, his face white and staring, his lower lip trembling.

'I was afraid of him and sorry for him,' Tanya later wrote. 'Never had I seen him in such a state.' He himself was alarmed by this moment of insanity and decided a few days later to go to Moscow and consult a specialist.

Distance had its usual effect, and on 18 June 1867, overflowing with tenderness, he wrote to his wife:

'Coming into Moscow yesterday, as soon as I saw the dust and the crowds, felt the heat and heard the din, I was so terrified that I wanted to run back and hide beneath your wing as quickly as possible. I always love you even more when I leave you!'

And on 20 June:

'I have just read your letter and I cannot describe the tenderness – to the point of tears – I feel for you, not only this minute, but every minute of the day. My little soul, my dove, the best in all the world!'

He had promised her to see Dr Zakharin. He went. The physician thumped and poked and prodded him with 'pedantic thoroughness' and then announced that his nerves were overstrained and he had gallstones. As he refused to take any medicine, a cure at Carlsbad was proposed as an alternative. But he had no intention of doing even that. At most, he might go on a special diet. Reassured on the score of his health, the question of the publication of his book remained to be settled. On Sonya's advice, he had decided to discontinue the instalments in the *Russian Herald*. The lukewarm response of both critics and readers, when the second part came out in 1866, had convinced him that the essence of a work of this type was in its totality and that by releasing it bit by bit in a periodical, he was distorting its meaning and weakening its impact. Now, therefore, he wanted to publish the book as a whole, and sell it directly through the bookshops.

After a number of unsuccessful attempts, he agreed on terms with a publisher, P. I. Bartenyev* and a printer, Riss. The first printing, without illustrations (Too bad for Bashilov and his drawings! 'There is something missing from them – the nerve of life!'), was to be 4,800 copies. The book would be published as it was set up, in six volumes. The series would sell for eight roubles. Tolstoy would advance 4,500 roubles to the printer,† in instalments, as his share of the printing costs. He allowed Bartenyev 10 per cent of the selling price, 20 per cent went to the booksellers, and he took the rest. If the book was a success, the enterprise would be highly profitable for him. Of course, now he would not only have to go on writing the book, he must also revise the two parts which had already come out in the magazine, in

* Publisher of *Russian Archives*.
† Or $12,700.

preparation for their publication in bound volumes. According to his contract with Bartenyev, the publisher would have the proofs checked over after the author had finished with them, to correct 'any mistakes in language or grammatical errors'.

He arrived at Yasnaya Polyana, highly pleased with his contract, to learn that Tanya was about to become engaged to her cousin Alexander Mikhailovich Kuzminsky, a good-natured, dull young magistrate. The engagement was nearly broken off because the girl – who was decidedly under her brother-in-law's influence – had the rash idea of showing Kuzminsky her diary, containing her account of her misfortunes with Sergey Tolstoy. But everything worked out in the end. Leo would have preferred Tanya to marry his friend Dmitry Dyakov, who had been much attracted to her since the death of his wife, but was prevailed upon to side with the others.* Sergey, moreover, had just legalized his situation by marrying his mistress, the gypsy Marya Shishkin.† On their way to find a country priest to celebrate their respective unions, the two couples had met in their coaches outside Tula. Tanya and Sergey exchanged embarrassed greetings and the horses bore them off to their separate destinies.

Tanya was married on 24 July 1867, and Tolstoy, 'patron of the ceremony', made an effort to appear pleased by the event, which was depriving him of his sister-in-law. But although he was losing her in real life, she still belonged to him in his work. Nobody could deprive him of Natasha Rostov. Unfortunately, he was now forced to stop writing while he corrected the proofs of the first part of the book. He received the galleys of the opening pages in mid-July. He scored out and revised in so many places that Bartenyev wrote back indignantly:

'God alone knows what you are doing! If you go on like

---

* Tanya, who had long been an intimate of the Dyakov family, went abroad with Dmitry after his wife's death.

† On 7 June 1867.

that we will be correcting and resetting forever. Anyone can tell you that half your changes are unnecessary. But they make an appreciable difference in the typesetting costs. I have asked the printer to send you a separate bill for corrections. ... For the love of God, stop scribbling!'[23]

'It is impossible for me not to scribble the way I scribble and I am firmly convinced that my scribbling is most useful,' retorted Tolstoy. 'Therefore, I am not afraid of the typesetter's bills which will not, I trust, be exorbitant. Those passages you say you like* would not have been as good if I had not scribbled all over them five times.'[24]

In the chapters telling of Pierre Bezukhov's initiation into a masonic lodge (Volume I, Book V, Chapters 3 and 4), he made so many changes that he doubted whether the corrector would be able to make them out and demanded a new set of proofs. Even so, the work went quickly. On 23 September Tolstoy returned to Moscow for another interview with his publisher, and also to visit the battlefield of Borodino, seventy-five miles away. His young brother-in-law Stepan Behrs (then twelve years old) went with him; Dr Behrs lent them his hunting wagon.

For two days they drove back and forth in a driving rain across the vast, muddy, misty plain, punctuated by hummocks and potholes, where, fifty years before, the most devastating of all Napoleonic battles had been fought. Victory of Borodino for the Russians, victory of the Moskva for the French: this hopelessly entangled encounter between the two armies came back to life in Tolstoy's eyes with frightening clarity.† He had studied the movements in books, but everything took on a new light at the actual scene of the battle. He questioned old peasants, who muddled everything up in their memories, took notes, consulted maps, verified troop movements, imagined his characters in different settings. The drizzly fog of 26 September 1867 dis-

* Bartenyev had written that he especially admired Pierre Bezukhov's scene with his wife and the chapter at Lysya Gory.
† The Russians also counted this battle as a national victory.

solved in the sunlight of 26 August 1812.* Fields of rye sprang from the bare earth. The landscape became peopled with phantom regiments, nightmare faces wavered past in the fog, flags snapped in the wind, the voice of the cannon thundered through the ground. Lost in his vision, Tolstoy told his inattentive little companion everything he saw. They spent the night in a convent inn and returned to Moscow the following morning after a final tour of the neighbourhood of Borodino. 'I am very, very pleased with the trip and the way I endured it, regardless of lack of sleep and inadequate food,' he wrote to his wife on 27 September. 'God grant me health and peace and quiet, and I shall describe the battle of Borodino as it has never been described before.'

When he got back to Yasnaya Polyana, he plunged into the mêlée, with Prince Andrey, Pierre Bezukhov, Napoleon and Kutuzov. ... And there were those accursed proofs to read. He was 'exhausted', he had a 'horrible fog in the head'. Would he hold out to the end? And the censor, what would the censor say? 'I am terrified at the thought that it may play some dreadful trick on us, now that the end is in sight.'[25] He hoped the first three volumes might come out before the end of the year. But what name should he choose? *The Year 1805* would not do for a book that ended in 1812. He had chosen *All's Well That Ends Well*, thinking that would give the book the casual, romantic tone of a long English novel, when he suddenly had an illumination. ... On 17 December 1867, the *Moscow News* published the following advertisement: '*War and Peace*. By Count Leo Nikolayevich Tolstoy. Four volumes (80 sheets). Price: 7 roubles. Weight parcel post: 5 pounds. The first three volumes delivered with a coupon for the fourth, by P. I. Bartenyev, Publisher.'

Proudhon's tract, published in 1861 and translated into Russian in 1864, had given Tolstoy a title worthy of the scope of his subject. The first edition of *War and Peace*

* 7 September 1812, according to the Gregorian calendar.

was sold out in a few days. In May 1868, when the fourth volume came out, the public acclaim was confirmed. Encouraged by the flattering echoes he heard on all sides, Tolstoy began to work still more quickly. He devoted the whole of 1868 to writing the next part of *War and Peace* and correcting proofs, allowing himself only a few days' holiday during the summer. On sunny days he hunted or fished, as always. He also gave some time to his estate, which had expanded (he had bought more land), made frequent visits to his brother Sergey, did a great deal of haphazard reading of philosophers and historians, thought briefly of translating the *Memorial de Sainte-Hélène* into Russian and founding a review to be called *The Non-Contemporary*, as a gibe, which would concern itself with 'whatever could not conceivably be successful in the nineteenth century but might be in the twentieth'. His relations with his wife were so warm and simple that she wrote, 'We still argue, but the causes of these quarrels are so deep and complex that they would not occur if we did not love each other as we do. I will soon have been married six years, and my love continues to grow. Lyovochka often says that it is no longer love, but a fusion of souls so complete that we could not go on living without each other. I still love him with the same anxious, passionate, jealous, romantic love as before. Sometimes his assurance and his self-possession annoy me.' [26]

This assurance and self-possession were only apparent. In reality, Tolstoy was 'hanging on' by his nerves. 'The poet skims off the best of life and puts it in his work,' he wrote in a notebook. 'That is why his work is beautiful and his life bad.' [27] Work on the proofs of the fifth volume was delayed by children's illnesses. In April 1869, the author was writing the second Epilogue. 'What I have written there,' he told his friend Fet, 'was not simply imagined by me, but torn out of my cringing entrails.' [28] And at last, on 4 December 1869, the sixth and last volume of *War and Peace* appeared on the booksellers' shelves.

Suddenly severed from his characters after living in intimate communion with them for six long years, Tolstoy felt tragically bereft. Bewildered, disconnected, he went on dreaming of the phantoms he had let loose in the world, whose fate he could no longer alter. Would he ever be able to write anything else, after this huge book into which he had poured all that was best in him? 'Now, I am simply marking time,' he confessed to Fet. 'I don't think, I don't write, I feel pleasantly stupid.'[29] That same year, on 20 May, a fourth child was born to him – a son, called Leo.

[16]

War and Peace

THE success of the six-volume bound edition of *War and Peace* far surpassed Tolstoy's expectations, based on the lukewarm response to the first chapters in the *Russian Herald*. Readers swept bare the booksellers' shelves, gave the book to their friends, wrote letters from one end of Russia to the other defending their opinions of the characters. In the literary world, emotion was at fever pitch. Everyone was aware that an event of major importance had taken place. Like a meteor fallen from another planet, the huge mass of words intrigued and bothered people, and caused them to erupt in indignation.

Tolstoy's friend Fet was jubilant at the end of the final volume, although he disapproved of the author's 'depoetization' of Natasha in the Epilogue. Botkin wrote to him: 'Apart from the section on freemasonry, which is uninteresting and in fact boring, the novel is excellent from every point of view. What animation and depth! What a quintessentially Russian work!'[1] Goncharov wrote to Turgenev: 'I've saved the most important thing for the last: the publication of Count Leo Tolstoy's *War and Peace*. The count has become a veritable literary lion.'[2] Another colleague, Saltykov-Shchedrin, ground his teeth: 'The military scenes are all falsehood and chaos. Generals Bagration and Kutuzov are made to look like puppets. ...' Dostoyevsky, whose *Idiot* had just been raked over the coals by the critics, took offence at Strakhov (a critic) for comparing Tolstoy with 'all that is greatest in our literature'. 'To arrive with *War and Peace*,' he wrote, 'is to arrive too late, after "the new word" of Pushkin; and however far, however high Tolstoy may go, he cannot change the fact that that new word was uttered before him, and the first time, by a

genius.'[3] As for Turgenev, after his fierce criticism of the
opening of *War and Peace*, he let himself be swept away
by the rest. 'There are scores of ceaselessly astonishing
pages in *War and Peace*, absolutely top quality; all the
description, the customs and manners (the hunt, the troika
race at night, etc.). The historical appendix, on the other
hand, which has brought the readers to such a pitch of
frenzy, is nothing but puppetry and charlatanism. ... Tolstoy makes his readers' eyes bug out by telling them about
the tips of Alexander's boots or Speransky's laugh, and
makes them believe he knows *everything* about these people
because he knows those specific things about them, when in
fact that is all he knows. ... However, there are things in
the novel that nobody but Tolstoy is capable of writing,
anywhere in Europe, things that made me shiver with a
positive fever of excitement.' (Letter to Annenkov, 14 [26]
February 1868.) 'There are passages in it that will live as
long as the Russian language.' (Letter to Borisov, 27 February [10 March] 1868.) 'Tolstoy is a giant among his fellow writers, he makes me think of an elephant in a menagerie. It's incoherent – absurd, even; but immense, and so
intelligent!' (Letter to Borisov, 12 [24] February 1869.)

However, although Turgenev knelt before Tolstoy's art,
he could not swallow his philosophy. 'It is a great misfortune,' he wrote, once again to Annenkov,[4] 'when a self-
educated man of Tolstoy's type sets out to philosophize. He
invariably climbs on to any old broomstick, invents some
universal system that seems to provide a solution to every
problem in three easy steps – historical determinism, for
instance – and forward march! When, like Antaeus, he
comes down to earth again, his strength is renewed: the
death of the old prince, Alpatich, the peasant uprising, all
that is remarkable.'

Old Pogodin was no less effusive: 'I melt, I weep, I rejoice,' he wrote to Tolstoy on 3 April 1868. And he went on,
the next day: 'Now look here, what is this? You've done
for me. ... You have turned me, in my dotage, into –

Natasha! ... And Pushkin not here to see it! How he would have applauded, how happy he would have been, how he would have rubbed his hands with glee!'

It is true that a few months later, on second thought, the same Pogodin expressed a far more critical view of the same novel in an article in *The Russian*: 'What the novelist absolutely cannot be forgiven is his offhand treatment of figures such as Bagration, Speransky, Rostopchin and Ermolov, who belong to history. To study their lives and then judge them on the basis of evidence is all well and good; but to present them, without any reason, as ignoble or even repellent, mere outlines and silhouettes of men, is in my opinion an act of unpardonable irresponsibility and provocation, even in an author of great talent.'

This criticism was typical of the views of the conservative writers' clique, headed by Vyazemsky and Norov. Prince Vyazemsky, an old friend of Pushkin and Gogol, was incensed by Tolstoy's rabid determination to knock the national heroes off their pedestals. 'In atheism, heaven and life after death become meaningless,' he wrote. 'In historical free-thinking, earth and life itself become meaningless, through belittlement of the events of the past and contempt for the idols of popular imagination. ... This is no longer scepticism; it has become literary materialism.'[5] And Norov, who had fought in the battle of Borodino in his youth, admitted that the author had portrayed the battle scenes with praiseworthy respect for detail, but bemoaned the fact that 'our generals, whose names are inseparable from our military history, and are still heard in every mouth in the new generation of officers, were presented as a set of blind and incompetent tools of fate'.[6] The reactionary critic of *Action*, curiously enough, attributed this deflation of the official embellishments of war to a perverted sense of patriotism in the author – even though, said the critic, judging by his family name, he was a true Russian. 'Some ascribe this phenomenon,' he went on, 'to the influence of the environment in which the author grew up; during his childhood or youth, he was undoubtedly surrounded by Jesuit-trained French governesses, whose views of the year 1812 penetrated so deeply into the impressionable mind of the baby or boy that even in his adulthood Count Tolstoy has been unable to divest himself of this muddled, unintelligent and Roman Catholic interpretation of events.'*

The monarchist heaped abuse on Tolstoy's head because he had flaunted national values, and the liberals wanted to send him to the stake because he had flaunted the people. In the progressive paper *The Affair*, Bervi stated that for Tolstoy, 'honour and elegance exist only among the rich and famous,' that all the characters in the novel were 'base'; that Prince Andrey, for one, was nothing but a 'dirty, vulgar, unfeeling automaton', that the author 'let no opportunity pass to glorify passion, vulgarity and inanity', and that in reading the military passages 'one continually got the impression that a narrow-minded but garrulous corporal was boasting of his exploits in some remote hamlet to a group of gawping hicks'.

This virulent attack set the tone for other radical writers. In the *Illustrated Gazette*, an anonymous critic reviled the characters of *War and Peace*, who were 'all infamous products of the age of serfdom' and held the entire book to be 'an apologia for gluttonous aristocrats, sanctimony, hypocrisy and vice'. Tongue-in-cheek, *The Spark* congratulated Tolstoy on his appetizing rendition of the battle scenes, proving that 'it was a pleasant and easy thing to die for the Fatherland'. And Shelgunov, taking over from Bervi in *The Affair*, raised the tone of the debate by solemnly declaring that 'Tolstoy's philosophy could have no European significance', that the author was preaching 'Eastern fatalism against Western reason', that he and his ideas were 'throttling all energy, initiative and desire in the individual to im-

---

*A singular comment on a novel in which patriotism in epic proportions looms out of every page, and the French can scarcely be said to be flattered!

prove his social condition and achieve happiness', and, in short, that the teachings he was propagating were 'utterly opposed to those of modern thinkers, and chiefly Auguste Comte'. 'Fortunately,' concluded Shelgunov, 'Count Tolstoy is not a great writer. ... If, with his lack of emotional maturity, he had the genius of a Shakespeare or a Byron, the direst curse on earth would not be too strong for him.'

The liberals' mistrust of Tolstoy could be explained by the fact that in those days, with his title of nobility, his estate at Yasnaya Polyana and his military background, he still appeared to a portion of the young intellectuals as an aristocrat playing at being a friend of the people. None of his novels dealt with the issues that inflamed public opinion: emancipation of the serfs, freedom of the press, reorganization of the courts, women's rights, government reform. It seemed as though, by living in retirement on his estate, he were trying to ignore the present. True, there had been the *Sevastopol Sketches*. But since then ...? The novels of Goncharov, Dostoyevsky and Saltykov-Shchedrin aroused impassioned debate because they were blows struck in a battle; for many people, those of Leo Tolstoy were mere works of art. 'Although everyone read *War and Peace* with great enjoyment,' wrote Lystsev in his reminiscences, 'I must confess that we were not very stirred by it because the period the great author was writing about was too remote from the problems which were tormenting Russian society at that time.'

Hooted at by left and right, Tolstoy received his just measure of praise from the moderate critics and what is commonly called the general public. In *Fatherland Notes* Pisarev spoke of 'truth, unadorned and unadulterated'; Mrs Tsebrikova, writing in the same periodical, praised the ruthless and unerring simplicity with which he transposed life in his novel; in the *European Herald* Annenkov devoted a substantial article to the book, 'which can be compared with nothing on earth'; Suvorin, in the *Army and*

Navy Gazette, confessed that he was left at a loss by qualities he could not define: 'Nothing spectacular, nothing
strained; this gifted writer has not resorted to a single trick.
This is a smooth-flowing epic, by a painter-poet'; and in
The Dawn, Strakhov wrote the following lines, which filled
Tolstoy to bursting with pride: 'What mass and balance!
No other literature offers us anything comparable. Thousands of characters, thousands of scenes, the worlds of
government and family, history, war, every moment of human life from the first mew of the newborn babe to the
last gush of sentiment of the dying patriarch. ... And yet
no person is hidden by any other, no scene or impression
is spoiled by any other, everything is clear, everything is
harmonious, in the individual parts as in the whole ...'

The avant-garde found this dithyrambic praise very offensive. 'Strakhov is the only one to believe that Tolstoy is a
genius,' said the *St Petersburg Gazette*. And in the *St Petersburg News*, Burenin affirmed that *The Dawn* must have
been attempting to compete with the humorous newspapers
when it said that Tolstoy's novel had 'universal significance'.
Satirical verses were circulating, in which Tolstoy was qualified as the 'world's greatest genius'. [7]

Amused by this critical controversy raging over *War and
Peace*, the novelist Leskov wrote, in the *Stock Exchange
News* (1869–70), that 'Long periods elapse between the publication of each volume of the series, during which, as the
saying goes, reeds are broken on the author's back: he is
called this and that, a fatalist, an idiot, a madman, a realist,
a troll; and he, in the following instalment, remains what
he is and intends to be. ... He paces along, a massive
charger borne up by solid legs, and iron-shod ...'

In general, Tolstoy paid no attention to the critics. 'Pushkin was greatly troubled by critics,' he said. 'One is better
off ignoring them.' [8] However, he could not resist the pleasure of reading and re-reading Strakhov's flattering articles,
and he was subsequently to say, with regal assurance, that
in his study of *War and Peace* Strakhov had perceived 'the

lofty significance the book has acquired and can never lose again'.

In a postscript to *War and Peace* Tolstoy said the book was not a novel, even less a poem, and still less a historical chronicle; it was a new form of expression, 'designed to suit what the author had to say'. Thus proclaiming his independence from every literary form, he invited his readers to abandon their old habits, too, and reach beyond the characters and plot to discover the overall structure of the work for themselves. And indeed, it is only when the eyes cease to focus on the thousand details in the picture that the grandeur of the whole becomes apparent. Then, far above the scramble and swarm of individual human destinies emerge the eternal laws that govern the universe. Birth, death, love, ambition, jealousy, anguish, vanity: the deep, calm respiration of mankind strikes us full in the face.

First we see the cream of Russian society in the last days of peace in 1805. Drawing-room conversations, fluttering of butterflies, pettiness of speech and intention. Among this little menagerie of insignificant, silly, deceitful, debauched, idle people, a few souls ring more deeply. Pierre Bezukhov, oafish and soft-hearted; Prince Andrey Bolkonsky, tense, sardonic and proud; Princess Marya, exuding sweetness and resignation in the shadow of her tyrannical father; the Rostov children, whose liveliness, spontaneity and youthful appeal are like a fresh, cool breeze blowing through the book; and among them, Natasha – passionate, devil-may-care, wilful and tender Natasha, a mixture of Tanya Behrs and Sonya Tolstoy.

War breaks out. The problems of each are swept away by the problem of all. History puts an end to stories. The Russian army invades Austria. Bloody battles are fought, as futile as they are inevitable. The real leaders are not the men who plot stratagems, like Napoleon, but those who, like Kutuzov, submit to 'circumstances, the will of their subordinates and the whims of chance'. In action, Prince

Andrey feels strangely relieved to be borne along by a flood over which he has no control. While he searches for the meaning of this tempest raging over whole nations, Pierre Bezukhov, far behind the lines, is contaminated by the artificiality of his circle and marries the lovely Elena Kuragin; and Elena's brother Anatol is refused by Princess Marya, whom he does not love. The war continues. Wounded at Austerlitz, Prince Andrey has a revelation of the absurdity and purposelessness of life. Lying on his back, he sees above him 'a sky that was somehow vague, but very far and high, immensely high, in which grey clouds were drifting'. And he says to himself, 'How calm and peaceful, how majestic. ... Everything is vain, everything is false, except this boundless sky. There is nothing, absolutely nothing, except-that. . . .' Life resumes its course, however, for him and for the others, with its horrors and errors and fruitless striving. Pierre Bezukhov suspects Elena of faithlessness, wounds his rival Dolokhov in a duel, separates from his wife, contemplates his existence with disgust, becomes involved in freemasonry, plans to emancipate his serfs. Prince Andrey, back home, finds his wife, the 'little princess', about to give birth. He has scant affection for her and treats her as a child herself; but she dies in childbirth, almost under his eyes, and her death depresses him. He seeks another source of affection and begins to grow fond of Natasha Rostov. She is moved, attracted; but, out of respect for family conventions, the marriage is put off for a year. For her, the delay is fatal: forgetting Prince Andrey, she becomes enamoured of handsome Anatol Kuragin and plans to elope with him, but the attempt ends ignominiously in scandal and dishonour. And once again the dreadful threat of cataclysm rises and towers over the frog-pond: 1812 – war breaks out again. Napoleon's troops invade Russia. Borodino. Prince Andrey is badly injured. On the table next to him in the field hospital, a leg has just been amputated – the leg of the person he hates most in the world: Anatol Kuragin. His hatred melts on the spot, into trembling pity. He weeps 'for all men, for himself, for their errors and his'. He thinks of Natasha. He dreams of seeing her again. Miraculously, he does see her again, during the retreat, and then he dies. But what is that one death among all those others that litter the Russian soil these days? Moscow in flames. National union. Napoleon hesitant, worried. Pierre Bezukhov schemes to slay the tyrant. He is arrested and deported by the French. In his convoy he meets a Russian muzhik, Platon Karatayev, a pious and resigned man who smiles at suffering. Partisans heckle the fleeing French. One of them is Petya Rostov, who is killed. But Pierre Bezukhov is liberated by the Cossacks. Back in Moscow, he meets Natasha Rostov again and, after a long struggle with his conscience, realizes that he loves her and finds the courage to propose. The couple appears again, older, more staid and sedate, in 1820, in the Epilogue. Pierre is still excited by liberal ideas. He joins a small political club that aspires to reform every institution; a few years more, and we will probably find him among the ranks of the Decembrists. The story stops before the heroes reach the end of their road – with the next wave swelling behind them, the young, thirsty for love and battle.

When he began his book, did Tolstoy know what adventures lay in store for his characters from the first line to the last? Everything inclines us to believe he did not: their destinies as well as their personalities were decided as he went along. And yet their behaviour corresponds to their personalities at every turn. The wildest schemes seem as matter-of-fact as if they were proposed by living beings. That is the miracle of Tolstoy: the gift of life that he transmits to hundreds of creatures, all different, lightly yet unforgettably sketched: soldiers, peasants, generals, great noblemen, young maidens and women of the world. He moves from one to the other, effortlessly changing age, sex and social class. He gives each a particular way of thinking and talking, a physical appearance, a weight in live flesh, a past, even an odour. There would be nothing so remarkable in it if these were exceptional people, whose features were etched in acid. But no: the protagonists of this drama are standard issue, who might not arouse our curiosity if we were to meet them on the street. Here, however, they are identified and animated with such skill that they continue to live and move in our memories after we have closed the book. We would recognize her in a thousand, Natasha Rostov, 'not pretty, black-eyed, with a wide, expressive mouth ... narrow shoulders, bare arms full of childish grace'. She dreams of Boris Drubetskoy, inflames Vaska Denisov, falls in love with Prince Andrey Bolkonsky and becomes engaged to him – which does not prevent her from being swept off her feet by Anatol Kuragin and ultimately marrying Pierre Bezukhov. Thus, as she pursues her hectic course towards happiness, she acts as a link between all the main characters of the book. Every one, at some point, draws near to her, is lit up by and glows in her flame. 'Whatever she did, she threw herself into it, body and soul,' wrote Tolstoy. Whether caring for the wounded, sitting with Prince Andrey on his deathbed, singing, dancing, dashing through the country or loving the fatuous, absurd Kuragin – she abandons herself utterly to her joy or duty or danger or sorrow. Not over-intelligent, perhaps, or very cultivated, but instinct does duty for wit in her. In his remarks Tolstoy noted, 'Prodigal ... Self-confident ... Loved by all ... Proud ... Musical ... She needs a husband, two husbands, she needs children, she needs a bed. ...' The war and the deaths of her brother and Prince Andrey make brutal inroads on the girl her intimates used to call the 'graceful little imp'. Badly shaken, she contemplates the world with new seriousness. In the Epilogue we see her happily married, basking in a fairly obtuse sort of felicity. 'She had grown so round and broad that it was hard to recognize the slender, quicksilver Natasha of old in this stout matron. ... Talk and argument on women's rights or the relations between married couples not only did not interest her, she did not understand them.' In the author's scale of values it was not wrong for a wife to be concerned exclusively with housekeeping and children. Unlike the avant-garde writers of his time who were preaching emancipation, he considered that women must remain in their rightful place, obedient to their husbands and tied to hearth and cradle, if the very structure of the family and hence of society were not to collapse.

And yet, as though to disprove his own theory, he created Princess Marya Bolkonsky, ugly and awkward but sensitive, dignified, devout, capable of total abnegation, who, far from losing her own personality in marriage, remained as before, her soul turned 'towards the infinite, the eternal, the perfect'.

Among the men, the two heroes, Andrey Bolkonsky and Pierre Bezukhov, are the two parts of Leo Tolstoy. Into one he put his appetite for life, his pragmatism, his brutality, and into the other his aspirations towards ideal peace and charity, his naïveté, his awkwardness, his hesitation. He brings them together in conversation at Bogucharovo, by the side of a lake, and at Lysya Gory – and it is Tolstoy conversing with himself in his private diary. Prince Andrey has a sceptical turn of mind; he mistrusts his heart and hides his feelings in irony. Ambitious, he sees the war as a means of proving himself in action. But his thirst for glory vanishes on the battlefield of Austerlitz, under the vast sky filled with drifting grey clouds. After his wife's death he determines to improve the lives of his peasants, but not at all out of compassion for their wretched lot. 'An excellent intention, to free the serfs,' he says to Pierre. 'But it will not be a good thing for you – who have never, I suppose, had anyone flogged or sent to Siberia – and still less for them. Besides, if they are beaten and flogged and deported now and then, I don't believe they are any the worse for it. In Siberia they go on living the same animal existence, the marks of the whip will be scarred over, and they will be just as happy as before.'

In a burst of patriotic enthusiasm in 1812, he momentarily

forgot his sorrow and disgust at Natasha's betrayal. But it takes a fatal wound at Borodino to bring about the moral rebirth he has been hoping for. The sky he had believed was empty leans down over him at last, the inner peace he had been seeking in vain begins to grow in his heart as his strength gradually fails. He, the atheist, suddenly thinks, 'Love is God, and to die means that I, a part of that love, shall return to the great whole, the eternal source of things ...'

Opposite him is Pierre Bezukhov – massive, ungainly, short-sighted – made of such permeable stuff that the wildest schemes pass through him without leaving a trace. His good-will is equalled only by his boundless naïveté. He plunges head-first into debauchery, marriage, duels, free-masonry, patriotism, heroism in civilian dress, schemes to murder Napoleon, communion with the people and love of Natasha. He says, 'We must love, we must have faith. . . .' But he doesn't know in what or whom. In the end it is he – uncertain, shifting, bewildered Pierre – who finds happiness on earth, just as the somnolent Kutuzov triumphs over the most wily strategists. Pierre's revelation does not come in a bolt of lightning on the battlefield, but in listening to the peasant Platon Karatayev. Thereafter, in moments of doubt, he need only think of the humble muzhik, killed by the French, to be reconciled with the world.

Tolstoy put much of himself into Pierre Bezukhov and Andrey Bolkonsky, but he also allotted a few of his features to Nicholas Rostov: his strength and health, his pagan love of nature, his exaggerated sense of honour and his passion for hunting. But Nicholas Rostov is a boy of very average intelligence, anxious above all to avoid doing anything contrary to the established rules. He wants to belong to his time and his circle. Natasha, who knows him very well, says, 'Nicholas has one fault: he cannot like a thing unless everyone else likes it first!'

Alongside these stars of the first magnitude, mention should be made of little Sonya, Anatol Kuragin, Dolokhov,

Petya Rostov, old Prince Bolkonsky, Denisov, and so many others! ... When, how, did Tolstoy describe them? Impossible to tell exactly. Each of their portraits is composed of a thousand separate strokes scattered throughout the book. The author does, it is true, have occasional recourse to internal monologue to document his characters' states of mind, but most of the time he suggests their thoughts by an attitude or gesture, or the play of facial expressions caught on the wing. His people never merely smile, they do so 'with sudden good-will', 'condescendingly', 'with a touch of melancholy'. The word 'shade' is often found in his writing, and proves the importance he attaches to the exact translation of an emotion. After his father's death, Pierre is re-received by Anna Pavlovna 'with a shade of mournfulness', Prince Andrey speaks of happiness 'with a shade of bitterness and irony', in Nikolenka's love for his uncle there is 'a barely perceptible shade of contempt'.

In spite of the monumental dimensions of the book, this preoccupation with detail never deserts Tolstoy for one moment. When he shows the surgeon coming out of the operating tent, he notes that 'he held his cigar carefully, between thumb and little finger, for fear of staining it'; Kutuzov, talking to the tsar, has 'a trembling of his upper lip'; when Anatol talks to Princess Marya, he 'slides one finger through the buttonhole of his uniform'. Minor characters are identified by some external feature that recurs whenever they appear. The first thing the author notes about the little Princess Bolkonsky is 'her short upper lip, slightly down-shadowed'. This 'short lip' is mentioned four or five times, and after the young woman's death the angel on the monument over her grave is also given 'an imperceptibly raised upper lip'. The lovely Elena, Pierre's wife, always appears with 'her smile', 'her plump hand', 'her marble shoulders and throat'. Dolokhov is identified by his light blue eyes and the lines of his mouth, the upper lip of which 'came down far over the large lower lip, forming an acute angle'. Vereshagin, a Moscow merchant turned over to the mob by

Rostopchin, has for distinguishing marks his 'fox fur jacket', his 'shaved skull', his 'long thin neck' and 'frail hands'. Bilibin the diplomat is noteworthy for the mobility of his face: 'Sometimes his brow would be grooved by broad wrinkles and his eyebrows would rise, and sometimes they lowered and deep furrows formed in his cheeks.'

One must not conclude that Tolstoy freezes his characters into immobility by this process. On the contrary, believing that human personality is multiple, dynamic and changing, he contrives to show his people in different lights according to their surroundings. Prince Andrey is not the same in 'society' as when he is alone with Pierre, or with Bilibin the diplomat, or among the officers of his regiment, or in his father's presence, or escorting his sister, or with Natasha. Each time we see him through the eyes of the people with him, and discover a new side of his character. But these psychological fluctuations do not affect the rock on which the individual's entire personality is built, always perceptible beneath the waves that occasionally engulf it. Even when the foundation contradicts itself, it does not cease to exist. What gives so much life to the protagonists in *War and Peace* is that they are all defined in terms of each other.

'Returning to Moscow from the army,' writes Tolstoy, 'Nicholas Rostov was welcomed *by his close relatives* * as the best of sons, a hero, the irreplaceable Nikolenka; *by the other members of his family* as a pleasant, easy-going and well-mannered young man; *by his friends* as a good-looking lieutenant of hussars, a first-rate dancer and one of the most eligible young men in Moscow.'

Prince Andrey, on the other hand, is much sought after by the high society of St Petersburg: '*The pro-reform party* opened their doors wide to him – first, because he was noted for his intelligence and culture, and then, because by freeing his serfs he had acquired the reputation of being a liberal. *The discontented old men* sought his favour because,

* Italics in this and the following two quotations by the author.

for them, he was first and foremost his father's son and as such, they thought, he must disapprove of the reformers. *The ladies* welcomed him with open arms because he was an eligible bachelor, rich, notorious and surrounded by an aura of romance because he had been thought dead at the front and had just lost his wife.'

Among Kutuzov's staff officers, 'Prince Andrey had *two conflicting reputations*. Some – a minority – realized that he was an unusual person and expected great things from him, listened to him, admired and imitated him. ... Others – a majority – did not like him and considered him insufferably haughty, cold and unfriendly.'

Through a thousand observations of this type Tolstoy creates a definite atmosphere around each of his characters. Each one is caught up in an extremely subtle net of sympathies and antipathies. His slightest gesture resounds in several other consciousnesses. Prince Andrey, Pierre, Natasha and Princess Marya are not flat images, always seen from the same side; the reader moves around them and feels their interdependence with all the other characters. They all obey the law of relativity.

The historical figures are painted 'in motion' like the fictional ones. For them, too, the author chooses a few physical traits that recur, rather like a leitmotiv, and assist in their rapid identification: Napoleon – his rounded belly and 'plump hands'; Kutuzov – his sleepiness, his fat neck, his one eye and his scar. But although Tolstoy remains remarkably impartial towards the products of his own imagination, he loses every semblance of self-control when Napoleon enters the scene. The rage he felt long ago in the crypt at the Invalides in Paris pours into his brain. Unconsciously, the veteran of Sevastopol is wreaking his vengeance on the French, pen in hand. His descriptive method serves him admirably in this work of demolition. To clear himself of the charge of partiality, he protests that he 'invented nothing', that he gleaned 'every detail' from contemporary memoirs. No doubt; but the only details he selected from the memoirs were those that would make the emperor of the French appear ridiculous. The description of Napoleon performing his toilette, for example, is exact: his 'fat and furry chest', his 'snorting', his 'yellow, bloated' face, his expression, 'Go to it!' 'Harder!' while his manservant is rubbing him with cologne water – all are confirmed by Las Cases, but the scene took place during the sinister period of idleness of St Helena, not on the eve of Borodino. Never mind! At all costs, the Latin tyrant, the profaner of Russian soil, must be made to appear grotesque. These few strokes, artfully applied, make him into an ageing, fatuous creature whose allegedly statesmanlike stratagems misfire because of a head-cold, who never forgets for one moment to act out his little play before his aides-de-camp, his soldiers, his mirror. No psychological intuition, no military genius, nothing but nervous twitches. The fate of the world hanging upon one man's digestion. 'An insignificant tool of history who never, anywhere, even in exile, displayed any human dignity,' one reads in *War and Peace*. And what he didn't put in his book, Tolstoy found room for in his diary – there, he calls Napoleon a 'poor rider', a 'robber of paintings and statues' who delights in strolling through battlefields, where he 'thrills at the sight of the corpses and wounded men'. 'He is not interesting, but the crowds around him are, those he affects. At the beginning, he is narrow-minded but fair, in comparison with Murat and Barras; then groping, complacent and happy; and finally, insane: *wanting to take the daughter of the Caesars into his bed*. Total madness, senility and incompetence at St Helena. The false grandeur simply because the field of action was so great, but as soon as it began to shrink – incompetence. And a shameful death!'[9] Next to this bloodthirsty monster, Alexander appears an angel of light: intelligent, kindly, sensitive, from the height of his great power he is seeking his way, he has set out in quest of virtue.[10] Where, in this portrait, is the scheming, weak and fickle prince of whom Pushkin wrote, 'In appearance and in action, he was a clown'?[11]

The person who profited most by this patriotic distortion of the truth was not Alexander I, as it happens, but Kutuzov. The superiority of the old one-eyed general drowsing through his staff meetings lies in the fact that, unlike Napoleon, he does not take himself for a genius, he is not eternally posing for the historians of future generations, he never makes a plan, he never gives an order; he lets himself be carried along by events. 'He plainly had no patience with book-learning and intelligence, he had some other and more decisive form of knowledge,' wrote Tolstoy. And he possessed that 'decisive' knowledge because he was Russian and therefore had a sense of fatality. At the opposite pole from Napoleon, he is not a 'strong personality', but an incarnation of the people; hence his modesty, his habit of taking his time, his superhuman sixth sense. 'The people, by strange ways, chose him [Kutuzov] because they recognized that the old man who had fallen out of favour possessed this sense; they chose him against the will of the tsar, and made him their representative in a people's war. It is this sense alone that raised him to the position of supreme power, in which, as commander-in-chief, he strove with all his might, not to slay and exterminate, but to save and spare.' Here the writer, the great exponent of the 'shade', is abruptly transformed into a hagiographer. Chauvinism gives him a heavy hand. Everything is rose-coloured on the Russian side, black on the French.

But he regains his stride when he turns from his critique of great men to describe great events. His battles are not observed and commented upon by a placid historian; they are lived – by three, five, a score of frightened, exhausted, uncomprehending participants. On all sides, the fearful din, death, helplessness, incoherence. Orders are lost on the way or arrive too late. The fate of an engagement hangs on one battery which may or may not hold out, a bridge which may or may not blow up, an officer who will or will not dare to lead his men out under fire. One bridgehead resists and another gives way, by chance. Nothing ever happens accord-

ing to plan. And after it is all over the generals invent
logical causes for the uncontrollable movements of their
men. The truth is that victory and defeat are determined
by the morale of the army, that is, the people. And the
Russian people are fighting to defend their desecrated soil.
Therefore, they cannot help but prevail over their enemies:
'Pierre saw that the latent heat – as they say in physics – of
patriotism animated everyone he saw and explained why
they were calmly and almost gaily going about their preparations to die.'

Thousands of soldiers file past the reader over the ruined
roads – the wounded on their stretchers, limping infantry,
straying cavalry, peasant militiamen in white blouses with a
cross on their caps: the people on the march, countless,
unconscious, obscure, overpowering. It should be noted, however, that they do not appear until late in the book. Throughout nine tenths of it, Tolstoy is hardly aware of their existence. Guided by caste, he chooses his heroes among the
aristocracy: senior officers, socialites, landowners. And, on
the whole, his people are not tormented by democratic
aspirations. The daydreams of Prince Andrey and Pierre
Bezukhov are mild stuff in comparison with the liberal
passion that was agitating some men's minds in Russia as
early as the beginning of the nineteenth century. Well
might Tolstoy say, 'A work cannot be a success unless one
loves its governing idea, and the idea I loved in *War and
Peace* was the people': of its two thousand pages, only two
hundred are concerned with commoners.[12] It is as though
the author had suddenly been reminded of their existence
at the last moment. They burst upon the scene, a thick grey
flood: the townspeople of Moscow, soldiers, peasants, heroic
partisans. . . . Pierre Bezukhov, as a prisoner, meets the real
Russia, the Russia of the eternal muzhik, in the remarkable
Platon Karatayev. And even Platon Karatayev did not exist
in the first two versions of Book IV of *War and Peace*. He
sprang to life in the third draft – patient, laughing, tireless,
talking in proverbs, 'able to do everything, neither very

badly nor very well'. Through him Pierre realizes that there is 'an inner freedom that is not controlled by circumstance'. Earlier, wandering through the deserted streets of Moscow, he had told himself that 'wealth, power, life, all the things men organize and protect with such care, are valueless except for the joy with which one is able to abandon them'. The Russian people strengthened this conviction. Another expression of their force is the partisan, Tikhon Sherbaty, robust, brave and skilful, able to split a wooden post with one blow of his axe or whittle a graceful spoon. Moral and physical resistance combined. An alloy stronger than bullets and bayonets.

The heroes whose names have gone down in history seem so tiny, alongside these unsung warriors. Inspired by this thought, Tolstoy turned his back upon the romanticism of Alexandre Dumas and Walter Scott and proclaimed himself the enemy of all great men. Throughout the book he scattered challenges to the idol-makers: 'The history-book hero does not command the mass; he is constantly commanded by them.' (Volume III, Book XIII, Chapter 1.) 'In historical chronicles, the so-called great men are mere labels used to designate events but having no closer relation to them than labels do.' (Volume I, Book IX, Chapter 1.) 'The king is history's slave.' (Volume II, Book IX, Chapter 1.) 'Throughout this entire period Napoleon was like a child holding a pair of ribbons attached to the inside of a coach and imagining that he is driving the horses.' (Volume II, Book XIII, Chapter 10.)

In his determination to debunk traditional history, Tolstoy was edging back to the ideas he held in his University of Kazan days. As the historian Shebalsky has said, this is 'historical nihilism'. But since individuals have no control over events, how does one explain war? After all, the people are not the ones who are lusting to cut each other's throats! An embarrassing question for the novelist. To admit that Napoleon is capable of setting a massacre in motion is to admit that he possesses some power over history, and the attractive theory of the total ineffectiveness of the hero no longer holds water. To insist that a lone man cannot 'compel five hundred thousand to die' is to admit that the five hundred thousand have determined, more or less consciously, to invade a neighbouring country; and so another, no less attractive theory – that of the fundamental goodness of the people – must also fall by the wayside. Tolstoy took the easy way out of his dilemma in his article, 'Some Words about War and Peace': fatality. 'Why did millions of men kill each other, when everyone has known since the beginning of time that it is morally and physically wrong to do so?' he writes. 'Because the thing was so inevitable that in doing so they were obeying the same elementary zoological law as the bees when they kill each other in the autumn, and all male animals who exterminate each other.'

Having thus disposed of one problem, the author fails to see that another danger is lurking in its place. His opposition to personality worship drives him into apersonality worship. In refusing the unqualified deification of a man, he is forced to accept the unqualified deification of the people. The attention to shading, so dear to him in his study of character, is utterly lacking in his study of ideas. Suddenly, with the turn of a page, the novelist becomes a polemist, a moralist, a strategist. But the moment he forgets his dissertations and returns to his story, the spell that was momentarily snapped begins to work again … a 'Russian spell', in his own words. It would be interesting to count the number of times the word 'Russian' occurs in *War and Peace*. The army marches 'with a murmur of Russian voices and Russian thoughts', Natasha dances 'Russian-style', the diplomat Bilibin describes the campaign in French, 'but with that essentially Russian candour that allows room for pitiless self-criticism and mockery'.

Tolstoy was deeply attached to the ideas in *War and Peace*. But it is not his ideas that have guaranteed the posterity of the book; it is the fact that, in spite of the historical, military and philosophical considerations that encumber it, the book is a hymn to man and nature whose like has not been seen in the literature of the world. If Tolstoy could give such a convincing portrayal of Natasha's delight at the ball, the discussions of the German generals, Prince Andrey's luminous musings as he lies on his back under the infinite sky, the jokes of soldiers on bivouac, the night-whisperings of young girls in front of an open window, the exuberant bounds of hunting dogs on the scent, the peasants' rebellion, the heroic thoughts of Nicholas Rostov, the somnolence of Kutuzov at staff meetings, Pierre's wedded bliss, Speransky's artificial laugh, a masquerade party in the country, a hair-raising troika race, the face of a little girl painted with a burnt-cork moustache, the eerie rites of the masons, Moscow in flames or the countryside under the snow, it is because his overwhelming love of life enabled him to experience every expression of it with equal intensity. And he treasures this many-faceted existence even more deeply when it is simple: to him, everything that is close to nature is good. He respects the attraction between man and woman, he respects marriage and the family. He admires ordinary people, soldiers and peasants, with their dances and dirt, their own peculiar speech and their bravery. The person in the book who best understands the sense of human destiny is not a scholar or philosopher but the illiterate Platon Karatayev. And the farther one strays from this bucolic reality, the more deeply enmeshed one becomes in the artificial and lecherous coils of the lords of society. There, in the glimmer of the candelabras, souls do not ring true. Tolstoy has nothing but contempt for these empty-headed puppets. 'Man was built to be happy,' thinks Pierre Bezukhov; 'he carries his happiness inside him, in the satisfaction of his natural desires. ... There is nothing really terrifying in life. ... There is no situation in which man cannot be perfectly happy and free.'

Begun as a novel of the aristocracy and completed as a national epic, the gigantic and disparate work seems unfinished in some places.* Even though it was read over a hundred times, by the author, his wife and professional proofreaders, the text bristles with errors. It is a little silver icon that Princess Marya gives her brother Andrey as he is going off to war, but it is a little golden icon that the French soldiers remove from his neck when they pick him up wounded at Austerlitz. Natasha Rostov is thirteen years old in August 1805, fifteen in 1806 and sixteen in 1809. After gambling away his money late in December, Nicholas Rostov leaves Moscow in mid-November. Minor characters change their first names from one chapter to the next. Pierre Bezukhov sees the comet of 1812 in February 1811. ... But the very fact that most readers fail to notice these lapses proves the power of Tolstoy's art as a storyteller.

His style is perfectly suited to his purpose. As his sole aim is to seize life in all its fullness and diversity, he pays no heed to the harmony of his sentences: he spins them out, cripples them with adjectives, loads them down with subordinates. His superabundant conjunctions are by no means a result of carelessness, but rather of a painstaking search for exactitude. By piling up his modifiers, the author laboriously but inevitably approaches the impression he wants to produce. He is like a painter trying to cover a wall with a three-haired miniaturist's brush. Nose to the canvas, he lays on his infinitesimal strokes with myopic doggedness,

* At the provocation of the critics who had complained of his digressions, Tolstoy deleted all the philosophical considerations at the head of each section of *War and Peace*, when preparing the third edition in 1873. The chapters on the theory of warfare were relegated to an appendix at the end, the long passages in French were replaced by Russian translations, and the book was divided into four parts instead of six. This order was maintained in the fourth edition (1880), but for the fifth (1886), Countess Tolstoy, with Strakhov's assistance, replaced all the deleted or displaced passages and the conversations and letters in French: it had become clear that the style of the work, and even its meaning, had suffered from such brutal cutting. Thus, except for the division into four parts, which was retained, the book reverted to its 1868-9 form. Four more editions were published during Tolstoy's lifetime.

covers them over, sharpens them, scratches them out, puts them in again; and when he has finished, the myriad dots of colour converge, at a distance, into a fresco. The margins of his drafts are full of trial adjectives, as a painter mixes trial colours on the edge of his palette. To portray Napoleon giving the order to begin the battle of Austerlitz, he writes on a sheet of paper: 'firm, refreshed, intelligent and light-hearted'; 'healthy, gay, refreshed'; 'light-hearted, happy, bright'; 'with something like a reflection of well-earned contentment on his face'. Then, with the help of these guidelines, he builds his sentence: 'Feeling refreshed and light-hearted, in that happy mood in which everything seems possible and everything succeeds, he [Napoleon] mounted his horse and rode out on the field. ... His cold face expressed the confident and merited happiness of young lovers whose passion is requited.' [13] Or he may jot down impressions on the wing, lest he forget the turn he wants the chapter to take later on: 'Sonya, the blood rushing to her face. Her dark eyes of a faithful dog, thick braids wound around her face like a hound's ears. ... The old lackey. . . . The old birch with drooping, motionless branches. ... Sound of the hunting horn. ... Baying of the dogs ...' And from these gropings emerge the admirable pages of the Rostovs' hunt.

In the dialogue, every character's language corresponds to his social position, temperament, associates and age. The landscape is never set up behind the characters like a cyclorama, but reflects their moods and takes part in their action. The impact of heart on heart, army on army: when he looks up from the last page of the book, the reader feels lost, as though the thread of his own life had been cut. And yet he is not blinded, he has had no revelation, heard no prophecy. Here, Tolstoy is not a visionary; he is not waving a torch above the abyss, like Dostoyevsky; he does not turn his people inside-out like gloves, he does not scare us with our own shadows. His exploration never goes beyond what is directly perceptible to ordinary mortals. But he responds more intensely than ordinary mortals to the appeal of beings and things. Instead of bringing us closer to the Beyond, he brings us closer to the Here-and-Now. Men and plants, stones and animals are on the same plane for him. He observes a piece of carrion as attentively as a flower. The fatigue in the eyes of an aged horse is as significant to him for the comprehension of the universe as the fatuous conceit shining in the captain's face. The paradox is that this pantheistic process of creation, binding together pure and impure, great and small, beautiful and ugly, animate and inanimate, suffuses the entire work with the majesty of a second Genesis.

The Night at Arzamas

THE long and laborious convalescence began: after being delivered of *War and Peace*, Tolstoy started reading gluttonously. His meditations in the course of writing his book, on human destiny, the role of the individual in history and the comparative merits of reason and instinct naturally turned him in the direction of the philosophers. He devoured Kant and Schopenhauer – and was blinded by the latter, then little-known in Russia. How could Fet dare to say that the German thinker was only 'so-so'? Never had anyone written anything more profound or true about the sufferings of man, struggling with all his 'will to live' against the forces of destruction – or about chastity, the negation of the species, as the means to perfect happiness. Ah, the bitter vigour of this Teuton, his savage pessimism, his aspirations to oriental serenity.

'Do you know what my summer has been?' Tolstoy said to Fet. 'One continuous roar of approval of Schopenhauer, a series of spiritual joys such as I have never known before. I wrote away for his complete works and I have read them and am reading them again. Certainly, no student ever learned as much in his entire course of study as I have in this one summer.'

And, true enough, he was rather like an old student who had fallen behind in his work and was filling in the gaps in his education, a chunk at a time, first-come-first-served, in greedy gulps. He momentarily thought of translating Schopenhauer into Russian so that his compatriots could discover him, too, and even asked Fet to help him with this labour of love; but in the end, he contented himself with buying a portrait of the great man and hanging it up in his study.* Now that his own characters had abandoned him, he was thinking more and more of the mystery of life-after-death. 'He engaged in long and laborious meditations,' wrote Sonya. 'Often he said his brain hurt him, some painful process was going on inside it, everything was over for him, it was time for him to die.'[1]

His mind had become used to such sombre preoccupations: there had been the death of his brother Nicholas nine years before, which he still remembered with mixed feelings of grief and horror; there were the more recent deaths of Dyakov's wife, of Elizabeth Tolstoy (Alexandra's sister), of his father-in-law, Dr Behrs, in 1868; and lastly, of course, there were the deaths of the characters of *War and Peace* – such as Prince Andrey, into whom he had put a great deal of himself. Had he been worn out or in poor health, he might have accepted the idea of his destruction more readily. But at the peak of physical and intellectual power he had now reached, his whole being shuddered at the thought of the gaping void. His expanding lungs, the powerful, regular thud of his heart, his iron muscles, the amorous resources of his loins, his keen mind, the success of *War and Peace*, the land he owned and the land he planned to buy, Sonya, the children, the house, the dogs, horses, peasants, trees, everything conspired to make him unable to accept death. To be sure, there were his headaches and his stomach pains, but these were the minute creakings of a prodigiously well-functioning machine. What was there to worry about? Of course: the very fact that he had nothing to worry about! He was afraid of being stabbed in the back. His fear was animal, visceral, chilling. It came upon him all of a sudden – he began to tremble, sweat broke out on his forehead, he felt a presence behind his back. Then the jaws

---

*Thirteen years later, in 1882, he made a violent attack upon Schopenhauer's pessimism in *Confession*. 'Pessimism, and that of Schopenhauer in particular, has always seemed to me to be not only a sophism, but a form of nonsense, and a vulgar form at that,' he wrote, in 1889, to Edward Rod.

of the vice loosened, the shadow passed on, life tumbled in upon him, the tiniest vein in his body rejoiced at the new surge of blood. But he knew that one day *it* would come back.

Perhaps it was in order to fortify his defences against this peril that he determined to buy still more land – as though by enlarging his domain, increasing his fortune, sending his roots down yet deeper into the world of the living, he might find security against death. He read a notice in a newspaper of an estate for sale in the government of Penza, and suddenly decided to go there and negotiate the purchase. He had a little money on hand from the sale of *War and Peace*. On 31 August 1869 he took the train to Moscow (a line had recently been put through from Tula to the capital), and from there he set out, still by train, for Nizhny-Novgorod, where he arrived on 2 September. For the remainder of the trip, some two hundred and thirty miles, he had to hire a coach. His favourite servant, Sergey Arbuzov, was with him – a cheerful boy, whose excitement at the sights of the country they were crossing communicated itself to his master. Looking out and laughing together, they rolled southward all day long.

At dusk, Tolstoy began to doze. His head was heavy, yet he was not sorry to have set out on this long ramble: 'I was very anxious,' he later wrote, 'to increase our property, and to do so in the cleverest way possible, that is, better than anyone else. ... I had made up my mind that income from crops or sale of timber ought to cover the purchase price, and so the farm itself should cost nothing. I was looking for a seller who was an imbecile with no business sense and it seemed to me that I had found one.' As he was calculating his coup, he was suddenly frozen by dread. The night, the jolting, the ghosts of ragged trees along the road. Yasnaya Polyana at the other end of the earth: five hundred miles away! What was he doing here? And what if he fell ill? Far from his home, his family, Sonya! To keep up his spirits, he exchanged a few words with his servant. But the boy laughed at everything, and his youth and excitability merely deepened Tolstoy's gloom. He suddenly wanted to be indoors, see a lighted lamp, a samovar, faces. ... They were coming into Arzamas. He decided to spend the night there.

The entire town was asleep – a silent, compact, inhospitable wall. The horses' bells rang out harshly between the crowded white houses. At last the inn, with its signpost, big dusty courtyard, dark windows. Sergey leaped out, pounded on the door, woke a servant snoring in the entry-way. 'The man,' wrote Tolstoy, 'had a spot on one cheek and this spot seemed somehow horrible to me'.* He asked for a room. The doorkeeper showed him the only one in the establishment. He was checked in the doorway by an uneasy foreboding. It was a large room, square and white. 'I recall that I was particularly disturbed by the fact that it was square.' The doors and woodwork were painted dark red, a colour of dried blood. A table in Karelian birch, an old imitation-leather divan, not very clean, two candles with smoking wicks. While Sergey busied himself with the samovar, Tolstoy stretched out on the divan, a travelling pillow under his head and a rug over his legs. Through the fog in his head he heard the boy calling him to drink his tea, but he no longer wanted to get up or talk or drink; his eyes closed, he let himself drift off to sleep.

He awoke a short time later, in an empty, black, unfamiliar room, full of the rancid smell of burnt-out candles. 'Where am I? Where am I going? What am I running away from?' The questions fell upon him like a flock of ravens. He went out into the hall. Sergey was asleep on a bench, with one arm hanging down, next to the doorkeeper with the sinister spot on his cheek. 'I had hoped to get rid of

---

*Eleven years later, in 1880, Tolstoy described this night in an unfinished story from which most of the quotations in this chapter have been taken. But fearing his readers' incredulity, he did not dare to present the text as a description of an actual experience, and entitled it *Notes of a Madman*.

the thing that was tormenting me in the room,' wrote Tolstoy. 'But it came out behind me and everything turned black. I became more and more frightened.' He usually managed to calm himself by making a conscious effort to think rationally. But this time all the tricks he tried in order to regain his self-control only increased his terror.

' "This is ridiculous," I told myself. "Why am I so depressed? What am I afraid of?"

' "Of me," answered Death. "I am here." '

'A cold shudder ran over my skin. Yes, Death. It will come, it is already here, even though it has nothing to do with me now. ... My whole being ached with the need to live, the right to live, and, at the same moment, I felt death at work. And it was awful, being torn apart inside. I tried to shake off my terror. I found the stump of a candle in a brass candlestick and lighted it. The reddish flame, the candle, shorter than the candlestick, all told me the same story: there is nothing in life, nothing exists but death, and death should not be!'

He tried to think about his project, his money, Yasnaya Polyana, his wife, his four children, *War and Peace*, what he would write next – but they all seemed utterly pointless to him. Horror spread over him, mixed with a deep despair, 'as though I were about to vomit'. A geometrical horror, implacable, 'a square, white and red horror', the horror of the box. What else is a room but a big coffin?

He went back into the hall, where he heard the regular breathing of the two sleepers, and was amazed at their indifference. How could they sleep with Death among them? He was the only person awake on a sinking ship. The boat was going down and the crew were snoring. 'I was in agony, but I felt dry and cold and mean. There was not one drop of goodness in me. Only a hard, calm anger against myself and what had made me. ...' He went back to the room and lay down again. 'But what made me? They say God did. ... God. ... I remembered my prayers. ... I began to pray. . . . I invented orisons. . . . I crossed myself, I fell on my face, looking sideways for fear that someone might see me. . . .' As he muttered, 'Our Father which art in Heaven,' he imagined death entering him through every pore of his skin, weakening and rotting his organs, binding his tongue, darkening his brain. No more! . . . He rushed out, shook his servant and the doorkeeper; ordered the carriage harnessed. He would not stay one minute longer in that cursed inn for all the money in the world!

While Sergey stumbled out to the stable, he let himself fall on to the couch, closed his eyes and dropped off to sleep. When he awoke it was broad daylight. Sergey, seeing him asleep, had not dared to disturb him. The white and red room had lost its mystery. Tolstoy, rested and calm, could hardly believe he had had his nightmare. A glass of scalding tea and he was himself again.

On the road his dread returned, but with less force; he managed to control it. 'I felt that some misfortune had befallen me; I might forget it for a moment, but it was always there, at the back of my mind, and it had me in its power. . . . I went on living as before, but the fear of this despair never left me again.'

On 4 September, when he arrived at Saransk, he wrote to his wife, 'How are you and the children? Has anything happened? For the last two days I have been wild with worry. . . . Something extraordinary happened to me at Arzamas. It was two o'clock in the morning, I was very tired, I was sleepy, but I felt perfectly all right. And suddenly I was seized by a despair, a fear, a terror such as I have never known before. I shall tell you the details . . .'

He looked at the property for sale and thought it very handsome, but did not have the courage to buy it after his ominous revelations at Arzamas. Everything he saw was tinged with ash. He had only one thought, to hurry home to Yasnaya Polyana. There, at least, on his own land, with his own furniture and family around him, his life would recover its meaning, or so he trusted. That was his home port, his haven of hope. When he saw the two entrance towers, he felt saved. Sonya rushed into his arms.

Some time afterwards he learned that his old friend Vasily Petrovich Botkin, the publicist, had died at his home on 4 October during a *soirée musicale* to which he had invited a great many people. How strange it was – all those preparations, the invitations sent out all over town, the orchestra, the gilded chairs, the baskets of flowers, decisions to make about the buffet, the wines, one's clothes, the seating arrangements, and, all of a sudden – blackout. And how would he die? Leafing through his notebook, he found some lines he had written four years before: 'I was expecting some people I was fond of. ... They arrived and were exactly as I had hoped they would be. I was happy. That evening I went to bed. I was in that half-waking state in which superficial agitation dies away and the soul begins to speak clearly. My soul was striving towards something, wanting something. "What can I want?" I asked myself in surprise. "My friends are here. Isn't that what I needed to regain my peace of mind? No, that is not it. ... What, then?" I went through everything in my mind. ... Nothing could satisfy this desire in me. And the desire persisted, it still persists and indeed it is the most important and strongest thing in my soul. I desire what does not exist in this world. But it exists somewhere, since I desire it. Where ... ? To be reborn, to die. That is the peace I yearn for, we all yearn for. ...' [2] Yesterday he was courting death, today he was running away from it. But isn't that the very essence of man, in every circumstance, to put hope in his fear and fear in his hope? For the rest of his life, he was to live like a man who had been hit by a bullet that cannot be extracted. It is always there, lodged in one's head. Impossible to forget it, although one hardly feels it at all.

Winter came, snow enveloped the house, the family huddled together around the glowing stoves and, little by little, Leo Tolstoy regained his confidence in the future.

PART V

—

CONFLICT

[18]

Interim

'ALL this winter,' Tolstoy wrote in February 1870, 'I have done nothing but sleep, play Bezique, ski, skate and run, but mostly lie in bed.'[1]

This vision of vegetation was not strictly accurate. At forty-two as at twenty, Tolstoy was incapable of doing nothing for a week on end. Between whirls around the frozen pond, where he made S-turns and cut figures of eight, gliding gracefully along with his beard streaming in the wind, he began reading again. That year the object of his curiosity was the theatre: he read and re-read Shakespeare – for whom he had scant affection – Goethe, Molière, Pushkin and Gogol, and planned to write a play on the reign of Peter the Great. However, when he began to look into the period more deeply, in Ustryalov's *History of Peter the Great*, he realized that a novel would give him greater scope. He immediately started making notes and drafting outlines, and even dashed off a chapter. But with the first ray of sunshine he dropped his pen and fled outdoors. His place was with the peasants. There was so much to be done on the estate in the springtime! 'I received your letter,' he wrote to Fet on 11 May 1870, 'as I came in from work, covered with sweat and carrying my axe and spade, and thus a thousand miles from any thought of art.' A month later, 'Thanks be to God, this summer I am as stupid as a horse. I work, chop, spade, mow and, luckily for me, do not give one thought to that awful lit-tra-tyure or those awful lit-try folk.' Nor did he give a thought to politics. The noise of the world died away at his doorstep. Neither the Franco-Prussian war of 1870 nor the Commune of Paris troubled his meditations. He did occasionally open his notebook, but only to inscribe philosophical maxims or make childish drawings to illus-

trate his *Reader*. Sonya, distressed by his inability to concentrate, blessed the return of the rainy season that drove
him back into his study. She so wanted to relive those arduous years of the creation of *War and Peace*.

That autumn, she thought, her prayers had been answered. 'Now our life has become very sober; we work all day
long,' she wrote to her brother. 'Leo sits behind a stack of
books, portraits and pictures, frowning and reading, examining, taking notes. In the evening, when the children are in
bed, he tells me his plans and what he wants to write. ...
He has chosen the period of Peter the Great.'[2] And a
month later, 'I think he is going to write another epic like
War and Peace.'[3]

She was wrong. Tolstoy suddenly abandoned his characters, almost before they were born. He didn't feel them, he
couldn't see them, it was hard for him to imagine the world
in which their story unfolded. To Strakhov, who was pressing him for the beginning of his next novel to publish in
The Dawn, he sadly replied that he could not promise anything: 'I am in a most exasperating state of mind, with
wild schemes, doubts of myself and hard mental labour all
intermingled. Perhaps this is the prelude to a period of
happy and confident work, and perhaps, on the contrary, I
shall never write another word!'[4]

A strong feeling of intellectual companionship had
bound him to this correspondent after Strakhov's glowing
article on *War and Peace*. Also, he was delighted with a
study Strakhov had just published in *The Dawn* on the
position of women. According to its author, woman was entitled by her physical and moral beauty to be considered the
queen of creation, as long as she did not forsake her mission. Born to give delight and bear children, she became a
monster the moment she turned aside from the path God
had traced for her. Feminism was a crime against nature
and it was man's duty to see that his helpmeet did not suc-
cumb to this temptation. Tolstoy was ready to enlist in
Strakhov's cause, but pointed out that some women might

be useful to society even though they were not wives or mothers: nurses, nannies, maiden aunts, unoccupied widows, 'all those who look after other people's children', and even 'loose women'! He had not yet developed his theory of prostitution as an attack upon human dignity. In 1870, the man who was to fulminate a few years later against the ignominy of paid love (in *Resurrection*) calmly wrote to his new friend Strakhov that 'prostitutes' were necessary for the safeguard of the family. Without them, in the cities, where large numbers of bachelors congregated, 'few wives and daughters would remain pure'. Without them, most husbands would eventually be unable to put up with their wives. 'These poor creatures have existed since time immemorial and they always will,' he said, 'and in my opinion it would be impious and unintelligent to pretend that God was wrong to tolerate this state of affairs and Christ had been wrong to pardon one of them.' When he read his letter over, however, his claims did not seem quite so self-evident, and he decided not to send it.

While he was thus meditating upon the role of women in general, his own wife was watching for the rebirth of his inspiration. 'Today, for the first time, he began to write,' she noted in her diary on 9 December 1870. 'I cannot understand what is going on in his head during his hours of inactivity. His lack of direction is a great trial to him. He is ashamed of it, not only with me but with the servants and everyone else. ... Sometimes he thinks he is losing his mind, and his fear of insanity is so intense that I am terrified when he tells me about it afterwards.' Tiptoeing back and forth before his study door, she yearned, as though for manna from heaven, to see the pages that illustrious hand would pass out to her to copy. She was eager to do something useful but she did not dare to interfere, for fear of disturbing the work in gestation. Days passed, nothing came, she grew impatient. Suddenly, instead of handing her the opening chapters of a novel, he announced that he was going to learn Greek. She thought he was joking. But he meant it. He sent for a theological student from Moscow to teach him the rudiments of the language. From the first day, the forty-two-year-old pupil threw himself into Greek grammar with a passion, pored over dictionaries, drew up vocabularies, tackled the great authors. In spite of his headaches, he learned quickly. In a few weeks he had outdistanced his teacher. He sight-translated Xenophon, revelled in Homer, discovered Plato and said the originals were like 'spring-water that sets the teeth on edge, full of sunlight and impurities and dust-motes that make it seem even more pure and fresh', while translations of the same texts were as taste-less as 'boiled, distilled water'. Sometimes he dreamed in Greek at night. He imagined himself living in Athens; as he tramped through the snow of Yasnaya Polyana, sinking in up to his calves, his head was filled with sun, marble and geometry. Watching him changing overnight into a Greek, his wife was torn between admiration and alarm. 'There is clearly nothing in the world that interests him more or gives him greater pleasure than to learn a new Greek word or puzzle out some expression he has not met before,' she complained. 'I have questioned several people, some of whom have taken their degree at the university. To hear them talk, Lyovochka has made unbelievable progress in Greek.'[5] He himself felt rejuvenated by this diet of ancient wisdom. 'Now I firmly believe,' he said to Fet, 'that I shall write no more gossipy twaddle of the *War and Peace* type.'

He sententiously proclaimed to Sonya, whose eyes bulged at his words, 'Writing is easy. The hard thing is not to write.' 'He wants to write something pure and elegant, from which not one word could be removed,' she noted, 'like the works of ancient Greek literature or art.'[6] He had half a mind to write directly in the language of Homer; after all, at the end of a few months of study he had held his own in an argument with Professor Leontyev of the University of Moscow and had even convinced him that he had made mistakes in translation. But in the end, such an undertaking, carried out at such a pace, could only add to his fatigue, and

Tolstoy's constitution began to suffer from his love of Greek. Sonya was pregnant, but he was the one who had dizzy spells, bouts of melancholy and irrational despair. She was more impatient to see him begin a new book than he was to see her delivered of her fifth child.

On 12 February 1871 she gave birth, after a difficult labour, to a delicate little girl with pale blue eyes, who was baptized Marya. Puerperal fever set in; the doctors feared for the mother's life. Tolstoy was badly frightened. Then her temperature fell, the pain diminished, and Sonya got up out of bed. Reassured to see her back on her feet again, Tolstoy returned to his worries over the state of his own health: rheumatism in one knee, a little hacking cough. ... He was not quite a hypochondriac, but he was always ready to believe himself seriously ill. It seemed to him that death was assuming all kinds of mysterious disguises in trying to worm its way into his body. 'I am ill,' he wrote to Fet, 'but I don't know what's the matter with me; at any rate, it looks bad or good, depending on one's attitude towards the end of it all.' [7] And to Urusov, 'My health is poor. I have never been so depressed in all my life. I have lost all joy in living. ...' [8] Persuaded that his hour was at hand, he began to treat his wife with increasing coolness. He had lost his appeal for her as well. 'Something in us has broken,' she wrote. 'I have lost my faith in happiness and life. ... I am afraid of the future.' And to drag him out of his apathy, she begged him to follow the doctors' advice and return to Samara for another *kumys* treatment, like the one he had had in 1862. Flattered to see that someone took his symptoms seriously, Tolstoy condescended to go. But, dreading a repetition of the nightmare of Arzamas on the way, he took along his sixteen-year-old brother-in-law Stepan Behrs, who had accompanied him to Borodino, and a manservant.

From Moscow they went to Nizhny-Novgorod by train, then down the Volga by steamboat. To reach the village of Karalyk they still had to travel eighty-five miles by road, from Samara. Upon reaching the Bashkir settlement, he was delighted to find that everyone remembered him, after nine years. He rented a felt tent from a mullah, which leaked at every seam. Their bed was a layer of hay, their furniture a chair, a table and one rickety buffet. Hens cackled and pecked at the ground in the doorway, and tethered horses whinnied. The diet was strict. No vegetables, no cereals, no salt. They ate nothing but mutton, tearing it apart with their hands, and drank *kumys*. The fizzy, invigorating milk was brewed in leather vessels by the women of the tribe. There were a few Russian summer visitors, in more or less acute states of decline, trying to convince themselves of the rejuvenating powers of the beverage. Consumed at the rate of six bottles a day, it produced a mild and pleasant state of inebriation. At first, however, Tolstoy was sorry he had come. Around six o'clock every evening, the mortal oppression of the night of Arzamas settled down on him. He could not repress the feeling, and relieved himself by describing it to his wife, with the perverse desire of tormenting her: 'It is like a fever, a physical feeling of dread, a sensation I can only describe by saying that the soul becomes separated from the body. As for my mental anguish on your account, I refuse to let it raise its head. I never think about you or the children, I forbid myself to think about them, for if I did I should head for home the next minute. I don't understand my condition at all: either I caught a cold in the *kibitka* the first chilly nights, or else this *kumys* is bad for me.'[9]

His consolation was the discovery, among the 'patients', of a professor of Greek at a theological seminary, with whom he read his beloved ancients in the original. Thanks to them, in spite of his discomfort, he began to find 'a touch of Herodotus' about the Bashkirs. 'If you keep slaving away at your Greek you'll never get well,' was Sonya's irritated reply. 'That is the cause of your anxiety and indifference to life here and now. It's not for nothing that Greek is a dead language: it puts the mind in a coma.'[10]

Tolstoy was touched by her naïve concern. Once again, at

a distance, his wife seemed a priceless pearl. 'Your letters do me more harm than my Greek, they disturb me so,' he wrote. 'I cannot read them without shedding tears, my whole body trembles, my heart begins to pound. You write anything that comes into your head, but for me *every single word*** is important, I read them over and over again. Right now I love you so much that I want to cry.'

However, when she had the curious idea of sending him a photograph of herself wearing a kerchief (her head had been shaved after the puerperal fever), he could not hide his disappointment: 'You looked old, too thin, and pitiful. Besides, after a separation, a portrait, even of the face of the person one more than loves (as I do you) is always a disillusionment. In my imagination I see you the way you are, only better. But reality is never perfect. However, now I am reconciled to your picture and it is a great source of comfort to me.'

Was it the *kumys*, the open air or the rough life in a tent? Little by little, he regained his balance. The heat was debilitating, but it was good to sweat under his shirt. He became friendly with his neighbours; urged on by him, the Greek professor became a devotee of rope-skipping; a surrogate judge told him law-court anecdotes; a young landowner entertained him with hunting stories. His old love revived, he bought a dog and a horse and began to amuse himself shooting bustard and wild duck – the steppe was full of them.

Then, with Stepan Behrs, he toured the surrounding villages and went as far as Buzuluk, where a fair was being held. All the tribes in the region were pouring into the trading post. Tolstoy mingled with Russian muzhiks, Cossacks, Bashkirs and Kirghiz in tribal costume, and talked to them all. Not far from there he met the members of a religious sect, the Molokhans, or milk drinkers; he also went to see an old hermit who lived in a cave and talked interminably about Holy Scripture. Suddenly he decided to buy

*Tolstoy's italics.

a piece of property in the district of Samara. The land was dirt-cheap, and the climate was so bracing! The whole family would come, every summer. And there just happened to be a 6,700-acre tract for sale. Price: twenty thousand roubles.* The temptation was too great. Tolstoy notified his wife that he was about to make a very good deal and gave instructions to the notary.†

Invigorated by the *kumys* and the option he had taken on the land, he returned to Yasnaya Polyana on 2 August 1871; but at the sight of his wife and children, all the good effects of his treatment seemed to go up in smoke. He was enveloped in tragic indifference. Confronted by his lifeless mask, Sonya did not know what to do. 'Lyovovchka keeps saying that everything is finished for him,' she wrote to her sister on 15 September 1871, 'that he is soon going to die, nothing gives him pleasure any more and he wants nothing more out of life.'

But then someone appeared to boost his morale: his admirer Strakhov arrived at Yasnaya Polyana, and Tolstoy blossomed anew under his shower of praise. This visit marked the beginning of an exalted correspondence between the two. 'A spirit of light radiates from you as from everything you write,' said Strakhov to Tolstoy. 'It is my only wish to know you are well and happily writing.' And, 'The more I see you, the fonder I grow of you. ... Be assured that even if you never write another word, you will still be the most original and profound author in all Russian literature. When the Russian empire is no more, new nations will learn what the Russians were by reading *War and Peace*.' Or, 'You will not often meet another man who loves and understands you as I do.' He said that for him, Yasnaya Polyana was 'like Mecca'.[11] Tolstoy, however, did not always agree with his admirer's theories. For Strakhov, who had just published a philosophical work entitled *The World as a Totality*, man was the centre of creation and the most

* Or $56,600.
† The sale was concluded on 9 September that same year (1871).

highly developed product of nature. 'The zoological perfection of man, on which you lay such stress,' wrote Tolstoy, 'is extremely relative, for the very reason that man himself is the judge of it. The housefly is just as much the centre and pinnacle of creation.' Also, he could not agree that the goal of man was a sort of organic supremacy, as Strakhov claimed. In his opinion, man's purpose on earth was to strive to elevate his soul by obeying ethical laws, practising the great religions (Christian or Buddhist) and seeking the good.

It was undoubtedly these ideas that led him back to his pedagogical schemes, which he had abandoned since 1863. While in Moscow in 1868, he had met Skyler, the American consul there, who had told him about the teaching methods employed in his country and given him some textbooks: *The First, Second and Third Readers.* From 1870 to 1872, using them as a basis, Tolstoy worked on a series of *Readers* of his own. This work, seven hundred and fifty-eight pages long, is divided into four parts and contains two hundred short, easy-to-understand stories (anecdotes about Tolstoy's dogs, adaptations of Chinese and Persian tales, translations of Aesop's *Fables*, folk legends, episodes based on *Les Misérables*, sample pages from Plutarch, etc.). As a supplement to the literary section the author presented a new method of learning arithmetic. ('The last few days I have worn myself out trying to finish the section on arithmetic. I have finished multiplication and division and am almost done with fractions.'[12]) He even developed a passion for astronomy, and spent whole nights examining the stars. This titanic labour in an unfamiliar field exhausted him. 'If these articles have any merit, they will owe it to the simplicity and clarity of the drawing, the line – that is, the language,'[13] he wrote to Strakhov. And to his aunt Alexandra, 'As for the *Reader*, my ambitious dream is as follows: for two generations every Russian child, imperial prince or muzhik, should learn with this book, should receive his first impressions of poetry from it, and I, having

written it, should be allowed to die in peace.'[14] As a
friendly gesture, Strakhov offered to correct the proofs. Tolstoy hoped the *Reader* would bring in more money, which
he needed to consolidate his family's position and buy more
land. But he was afraid that professional teachers would be
exasperated by the book, which was so contrary to all their
traditions. If he did not sell 3,600 copies by the end of the
year, it would be a 'financial fiasco'.

'When I brought out *War and Peace*,' he wrote to Strakhov, 'I knew the book was full of faults, but I was sure it
would be exactly as successful as it was; now, publishing my
Reader, I know it has hardly any faults and is far superior
to every other textbook of the same type, but I am not expecting it to have anything like the success a textbook ought
to have.'[15] He was right. Most critics were opposed to the
'aberrant' educational system he advocated. His daring to
condemn phonetic reading, which was just beginning to become popular in Russian schools, caused much indignation.
P. M. Polevoy, in the *St Petersburg News*, said it was criminal to affirm that a pupil who was sincerely convinced that
the earth was held up by 'water and fish' showed sounder
judgement than one who knew the earth turned on its axis
but was incapable of understanding or explaining the phenomenon. 'It is a pity,' he wrote, 'that the talented author of
so many admirable works, the pride of Russian literature,
should waste his energy composing a *Reader* such as this,
which must have taken him a long time and will certainly
not be used in our schools.' Other journalists were scornful
of the false simplicity of the subject matter, the lack of
style, the moralizing pretentiousness of the whole book.
However, public, tutors and families gradually began to take
an interest in it, new printings followed in rapid succession
and, when he was taking stock at the end of his life, Tolstoy
found that nearly a million copies of this much-maligned
book had been sold.

Before he had even completed his *Readers*, he wanted to
try out his new system of education on his usual guinea-

pigs: the little muzhiks of Yasnaya Polyana. He opened a school, this time inside the main house instead of the nearby pavilion. Thirty-five local children attended. The teachers were himself, his wife, his son Sergey (age eight) and his daughter Tanya (age seven). The countess soon produced another son (13 June 1872), Petya. Tolstoy had become a habitué of the delivery room and was quite unmoved by this succession of births – he told the news to Strakhov between parentheses: 'I am deep in my papers and would have finished today except for my wife's confinement (she gave birth yesterday, a boy). I shall send you the manuscript, etc., in the next few days.'[16]

No mere family occurrence seemed able to tear him away from his teaching. The flock of peasant children gathered anywhere, in the hall, the dining-room, under the stairs, in the new study the author had built for himself. A characteristic odour of greased leather and damp goatskin rose from the squirming little group. As he had done ten years before, the count reigned in wide-eyed wonder over his covey of cherubs with runny noses and dirty hands. The same lack of constraint as in the past, the same familiarity in relations between teacher and pupils. They all talked at once, answered at random, laughed and enjoyed themselves, and learned like birds pecking seeds. 'When I see these tattered, underfed, unwashed youngsters with their candid eyes from which the soul of an angel often shines out, a feeling of apprehension and horror comes over me, as though I were watching someone drown,' he said.

To demonstrate the virtues of his method, he invited a dozen school-teachers to spend a week at the school. A group of totally illiterate children were imported for the test from the hamlets of Telyatinki and Grumond. The object was to see how long it would take them to learn to read and write, using the *Reader*, and the results were apparently conclusive. Encouraged, Tolstoy began to think seriously of founding a sort of secondary school for peasant children who wanted to continue their education without changing their way of life – a *laptis* university, was the expression he used : * higher mathematics and foreign languages for every farmhand. The only thing he lacked was capital. The marshal of nobility of the province, D. F. Samarin, whispered in Tolstoy's ear that the local *zemstvo* had a grant of thirty thousand roubles for educational purposes. Allured by the prospect of a subsidy, the author-teacher, who had hitherto strenuously avoided all administrative functions, stood for and was duly elected to the *zemstvo*. But the actual amount of the grant was only ten thousand roubles and the majority voted that it should be used for fellowship pupils at the Tula Girls' School in homage to Catherine the Great, civilizer of Russia.†

Tolstoy was undaunted by this setback. Going over his opponents' heads, he decided to defend his educational system before the Moscow 'Society for the Education of the People'. On the day of the debate he marched into the committee room, where thirty-one professors were seated, as though it were the lion's den; the lions, however, were an elderly and, for the most part, affable lot. After a few growls of protest at the disturbance, they decided that his method would be 'tried out' on illiterate factory workers in a Moscow school. But it was so hot on the day of the test that the labourers, dripping with perspiration, remained deaf to all their instructor's exhortations. This experiment having proved inconclusive, two factory schools were then selected; the phonetic method was taught in one and the Tolstoy method in the other. At the end of seven weeks a special committee found that the first group was, on the whole, 'more advanced' than the second. But no decision was taken, the question was left in mid-air, and Tolstoy resigned himself to continuing his crusade in the press. His 'Open Letter

* *Laptis* are shoes made from woven linden-bark, worn by Russian peasants.

† Tolstoy's first biographer, Biryukov, was mistaken when he said the sum of thirty thousand roubles coveted by the author had been used for a statue commemorating one of the empress's edicts.

to Chairman Shatilov', affirming that 'freedom is the sole criterion in pedagogy', appeared in *Fatherland Notes* and provoked the ire of some and the admiration of others. At the same time, he was working on a second *Reader*, the purpose of which, as he stated in the preface, was to 'give the pupils, for the smallest price, the greatest quantity of comprehensible material, arranged progressively …' He felt as though he were waging a single-handed battle with every bureaucrat in the empire. In 1872 he had time for only a short trip to Samara, to inspect the farm he had bought the previous year and gulp down a few bowls of foaming *kumys*.

Upon his return, there was a fresh collision with the administration. While he was away, a Yasnaya Polyana shepherd had been killed by a young bull. Thereupon, some little greenhorn 'who pretended to be an examining magistrate' came to interrogate Tolstoy on the circumstances of the incident and even on the particulars of his identity and marital status. Tolstoy took on a rather haughty tone, whereupon the greenhorn had the effrontery to ask him whether he was the legitimate son of his parents and presented him with a statement to sign, to the effect that he promised on his honour not to leave Yasnaya Polyana until the investigation was over. To hear this underling talk, it was the owner of the bull who was responsible for the shepherd's death. The judge's deputy was to decide within a week whether to maintain or drop the charge. Tolstoy saw red. A week! Everyone knew that week could go on for months, years! He, Count Leo Tolstoy, confined to his estate for years! Or, worse yet, dragged into court! He already saw himself in a tattered shirt lying on the straw pallet in his cell. A miscarriage of justice. A scandal. A crime against humanity! In his fury he forgot all about the dead shepherd. If anyone was to be pitied in this business, it was he, Leo Tolstoy, and he alone. As usual, Alexandra Tolstoy, as representative of the court, was the first to hear his grievances.

With my grey beard and my six children, [he wrote] with my consciousness of living an industrious and useful life, with my firm conviction that I am not guilty, with a contempt I cannot hide for the modern form of justice, with my sole desire to be left in peace as I leave others in peace, I consider it impossible for me to remain in Russia. ... You will read the whole story in the press; I shall die of rage if I cannot relieve myself by making it public. ... If I do not die of rage and grief in the prison into which they are undoubtedly going to throw me (I have had proof of their hatred of me), I have decided to emigrate to England for the rest of my days, or at least for as long as personal liberty and honour are not safe here. My wife approves of my plan. She loves everything English. It will be ideal for the children. I shall have enough money: if I sell everything, I shall have nearly two hundred thousand roubles.*

And he enlarged upon his scheme, in deadly earnest: first, the family would settle near London; then they would choose some pleasant little town by the sea and buy land somewhere in the vicinity, as in Russia. English peasants would do the farming, just as the muzhiks did here. The main thing was to have an entry into the aristocracy. 'For that you can be very useful to me,' he went on to Alexandra. 'Two or three letters of recommendation would suffice to open the doors of English high society to us. It is essential for the children, who will grow up there.' [17]

To impress the pious Alexandra, he added that he was suffering from his own anger and had just tried to calm himself by reciting a paternoster and thirty-seven psalms, but to no avail. Knowing her nephew's penchant for exaggeration, the old maid of honour did not attach too much importance to his fulminations. Besides, she had little time to act, for a second letter from Tolstoy arrived four days later, announcing that everything had been cleared up: he had been given assurance that the charge would not be pressed, the president of the court had apologized for the incident and, in short, everything was back to normal;

* Or \$566,300.

Russia had become habitable again. 'Forgive me if I have worried you,' he wrote to Alexandra, 'but it wasn't my fault. This month I have been tormenting myself as never before in my entire life and, with proper male selfishness, I wanted everybody else to be tormented along with me.'[18] A few months later, a second shepherd was fatally injured at Yasnaya Polyana by a mad bull. This time Tolstoy himself nursed the man for three days, but in vain, and he confessed that the man's death weighed on his conscience.

When the shepherd had been buried, the bull sacrificed, and the matter was at an end, he went back to his *Reader* and his pupils. At first, Sonya also showed an interest in the education of children. After all, she had received her teacher's certificate before she married, and she personally was teaching her sons Leo and Ilya and her daughter Tanya to read and write; they learned foreign languages from the English Miss Hannah and Mr Rey, a Swiss, and Tolstoy himself was to instruct them in arithmetic and Greek. But although he was a paragon of mildness and patience with the little muzhiks, he became exacting, irritable and unfair where his own progeny were concerned. What was endearing in ignorant creatures destined to oblivion became intolerable in the descendants of Count Tolstoy.

Sonya deplored her husband's sternness, but her chief source of anxiety lay in the fact that he was now totally immersed in his pedagogical experiment and was increasingly neglecting literature. At first she was touched by his concern for the education of the poor, but then it began to exasperate her to see the author of *War and Peace* frittering away his time on the three Rs. 'I am sorry,' she wrote to her brother Stepan Behrs, 'that Lyovochka is wasting his energy on such occupations instead of employing it to write books. I do not see the point of all this, since his efforts must be confined to one tiny corner of Russia, the district of Krapivna.'[19] It would be a different matter if the publishers would leave her Lyovochka alone; but he was receiving the most mouth-watering proposals from all sides for the publication of a new book: ten thousand roubles in advance and five hundred roubles per sixteen-page sheet.* A fortune! And he was playing deaf. 'It isn't so much the money,' she wrote to her sister Tanya, 'but the main thing is that I love his literary works, I admire them and they move me. Whereas I despise this *Reader*, this arithmetic, this grammar, and I cannot pretend to be interested in them. Now there is something lacking in my life, something I loved – it is Leo's work I am missing, that has always given me so much pleasure and filled me with such respect. You see, Tanya, I really am a writer's wife, I take his work so much to heart.' [20]

She clung all the more fiercely to her mission as 'writer's wife' because she was afraid she had failed in her role of just plain 'wife'. There was no doubt about it; after singing her praises as an ideal helpmeet, capable of satisfying both spirit and flesh, Tolstoy was now discovering that she was 'separate' from him. Apart from brief moments of physical pleasure, no fusion was possible between two such strong characters. Both, walled up in their own natures, felt alone and misunderstood. Obsessed by his own work and worries, Tolstoy refused to believe that Sonya, too, might be having difficulties. He saw her as a fertile mother, secretary, manageress, housewife; he loved her out of habit, because he needed her, because he had chosen her to play a certain role; he did not even notice her any more. And she was scarcely thirty. All those pregnancies! Year after year, she wrote in her diary: 'I am pregnant ...' 'I am afraid I am pregnant again ...' 'I wish I were not pregnant ...' What had she got out of life, apart from housework and childbearing? A pitiful coquetry awoke in her. Hiding in her study, her eyes full of tears, she wrote, 'I need gaiety, idle chatter, elegance. I would like to be liked, to hear people tell me I am beautiful, and I would like Leo to see and hear them too. He ought to abandon this isolation – sometimes he wearies of it – and live with me the way ordinary mortals do.'

* Or \$28,300 in advance and \$1,400 per sheet.

A look in the mirror turned her to stone: an ageing woman with thickened waist and a double chin, her hair parted in the middle, her weary eyes. ... Oh, no! She was not beautiful!

I never thought I was before, and time is growing short. Besides, what good would it do me to be beautiful? My darling Petya loves his old nursie as much as he would have loved a great beauty, and Lyovochka would have grown accustomed to the ugliest face alive, provided that his wife were obedient and contented herself with the life he had chosen for her. ... I feel like curling my hair. Nobody will see, but it will be pretty all the same. Why should I need people to see me? I like ribbons and bows. I should like a new leather belt; after writing that, I feel like crying.[21]

With the birth of the sixth Tolstoy child, Petya, the house had become too small. A wing was added, in which the master installed his study. When he withdrew to this book-filled room, the children were ordered to cease all noise. For them their father was a mysterious, remote and powerful being; they did not really understand what it was he did in there with a pen in his hand. One day Ilya asked his mother who had written the poetry she had just recited to him, and she replied that it was by a great author named Pushkin. The child was miserable because he was not the son of an author, but his mother told him that his father was also a famous writer, and then Ilya cheered up again. For him and his brothers and sisters, the most important person in the house was Maman. Everything depended upon her. She was tireless. She was forever nursing 'some little one', and she was on the go from dawn to dark, ferreting about and organizing things: she bullied the servants, laid in stores for the winter, cut and sewed shirts for her husband and sons, told the cook Nicholas Mikhailovich what to prepare for dinner, sent everyone out for a walk or ordered them to stay indoors because it looked like rain, insisted that they speak French at table and come with clean hands, and administered 'the King of Denmark's drops' when they had sore throats. When someone wanted a 'treat' he went to see Dunyasha, the steward's wife, who would give him jam in a thin, battered old silver spoon. 'We knew why the spoon was like that,' wrote Ilya.[22] 'It had been thrown in the garbage pail and a sow had chewed on it.' Even more highly prized as sweets were the hot, sugary pastries concocted by Mikhailovich. To make them nice and round, he injected air into them through a little hole, but he could not be bothered to use a straw and simply puffed away with his mouth. They were called 'Nicholas's sighs'. He was very dirty and drank hard. The children adored him.* They were also fond of Agatha Mikhailovna, tall and scrawny, with white witches' locks and a sour smell in her clothes, surrounded by every dog on the estate; and old Aunt Toinette, who was almost always in bed in her room, in which there was an imposing silver-sheathed icon that gleamed; and Hannah the nurse, and Natalya Petrovna. ... Papa, of course, was the most severe. 'He almost never punished us,' wrote Ilya. 'But if he looks me straight in the eyes, he guesses everything I am thinking and I feel uneasy. I can lie to Maman but not to Papa. He knows all our secrets.'

And yet sometimes he could be so jolly, this dreaded father! He told his children wonderful tales, about his dogs, Bulka, Malish and Sultan, or a horse he had trained, or the grouse he flushed over by the bog. He took them out sledding and ice-skating in the winter and bathing in the Voronka in the summer, played football and croquet with them. He took them hunting with the hounds and on foot, dressed himself up in disguises and composed charades that made them laugh. Or he read to them: *Twenty Thousand Leagues Under the Sea, Captain Grant's Children, The Three Musketeers.* He skipped over the 'love scenes' in the latter, which made the story incomprehensible. There were no pictures in *Around the World in Eighty Days*, so he

---

* After his death he was replaced by his son Simon, who prepared vegetarian meals for Tolstoy.

illustrated it himself; his young audience crowded around him as he sketched, tumbling to the floor and crawling over the round table. And he invented new games that immediately caught their childish fancy. For example, he would stuff one of them into the laundry basket and drag it all over the house, making him guess at every stop which room he was in. Or, seeing the family bored at tea-time, he would leap up from his chair, raise one arm as though holding a pair of reins, and gallop around the table. That, he said, was 'the charge of the Numidian cavalry'. The children, dizzy with laughter, clattered after him under their mother's mournful, tender gaze.

Every year at Christmas a party of friends gathered around the lighted tree, presents were distributed and a masquerade held. On one of these festive occasions a gypsy arrived, leading a bear and a goat; the goat was Leo Tolstoy.

One great source of delight was the weekly steambath. This took place in a wooden cabin with a thatched roof. Every Saturday the floor was covered with fresh straw. A servant heated the stove red-hot and then threw buckets of water over it to make steam. The children waited until they were dripping with sweat, then rushed outside to roll in the snow and came running back to the cabin. Sonya believed this was an excellent 'health-building' activity for the young. Besides, there was no running water in the house. Whenever anyone wanted to take a bath a servant had to fetch water from the river in buckets.

It was forbidden to buy toys in the shops, for, said Tolstoy, they stifled a child's imagination. (Those they made themselves out of three scraps of wood were so much more precious and fun!) To spare their tender souls from humiliation, no punishment was ever administered. Even if the offence was serious, nobody forced the culprit to apologize; he came to see the error of his ways himself, by observing that his parents were treating him coldly. Consideration for the servants was compulsory, as well as continual striving for simplicity, culture and cheerfulness.

Vigilance relaxed a little with the arrival of summer guests – pretty Aunt Tanya and her husband, the boring Kuzminsky. There were picnics, hikes, croquet tournaments, bathing. ... They played 'postbox'. The postbox sat on the staircase landing near the clock, and everybody, grownups and children alike, contributed what he had written during the week: poems, caricatures, anecdotes, comical accounts of happenings at Yasnaya Polyana. On Sundays the box was opened in the presence of the entire family and Tolstoy read out the notes; none of them were signed, but all could be identified by the style or the handwriting. At one point in the game, it was decided to make a survey of 'the ideals of the inhabitants of Yasnaya Polyana'. Some of the anonymous replies were noteworthy. Tolstoy's ideal was expressed as follows: '1. Poverty, peace and concord. 2. Burn everything he had worshipped and worship everything he had burned.' Sonya's was 'to have one hundred and fifty children, who never grow up'. Tanya's was 'eternal youth, and freedom for women'.

Another question to which everyone had to reply was, 'What is the *raison d'être* of the people at Yasnaya Polyana?' Replies: 'For Sofya Andreyevna [Countess Tolstoy], it is to be the wife of a famous man and to find enough trivia over which she can wear herself out.' 'For Tatyana Andreyevna [Tanya], it is the ability to please, entertain and be loved.' 'For Leo Nikolayevich [Tolstoy], it is to believe he has found a solution to life.' A series of comic portraits entitled 'Distressing register of the mentally deranged inmates of Yasnaya Polyana' made a great hit with the family: 'Patient No. 1. Leo Nikolayevich Tolstoy. Sanguine temperament. His delusion is that he can change others' lives with words. General symptoms: dissatisfaction with the present scheme of things; blames everyone except himself; voluble irritability, no consideration for his listeners; often goes through phases of manic excitement, giving way to exaggerated and lachrymose sentimentality. ... Particular symptoms: indulges in irrelevant activities: polishes and repairs shoes, mows hay and so forth.' 'Patient No. 2: Sofya Andreyevna Tolstoy. Her delusion is that everybody is in continual need of quantities of things, and that she doesn't have time to satisfy them all. ... Treatment: hard work.' 'Patient No. 6: Tanya Kuzminskaya. Causes of illness: popularity in her youth, being accustomed to having her vanity flattered; but no moral foundation for either case. Symptoms: fear of imaginary personal demons, inability to withstand all sorts of temptations: luxury, maliciousness, idleness. ... Prescriptions: truffles and champagne, gowns entirely covered with lace; three changes of dress every day.'

These comments are so perceptive that Tolstoy might as well have signed his name to them; moreover, he carried the game into the open one day by sending a long letter to his *babushka* Alexandra, in which, with mocking affection and indulgent pride, he sketched the characters of his six children.[23] Sergey, the eldest, was rather a pretty lad, clever, with a penchant for daydreaming, attracted to the arts; he was said to be like his dead uncle Nicholas ('That would be too much to ask!'). Behind an engaging façade, Ilya, 'pink, blond, glowing', had a passionate, violent and sensuous nature ('When he eats currant jelly it tickles his lips'); Tanya ('They say she resembles Sonya and I believe it!') was good behaviour personified, she loved to take care of the younger ones and would make an excellent mother; Leo, graceful and clever with his hands, had a natural elegance ('Whatever clothes they put on him look as though they were made for him'); Marya, with her milk-white skin and big blue eyes, displayed a keen and restless mind ('All her life she will suffer and try to reach the inaccessible'); Petya, the big fat baby, only a few months old, was appetizing and incomprehensible. 'I do not care for children until they are two or three years old; I don't understand them,' wrote Tolstoy. 'There are two types of men: hunters and non-hunters. Non-hunters love babies and can pick them up and hold them in their arms; hunters are terrified, sickened and filled with pity at the sight of a baby. I know of no exception to that rule.'

In June 1873 Tolstoy decided to transport his entire family to the vast tract of land he had bought eighty miles from Samara. Governesses and servants would follow the family. The wooden house was tumble-down, inconvenient and ill-furnished. The wind from the steppe blew through the cracks between the boards. *Kisyak* – dried horse-dung – was used for fuel in the stoves, and its sharp tang impregnated the rooms. Clouds of blue flies droned beneath the ceiling, and at night, scurrying regiments of rats kept Sonya from sleeping. She did not like this wild place and, ever concerned for the health of her children, complained that there was no doctor within reach. But Tolstoy was entranced with their primitive way of life, and declared it was far more healthy than all the contraptions invented by civilized peoples. In order to give them all a *kumys* treatment without leaving the farm, he hired a Bashkir, who arrived with wives, mares and foals, and pitched his tents just outside the farm. The foals were tethered during the day so that they could not drink their mothers' milk, which was reserved for the distinguished summer visitors. Morning and evening, the veiled women milked the mares. Then, hidden from the men behind cotton curtains, they prepared the *kumys*. Tolstoy and his sons entered the tent and sat cross-legged on cushions across from the smiling Bashkir. Soon a woman's arm parted the curtains and thrust out a leather jug. The Bashkir stirred the liquid with a whisk and ladled it into cups made of Karelian birch. Tolstoy and his eldest son smacked their lips over the sourish brew, but the other children grimaced.

The only thing that seriously marred their otherwise happy stay on the steppe was the great poverty around them. A dreadful famine had devastated the province that year. The ruined peasants were selling off their emaciated livestock and going to hire themselves out elsewhere. Women and old people begged by the roadside. The administration was helpless to cope with a disaster of such magnitude, and did not know where to begin. With Sonya's approval, Tolstoy investigated the situation in the neighbourhood, toured farms and villages, evaluated the remaining food supply and calculated requirements. Then he published an appeal on behalf of the victims in the Moscow papers. His article, written in the simplest terms, had a considerable impact: a donation from the empress headed the list, and nearly two million roubles were collected within a few months.

The next year only Sergey went to the Bashkir country with his father, but in 1875 Tolstoy took the whole family again, this time to set up the stud farm. He soon had four hundred head: English thoroughbreds, Rostopshins, Kabardian trotters. To establish good relations with the natives, he organized a race meet. The track was circular, three and three-tenths miles long. First prize: a shotgun; second: a gown of Chinese silk; third: a watch bearing the emperor's portrait. Bashkirs and Kirghiz flocked to the race. A motley encampment sprang up around the farm. Beside every tent the natives dug a hole in the ground – their oven – and drove stakes to tether their horses. The festivities continued for two days: singing, dancing, banquets. Incredible quantities of *kumys* were drunk, fifteen sheep eaten as well as one horse and an 'English colt that had bad legs'. In the evening the veiled women disappeared into the *kibitkas* and the men, in multicoloured costumes and embroidered bonnets, gathered to wrestle. Tolstoy beat them all in the club pull: the two opponents, sitting opposite each other on the ground with the soles of their feet together, tugged at a club until one forced the other to his feet. A large body of spectators assembled along the track for the horse race, the women in closed wagons and the men on horseback. Twenty-two riders started, uttering hoarse cries. The wind ballooned in their clothes and sharpened their profiles; whiplashes rained down. The count's horse won second prize.

Tolstoy returned to Samara every summer for seven

years, sometimes alone, sometimes with his wife, children
and friends. But the herd was not kept up and deteriorated
from year to year. The last Kabardian horses were shipped
to Yasnaya Polyana, where they ended their days in-
gloriously, working in the fields.

After finishing his *Readers*, Tolstoy remembered his plan
to write a historical novel. He went back to his notes and
books and tried once more to take up with the ghosts of the
past. Every morning he left his corner room on the second
floor and came downstairs in a dressing-gown, with his
beard in a tangle and his hair on end, to dress in his study
on the ground floor of the new wing. He soon reappeared,
neat and clean, wearing a grey blouse, and went to the dining-room to eat with the family. A light breakfast, and he
was back on his feet. With one hand stuck through his
leather belt and the other holding a glass of tea in a silver
stand, he exchanged a few words with his wife and children and went back to the study, while the brood lowered
their voices in order not to disturb him. The little ones retreated to their rooms, or to the garden in the summer, and
Sonya, alert to every sound, stayed behind sewing shirts or
copying manuscripts in the jam-scented dining-room.

Around three or four in the afternoon the master
emerged, weary and morose, and climbed on his horse or set
off on foot with a gun slung over his shoulder and a dog at
his heels. At five, the bell hanging from an old elm rang to
call the family together. The children ran to wash up.
Everyone waited for the paterfamilias before going to dinner. He came in late, apologized, poured a measure of vodka
into a silver goblet and tossed it down with a gulp, heaved
a sigh, made a face and went to the table. His walk had
whetted his appetite, and he tore into his food. Sonya told
him not to 'stuff himself on porridge' because the 'meatballs
and vegetables' were coming afterward.

'You're going to upset your liver again,' she would say.[24]
After dinner he returned to his study and did not come

out until eight o'clock, for tea. After that, the grownups conversed among themselves, read aloud or played the piano, while the children, crouching in the corners, hoped they would be forgotten. But the clock on the landing struck ten in its rusty voice, and the young ones were ruthlessly ordered to bed. Sometimes Tolstoy went back to his 'lair' to pore over some history book. He was fond of the room, which Sonya had lovingly furnished for him. Book-filled cabinets supported by cross-bracing cut the room in two. Behind the desk, littered with papers and pamphlets, stood an old barrel chair. The walls were decorated with stag-antlers brought back from the Caucasus, and the antlers of a stuffed reindeer-head served as clothes hooks. Beside them hung portraits of Dickens, Schopenhauer and Fet. A bust of Nicholas stood in a recess, sculpted abroad from his death mask. Opposite it was a photograph, dating from 1856, of the contributors to *The Contemporary*: Turgenev, Ostrovsky, Goncharov, Grigorovich, Druzhnin, and Leo Tolstoy in uniform.

Despite the comfort and charm of his surroundings, Tolstoy still did not feel ready to begin his book. 'Thus far I am not really working,' he wrote to Strakhov on 17 December 1872. 'I am surrounded by books on Peter I and his period, I read, I take notes, I want to write, and I *cannot*. But what a period for a painter! Everywhere you look – a mystery, which can only be penetrated by poetry. The whole secret of Russian life is there. I begin to feel that nothing is going to come of all my preparations: I've been trying and fretting for too long now! Besides, I wouldn't care if nothing did come of them.'

In one notebook he methodically recorded everything relating to the customs, dress, manners and dwellings of the people; in another, everything connected with the tsar and his court; in a third, the characters, general ideas, crowd scenes, the crucial episodes. ... 'It's like making a mosaic,' noted Sonya. 'He is going into the most minute details. Yesterday he came back from hunting early and tried to find out from various documents whether it was not wrong to say that high collars were worn with short caftans [tunics with long, hanging sleeves]. He thinks they were only worn with long caftans, especially among the common people.' [25]

Every book he read about Peter the Great made him want to read another one. He had them shipped out from Moscow by the cartload. But the more deeply he delved into the period, the more he was afraid of getting lost in it. 'I have now reached the point in my research at which I am beginning to go round in circles,' he wrote to Golokhvastov, the historian, on 24 January 1873. And a week later, to Fet, 'I am in a very bad mood. Making no headway. The project I have chosen is incredibly difficult. There is no end to the preliminary research, the outline is swelling out of all proportion and I feel my strength ebbing away.' The very figure of Peter the Great, whom he so admired when he began, had become repulsive to him. It was perfectly plain that his famous reforms, copied after the tyrannical Grand Duke of Saxony, had not been inspired by a concern for the salvation of the State, but by a desire to add to his own comfort. He had not founded St Petersburg in order to escape from the plotting of the boyars, but in order to lead an immoral life with his fellow rakes. He had disfigured Russia by introducing decadent Western manners. He had made the Church subservient to the State, undermined tradition, ordered the boyars to cut off their beards. Tolstoy, a Slavophil in his heart of hearts, sided staunchly with the boyars and the beards. Then, too, he could not forget that the man had had his son Alexis put to death for the crime of not sharing his ideas. If he had to describe the monster, he would give him the same treatment as Napoleon. He was a past master at the sport of shattering pedestals and upending idols. But this time the idol was Russian, and in spite of everything, it hurt him to demote a national hero. Perhaps he would have better luck with Peter's successors: Catherine II and her favourites. How about taking the officer, Mirovich, as his hero – the one who had tried to free the dethroned Tsar Ivan VI? He had looked so hard that he was growing desperate. 'The period is too far removed from me,' he said. 'I can't put myself inside the people, they have nothing in common with us.' During the month of March 1873, he tried seventeen times to begin the book and seventeen times he gave it up. 'My work is not progressing,' he wrote to Alexandra Tolstoy. 'Life is so beautiful, so light, so short, and a representation of it is always so ugly, so heavy and so long.'[26]

Suddenly he had an illumination. He remembered an occurrence that had deeply affected him the previous year. A neighbour and friend of his, Bibikov, the snipe hunter, lived with a woman named Anna Stepanovna Pirogova, a tall, full-blown woman with a broad face and an easy-going nature, who had become his mistress. But he had been neglecting her of late for his children's German governess. He had even made up his mind to marry the blonde *Fräulein*. Learning of his treachery, Anna Stepanovna's jealousy burst all bounds; she ran away, carrying a bundle of clothes, and wandered about the countryside for three days, crazed with grief. Then she threw herself under a freight train at the Yasenki station.* Before she died, she sent a note to Bibikov: 'You are my murderer. Be happy, if an assassin can be happy. If you like, you can see my corpse on the rails at Yasenki.' That was 4 January 1872. The following day Tolstoy had gone to the station, as a spectator, while the autopsy was being performed in the presence of a police inspector. Standing in a corner of the shed, he had observed every detail of the woman's body lying on the table, bloody and mutilated, with its skull crushed. How shameless, he thought, and yet how chaste. A dreadful lesson was brought home to him by that white, naked flesh, those dead breasts, those inert thighs that had felt and given pleasure. He tried to imagine the existence of this

* The little station of Yasenki was on the Moscow–Kursk railway line that passed through Tula.

poor woman who had given all for love, only to meet with such a trite, ugly death.

Her image haunted him for a long time, but not specifically as material for a book. But in 1870, he had had an idea for a novel about an upper-class woman guilty of adultery. Sonya had even made a note in her diary, on 23 February 1870: 'He told me that the whole problem, for him, was to make the woman pitiable but not contemptible, and that when this creature came into his mind as a type, all the masculine characters he had previously invented immediately grouped themselves around her.' Yet when Anna Stepanovna's suicide occurred two years later, he did not immediately link the incident to the story of the unfaithful wife. For over a year the two subjects – infidelity and violent death – had co-existed in his mind without connecting. Then, by some mysterious process, each began to round out the other. The real-life woman gave her tragic ending and her name to the fictional one. At the very moment Tolstoy was brooding over Peter the Great, Tsarevich Alexis and the boyars, men and women in modern dress were flitting through his historical vision: the figures who became Anna Karenina, Vronsky, Levin, Kitty, Oblonsky ...

Although he refused to follow literary fads, Tolstoy could not remain oblivious to the vogue for the psychological novel abroad. World opinion was all agog with the problems of marriage and women's rights. In France, Alexandre Dumas *fils*, who had become famous in 1852 with the resounding success of *La Dame aux Camélias*, had just published a study of conjugal infidelity: *L'Homme-Femme*. On 1 March 1873 Tolstoy wrote to Tanya Kuzminskaya: 'Have you read *L'Homme-Femme*? I was staggered by it. One would not expect a Frenchman to have such a lofty concept of marriage and relations between men and women in general.'

A few days later, on 18 March, he went into his son Sergey's room and noticed a book lying on a table, which the boy had started to read: Pushkin's *Byelkin Tales*. He leafed through it and was as charmed as ever by that lively prose. The story called *Loose Leaves* began with the sentence, 'The guests were arriving at the country house. . . .' For Tolstoy this leap into the heart of the matter was the summit of artistry. He thought of it in relation to his own characters, and his desire to write returned at last, after months of indecision – irresistible, dizzying, painful as thirst. He rushed into his study, seized a pen and wrote down the first words of an opening chapter, 'After the opera, the guests reassembled at the home of the young Countess Vraski.'*

The next day, 19 March, Sonya wrote in her diary, 'Yesterday evening Lyova suddenly announced, "I have written a sheet and a half and I think it's coming all right." Assuming he had been trying once more to write something on the period of Peter the Great, I did not pay much attention; but then I learned that he has begun a novel on the private lives of contemporary people.' That day she let her joy overflow in a letter to her sister: 'Yesterday Leo suddenly started to write a novel on contemporary life. The subject is the unfaithful wife and all the ensuing tragedy. I am very happy.'

The first chapters were dashed off in a state of elation. As with *War and Peace*, he took his models from the people around him. He gave some of Sonya's features to Kitty, put a great deal of himself into Levin, borrowed from various friends to portray Oblonsky, Koznyshev, Varenka, Mikhailov; he made Levin's brother a replica of his own brother Dmitry, who had died of tuberculosis. Vronsky probably owed a good deal to Sonya's first suitor, Mitrofan Polivanov, and Karenin was compounded of the minister of finance Valuyev, Tanya's husband Kuzminsky, and Sukhotin the chamberlain; physically, Anna Karenina her-

---

*In the final version this sentence, somewhat altered, appears at the beginning of Chapter 6 of Part II. It was a long-standing and erroneous family tradition that Tolstoy had begun his book with the sentence, 'Everything was topsy-turvy in the Oblonsky house.'

self was said to resemble Marya Alexandrovna Hartung, the poet Pushkin's daughter. The Karenins were actually called Pushkin in the first draft. Tolstoy had met Mrs Hartung at General Tulubyev's home in Tula, and had been impressed by her beauty, 'her smooth gait', 'the Arabian ringlets that betrayed her ancestry'. There was African blood in her father's family, her mother was Natalya Niko-layevna Goncharov, the most beautiful woman in Russia. Fascinated by this handsome creature, Tolstoy looked for a soul to put inside her. Anna's personality was thought to be based on that of another woman famous for her learn-ing and intelligence: Countess Sofya Tolstoy, wife of the poet Alexis Konstantinovich Tolstoy and friend of the philosopher Vladimir Solovyev. Other details of the novel he was to find around him, in the story of his friend Dyakov's sister, for one, who had remarried after divorcing S. M. Sukhotin. He also made use of the open liaison be-tween Kiselev and Princess Golitsin, who had deserted her husband and caused a scandal in high society.

He worked so quickly that on 11 May 1873, eight weeks after starting to write, he announced to Strakhov: 'I am writing a novel that has nothing to do with Peter the Great; I started it over a month ago and have finished the first draft. This is my first real novel and I am taking it very much to heart. I am completely wrapped up in it. ... I wrote to you about it in a letter I never sent, telling you how it came upon me in spite of myself, thanks to the divine Pushkin, who fell into my hands quite by accident and whom I have reread *in toto*, with renewed admiration. ... I beg you not to repeat this to anyone!'

His draft was far from finished though, and Tolstoy knew it. Early in June he stopped work to go to Samara with his family. When he returned, on 22 August, his first gust of energy had spent itself and fresh doubts assailed him. Sonya was copying again, as in the days of *War and Peace*. For the children, she was the writer in the family.

He was still not quite back in his stride when the painter

Kramskoye, who had vainly begged for the honour of being allowed to paint him on several occasions, made another attempt. The portrait was to go into the Gallery of Famous Russians, founded in Moscow by the Tretyakov brothers. Tolstoy protested that he had no time to waste in posing, which was a useless occupation and unworthy of a solitary and studious man such as he. But Kramskoye came to Yasnaya Polyana to talk to the master in person and argued that if he did not let himself be painted during his lifetime, strangers would make portraits of him afterward, from photographs; but this was not enough to weaken Tolstoy. Kramskoye then offered to paint a second portrait, for a very low price, that he could keep himself. Sonya was delighted and undertook to persuade her husband. They talked money. Without batting an eyelid, Sonya proposed two hundred and fifty roubles.* Kramskoye usually asked one thousand roubles for a commission. Canvas, paint and frame alone cost fifty roubles. Nevertheless, he agreed. Sonya turned victoriously to her husband. Surely he would not refuse now. Pecuniary considerations triumphed over principle, and Tolstoy consented for the first time in his life to sit for his portrait. Kramskoye painted him seated, his grey full-sleeved blouse buttoned down the front, his head cocked slightly, with a full beard, imposing brow and a calm, clear, keen expression under his frowning eyebrows. 'The two portraits are remarkably alike; it almost frightens me to look at them,' Sonya wrote to her sister on 14 September. During the sittings the two men chatted amicably about art, morality, politics and religion. Kramskoye did not dream that while he was painting the portrait of the author of *War and Peace*, Tolstoy was doing as much for him, and that he would reappear in *Anna Karenina* as the painter Mikhailov. As usual, Tolstoy was making capital out of everything that crossed his field of vision. Nothing could happen to him that would not in some way be essential to his work, he thought.

* Or $700.

And yet, on 9 November 1873 a tragedy occurred that almost made him forget literature for a while. His youngest son, Petya, the pink and blond baby, was carried off in two days by the croup. Grief-stricken, Sonya wrote in her diary: 'He died peacefully. I nursed him fourteen and one-half months. He lived from 13 June 1872 to 9 November 1873. A gay, healthy child. The darling, I loved him too much! They buried him yesterday. What an emptiness now. I cannot reconcile the images of Petya living and Petya dead. They are both precious to me, but what is there in common between that being full of life, light and affection, and this other, motionless, solemn and cold. He was very attached to me. Did it hurt him to leave me?'

Tolstoy managed to restrain his emotions; he had said that Petya was too young to interest him. After the burial, while his wife was wandering tearfully about the silent house, he wrote to his brother Sergey:

'Petya is dead and has just been buried. ... This is something new for us, and very painful, particularly to Sonya. I have just received a letter from the typesetters, telling me that the edition [of my works] will come out on the twelfth of this month. The Dyakovs arrived today. Dyakov is going to Moscow and will leave Masha [his daughter] and Sofya [her governess] with us. I think I ought to go to Moscow too; Sonya would not be completely alone in the house. If you can manage it, let us go the day after tomorrow, the twelfth. Will that be all right? Let me know.'[27]

Two lines on the death of his son, the rest on the publication of his books and a forthcoming trip. To be sure, the death of a child was a common occurrence in those days and it was natural for a mother to be more deeply afflicted by the sight of an empty cradle than a father. But how is one to explain the fact that this model head-of-family, this vast compassionate heart, open to all the sufferings of mankind, had only one thought after the funeral: to get away from the house, out of earshot of his wife's lamentations? Two days later he was in Moscow, supposedly in order to see his publisher; but what really drove him away from Yasnaya Polyana was the fear of death. Death had entered his house; he must wait until the noxious vapours of its passage had been dispelled. Ever since the night at Arzamas, he had been playing hide-and-seek with death. A sneeze, a pimple on his nose, and he was a doomed man. As soon as he returned to Yasnaya Polyana he wrote to Fet to explain:

'This is the first death in the family in eleven years, and the thing is extremely hard for my wife. There is some consolation in the fact that of the eight of us, his death was certainly the easiest for us all to bear; but the heart, and especially the heart of a mother – that astonishing, sublime manifestation of the divine on earth – cannot reason, and my wife is plunged into grief.'[28]

All things considered, he told himself, there was another consolation in this bereavement: death could not strike the same family twice in succession. They would be left in peace for a while. Tolstoy went back to work and Sonya 'wore out' her grief through the long nights, copying manuscripts that were black with corrections.

The first part was finished in March 1874. 'I like the book,' he wrote to Alexandra, 'but I doubt that others will, because it is too simple.' Nevertheless, he was in such a hurry to publish it that he took the beginning (seven sixteen-page sheets) to Katkov, editor of the *Russian Herald*. While the proofs were being set up in Moscow, the author, after being eager to see them, suddenly lost interest in his characters. His teaching mania had taken hold of him again, and he began to neglect Anna Karenina and Vronsky and Levin for the little muzhiks at Yasnaya Polyana. 'I love them again, as I did fourteen years ago, these thousands of youngsters I work with,' he wrote to Alexandra. 'The only reason why I want the people to be educated is in order to salvage the Pushkins, Ostrogradskys,* Philaretuses† and Lomonosovs‡

---

* M. V. Ostrogradsky, a mathematician (1801–61).
† Philaretus, son of a deacon who became metropolitan of Moscow.
‡ Lomonosov, author and scholar (1711–65).

in the lot. Every school is crawling with them. ... I have promised my book to the *Russian Herald*, but I simply cannot tear myself away from living beings to bother with imaginary ones.'[29] And to Strakhov, 'My novel has gone to sleep. Katkov's typesetter is about as speedy as a turtle. One sheet a month – which is fine with me, I'm delighted!'[30]

On 22 April 1874 Sonya, still in mourning for little Petya, gave birth to a fifth boy, Nicholas. A ray of joy crept into the house. But there were fresh alarms early in June. Old Aunt Toinette was at death's door. She was seventy-nine, and had long been confined to her bed; her faithful servant Axinya had preceded her into the grave. Half-deaf and half-blind, she had begun to mix past and present together. When Leo sat down at her bedside, she mistook him for his father, whom she had loved so deeply and yet refused to marry. She smiled at him in senile flirtatiousness, she called him Nicholas; obscurely frightened, he beat a retreat. Some days he could not bring himself to go to her at all. Did she realize that her end was near? She asked if she might leave her room on the upper floor and move to a wood-panelled recess on the first floor. 'I don't want to spoil your lovely upstairs room with my death,'[31] she said. Then she began to suffer, complain, struggle. ... She died on 20 June 1874. Tolstoy felt remorse, at having too often shown his irritation or been inconsiderate of her, and also relief, because he could not bear the presence of sickness under his roof. But both feelings were dominated by a third: sorrow at the loss of another witness of his childhood. Who would love him as she had done? In the end, it was himself he felt most sorry for. Moved as he had not been by his son Petya's death, he wrote to Alexandra:

'She ceased to exist for me about three years ago. So (right or wrong? I cannot say) I avoided her, and could not look at her without suffering. Now she has really ceased to exist (her death-agony was long and painful, as a long labour in childbirth), and my heart goes out to her more strongly than ever before. She was an admirable person ...'[32]

A little later, he told his sister:

'When death came, her features cleared, and all my memories of her returned; I miss her; one of my most important ties with the past has been broken. You and Sergey are all I have left.' [33]

Mourning, travel, work on the second *Reader—Anna Karenina* suffered from this irregular life. Tolstoy already had a new project in mind: to found a primary teacher training school in his home. He had desks and benches put into the pavilion in which the Kuzminskys usually spent the summer holiday: 'Instead of your dear faces,' Sonya wrote to her sister, 'we shall be seeing unknown muzhiks and theological students.' But the local administration showed little interest in the project, there were few applicants (a dozen) and Tolstoy abandoned the idea.

Anna Karenina was no consolation for his academic fiasco. He was fed up with the book and wanted to rewrite the beginning, 'everything that has to do with Levin and Vronsky'. Strakhov, who had read the opening chapters, begged him not to be too severe: 'I can't get your book out of my head. Every time you write something I am stupefied by the freshness, the utter originality of your creation. It is as though I leaped from one period of literature into another. The growth of Anna Karenina's passion is a divine miracle! ...'

Chapters 1 to 14 came out at last in the *Russian Herald* of January 1875. Willy-nilly, Tolstoy had to sit down and produce the rest, for which Katkov was clamouring. The public was enthusiastic. 'It's nothing less than delirium!' Strakhov wrote to the author. 'I have seen solemn old bodies hopping up and down in admiration: "Ah, how beautiful! Ah, how beautiful!" they said. "How can he write like that?" And it's true, the story is pure as crystal.' [34] With this incitement, Tolstoy redoubled his speed, but did not give up his educational activities. 'Not only did I not expect [*Anna Karenina*] to be a success,' he wrote to Strakhov, 'but, I must confess, I was afraid I would lose my name as a writer for ever on account of the book. . . . This winter I am very busy. . . . I am directing the seventy schools that have opened in our district; all are working to perfection. I am continuing the educational research I wrote to you about, teaching my older children myself, supervising the printing of the book, correcting the proofs of the second *Reader* and going through a family crisis to boot.'

The crisis was the illness of their last-born, Nicholas, who had water on the brain.

'In the last four months he has gone through every phase of this incurable disease,' Tolstoy continued. 'My wife is feeding him herself. Part of the time she is in despair at the thought that he is going to die, and part of the time she is in terror lest he live and remain an idiot.'

And with devastating frankness he went straight on, without transition:

'As for myself, it is curious, but I have never wanted to write as intensely, as joyfully as I do now.'[35]

Four days later, on 20 February 1875, the child died in dreadful agonies.*

'I am deeply upset because of my wife,' Tolstoy wrote to Fet; 'for her, after nursing the child, it was awful. You speak highly of *Anna Karenina*, and that is music to my ears; the book is a success, from what I hear on all sides; but I am sure there has never been a writer more indifferent to success than I am, if it is success.'[36]

Still stunned by this latest death, Sonya had to continue caring for several of the other children, who had whooping cough. They all recovered, but she caught the disease from them, and peritonitis followed. And she was pregnant. Utterly exhausted, she gave birth prematurely, on 30 October 1875, to a baby girl who died after half an hour. Tolstoy was terrified by this new onslaught of death in the family. Why was fate dogging his heels like this? He felt as though he were skirmishing with some animal – intelligent, power-

* It was on this death that Tolstoy based his short story, *The Prayer* (1905).

ful and vindictive – that had been trained to snap at him. In
a moment of abandon, he wrote to Fet: 'Fear, horror, death,
the children laughing and gay. Special food, agitation, doctors, lies, death, horror – it was torture!'[37] Death was there;
and he had to eat and sleep, teach the children, tell them
to keep their voices down, command them to learn their
lessons, write letters, read proofs, cut his nails, brush his
beard ...

Soon after Aunt Toinette died her former rival, Aunt
Pelagya Ilinishna Yushkov, left the convent in which she
was perishing of boredom and moved in, bag and baggage,
to Toinette's little wood-panelled room. In spite of her
seventy-six years, the new arrival was alert, sharp-witted
and dictatorial. She had been nursing her dream of usurping
Aunt Toinette's place in her nephew's home for twenty-
eight years; but her triumph was short-lived. A few months
after moving in, she fell ill. Aches and pains everywhere,
legs, chest, stomach. The vast piousness that had sustained
her throughout her life suddenly fled. Terrified at the
thought that she, too, was about to disappear, she struggled,
refused to see a priest, accused the family of not knowing
how to take care of her. She whined, in French: 'I am so
happy with you! I don't want to die!'[38] Sonya, still extremely weak from her latest delivery, had to nurse her as
though she were a child.

Pelagya Ilinishna Yushkov passed away on 22 December
1875. The same men who had delivered a miniature coffin
for the dead baby seven weeks before returned with a larger
one for the old woman who lay waiting for them, stiff and
white, with an aristocratic pout on her lips and her hands
clasping an icon. And once more there were the hymns,
the odour of incense, the trip to the cemetery, the muzhiks
baring their heads in their doorways. In three years, 1873 to
1875, Tolstoy had lost three children and two dearly loved
aunts.

'It is a strange thing,' he wrote to Alexandra, 'but the
death of that eighty-year-old woman has affected me more

than any other; I was sorry to see her disappear, to see disappear the last memory to recall my father's and mother's generation, and also sorry to see her suffering; but there was something else in this death that I cannot describe . . .'[39] And to his brother, 'This winter has been very hard for me emotionally; Aunt's death has depressed me terribly. . . . *It is time to die!* That is not true. What is true is there is nothing else to do in life but die. I feel it every instant. I am writing, I'm working very hard, the children are healthy, but there is no happiness for me in any of it.'[40]

In the meantime his sister-in-law Tanya had lost a daughter, Dasha, five years old, and his brother Sergey a two-year-old son, Alexander.*

Sonya was a long time recovering from her deaths, deliveries and illness. She had lost weight; she suffered from migraines; she coughed and spat blood. Yet she would not give up her role as mistress of the household, and scurried about, ordering and scolding from morning to night. More than ever, she needed to feel her husband beside her, but it bothered him to see her so tired. 'There is no worse situation for a healthy man than to have a sick wife,' he said.[41] One night young Sergey, who slept downstairs, heard a cry in his sleep: 'Sonya! Sonya!' His father's voice. Frightened, he got up and opened the door. The hallway was pitch dark. The anguished cry rang out again: 'Sonya! Sonya!' She appeared at the top of the stairs, holding a candle, and asked:

'What's wrong, Lyovochka?'

'Nothing,' he answered. 'I don't have any matches. I got lost in the house.'

Sonya was so startled that she had a coughing fit and stood there, gasping and wheezing. Afterwards, her husband explained that when he came out of his study to go to his bedroom, he suddenly could not remember where he was. What were those walls? Where did those steps lead? Panic

* Tanya's daughter died on 3 May 1873 and Sergey's boy in January 1873.

gripped him to the roots of his hair. 'I can give no explanation of this event other than a pathological condition,' his son Sergey later wrote. 'In my opinion the terror he felt that night was the same as what he used to call the "anguish of Arzamas".' No one in the family dared to pronounce the word hysteria but Sonya must have thought it at the time. She was increasingly worried by her husband's condition. Moreover, she was not in a normal state herself. 'I don't sleep, I eat almost nothing, I choke back my tears or hide and cry,' she wrote in her diary on 16 September 1876. 'I have a low temperature every day and chills in the evening. I am so tense that I feel my head will burst.'

At the beginning of 1877 she was no better, and went to Moscow to be examined by Dr Botkin, a court physician.* He reassured her. The cause of all her troubles was her nerves, nothing serious. Back at Yasnaya Polyana, she resumed her secretarial duties with renewed zeal. She hoped Leo would finish the book in the next few months. But he was writing slowly, in snatches, and without real conviction. 'I'm sick and tired of my *Anna K.*,' he wrote to Alexandra. And to Strakhov, 'Don't praise my book! Pascal had a nail-studded belt he used to lean against every time he felt pleasure at some word of praise. I should have a belt like that. I ask you, be a friend; either do not write to me about the book at all, or else write and tell me everything that is wrong with it. If it is true, as I feel, that my powers are weakening, then, I beg of you, tell me. Our profession is dreadful, writing corrupts the soul. Every author is surrounded by an aura of adulation which he nurses so assiduously that he cannot begin to judge his own worth or see when it starts to decline.' [42]

However, he laboured away at his manuscript, full of mistrust, anger and weariness. He made revision after revision. He felt that he was taking two steps backward for every step ahead. 'There are days when one gets up feeling re-

*It was on this trip that she made the acquaintance of Alexandra Tolstoy, of whom she received, she said, an excellent impression.

freshed and clear-headed,' he said. 'One begins to write; everything is fine, it all comes naturally. The next day one reads it over, it all has to go because the heart isn't there. No imagination, no talent. That *quelque chose* is lacking without which our intelligence is worthless. Other days one gets up hating the world, nerves completely on edge; nevertheless, one hopes to be able to get something done. And indeed, it doesn't go too badly; it's vivid, there is imagination by the carload. Again, one reads it over: meaningless, stupid; the brains weren't there. Imagination and intelligence have to work together. As soon as one or the other gets the upper hand, all is lost. There is nothing to do but throw away what you've done and start over.'

One evening he told Strakhov in anger, 'Ah, if only somebody else could finish *Anna Karenina* for me.' [43]

The summer of 1876 was especially sterile: 'Summer has come, wonderful! I go out for a walk, I admire, I don't understand how I was able to sit there and write last winter.' [44] Towards autumn his energy finally returned and on 9 December 1876 Sonya triumphantly announced to her sister: 'At last, we are writing *Anna Karenina* for good, that is, without interruption. Lyovochka is tense and excited; he writes another chapter every day; I am copying feverishly.'

When the children were in bed and the house fell silent, she sat down at her little mahogany writing desk and, with loving pen, neatly copied out the pages her husband had left for her, still smoking with the heat of creation. One day he came up to the desk, leaned over her shoulder and said, pointing to the notebook:

'Oh, let me hurry and finish this book so I can start another. Now I see it clearly. If a book is to be any good, you have to love the central idea it expresses. In *Anna Karenina* I love the idea of the family, in *War and Peace* I loved the idea of the people, in my next book I shall love the idea of the Russian nation, as a rising force.' [45]

When the proofs of *Anna Karenina* began to come back in the mail, Tolstoy forced himself to read every word, and in every line a mistake leaped up before his eyes. He was disgusted by his carelessness. 'In the margins,' Ilya Tolstoy later wrote, 'the proofreader's corrections appeared first – punctuation, letters omitted; then my father began to change words, then whole sentences; he crossed out one line and put in another, and in the end the proofs were smudged all over and some passages were so black that it was impossible to return them in that state, since no one except Maman could decipher them. Maman spent whole nights copying over the corrections. In the morning the new pages, covered with her fine, clear writing, were laid, carefully folded, on his desk, to be sent off in the mail when Lyovochka got up. Papa would pick them up for one last glance. But when evening came it was the same thing all over again: everything altered, everything crossed out and written over.

'"Sonya, darling, forgive me; I've spoiled all your work again; this is the last time," he would tell her, shamefacedly pointing out the places he had changed. "Tomorrow we'll send it all off."'

Sometimes, after the proofs had already gone he would remember a sentence that was wrong or a weak adjective and have to telegraph the correction.

He went to Moscow several times that winter, and met Peter Ilich Tchaikovsky, who had been worshipping him from afar. 'I was frightened and self-conscious when I found myself face to face with him,' the composer wrote in his diary. 'It seemed to me that none of the filth that lies hidden in the heart of man could be kept secret from this great authority on the subject. ... But ... his manner was very straightforward and open and showed little of that omniscience I had feared. With me, he only wanted to talk music, in which he was very interested at that time. He liked to belittle Beethoven and was sceptical of his genius.' Tchaikovsky asked Rubinstein to arrange a recital for his favourite author at the Conservatory, and was most flattered to see the author of *War and Peace* shedding tears when the orchestra played the andante of his D Major Quartet.

Tolstoy had always been sensitive to music. It acted on him like a drug. It unstrung his nerves and made him lose control of his reactions. Sometimes he even grew angry with the artist for destroying his peace of mind. Stepan Behrs observed that when his brother-in-law was listening to his favourite melodies, he would suddenly turn 'very pale', and 'he winced, almost perceptibly, in a way that seemed to express fear'.[46] When he returned to Yasnaya Polyana, Tolstoy sent Tchaikovsky a series of folksongs and asked him to arrange them 'in the style of Mozart or Haydn'.

Soon afterwards, however, the composer's ardour cooled towards the novelist, whose theories on music were really too outlandish. Tchaikovsky accused Tolstoy of saying 'very commonplace things, not worthy of a genius'. He did not even like *Anna Karenina*, of which he had read the opening chapters. He wrote to his brother, 'Aren't you ashamed to admire this disgusting non-entity, who pretends to be performing profound psychological analyses? ... What value can there be in this aristocratic babbling ...'

On the whole, however, readers and critics alike continued to rave over Tolstoy's new book. He was sincerely amazed at this, and wrote to Strakhov on 26 January 1877: 'The success of the last section of *Anna Karenina* pleased me greatly, I must confess. It was so unexpected: I am astonished to see that something as ordinary and insignificant as that can please the public.'

In March of that year Strakhov sent him two articles praising his book to the skies and, proudly testing himself, Tolstoy burned them. 'I was too afraid,' he wrote to Strakhov, 'that those articles would turn my head.'[47] Whereupon the good disciple chortled, 'I admire you for burning the reviews by Markov and the anonymous critic. That is not what Turgenev, Dostoyevsky and Stasov would have done. They read every line written about them and take up their own defence if no one else will.'[48]

While the final chapters of *Anna Karenina* were being published, the public was badly shaken by news of the uprising of the Serbs and Montenegrins against the Turks. Could the tsar turn a deaf ear to this, could he abandon his traditional role as protector of the faithful in the Balkans? Aroused by the journalists' call to arms, scores of Russians volunteered to serve under General Chernayev and defend their 'little Slavic brothers'. Collections for the downtrodden rebels were taken up at church doors. The officers of the guards had visions of a short military tour through the land of the miscreants, complete with distributions of the St George Cross. Tolstoy, who was writing the Epilogue to *Anna Karenina*, dared to express his disapproval through the mouth of his hero Levin, who said the volunteers for the front were 'misguided ... hotheads', always itching for a fight on the first pretext that came along; nothing could be more scandalous than 'these ladies in sable capes and trains behind their dresses going to extort money out of the peasants, when their total collection amounts to less than the price of their train'; he even proclaimed that 'the good of society is dependent upon scrupulous obedience of the moral law engraved in every human heart' and that 'no one, therefore, should desire or advocate war, whatever generous aim it purports to serve'.[49]

On 12 April 1877, after much beating around the bush, Russia declared war on Turkey. Tolstoy's dismay was equalled only by the enthusiasm of most of his fellow countrymen. Katkov, director of the *Russian Herald*, was a confirmed partisan of the Russian intervention on behalf of Serbia and Montenegro. He would not publish the Epilogue in his magazine without revision and he told Tolstoy so, to the latter's surprise and indignation. 'Leo has a strange attitude towards the Serbian war,' Sonya wrote to her sister three days after war was declared. 'I don't know why, but he does not see it as we do; it is a personal, religious question for him. He says he is very worried about this war.'

At Katkov's insistence, he made several unsuccessful attempts to rewrite the end of *Anna Karenina*; then, on Strakhov's advice, he decided to publish the Epilogue separately. The editors of the *Russian Herald* prevaricated about the real reason for the change, and printed the following notice in the July issue: 'The instalment of *Anna Karenina* in our last issue was followed by the words "To be concluded in the next issue". But the novel itself ends with the hero's death. According to the author's plans, there is to be a short epilogue – some thirty-five pages – informing the reader that Vronsky, feeling lost and miserable after Anna's death, leaves for Serbia as a volunteer; all the other characters live on in good health, and Levin remains on his estate and condemns the Slavic Committee and the volunteers. The author may expand this chapter in a special edition of his book.'

Indignant at this manoeuvre, Tolstoy sent a telegram to Katkov demanding the return of the manuscript of the Epilogue and announcing that he would have nothing further to do with the *Russian Herald*. The Epilogue came out in booklet form in January 1878. As Tolstoy expected, the Panslavists called him unpatriotic. Dostoyevsky, in his *Diary of a Writer*, went so far as to express his regret that an 'author of his stature should so deviate and cut himself off from the rest of the Russian community in a matter of such importance'. It was, he said, 'a mental aberration' and 'vulgar sentimentality', and a 'crime against nature' to be afraid of killing a Turk who was about to impale a child on his sword. Ignoring these appeals to his patriotism, Tolstoy continued to be tormented by the war. 'As long as it lasts,' he told his wife, 'I shall not be able to write. It is as though the city were burning. One doesn't know what to do. One can think of nothing else.'[50]

He followed events in the newspapers and gradually, unconsciously, began to side with Russia. Still hating the war, he came to rejoice at a Turkish defeat; the officer of Sevastopol began to stir within the apostle. 'Thank God Kars has been taken,' he wrote to Fet on 12 November 1877. 'I have ceased to feel ashamed.' A few days later (6 December), a new source of joy, non-military this time: Sonya gave him another son – Andrey. 'Even though it has come to be a sort of routine for me, I am stirred and moved and filled with happiness every time,' he wrote to V. Islenyev. At his feet, his children were playing war with lead soldiers in Russian and Turkish uniforms and collecting the pictures of generals printed on candy wrappers. Some Turkish prisoners had been transferred to Tula, and he wanted to show them to his sons. They entered the courtyard of an abandoned sugar refinery, which was filled with tall, handsome men with mournful faces, all wearing blue trousers and red fezzes. A few of them spoke Russian. Tolstoy gave them cigarettes and money and asked them about themselves, and was surprised to learn that every one carried a Koran in his pack. As he left he said, 'What splendid fellows, gentle and charming.' His sons, for whom the Turks were slayers of Christians, stared at him in bewilderment.

During the summer of 1877 Strakhov, who was staying at Yasnaya Polyana, helped to prepare *Anna Karenina* for hard-cover publication. It was agreed that he would read the text, correct the most obvious errors and mark questionable passages, and Tolstoy would then take over and adopt or reject his proposals. But the author quickly became so involved in the work that he caught up with his corrector and they continued working side by side. At four o'clock in the afternoon – an hour before dinner – the master emerged from his study and the disciple from his, and they set off together for a walk. With his big head planted on top of his narrow shoulders, his sparse beard and prominent forehead and wide-set eyes, Strakhov did not seem real – a being nourished on ink and paper – alongside the stocky, robust and red-cheeked lord of Yasnaya Polyana, who breathed through flaring nostrils and looked around him with a proprietary eye. As they walked, they talked about the book. Strakhov, paralysed with admiration, would sandwich a timid criticism between two enormous compliments. Tolstoy listened and usually objected; but occasionally he was converted to his guest's opinion and, following his advice, rewrote a few pages and deleted certain episodes.

'With regard to my corrections, which almost always related to questions of language,' wrote Strakhov, 'I found ... that Leo Nikolayevich would defend his choice of words to the death and refused to make the slightest alteration. I could see from his remarks that he cared a great deal about what he had written and that in spite of the seeming carelessness and awkwardness of his style, he had weighed every word and phrase as carefully as the most exacting poet.'

The final version was published in three volumes at the beginning of the following year. The chorus of praises redoubled around him. The bookseller's stocks shrank; every woman in society felt some tie with the hapless Anna. But her scowling creator would grumble to all and sundry:

'What's so difficult about describing how an officer gets entangled with a woman? There's nothing difficult in that, and above all, nothing worthwhile. It's bad, and it serves no purpose.'[51]

[19]

Anna Karenina

AT first, Tolstoy thought of calling his novel *Two Couples* or *Two Marriages*, since in an early version Anna Karenina was supposed to get her divorce and marry Vronsky. Then, when the characters began to impose their own wills on the author, the theme veered off in another direction. But it was a theme of the utmost simplicity. Oblonsky, the *bon-vivant*, has had a stupid affair with his children's former French teacher, and appeals to his sister, Anna Karenina, to try to patch things up between him and his wife. And Anna, who is grace, sweetness and integrity personified, manages to reconcile the couple. She herself is married to Karenin, an important government official in St Petersburg, twenty years her senior, a dry, self-satisfied man and a slave to etiquette. At her brother's house she meets a swashbuckling officer, Count Vronsky, with whom Kitty, Mrs Oblonsky's sister, is infatuated. Levin, a sober, introspective young man who is deeply in love with Kitty, goes off in despair to live on his estate when he sees that the girl has eyes for no one but the dashing soldier. Vronsky, however, pays scant attention to Kitty: it is Anna who attracts him. And she, despite her steadfast heart, cannot resist.

After the deed is done, she confesses to her husband. His first thought is to save appearances at all costs, and when his wife falls ill, he is even ready to forgive her. But she recovers and leaves the country with her lover. Then, when the novelty has worn off, her sufferings begin. Vronsky misses his military career, which he had to abandon to follow her. And she is miserable at having left her son in Karenin's care. She returns to see the boy in secret. Far from pacifying her, their meeting only sharpens her despair. She goes from disillusionment to disillusionment and in the end her life becomes intolerable and she throws herself under a train. Vronsky is consumed with remorse and enlists to fight the Turks. In counterpoint to this dark, violent story, there is the light-flooded relationship of Kitty and Levin. After rejecting her suitor Kitty returns to him, won over by his integrity and strength. They marry, settle down in the country and enjoy the perfect happiness of simple souls, in accordance with Tolstoy's golden rule.

In *War and Peace* the author had created so many characters, invented so much action and debated so many ideas that one might reasonably fear he had exhausted the psychological resources of a normal artist's entire career in that one work. But with prodigious ease, never once repeating himself, he created a new galaxy of characters in *Anna Karenina*, all as alive and convincing as those in his historical epic. This great power of self-renewal was undoubtedly due to the fact that he himself was continually being enriched by life as it passed him. Had he been less open to the world, less changeable and diversified, the range of his imagination would have been smaller. Once again, he had made good use of meetings with friends, current events, his own sensations, in brewing the 'juice of fiction'.

His attitude towards Anna Karenina, moreover, changed in the course of the book, almost as though the creator had gradually been seduced by his creature. Behind the love story of Anna and Vronsky lay the love story of Tolstoy and Anna. At first, Tolstoy did not like his heroine: he condemned her in the name of morality. He saw her as an incarnation of lechery and, oddly enough, did not even make her beautiful. His first notes on the woman who has become the quintessence of charm and elegance for generations of readers describe her in the following terms: 'She is unattractive, with a narrow, low forehead, short, turned-up nose – rather large. If it were any bigger, she would be deformed. ... But, in spite of her homely face, there was something in the kindly smile of her red lips that made her

likeable.' So much for appearance. Her personality is that of
a man-killer. One whole chapter in one of the early drafts
of the book, devoted to a description of Anna, is entitled
'The Devil'. She is the agent of evil in the world. Both husband and lover are her victims. Hence Karenin, the government official, is initially portrayed as a warm, sensitive
soul, cultivated and kind. His main fault is sentimentality.
When he suspects his wife of infidelity, he tells his sister,
'I feel like sobbing, I want sympathy, I want to be told what
to do!' And the first model of Vronsky is 'firm, kind-
hearted and sincere'. In a word, two choice characters, in
contrast to whom the diabolical Anna stands out blacker
than ever.

However, Tolstoy unconsciously begins to be intrigued by
his sinner. She moves him, disturbs him, disarms him. He is
on the verge of declaring his love. Suddenly he can no
longer deprive her of beauty. Plastic surgery is called for:
the operation is a resounding success. The troll with the
turned-up nose emerges a *sylphide*: 'Vronsky was drawn,
not by her beauty, although she was a very beautiful woman,
nor by the unobtrusive elegance she radiated, but by the
expression of utter sweetness in her charming face. ... For
an instant her grey keen eyes, which seemed darker than
they were because of her thick eyelashes, paused to give
him a friendly glance, as though she recognized him. Then
she began looking for someone in the crowd. ... Her eyes
and her smile revealed vast stores of repressed vitality.'
Further on, the author tells us of 'her brisk step, which gave
a curious air of lightness to her full body.' Little Kitty was
enamoured of her, 'as inexperienced girls often become
enamoured of older married women'. 'There was nothing in
Anna that betrayed the society matron or the mother of
an eight-year-old boy; from the relaxed ease of her movements, her fresh complexion, the spontaneous shifts of her
expression and smile, one would not have believed her to be
more than a girl of twenty, were it not for the serious, even
melancholy light in her lovely eyes. This feature was what

struck and attracted Kitty.' Even the children fall under her spell and quarrel over who is to be allowed to touch her hand or play with her wedding ring. At the ball she out-shines everyone else. Tolstoy describes her arrival with a lover's eyes: 'A very low-cut black velvet gown revealed her bosom and ivory sculptured shoulders, and her fine rounded arms and slender wrists. ... A delicate garland of pansies crowned her black hair, all her own; another just like it was pinned on the black ribbon of her belt, in the middle of a white lace ruffle. Her hair was dressed very simply, the only thing one noticed were the little ringlets escaping at the nape of her neck and temples. She wore a necklace of pearls around her full throat.' From this moment on, there can be no doubt. Anna's appeal owes nothing to the artifices of coquetry. A charm she is unaware of radiates from her body. '"Yes," Kitty said to herself as she watched her dancing, "there is something strange in her, wonderful, demonic."'

But Anna Karenina is not the conscious cause of the tragedies brought about by her implacable beauty: she was born under an evil spell, and at a moment chosen by fate, the spell simply begins to work. As the author continued, with infinite pains, to model each contour of this lost soul, he became increasingly irritated by the healthy, ordinary mortals around her. In the beginning she was the assassin and Karenin and Vronsky her victims. Now the tables were turned. Neither of the two men was worthy of her. With cold rage Tolstoy divested them, one by one, of the quali-ties he had freely bestowed upon them. He debased them in order to elevate and justify Anna.

Karenin becomes a dried-up, self-centred, narrow-minded man, a pure product of Petersburg bureaucracy. Life is hid-den from him by administrative regulations; every gesture he makes is an expression of the law, of convention; he para-lyses and disfigures everything he touches; for him, his wife is simply one item of his establishment. Not until the storm is about to break does he actually concede that she 'might have her own destiny, thoughts, desires,' and as this possibility terrifies him, he prefers to dismiss it from his mind. Just as some people hate the countryside and can only walk on concrete pavement, so Karenin, when life rushes in upon him in all its brutal nakedness and no longer in the form of an official report, utterly loses his grip. 'What she feels, what goes on in her soul, is no concern of mine,' he tells himself. 'That is between herself and her conscience, it is a question of religion.' And further on, 'I made a mistake when I linked my life to hers; but there was nothing shameful in my mistake and therefore I do not need to be unhappy.' A mixture of sham dignity, official piety, self-righteousness, cowardice, rectitude and sanctimoniousness, the reactions he causes in people are the exact opposite of those aroused by his wife. The mere sight of Anna warms people's hearts; he, involuntarily, chills them. At a dinner at the Oblonskys', 'he was the chief reason for the pall that fell over the party'.

Faithful to his style of 'contrasts', however, Tolstoy refuses to cut any character out of a single piece of cloth. When his wife is ill, Karenin suddenly becomes human. His carapace cracks. He becomes drunk with sympathy, dazzled by his own generosity. He even allows Anna's lover inside the house. 'Remorse at having wished for Anna's death, the compassion she inspired in him and, more than anything else, the joy of forgiving, had transformed his moral torments into a profound sense of peace.' The lull is short-lived. As soon as Anna recovers, he becomes as hard as before. What was sublime at the bedside of a dying woman is ridiculous in the presence of a healthy one. As a member of society, he does what society demands. This he can have nothing to reproach himself with afterwards. But she wants 'to tear apart this spiderweb, sticky with lies, in which he was keeping her prisoner'. 'Whatever happens,' she says, 'anything is better than dissimulation and deceit.'

She believes that in Vronsky she has found an ally as well as a lover. But he, whose heart was crystal-pure in the first

draft, is subjected to the same process of degradation as
Karenin, in order to highlight the figure of Anna. Tolstoy's dislike of his hero grows with his infatuation for his
heroine. True, he is not just a handsome, vain and foolish
officer, he belongs to the 'gilded youth' of the capital for
whom amorous intrigue is closely akin to the pleasures of
the hunt. 'In his Petersburg universe,' wrote Tolstoy, 'people
were divided into two totally different types. The lower type
was composed of vulgar, stupid and ridiculous people who
believed tha⸍ a husband should sleep only with his wife, a
maiden should be pure, a married woman chaste, one must
bring up one's children, make money, pay one's debts and
other nonsense of that sort.' On the other side there was 'a
world in which the rule was to appear elegant, handsome,
free with money, bold and high-spirited, to abandon oneself without scruple to every passion, and to laugh at everything else'. Vronsky, a bachelor, feels much more at home
in the second. But when he meets Anna his self-assurance
falters; he is gripped by a passion of unwonted violence.
Even after the charm of novelty has worn off, he sometimes
feels a superstitious fear of her grace and elegance and the
intensity of the emotions that course through her. The thing
he is least able to understand is her aching love for the son
from whom she is separated. He refuses to think of her as
a mother, and she is so aware of this that she prefers to
hide from him the almost physical pain she suffers after
seeing her little Sergey again. Vronsky's failure to understand this condemns her to solitude. 'Her sorrow was all the
greater for being unshared,' Tolstoy wrote. 'She could not,
nor did she wish to confide in Vronsky. ... She knew he
would never be able to understand the depth of her anguish;
she knew a cold comment would be his only response to any
allusion to her distress and she knew she would hate him
for it, and was afraid...'

With clinical exactitude, Tolstoy observes the slow
poisoning of their liaison. Every phase of the disease is ex-
haustively described. More than their relations as lovers,

the very structure of their personalities is infected, unable to withstand the trial of living together. They are ostracized by society, which will not forgive them for flaunting its rules, and they float in an artificial vacuum, with nothing to support them, no friends, nothing to plan for. Though she is strong enough to brave public opinion, Anna feels that a moral structure she has possessed since childhood is bending and giving way beneath her, and she had never realized how useful it could be. Of her two sources of support, her son and her lover – the first has been taken away from her and she may lose the second as well if she is not careful. She becomes anxious, she convinces herself that Vronsky must be pining for his carefree life of old, she accuses him of secretly seeing people whose doors are closed to her; she begins to think he has tired of her and is being unfaithful; she is tortured by jealousy; soon her only aim in life is to keep her hold over her lover, and as her fear that he will desert her increases, her efforts become more and more strained, nagging, awkward. Before long, her beauty and the physical pleasure she gives him are all she can rely upon to hold him. But Vronsky is no longer affected, even by her beauty. When he looks at her, magnificently attired on her way to the theatre, a shudder of repulsion runs through him. 'He raised his eyes,' wrote Tolstoy, 'and saw her beauty and the adornment that set it off so well; but just then it was her very beauty and elegance that irritated him.' And later, 'There was no longer anything mysterious in the feelings her beauty aroused in him; and so, although he was more aware of her appeal than ever before, he was almost offended to see her so beautiful.' Sensing that this weapon, too, will soon be useless to her, Anna begins to flirt with other men, but she cannot arouse Vronsky from his apathy. Then she grows desperate: she has nightmares, takes drugs, finally sees that death is the only way out. 'Why all these churches and bells and lies?' she thought. 'To hide the fact that we all hate each other like those scrapping cabdrivers!' Her inner monologue continues, jerky, compulsive, relentless, until the moment she throws herself under the train.

When shading his vast composition, Tolstoy wanted to save the brightest light for the legitimate couple, Kitty and Levin. Kitty is a pure, ardent and secretive girl in whom marriage suddenly reveals practical qualities of the highest order. Her husband is flabbergasted by her. 'How can this poetic, admirable Kitty, in the first weeks and even the first days of our married life, cope with tablecloths and furniture and mattresses for guests, and trays, and the cook, and the dinner?' This cry of wonderment was not uttered by Konstantin Levin, but by Leo Tolstoy. As always he had great respect for a woman's virtues as a housewife. A wife's universe should be bounded by bed, kitchen stove and cradle.

As he progressed in life, he identified himself more and more with his own characters. After disguising himself as Nicholas Irtenyev, Nekhlyudov, Olenin and Pierre Bezukhov,* here he was again, body and soul – and with what gusto! – in Konstantin Levin. He shamelessly attributed to him the events of his own life, fed him with his ideas, the books he read, his own blood. The relationship between Levin and Kitty – the declaration scene using the first letters of words, the wedding ceremony, including the last-minute hesitation and the incident of the forgotten shirt in the trunk, the young couple's first days in their country home, the birth of their first child – were one and all transposed from the author's past. Sonya must have been deeply moved as she copied over the passages in which the early days of her life with Lyovochka were described with such accuracy and delicacy. Similarly, the death of Levin's brother is an exact replica of the death of Dmitry Tolstoy. Levin's relations with his muzhiks are drawn directly from Tolstoy's experience at Yasnaya Polyana.

Levin personifies the quandary of the landowner. With

* Heroes of *Youth*, *A Landlord's Morning*, *The Cossacks* and *War and Peace*, respectively.

his democratic turn of mind, it seems only fair to him that the peasants should have the land, 'since the lord does nothing and his muzhiks work – thereby eliminating one unproductive element from the soil'. But the aristocrat in him will not die and it hurts him to see the great estates breaking up, the nobility fleeing to Nice and abandoning priceless fields and forests behind them in the heart of Russia for a mere pittance, and crafty stewards speculating at both their employers' and the farmers' expense, as, 'inexorably, on all sides, the impoverishment of the nobility pursued its course'. He seeks to reconcile the interests of both parties, for he has 'the love of the muzhik in his blood'. 'The entire agricultural system must be reorganized, and the living conditions of the people changed in every respect,' he thinks. 'In place of poverty, prosperity for all; in place of mutual animosity, understanding in the interest of all. In a word, a revolution, bloodless but on a grand scale, beginning in the little circle of our district and widening to include our government, then Russia, then the whole world.'

However, it is a far cry from theory to practice. When more and more flesh and blood beings lean with all their weight against the current of ideas, the stream is finally blocked; piled on top of each other, one hundred exceptions ultimately disprove a rule. In spite of his enormous effort, Levin fails to give his peasants a share in their master's profits.

In addition to his problems as a landowner, there are his metaphysical doubts. In the early days of his marriage he thinks he has gone beyond the reach of sorrow and fear. But love is a frail bulwark against the spectre of death. After witnessing his brother's death agony, Levin becomes obsessed by his own ignorance of the most urgent problem of all, the end of life on earth. The birth of his child renews his fascination with the unfathomable mystery. It seems to him that, by living like other people, he is neglecting the essential for the trivial. 'Like a man who trades a warm fur coat for a muslin shirt in midwinter,' Tolstoy wrote, 'Levin felt naked, not in his mind but in his whole being, and condemned to perish miserably.' He read the Bible and the philosophers and hovered between doubt and prayer, and added to his distress by attempting to explain it. While everyone else sees him as a strong, well-balanced man and a happy father, he turns away at the sight of a piece of rope and leaves his gun behind when he goes walking, for fear of yielding to the temptation of suicide. To escape from such depressing meditations, there is only one remedy: manual labour, and he hurls himself into it. Fatigue prevents him from thinking. 'Now, against his will, he sank deeper and deeper into the ground like a ploughshare, until he could not pull himself out without first ploughing his furrow,' Tolstoy went on. From associating with the peasants, Levin gradually absorbs their wisdom. One of them says to him, 'Some people live only for their bellies, and others live for God and their soul.' These simple words strike the young lord at his sorest point, and all his doubts are dispelled. What no philosopher or Church Father had been able to accomplish, a humble peasant does unwittingly: he brings a lost soul back to God. To what God? Levin doesn't know: 'Just as the conclusions of the astronomers would be useless and inaccurate,' he thinks, 'if they were not reached through observation of the visible sky in relation to a fixed meridian and a fixed horizon, so would all metaphysical deductions be absurd if I did not base them on this knowledge of the innate goodness of every human heart which Christianity has revealed to me and of which I shall always be able to find proof in my own soul.' At this point, he believes he has attained the inner peace he has so long aspired to, but the ambiguity of his religious feelings is a warning of fresh storms ahead.

During the four years (1873–7) it took him to write *Anna Karenina*, Tolstoy debated every one of the questions that were bothering him in his book. On the slightest pretext the novelist hands over the pen to the essayist, and the action halts to let the author express his views on rural husbandry, the meaning of life, the education of children or the relations between psychology and physiology. In the world of Levin and Anna, as in Tolstoy's own world, conversation centres on Gustave Doré's illustrations of the Bible, the novels of Daudet and Zola, the physicist Tindall's theories on radiant heat, the teachings of Spencer and Schopenhauer, Lassalle's scheme for workers' unions. Anna dips into Taine's *Ancien Régime*, her husband reads an article by Bréal in the *Revue des Deux Mondes*, there is a debate at Princess Betsy's on compulsory military service. ... Tolstoy might be said to have used the novel as an outlet for his own intellectual preoccupations. In fact, he said as much himself twelve years later, in a letter to Rusanov: 'Sometimes I still have a desire to write, and, do you know, what I would like to write is a big, loose novel like *Anna Karenina*, one in which I might easily find room for all the things I have understood in an original way and that might be useful to others.'

Unlike *War and Peace*, however, where the author intercedes directly to present his view of some point of history, strategy or politics, in *Anna Karenina*, he hides behind his characters and attributes to them the opinions he holds himself. For the sake of impartiality, he even invents contradictions for them. One day, telling a friend of the difficulties he was encountering in his work, he said he had rewritten the conversation between Levin and the priest (Part V, Chapter 1) four times, so that it would be impossible to tell which of the two he favoured. 'I have found,' he said, 'that a story leaves a deeper impression when it is impossible to tell which side the author is on.'[1] He also became increasingly aware of the interdependence of the parts of the book. In a mass of such dimensions everything hung together, the glitter and the tarnish were equally essential. As to the progression of the scenes, he believed it was the result of some mysterious process over which the author had no control. 'I had proof of this,' he wrote to Strakhov, 'with Vronsky's suicide. I had never clearly felt the necessity for it. I had begun to revise my rough draft and suddenly, by some means that was totally unexpected but ineluctable, Vronsky determined to put a bullet through his head, and it later became clear that that scene was organically indispensable.'[2] To his close friends he also said, 'Do you know, I often sit down to write some specific thing, and suddenly I find myself on a wider road, the work begins to spread out in front of me. That was the way it was with *Anna Karenina*.'[3]

It is precisely this 'spreading out', these digressions, this profusion of gratuitous ideas that an impatient judge might hold against Tolstoy. Some passages are definitely too long: the descriptions of the Levins' life in the country, the debates on serfdom and emancipation, the rut in which the peasants live and their unwillingness to change, the county justices of the peace. But the author's skill as a storyteller is so great that just when the reader is about to lose patience, he is caught up and delighted anew. Scenes such as the hay mowing, drenched in sunlight and pagan joy, or the race and the fall of the mare Froufrou, or Anna's secret meeting with her son, or the death of Nicholas, or the suicide in the little railway station, are marvels of precision, fullness of design and controlled emotion.

Here, as in *War and Peace*, it is accuracy of psychological observation combined with a felicitous choice of detail that carries conviction. Returning to St Petersburg after first meeting Vronsky, Anna suddenly notices that her husband's ears are very big, and she is annoyed because his habit of cracking his knuckles seems to be growing worse. On her wedding day, Kitty's friends find her 'much less pretty than usual' in her white dress. Under the strain of her false position after she has left her husband, Anna acquires a habit of screwing up her eyes slightly when she speaks. Oblonsky has a disarming smile that appears at the most unexpected moments and wins people's sympathy. Looking at herself in a mirror on her way to the ball, Kitty is entranced by the black velvet ribbon around her neck. 'She might entertain some doubt about the rest of her attire, but as for the velvet ribbon, no, decidedly, nothing could be said against that. She felt on her shoulders and arms that marble coolness she so loved.'

But although the same descriptive process is used in *Anna Karenina* and *War and Peace*, the general tone of the two works is very different. After dealing with a historical conflict between peoples in *War and Peace* Tolstoy narrowed his field of vision in *Anna Karenina*, to concentrate on a few persons and forage into their darkest recesses. What the picture loses in scope, it gains in depth. The epic is no longer played out in the open air, but within, in the dark shadows of the conscience. The battles are those of emotions, and they rage with the same incoherence and fury as the others.

Just as the outcome of military encounters is not determined by the strategists, so the fate of the individual most often escapes his own will. Actions are determined by circumstance, by the circles in which people move, the friends around them, a thousand imponderables collected together under the name of fatality. The fatality that presides over *Anna Karenina* is not, as in *War and Peace*, the god of war, bloated by politics and reeking of carrion and gunpowder, but the breathless god of passion. There are a hundred times more corpses in *War and Peace* than in *Anna Karenina*, yet the first seems a broad, optimistic, sun-filled work, while *Anna Karenina* is enveloped in grey, troubled clouds. *War and Peace* is an act of faith in life, a poetic glorification of the couple, the family, patriarchal traditions, a hymn to the triumph of the Russian armies over the invader. Victory ennobles all the sacrifices made to obtain it, and the heroes emerge purified by the sufferings they have undergone in the defence of their native soil. None of this is true of *Anna Karenina*, where the air is weighted down with ominous dreams, forebodings, hallucinations and supernatural presences. The very first meeting between Vronsky and Anna at the Moscow railway station is marked by the death of a switchman, crushed beneath a train. After the accident, Oblonsky sees his sister's lips quivering and tears glittering in her eyes.

'What's the matter, Anna?' he asks.

And she answers:

'It's a bad omen.'

Later, leaving the train, she is seized by a feeling of anguish and chaos as she steps out on to the platform in the snowstorm. After Vronsky's decisive words – 'I am going to St Petersburg to be where you are!' – the night, the cold and noise and the fleeting silhouettes of the passengers all conspire to plunge the young woman into a world of fantasy. 'The wind, as though it would overcome all obstacles, beat the snow from the carriage roofs and triumphantly brandished a sheet of metal it had ripped loose, and the locomotive's whistle emitted a demented howl. Anna became even more exhilarated by the tragic splendour of the storm: she had just heard the words her reason dreaded and her heart longed for.'

A still more awesome menace is Anna's famous dream, in which a little muzhik in rags appears, bending over an iron plate and mumbling incomprehensible words in French, 'and she sensed that he was performing some strange ritual over her with this piece of iron, and awoke drenched in cold sweat'. She had this nightmare several times; Vronsky himself was affected by it through a kind of telepathy; and the moment Anna throws herself under the wheels of the train, she sees, in a flash, 'a little man, muttering to himself and tapping on the iron above her'.

Another symbol: the death of the mare Froufrou. Through Vronsky's fault, she falls and breaks her back during the steeplechase, prefiguring Anna's suicide, to which she was driven by her lover's indifference. Even the words Tolstoy chooses to describe the fallen mare and the fallen woman are oddly similar. Here is Vronsky with Anna, who has finally yielded to him: 'Pale, his lower jaw trembling, he urged her to be calm.' And here he is beside his fatally wounded horse: 'He was pale, his lower jaw trembling, his face transfigured by rage.'

The evil omens become more clearly defined when Anna, returning to the hotel after her meeting with her son, removes from an album the photographs she had kept of him: 'There was only one left, the best. ... Her quick fingers, more nervous than ever, vainly tried to prize it out of the frame; there was no paper cutter near by, so she poked at the stiff paper with another photograph she had picked up without looking, a portrait of Vronsky, taken in Rome.' This incident strikes her as a warning from God: her lover driving out her son ...

Equally significant is the symbol of the candle that burns brighter just before going out. The first time she watches the wavering flame, Anna is seized by an irrational, morbid dread, and quickly, her heart pounding, lights another candle as though by doing so she might ward off the shadow of death. The second time is in the instant she loses consciousness under the wheels of the train: 'And the candle by whose light she had read the book of life, full of conflict, treachery, sadness and horror, flared up more brightly than ever, lighting all the pages that had remained in darkness before, and then sputtered, flickered and went out for ever.'

Anna is not the only person to be affected by dread. Oblonsky's wife Dolly fears for her children's future; Princess Sherbatsky is beset by funereal presentiments at night; Levin's brother Nicholas is haunted by fear of what lies beyond life; the only chapter in the book that bears a title is Chapter 20 of Part V: *Death*. All the characters' struggles to achieve happiness end in failure. Even Kitty and Levin are not exempt from the curse hanging over all couples who are bound by the flesh. In telling their story, the author tried to contrast the blessings that flow from conjugal love and the havoc caused by unsanctified love; but even the bliss of family life proves to be only a snare and a delusion. The happily married Levin is equally consumed by doubt. All his efforts at social improvement fail, and he saves himself *in extremis* only by grasping at the primitive faith of the muzhik. All in all, the hell of forbidden passion in which Anna and Vronsky are consumed is scarcely less perilous than the heaven of family affection in which Kitty and Levin slowly decompose.

One strange thing: in both *Anna Karenina* and *War and Peace*, it is the exceptional, glittering beings, those marked by some metaphysical sign, who disappear, and the average, even insignificant ones who survive and trudge on along their little paths, halfway between good and evil. After the death of Prince Andrey – with his dreams, his doubts, his pride – we are left with the placid Bezukhov and Rostov families, for whom every imaginable felicity lies in store if they will only be content to stay out of the limelight. Anna Karenina and Vronsky are swept from the scene, leaving behind them the mighty conquerors in the battle of life: Kitty and Levin, fine, upstanding, dull young folk, held up as an example by all their neighbours. Is this Tolstoy's plea for mediocrity? No; he simply feels that mankind needs, now and then, these extraordinary beings to shake up the dozing masses; but in the final analysis, it is the conjunction of innumerable ordinary destinies that carries history forward. Whether we like it or not, the future belongs to the Rostovs and Bezukhovs and Levins, to the shuffling mob of men of good-will. As landowner and father, Tolstoy considers himself among their number. In justifying them, he justifies himself. And even if he is occasionally tempted to desert to the camp of the idealist-in-revolt, he never tarries there. He is still at the stage of condemning private property with one hand while buying more land with the other, and inviting judges to his home while he reviles capital punishment.

But, contrary to his intentions, it is the damned, in this bitterly pessimistic novel, who arouse our sympathy and the virtuous who disappoint us. Saddled with every curse that could be laid upon her, Anna Karenina towers so far above

all the other characters that the author was forced to give
the book her name. The inscription, 'Vengeance is mine; I
will repay,' bears out the idea that Anna's fall proceeds
from a decision by some higher authority, divine and without appeal. Everything in this superficially realistic tale is
magical. Even objects – the candle, the snowy windowpane,
Anna's little red bag – are invested with occult powers. Tolstoy invited his readers to contemplate the implications of a
vast, disturbing, gloomy tragedy.

And they flung themselves upon it voraciously, titillated
by the portrayal of 'high society', spellbound by Anna's
illicit love affair, shocked by the daring scenes of her 'fall'.
As the issues of the *Russian Herald* succeeded each other,
Strakhov, in the front ranks in Moscow, dispatched regular
communiqués to headquarters at Yasnaya Polyana: 'Excitement keeps mounting. ... Opinions are so divergent that it
is impossible to summarize them. ... Some complain that
you are too cynical; others – more intelligent (Danilevsky, for
one) – are in ecstasy.' (21 March 1875.) 'Everyone is dumb
with admiration of the February issue. The January one was
less popular. ... Now there is a roar of satisfaction. It's as
though you were throwing food to starving men.' (5 March
1876.) 'Everyone is fascinated by your novel, it's incredible
how many people are reading it. Only Pushkin and Gogol
have ever been read like this, with people scrambling for
every page and paying no attention to what anybody else is
writing.' (February 1877.) 'Dostoyevsky is waving his arms
about and calling you a god of the art; I am surprised and
delighted – surprised, because I know how intensely he dis-
likes you.' (18 May 1877.)

Alexandra Tolstoy was also in raptures: 'Every chapter
has society rearing up on its hind legs,' she wrote, 'and there
is no end to the commenting and praise and gossip and
argument, as though it were something that affected every
individual personally.'[4]

Friend Fet hailed him as a genius: 'What artistic insolence in the description of childbirth! Nobody since

the world began has ever done it before, and nobody will ever do it again. The fools will go on about Flaubertian realism, when everything here is idealism!'[5]

Professional critics were no less stirred by the publication of the novel. Comparing Tolstoy and Stendhal, V. V. Chuyko, in *The Voice*, pointed out that whereas Stendhal always began with a psychological postulate and only gave a semblance of reality to his characters by the 'extraordinary logic' with which he followed up the consequences of a given situation, Tolstoy was all instinct, inseparable from life, owing nothing to any process.

Another critic in the same period affirmed that 'Count Tolstoy has no equal in any foreign literature' and that 'in our country, Dostoyevsky alone can come near him'.

'The author,' Suvorin wrote in *New Times*, 'has spared nothing and no one. He portrays love with a realism that no one in our country has yet approached.'

And Stasov chimed in, 'Count Tolstoy alone is forging ahead, while all our other writers are beating a retreat or falling silent or fading away or losing face . . .'

Dostoyevsky himself, although he disapproved of the last part of *Anna Karenina* out of loyalty to the holy war against the Turks, paid homage to the rest of the book in *Diary of a Writer*:

'*Anna Karenina* is a perfect work of art, appearing at exactly the right moment, utterly unlike anything being published in Europe; its theme is totally Russian. There is something in this novel of our "new word", a new word that has not yet been heard in Europe, although the peoples of the West have great need of it, however proud they may be.'

In a burst of national pride the author of *Crime and Punishment* explained that in Europe – the seat of logic, materialism and the narrow view – humans who violated the laws of society were punished by human justice, but for a Russian writer like Tolstoy, the true seat of judgement was in the heart of the individual. 'The human judge must know that he is not a final judge, being a mere sinner like the rest, that it is absurd for him to pass judgement except through the only means of understanding that exists: charity, and love.'

Along with these distinguished expressions of approval, Tolstoy received, as usual, a volley of snide comments and insults. Skabishevsky wrote, in the *Stock Exchange News*, that the entire novel was 'permeated with an idyllic aroma of diapers' and that Anna's suicide was 'a melodramatic piece of nonsense in the manner of the old French novels, and a fit conclusion to a vulgar love affair between a snob and a lady of Petersburg society with a weakness for frogged coats'. Tkachev, in *The Affair*, accused Tolstoy of seeking 'to degrade public morality', swore that *Anna Karenina* was 'an epic of baronial passions' utterly 'devoid of meaning' and, parodying its author, suggested that he write a book on the pastoral bliss of Levin and a cow. The anonymous critic of the *Odessa Courier* announced that 'food, drink, hunting, balls, horse races and love, love, love in the most naked sense of the word, without psychological ramifications or moral interest of any sort – that is what the novel is about, from start to finish.' He concluded, 'I challenge the reader to show me one page, nay! one half-page, that contains an idea, or rather the shadow of an idea.'

Nor did Ivan Turgenev like *Anna Karenina*. 'He has gone off the track,' he wrote to Suvorin on 1 (13) April 1875. 'It is the fault of Moscow, and the Slavophil aristocrats and Orthodox old maids, and his isolation and lack of perseverance.' And to Polonsky, on 13 (25) May: 'I do not like *Anna Karenina*, despite some truly magnificent pages (the horse race, the hay-making, the hunt). But the whole thing is sour, it smells of Moscow and old maids, the Slavophilism and the narrow-mindedness of the nobility.'

Tolstoy returned the compliment, when Turgenev published his *Virgin Soil*. 'I haven't read the Turgenev yet,' he wrote to Strakhov, 'but, judging from what I have heard about it, I am deeply sorry that this well of pure and wonderful water should have become sullied by such filth. If he would simply choose a day in his life and write about it, everybody would be delighted.'[6]

He felt even more aloof from praise and censure alike than he had after *War and Peace*. Without setting foot outside Yasnaya Polyana, he had conquered Russia. Sitting at his desk in his peasant blouse, he glanced through the press clippings sent by Strakhov. One, signed W –, was especially dithyrambic: 'New generations will come, society will be transformed, Russia will turn down other paths, but these works [*War and Peace* and *Anna Karenina*] will continue to be read and re-read by all because they are inseparable from Russian life and Russian culture. They will be eternally new.'[7]

How did Tolstoy respond to these glowing prophecies? With pride, scepticism, indifference? Whatever he said, he must have been touched by the understanding and love of so many people. But for him fulfilment, true fulfilment, was not to be found in newspaper articles, however flattering they might be. He must seek it in himself. And when he looked there, he saw nothing but darkness, uncertainty and confusion.

[20]

Art and Faith

THE royalties from *Anna Karenina*, added to those from *War and Peace*, exceeded twenty thousand roubles a year; in addition, the farms were bringing in nearly ten thousand roubles.* This more than covered the family's expenses. Once again, Sonya had taken full charge of the administration of the estate, releasing her husband from all material cares. All he had to worry about was writing.

The increase in his income led to the purchase of more land, but also to the enlargement of his domestic staff. Alongside the regulars – onetime serfs in caftan and bark shoes, dedicated to the family, with their own familiar way of addressing the masters – appeared liveried footmen (in red waistcoats and white cotton gloves), 'trained' chambermaids, seamstresses, governesses, French and German tutors. Little Tanya, who at the age of fourteen was also keeping her diary, wrote on 11 November 1878:

I have a governess, Mlle Gachet, but Masha has an Englishwoman, Annie; the boys have M. Nief; Andrey has a *nyanya*; we also have a Russian teacher, B. A. Alexeyev; he lives in a wing of the house with his wife, his son who is one year and two months old, and his stepdaughter Lisa, aged eight. M. Nief's wife also wants to live here; he has already taken a little isba for her and his son. Other teachers come to the house; the drawing teacher, Simonenko: he is short and humpbacked. Then the Greek teacher, Ulvansky. The priest, the music teacher Michurin, the German woman Amalya Fedorovna . . .

The most striking figure among this large staff of intellectuals was the Frenchman, M. Nief. 'Nief' was a pseudonym, masking a certain Jules Montel, onetime supporter of

*Or a total (royalties and income from the estate) of $84,900.

the French Commune, who fled the country after the 'Versaillais' had crushed the rebellion and did not reveal his true identity until 1880, when an amnesty was proclaimed in Paris. Alexeyev, the Russian teacher, was also a militant socialist. At first he was offended by the material comforts of the inhabitants of Yasnaya Polyana, but he ultimately fell under Tolstoy's spell and liked to say he was his debtor and his friend. Both tutors and pupils took part in all the family festivities. A picnic in the forest was planned for Tanya's birthday, on 4 October 1878. 'M. Nief rolled up his sleeves and made an omelette and hot chocolate,' Sonya wrote in her diary. 'Four fires were burning. Sergey roasted shashlik. The party was very gay, we ate a great deal and were fortunate enough to have a magnificent day.'

The house had been enlarged in 1871 but the new quarters were already cramped: guests were assembling at Yasnaya Polyana with increasing frequency. The disciples had not yet begun to come, but there were relatives, friends and neighbours. According to the Russian tradition, they said they were coming for the day and stayed for a week or a month. As the nearest station was three miles away and there was no hotel in the vicinity, Sonya offered bed and board to all comers. Tolstoy was not averse to this hum of guests, servants and children. He loved to feel himself surrounded by a noisy, simple life. It was his overcoat, to shield him from cold and death. Sometimes, in his study, he heard the laughter of croquet players under the larches and the crisp taps of their mallets against the balls. But did you have the right to make merry when a trap-door was about to yawn beneath your feet? He looked at himself in the mirror. A fifty-year-old face: hair cropped short above a high furrowed brow, broad bushy eyebrows overhanging two sharp grey eyes sunk deep in their sockets, a shapeless nose, fleshy ears, a sensuous mouth, and, framing the whole, a forest of stiff, tangled greying hair, thick as wire. He had never been in better condition. In spite of his headaches, he could easily work eight hours on end. Hiking, galloping through the brush, cutting hay or sawing wood, nobody could keep pace with him. Was there any more healthy, better-balanced life in the world than his? Everything he had wanted when he was young he had obtained, and in the prime of life. He had wanted literary fame, and he shared with Dostoyevsky the honour of being universally acclaimed as the greatest living Russian author; he had hoped to spend calm years working in the home of his ancestors, surrounded by a loving wife and many children, and thanks to Sonya, he was savouring this family happiness to the full. He had dreaded being forced to write in order to earn a living, and his financial circumstances allowed him to work in total freedom.

And yet, he was not happy. Or rather, the form of happiness that had become his lot did not content him and he wondered whether there might not be some other kind. His thoughts were haunted by the night at Arzamas. Sometimes he did not read a single page or write a line for days on end. Along with mental paralysis came physical indifference. An automaton went through the motions of everyday life in his place. Then, suddenly, he awoke and began to ask questions, and apathy would give way to anguish.

'I would be deep in my problems of estate management,' he writes in *Confession*, 'and a question would come to me: "All right, so you have 1,350 acres of land in the government of Samara, and 300 head of horses; so what?" Or, thinking of my children's education, I would ask myself, "What for?" Or, meditating upon the best way of making people happy, I would conclude, "What does it have to do with me?" Or again, thinking of the celebrity my books had brought me, I told myself, "Fine, you will be more famous than Gogol, Pushkin, Shakespeare, Molière, and all the writers in the world, and then what?"'

At that moment, if anyone had offered to grant his dearest wish he would not have known what to ask for; he wished for nothing. He wished for nothing because he had discovered the futility of human enterprise. He had walked along the road for fifty years, his eyes distracted by a moving leaf or a passing face, and suddenly he saw the chasm. 'And you can't stop and you can't go backward and you can't close your eyes in order not to see that there is nothing ahead but the lie of freedom and happiness, nothing but suffering, real death, complete annihilation.'

When he reached this point in his brooding, he thought he heard a sort of distant laughter. *Someone* was making fun of him, someone who had worked everything out beforehand, a long time ago.

'The *someone* was enjoying himself, watching how, after growing up, after cultivating my body and mind for thirty or forty years, after attaining the summit of my powers, reaching the height from which one looks out over the whole of life, there I stood like an idiot, realizing at last that there was nothing and never would be anything in life. And *he* thinks it's funny!'

If life was a nasty joke, the only thing to do was refuse it. Just as powerfully as he had once longed to fight, Tolstoy now wanted to die. The void attracted him as strongly as the prospect of new land to buy had done before. A simple and profitable operation. The rewards were certain. He was not troubled by the thought of his wife or children: he had never been concerned with them except in relation to himself. With him dead, they would manage, living on the income from the estate and his books. The question was when and how he would destroy himself. He was in no hurry – there was a glimmer of common sense in his delirium. No sooner had he let himself be swept away by the temptation of obliteration than he caught himself up again, his reason alerted, with a delicious shiver running down his spine.

The need to make an end of it all was strongest at night. He slept alone, in his study. As he undressed for bed, he looked at the crossbar between the two cabinets loaded with books. A slipknot, a chair kicked away, a body that jerks, sways back and forth and then stops. ... No more Leo Tolstoy! 'Then I, the happy man,' he wrote, 'removed the rope from the room ... and stopped taking my gun when I went out to hunt, so that I could not yield to the desire to do away with myself too easily.'[1]

This alternating boldness of purpose and prudence of action was in keeping with the rest of his personality. No one could be more preoccupied by the state of his health than this permanent suicide candidate. He was fond of re-calling an oriental fable: A man pursued by a tiger climbs down into a well. At the bottom of the well he sees the gap-ing jaws of a dragon. Unable to go either up or down, the poor man clings to a bush growing between the loosened stones. As his strength begins to fail he spies two mice, one white and one black, gnawing at the branch he is hanging from. A few seconds more and he will fall. Knowing him-self about to die, the man makes a supreme effort, and licks the drops of honey from the leaves. Tolstoy would have been glad to do the same; but the two drops of honey – love of family and love of literature – that had formerly helped him to accept reality had now lost all their savour for him.

The family, I told myself, my wife, my children, are also human beings and therefore ruled by the same conditions as myself: either they must live a lie or face up to the ghastly truth. Why do they have to live? Why do I have to love and protect them and help them to grow up and safeguard their in-terests? To lead them into the despair in which I am myself, or to keep them in a state of imbecility? As I love them, I cannot hide the truth from them. ... And the truth is death. As for art and poetry – for a long time I managed to convince myself, under the influence of success and praise, that they were a pos-sible form of activity, even though death would destroy all, both my work and the memory of it. Then I realized that this activity was also a lie.[2]

The despair he thought he alone suffered was in fact be-ing shared – and indulged in – by a good many intellectuals in Russia. In *Fathers and Sons* Turgenev had given a name to this *mal du siècle*: nihilism. And he had made it the sub-

ject of his last book, *Virgin Soil*. As defined by Turgenev,
the nihilist was 'a man who would accept no authority and
adopt no principle as an article of faith, no matter how
highly esteemed that principle might be'. A steadily growing number of young people, having rejected family, art,
religion and all existing social structures in general, were
finding themselves alone in a great emptiness, and losing
their heads. Some began to dress as muzhiks, 'going over to
the people' and coming back misunderstood. A suicide epidemic was raging among the students and wealthy classes.
People were killing themselves out of lassitude, nausea, imitation, braggadocio or plain curiosity.

But the true nihilists, those who resisted the call of 'nir-
vana', were the confirmed materialists who preached the mes-
sianic future of the Russian people and saw salvation for the
country in the abolition of the monarchy and the institution
of a republican government based on the rural commune.
This revolutionary movement was very foreign to Tolstoy,
who tended towards idealism and non-violence; but both
attitudes were the result of the same fundamental disillusionment, the same desire to challenge official doctrine
and the same trust in the wordless wisdom of the
peasant. After admiring Bakunin and Herzen, Tolstoy
turned away from them in disgust. All those two cared
about was the material side, and for him the welfare of the
soul was more important than that of the body. His personal torment had overleaped the social phase and ripened
into full flower in the metaphysical realm. In search of a
reliable opinion, he read or reread Plato, Spinoza, Kant,
Schelling, Hegel, Schopenhauer, all the philosophers who
had given a spiritualist explanation of life. But their enlightened minds had all tripped over the same obstacle.
'The life of the body is an evil and a lie,' said Socrates. 'And
that is why we should desire its destruction as a blessing.'
'Everything in the world – folly and wisdom, riches and
poverty, joy and grief – is nothing but empty agitation and
vanity,' Solomon went on. 'Man will die and nothing will

remain of him.' 'Life should not be,' said Schopenhauer, 'and the sole good is the passage from being to nothingness.' 'To live, conscious of the inevitability of suffering, weakness, age, death, is impossible,' added Buddha. 'We must free ourselves from life, from all possibility of life.'[3]

Not having found what he was looking for in the great thinkers, Tolstoy came down a few levels, and tried to understand how ordinary mortals made their peace with the human condition by observing those around him. If death were preferable to life, why did the majority of the people not commit suicide? Upon reflection, he concluded that his fellow men adopted one of four attitudes towards the problem: some were honestly unaware of the tragedy of life and death, but this implied a mental lethargy bordering upon idiocy; others, related to the epicureans, were aware of their desperate situation but continued licking the honey off the leaves of the bush while they waited to fall into the dragon's jaws; still others, realizing the absurdity of their destiny on earth, made it a point of honour to destroy themselves; and the last group, too weak to carry out this act of deliverance, went on eating, drinking, dressing, procreating, buying land and making money, in a state of insurmountable revulsion. Tolstoy belonged to the last category. He hated himself for his cowardice. Sometimes, however, his certainty wavered.

'If there were no life, there would be no reason,' he suddenly said to himself. 'Therefore, reason is the child of life, and being the child of life, reason cannot deny life.'

He was trapped in an infernal circle. His notebooks were filling up with observations on the relationship between intelligence and faith, man and space, matter and motion. The most self-evident concepts now seemed debatable to him. His new-found ignorance was comparable to that of the muzhik. The muzhik. Why hadn't he thought of him before? There was the source of light.

'I turned my eyes to the huge masses of simple, ignorant,

poor people, and I saw something altogether different,' he wrote.

These people accepted poverty, hunger, ill-treatment, disease, suffering and death with tranquil resignation. Some, in the direst circumstances, even looked happy. And few, in any event, thought of hanging themselves. Was it reason that helped them to bear the burden of their existence? Assuredly not. They drew their courage from the most simple blind faith, as taught by the pope in the little country church with the tarnished gilt cupola. Faith like theirs could only be accepted, without question or argument. God, like vodka, was to be swallowed at a gulp, without thinking. 'As soon as man applies his intelligence and only his intelligence to any object at all, he unfailingly destroys the object,' Tolstoy wrote in his notebook.[4]

One spring day when he was walking in the forest, his mind suddenly felt lighter and his whole body began to move more freely through the light-spattered dimness. Intrigued, he observed that he was always sad when he rejected God with his reason and always cheerful when he accepted him like a child.

'At the thought of God, happy waves of life welled up inside me,' he wrote. 'Everything came alive, took on meaning. The moment I thought I knew God, I lived. But the moment I forgot him, the moment I stopped believing, I also stopped living. ... To know God and to live are the same thing. God is life.'[5]

He had found faith. A faith within reach of all. Like a shipwrecked man at the end of his strength, Tolstoy clung to this raft.

First, he saw that he could only remain in his state of grace by accepting it unconditionally. Even if certain rituals seemed silly and unjustifiable to him, even if the behaviour of the faithful resembled blind superstition, he must obey the law of the flock or be lost. God, as creator of the entire world, could only have revealed his truth to all men, united by love. To pray to God by oneself was an absurdity. It was

1. Nicholas Tolstoy

2a. Tolstoy and his brothers

2b. The house at Yasnaya Polyana

3. Sofya Behrs

4. Tolstoy while he was working on War and Peace

5. *Tolstoy and his family*

6. Tolstoy at his worktable

7. Tolstoy and Maxim Gorky in the Crimea

8. Tolstoy on his birthday, 1908

necessary to pray to him among the masses, through the masses.

With the same energy he had formerly applied to reviling the dogma of the Orthodox Church, Tolstoy now threw himself into piety. He who had even refused to attend the services in the house organized by Sonya for feast days now began to say his prayers morning and night without any prompting from anyone; he got up early for mass on Sunday, confessed and took communion, fasted on Wednesdays and Fridays.

'I know that what I am doing is right,' he said, 'if only because, in order to mortify the pride of the spirit, be united with my ancestors and fellow men and continue my search for the meaning of life, I am sacrificing my physical comfort.'

To tell the truth, his mortification of the spirit was greatly attenuated by the feeling that he was being united, not only with the people, but with his own youth. He was not prospecting new ground, he was turning back into an old familiar path. The appeal of religion was heightened by the appeal of his childhood memories. The trembling flame of the vigil light in front of the icon was the same one that had fascinated him as a child. And when he made the sign of the cross, it was not a bearded fifty-year-old his protective gesture was shielding, but a nervous, sensitive boy, dreaming of the kingdom of the Ant Brothers.

'It was a strange thing,' he admitted, 'but the life force I rediscovered then was not new to me; it was the oldest of all, that of the very beginning of my life.'

Was there a shade of ostentation in his repeated genuflections in the little country church? Did he think it rather admirable of himself to return to this simplicity after studying the philosophers? In any case, he made no secret of his reconversion. He spoke of it at the dinner table with his wife and children, as though it were something that concerned them all. Sonya, who had so often bewailed his scepticism, was overjoyed at his new devoutness. Following his example, everyone in the family became possessed of renewed zeal. For Lent, they fasted not only in the first and last weeks, but for seven consecutive weeks.

When a guest arrived at Yasnaya Polyana, Tolstoy invariably led him to state his position on the problem of religion. Count Bobrinsky, founder of the 'Society for the Promotion of Religious and Moral Reading' and partisan of Lord Radstock's theories, pleased him immensely by the intensity of his faith. 'He cannot be contradicted,' Tolstoy wrote to Alexandra, 'because he is not trying to prove anything. He simply says he believes and, listening to him, one feels that he is happier than those who do not believe, one feels above all that belief such as his cannot be achieved by an effort of the mind, but that it must be received as a miraculous gift. And that is what I desire.'[6]

He read passages from his philosophical meditations to his friend Urusov. He had weighty discussions on materialism with Ushakov, the governor of Tula, and with Dr Sakharin. Alexeyev, the Russian teacher, affirmed that in the United States, where he had spent some time in a Russian communist colony, the pioneers had been forced to abandon their social reform until they had established their 'religious foundations'. This convinced Tolstoy that a society without God was inconceivable. His letters to Fet, Strakhov and Alexandra began to sound like metaphysical dissertations; he read nothing but religious works; he abhorred Renan's *Life of Jesus*, which Strakhov had sent to him, and said everything in it was false, dry and ridiculous; he was in seventh heaven, on the other hand, over Pascal's *Penseés*. How had this seventeenth-century Frenchman managed to understand his torment so completely, and even point the way to a remedy? 'Their method is to do everything as though they believed, to sprinkle holy water and hear masses said. ... Quite naturally, simply by going through the motions, you will come to believe and cease to reason.' There was an admirable piece of advice! The way it gave preference to feeling over reason, it might almost have been written by a Russian! Pascal approved of the faith of the muzhik. On the map of Christian thought, Port-Royal was next door to Yasnaya Polyana. Hurry, hurry, run to the people, down into oblivion, down into ignorance!

The highway to Kiev passed not far from the estate. In the springtime the pilgrims filed through the dust, pack on back and staff in hand, some going to the sanctuaries in the south, some to the north. It was like a river of folk-faith flooding his land. Every day, drawn by this flow of fresh water, Tolstoy donned his peasant blouse, pulled on his boots and stationed himself by the roadside. 'I am going out to the Nevsky Prospect,' he would say, taking up his walking-stick. He admired and envied these simple folk, who had left their villages weeks before with a few kopecks in their pockets and begun walking, never swerving from their course, with sunburned faces and bleeding feet, sleeping out under the open sky, living on whatever sustenance charitable souls provided as they passed, praying in every church, borne up in their weariness by the desire to kiss some icon or drink some holy water or touch the tomb of some miraculous monk.

Now and then the count would stop one of these visionaries and sit down in the grass with him, to question him about the goal of his journey and the nature of his faith. One day Strakhov, who was visiting at Yasnaya Polyana, accompanied him to a pilgrims' inn. There were a dozen people inside, men and women in rags, dirty and exhausted. Some slept, others were praying, and others were eating black bread and cucumbers. Tolstoy eagerly began to question one of them. 'It was most curious to listen to them,' Strakhov wrote to his friend Danilevsky. 'Tolstoy is very interested in the language of the people. He finds new words every day.'

Indeed, it was not only the naïve piety of the pilgrims' tales that delighted him, but the tellers' quaint turns of speech as well. He came for a lesson in faith and went away having learned a lesson in style. An incorrigible professional, he would have jotted down his impressions under the very nose of God. The pages of his notebook were soon covered with strange words, rhymes, adages and proverbs, the age-old lore of the common people. He brought tale-tellers to the house, chief among them, Shchegolenok, whose corkscrew beard fascinated the children; he used some of the old man's tales as a basis for lovely stories, such as that of Michael the cobbler (*What Men Live By*) and the men who find salvation on an island (*Three Old Men*).

In July 1877 he made a pilgrimage with his friend Strakhov to the monastery of Optina-Pustyn in the province of Kaluga, deep in the heart of Russia. Nicholas Gogol, the publicist Kireyevsky, the author Konstantin Leontyev, the philosopher Solovyev, even Dostoyevsky himself, had been there before him. The place was famous throughout the country for the devoutness of its monks and the authority of its starets, the spiritual leader of the brotherhood.

Following Leonid and Makarios, starets Ambrose was then head of the hermitage, and he was reputed to be something of a saint.[7] Persons suffering in body or soul, illiterate peasants and tormented intellectuals, wealthy merchants, military officers, great ladies, unwed mothers and starveling beggars, all came in search of enlightenment from the admirable old man. His advice was solicited with regard to a job to take or turn down, a projected marriage, a religious vocation, a family feud, a love betrayed, a hidden crime. Sometimes starets Ambrose guessed the trouble before the suppliant even had time to confide in him, and banished it with a soothing word.

Tolstoy had high hopes for their meeting. The travellers reached Optina-Pustyn at night and slept in the convent hostelry. Early next morning Prince Obolensky dropped over from his nearby estate to invite them to dinner the following day – to what desert did one have to flee to escape one's social obligations? This disappointment was followed by a much larger one: Tolstoy took an immediate dislike to starets Ambrose, who received them in his cell. He was a tall, stooped, lean man with keen eyes and a deeply lined face ending in a little beard. He had not read the count's books, but he had heard of Levin's confession to the priest in *Anna Karenina*. It had been spoken of most highly. Emboldened by the compliment, Tolstoy plunged into an interrogation of the Gospels. Perhaps his questions were too aggressive: the starets became withdrawn and curt and replied evasively. They parted in mutual dissatisfaction.

This unfortunate occurrence did nothing to weaken Tolstoy's religious beliefs and may even have strengthened his conviction that it was the common muzhik and not the exceptional being who was best qualified to perceive the mind of God.

A few months later, on 26 December 1877, Sonya noted that her husband had begun to write a philosophical-religious work in a large bound notebook. 'The object of what I am writing in this big book,' he told her, 'is to demonstrate the absolute necessity of religion.' To those who claimed that social laws, 'and especially socialist and communist laws', were superior to Christian laws, he replied: 'If the Christian doctrine, which has been implanted among us for centuries and is the basis of our society, did not exist, then neither would there be any moral law or law of honour or desire for a more equitable distribution of earthly wealth, or aspiration to goodness and equality, all of which exist in all men.'

This might almost be an echo of Pascal's remark: 'The Christian religion alone, being a mixture of internal and external, is proportionate to all. It elevates the lowly within and humbles the proud without.'

But while Sonya was under the impression that her husband was wholly engrossed in inscribing his theological reflections in 'the big notebook', he was still consigning more secular observations to his private journal. The novelist was continually tugging at the coatsleeve of the thinker. Country life supplied material for comment and sketches. At first these were only thumbnail descriptions of nature, in telegraphic notation: 'Vaporous heat. Towards evening, luminosity in the air. Hurts the eyes. Eyes go for rest to the dark green line of the forest. Mosquitoes spin, whining.' (23 June 1877.) 'A downpour, the wind at a sharp angle. A linden uprooted. Mud and dirt. Puddles on the road gleam blue.' (8 July 1877.) 'Sparkling day. Cold. Rain. It smells of wet straw.' (25 August 1877.)

Then he began to embroider and improvise upon these practice scales. Names appeared, dates, embryonic outlines. Once again Tolstoy wanted to write a work of fiction, although he did not abandon his mystical daydreams. But what would be the theme? It would have to be sufficiently serious and vast to stand comparison with *War and Peace* and *Anna Karenina*. After letting his mind roam in all directions, he returned to the idea of the Decembrist uprising.

In January 1878 he asked Alexandra Tolstoy to send him information about General Perovsky, whom she had known personally; he was a former military governor of the province of Orenburg and a confidential friend of Nicholas I.

Now I am deep in my readings on the 1820s and I cannot tell you how much pleasure I derive from them [he wrote to Alexandra]. It is both odd and appealing to me to think that a period I can remember – 1830 – is already part of history.[8] The figures in the picture suddenly stop wavering and shifting, and everything freezes into the solemn immobility of truth and beauty. I feel like a (mediocre) cook wandering through a loaded marketplace, eyeing the huge choice of vegetables, meat and fish, and dreaming of the dinner he is going to serve! ... This is so important to me! ... As important as your faith is to you. I am tempted to say, even more important. But nothing could be that![9]

In fact, the theme was still not clear in his mind. He admired the Decembrists for their noble aspirations and disapproved of their trying to impose them by force. He hated Nicholas I for putting down the insurrection so brutally, but recognized that maintaining order was essential to society.

Also, he wanted to bring the common people into his book, but they had played a very small part in events. One day he said to Sonya,

All these things will take place on Olympus. Nicholas Pavlovich [Tsar Nicholas I] will live among the aristocrats like Jupiter among the gods; the muzhiks will be transported to the governments of Samara and Irkutsk. One of the conspirators of 14 December will be living with these emigrants, and that will make the connection between the simple life and the aristocrats. Like a drawing, my book must have a background, and that will be provided by my present religious position. ... For instance, one could treat the uprising of 14 December without judging anyone, either Nicholas Pavlovich or the conspirators, simply understanding both sides and portraying them.

In his letters he often spoke of this desire for impartiality. 'In this story there must be no guilty party.' (Letter to Alexandra Tolstoy, 14 March 1878.) 'It is a great blessing that I do not take sides, and can love and sympathize freely with all.' (Letter to Alexandra Tolstoy, 5 September 1878.)

With this principle as his point of reference, he began the first chapter, twice. 'Yesterday morning,' Sonya wrote in her diary, 'Lyovochka read me the beginning of his new book, which is conceived on a scale as vast as it is fascinating. The action begins with a trial about land between an owner and his muzhiks, the arrival in Moscow of Prince Chernishev and his family, the laying of the cornerstone of Holy Saviour Cathedral, and the apparition of a pious old man. ...' [10] But to write the next part, he needed more than printed documentation. There were still survivors of the conspiracy around; he wanted to meet them and hear in their own words the story of the aborted coup d'état, their imprisonment, their exile to Siberia ...

In February 1878 he went to Moscow to meet two Decembrists, Svistunov and M. I. Muravyev-Apostol, who had been imprisoned in Sts Peter and Paul Fortress and sent to the convict colonies at Chita and Petrovsk. The old men recounted their ruined lives with a mixture of nostalgia and pride. Some people justify their lives by their work; theirs were justified by their sense of the ill-treatment they had suffered.

From Moscow, Tolstoy went to St Petersburg, where he saw his old and dear friend *babushka* Alexandra. They had long, mystical conversations, no doubt, and Alexandra was very happy to see Leo back in the Church. However, there was something impetuous and insistent in the neophyte's zeal that gave her cause to fear he would soon abandon the rank and file of the faithful. They also talked about the 1820s and the prominent figures of the day, whom the maid of honour had had the good fortune to know at first hand. Tolstoy took advantage of his trip to the capital to ransack the libraries. He was refused permission to examine the secret files of the Third Section, but he was allowed to visit Sts Peter and Paul Fortress, where most of the Decembrists had been incarcerated, with his brother-in-law Stepan Behrs. Baron Maidel,* the prison governor, showed the author the irons in which some of the prisoners had been shackled fifty-three years earlier, and told him how one of them (Svistunov) had tried to kill himself, first by leaping into the Neva and then by eating broken glass. When Tolstoy said he would like to take a closer look at the cells in the Alexis ravelin, Baron Maidel shook his head and said with a smile that, 'Anyone could enter the ravelin, but only the emperor, chief of police or governor of the prison could leave it, and every guard in the place knew it.'[11] Then, with professional pride, he explained to his guests the new features adopted in the cells. Tolstoy left him in a fury. As they passed the monument of Nicholas I on Great Morskaya Street, he looked away and said to Stepan Behrs that it was unpardonable for the tsar to have punished the Decembrists so harshly and that by his fault Russia had lost the cream of a generation at one blow.

Always ready to deplore the cruel fate of rebels past, pre-

* Baron Maidel was Tolstoy's model for Baron Kriegsmuth, the prison governor in *Resurrection*.

sent and to come, he was nevertheless stupefied, on 31 March 1878, to learn the verdict of the trial of the revolutionary Vera Zasulich. Two months before, she had seriously injured General Trepov, St Petersburg commissioner of police. Indeed, Trepov was a notorious brute, but who could have foreseen that the tables would be turned in the courtroom and the accused become the accuser, that the jury, bewitched and subjugated, would acquit the defendant and that the public would greet their verdict with applause? Far from rejoicing at this victory for the partisans of revolution, Tolstoy saw it as a dangerous incitement to fresh violence. He later wrote in his notebook:

'Revolutionaries are specialists. They exercise a profession like any other, like the military profession, for example (the analogy is perfect). It is a mistake to believe their profession nobler than any other.'[12]

Back at Yasnaya Polyana, surrounded by the peaceful fields, he found it even more inconceivable that politics should lead to crime. 'Living at a distance and having no part in the conflict, I can see plainly that hatred between the two extremist parties has reached the point of bestiality,' he wrote to Alexandra Tolstoy on 6 April 1878. 'For Maidel and those like him, all these Bogolyubovs * and Zasuliches are so low that they cannot recognize them as human beings or feel any sympathy for them; for a Zasulich, Trepov and his like are wild animals that can and should be cut down like dogs. This is not indignation, it is open war. Every one of those who acquitted the assassin and every one of those who approved her acquittal know full well that for their own personal safety a murderer must not be allowed to go unpunished; but in their eyes the question is not who is right but who, in the long run, will prove strongest. All of this seems to me to bode much misery and sin. And yet there are fine people on both sides. ... Since reading the account of the trial and all this commotion about it, I can think of nothing else.'

* Pseudonym of the revolutionary Emelyanov, arrested in 1876.

To Strakhov the next day: 'The Zasulich business is no joking matter. This madness, this idiotic capriciousness that has suddenly seized hold of people is significant. These are the first signs of something not yet clear to us. But it is serious. The Slavophil madness was the precursor of war, and I am inclined to think that this madness is the precursor of revolution.'

He returned to his novel, but without conviction. These Decembrists he was preparing to immortalize may well have been the distant source of inspiration to a Vera Zasulich, whose violence he could not condone. In keeping with his main idea, should he not show what brought men together, rather than what drove them apart? Religion alone could help him out of the dilemma in which he was caught in the conflict between his love of the downtrodden masses and his love of peace.

Under the influence of his new Christian sentiments, he felt a need for tolerance in life as well as in literature. And to prove how merciful he could be, he chose to humble himself to the person he held in least esteem: Turgenev. The mere thought of that over-refined and pettish European sent a shiver of disgust down his spine. With morbid delight he determined to write to him, out of the blue, on 6 April 1878:

Ivan Sergeyevich, these past few days, I have been thinking back over our relationship and I was surprised and happy to find that I had lost all my animosity towards you. Please God you feel the same. In fact, knowing how kind-hearted you are, I am almost certain that your hostility died long before mine. If this is true, shall we shake hands, and will you consent to forgive me entirely and completely all the wrong I have done you? It is natural for me to remember only your best features, for you have been very good to me. I do not forget that it is to you that I owe my literary success and I also remember that you used to like what I wrote, and myself too. Perhaps your memory of me will be the same, for there was a time when I loved you sincerely. Honestly and openly, if you can forgive me, I offer you all the friendship of which I am capable. At our age there is only one thing of value: the love we can share with our fellow men; I should be very happy if you and I could have such a relationship.

After seventeen years of vindictive silence, this declaration of affection stupefied Ivan Turgenev. There was the Russian temperament, all right, quick to anger, confession, debasement and embrace. Not even the most extravagant of his French acquaintances would have been capable of such an about-face. From Paris, where he was still languishing in the shadow of the Viardot family, he replied, on 8 (20) May 1878:

Dear Leo Nikolayevich, the letter you sent to the post office to be left until called for did not reach me until today. It touched me deeply and made me very happy. It is my fondest wish to renew our former friendship and I most warmly shake your outstretched hand. You are quite right to believe I have no hostile feelings towards you. If I ever did, they vanished long ago; all that is left is a memory of a man to whom I was sincerely devoted, an author whose first works I had the good fortune to applaud before anyone else, and who continues to arouse my keenest interest with every new publication. I rejoice with all my heart and soul to see the end of the misunderstanding between us. I hope to go to Orel this summer and if I do we will surely meet again. In the meantime, I wish you all good things and, once again, cordially shake your hand.

On 8 August, having written to announce his arrival, Turgenev steamed into the Tula station. Tolstoy and his brother-in-law Stepan Behrs were waiting for him on the platform, and the three set off in a carriage for Yasnaya Polyana, where Sonya, delighted, intimidated and anxious, was preparing to welcome this remarkable guest of whom her husband had said so much good and so much evil.

She was immediately charmed by the tall man with the regular features crowned by a thick crest of silver hair, and the gentle, oily, feminine eyes. His grey beard was yellowed around the lips. His movements were graceful, he swayed as he walked, and he had a thin little voice that contrasted with his imposing stature. Beside him Tolstoy seemed small, clumsy and unbelievably young. The children were agape with admiration at the traveller's suitcases, his velvet jacket and waitcoat, his silk shirt, his paisley cravat, soft leather pumps, gold chronometer and precious snuff-box, and they sniffed the air of Paris all around him.

At dinner he dazzled them with his eloquence. In front of Tolstoy, who was making a strenuous attempt to be amiable, he talked about his pet dog Jack, the hectic and futile life of Paris where the French dismissed everything as '*vieux jeu*' – the latest fashionable expression – the villa he and the Viardots had bought at Bougival, near which they had built an orangery costing ten thousand francs, and the cholera, of which he was in deadly fear. Whereupon, observing that they were thirteen at table, he said, 'Whoever is afraid of death raise his hand!' And he raised his own, laughing. No one followed suit, for fear of offending the Christian sentiments of the master of the house. 'I seem to be the only one,' Turgenev resumed. Since the night at Arzamas Tolstoy was too familiar with this elemental dread to deny it any longer, but he did not want to resemble his old enemy in anything, not even in this; at last, spurred by honesty or hospitality, he stuck up his hand and growled, 'Well, I don't want to die either!' Then, to change the subject, he affably inquired of his guest:

'Why don't you smoke? You used to.'

'Yes,' Turgenev answered. 'But two charming young ladies in Paris told me that they would not allow me to kiss them if I smelled of tobacco, and so I have stopped.'

Acutely embarrassed, Tolstoy looked around at his family, but no one dared to smile.

After dinner the two men withdrew to Tolstoy's study where, in privacy, their conversation turned to more serious matters. Neither alluded to the quarrel that had divided them. But they talked at length of literature, poetry, philosophy. Once again Tolstoy was appalled by his guest's indifference to questions of morality and religion. Turgenev, then engaged in writing his delightful *Prose Poems*, placed art above all else. For him God, the salvation of the soul and life after death were meaningless concepts, since the human mind was incapable of penetrating the mystery of creation; the worship of beauty, on the other hand, could illuminate an entire life. To Tolstoy, this adoration of the aesthetic was the height of irresponsibility. Sitting across from him in an armchair he saw his ideal opponent – in the form of a well-groomed, roguish, garrulous old man. Everything he most loathed – the music of words, intellectual *divertissements*, artificial courtesy, Western culture – combined in a single man! What self-control it must have required for him to refrain from turning him out of the house! As a good Christian, he dedicated his patience to God.

It was a fine day, so they went outdoors, where the rest of the family were waiting for them. There was a seesaw near the house, formed by a plank laid across a chopping block. Tolstoy climbed on one end and proposed that Turgenev sit on the other and then, to amuse the children, the two writers began to bounce up and down in alternation. Did Tolstoy think of the literary symbolism of their game of teeter-totter? The author of *Smoke* counterweighting the author of *War and Peace*, the descent of one causing the rise of the other …

They stopped, out of breath, and Tolstoy urged his guest to come with him for a walk in the country. Turgenev, who was a keen hunter, could identify the birds by their song: 'There's a flicker,' he said. 'A linnet! A starling!' But even he who knew nature so well, was amazed at Tolstoy's more profound understanding of animals. There was more than a familiarity between them – something like an organic intimacy. He stood by a bony, mangy old nag, stroking its back and whispering gently into its ear, while the horse listened with evident interest. Then he translated the animal's feelings to those around him. 'I could have listened forever,' Turgenev later said. 'He had got inside the very soul of the poor beast and taken me with him. I could not refrain from remarking, "I say, Leo Nikolayevich, beyond any doubt, you must have been a horse once yourself!" ' [13]

In the evening everyone assembled in the drawing-room and Turgenev read aloud one of his stories, *The Dog*. His audience's response was lukewarm and their words of praise halfhearted, but the author did not seem to notice. As he said good-bye the following day, he thanked his hosts with genuine emotion, and said to Tolstoy, in front of Sonya who blushed with pleasure, 'You did admirably well, old man, when you married your wife!'

He wrote to Tolstoy from his Spasskoye estate, 'I cannot help saying once more how good and enjoyable it was for me to be at Yasnaya Polyana, and how happy I am to see that the misunderstanding between us has vanished without a trace, as though it had never existed. I felt very strongly that the years which have aged us were not lived in vain and that both of us have become better than we were sixteen years ago.* I need not add that I shall certainly stop by to see you again on my way back.'

On 2 September 1878 Turgenev returned to Yasnaya Polyana for three days, accepted his host's forced cordiality at face value, and sent an enthusiastic letter to Fet:

'It was a great joy for me to renew relations with Tolstoy. ... His whole family is most likeable and his wife charming. He himself has calmed down considerably and matured. We Russians know he has no rival.'

Tolstoy, more perceptive, measured the full width of the gulf between them and foresaw that their views of life could only drive them apart as they grew older. The day after Turgenev's departure, he also wrote to Fet, their mutual friend:

'Turgenev is the same as ever, and we have no illusions as to the degree of intimacy that is possible between us.'

And to Strakhov:

*In fact, it was seventeen years since Tolstoy and Turgenev had seen each other.

'Turgenev has come back among us, amiable and brilliant as ever. But, between you and me, he is a little like a fountain of water that has been piped in: one is continually afraid it will run dry and there will be nothing left.'

Unaware of this harsh judgement, Turgenev generously devoted his energies to serving his compatriot in France. On 1 October 1878 he wrote from Bougival to announce the success of the English translation of *The Cossacks* and the publication of the same work, in French, in the *Journal de St Petersbourg*, in an adaptation by Baroness Mengden. He was rather annoyed by this, moreover, as he had wanted to translate *The Cossacks* himself, with the help of Mme Viardot. 'I don't know whether you have already made arrangements to publish it in book form in Paris,' he wrote to Tolstoy, 'but I should be very happy to assist the French public to appreciate the best story ever written in our language.'*

His letter came just as Tolstoy was going through a crisis of literary humility, which paradoxically took the form of exacerbated sensitivity about everything. Instead of thanking Turgenev for his generosity, he flared up and replied:

Skyler has sent me his English translation of *The Cossacks*. I think it is very good. Baroness Mengden's French translation (you met the lady at our home) is certainly bad. Please don't think I am putting on airs, but sincerely, it gives me an extremely disagreeable and confused feeling – the main ingredients of which are shame and the fear of being made fun of – to reread what I have written, and even to skim it or hear it talked about. ... In spite of all my affection for you and my assurance that you wish me well, I feel as though you, too, are making fun of me. Therefore please let us not talk any more about my writing. You know every man has his own way of blowing his nose, and believe me, I blow mine exactly as I see fit.

After this outburst, a resurgence of Christian charity prompted him to add, 'I continue to admire your active old

* Turgenev's plan to translate *The Cossacks* with Pauline Viardot never materialized.

age. During the sixteen years since we last saw each other, you have done nothing but improve in every respect, even physically.'[14]

Justifiably surprised, Turgenev wrote back immediately:

Though you ask me not to speak of your writing, I cannot help pointing out that I have never, in the slightest degree, made fun of you. I have liked some of your books immensely, disliked others intensely and derived keen pleasure and genuine astonishment from still others, such as *The Cossacks*. But why should I have laughed at them? I thought you had long since gotten rid of such 'centripetal' feelings. Why do they affect only authors, and not painters, musicians and other artists? Probably because a larger share of that region of the soul which it can be embarrassing to expose goes into a literary work. No doubt; but at the stage we have reached in a writer's career, we should no longer be bothered by this.[15]

This letter, courteous as it was, nevertheless seemed the height of insolence to Tolstoy and he complained to Fet: 'Received an epistle from Turgenev yesterday. You know, I have decided to keep away from him and temptation. He really is an unpleasant trouble-seeker.'[16]

This curious association of Ivan Turgenev and 'temptation' provided Tolstoy with one more reason for hating the man who was morally and physically irritating to him.

Turgenev, however, continued his efforts in France on his friend's behalf. *War and Peace* appeared on the Paris booksellers' shelves in 1879, in a translation by Princess Paskevich.[17] Turgenev immediately began to sound the drums, send copies to the most important critics (Taine, Edmond About) and call on his friends to create a wave of enthusiasm.

'One must hope they will grasp all the power and beauty of your epic,' he wrote to Tolstoy. 'The translation is somewhat faulty, although conscientious and faithful. I have been rereading your very great work for the fifth or sixth time, and with renewed pleasure. Its structure is very foreign to everything the French are fond of and look for in a book, but truth ever prevails. I trust there will be, if not a smashing triumph, at least a slow but sure invasion.' [18]

A fortnight later he sent Tolstoy an extract from a letter Flaubert had written after reading *War and Peace:*

'Thank you for giving me Tolstoy's novel to read,' he wrote. 'It is first-rate. What a painter, what a psychologist! The first two volumes are *sublime*, but the third falls off terribly. He repeats himself! And he philosophizes! At last we see the man – the author and the Russian – whereas until then we had seen only Nature and Mankind. There are some things in him that remind me of Shakespeare. I uttered cries of admiration as I read, and one is a long time reading! Yes, it is powerful, very powerful.'

Turgenev added: 'I think, on the whole, you will be satisfied. ... There have not been any individual reviews yet, but three hundred copies (out of five hundred) have already been sold.'

But once again, Turgenev and his congratulations came at the wrong time. Just then, Tolstoy did not want to hear another word about his novels. *The Decembrists*, for which he had compiled a vast documentation, appealed to him less and less. After starting over ten times and telling Sonya that the characters were beginning to come to life in his mind at last, he shut the manuscript up in a drawer, for good.

'My *Decembrists* are God knows where now,' he wrote to Fet on 17 April 1879, 'and I have forgotten all about them.'

Was it fear of being asphyxiated under the mountain of historical detail, or lack of sympathy for the characters' political ideas, or the difficulty of writing objectively about a period so close to him, or discouragement in the face of the sheer size and complexity of the undertaking? All these were behind Tolstoy's refusal, but even more, there was his growing desire to renounce the pleasures of the pen and devote himself to the mysteries of religion. For they had not seen the last of each other! His first step had been to return to the Church and adhere blindly, à la muzhik, to the Orthodox ritual. This phase of obedience had lasted nearly two years, to the satisfaction of Sonya and Alexandra. Tolstoy's children marvelled at the athletic ease with which the model penitent prostrated himself in front of the icons. Yet, at the very moment his forehead touched the dusty floor of the little church of Yasnaya Polyana, a seed of doubt began to sprout in his heart. Perhaps he had taken a wrong turning. He had never been one to follow in the footsteps of the common herd or submit to a rule that he had not invented. He had questioned everything he had ever learned, before teaching it to others in his own way. This spirit of dissension, independence and domination ill accorded with the self-effacement demanded of the faithful. No matter how sternly he ordered himself to respond automatically in thought and deed, his intelligence rebelled.

On 22 May 1878 he wrote in his diary, 'Went to mass Sunday. I can find a satisfactory explanation for everything that happens during the service. But wishing "long life" [to the tsar] and praying for victory over our enemies are sacrilege. A Christian should pray for his enemies, not against them.' This was the beginning of schism.

Other parts of the service gradually began to come into conflict with his common sense, and even with the teachings of Christ. After refusing to let himself question a single word of the dogma, he now began to pick it to pieces, word by word, not as a sceptic but in the manner of one of the early Christians, still illuminated by the *historical* proximity of the Lord. He admired the ethical laws preached by the apostles, but he did not believe in the resurrection of Christ because he could not imagine it actually happening. He also balked at the celebration of the miracles – Ascension, Pentecost, the Annunciation, the Intercession of the Blessed Virgin. To his mind all that was a product of cheap imagery, unworthy of the cause of God. 'To reinforce the teachings of Christ with miracles,' he wrote in his notebook, 'is like holding a lighted candle in front of the sun in order to see it better.' [19]

Still more absurd and pointless, in his opinion, were the mysteries, especially baptism and Eucharist. And besides, why did the Orthodox Church, whose mission should be to bring about an alliance between all men, treat the Roman Catholics and Protestants – who worshipped the same God – as heretics? Why, in the same breath as it commanded the faithful to be charitable and forgive those who trespassed against them, did it pray for the victory of the Russian army over the Turks? Why was the Church, champion of the poor and disinherited, swathed in gold and precious stones and damasks?

Hereafter, every time Tolstoy went anywhere, he made a pilgrimage to see some ecclesiastical dignitary. In June 1879, he went with Fet to the holy city of Kiev, ran from cell to cell and hermitage to hermitage, confided all his doubts to the monks, to the anchorite Anthony, to Metropolitan Makarios of Moscow, to Bishop Alexis of Mozhaysk, to Leonid the archimandrite. These eminent personages sympathized with his desire to raise himself to a higher level of spirituality at which all the inconsistencies and implausibilities of the different churches would melt away, but they warned him against undermining, by ill-considered criticism, a tradition that had been tried and accepted by the people. All too often, they told him, setting one angle straight will throw a whole edifice out of kilter, especially if the house is an old one. The imperfections of the Orthodox religion were of small consequence; the main thing was that it remain intangible throughout the centuries. 'What have they done?' wrote Tolstoy. 'They have cut up the teachings into shreds and tacked their idiotic, vile explanations – hateful to Christ – on to every morsel. They have blocked the door for others and won't go inside themselves.'[20]

He wrote to Strakhov:

'They are all admirable, intelligent people; but my convictions are growing stronger and stronger, I am straining my brains, thrashing about, struggling with all my soul and I am suffering, but I thank God for my suffering.'[21]

The bishop of Tula, with whom he had a conversation in December 1879, was much surprised to hear him say he would like to become a monk. Despite his visitor's resolute air, he dissuaded him from this project. Next, Tolstoy informed him that he was thinking of giving all his possessions to the poor. Kissing him on the forehead, the holy man mildly replied that this was 'a dangerous course'. Tolstoy withdrew, at once disappointed and relieved.

Less than ten days later the decidedly indefatigable Sonya gave birth to her seventh son, Michael.

'Although it no longer gives me the same sensation of wonder as when my first children were born, I am grateful that this time there were no complications,' he wrote to his brother on 21 December 1879.

One morning a short time later, as he was preparing to take communion, the priest called upon him to affirm that the body and blood of Jesus Christ were literally present in the consecrated bread and wine. He was suddenly disturbed and annoyed by this ritual question he had heard hundreds of times before; he felt something like a knife-thrust near his heart, and stammered out a faltering 'yes'; but he knew as he came out of the little country church that he would never touch the bread of life again. One Wednesday – a fast-day – when the whole family was sitting down together for the evening meal, he pushed away his porridge and, pointing to a dish of meatballs that had been prepared for the two non-fasting tutors, frowned at his son Ilya and growled aggressively, 'Pass the meat!' No one dared to express surprise. Before the entire mute but smirking table, the master of Yasnaya Polyana defiantly began to chew the forbidden food.

It was the declaration of war on orthodoxy. Tolstoy was not content with repudiating the Church. He felt as resentful as a deceived husband; he was itching to revenge himself, by word and pen, for the two years he had wasted believing in it. He covered the pages of his notebooks with vindictive entries: 'From the third century to the present,' he wrote on 30 September 1879, 'the Church has been nothing but lies, cruelty and deceit. In the third century something great was still lying hidden. But what? Is there really anything? Let us examine the Gospels. If the soul exists, then God's commandments exist. The question of the soul is the only question. What did the others have to say about it?'

And on 28 October: 'In this world there are heavy people, without wings. They lurch about here below. Among them there are strong men like Napoleon, who leave terrible marks on mankind, and sow discord among men, but all this happens at ground level. Then there are men who let their wings grow, who rise slowly from the earth and soar above it: the monks. And then there are lighter men, who spring easily from the ground and fall back again: the good idealists. And there are men with broad, powerful wings who let themselves come to rest in the thick of the human crowd for the sheer pleasure of it, and then their wings are torn: I am one of those. Afterwards the wounded wings beat the air, thrust upward and fall back again. My wings will heal. I shall fly very high. May God help me! And then there are men with celestial wings, who come down to earth on purpose and fold their wings out of love for their fellows, in order to help them learn to fly. Then, when they are no longer needed, they go back up into the sky: Christ.'

On 30 October the government came under his fire: 'Religion, as long as it is religion, cannot, by its very essence, be subject to authority. . . . Religion negates temporal authority (war, torture, plunder, theft, everything bound up with government). That is why a government must make certain of its control over religion. If it does not lock up this bird, the bird will fly away.' [22]

At last he saw plainly what it was he had to do. Starting with the texts of the Gospels, he must think religion through again, separating the true from the false. 'Now it is all clear,' he told Sonya, 'and, God willing, what I write will be very important.' But it worried Sonya to see him continually plunged into books on theology. 'His eyes are strange and staring,' she wrote to her sister. 'He hardly speaks. He seems not to be in this world and he is incapable of taking any interest in ordinary matters.' He attacked the Church violently at table, to his wife's consternation. The most ordinary incidents of daily life were pretexts for vituperation and parable. 'He often quarrelled with Maman,' his son Ilya later wrote, 'and from the fun-loving, lively head of our family he was transformed before our eyes into a stern, accusatory prophet. ... We would be planning an amateur play, everybody was animated, chatting away, playing croquet, talking of love, etc. Papa appeared and with one word, or worse, with one look, everything was spoiled: the gaiety was gone; we felt ashamed, somehow. It would have been better for him to have stayed away. The worst of it was that he felt it too.' Yes, he would have preferred not to deflate this childish joy. But he could not resist: he had never been able to hide what he felt. He was doomed to be a kill-joy.

On a brief trip to St Petersburg in January 1880, he called on Alexandra to explain his new position to her. The old spinster was aghast when she heard this rabid evangelist, his eyes like marbles and his face aflame, reviling the popes who had perverted the message of Christ and exhorting her to break with the aristocratic and pious circle in which she had been living blindly for so long. She demurred, became angry, he raised his voice, the discussion degenerated into an argument. Disrespectful words tumbled out of Tolstoy's mouth. In a paroxysm of rage he rushed out, slamming the door behind him, went home and was unable to sleep all night. The next day he set out for Yasnaya Polyana without seeing his dear aunt again, although he sent her a letter of apology: 'To you, I cannot talk any other way than with my whole heart. I think you truly love God and goodness, and therefore you must understand where He is. I ask your pardon for my bad temper and rudeness. ...' [23]

She replied the same day:

'Your precipitous departure annoyed, offended and pained me to the depths of my soul. There was cruelty in your action, and enmity, and I would almost say a desire for revenge. Such behaviour would be unseemly in the young, but at our ages, when every parting may be our last, it is unpardonable to separate on such terms, and it will be hard for me to forgive you.'

Six days later, on 29 January, she had recovered her serenity and wrote to tell him that she wanted to forget their quarrel, but would never change her mind because she was too happy in the peace she derived from her allegiance to the Orthodox Church. 'Not one stone can be removed from the holy edifice without destroying the harmony of the whole.' Touched by the conciliatory tone of this letter, Tolstoy elaborated upon his views:

'I can believe in something I can neither understand nor refute. But I cannot believe in something that seems to me to be a lie. Or better still: to persuade myself that I believe in something I cannot believe, something that is no use to me in understanding my soul and God and the relations between them, to persuade myself of that, I say, is an attitude diametrically opposed to true faith.'

He went on to affirm that he was quite ready to respect the beliefs of Alexandra and the muzhiks, if they enabled them to accede to a knowledge of God. The only thing was, he was afraid his dear friend was looking towards God through spectacles borrowed from the Church, which were not right for her eyes: 'Do those spectacles bother you or not? I cannot tell. A man as cultivated as you are could not tolerate them, that I am sure of, but a woman, I don't know. That is why I am sorry I said all those things. ... The sense of my words was this: "Look at the ice you are walking on; it might be wise to try to make a hole in it and test whether it is firm. If it gives way, it would be preferable to return to more solid ground."'

For him, solid ground was the Gospels, and not another word:

I and all the rest of us live like animals, and we will die the same way. To escape from this excruciating situation, Christ offered us salvation. Who is Christ: a God or a man? He is what he says he is. He says he is the Son of God, he says he is the Son of Man, he says, 'I am what I tell you I am. I am the truth and the life. . . .' And from the moment they began to mix it all up together and say he was God and the second person of the Trinity, the result was sacrilege, falsehood and nonsense. If he were that, he would have been capable of saying so. He offered us salvation. How? By teaching us to give a meaning to our lives that is not destroyed by death. . . . For me, the foundation of his teaching is that to achieve salvation it is necessary, every day and every hour of every day, to think of God, of one's soul, and therefore to set the love of one's neighbour above mere bestial existence.[24]

Not content to profess his new faith in letters to his friends, he decided to bequeath it to Russia and the world, in a series of books: first, his *Confession*, begun in 1879, then a *Criticism of Dogmatic Theology* (1880), *Union and Translation of the Four Gospels* (1882) and lastly, *What I Believe* (1883). In these four complementary books, he sought to define the origins of his torment and the outcome of his reflections. 'Leo is still working, as he calls it,' Sonya wrote to her sister on 7 November 1879, 'but alas! all he is producing are philosophical disquisitions! He reads and thinks until it gives him headache. And all in order to prove that the Church does not accord with the Gospels. There are not ten people in Russia who can be interested in such a subject. But there's nothing to be done. My only hope is that he will soon get over it, and it will pass, like a disease.'

Far from passing, the 'disease' was developing complications. By thinking about it night and day, Tolstoy was aggravating his case. His *Confession* was the tale of the internal struggle that led him to leave the Church. To be sure, the desire for total honesty that prompted it is praiseworthy, and many of its pages are remarkable for their tragic beauty, but the general impression created by the book is an unhealthy one of public exposure and flagellation. One continually feels that the author is burrowing into his dung-heap with too-evident relish. The extravagance of his language casts doubts on the nobility of his purpose. At the end of the book one wonders whether this display of Christian humility is not rather an orgy of masochistic pride, for self-criticism, when performed in broad daylight, can produce a kind of intoxication, and setting oneself up as an example not to follow may be another way of attracting attention.

'I killed men in the war,' he writes, 'I fought duels; playing cards, I squandered money extorted from the peasants, and I punished them cruelly; I fornicated with women of easy virtue and deceived husbands. Lies, theft, adultery, drunkenness and brutality of every sort, I have committed every shameful act; there is no crime I am not acquainted with.' Elsewhere he calls himself 'a base and criminal man' and a 'vermin' – flashy eloquence and greasepaint. He struts in his rags, he wallows in sham humility, and more than ever, reviling himself, he adores himself.

In the *Criticism of Dogmatic Theology* he wages a frontal attack on the teachings of the Orthodox Church. In the name of reason he rejects all that is beyond his understanding, beginning with the dogma of the Trinity: 'Let us suppose that God lives on Olympus, that God is made of gold, that there is no God, that there are fourteen gods, that God has several children or one son. All these affirmations may be strange and barbaric, but each of them is based on one idea, one concept. But that God is one *and* three can be based on no concept or idea.' Further on, he refuses to accept that Jesus is 'the second person of God who became incarnate in the womb of the Virgin Mary through the intervention of the Holy Ghost'. Demons and angels, the creation of the world in six days, the story of Adam and the serpent, salvation and eternal damnation are just so many primitive legends. At times his refutation of the traditional trappings of religion reveals the author's fragmentary knowledge and specious argumentation, ill-hidden by the polemicist's fervour.

Still more singular is his claim to offer a personal and
original version of the divine message, in the *Union and
Translation of the Four Gospels*. His knowledge of Greek
is insufficient, so he hastily learns Hebrew in order to penetrate and compare the sacred texts. He attempts to throw
light on what he cannot understand through the works of
the exegetes: Dom Calmet, Reuss, Griesbach, Tischendorf,
Meyer, Lücke, etc. By good fortune, his children have a new
tutor, the young philologist Ivakin; whenever Tolstoy encounters some difficulty in translation, he runs to him and
thrusts the Greek Bible under his nose. 'I translated the
passage he pointed out to me,' Ivakin recounts in his reminiscences, 'and most of the time my translation concurred
with that of the Church.' Tolstoy was greatly vexed at this.
He would have liked the text to say exactly what he thought
it ought to say: ' "Can't that be interpreted to mean this
or that?" he would ask. And he told me what he wanted.
I pored over the lexicons and did the impossible to satisfy
him.' Thus, carried away by his passion to convince, he
sometimes lost sight of the truth in his efforts to impose his
version of it at all costs. In a fever of excitement, he would
cry out, 'What do I care whether Christ is risen! Is he risen?
Well, God be with him! What I care about is to find out
what I must do, how I must live!' [25]

He relied on his intuition, his heart, to rediscover the
sources of Christianity. Starting with the idea that all four
Gospels were describing the same events, he rearranged
them in chronological order into a single text. The Gospels
according to St Matthew, St Mark, St Luke and St John
were superseded by the Gospel according to St Leo, which
is no more nor less than another of his rules of life. It is
embodied in the fourth part of his mystical series, *What I
Believe*. The entire foundation of the Tolstoyan faith is in
the Sermon on the Mount. Six commandments: 'Thou
shalt not be angry, thou shalt not commit adultery, thou
shalt not swear, thou shalt not resist evil by evil, thou shalt
have no enemies, thou shalt love God and thy neighbour

as thyself.' With prodigious naïveté Tolstoy observes, 'Strange as it may seem, it was necessary for me to discover these rules after eighteen centuries, as though for the first time.' What Tolstoy really wanted was to believe in God and to live according to Christian morality, while denying the divinity of Christ.

It required courage to adopt a position in open opposition to the Church, in a country in which the Church was a State institution. Since the publication of such inflammatory religious writings was out of the question, Tolstoy had a number of manuscript copies made and circulated among the public. Later he published a printed edition of *What I Believe*, limited to thirty copies, which could be done without authorization from the censor. Even so, the police seized every one.* *Union and Translation of the Four Gospels* was first published in Geneva in Russian, and French and German translations soon appeared elsewhere abroad.

'You used to be worried because you had no faith; why aren't you happy now that you have it?' Sonya sighed. Even Fet was unable to go along with his friend's newest passion. Strakhov, however, continued to sing the master's praises: Not only have you amazed me, inestimable Leo Nikolayevich, as you have often done in the past, but this time you have given me peace and warmed my heart. ... My God, it's good! When I think of you, your tastes, your habits, your work, when I remember the horror of every form of deceit that is expressed in all your books and permeates your life, then I can understand how you arrived where you are now. ... Please, do not chide me for these words of praise. I need to believe in you; that belief is my sole support. ... I shall cling to you and, I hope, be saved.' [26]

And as, in spite of these clouds of incense, Tolstoy still complained that he was unhappy, the good disciple protested, 'You are in the prime of life; you are not suffering from any illness; why are you so sad and why do you talk

* This took place on 18 February 1884. See following chapter.

of death? Of course, you lead an appalling life. You drive yourself unmercifully.' [27]

Now that he had become the prophet of his own religion, Tolstoy began to wonder when and how he could put it into practice.

At the end of April 1880, Russia's foremost writers gathered in Moscow in preparation for the unveiling of a monument to Pushkin. Turgenev, a fervent admirer of the poet, returned from France for the occasion and resolved at all costs to persuade Tolstoy to take part in the celebration. He came to Yasnaya Polyana on 2 May 1880, and was received with open arms. Spring was warming the air, a green mist of new leaves shimmered around the birches, the nightingale sang through the heart of the night. Tolstoy arranged a hunt and posted his colleague in a choice clearing, where the snipe usually came. But just then, there was not a bird in sight. Sonya, who had stayed behind with her guest, asked why he had stopped writing. He smiled wistfully and murmured:

'No one can hear us, so I shall tell you. I can't write any more. Whenever I felt the desire to write, in the past, I was trembling in an absolute fever of love. Now that's finished. I am an old man, and can neither write nor love any more.'

At that moment a shot rang out and Tolstoy, invisible, called to his dog to retrieve the bird he had brought down.

'There, we're off,' said Turgenev. 'Leo Nikolayevich is already hard at work. Now there's a man of many blessings. Fortune has smiled on him his whole life long.' [28]

True enough, all the snipe were flying Tolstoy's way. Turgenev only managed to bring down one, and it caught in a branch and was not found until the next day.

After the hunt the two men withdrew to an isba that had been converted into a study, not far from the house. There Turgenev tried to persuade Tolstoy that in his position as a great Russian author it was his duty to make a speech at the forthcoming ceremony in honour of Pushkin. But Tolstoy categorically refused to appear in public. True, he had always loathed official occasions: but this time his bashfulness was coupled with pride – in a way, the evening would almost be a kind of contest between him and Dostoyevsky, and he did not want to run the risk, by going to Moscow, of finding himself less popular than his rival. When Turgenev had exhausted his store of arguments he could hardly hide his vexation at his host's obstinacy. He packed his bags and left the same day. In Moscow he saw Dostoyevsky, who had just arrived for the unveiling and was planning to go to Yasnaya Polyana to meet Tolstoy. Turgenev talked the author of *The Brothers Karamazov* out of making the trip. It was rumoured in the literary world that Tolstoy was going through a mystical crisis. Dostoyevsky wrote to his wife: 'Grigorovich told me today that Turgenev fell ill upon his return from Tolstoy's place and that Tolstoy is half-mad and maybe completely mad.'[29]

The festivities in Pushkin's honour concluded with an apotheosis for Dostoyevsky: at the end of his speech the audience burst into wild applause, women flung bouquets of flowers on to the platform, enemies embraced each other and one student fainted. Upon hearing the news of this triumph, Tolstoy must have congratulated himself for sitting tight at home.

He and Dostoyevsky were destined never to meet. That summer he reread *The House of the Dead* and, struck with admiration, wrote to Strakhov: 'I know of no more beautiful book in modern literature, not excepting Pushkin. I am not so much impressed by the style as by the author's point of view – wonderfully sincere, natural and Christian. It is a good book, uplifting. … If you see Dostoyevsky, tell him I like him.' Strakhov did more than pass on the compliment; he gave Dostoyevsky the letter. A few months later, on 28 January 1881 Dostoyevsky died. When he read the news in the papers, Tolstoy felt a sharp, profound blow, which surprised him.

How I should like to be able to say all I feel about Dostoyevsky [he wrote to Strakhov]. I never saw the man, never had any direct contact with him, and suddenly, at his disappearance, I realized that he was the closest of all to me, the most precious and essential. ... I was a writer and all writers are vain and envious, or at least I was. But it never occurred to me to compete with him. Everything he set out to do was so good, so sincere that the more he did the happier I was. Artistry can make me jealous, and so can intelligence, but actions that spring from the heart give me nothing but joy. I always thought of him as a friend, and was convinced that one day we would meet. ... And all of a sudden, during dinner – I was dining alone, late – I read of his death. It was as though one of my supporting pillars had suddenly buckled. I had a moment of panic, then I realized how precious he was to me and I began to cry, I am still crying.[30]

When his emotion subsided, Tolstoy's critical sense returned and he abandoned himself to his natural animosity to anyone who did not share his opinions. Some time later Rusanov, an admirer of his, asked what he thought of Dostoyevsky and he unhesitatingly replied:

'*The House of the Dead* is a fine thing, but I do not set great store by his other books. People cite passages to me. And indeed there are some very fine parts here and there, but, on the whole, it is dreadful stuff! His style is turgid, he tries so hard to make his characters original, and in fact they are hardly outlined. Dostoyevsky talks and talks and in the end all you are left with is a sort of fog floating above what he was trying to prove. There is a peculiar mixture in him of the most lofty Christian concepts and panegyrics on war and submission to emperor, government and the popes.'

'Have you read *The Brothers Karamazov*?' asked Rusanov.

'I couldn't stick it out to the end,' confessed Tolstoy.

'But *Crime and Punishment*? It's his best book! What do you think of it?'

'Read a few chapters at the beginning and you can guess everything that's going to follow, the whole novel.'[31]

Above all, Tolstoy disliked Dostoyevsky's exaggeration,

his implausibility, his 'shapeless style', his grammatical errors, his mania for crowding the stage with epileptics, alcoholics and paranoiacs. 'If Prince Mishkin had been a healthy human being, his innocence and fundamental decency would have moved us deeply,' he said. 'But Dostoyevesky lacked the courage to make him healthy. Besides, he did not like healthy people. Since he was sick, then he wanted the whole universe to be sick with him.'[32] Dostoyevsky, on the other hand, had written about *Anna Karenina*, 'A boring book, by and large, and nothing out of the ordinary at all. What do they all find that is so wonderful in it? I don't see it!'[33] There was a chasm between these two giants, one of whom had lived a martyrdom while the other sought the tranquil wisdom of the prophets.

Later, after publishing a biography of Dostoyevsky, Strakhov wrote an extraordinary letter to Tolstoy:

All the while I was writing the biography I had to fight off a revulsion that kept rising within me, and I have tried to stifle this evil feeling. Help me to find some solution. I cannot regard Dostoyevsky either as a good man or as a happy one (in reality they are the same). He was vicious, envious, depraved and spent his entire life in a state of emotional upheaval and exasperation that would have made him appear ridiculous had he not been so malicious and so intelligent. . . . He was attracted by base actions and gloried in the fact. . . . Viskovatov told me that he bragged one day of having . . . with a little girl whom his governess had brought him, in the public baths. . . . Note that along with his bestial sensuality he was utterly lacking in taste, and had no sense of beauty or feminine charm. . . . The characters most like him are the hero of the *Notes from Underground*, Svidrigailov in *Crime and Punishment*, and Stavrogin in *The Possessed*. . . . He was a truly wretched and truly evil man, who thought he was noble and happy, and never had any real affection for anyone but himself.[34]

Strange rejection on the part of a man who had long been Dostoyevsky's protégé, confidant and intimate friend. Why did he not refuse to write the biography, if it 'revolted' him to think of the man? Seeing how easily Strakhov turned coat, Tolstoy might have feared for the future of his own relations with him. But he was so habituated to the adoration of this envious, petty, prolix little writer that the idea of being betrayed by him never entered his head. He answered:

I believe you have been victim of a false and erroneous opinion of Dostoyevsky. This opinion, which is not really yours at all but is universally held has exaggerated the man's importance and raised him to the rank of a prophet or a saint, a man who died in the throes of a fierce struggle between Good and Evil. He is moving and interesting, no doubt, but an individual who was all conflict cannot be put on a pedestal as an example for future generations. ... There are horses which are splendid to look at (thousand-rouble trotters), until suddenly one sees their 'flaw'. Then the most handsome and strongest horse in the world is worth nothing. ... Pressensé and Dostoyevsky both have flaws. One sacrificed wisdom, the other intelligence and heart, and both for nothing! Turgenev will outlive Dostoyevsky, not because he is a greater artist but because he has no flaw.[35]

On Monday 2 March 1881, one month after Dostoyevsky's death, Tolstoy was taking his customary walk along the highroad to Kiev, rutted and flooded by the spring thaw, when he saw a young itinerant musician splashing towards him through the puddles, carrying a hurdy-gurdy over his shoulder and some birds in a cage. The boy had pronounced Italian features and was presumably on his way from Tula. Owing to the state of the roads, the family at Yasnaya Polyana had been unable to send anyone to town for the newspapers for some time. Tolstoy asked the traveller what was going on in the world.

'Bad business,' the boy managed to articulate. 'Tsar murdered.'

'What tsar?' cried Tolstoy. 'Who murdered him? When?'

'Russian tsar. Petersburg. Bomb!'

The next day the papers arrived to confirm the news. Tsar Alexander II was going along the Katerina Canal in his carriage on his way back from reviewing the guard, which he did every Sunday in the riding school, when someone threw a newspaper-wrapped parcel under the horses' feet. A violent explosion killed the horses and injured two Cossacks in the escort and a passing child, but by some miracle the tsar was unharmed. However, instead of leaping into another carriage and riding away post-haste, he stopped to question the author of the attempt upon his life, who had also been injured. At that moment a second bomb, thrown by an accomplice, finished the work of the first. His legs crushed to a pulp, his face torn to shreds, the emperor collapsed, his blood pouring out in the snow. He was taken to the Winter Palace, where he died during the night. This was the Nihilists' seventh attempt upon his life. Their persistence was incomprehensible, especially as Alexander II had abolished slavery, recalled the exiled Decembrists, ended the disastrous Crimean War and, at the instigation of General Loris-Melikov, was about to give Russia a sort of constitution as a first step towards more far-reaching structural reforms. It was presumably in order not to be outdistanced by a liberal monarch that the conspirators had determined to make an end of him on the eve of the publication of his manifesto: by granting more than the people were asking for, Alexander II might well have drawn the teeth of the opposition and, by his last-minute action, rendered a revolution pointless or simply inopportune. In politics your worst enemy is the one who uses your ideas to achieve his own ends. Alexander II had to contend with both the liberals, who reproved terrorist methods but wanted him to hasten the country's administrative reorganization, and the reactionaries, who were afraid of losing their few remaining privileges in the renovation that had been in progress since the beginning of his reign.

Tolstoy, absorbed in his own battles of conscience, had paid scant attention to politics. True, 'shady-looking characters' with long dirty hair and demented eyes were occasionally seen going into his study, arriving from St

Petersburg with their pockets full of subversive tracts – they wanted a cataclysm of fire and blood, from which Russia would emerge torn, impoverished and ready for her new destiny; they were proud of the assassinations perpetrated by the 'People's Will' group, and wanted official support from Tolstoy. Gently but firmly, however, in the name of Christian morality, he sent them away. 'The revolutionary and the Christian,' he said, 'are at opposite ends of an open circle. Their proximity is only apparent. In reality, no two points could be farther apart. To meet, they would have to turn around and travel back over the entire circumference.' [36]

He was horror-stricken at the murder of Alexander II. Steeped in his evangelical doctrine of love and forgiveness, he was unable to understand this crime, committed without hatred, without real necessity, as part of a programme, by cold-blooded, iron-nerved theorists. But he was even more tormented by the thought that the killers would themselves be sentenced and executed. Blood for blood. By going on in this way, from crime to vindication, the whole country might soon find itself being propelled towards the slaughter of civil war. To stop this chain reaction, one act of mercy by the new sovereign would suffice. A week after the assassination, when Tolstoy was taking an after-dinner nap on his leather sofa, he had a dream : in the courtroom, it was himself, not the murderers, who was standing trial; and he was the judge, too; and Alexander III; and the executioner. He pronounced, carried out and was victim of the sentence.

He awoke drenched with sweat. He now knew that if he had been in the new emperor's place, it would have been a divine joy for him to pardon the assassins. Inspired by this idea, he decided to write to Alexander III forthwith. Perhaps it might appear presumptuous on his part. But he told himself that under divine law, human hierarchies ceased to exist; there was no difference between him and the monarch. In fact, with his eternal need to teach others, be they muzhik or prince, he felt that he was an ideal person, by virtue of his experience and fame, to preach clemency to the young sovereign. After all, potentates need *Readers*, too. His eyes brimming with tears, he appealed – as subject, friend and prophet – to the son of the assassinated tsar:

Sire, your father, the emperor of Russia, an old and good man who did much that was good himself and always wished for the welfare of his people, has been cruelly tortured and slain. And he was not killed by personal enemies, but by the enemies of the established order, who destroyed him, so they claim, for the good of mankind. You have succeeded to his place and before you stand the enemies who tormented your father during his lifetime and then murdered him. Now they are your enemies, too, because you have taken your father's place and because, in order to achieve that good of mankind which they claim to be seeking, they must also wish to do away with you. Toward these men, your father's murderers, you feel a desire for vengeance, mingled with a sense of horror at the act you are about to commit. ... Your position is a dreadful one, but the doctrine of Christ is necessary precisely in order to guide us through such moments of dire temptation which befall every man. ... It is true that it is presumption and folly on my part to demand that you, the emperor of Russia and a loving son, should pardon your father's murderers in spite of the pressure of those around you, returning good for evil. It is folly, yet I cannot do otherwise than wish it. .... About twenty years ago a little group of young men banded together, full of hatred for the established order and the government. These young men aspire to heaven only knows what new order, or rather to none at all, and, by the basest, most inhuman methods, fire and robbery and murder, they are destroying the structure of society. ... People have tried, in the name of the State and for the welfare of the people, to suppress, deport and execute them; people have also tried, in the name of the same State and the same welfare of the people, to treat them humanely. The result has been the same in both cases. Why not try, then, in the name of God, to carry out His law, thinking neither of the State nor the people? ...

Sire, now you stand pure and innocent before yourself and before God, but you are at a crossroads. A few days more and, if the victory goes to those who think and say that Christian truths have no value except in words and that in life, blood must flow and death must reign, then you will lose forever your blessed state of purity and communion with God, and you will set forth along the dark road of 'reasons of State' that justify everything, even the violation of divine law. If you do not pardon, but execute the murderers, you will have done away with three or four individuals out of hundreds; but evil breeds evil, and thirty or forty more will spring up to replace those three or four. ... But forgive, return good for evil, and out of a hundred wrong-doers ten will be converted, not to your side but to the side of God, whereas before they were on the side of Satan. And thousands, millions of your subjects will thrill with joy and affection at this act of mercy from a throne, at a moment so painful for the son of a murdered father. Sire, if you did that, if you called these men before you, gave them some money and sent them away somewhere, to America, and wrote a manifesto beginning with the words, 'But verily I say unto you, love your enemies,' I do not know what others would feel, but I, who have not been a model subject, would become your dog, your slave, I would weep with love – as I am weeping at this moment – every time I heard your name. What did I say: that I do not know how others would feel? I know with what torrential force good and love would pour over Russia at those words. ... The death penalty is useless against revolutionaries. Their numbers are not what counts, it is their ideas. To fight them, you must meet them on the ground of ideas. Their ideal is universal well-being, equality, liberty. To combat them some other ideal must be advanced, superior to theirs, larger than theirs. There is only one ideal that can be opposed to them: that to which they turn for support without realizing it, and in blaspheming it, the only ideal that is larger than their own, the ideal of love and forgive-ness. ... Then, as wax melts in the fire, the revolutionaries' opposition will melt in the deed of their emperor, the man who fulfils the law of Christ.

After writing out his plea, Tolstoy read it to his family. Sonya was furious that he could dare to intervene on the murderers' behalf. She was afraid he would anger the young tsar by preaching a form of mercy that was unnatural. In her anxiety she even threatened to dismiss Alexeyev, her children's tutor, who was guilty of approving her husband's

latest folly.* Under the storm of reproach, Tolstoy held his
ground as far as the principle was concerned, but agreed to
tone down some of the more inflammatory sentences. Then
he sent to Tula for some best-quality paper and his copyist
Ivanov wrote out the epistle in the proper calligraphic
form.

It was sent to Strakhov on 17 March 1881, to be given to
Pobyedonostsev, the tsar's minister to the Holy Synod, who
had been the monarch's tutor and had great influence over
him. If he presented the request in person, Alexander III
would certainly consider it favourably. In a postscript to
Tolstoy's note to Strakhov, Sonya reiterated her misgivings:

'Despite my advice and entreaties, Leo Nikolayevich has
decided to send his letter to the emperor. ... Read it, judge
for yourself and ask Pobyedonostsev's opinion. Won't it be
likely to arouse the tsar's displeasure or animosity toward
Leo Nikolayevich? If so, I beseech you to see that it does
not reach him.'

Wasted effort! Thrilled by Tolstoy's gesture, Strakhov
immediately went to see the minister, who glanced through
the letter and refused to show it to the emperor on the
ground that in a matter of such consequence he was bound
to follow his own views of Christianity, which were
diametrically opposed to those of the writer. His visitor bemoaned this fresh recourse to violence, so Pobyedonostev
assured him that although he personally was a confirmed
partisan of capital punishment, he would see that the
criminals were executed privately. Strakhov withdrew in
despair.

After he left, Pobyedonostsev began to fear that copies of
the letter might be circulated in the city, and the emperor
would hear of it from some other source. That evening he
learned that the philosopher Solovyev had just made a public address on capital punishment and that in his peroration
he, too, had exhorted the heir to the throne to pardon the

---

* Although she later apologized to him for this outburst, Alexeyev
and his family left the house and went to live on the Samara farm.

assassins. That was too much! On 30 March 1881 the minister dashed off the following note to Alexander III:

An idea that fills me with horror has just begun to circulate. People are capable of such mental aberration that some of them think it possible not to execute the murderers. The Russian people are already beginning to fear that monstrous schemes may be submitted to Your Majesty to incite you to pardon the criminals. ... No, no, a thousand times no; in this moment, with the eyes of the entire Russian nation upon you, it is unthinkable that you should pardon the murderers of your father, the emperor of Russia – that you should forget the blood that has been shed, for which everyone (apart from a few weak-hearted and feeble-minded individuals) is crying vengeance, and people are already demanding to know why the sentence is so long in coming. ... I am a Russian, I live among Russians, and I know what the Russian people feel and want. At this moment, they are all eager for punishment. If one of these wretches should escape death, he will immediately begin to hatch new plots for undermining the government. For the love of God, Sire, do not listen to misguided sycophants.

With a firm hand Alexander wrote across the page: 'Rest assured, no one will dare to come to me with such a request, and I promise you that *all six of them will hang*.'*

When he learned that his first attempt had failed, Tolstoy telegraphed to Strakhov asking him to give the letter to Professor Konstantin Bestuzhev-Ryumin, who would pass it on to Grand Duke Sergey, one of the monarch's four brothers. This time the contact was the right one: the document reached the tsar's desk within forty-eight hours. But Alexander III, a clear-sighted, intransigent man imbued with the doctrine of the divine right of kings, did not alter his decision.

On 3 April 1881 the six murderers were hanged. The rope broke twice under one of them, Mikhailov, who had to be hanged a second time with his legs broken.

* Six conspirators were arrested: 'Rysakov, Sofya Perovsky, Zhelyabov, Jessya Helfmann, Mikhailov, Kibalchich ...'

Two and a-half months later, Tolstoy received a letter from Pobyedonostsev telling him why, in good conscience, he had been unable to support his appeal:

'When I read your letter I saw that your faith had nothing in common with mine, which is that of the Church, and that my Christ was not your Christ,' wrote the minister for religious affairs. 'My Christ is a man of strength and truth who heals the weak, and yours seemed to me to be a weak man himself in need of healing.' [37]

Tolstoy choked down his anger and did not reply to this lesson in Christianity administered by the highest official of the empire, the man in charge of relations between Church and State.

Now he was certain that he found Christ by rejecting the priests. In this spirit, he began to draft his *Notes of a Christian*: 'I have been on earth for fifty-two years and, apart from the fourteen or fifteen years of more or less total unconsciousness of my childhood, I have lived, for thirty-five years, not as a Christian, Mohammedan nor yet as a Buddhist, but as a nihilist, in every sense of the word, that is, someone who believes in nothing. Two years ago I became a Christian. And from that moment all I hear, see and feel has appeared to me in a new light.'

He also took up his diary again. The first entry, dated 17 April 1881, is significant:

'Conversation with Sergey on non-resistance to evil.' [38]

And further on:

'21 May. Discussion: Tanya, Sergey, Ivan. Good is a convention. In other words, good does not exist. There is nothing but instinct.'

'22 May. Continuation of discussion: the good I am talking about is what you regard as good for yourself and everyone else!'

'29 May. Conversation with Fet and my wife. The Christian doctrine cannot be lived. Then, is it nonsense? No, but it cannot be lived! Yes, but have you tried? No, but it cannot be lived.'

Fet seldom agreed with Tolstoy, but the author's sons could not help feeling that the poet was a sensible and likeable man. He had pronounced Semitic features, a long brown beard already going grey, and small womanly hands with well-manicured nails. His speech was interspersed with sighs resembling little moans. When his audience was least expecting it, he would toss out some witticism and disarm the most sullen among them. (One day Igor, the man who served at table in white gloves and scarlet vest, could not help laughing out loud at one of the poet's jests and, setting his dish on the floor, scuttled away to the kitchen.) Now even more than before, Tolstoy criticized his friend for preaching art-for-art's-sake and refusing to enter into the torments of the conscience. He, on the contrary, was not at all loath to engage in evangelical exhortation at table. He claimed to despise earthly blessings; and when he argued with a guest, he begged his pardon immediately afterwards.

'I often have little quarrels with Leo now, and once I even wanted to leave the house,' Sonya wrote to her sister. 'It must be because we have begun to live as Christians. In my opinion, everything went much better before, without the Christian manner.'[39]

And to her brother:

'You should see and hear Leo now! He has changed a great deal. He has become the most convinced and earnest of Christians. But he has grown pale, his health is poor and he is more subdued and sombre than before.'

In order to become more actively involved in the misery of the world, Tolstoy made several visits to the prison at Tula, comforted the prisoners, accompanied them to court and stood on the platform when trains of deportees left for Siberia. 'Their heads are shaved and their feet chained together. One man, almost at death's door, and a little boy, crippled. One hundred and fourteen persons sent away for failure to possess a passport. Some very corrupt. Others simple, delightful. One old man, very weak, just out of hospital; a huge louse on his cheek. Some deported by their commune. Two accused of nothing; they're just being deported. Another on a complaint by his wife ... A strapping soldier who has been in prison for four years ... Two convicts sentenced to hard labour for life, for brawling and manslaughter ... They were crying. A pleasing face. Appalling stench ...' [40]

The sight of such wretchedness confirmed his feeling that the mission of a man such as he was not to devote himself to his family. 'The family is the flesh,' he wrote as early as 5 May. 'Abandon the family. That is the second temptation. Commit suicide. The family is only a body. But do not yield to the third temptation: live not for the family but for God.'

A plan had been nagging at him for some time: to make a second pilgrimage to Optina-Pustyn. This time, it was not the desire to reconcile himself with the Church that was driving him, but the hope that by mingling with the muzhiks, the sick and the sanctimonious old women, he might renew his own faith in mankind. Although he considered their piousness false, crude and ridiculous, he continued to admire the fervour with which they believed the unbelievable. Perhaps, in order to accede to their inner beatitude, one must spurn carriages and railroad cars and set off like them, on foot, walking along the highways for days on end across the unchanging plains, sleeping under the open sky or in some filthy inn, begging for alms. ... Nothing can prepare the soul to meet God like the infinite flatness of the Russian steppe, where the eyes skim and wander and lose their way and find no obstacle to stop them.

On 10 June 1881, dressed muzhik-fashion with a pack on his back, bark shoes and a staff in his hand, Tolstoy took leave of his wife and children, who were mortified by this masquerade, went down the front steps and turned on to the road. Two bodyguards trudged along behind him, also in disguise: Vinogradov the schoolmaster; and a valet, Arbuzov, who had red sideburns and a comical countenance, lugging a suitcase full of clean clothes. Tolstoy was enchanted by this escapade. However, as he was not used to the plaited bark shoes his feet were soon covered with blisters. Arbuzov had to teach him how to wrap strips of cloth around his burning toes. At Selivanovo, the first halting-place, the trio slept on the floor of an old peasant woman's house. The next day at Krapivna, the vagabond count bought heavy socks to protect his sensitive feet and prunes to purge himself and wrote to his wife: 'One cannot imagine how new, important and useful it is to the soul to see how God's world lives, the true world, the great world, not the one we have arranged for ourselves and never stepped outside of.' [41]

They continued their trek, shuffling along, stopping for a snack at the roadside, napping in the shade of a copse, spending the night in an isba, getting up at dawn. On the evening of the fourth day they reached the monastery of Optina-Pustyn. It was mealtime and the bell was ringing. A rich aroma of soup wafted out of the kitchens. At a glance the monks summed up the three hairy and dust-covered pilgrims as beggars and would not allow them inside the travellers' dining-room. Relegated to the common refectory, they went inside with their packs on their backs, crossing themselves.

Tolstoy was in seventh heaven. At last he was a muzhik among muzhiks. Men and women were sitting together around a long table, elbow to elbow in the dim light, gulping down food and drink and breathing heavily in a fog of cabbage, sweat and dirt. Pulling a notebook from his pocket, Tolstoy jotted down an aside:

'Borscht, kasha, kvass. One cup for four people. Everything is good. They eat hungrily.'

After supper he and his two companions followed the crowd towards the third-class dormitory. In the doorway of the stinking hall with its dubious straw pallets and walls encrusted with squashed insects, the stomach of the lord of Yasnaya Polyana heaved. Perhaps he was carrying humility too far. ... His manservant rushed over to one of the hostelry monks, thrust a rouble into his hand and asked him to provide some more decent accommodation for them. The monk let them sleep in a little room already occupied by a cobbler from Bolkov. The man, about to drop off to sleep, must have been amazed to see one red-whiskered muzhik pull a clean sheet and pillows out of a bag, arrange them on a bench and, with obsequious airs, assist another muzhik, grizzled, tanned and bearded, to settle himself comfortably for the night. After putting his master to bed, Arbuzov himself stretched out on the floor. As soon as the candle was blown out, the cobbler began to snore so loudly that Tolstoy sat up in alarm and whispered:

'Wake up that man and ask him not to snore.'

Arbuzov shook the cobbler by the shoulder and said:

'Old buddy, you're snoring too loud, you've scared my old man, it frightens him to hear somebody snoring in his sleep in the same room.'

'So on account of your old man I'm not supposed to sleep all night?' growled the cobbler.

He turned to the wall and went back to sleep, but snored no more.[42]

At ten the next morning, after drinking a few glasses of scalding tea, Arbuzov went to mass while his master, the enemy of the Church, watched the monks working in the fields. A little later a rumour began to spread through the convent that Count Leo Tolstoy was there incognito, among the pilgrims. Some monks questioned Arbuzov, who confessed the truth with a sigh of relief.

A great commotion ensued among the brotherhood. Excited palavering of black habits, whisperings into the superior's ear. The illustrious guest's baggage was carried forthwith into the first-class hostel, where the walls were hung with velvet. Tolstoy protested that he wanted to remain with the poor. But his eyes were already feasting upon the clean bed, polished flooring, deep armchairs. There were monks bowing to him and calling him 'Excellency'.

'Hopeless,' he sighed, and, turning to Arbuzov: 'Give me my boots and my good shirt.'

After removing his beggar's garb, he went to call on the superior, who, meanwhile, had invited him to dine. He spent nearly two hours with him. Then, as on his previous visit, he requested an audience with Father Ambrose. Thirty or more poor wretches had been waiting five or six days at the hermitage door for the starets to condescend to receive them, if only for one minute, and give them his blessing and counsel. Grouped according to category, they milled about mumbling prayers: the men just outside the door, the women behind the house, the nuns in the entry. Tolstoy asked a few pilgrims their reasons for coming to Optina-Pustyn, and wrote down their answers in his notebook: 'Will my daughter marry soon?' 'I am starting to build a house: is this a good thing?' 'Should I go into trade or open a cabaret?'

As befits a lord, he swept by in front of this hoi-polloi and was admitted at once. He spent four hours with the hermit, who was aware of Tolsty's religious opinions and wanted to persuade him to return to the Church. Wasted effort: Tolstoy was immovable. He even caught the starets in a flagrant misconstruction of a passage from the Gospels. As he came out of the cell, much agitated, he saw the pilgrims still waiting humbly, and distributed his small change among them.

The next day he donned his muzhik's costume again and, with his two companions in tow, set off on foot. But he did not feel up to going all the way to Yasnaya Polyana; at Kaluga, he decided to finish the trip by rail. But in a fresh burst of Christian humility, however, he ordered his man-servant to buy third-class tickets. His place was among the dispossessed. Smiling sarcastically, he recoiled before the fine gentlemen in their white false collars who were climbing into the first-class cars. Ah, the charms of temporary poverty! Before the train pulled out, he wired Sonya the time of their arrival, and spent the entire trip chatting with the peasants sprawling about him on the benches. They were all his brothers!

Nevertheless, at Tula he greeted the coachman Philip, who was waiting for them with a carriage and a handsome pair of horses, with unmitigated pleasure.

No sooner had he arrived at Yasnaya Polyana than he received a letter from Turgenev inviting him to spend a few days at his home at Spasskoye. He went on 8 July 1881, but he had got the date wrong and was not expected until the following day. Late at night the poet Polonsky, also Turgenev's house guest, heard footsteps, barking, a shrill blast on a whistle. 'In the light of the candle I saw one tanned and greying muzhik in a blouse giving money to another muzhik. I looked at him more closely, but I did not recognize him. Then the muzhik looked up and saw me and said, "Are you Polonsky?" Only then did I realize that it was Count Tolstoy.' [43]

Turgenev had not gone to bed and greeted his guest with joy. He proudly showed him his remodelled, freshly painted house, but Tolstoy was insensitive to the charm of physical surroundings. He wrote in his diary, 'At Turgenev's. Nice Polonsky, peacefully occupied with painting and poetry, judging nobody, perfectly untroubled. Turgenev fears the name of God, although he believes in him. But he, too, is naïvely peaceful and untroubled in the midst of his life of luxury and idleness.'

To inject a little seriousness into this gathering of aesthetes, Tolstoy told them about his trip to Optina-Pustyn and the new religion he had founded. They listened politely, they offered timid objections, Turgenev's face bore an expression of commiseration and tenderness. Some time before he had written to a friend, 'I am very sorry for Leo Tolstoy, but after all, as the French say, everyone has his own way of killing his fleas. ...' [44] His entire being now radiated the same sentiment.

Tolstoy remained only two days at Spasskoye. On 12 July

he was back at Yasnaya Polyana, and on the thirteenth, with his eldest son Sergey, he started off for Samara, where he had not been for two years. Sonya was very sad as she went out on to the steps with him. But the huge estate, the forests and the stud farm could not wait any longer for the master's tour of inspection. And then the *kumys* treatment was essential to his health. Once again (All very well to be a big landowner, but one must be able to get along with the common people!) he bought third-class tickets. At every station there were crowds milling about on the platform, shouting 'Hurrah!' But not for Leo Tolstoy: Grand Duke Nicholas Nikolayevich was travelling in a special car in the same train.

When he first reached Samara, Tolstoy's conscience reeled at the wretchedness of the people in comparison with his own prosperity: 'July 16. Went to see the horses. Unsurmountable anguish. Idleness. Shame . . .' 'July 24. The husband of a woman from Pavlova died in prison, her son died of starvation. Gave milk to the daughter. Patrovsky, used to be a herdsman – now destitute. Pale, grey hair ... Conversation with A.A. about the owners: those who do not want to give the land and those in favour of division.'

On his land, at any rate, the workers were not idle. Three hundred husky fellows, burnt black by the sun, were scything, harvesting, putting up hay, threshing wheat. The price of horses was rising at the fairs. Tolstoy counted on asking one hundred roubles for a good colt, one hundred and twenty for a full-grown horse of average quality. According to his calculations, the property would bring in between ten and twenty thousand roubles that year.* He triumphantly informed Sonya of this fact, but a prick of conscience prompted him to add, in the same letter, 'The only sad thing would be if one could do nothing at all for the people around one. There are too many poor in the village. It is a shameful kind of poverty, they are not even aware of it.' [45] Sonya made her usual commonsense reply: 'You know what

* Or between $28,300 and $56,600.

I think about giving help to the poor. It is impossible to feed the entire population of Samara, which is thousands. ... But if you see or hear of some man or woman who has no bread or cow or horse or isba, you must give them to him right away.'[46]

Whether engaged in increasing his income from the estate or in pitying those who had nothing, Tolstoy never lost sight of his religious pursuits. Having broken with the Church, he was being increasingly drawn to the sectarians. There were many of them in the region, mostly Molokhans. Tolstoy went to see them one Sunday, and noted: 'To prayer with the Molokhans. Heat. They wipe off the sweat with handkerchiefs. Very loud voices. Necks brown and rough as rasps. Greetings exhanged. Dinner: 1. Cold plate. 2. Cabbage soup with thistles. 3. Boiled mutton. 4. Noodles. 5. Walnuts. 6. Roast mutton. 7. Cucumbers. 8. Noodle soup. 9. Honey ...' These half-literate people amazed him by the simplicity of their customs and the soundness of their reasoning. He discussed the commandments with them and the meaning of the Feast of Cana; he read them passages from his theological studies and was proud to find that nearly all of them understood and approved of his ideas.

As always, *kumys*, rest and separation from the family restored his equilibrium. Calm, relaxed, full of love for the human race, he was already beginning to consider spending the remainder of his life in meditation while his wife assumed, single-handedly, the heavy burden of raising the children and managing the property.

'You cannot imagine how it upsets me to think that you are working too hard, and how sorry I am to help you so little, or in fact, not at all,' he wrote to Sonya on 2 August 1881. 'Now I see things differently. I still think and feel as before, but I am cured of the error of believing that other people can and must think as I do. I am very guilty towards you, my darling; involuntarily and unwittingly, you know that, but guilty all the same. My excuse is that in order to work under such tension, and really create something, one must forget everything else. And I have forgotten too much, and I am sorry. In the name of God and our love, take care of yourself. Put off as much of the work as you can until I come home; I shall do it joyfully, and not too badly; I shall apply myself.'

And on 6 August:

'Please God let me come home safe to you all, and you'll see what a good boy I will be, exactly as you want me!'

These letters poured balm into Sonya's heart. At the news that her husband was planning another novel, she could not contain herself:

'I felt such a surge of joy when I read that you want to return to poetical writing. You know how long I have been waiting and longing for that! It is salvation and happiness. That is the thing that will bring us together again. That is what will console you and light your life. That is real work! Away from it there can be no peace for your soul. I know you cannot force yourself, but may God keep you in the same state of mind, so that the divine spark may kindle in you again!'

Tolstoy's good resolutions did not outlast his treatment. When he had emptied his last bowl of *kumys*, his optimism and forbearance vanished as though by magic. On 17 August 1881, returning to Yasnaya Polyana, he found the house full of relatives, guests and neighbours. The young people were dancing and chattering and racing about in all directions, pawing through the closets: an amateur play was in preparation. Irritated by all this racket, the master took refuge in solitary and morose meditation. No more thought of writing novels or doing his share of the family chores. He wrote in his diary, 'Theatricals. Non-entities. ... The days of 19, 20 and 21 are stricken from my life.'

The next day, 22 August, Turgenev came to Yasnaya Polyana for Sonya's birthday and was swept away in the general hilarity. Tolstoy glowered at the elegant and garrulous old man trying to share in the amusements of youth. The newcomer proposed that each person should recite the happiest moment of his life. Among the group were Tanya and Sergey, whose romance had once been a major topic of interest in the family and who had since married separately – she to Kuzminsky and he to his gypsy. Sergey whispered something into the young woman's ear; she blushed and murmured, 'You are impossible, Sergey Nikolayevich!' and forbade him to tell 'his most wonderful memory'. Then they all turned to Turgenev, who smiled dolefully, assumed a languid expression and confessed: 'The most shining moment of my life naturally has to do with love. It is the one in which your eyes meet those of the woman you love and you guess that she loves you, too. That happened to me once ... perhaps twice.'

It was hard for Tolstoy to hide his scorn; and he was forced to redouble his efforts when his colleague, yielding to the pleas of the young, demonstrated how the cancan was danced in Paris. As Turgenev hopped nimbly about with his thumbs stuck through the armholes of his waistcoat and a gasping leer on his face, the whole household applauded and laughed. At last he collapsed, breathless, into an armchair. They flocked around, plying him with questions about France. He told them that he had attended classes in 'pornography' in Paris, with demonstrations 'on live subjects'. The ladies gasped. Tolstoy scowled. An air of debauchery had entered his house. To change the subject, someone began to talk of French literature. Turgenev was very well acquainted with Flaubert, Zola, Daudet, Goncourt, Maupassant. ... Once again he entertained his audience with his recollections of the great foreign authors. He said he disapproved of the excesses of realism. Then, carried away by his eloquence, he turned to Russian literature, and began to pick Dostoyevsky to pieces. Tolstoy immediately pricked up his ears. The expression on Turgenev's face was mocking and mean.

'Do you know what a backward cliché is?' he said. 'When a man is in love his heart pounds; when he is furious he turns scarlet, etc. Those are ordinary clichés. But with

Dostoyevsky it's all the other way around. For instance, a man meets a lion. What does he do? In the normal course of events, he turns pale and tries to run away or hide. In any ordinary story, in Jules Verne for example, that's the way it should happen. But in Dostoyevsky it's all the opposite: the man sees the lion, he turns red, and he stays put. That is a backward cliché. It is an easy method of being thought original. And then, in Dostoyevsky, the heroes are always in a state of delirium, frenzy, fever every second page. No, really, that is not how things happen in real life!'[47]

Tolstoy was jubilant to hear such lively criticism of the writer whom some, in the press, had dared to place on a level with himself. He might almost have forgiven Turgenev his well-cut vests and his fancy manners with the ladies. However, he could not forget that ridiculous cancan. That evening he wrote in his diary: 'August 22. Turgenev – cancan. Pity.'

The Horrors of the City;
the Appeal of the
'Dark Ones'

As the years went by, Tolstoy felt a growing need to be
alone. He even began to fear the coming of summer, with
its noisy guests, dinner-table chatter, croquet and tennis
matches, organized walks and picnics. With the first rain,
his private sky cleared. He waited impatiently for the dry
white frost that drove away the importunate guests, brought
the family together under one roof and restored propitious
conditions for meditation. Sonya, on the contrary, dreaded
the approach of winter. When the house was walled in by
snow she dreamed ruefully of city lights, receptions, balls,
theatre. ... If only she had a novel of Lyovochka's to copy,
she might have peopled her own empty existence with the
sentimental life of his heroes. But he showed no inclination
to go back to fiction. The more she urged him, the less he
hastened to obey. He wasn't bored, in his study surrounded
by his philosophers. But her only distractions were the children's education, household accounts, needlework, the dinner: 'I am going down to dine, I will eat pike, then I will
nurse the baby and go to bed. ...'[1] 'I drank tea and ate
chocolate. ...'[2] Lyovochka went hunting every day, and
she feverishly awaited his return. 'He went out after hare,
but saw no game. ...' 'He came back with four hares and a
fox. ...' 'Yesterday, with the pointer, he took six hares, and
today, with the hounds, one fox. ...'[3] One child had diarrhoea, another a sore throat, Andryusha's fontanels were
late in hardening. ... Worries of this kind were soul-
destroying. Sonya complained, alone with her notebook.
For a while she became engrossed in a job her husband had

given her, at Strakhov's instigation: the preparation of a short biography of Lyovochka for an anthology of selected works, *The Russian Library*. 'It is not easy to write a biography,' she noted. 'I have written little and badly. I was interrupted by the children, nursing, noise. And in addition, I do not know the details of Lyovochka's life before his marriage.'⁴ Later, she wrote, 'In the evening we went over Lyovochka's entire life together for his biography. He talked and I wrote. We worked cheerfully and amicably.'⁵

Brief interlude. Once the biography was written, revised and sent off to Strakhov, Sonya relapsed into lethargy: 'The autumn has brought back my morbid melancholy. I spend all my time embroidering a rug in silence or reading. I feel nothing but coldness and indifference towards everyone and everything. Everything seems tedious and sad, and ahead – the shadow of darkness.'⁶

On 30 January 1880 she wrote to her sister Tanya, 'Sometimes I find this cloistered existence extremely hard. Think, Tanya, that since last September I have not set foot outside the house. It is a prison, though everything inside it is light enough, both morally and materially. Nevertheless I often feel as though someone is fencing me in, shutting me away, and I want to knock everything down and smash everything around me and run away somewhere, but quickly, quickly!'

Of course, if her husband had the only say in the matter, she would never have returned to the city to live. But there were the children. They could not go on studying indefinitely with tutors in the country. In 1881 the eldest boy, Sergey, was eighteen and it was essential to enroll him at the University of Moscow; Ilya and Leo, aged fifteen and twelve, were old enough to attend classes at the lycée; Tanya, seventeen, had a flair for drawing and would study painting and make her début. Sonya had long been preparing Lyovochka for this great step. They had discussed it together a hundred times. Tolstoy was unwilling to oppose the move to town since the children's education was at stake; but while everyone around him was looking forward to it with delight, he contemplated with loathing the new life, so contrary to his principles, that he would be compelled to lead there.

While he was imbibing *kumys* at Samara, Sonya, pregnant again, went to Moscow to rent a house and make preparations to move the entire family. It was decided that they would leave Yasnaya Polyana early in September. Soon suitcases, trunks and wicker hampers appeared in all the rooms. The servants counted linen and sorted it into piles. In the children's rooms all was laughter and clatter and joyous whispering. Neglected, misunderstood and morose, Tolstoy prowled about the grounds and bade farewell to the trees and animals as though he were never to see them again. On 28 August 1881 Yasnaya Polyana was in such a ferment that neither his wife nor his sons nor his daughters thought to wish him a happy birthday. He was fifty-three years old. That evening he wrote in his diary, 'I could not help feeling sad that nobody remembered.' And on 2 September, 'I often want to die. I cannot get caught up in my work.'

At last, on 15 September 1881, the whole family removed to Moscow, to a house rented from Prince Volkonsky in Denezhny Street. It was a huge place full of echoes, the partitions were too thin. 'A cardboard house,' Sonya said. Leo's study was so imposing that he felt lost in it. No possibility of peace and quiet here: the slightest tremor reverberated between the walls as in a drum. Sonya, in dismay, ordered the servants and children to talk in whispers. She wrote to her sister, 'Leo says that if I loved him I would have shown more consideration for his state of mind, I would not have chosen for him this enormous room in which he cannot have a minute's peace, in which every armchair would be the answer to a muzhik's prayers because with the same twenty-two roubles the muzhik could buy a horse or a cow, that he feels like crying, etc.'

And indeed, he did cry. His wife wept beside him.

But she soon recovered. Since Lyovochka was going to fail

her, she would have to cope alone. Two weeks before her confinement she plunged into sorting and storing, arranging, buying furniture. Following her lead, the family found its second wind. Sergey, now a sober young man, reserved, awkward, brutally frank, donned the student's uniform and entered the University. He admired his father and, considering himself also to be an intellectual, despised the government, all civil servants and rich people, and the Orthodox Church. Pretty, sweet Tanya, who had been brought up as a hoyden, swooned with joy at her first trip to the dressmaker. She was clothed from head to foot, enrolled in a painter's studio, presented with a schedule of social engagements. Their father proceeded to enroll Ilya and Leo, the younger boys, in a *gymnasium*. At the last minute, however, a difficulty arose. In order for a child to be admitted to a State institution, his parents had to vouch for his good behaviour in writing. In front of the open-mouthed principal, Tolstoy categorically refused to assume such a responsibility. 'How,' he cried, 'can I vouch for the conduct of someone other than myself?' He enrolled his two sons in the Polivanov School, a private *gymnasium* where pupils were admitted with no other formality than an entrance examination.

The more his family rejoiced in their new style of life, the more he abhorred the city, its falsehood and artificial pleasures. On 5 October 1881 he wrote in his diary: 'Moscow. A month has gone by, the hardest month of my life. The move to Moscow. Everybody is settling down. But when are they going to start living? Everything they do is done not in order to live, but because somebody else is doing it. Poor wretches! And there is no life here! Stench, stone, opulence, poverty, debauchery. The robbers have banded together and despoiled the people, assembled an army, elected judges to sanction their orgies, and now they are feasting. There is nothing left for the people to do but take advantage of other men's passions, to get back what has been stolen from them. The muzhiks are best at this game. In town, the women do housework and the men polish floors or bodies in the steam-baths, or become cab drivers.'

At Yasnaya Polyana, social injustice was camouflaged by country quaintness, the poor were scattered far apart, and sun and wind drove away the bad smells; but in Moscow poverty was walled in and concentrated, and it exploded in your face like a boil. Impossible not to see it. In this city, merely having food to eat was enough to make you feel guilty. Stricken by remorse at the comfort in which he and his family were living, Tolstoy could not sleep, refused to eat, groaned, wept and pined for the solitude and peace of his country estate. On 31 October 1881 Sonya gave birth to her eleventh child, a boy, Alexis.

This event brought no joy to the father. He rented two small, quiet rooms in the adjoining villa for six roubles a month and shut himself up to work on his philosophical studies in peace. Around two or three in the afternoon he would slip surreptitiously out of the house dressed as a workman, cross the frozen river and climb the hills on the other side – the Sparrow Hills, white with snow – and there, with voluptuous pleasure and gratitude, he helped the muzhiks to chop and saw wood. In the evening he drew the water from the well himself. Sometimes, as if to impose a penitence upon himself, he went walking in the grimmest districts of Moscow, or to the Khitrovka Market, inhabited by beggars, thieves and escaped convicts. Twisting alleyways led down to a sort of pit surrounded by flophouses and gambling dens. Gaunt creatures, half-man, half-beast, each with his own tragedy, his mortal wound, his madness, swarmed in the murk. Tolstoy inhaled the gamy smell of the five-kopeck-a-night flophouses, stumbled over sleeping drunks, brushed against ragged, filthy cripples, handed out his small change and went home, sick with horror and pity. His guilt deepened at the sight of the carpeted stairway, chandeliers, white-gloved lackeys, well-dressed, healthy children and wife, set table, silverplate, five-course dinners.

'It is very hard for me to live in Moscow,' he wrote to

Alexeyev on 15 November 1881. 'I have been here for two months and it is not becoming any easier. I know now that, although I was aware of the enormity of the evil and temptations around us before, I did not really believe in them, I did not really see them as they are. ... Now the enormity of the evil is crushing me, driving me to despair, driving me to doubt everything ...'

How to get out of this dilemma? Fold his arms and whimper? Deceive himself playing cards or talking? No!

'I see one way: propaganda, spoken and written, but I am afraid this is nothing but vanity, conceit and possibly delusion. Another way would be to give help to people. But the infinite numbers of the destitute are disheartening. It isn't like in the village where a little circle forms naturally. The only way I can see is to live honestly and always show one's good side to others.'[7]

His own 'good side' was shown increasingly seldom to his wife and children; he was keeping it for the poor, who alone could understand him. At home, he was a stranger. When she had recovered from her confinement, Sonya flung herself into the social season with a vengeance. Accompanied by Tanya, she went calling, shopping, to the theatre and the concert. She even chose an 'at-home' day, Thursday, to which all the smartest people came in droves. It was impossible for Tolstoy to avoid his wife's guests all the time, but he insisted upon appearing in his grey peasant's blouse, and categorically refused to dress up in city clothes. The very thought of putting on a jacket and stiff collar, knotting a tie, putting his feet into fine leather shoes, revolted him as a form of treason. He stood by his dress as he stood by his principles. 'However,' wrote his son Sergey, 'he eventually accepted a compromise. He had a sort of black tunic, which he put on over a starched shirt and buttoned up to the throat. This black tunic was neither a blouse nor a jacket. He wore it one winter, then went back to his usual blouse.'[8]

Deep in his own social preoccupations, he was filled with

eager anticipation by the announcement that the city administration was to make a census of the population, in
January 1882. The project was being directed by civil servants, with the help of sociologists, students and other interested persons, and would last three days. Tolstoy decided
to volunteer. He hoped to make use of this sally into the
lower depths to devise a scheme for relieving the under-
privileged. In all likelihood there was, mingled with his
official and disinterested intentions, the artist's ever-present
desire to document himself on a little-known fauna and put
his sensitivity to the test. He would certainly get a closer
look at human destitution during this survey than on his
solitary walks in the Khitrovka district, where he could only
go as far as people were willing to let him. He obtained permission from Professor Yanzhul, the census director, to
cover the district beyond Smolensky Market, which contained the grimmest slums, flophouses and dives in the entire city.

Tolstoy spent the days of 23, 24 and 25 January moving
about in this skid row swarming with thieves, prostitutes,
drunkards and starveling children. At the sight of the
census-takers, they all tried to run away. The exits were
blocked and the poor wretches were assured that no one was
going to ask them for their papers.

'Terrified and frightening in their terror,' wrote Tolstoy,
'they clustered together by the reeking cesspool, listened to
our explanations and did not believe a word we said. ...
Every dwelling was full, every bunk occupied. ... All the
women who were not dead drunk were lying with men.
Many of those who had babies with them were wallowing
on narrow bunks with total strangers. After this place a
second, identical, then a third, tenth, twentieth and on forever, and everywhere the same suffocating stench, cramped
quarters, mingling of the sexes. Men and women drunk to
the point of idiocy, and on every face the same alarm, the
same docility, the same guilt.'

Swallowing his nausea, Tolstoy questioned this human

debris, trying to find out what they lived on and how they had fallen so low. Their answers revealed a degree of stupidity, cowardice, bad luck, cunning and vice that left him speechless. No collection, no charitable bequest, no State relief would be enough to save these souls from the abyss. Such need could only be repaired by love, not money. Public opinion must be awakened, the eyes of the rich must be opened to the hell outside their doors, they must be forced to share their fortunes with those who had nothing. To gain support in the wealthier classes, Tolstoy published a poignant article entitled *On the Moscow Census*.

This appeal to Christian charity went unheeded. The voice of one writer, be he the author of *War and Peace*, could not shake the foundations of the established order. Tolstoy saw that he would have to content himself with a few disciples, rather than the hordes he had hoped to draw into the paths of righteousness. Quality would take the place of quantity. Well: the worshipful Strakhov was still at his side, and this stammering sycophant had recently been joined by Alexeyev, his sons' former tutor, who, after being arrested for his progressive ideas, had emigrated to Kansas with some other socialists to found an agricultural community and then returned to Russia disenchanted. He had abandoned Marxism in 1878 and had been seeking some religious foundation for his morality ever since. He was an excellent teacher, but after his quarrel with Sonya over Tolstoy's letter to Alexander III, he had left Yasnaya Polyana and settled with his family on the Samara estate. In his letters, Tolstoy poured out his heart to him as to a member of the same church.

He would have been pleased to number Ivanov, the scribe, among his followers; he had picked him up starving on the road to Kiev and employed him to copy his manuscripts for the last three years. But Ivanov, a mild little man with a pockmarked face and a goat's beard, had two obsessions – alcohol and vagabondage. One spring day he would get drunk and start off along the highroads, going nowhere in particular, 'Russian-style', begging his food, writing a letter or giving a lesson in grammar to earn a few kopecks. He returned with the autumn, repentant and tearful, and the Tolstoys took him in with open arms. In Moscow Tolstoy had found him a job as secretary of a district court judge, and arranged for his marriage to a seamstress. Within days, Ivanov abandoned the conjugal hearth. Some ragged urchins brought the count a note from the fugitive, beseeching him to settle his account with the owner of a Khitrovka flophouse, so that he could leave. He had run through the money he had received from the judge and sold all his clothes. Tolstoy bailed him out of that predicament, but gave up any hope of elevating him to the ranks of the faithful.

He had better luck in his friendship with two remarkable men he had met in Moscow: Fyodorov and Orlov. Old Fyodorov, librarian of the Rumyantsev Museum, was a learned, ascetic scholar, who lived in a bare cell, slept on a pile of newspapers, ate almost nothing and gave what little money he earned to the poor. His extraordinary memory made him a 'walking encyclopedia'. He believed that scientists would soon be able to resurrect the dead in flesh and blood, and it was therefore the duty of the Christian community to preserve all that men left behind them after giving up the ghost. Whenever he saw Tolstoy he exhorted him, in a voice quivering with emotion, to spread the new words of physical resurrection, and was offended when the author expressed doubts as to the future of his doctrine of 'mystical and scientific immortality'. Orlov was a professor at the Railways School, but there was no one like him for the interpretation of the Gospels. He worked himself into a state of collapse to support his nine children and, in spite of his poor health and slender resources, never complained of his lot.

These two fellow-thinkers paled, however, before a third, a certain Syutayev. Tolstoy had heard of him the previous July during his *kumys* treatment in Samara, from another

patient named Prugavin, who wrote histories of Russian
religious sects. According to Prugavin, Syutayev, a peasant,
herdsman and stonecutter, raised in the faith of the Old
Believers, was a man of supernatural goodness and wisdom.
He was said to live in a village near Tver. Shortly after his
arrival in Moscow in autumn 1881, Tolstoy had gone to see
an old friend of his, Bakunin, whose estate was five miles
from the hamlet of Shevelino where Syutayev lived. The
temptation was too great; the next day, the count went to
call on the muzhik. Of the two, the count was the more intimidated. Syutayev willingly explained the substance of his
doctrine: pool everything in the family – land, implements,
food, animals, clothes, women! He would have no commerce, courts, taxes or army. He wanted the whole world to
have but one heart. Tolstoy was overcome with admiration
for the little old shepherd with the illuminated eyes, melo-
dious voice and dirty beard. In the evening Syutayev accompanied his guest back to Bakunin's home in a telega. As it
was against the Old Believer's principles to use a whip, his
horse ambled along at a snail's pace. Unnoticed by driver
and passenger, who were deep in their theological discussion, the wagon gradually edged off the road and all of a
sudden, they found themselves head over heels in a
ditch.

Back in Moscow, Tolstoy continued to think of Syutayev
as a second self, simpler, less educated and, consequently,
closer to God. He even invited him to call on him at
Denezhny Street if ever he came to town, and at the end
of January 1882, when he was still in a state of shock after
the census-taking, he received an unexpected visit from the
old shepherd. He dragged him into his study, told him of
his sufferings and explained his plan to succour the unfortunate. Syutayev, hunched up in a short black sheepskin
cloak which he wore, peasant-style, indoors and out, seemed
to be thinking of something else. Suddenly he broke in:

'That's all nonsense!'

'Why nonsense?' asked Tolstoy. 'Is it wrong to clothe

those who are naked and feed those who are hungry, as it says in the Gospel?'

'I know, I know. ... You see a man, he asks you for twenty kopecks, you give them to him. Is that charity? No; all you want is to get rid of him!'

'Then is one supposed to let him die of hunger and cold?'

Syutayev's little grey eyes sparkled and he murmured, 'Let us divide up these unfortunate people between us. I'm not rich, but I'll take two right away; even if there are ten times as many, we will take them all. ... We will all go to work together. ... We will sit down at the same table. One of them will hear a good word spoken by you or me. He will learn the right way to live. That is real charity; but your scheme is just a game of seesaw.'[9]

This Christian communist, who rejected government in any form and relied on love alone, was a perfect expression of Tolstoy's ideas. Overjoyed, he saw that he had invented nothing new, that it had all existed before him in the head of an old shepherd, that he was at last becoming one with the people!

He talked about Syutayev to his wife, his friends and acquaintances. The hard core of the countess's Thursdays also wanted to meet the prophet of Shevelino. Tolstoy consented to exhibit his 'discovery' to society. 'These evenings are always dull,' Sonya wrote to her sister, 'but we were saved by the presence of a sectarian named Syutayev, who is now the talk of Moscow and is being introduced everywhere and is spreading his ideas everywhere.'[10]

Not in the least intimidated by his brilliant audience, Syutayev preached in a singsong voice, drawing out his 'o's' like the peasants of the north. His sheepskin jacket gave off an odour of tallow. Tolstoy's attitude towards him was both fatherly and deferential. Young Tanya, attracted by the picturesqueness of the old prophet, painted his portrait in oils.

After several of these evenings had taken place, Prince Dolgorukov, governor general of Moscow, became alarmed at the thought that people of the best society were gathering in Tolstoy's home to listen to the ranting of a muzhik. He sent an officer of the gendarmerie to ask the count what was the meaning of these lectures and, as on every other occasion when the administration had the effrontery to meddle in his affairs, Tolstoy reacted like an offended boyar. White-faced, his beard trembling and his eye dreadful to behold, he pointed to the door and snarled at the governor's emissary:

'Get you gone in the name of God! And on the double!'

But Prince Dolgorukov was not to be so easily repulsed, and dispatched a government official to persuade Tolstoy to reply to his questions. Luckily, Syutayev had already gone back to his village by then.

He left his fellow believer convinced that any effort made by an individual to help the poor was futile in practical terms, and an offence to human dignity, in moral ones. This view was corroborated by the failure of Tolstoy's appeal in the press. Tolstoy distributed the money he had begun to collect and gave up his 'nonsense'.

Because he was stifling in Moscow, he went to Yasnaya Polyana on 1 February 1882. Back in his childhood home, with the snow-covered grounds and the ageing servants and the silence, he felt new strength surge up within him. 'I think there is no place where I shall feel better or more at peace than here,' he wrote to Sonya on 4 February. 'Eternally occupied as you are by the household and the family, you cannot understand what a difference there is for me between town and country. ... The main thing wrong with life in town, for me and any thinking man, is that one is constantly compelled either to argue and refute mistaken opinions, or to accept them without an argument, which is worse.'

Divested of his wife, his sons, his daughters and the Thursday crowd, he wrote an essay: *What Then Must We Do?*, savoured the rough and hearty peasant fare (blinis, salt meat, kasha), and thought 'no more of man, but only of

God'. Looking at him, the old servant Agatha Mikhailovna shook her head and grumbled, 'You've left the countess back there to carry on alone with eight children, while you sit here pulling at your beard!'

And although Sonya agreed that her husband needed a rest, she could not forgive him for such an ostentatious lack of interest in his family.

'You and your Syutayevs,' she wrote on 3 February, 'maybe you can remain above all feelings of affection for your own children, but mere mortals like me cannot. Or maybe it's that we don't try to justify our lack of any profound love by pretending to love the whole universe.'

And the following day:

'Even when you are in Moscow I hardly ever see you. Our two lives have separated. Is this still a life at all?'

Remorse-stricken, Tolstoy returned to Moscow, talked to his wife and, unfortunately, had another religious quarrel with Alexandra Tolstoy who had made a special trip from St Petersburg to see him. Once more, the old maid of honour tried 'to bring him back to Christ' and once more he lost his temper, denied that she had any right to give lessons in Christianity to anyone and left her, not on speaking terms. He was so angry that he struck out for Yasnaya Polyana again, to calm himself. The moment he reached the country, he wrote a letter of unprecedented violence to his incorrigible *babushka*:

'Right or wrong, I regard your faith as the devil's work, designed solely to deprive mankind of the salvation promised by Christ. ... In my book and in person, I denounce all liars and false prophets in sheep's clothing. ... Those liars will do as they have always done, they will be silent. But when they can be silent no longer, they will kill me. I am expecting it. And you are helping them in their task, for which I am grateful to you!'[11]

Having signed his name at the bottom of the page, he called for a horse and galloped off at full speed to post his vindictive epistle in person from the Yasenki station. But when he got back to the house, his fever began to abate. Fearing he had gone a little far, he sent a servant to recover the letter in the mailbag, with a word of apology to the mail clerk.

The next day he wrote what he hoped was a milder letter to Alexandra, although in fact it was hardly less violent:

'Do stop talking about Christ, in order to avoid the inanity that is so prevalent among ladies of the court, with their sermonizing and preaching and converting. Is it not laughable that ladies of the court such as you, or the Bludovs or the Tyutchevs, should feel called upon to preach Orthodoxy? I can understand that any woman should desire salvation, but then, if she is a true Christian, the first thing she will do will be to leave the court and society; she will go to matins, and fast, and do the best she can to save her soul. Why has the position of courtier become tantamount to a degree in theology? Nothing could be more absurd!'

At this point he could not forgo the pleasure of imagining himself a martyr again, falling beneath the blows of the false prophets. Although no one was threatening his life, he repeated the terms of his first letter with evident relish:

'They will be silent as long as they can, and then they will kill me. And you, talking to me about your Christ, are helping them in their work. You and I have as little in common as Christ and the Pharisees. My body can perish, but the teachings of Christ will not perish.'

This was the first time he had compared himself with Christ, and consigned his enemies to the status of Pharisees. He so wanted to suffer for the faith! The pain, the spilling blood, the wondering crowds. . . . Ah, but it was sweet to imagine his torture, sitting in his warm study at Yasnaya Polyana with a shawl over his shoulders and woollen slippers on his feet.

Having settled Alexandra's hash, he turned to his wife. As always, after an outburst, he was full of guilty affection for her. He wrote to her that he needed the country 'to thaw out morally' and 'recover [his] self-possession', that he was planning 'poetical works', that he was playing solitaire and dreaming of his beloved helpmeet, but that he was crushed by his consciousness of the evil that dominated the world. Sonya answered:

'I begin to think that when a happy man suddenly notices that life is dreadful and closes his eyes to everything good in life, that man is sick. You should undergo treatment. I say this without any ulterior motive, I am simply noting a fact. I am very sorry for you, and if you were to think over what I say with an open mind you might find a remedy for your troubles. ... Have you only just discovered that there are starving, sick, miserable, wicked people in the world? Look again; there are also cheerful, healthy, happy and good people. May God help you! As for me, what can I do? ... You don't need my love any more now. What do you need, then? If only I knew!'

This appeal moved Tolstoy to tears.

'Don't worry on my account,' he wrote, 'and above all, don't accuse yourself. ... I have forgotten why I was so unhappy. Maybe it's age, or poor health. But I have nothing to complain about. I learned a great deal from life in Moscow. It showed me the path to follow if I want to continue my work, and it has brought us closer together. ...

'I cannot live apart from you. Your presence is absolutely necessary to me. ... You say, "I love you, but you don't need my love any more." On the contrary, that is all I do need. And nothing can revive me like your letters. A liver ailment is one thing, the life of the soul another. I had a desperate need of solitude; it has refreshed me; and your love gives me the greatest joy in the world.'

Sonya had to stay in the city because of the children's studies, so he made several quick trips to Moscow that spring to keep in touch with his family. Between trains, he visited picture galleries, chatted with writers and journalists and supervised the publication of *Confession* in *Russian Thought*. But by order of the censorship committee, the police confiscated the first issues of the review. However, handwritten and typed copies of the book circulated secretly, and it was later published in Geneva.

The violence with which the author denounced his own errors, criticized the Christian religion and proclaimed the need for a new rule of life provoked moral crises among his readers. Strangers wrote to insult him; others to congratulate him or ask him for advice. Gay, a well-known painter, was enthralled by the article *On the Moscow Census*, caught the first train to Moscow, rushed to Denezhny Street and found no one at home, paced back and forth outside the door for three hours, came back the next day and at last saw the master, fell into his arms and begged to be allowed to paint his portrait or that of his daughter. 'Do my wife instead,' said Tolstoy, and Gay, who was a gentleman, hid his disappointment and set to work forthwith. 'I have been posing for a week now,' Sonya wrote to her sister. 'He is doing me with my mouth half-open, in a black velvet top with Alençon lace and my hair loose.'

A few days were all that the painter needed to fall in love – not with the wife, but with the husband. He had admired Tolstoy as a writer before meeting him. Once admitted to his inner circle, he resolved to devote himself to the author for life. 'I loved that man beyond words,' he said to Stasov. 'He revealed everything to me.' [12] Gay carried a New Testament in his pocket and was forever pulling it out to cite a passage; the fifty-year-old man with his grey beard, bald pate and blue eyes was transfigured. Tolstoy said he was 'an elderly child, brimming over with affection for everything and everyone'. [13] Gay was a severe critic of his own work, however. He did not like his portrait of Sonya: 'I painted a lady in a velvet dress who has forty thousand roubles in the bank,' he said. Or, 'I painted a woman of the world and Sofya Andreyevna is a mother.' [14] He finally destroyed it. He made a second portrait of Sonya later, holding her youngest daughter in her arms, and another, very good one, of Tolstoy at his desk.

Early in the summer of 1882 the entire family returned to Yasnaya Polyana; as usual, the Kuzminskys moved into their special pavilion, other guests flocked in and the youngsters were hard at play around the swings, along the paths and on the croquet lawn. Sergey and Ilya were grown up now and had their own horses and guns and dogs and their own ideas, and talked with men's voices. Tolstoy, who had just given up hunting, looked on and gritted his teeth as his sons strode off to shoot snipe and hare. He found them heavy and rather oafish, as he himself had been at their age. There was no communion of thought between him and any of his family. His true sons were Syutayev, Alexeyev, Fyodorov, Strakhov . . .

'The folly of the people I live with saddens me,' he wrote to Alexeyev. 'Often they fail to see how I can perceive their insanity so clearly when they are utterly lacking in the capacity to understand the error of their ways. And so there we stand, staring at each other and not understanding, astonished by each other and each holding the other to blame. Only, there are untold hordes of them and I am alone. And they look happy and I look sad . . .'[15]

His coldness towards his children could not fail to affect Sonya, especially as Ilya had just fallen ill. She was afraid he had typhus. The doctor prescribed frequent small doses of quinine. He lay in the drawing-room shivering with fever. At her wit's end with worry, Sonya complained that Lyovochka was no help to her in nursing him and, in general, never lifted a finger in the house. He turned white with anger and shouted that his fondest desire was to run away from his family. 'As long as I live I shall remember the sincerity of that cry which broke my heart,' Sonya wrote on the evening of 26 August 1882. 'I yearn for death with all my strength, for I cannot live without his love. I cannot prove to him how deeply I have loved him these twenty years, no less today than on the first day. My love weighs me down, but it only irritates him. He is filled with his Christian ideal of self-perfection. I am jealous of him.'

After this explosion he had fled to his study, intending to sleep alone on the sofa. Sonya, choking with sobs, stared at the empty bed and refused to get into it. Carried away, as always, by her romantic imaginings, she told herself that Lyovochka had been seduced by another woman. She went to her son, gave him his medicine, passed in front of the study door hoping her husband would call to her, heard nothing, went back to her bedroom, waited, motionless, her eyes blank, under the round circle of lamplight. He came back at dawn, but their reconciliation was not immediate. At last, tears gave way to kisses. Worn out by emotion, lack of sleep and her husband's final caresses, Sonya made her way along the path through the woods to the bathhouse early in the morning. 'I shall never forget that glorious morning, light and cool, and the silver-gleaming dew.' Nor was she to forget her husband's *cri du coeur*, threatening to abandon her. Half-joyful, half-anxious, she dived into the chilly water and stayed longer than she should have. 'I would have liked to catch cold and die,' she wrote in her diary. 'But I did not catch cold. I came back to the house and nursed Alyosha, whose smile filled me with joy.'

When summer came to an end, Tolstoy left his wife at Yasnaya Polyana and went to Moscow with the two older boys to prepare for the family's return. Four months before, he had bought a house that was more to his liking – as a measure of economy, he said. In fact, he had paid 27,000 roubles* for it and thought to himself that it was cheap at the price. Naturally, with his simple tastes, he had not chosen to live in one of the luxurious parts of town, but in the industrial outskirts in the southwest, on Dolgo-Khamov-nichesky Street.† Close by were a sock and stocking factory, a perfume distillery, a spinning mill and a brewery. Each had its own whistle, its special smell and its muffled, cease-less, daily noise. The chief attraction of the new residence was a big walled garden (over two acres), with a row of lime

* $76,400.
† In 1920, this house became the Tolstoy Museum.

trees, impenetrable thickets, a dozen apple trees, thirty or so cherry trees, a few plum trees and barberries, a little hummock covered with stiff grass, a pavilion for solitary daydreamers, a wide raised walk that could be used as a croquet lawn in summer and a skating rink in winter. The outbuildings (caretaker's house, coach house, stables, barn and cowshed) stood around the main house, which was built all of wood, two storeys high. The façade was painted ochre and the shutters green. There were twenty rooms inside, all badly in need of redecoration. No running water, but they were used to that in the country. Besides, there was a well in the garden.

With surprising energy in a man who declared himself the enemy of all material contingencies, Tolstoy directed the renovation. The roof needed repairs, new floors had to be laid, the woodwork repainted, the wallpaper changed. A mere trifle! He had decided that they would move in at the beginning of October. Racing to meet his deadline, he bullied the contractor, heckled the workmen, raced through the shops in search of antique furniture (preferably mahogany), brought everything he could from the Denezhny Street house and dispatched daily bulletins to Sonya: 'Yesterday, to my great despair, the contractor announced that we would not be able to move in before 1 October! ... The four downstairs rooms will be ready on Tuesday. ... The wallpaper has been hung, but the doors and woodwork still have to be repainted.' (12 September.) 'The main reason for the delay is that it is taking the plaster so long to dry. They heat and heat, but not everywhere. ... The ceilings and one wall are already dry in the big hall and the drawing-room, and have turned from grey to white. ... The wallpaper in the corner room is too light, and too dark in the dining-room, but in your room and Tanya's it is perfect!' (14 September.) 'The banister is very handsome, but the rails are so far apart that a baby could easily squeeze between them. I shall talk to the contractor about it tomorrow.' (28 September.) 'My dream of stunning you with my remodelled house will not come true. I am afraid you will be disagreeably surprised by the disorder you will find when you arrive. But we can all move in, warm and dry.' (29 September.)

At first Sonya was amused by these technical reports, but she soon began to worry at the lack of affection in her husband's letters.

'You write of nothing but practical things,' she said. 'Do you think I am made of wood? Floors and toilets are not the only things in the world that interest me.'

On 8 October, the rest of the family arrived in the new house, where the table was laid for the travellers: cold meat, tea, fruit. Sonya went from room to room admiring her husband's taste; but the garden was the chief subject of enthusiasm.

It required a few weeks for the little tribe of eight children and twelve servants to divide up the rooms, unpack their belongings and adapt their habits to the new walls, furniture and echoes. Order was established. Lunch at one o'clock, dinner at six, evening tea at nine. There was a chef for the family and a woman cook for the staff. Each member of the family had his own place at the big table in the dining-room with its yellow walls and brown woodwork. Sonya presided; a voluminous soup tureen steamed on her right and a pile of soup plates mounted on her left; she filled them one after the other and a footman set them in front of each person in order of seniority. No wine, but a carafe of water and a jug of home-made kvass. Tolstoy had resolved to go on a vegetarian diet, as far as possible, and lived on oatmeal porridge, fruit jelly and preserves. This special menu suited both his philosophy and his lack of teeth. Conversation was always animated. The children whispered and teased each other. Chewing his bread in his toothless mouth, their father told a funny story, began to laugh before anyone else, and carried the whole table with him. Then, at a moment's notice, the grown-ups would begin to 'philosophize' and the youngsters to ache with boredom. At regular intervals a cuckoo clock on the wall uttered his wheezy hiccough.

When there was company, evening tea was served in the big white-walled drawing-room with its outsize table and massive mahogany chairs. Not one picture, not one rug on the bare, gleaming floorboards, and, in the place of honour, a piano, at which Tolstoy and Sonya sometimes sat to play four-hand duets. On reception days, forty-four candles in the hanging chandeliers and wall-sconces were lighted, in addition to the three kerosene lamps. Famous musicians and singers came to perform for the master. A few years later Chaliapin sang his greatest arias for him – 'Midnight', 'The Miller's Return', 'The Flea' – which he did not like as well as the folksongs sung by the same artist.

Tolstoy often left his wife and Tanya to receive their friends and hid himself away in his study, a little room half-way between the first and second floors, with bare walls painted pale green. To the left of the door stood a deal table covered with dark green felt, with three drawers and a railing around the top. No bric-à-brac, but two wooden-shafted penholders, a marble paperweight, a crystal ink-well, a goblet of ink, pen-wipers, folders and two bronze candlesticks. Tolstoy wrote by the light of a single candle. The corners of the room swam in darkness. He boasted that he didn't need glasses, but as he was really quite myopic he had his chair legs sawed off to bring the paper closer to his eyes. When he tired of working seated, he would get up, open a folding writing-desk and continue standing. Or else he would settle himself among the brown silk pillows on his imitation leather sofa and read and take notes with his legs tucked under him. A litter of papers and books in Russian, French, English and German spread all around him. More books were stacked inside the glass-front book-case.

Tolstoy had never felt more remote from Sonya. While she splashed about on the surface, he, or so he thought, was probing the lower depths. He listened to the jolly drawing-room gabble going on over his head, and wrote to an almost unknown correspondent, the young revolutionary Engelhardt:[16]

You cannot imagine how alone I am, how my true self is scorned by everyone around me. ... I am guilty, I live in sin, I deserve contempt because I do not practise what I preach, but I will say to you in reply, less to justify than to explain my weakness: look at my past life and look at my life now, and you will see that I am attempting to do what must be done; I have not achieved the thousandth part of it, true, not because I have not wanted to but because I did not know before. ... Judge me if you like; I judge myself severely enough! But do not judge the path I have chosen. I know which is the road that leads home and if I weave like a drunken man as I go down it that does not mean the road is the wrong one.

In order 'to weave as little as possible' going down his road, he got up in mid-winter while it was still dark, to the cry of the whistles summoning their workers to the nearby factories, did a few callisthenics with his dumbbells, dressed himself in peasant clothes, went down to the courtyard to draw the water, drag the huge tub through the snow on a little sled and fill the water pitchers; he split wood for the stoves, cleaned his room and then, sitting in the entryway, pulled open a drawer under a bench, took out wax and brushes and waxed his boots, proudly reminding himself that he had twelve servants and was taking care of himself. Moreover, it was his opinion that such menial tasks put one in a proper frame of mind for lofty thought. His mind bubbled and soared while his hands stayed earthbound, slaves to routine. He had become infatuated with Hebrew, which was to help him to a better understanding of the Gospels, and was taking lessons from Rabbi Minor. 'Leo is learning the Hebraic language, to my intense regret,' said Sonya. 'He is wasting his energy on foolishness.' And, 'This is the end of his literary career and it is a shame, a great shame!'

She unconsciously knew that whenever he began to write

a work of fiction, he drew closer to her. It was all this cloudy theology, this striving for a superhuman perfection, that separated them. She did not have what it took to be the wife of a saint. With objectivity and humility, she wrote to Tanya Kuzminskaya on 30 January 1883:

'Leo is very calm. He's working, writing articles and only occasionally showing his aversion to town life, especially that of the aristocracy. It is painful for me, but I know he cannot do otherwise. He is a man ahead of his time, he marches in front of the crowd and shows the way it must follow. And I am one of the crowd, I live with it and, with it, I see the light in the men ahead of their time, like Leo, and I say yes, that is the light, but I cannot walk any faster than the crowd to which I am bound; I am held back by my environment, by my habits.'

He, meanwhile, was writing in his diary:

'Again in Moscow, and again, for more than a month, enduring atrocious moral agonies, but not without progress. ... What you have done will not be truly good until you are no longer there to spoil it. ... One sows, the other reaps; you, Leo Nikolayevich, will not reap. ... I used to think it unfair that I should not be allowed to see the fruit of my labour, now I realize that it is not unfair, it is good and reasonable. ... Now it is clear: what you do out of love, without reaping any reward, is certainly the work of God.' [17]

For the New Year, 1883:

'Property defended by force – a policeman armed with a pistol – is bad. Make yourself a spoon and eat with that spoon as long as no one else needs it. That is what is certain. ... We live, therefore we are dying. To live well means to die well. The New Year. I make a wish, for myself and for all, that we may die well.'

Every minor illness, every death among his acquaintances, brought him back to the thought of his own end. The previous year he had been particularly distressed by the news that Ivan Turgenev was seriously ill in France. With his usual tact, he had hastened to inflict his compassion upon his unfortunate colleague: 'The news of your illness has caused me much sorrow ... especially when I was assured that it was serious. I realized how much I cared for you. I felt that I should be much grieved if you were to die before me.'[18]

Touched by this letter, Turgenev immediately replied, saying that, according to his doctors, he was suffering from 'angina pectoris with gout' – not, he believed, a dangerous disease. In fact, he had cancer of the bone marrow, which had momentarily subsided after the first warning signs. Between spoonfuls of medicine he still took an interest in literature. Much intrigued by Tolstoy's *Confession,* he asked him to send a lithographed copy; but after reading the book, so remote from his own convictions, he could not bring himself to enthuse to the author, and wrote to Grigorovich: '*Confession* is astonishing in its sincerity, truthfulness, persuasiveness; and yet it is built upon false premises and leads in the end to the most sombre negation of all human life. ... It is a sort of nihilism. ... This does not alter the fact that Tolstoy is, without doubt, the most remarkable man in Russia today.'[19]

Turgenev's condition grew worse at the beginning of 1883. He was tortured by excruciating pains shooting through his back. Nothing helped – poultices, chloroform or morphine; he screamed in agony. He had become cadaverously thin, and entreated Mme Viardot, who was nursing him devotedly, to heave him out the window. As soon as the warm weather came, he was carried – 'the patriarch of the molluscs', as he said – to Bougival, to the villa 'Les Frênes'. On 27 June, summoning his last remaining strength, he pencilled on a scrap of paper:

My good and dear Leo Nikolayevich, I have not written to you for a long time because I was and still am, to tell the truth, on my deathbed. I cannot get well, it is useless even to think it, I write you chiefly in order to tell you how happy I am to have been your contemporary and to make one last, sincere appeal to you. My friend, return to literature! That gift came to you from the same source as all the rest. Oh, how happy I should be to think that this letter might have some influence upon you! I am done for, the doctors don't even know what name to give my illness. Gouty stomach neuralgia! I can neither walk nor eat nor sleep. It bores me to talk about it. My friend, great writer of the Russian land, hear my prayer. Let me know you have received this scrap of paper, and allow me to embrace you once more, *hard*, very hard, you, your wife and all your family. I cannot go on, I am tired . . .

Tolstoy did not read this poignant letter until long afterwards. When it reached Moscow he was in Samara for his *kumys* treatment. Before that, he had gone to Yasnaya Polyana where, finding the village half-destroyed by fire, he directed emergency relief operations. Decidedly, however, he had no desire to handle his affairs alone. On 21 May 1883 he signed a power of attorney authorizing Sonya to manage all his property. Then he set off, at peace. Three days later he was in the old wooden house among the Bashkirs. What a disappointment! The farm was being badly mismanaged, half the colts had died during the winter and the harvest would be worthless. Discouraged, Tolstoy decided to sell the stock and stud farm and farm out the land. But he could not bear to witness the 'bargaining' between the steward and the prospective buyers.

On the other hand, he engaged in lengthy conversations with the Molokhan sectarians and his friends Alexeyev and Bibikov,* whom he liked less and less, and two militant socialists who had come to stay with them. These men had been involved in an important political trial; they bitterly defended the right to use violence and this infuriated Tolstoy, who did not agree. He was relieved when they left. The treatment was prolonged, he began to feel better. 'Although I am ashamed and disgusted to think of my base body, I know the *kumys* will be good for me, principally because it will regulate the functioning of my stomach, the

* Alexis Alexeyevich Bibikov; not to be confused with Alexander Nikolayevich Bibikov, Tolstoy's neighbour at Yasnaya Polyana.

effect of which will be to improve my nerves and put me in a better frame of mind,' he wrote to his wife.[20]

Once again the benefits of the *kumys* evaporated in the superficial and agitated atmosphere of Yasnaya Polyana in the summer. Back with his family in July 1883, he began again to suffer from nothing and everything. He had refused to serve as marshal of the nobility for the Krapivna district, in order to avoid even the slightest temptation to collaborate with the authorities. One day, returning home after a visit to an old muzhik on his deathbed, he heard his son Sergey playing Brahms's 'Hungarian Dances' on the piano. Startled, he hesitated for a moment, then flew into a red-hot rage: 'It isn't that particular thing I hold against him,' he said, 'but how strange: by our side are wretched souls lying ill and dying, and we don't even know they are there, we don't want to know it, we are playing joyful music!'[21]

Another day the guests suggested resuming the old game of 'post-box', and he proposed this thorny question for their meditation: 'Why must Ustyusha, Alyona, Peter, etc. [the servants] cook and prepare things, sweep, clear away and serve at table, and the gentlemen eat, gorge themselves, defecate and eat again?'

He made himself clearer in his next note, which also went into the 'post-box':

'Today, July 7, thirteen chickens were killed in the two houses;* July 8, one sheep was delivered to one house, salt-meat to the other; July 10, 11 and 12, thirty pounds of roast beef were brought to the two houses, forty pounds of beef for soup, two hens, seven chickens and a seventy-pound lamb ...'

Another variation:

'Timetable of activities at Yasnaya Polyana: 10 to 11 a.m., coffee indoors; 11 to noon, tea on the croquet lawn; noon to 1 p.m., lunch; 1 to 2 p.m., tea on the croquet lawn; 2 to 3 p.m., study; 3 to 5 p.m., swimming; 5 to 7 p.m, dinner;

* The main house at Yasnaya Polyana and the pavilion in which the Kuzminsky family stayed.

7 to 8 p.m., croquet and boating; 8 to 9 p.m, low tea; 9 to 10 p.m., high tea; 10 to 11 p.m., supper; and 11 p.m. to 10 a.m., sleep!'

The only work he could really enjoy was manual, so for several days he helped the peasants with the haying. His children brought him food in the fields, like a real muzhik. 'He is so free and gay, he has come back to us again!' his daughter Tanya gratefully noted. But he told a guest, Rusanov, 'I wish they would exile me or lock me up somewhere!' Once again, his eternal shame of his physical comfort, his yearning for some form of bodily suffering to crown and give substance to his mental anguish, his greedy envy of all who had the good fortune to be unfortunate.

On 2 September 1883 he learned that Ivan Turgenev, at the end of his strength, had died at Bougival on 22 August. He was instantly sorry he had not answered his colleague's last letter, so mournful and so tender. To be sure, Turgenev's pretensions to lead him, Leo Tolstoy, back to the paths of literature were absurd, but his intentions had been good. How death blots out all imperfections in the individual, and places him in a favourable light. Now that the author of *Smoke* was no more, Tolstoy was suddenly possessed of a consuming passion for him. He reread his complete works, sighing and weeping. 'I think of Turgenev continually, I love him terribly, I pity him, I read him, I live with him,' he wrote to Sonya, who was in Moscow. 'I have just finished his *Enough!* Read it! Magnificent!'

Could he recall that, some eighteen years before, he had abhorred the book for being 'full of false suffering'? [22]

Turgenev's body was brought back to Russia. Edmond About and Ernest Renan made speeches on the platform in the Paris railway station. In Moscow, the Society of Lovers of Russian Literature decided to organize an official ceremony in honour of the late, great author, and scheduled it for 23 October 1883. Tolstoy was approached to speak. What he had refused to do for Pushkin, he agreed to do for Turgenev. True, Dostoyevsky had died in the meantime, so there was no rival speaker on the programme. He conscientiously prepared to inter under posthumous praise the man he had so often buried in sarcasm during his lifetime. He recalled their first meetings, their conversations, their disputes, and in his memory everything became noble, beautiful and serene. Sonya was very excited at the prospect of this glorious occasion: 'All Moscow is already in an uproar,' she wrote to Tanya. 'They say there will be a huge crowd in the great hall of the University.' [23]

The powers-that-be thought so too, and took a very dim view of all this fuss and bother. Tolstoy had been under police surveillance for the past year. Spies reported that he had been to see the Molokhans in Samara, that he was inculcating false and dangerous notions about the equality of men into the muzhiks of Yasnaya Polyana and had publicly proclaimed that the Orthodox Church had distorted the teachings of Christ. On 28 September 1833, having been called to jury duty at Krapivna, he refused to serve on the pretext that his religious beliefs would not allow him to take part in an act of punishment. Cost of this offence: two hundred roubles. A trifle, in comparison with the moral satisfaction he felt as he walked, head high, out of the courtroom. But on 18 October the minister of the interior, his homonym Count Dmitry Andreyevich Tolstoy, submitted a paper to Alexander III on measures to be taken against the writer whose activities were in danger of 'undermining the people's confidence in justice and arousing the indignation of all true believers'. The tsar had not replied when the head of the department of press affairs notified the minister of the interior that Tolstoy was to make a speech at the ceremony in honour of Turgenev. 'Now,' pursued this well-informed official, 'Count Tolstoy is a madman; he is capable of anything; he may say all manner of outlandish things; and the scandal will not be a small one!' The minister of the interior immediately sent off a coded telegram to Prince Dolgorukov, governor general of Moscow, ordering all memorial speeches for Turgenev to be submitted for prior approval. Prince Dolgorukov sent for the president of the Society of Lovers of Russian Literature and strongly 'advised' him to postpone the ceremony, indefinitely. And so, because of Tolstoy, Turgenev was deprived of the homage his fellow citizens had wanted to pay him. The friendship of these two men had been decidedly star-crossed.

In Ivan Turgenev, Tolstoy had lost one steadfast and sincere admirer; but another, of a very different sort, was to emerge from the autumn mists that same year, 1883. The newcomer was named Vladimir Grigoryevich Chertkov, and belonged to the St Petersburg aristocracy. His father, a general and aide-de-camp to the tsar, had a huge fortune; his mother, née Chernishev-Kuglikov, was an intimate friend of the empress. He himself, after graduating from the military academy, had chosen to make his career in the army. Handsome, rich, elegant, impeccably educated, he could expect, thanks to his parents' connexions, a brilliant future in uniform. Yet, as early as 1879, he contemplated resigning his commission to devote himself to social work. At his father's behest, he agreed to confine himself to applying for a year's leave of absence and, after a long stay in England, he returned to his horse guards, albeit with heavy heart. Before, he had played cards, drunk and flirted with the girls, but he no longer derived the slightest pleasure from joining his comrades in their debauchery. His dream now was to retire to his family estate in order to live in closer union with the peasants. He had already read the works of Tolstoy. He felt there must be a communion of thought between them. He went to call on him in Moscow.

At first, Tolstoy was flattered to see that his philosophy had touched not only the 'Dark Ones' of town and country – the ragged sectarians and dishevelled nihilists – but also a man of the best society, a landowner and guards officer. He looked with friendly approval upon the tall thirty-year-old man with the receding hairline, aquiline nose and well-tailored uniform, who was telling him how he wished to leave the army. Master and disciple agreed that military service was incompatible with the doctrine of Christ. Then Tolstoy read his visitor passages from *What I Believe*, which he had just finished. 'The realization that my period of moral isolation was over at last gave me such joy,' Chertkov later said, 'that, lost in my own thoughts, I paid no attention to the passages he was reading to me; I only came to my senses when, after reading the last lines of the work, he pronounced the author's name with peculiar emphasis: "Leo Tolstoy".'

Then and there, with radiant vanity, Chertkov announced that he was his host's 'co-thinker'. He was certain that his fervour was as necessary to Tolstoy as Tolstoy's teachings were to him. The two men parted company affectionately.

A short time later, Chertkov resigned from the army. Tolstoy's first letter to him began with the words: 'Very dear, very kind and very close to me Vladimir Grigoryevich ...' It was as though he were writing to his spiritual son. Sonya herself admitted that, for the first time, one of her husband's followers had some class and decent manners, and when he came back, she received him cordially. She soon observed, however, that this new type of disciple was more intransigent than his master on questions of doctrine. Chertkov had a narrow, systematizing mind, and was so attached to Tolstoy's ideas that he would not suffer him to depart one iota from them himself. On any and every matter, however trifling, he would respectfully call the master to order in the name of Tolstoyism. Instinctively, he sided with the thought against the thinker, with the work against the man. At first, the family was amused by his stern application of the rules. Then Sonya dimly began to sense that a rival had crept under her roof and, uneasy and uncertain, she put up her guard.

On 18 February 1884 the police seized all the copies of

What I Believe at the Kushnerev printing-works. 'I hope after this he will calm down and write nothing more in this vein!' Sonya wailed to her sister. Urged on by Chertkov, however, Tolstoy was working furiously away at his new essay, *What Then Must We Do?*

PART VI

===

THIS LOATHSOME
FLESH

[22]

The Temptation of Sainthood

ON 30 January 1884 Countess Tolstoy and her eldest daughter, in full evening dress, attended the ball given by Prince Dolgorukov, governor general of Moscow – the man who, three months before, had decreed that the ceremonies in honour of Turgenev could not take place because Leo Tolstoy was to speak. 'The governor general had a chair brought and sat next to me,' the dazzled countess wrote to her husband, 'and for one whole hour he talked to me as though he wished to show me a mark of special favour. ... He also paid thousands of compliments to Tanya.' Sonya's letter, bubbling over with socialite vivacity, crossed one from Tolstoy at Yasnaya Polyana, proudly announcing that he was making a pair of shoes for their old servant Agatha Mikhailovna, whose feast-day was on 5 February.

Every evening he went to the isba of Arbuzov or Mitrofan, the village cobbler, and humbly drove pegs and punched holes with his awl under the half-amused, half-fearful eyes of the muzhiks. 'How clean, how morally elegant everything is in their dirty, dark hole!' he said. And, 'All it takes to give new life to the soul is to enter the dwelling of a workman!'[1]

Back in Moscow, he wanted to continue his apprenticeship and had a workshop set up next to his study. He bought tools and leather. A pensive, bashful cobbler with a thick black beard came to give him regular lessons. An oddly-shaped stove stood by the window against the bench, intended both to heat and ventilate the room. In spite of this device, a cloying odour of leather and tobacco assailed one in the doorway. The cobbler came at fixed hours and was admitted by a white-gloved, liveried lackey; walking on tip-toe, his head screwed down between his shoulders and his eyes darting off into the corners, he joined the count in his grey blouse and sat down beside him on a stool. Work began: wax the thread, stitch, shape the quarters, nail on the sole, mount the heel. ... Humped over his bench, Tolstoy grunted and cursed, trying to drive the wooden pegs into the soles.

'Let me do that, Leo Nikolayevich,' the cobbler would say.

'No, no! You do your job and I'll do mine!' growled the pupil.[2]

Friends and admirers came to see the writer in action and were amazed at his perseverance in a trade at which, try as he like, he could never excel. He explained to the sceptics that no one had the right to profit from the labour of the poor without giving them as much in return. He made a pair of boots for his friend Sukhotin, who stood them up in his bookcase next to the first twelve volumes of Tolstoy's works, bearing the label 'Volume XIII'. And Fet, in exchange for a pair of shoes, gave the cobbler–author a certificate stating that they had been made 'to order, by Count Leo Tolstoy, author of *War and Peace*'.

The joys of bootmaking were soon augmented by the discovery of Chinese philosophy. He read Confucius and Lao-tzu and recognized his own ideas in oriental disguise. 'One must make a circle of reading for oneself,' he wrote, 'Epictetus, Marcus Aurelius, Lao-tzu, Buddha, Pascal, the Gospels. Everyone should do it.' What would he have given to see his wife following him in this praiseworthy enterprise. But she refused to leave the flock. When he needed her, he had to look for her in the world of other people. Every time, he came back from the country with a renewed appetite for her. Even though, at forty, she was matronly and faded, she remained extremely desirable. After weeks of privation he could not contain himself, he took her, roughly, rapidly, to relieve himself and exorcise the evil spirit, and when it was over he went back to his philosophy, pacified.

Early in 1884 she found to her despair that she was pregnant for the twelfth time. This succession of pregnancies now humiliated her. She was no longer a woman, she thought, she was a brood mare, a vase, good only to receive the master's seed and germinate his progeny. 'It's too bad,' she wrote to her sister Tanya on 5 February 1884, 'that I won't be confined before we go to Yasnaya Polyana. I should so like to get this ghastly thing over with in solitude.' And on 22 March, 'This year I am going to Yasnaya Polyana to be tormented instead of happy. The best season – swimming, haying, long days, wonderful moonlit nights – I'll be spending in bed in the company of a squawling baby. I'll take a wetnurse.' She complained to Tolstoy, and he was incensed at her for daring to disparage the holy state of motherhood. 'Her nerves are badly strained,' he noted. 'Her pregnancy is an obsession with her. It is a great, a very great sin. A shame!'[3]

The truth is that he could not have approved her without condemning himself to continence, since for him conception was the sole justification of physical relations between couples. With a woman who refused to have children the act of love became a lewd farce. No concern for mere beauty could prevail against divine law. Nor any fatigue. So long as the male could procreate, the female must lend him her womb. And Tolstoy was full of sap, eager to spread and multiply. How admirable that religion and nature agreed on this point.

Without telling her husband, Sonya went to Tula to be aborted by a midwife. But when the woman heard her caller's name she became frightened and refused the job. Then Sonya tried to abort herself by taking scalding baths and jumping off the top of a dresser with her feet held together.[4] To no avail.

Meanwhile Tolstoy, busy with his own thoughts, daily noted in his diary all his grounds for dissatisfaction with his family life. 'It distresses me greatly, but I cannot approve of them. Their joys – success at school or social success, music, physical comfort, shopping – I consider them all bad for them, but I cannot say so out loud. I might, but nobody would pay any attention to me. What seems to count for them is not the meaning of my words but the fact that I have the deplorable habit of repeating them. In my moments of weakness – this is one now – I am amazed by their lack of pity. How can they fail to see not only that I am suffering, but that I have ceased to live at all for the last three years? I am condemned to play the part of a grumbling old man and as far as they are concerned I can play no other; but if I joined them, I would be deserting the truth, and they would be the first to let me know I had defected!' (4 April.) 'Poor creature [Sonya], how she hates me! My God, help me! I don't mind bearing a cross, so long as it demolishes me completely. But this emotional tug-of-war is awful, painful and sad.' (3 May.) 'I saw in a dream that my wife loved me. Everything immediately became light and sunny. The truth is nothing like that. It is poisoning my existence. It would be so good to die.' (5 May.) 'I am suffering atrociously. Her soul is obtuse and dead; that I could bear, if that were all; but she is insolent and self-assured. ... I ought to be able to put up with her out of pity, at least, if not love.' (20 May.) 'I have the feeling that I am the only sane man in a madhouse run by a madman. ' (28 May.) 'The dreadful thing about it is that the luxury and sin in which I live were created by me; I am corrupt myself and incapable of doing anything about it. I cannot break the habit of smoking, I cannot devise a way of treating my wife without offending her and I cannot allow her to go on without any restraint. ... I keep looking. I try. ...' (29 May.) 'Why, really, am I necessary to them? What is the use of all this brain-beating? However hard the life of a vagabond (and it is not so hard as all that!), it cannot be anything like the agony I endure.' (4 June.)

He had cut down his cigarette ration and given up eating

meat and white bread, and tried to steady his nerves by working in the fields with the muzhiks. But he need only enter the house to return to the 'life of debasement' in the person of his sons, sprawled about in armchairs, his too well-dressed daughter, Sonya with her swollen stomach, her face drawn by her pregnancy and her eyes full of resentment. On the evening of 17 June he had a stupid quarrel with her in the garden over the sale of some horses, which he had carried out without consulting her. As her voice began to rise, he suddenly felt that his cup was running over, the camel's back was breaking, he had to get away. He ran to his bedroom, grabbed up a knapsack, threw some clothes and his toilet articles into it, slung it over his shoulder and came out shouting that he was going to Paris or America. His daughter Tanya watched him go down the drive towards the Tula road. Sitting in front of the house, Sonya, her labour pains beginning, clutched her stomach and sobbed hysterically. Her second son Ilya came running, helped her to her feet and half-carried her to her room.

Tolstoy strode along the road under the moonlight at a furious pace. He had thought of leaving his wife before, since she kept saying how tired she was, of taking some broad-hipped young peasant woman with a bosom made for nursing and setting off for parts unknown, joining some group of emigrants. Once, in a burst of honesty, he had even told Sonya of his plan. She had not believed him. Now he was going alone. Without preparation. Besides, he didn't know where he was going. Halfway to Tula his conscience began to nag. Did he have the right, morally, to leave his wife just when she was about to give him another child? In his wrath he had forgotten this detail. Reluctantly, he turned back. He became gloomier with every step that brought him closer to the entrance towers of the estate. 'In the house,' he wrote, 'I saw two bearded muzhiks playing *vint* – my two young sons. Their sister Tanya said, "Have you seen her? . . ." I answered, 'I don't even want to see her!' And I came into my study to sleep on the couch. But I am too weighed down with sorrow to sleep. It's too painful. Now I feel sorry for her. I cannot believe she is made entirely of stone.'

At three in the morning, just as he was about to drift off, Sonya, distraught and haggard, dragged herself to his room: 'Forgive me,' she said. 'The child is coming. Maybe I shall die! ...' He did not say a word, but stared fixedly at her and helped her to her room. The pains were coming faster. The midwife – the one from Tula? – sent the count out of the room.

In the morning of 18 June 1884 Sonya gave birth to a daughter, Alexandra, called Sasha. While the exhausted mother lay in her bed, Tolstoy was writing: 'This event, which should have filled the family with joy and happiness, resembled some pointless and painful ordeal. A wetnurse was engaged. If there is someone directing the course of our lives, I feel like complaining to him. It's too hard and too cruel. ... Cruel for her. I see her heading for her ruin, and dreadful moral suffering. ... I have stopped drinking wine, I drink tea and suck on a lump of sugar, I eat no meat, I am still smoking, but less.' (18 June 1884.)

For the first time he confessed – to his brother Sergey who had come over from Pirogovo to congratulate the mother – that he was unhappy in his marriage and did not know what to do to get out of this 'dreadful predicament'. He also confided his grievances, by letter, to his new 'co-thinker' Chertkov. Now there was a wonderful disciple, understanding, dedicated, uncompromising! 'He coincides uncannily with me!' he wrote.[5] He had a nightmare, however, that was as disturbing as an evil omen: 'I saw Chertkov in my dream. Suddenly he began leaping about, he was nothing but skin and bones, I realized that he had gone mad!'[6] What a pity that Chertkov's soul and Sonya's body could not be joined together to form one person. Many times, simply looking at her, with her round neck and broad waist and red mouth, he was on the point of forgiving her everything, even the fact that she refused to nurse the baby.

Then one remark led to another; his patience at an end, he stormed out, slamming the door; she ran after him, wheedling, begging his pardon. 'She tries to win me with her body,' he wrote. 'I struggle to resist, but I know I cannot, the way things are now. And living with a woman who is a stranger to your soul is horrible!'

On 7 July, another scene. Tolstoy, beside himself, wrote some ominous sentences in his diary: 'Until the day I die she will be a stone around my neck and the necks of my children. I must learn not to drown with this stone around my neck.'

Later, lying beside her in bed after the light was out, desire awoke in him again. A certain warmth, something in the odour of her skin and hair made him dizzy. He wanted to hurl himself upon her as he used to do, drown his sorrows in the pleasures of his senses. She refused him. It was hardly a month since the baby was born. It was too soon, she told him. He was hurt by the tone in which she rebuffed him – cold, 'wilfully mean'. She was simply provoking him, of course. He could not sleep all night. He wanted to run away again. He got up and packed his knapsack, woke up his wife and, trembling with desire, disgust and resentment, poured out everything he had on his mind: 'I told her she was no longer a wife to me. A helpmeet for her husband? She ceased to be a help to me long ago, she is a hindrance! A mother to her children? She refuses. A nurse? She won't. The companion of my nights? She provokes me, she makes it into a game. It was very unpleasant, and I felt how weak and pointless it was. I was wrong not to go. I think it will happen, sooner or later.'[7]

That night, or another soon afterwards, she yielded to his importunities. Complications and pains followed, and Tolstoy became alarmed. The midwife came to the rescue, and forbade 'intimate relations between husband and wife'. In dismay, the fifty-six-year-old husband rebuked himself for his brutality and raw schoolboy haste. 'The midwife prescribes a strict *diet* (you can guess what I mean!) for a month

at least,' Sonya wrote to her sister on 23 September 1884. 'I
have been ordered to remain seated or lying down, not to
walk, not to go out driving, not to get upset – nothing! It's a
nuisance, but what can I do? I did not take care of myself
before my confinement and I was not spared by others after
it. ... Lyovochka is quite alarmed and full of consideration
for me, although he is unpleasantly surprised by my condition.' This enforced chastity so tormented Lyovochka that
he advanced the date of his wife's departure for Moscow,
hoping to kill temptation by removing it.

Left alone at Yasnaya Polyana he thought of her constantly – as a male, 'as a muzhik', he confessed in his letters.
He begged her not to pay too much attention to what the
Moscow doctors would say, as 'they can only ruin our lives'.
And with what huge satisfaction he described his healthy,
simple life in the country, working with his hands, striving
for humility and talking to no one but the peasants. A little
irritated by this homily, Sonya tartly replied:

I see you have stayed on at Yasnaya Polyana to play at Robin-
son Crusoe, not to do the intellectual work I value above
everything else. ... No doubt you will say this is the life that
corresponds to your convictions and you enjoy it. That is another
matter. All I can say is, 'Be happy, much good may it do you!'
All the same, though, it makes me sad to see such intellectual
power as you have going to waste chopping wood, heating the
samovar and making boots. These may be ideal as relaxation
after work, but not as occupations in themselves. Ah, well, we'll
speak no more of that! ... I comfort myself with the saying,
'Never mind what game the baby plays, as long as it keeps him
from crying.'

She was afraid her sarcasm might sting too sharply,
however, and ended her letter on a conciliatory note:

'Farewell, my beloved, I kiss you tenderly. Suddenly I can
see you clearly, and I feel my heart swelling with love.
There is something wise and good in you, innocent and
obstinate, that no one has but you, and it is illuminated by
your affectionate solicitude for everyone around you and

your look that pierces straight to the depths of every soul.'[8]

Still under the effect of this wifely homage, Tolstoy learned the following day that Dr Chizh had confirmed the midwife's fears and recommendations. Dismayed, he gave free rein to his remorse:

'Yesterday I received the letter you sent after seeing the doctor, and it has grieved and pained me, and above all, disgusted me with myself. All this is nobody's fault but my own, brutal, selfish beast that I am! And I set myself out to judge others and ape righteousness! I cannot tell you how upset I am. Yesterday I saw myself in a dream, full of contempt for myself.'[9]

'Why, my beloved, do you worry so about my condition?' she answered. 'You are absolutely not to blame; we are both at fault; perhaps it is the result of some mechanical thing that went wrong when the baby was being born. Yesterday I was in great pain, something was flowing inside me as though an abscess had burst, but today there's not a drop and the pain is much less.'[10]

And two days later: 'Oh, Lyovochka, if I were to write to you at the times when I want to see you so badly, and tell you all I feel for you, I should burst into such a torrent of passionate, demanding words that you would be submerged by them. Sometimes I suffer from your absence more than I can tell. ... But as I have told you before, I would suffer more to see you miserable in Moscow than not to see you at all. And just now you are in such a good mood! Your love of music, your impressions of nature, your desire to write, those are you, the *real* you, the one you want to kill; but in spite of everything, that one remains wonderful, full of poetry, and so good, the one all your friends love in you. And you will not kill him, no matter how hard you try.'

While these protestations of love, hyperbolic praise and tender counsels were flying back and forth between Moscow and Yasnaya Polyana, Sonya was not losing sight of the material side of the household. Since her husband was absorbed in his meditations and would not stoop to glance at the accounts, she was forced to replace him as master of the house. And its steadily mounting expenses worried her. According to her calculations, they needed 910 roubles a month* to manage; 203 for the children's education (including the salaries of two governesses and two schoolmistresses), 98 for the servants and 609 for expenses and food. She informed Tolstoy of this and added that it was impossible to reduce these expenses and she wondered how much longer they would be able to meet them.

From the depths of his retreat, the philosopher smiled. How could Sonya, his wife, fail to realize that such trivialities merited no more than the contempt of the righteous?

Don't be angry, my darling, I simply cannot attach any importance to these money problems [he wrote to her]. These are not events, such as an illness, for example, or a marriage or birth or the acquisition of new knowledge or a good or bad deed or the praiseworthy or blameworthy habits of beings near and dear to us; this is a matter of our personal arrangements, and if we arranged things one way before, we can always arrange them differently now, in a hundred different ways. I know it annoys you often and the children always, but I must repeat that our happiness or unhappiness does not depend upon whether we spend or earn money, but upon what we make of ourselves.[11]

Had she been able to read the outline for an ideal existence for himself and his family which her husband had conceived and inscribed in his notebook that very summer, Sonya would in all likelihood have been appalled:

Live at Yasnaya Polyana. Give the income from the Samara farm to the poor. Same for the money from Nikolskoye, after distributing the land to the muzhiks. For us, that is for my wife, myself and the younger children, keep two thousand to three thousand roubles† of the income from Yasnaya Polyana as a provisional measure. ('As a provisional measure,' i.e., with the ultimate design of turning the money over to others later and restricting our own needs as far as possible; in a word, give

---

* Or $2,600 – $570 plus $280 plus $1.700.
† Or $5,600 to $8,500.

more than we take, which is the supreme goal of all our efforts and the joy of our existence! ...) Keep only those servants who are necessary to teach us their work and transform us, after which, having learned what to do, we will dispense with their services. All live together, the men in one room, the women and girls in another. One room must be a library for intellectual work, another must be a workshop. As an indulgence, we might also provide a separate room for those who cannot resist. ... On Sunday, dinner for us and the poor, readings, conversation. Our life, food and clothes will be of the utmost simplicity. Everything superfluous, piano, furniture, coach horses, will be sold or given away. Concentrate exclusively on the sciences and arts that can be understood by all. Equal treatment for all, from governor to beggar.

When, captivated by this mirage, Tolstoy returned to Moscow on 3 November 1884 and found the big house with its servants, schoolmistresses, indolent children, shiny new furniture, polished floors and white tablecloths, he had a rude awakening. He was forced to admit that Sonya had reason to be alarmed by the growing strain on the family budget. Since it was out of the question to change their style of life overnight, literature would have to fill in the gaps left by agriculture. But since Lyovochka had stopped writing novels his royalties had fallen off considerably. He couldn't care less, of course; but it kept Sonya awake at night.

Suddenly she had an idea that would save them all! Why should the profits from the sale of his books go to others? Following the example of Dostoyevsky's widow, Countess Tolstoy would publish her husband's works too.

At first Tolstoy was horrified at this mercenary scheme, but he eventually admitted that in the present state of their finances he had nothing better to offer. He, who devoutly desired to abandon his land to the muzhiks, refuse the income from his writing and live half-naked – here he was, literally about to sell his soul in order to please his family. To avoid compromising his principles entirely, he decided to sign over to Sonya the right to manage his copyrights as

well as his property, which she was already handling. That
way, at least, he would not have to soil his own hands in
these diabolical affairs of money. As a matter of form, she
protested that he was trying to push over on to her what he
regarded as a foul sin, but at heart she was delighted. As a
limitation upon this concession to filthy money, he decided
to restrict his wife's rights to the titles published prior to
1881, the year of his 'rebirth'. But the titles published before
1881 included *War and Peace*, *Anna Karenina*, *The Cossacks*, *Childhood*, *Boyhood*, *Youth* and the *Sevastopol
Sketches*: the cream of his literary production.

Sonya immediately saw the enormity of the task that lay
before her, as well as the profits that could accrue to the
family from it. Overworked as she was, as wife, mother and
head of the household, she valiantly launched out in her
new business venture. Capital was needed. She borrowed ten
thousand roubles from her mother and fifteen thousand
from Stakhovich, a landowner and friend of the family. In a
pavilion next to the main house on Khamovnichesky Street,
she opened the 'Publishing Office for the Complete Works
of Leo Tolstoy'. Every time he passed the sign Tolstoy glowered. It was himself they were selling in there. He, whose
writing should have been a gift to mankind! After publicly
proclaiming his indifference to worldly goods, he might well
be taken for a hypocrite now, incapable of practising what
he preached. And all this in order that his daughter could
buy more dresses and his sons stuff their faces! Soon piles of
books mounted inside the shed. A clerk was hired to take
charge of their distribution to booksellers. The money began to come in ...

Fortunately, to offset the degrading effects of this commerce, the pure, the irreplaceable Chertkov had suggested
another, perfectly in keeping with the master's principles.
Together they would found a publishing company, the Intermediary, to produce small, inexpensive, high-quality
books for the common people. A publisher, Ivan Sitin,
agreed to print and sell these booklets. The secretarial work

was entrusted to a friend of Chertkov's named Paul Biryukov, a cultivated young aristocrat who had abandoned a
career in the navy to devote himself to the ideas of Leo
Tolstoy.* Together, Tolstoy and Chertkov selected the
texts. The first series included three stories by Tolstoy: *A
Captive in the Caucasus*, *What Men Live By*, and *God Sees
the Truth but Waits*, and a story by Leskov: *Christ Visits a
Peasant*. Other 'popular' stories by Tolstoy followed, works
by Russian and foreign authors, translations of the classical
philosophers.

At the helm, Chertkov proved a remarkable organizer
and a stern defender of the Tolstoyan faith. He cared less
for the artistic value of the works than for their potential
influence upon the masses. Often, to point some moral lesson
more strongly, he demanded that Tolstoy revise sentences
that might create confusion in a simple mind. Although
annoyed by this uncompromising rigour, the author ultimately yielded to the arguments of the critic. Little by little,
Chertkov was becoming a cumbersome incarnation of Tolstoy's own conscience. However, the little books of the Intermediary series – costing five kopecks apiece – were selling
by the thousands all over Russia. The author gained nothing from them, except greater fame. In six years, more than
twenty million copies were printed.

Not to be outdone, Sonya, too, printed, published and
sold. But her firm, unlike the Intermediary, was distinctly
profit-making. In February 1885 she went to St Petersburg
with her daughter Tanya, to apply to the administration
for authorization to include in her husband's *Complete
Works* such hitherto unapproved titles as *Confession*, *What
I Believe* and *What Then Must We do?* Permission was refused. However, she took advantage of her stay in the capital to call on Dostoyevsky's widow. The two authors'
wives-turned-businesswomen amicably compared notes. Mrs
Dostoyevsky, who had more experience, gave Mrs Tolstoy

* Paul Biryukov, introduced to Tolstoy on 21 November 1884, later
became his devoted biographer.

some sound advice. They talked cost price, handling expenses, registration and profit margins as they sipped their tea. 'In the last two years she has netted 67,000 roubles,' Sonya enthused. 'I was very surprised when she told me she only gives five per cent to the booksellers.' [12]

She was even more affected by another encounter. While she and Tanya were paying a social call to her aunt Shostak, the empress was suddenly announced. Flutter in the drawing-room. The hostess snatched up her cane and limped hastily to the door. The ladies sank into deep curtsies. 'I came forward,' Sonya wrote to her husband, 'and Mrs Shostak presented me to the empress. Then she presented Tanya. I said, *"Ma fille"*. I frankly admit that I was in a dither, but I kept my wits about me.'

Amiable and languid, the empress began a conversation with Sonya, in French:

'Have you been here long?'

'No, Madame, only since yesterday.'

'Is your husband well?'

'How kind of Your Majesty to inquire. He is very well.'

'I hope he is writing?'

'No, Madame, not just now; but I believe he is planning something for the schools, along the lines of *What Men Live By*.'

At that point, old Mrs Shostak intervened with a honeyed smile:

'He will never write another novel. He said so to Countess Alexandra Tolstoy.'

Turning to Sonya, the empress murmured:

'And do you not wish him to? That surprises me!'

Sonya, taken aback, could not think what to answer and, with a naïve ignorance of etiquette, suddenly said:

'I hope Your Majesty's children have read my husband's books.'

The empress nodded magnanimously and uttered, with a smile:

'Oh, I believe they have.'

After reporting this conversation word for word in her letter to Lyovochka and the children, Sonya bubbled:

'I can hear you now. You're saying, "Maman's head's been turned." Truly, this meeting was the last thing in the world I was expecting.'[13]

Lyovochka's answer was acid:

'That certainly was a stroke of luck! You wanted it so badly, that meeting. I am highly flattered by your account, but I dislike it. Nothing good can come of this. I remember there always used to be a man in the Pavlovsk Park, sitting among the bushes imitating the song of the nightingale. One day I struck up a conversation with him and from his unpleasant way of speaking I gathered he was connected with some member of the imperial family. Take care that the same thing doesn't happen to you.'

And he added:

'Why did you speak to her of what I am not writing instead of what I am writing? Were you too timid?'[14]

Sonya returned to Moscow at the end of February 1885, and on 12 March Tolstoy left for the Crimea with his friend Leonid Urusov, vice-governor of Tula, who was in the final stages of tuberculosis.

He was moved to see Sevastopol again – the heights where he had camped, the sites of the enemy cannon, all those places where violence and terror had once reigned. As he went over his war memories in his mind he felt, to his own astonishment, 'a flush of energy and youth'. Finding a half-buried cannonball, he even persuaded himself that it had been shot by a cannon from his own regiment, and was childishly pleased at the thought. Everything that belonged to his past – even his soldiering days – was pleasant; everything that belonged to his present – even his children – was a burden.

The moment he returned to Moscow, he wrote in his notebook:

Today I thought about my poor family: my wife, my sons, my daughters, who live with me and carefully erect screens between themselves and me in order not to see what is true and good. . . . If only they could understand that there can be only one justification for idleness made possible by others' labour: to devote all their leisure to thinking and understanding themselves. Instead of which, they spend it in futile rushing about, with the result that they have less time for thinking about themselves than labourers burdened by overwork. . . . I have wondered why so many intelligent and good men live so blindly and badly. The reason lies in the power that women have over them. They let themselves be carried along by the current because that is what their wives or mistresses want. The whole story is told in bed.[15]

He, at any rate, did not intend to be the victim of woman's wiles, the victim of a bed. He might occasionally give in to sensuality, but he immediately caught himself up again. He spent the entire summer at Yasnaya Polyana, working in the fields and writing stories for the Intermediary,* revising his essay *What Then Must We Do?* and working on a long story, *The Death of Ivan Ilich*, which was moving ahead by fits and starts, depending on his mood. Chertkov and Biryukov came to see him, and it seemed to him that they had a most beneficial influence on his daughters. In October 1885, having stayed on alone, he received a letter from the eldest, Tanya, that was so reasonable he could hardly believe his eyes. In spite of Sonya, the girl was timidly beginning to turn towards her father's ideas.

'For the first time you acknowledge that your view of the world has changed,' he replied on 18 October. 'My only hope, the only joy I dare look forward to, is to find brothers and sisters among my family instead of what I have seen in it thus far: remoteness, systematic disparagement and contempt, not for me but for the truth – unless it is a fear of something, I don't know what. And what a great shame it is! Death will come tomorrow. Must I take away with me this vague sense of misunderstanding between myself and mine, worse than between strangers? I am afraid for you,

*In particular, *Three Old Men* and *Ivan the Fool*.

because of your weakness, your natural tendency to indifference, and I would like to help you.'

In Moscow, however, the smiles of his two elder daughters were not enough to reconcile him to his family's way
of life. He suspected Sonya of sabotaging his theories behind his back, in her relations with the children. With remarkable candour, she had written what she thought of him
the previous year. He had kept the letter, and every time he
read it he received a chilling impression of narrow-mindedness and defeat.

Yes, you and I have been following different paths since childhood. You love the country, the people, the peasant children,
you love the primitive life you abandoned when you married
me. I am a city dweller, and no matter how I try to reason with
myself and force myself to love the country and the common
people, I shall never be able to devote myself to them body and
soul. I do not understand and never shall understand the
peasants. What I love is nature and nature alone, and with
nature I could joyfully spend the rest of my days. Your description of the little muzhiks, the life of the people, etc., your tales
and your conversations – it is all exactly the same as in the days
of your school at Yasnaya Polyana. But it is too bad that you
care so little for your own children. If they belonged to some
peasant woman it would be a different story! [16]

That woman certainly did not understand him. She
nursed him, copied his manuscripts, published his works, ran
to St Petersburg to plead with the censorship committee, but
she was not, really, an ally. What bothered him most was
that she was making so much money from his books. She
had just placed an advertisement in the newspapers, to
bring in more subscribers. He was ashamed. And yet he
could not deny that he, like the rest of his family, lived on
the profits. Exasperated beyond endurance, he began to
write to Chertkov:

At the *gymnasium* (and the younger ones at home), the
children learn things – in particular a catechism – that they will

need to know later at school. . . . Not one of them reads what I have written on these subjects; either they don't listen to what I say or they make some sharp retort; they don't see what I am doing, or they refuse to see. . . . During the last few days, the subscription and sale of my books has begun, on terms that are very advantageous for us and very hard on the booksellers. I go out and see a buyer looking at me, the humbug, the man who writes against property and, through my wife's business, extorts every cent he can out of the people who read him. Ah, if only someone could trumpet the ignominy of it all in the newspapers, loud and clear and devastating! . . . In the family, my daughters are my one, slender consolation. They love me as I should be loved and they love what I love.[17]

He did not have the heart to send this letter; it became irrelevant before he had finished writing it. After supper on 18 December 1885 a quarrel broke out between him and his wife, presumably on the subject of the 'lie' of their life together. Frightened by the loud voices, the older children came running and froze at the foot of the stairs leading up to their parents' room. Sitting side by side in the hallway Tanya, Ilya, Leo and Masha[18] (aged twenty-one, nineteen, sixteen and fourteen, respectively) listened to the family tempest, the most violent their ears had recorded to date. Their father was announcing to their mother that he had had enough, he meant to leave her and, once again, set off for Paris or America! 'When you overload the cart the horse just stops, he can't pull any more!' he shouted. And, with fearful violence: 'You poison the very air around you!' The walls were shaking. No one dared interfere. 'Neither of them,' Tanya wrote later, 'would give an inch. They were both defending something more important to them than life: for her it was her children's welfare, and she loved them to distraction; he, in defending his soul, was fighting for what he loved above all else: truth.'[19] A little later the children saw a servant go by carrying an empty trunk. They realized that their mother was getting ready to leave home. They rushed up the stairs and flung themselves upon her, weeping, 'Stay, Maman, stay!' Sonya, her eyes hot with tears, let herself be persuaded. But the moment she calmed down, it was Lyovochka's turn to become hysterical. 'He was trembling and shaking all over with sobs,' she wrote her sister on 20 December. 'I felt sorry for him.'

The next day Tolstoy, too unnerved to resume his regular life with her, decided to take his daughter Tanya to the estate of some friends of his, the Olsufyevs, forty miles outside Moscow. Tanya was delighted by this escapade and bursting with pride to take her mother's place beside her father. On his desk he left a letter, no more nor less than an open indictment of his wife, who was stunned by it:

For the last seven or eight years every conversation between us has ended, after painful conflict, with this: I tell you there can be no understanding or love between us until you have reached the same point as I have, whether out of love for me, or instinctively, or by personal conviction. ... If my conscience and reason command me to do something, I cannot disobey them and remain at peace; nor can I calmly look on while those I love, who know what conscience and reason command, disobey them too. ... By some tragic misunderstanding you failed to realize the depth of the crisis that has altered my entire life, and you responded to it with open hostility, or as though it were some abnormal, clinical phenomenon you had to deal with. ... Everything that was important and precious to me became hateful to you; our quiet, modest, admirable life in the country, the people in it. ... Then you began to treat me as though I were mentally unbalanced. You have always been bold and resolute, but from that moment on your determination became hard as rock, as happens with people who are nursing patients whom everybody knows to be deranged. ... Our move to Moscow, the organization of our new life, our children's education, all of that was so alien to me that I was not even able to protest against what seemed to me to be evil. ... And thus a year went by, two years, five years. The children have grown and their corruption with them, we have drifted steadily apart and my position has steadily become more false and painful ...

I can see only three alternatives: 1. Act upon my rights and distribute all my property to those to whom it rightfully be-

longs, I mean the workers; in a word, give it to anybody, simply
to deliver my children, big and little, from temptation and
damnation; but I would be forcing this upon them, and that
would provoke their anger and irritation and frustration and the
result would be even worse. 2. Abandon my family; but then I
would be leaving them to their fate and depriving them of my
influence, which I believe ineffectual but which does, perhaps,
make some slight impression upon them; I would be condemning
my wife and myself to live apart, and in so doing would be dis-
obeying God's commandments. 3. Continue to live as I have
done, trying to fight evil with love and kindness. . . . Is that what
must be done? Is it possible that I am to endure this torment
until I die? . . . My children do not even see fit to read my books.
They think my literature is one thing and I another. But every
inch of me is in what I write. . . . You are looking for the cause,
look for the cure instead. If the children were to stop gorging
themselves (vegetarian diet) I should be happy and gay, and not
mind the petty affronts and snubs. If the children were to keep
their rooms neat, stay away from the theatre, show some feeling
for the peasants and women of the people, read serious books,
you would see me in a transport of joy and all my ailments
would vanish at once. But this is not what happens, no move is
made in this direction, wilfully, out of sheer stubbornness. A
fight to the finish has begun between us . . .

To this diatribe Sonya might have replied that after
marrying her when she was eighteen, taking her to live at
Yasnaya Polyana, associating her in his writing and the
management of all his affairs, and begetting a dozen children upon her, nine of whom were still living, he did not
have the right to demand that she give up every comfort
in life overnight in obedience to 'God's commandments'.
And besides, which God? He changed them so often! Had
he forgotten what he once said about the family? Love,
marriage, childbearing, the education of children, respect
for ancestral traditions, affection for parents – they were
all themes he had glorified in his early books. And now,
after summoning his wife to join him at the altar of the
self-sufficient little family unit, he would compel her to
forswear her role as guardian of the hearth. Furthermore,

there was not one idea in his whole arsenal that he had not contradicted at some point in his career. Sonya was not sharing the destiny of one man but of ten or twenty, all sworn enemies of each other: aristocrat jealous of his prerogatives and people's friend in peasant garb; ardent Slavophil and Westernizing pacifist; denouncer of private property and lord aggrandizing his domains; hunter and protector of animals; hearty trencherman and vegetarian; peasant-style Orthodox believer and enraged demolisher of the Church; artist and contemptuous scorner of art, sensualist and ascetic. ... This multiplicity of psychological impulses made it possible for Lyovochka to put himself inside the skins of many characters and hence to be a matchless writer of fiction, but it also complicated his partner's task. So many husbands had succeeded each other beside her inside the same skin that in order to preserve some semblance of stability in her life she was forced to oppose the ever-shifting course set by Leo Tolstoy.

'With all my children around me,' she was to write, 'I really could not turn myself into a weather vane, spinning around to point wherever my husband's fickle mind led him. In him, it was an ardent and earnest search for the truth, in me it would only have been blind mimicry, and bad for the whole family.'

She was convinced that by adopting Lyovochka's ideas but without carrying them to extremes, she would ultimately shape their lives into something at once Christian and reasonable. But this moderate policy could not content a nature enamoured of cataclysms like that of the master of the house. He complained that his wife did not love him enough to accept the poverty he was yearning for with his whole being. As a mother she could not bring herself to make such a sacrifice, which she might have accepted at the beginning of their marriage. When she fought for her inheritance she was not thinking of her personal comfort, but of the future of those she had brought into the world. She would never be able to dispossess them of everything, deprive them of a proper education, turn them into labourers, peasants and beggars. The vow of poverty could not be imposed from without. The soul had to be predisposed to it and hers was not. Since tolerance was the essence of the Christian, Lyovochka ought to respect the views of his family. His behaviour in trying to force them to adopt his ideas was that of a sectarian. What mattered to him was not that his family should be happy, but that everybody should think the way he did. His altruism was simply another form of selfishness. Didn't he keep saying that a real wife was one who had the 'ability to absorb and assimilate ideas until she saw everything through her husband's eyes'? Indeed, to Christ all humans were equally precious. So why should Sonya give in to him? She felt as imperturbably at peace with her conscience defending the *status quo* as he did preaching against the bourgeoisie. Which was the greater sin : to conform to the law obeyed by all or to pretend to be God's messenger on earth? Sonya saw the intervention of divinity, not in her husband's vaticinations, but in the enormous powers he had been given as a teller of tales. In her eyes, he served the Almighty by accomplishing what he had been set on earth to do, and he betrayed Him by philosophizing and making boots, and no demonstration by Lyovochka, no speech, no threat could make her see otherwise. She was sure that by opposing him, she was protecting him from himself. After all, if he had not written *War and Peace* and *Anna Karenina*, who would have paid any attention to his philosophical and social writings? His message would never have got beyond a tiny circle of disciples; he would have been a peasant preacher, a visionary heretic, like hundreds of others in Russia. The thinker's ever-growing public had been won for him by the novelist. Didn't he realize, he of all people, with his hatred of misunderstandings, that his importance as an apostle rested on a *quid pro quo*? She might have written all these things to him in reply to the letter he had left for her, but where would that get her? She opted for a softer treatment:

'I would give anything to know how you are. But I'm afraid to touch these painful wounds which are not only unhealed but, it seems to me, have started to bleed again. ... I am happy to think that away from me your shattered nerves have been calmed. Maybe you will even be able to do some work. ... Give the Olsufyevs all my blessing. ... You are comfortable with them. You don't hate and condemn them as you do me. You see? *I* was the one who wanted to go away and it was *you* who left. As always, *I* am the one who stays behind, with my worries and my hurt feelings.' [20]

Restored to reason, Tolstoy admitted his guilt:

'I do not tell you this to pacify you, but, truly, I see how badly I have wronged you. The moment I understood this and expelled from my soul all sorts of imaginary grievances, and resurrected my love for you and Sergey, I felt well again!'

He returned to Moscow, determined to accept a compromise between the life according to society advocated by his wife and the life according to God which was becoming increasingly necessary to him. Three weeks later a sudden death deepened the household gloom. On 18 January 1886, little Alexis, age four and a half, the youngest Tolstoy son, died of quinsy after thirty-six hours of gasping, rattling agony. 'Dear Tanya,' Sonya wrote to her sister, 'can heart imagine my sorrow? I buried Alyosha today.' Tolstoy took a more lofty tone, as was his wont: 'All I can say,' he wrote to Chertkov, 'is that the death of a child, which I once thought incomprehensible and unjust, now seems reasonable and good. Through this death we have been united in a closer and deeper affection than before.' [21] And to a distant cousin, Mrs Young: 'My wife has been much afflicted by this death and I, too, am sorry that the little boy I loved is no longer here, but despair is only for those who shut their eyes to the commandments by which we are ruled.' [22]

For a few months things went more smoothly between

the two, each trying to make allowances for the other. Tolstoy finished his essay *What Then Must We Do?* and his long story, *The Death of Ivan Ilich*, and wrote more stories for the Intermediary, a virulent attack upon Nicholas I – *Nicholas Stick* – and a short play – *The First Distiller*.

That summer at Yasnaya Polyana, he rejoiced to see his children rallying around him. Following their father's example, they all set to work to help the muzhiks in the fields. Even Sonya, in peasant costume, occasionally joined them with a rake over her shoulder. The men's team, which included Tolstoy and his two sons Ilya and Leo, began haying at four in the morning. 'My father was good at scything,' wrote Ilya, 'but he perspired a great deal and one could see it tired him.' The other team were not such early risers: the girls, the French governess, Sergey. 'The women,' Tanya recounted, 'lined up in a row, spread the swaths of hay out in the sun, raked them into heaps and carried them to the "lord's court". But we were not working for the lord; we worked for the peasants, who received half the harvest in return for cutting the hay in the "master's" fields.' After a noonday snack in the shade of the trees, the men took up their scythes again and went back into the tall grass under the blazing sun. At dusk, escorting a dishevelled and dog-happy Tolstoy, the company made its way back to the house, singing. Sometimes Masha dropped her rake, beckoned to one of the peasant girls and broke into a wild dance. 'Of course,' Ilya Tolstoy observed, 'everybody did not share Father's ideas, and we did not all have our hearts in the work.'

The 'little lords' and 'little ladies' also harvested the crops. For a time every member of the family was vying to see who could do the most good deeds. Tanya went to visit sick peasants and wrote in her diary, 'It was not at all difficult for me to dress and bandage Alyona's dirty foot.' Ilya worked the plot of the mother of a large brood of children. Tolstoy repaired a widow's isba. He himself admitted, moreover, that this charity campaign was a form of play-acting. Children and guests dressed themselves up in coloured kerchiefs and boots; they worked as though playing a sport, and showed each other the blisters on their hands with tender self-concern. But the main thing, thought Tolstoy, was to act right, and the right feeling would come later.

The peasants were only amused by these bucolic distractions; but they were perplexed when Tolstoy gave them a lecture on drunkenness and asked them to sign a pledge not to drink any more. He also exhorted them to give up smoking, since he had given it up himself. At his order, they threw their tobacco into a pit he had dug for the purpose. But behind his back, they continued to puff at their cigarettes and befuddle their brains on vodka. He knew this and it made him as miserable as a lie told by someone he loved. When he asked Chertkov to join the 'Anti-Alcoholism League', of which he was proud to be a promoter in Russia, Chertkov replied that he could not take the oath because Christ had said, 'Thou shalt not swear'; Tolstoy was unconvinced.

In the midsummer heat, he accompanied Ozmidov, his daughter and another disciple to the Tula station, from which they were setting out to the Caucasus to found a 'Tolstoy colony'.* Shortly afterwards, while he was trying to set an example of the joys of physical labour, he had an accident: he was carting hay for a muzhik's widow, was thrown off balance by a false movement, fell from the telega and hurt his leg. He paid no attention to the wound and it became infected. Periostitis developed. Bedridden, the patient reverted to his wife, who set rapturously to work nursing her bearded baby as he lay shaking with fever. She delighted in the most intimate and repugnant tasks, and in his weakened condition he found her touching and let her do as she pleased. For the first time, he was not afraid of death: 'I am dying of a leg injury,' he wrote to Ozmidov. 'The river of life has dwindled to a tiny rivulet.'[23]

* This colony failed after five months.

And to Alexandra Tolstoy, 'Feeling myself within the house of God is excellent. I should like to remain there always and, for the moment, have no desire to leave.'[24] He mockingly told his son, 'I lie here and listen to the women and have become so completely possessed by their feminine world that I catch myself saying, "I must have dropped off."'

He did not really believe he was dying, but it was fascinating to imagine death, to smell it up close, to hazard a peek into the tomb, knowing he could pull back in time; he compared his present thoughts with those he had attributed to Ivan Ilich. As soon as he was better, he drew away from his wife again.

'Now that he is almost well and can go outdoors, he has given me to understand that I am no longer necessary to him,' Sonya lamented on 25 October 1886. 'Here I am, rejected again, like some useless object.' It annoyed her, when both the children and their father began coming to her, 'wearing their masks of self-righteousness', 'looking cold and stiff', to demand flour or clothing or money for the peasants. When Lyovochka asked her for a few roubles for 'Ganka the Thief', a revolting, foul-smelling woman who lived in the village, she refused, saying her moneybox was empty. Then, at a frosty stare from Tanya, who was siding increasingly often with her father, she yielded, grumbling and humiliated, and Ganka the Thief went off bearing her pittance.

Sonya had some compensation for these little blows to her pride; at least Lyovochka was no longer neglecting her only for his muzhiks and his philosophy. He had begun to write a play about the peasants. The first act was finished on 26 October 1886, the second three days later. Sonya recopied the manuscript in a flush of victory; but she was not blinded by love. 'It is good, but flat; I told Lyovochka there were not enough dramatic effects,' she wrote. He listened, revised, went on writing. All five acts were finished within a fortnight. Title: *The Power of Darkness*. Stakhovich, who happened to be staying at Yasnaya Polyana, had real talent as an actor, and Tolstoy asked him to read the play to the peasants. Since the action took place in the country, he thought it would be interesting to observe their reactions. Some forty muzhiks were assembled in the main room and the reading began. They listened silently, hanging their heads and looking blank. Only Andrey, who ran the Tula station buffet, occasionally broke into a loud guffaw. His bursts of merriment became even more inappropriate as the story of Nikita and Akulina unfolded, each scene more grisly than the one before. At the end, an exasperated Tolstoy asked his public what they thought of the play. The spectators looked at each other uncertainly. What could they tell the master, seeing they hadn't understood a word of it? At last, one of the ex-pupils of the Yasnaya Polyana school mumbled:

'It seems to me, Leo Nikolayevich, that in the beginning Nikita was doing all right. But afterwards, he went wrong.'

Tolstoy could get nothing more out of these people whom he held to be the best judges of art. That evening he raged to Stakhovich:

'It was all that Andrey's fault! Until now he looked up to you as a sort of general, you tipped him three roubles at the station buffet. ... And all of a sudden you begin to shout and imitate a drunkard. How could he help laughing? ... And his laughing prevented the others from understanding the meaning of the play.' [25]

He sent *The Power of Darkness* to Chertkov to be printed in the Intermediary collection, and began a comedy, *The Fruits of Enlightenment*. Passing the year's work in review, Sonya could proudly tell herself that apart from the essay *What Then Must We Do?* and a few minor articles, her husband's entire output had been, as she hoped, literary.

In the first part of *What Then Must We Do?* Tolstoy describes the Moscow slums he had seen during the census-taking. Here his accuracy of observation and the unfaltering logic of his discernment are remarkable. From page to page the shocked and horrified reader breathes in the stink of cesspools, blinks in the gloom and feels his skin itching from head to foot. But the novelist soon yields to the moralist, and the emotion he aroused in describing the evil is dissipated when he begins to set forth the remedies for it. As disorderly in manipulating ideas as he is incisive in describing facts, he rants, threatens and promises with the naïve self-assurance of an autodidact. The root of all evil, as others had said before him, is property. The rich, who produce nothing and revel in vice, luxury and idleness, attract the poor to the towns and enslave them. 'The poor come to feed on the crumbs of wealth,' writes Tolstoy. 'It is surprising that some of them continue to work, and do not begin to seek easier means of making money: commerce, hoarding, beggary, debauchery, swindling and even robbery.' Wage-earning and slavery are synonymous. And whoever says slavery says deprivation. The reason the rich can get away with such scandalous conduct is that they are protected by State and Church. The State is a murderous vehicle devised by the violent to dominate the weak. In a mankind-according-to-Christ, there should be no State. Nor any Church. For the Church deforms the teaching of Christ in order to adapt it to the demands of the State. It is aided and abetted in this devil's work by science and art. The true scholars and artists are not those who are supported by State and Church, but those who 'claim no rights, and recognize only duties', those who fight, suffer and die for the truth. 'There are no fat, self-indulgent and self-satisfied artists,' Tolstoy concludes.

How to combat the evil to which mankind is sinking ever more deeply? First, by rejecting all the machinery on which society is now founded. Turn one's back on the State, refuse to serve it in any way, take no share in the exploitation of others, give up money and land, abolish industry – a source of pauperism – flee the corrupting cities, tear the conceit of education out of your heart and return to a healthy rural existence. God wants everyone to work with his hands and be self-sufficient. The mind is improved by the body's fatigue. The truly wise are the 'peasant thinkers' on the Syutayev model, the muzhik in sheepskin jacket. Down with intelligence! Long live simplicity!

The thing that immediately strikes one about this sermon is the enthusiasm the author feels for religious ideas which he believes to be new but which in fact go back to the heart of the Middle Ages – the Waldensian, the Lollard and Anabaptist brotherhoods, who taught the indivisibility of the Church and the uselessness of the sacraments and preached that the people should be free in relation to kings, magistrates and priests. On the social side, advocating a sort of communism in Christian sheep's clothing, he errs through over-confidence in man. If everyone loved other people more than himself and the world were inhabited exclusively by followers of Leo Tolstoy, there would obviously be no need of laws, courts, police or government. If all people were equally intelligent, strong and skilful, everyone would work for himself and it would not be necessary to divide labour according to individual capacities at the risk of establishing further noxious inequality. If mere non-resistance could convince and ceasing to fight could convert, we might demobilize the army and throw open the frontiers.

Unfortunately, human nature is not made of such delicate stuff. Aggressiveness, jealousy, sloth, falsehood and violence are solidly anchored in our hearts. To pretend that abolishing evil's outward means of coercion will do away with evil itself is putting the cart before the horse. Once again, in presenting his doctrine, Tolstoy assumes that the problem has been solved so that he will not have to solve it, and replaces reasoned argument with prophetic but haphazard intensity. In his anger, he hurls himself against everything his contemporaries might be tempted to venerate. The more universally an idea is accepted, the more it infuriates him. He would impose a whole new scale of values upon the mass, reject all that has been said and done before him; if need be, recreate the world. In passing, he doles out a lesson in conjugal meekness to his wife: a mother is the only woman entitled to man's respect, all others are prostitutes and that's that. (The days when he recognized their usefulness to society are long past.) 'The mother will not urge her husband to engage in false and misguided strivings whose only aim is to profit from the work of others; she will regard all such activities, which might tempt her children, with loathing and contempt. . . . Such are the women who dominate men and act as their guiding light.'

Upon reading this paragraph Sonya must have felt that she could never be a 'guiding light' in the sense Lyovochka meant. However much he insisted that his philosophizing was more important than his novels, she would never believe it. Besides, if she had begun to doubt her judgement, this year's admirable *Death of Ivan Ilich* was proof that she was not mistaken. After so many volumes of woolly philosophy, the simple, profound, piercing story showed that at fifty-seven, Tolstoy's creative powers were still intact.

The idea for the story, originally entitled *The Death of a Judge*, was given to him by the death of a man named Ivan Ilich Mechnikov, a judge at the court of Tula, in 1881. He had heard the details from Mechnikov's brother. His original idea had been simply to write a diary of a man struggling with and then abandoning himself to death. But gradually he saw what the story might gain in tragic depth by being told in the third person, particularly in changes of lighting effects and camera angles. And the diary grew into a novel.

Ivan Ilich is a perfect specimen of the conscientious official, who has no religion but is supported by a few principles handed down from his parents; he does not steal, he does not take bribes, he is not unfaithful to his wife, he lives an 'easy, agreeable, honest' life. His rise through the ranks of the administration keeps pace with the gradual disintegration of his marriage. Indifference soon settles in, followed by irritation and sullen anger. 'At rare moments amorous impulses still drove them towards each other, but not for long,' writes Tolstoy. 'They were little islands, brief ports of call before sailing back out on to the high sea of their latent hatred.' The hero's material circumstances are so vastly improved by an unexpected promotion that he is able to move into a luxurious apartment, perfectly suited 'to his rank', and he becomes totally absorbed in decorating and furnishing it. Antique furniture, bronze figurines, plates on the wall. ... An echo of Tolstoy's joys and tribulations while he was supervising work on the new house in Moscow? 'When there was nothing left to decorate, they began to be a little bored.' But Ivan Ilich had fallen from a ladder while hanging curtains and, after a time, the pain began to grow worse instead of better. This is the prelude to a period of unremitting anguish for the judge. He senses that something dreadful is going on inside him, 'something more important than everything that had happened to him until then'. He consults doctors, who reassure but cannot cure him. His wife and daughter refuse to take him seriously, or feign cheerfulness in order to keep him from worrying even more. A chasm opens up between him and all people in good health. They are only play-acting; he, for the first time, has touched the essence. Condemned to his bedroom, he faces the thought of death. 'I was alive and now my life is going away. It is going and I cannot stop it. ... Where shall I be when I am no more?' As his illness wears on, he begins to feel more alone, less understood, less loved. His presence is a weight upon the living, he is preventing them from being happy, amusing themselves, going about their business. His wife and daughter stop in to see him one evening on their way to the theatre. He hates them for looking so strong and clean and healthy, with the loathing of a diseased body for all cool, white, sweet-smelling flesh. His only friend is a servant, Gerasim, who wipes and washes him and sometimes holds up his feet, which relieves the pain a little. He feels sorry for himself, he bemoans his fate, he tries to recall his former pleasant life, and he is appalled to discover that all the memories he took for gold are nothing but false coin. 'The closer he came to the present, the more uncertain and empty seemed the joys he had known. ... Perhaps I have not lived as I should have lived, he thought.' No matter how he rationalizes, his failure becomes more and more patent. Now he knows that all the time he thought he was succeeding in his career, he was actually failing in his life, and his 'service, well-ordered existence, family and social interests were nothing but lies'. Then what is man's purpose on earth? Why live? Why die? His wife entreats him to have extreme unction. He submits. Then he is seized with terror. He screams. He grows calm again. He begins to listen attentively. 'Where is death? What death? He was not afraid any more, because there was no death any more. Instead of death, there was only light.'

Beyond any doubt, this double story of the decomposing body and awakening soul is one of the most powerful works in the literature of the world. The author employs the same precision in his clinical analysis of the disease (cancer of the abdominal region) as in his description of the successive stages passed through by the dying man's soul. A dying man who is in no way exceptional, or even likeable, and yet we identify with him because through him we imagine what our own death will be. We think of ourselves while Ivan Ilich moans in pain in his bed; we pass our own lives in review as he draws up the balance sheet for his. At the end of his torment, two things dominate: the terror of what is coming and the emptiness of what has been. No philosophical dissertation can ever equal in depth this simple 'documentary' – unemotional, sharp, cruel, devoid of all artistic effect – of a sickroom. The most fervent challenger of modern society, the world of officialdom and middle-class marriage is not the author of *What Then Must We Do?* but the author of *The Death of Ivan Ilich.*

The first persons to read it were overwhelmed by its

cynicism and grandeur. Stasov wrote to Tolstoy: 'No nation anywhere in the world has a work as great as this. Everything is little and petty in comparison with these seventy pages.'[26] On 12 August 1886, Tchaikovsky wrote in his diary, 'I read *The Death of Ivan Ilich*. More than ever, I am convinced that the greatest author–painter who ever lived is Leo Tolstoy. He alone can keep the Russians from bowing their heads in shame when all the great things that have come out of Europe are lined up in front of them. But patriotism has no part in my belief in Tolstoy's immense, almost divine importance.'

Tolstoy's toughness, in this story which he wrote for the cultivated classes, is equalled only by his gentleness in the simple tales he was writing during the same period for the common people to illustrate his catechism: love of God, love of one's neighbour, charity, poverty. Some of these 'moralities', such as *What Men Live By* and *Three Old Men*, have a biblical purity of inspiration. Written in the words of everyday life, they can be understood by children. And yet grownups find in them, if not a specific lesson, at least an impression of freshness, a taste of spring – which may be more important.

If Tolstoy idealizes the common people in these delightful tableaux, he unveils all their hideous reality in *The Power of Darkness*. Why this shift from moderation to violence, admiration to execration? The reason is that although he honours the superior 'wisdom' of the muzhiks and exhorts all intellectuals to follow in their footsteps, he is sometimes overcome with aristocratic revulsion at the physical and moral filth in which these primitive beings live. True, the capitalist civilization is the only thing that keeps them in their bestial condition. But in the present state, most of them cannot serve as examples to the bourgeois. In *The Power of Darkness* the author unconsciously contradicts *What Then Must We Do?* But who cares? One ambiguity more or less was not going to make any difference to Tolstoy!

The subject of *The Power of Darkness* was furnished by an actual occurrence, on 18 January 1880, in a village in the government of Tula: after murdering a child born to him and his daughter-in-law, Koloskov, a muzhik, was stricken with remorse and publicly confessed his guilt. Out of this unremarkable material Tolstoy wove a work of black, brutal despair. All the characters are heavily underscored and lean on their shadows. Nikita the farmhand, handsome and weak; Anisya – hot-blooded, completely dominated by wild sensuality; old Matryona, who encourages her son Nikita to commit adultery; Akim, Nikita's father, a muzhik with a stutter who aspires to saintliness. The sin of the flesh begets crime. Anisya poisons her husband in order to be free to love Nikita. But Nikita, not content with sharing Anisya's bed, also seduces her sixteen-year-old stepdaughter, Akulina. A child is born. Going berserk, Nikita crushes the tiny bastard between two boards, while Matryona and Anisya look on. But he does not have their strength of character. He appeals to them: 'I can't go on! Where can I hide?' He thinks he hears the child whimpering. To atone for his crime, he waits for Akulina's wedding-day and then, kneeling down in the middle of the crowd, tells the whole story, urged on by Akim, his stammering father, who sighs, 'God! Ah There, God! . . .'

To add credulity to this tragedy of the downtrodden, Tolstoy pored over his pocket notebooks, veritable dictionaries of the peasant language, and sprinkled his dialogue full of the popular expressions, the old, flavourful, crude proverbs that were his delight. He admitted that he enjoyed himself enormously writing these speeches; they virtually wrote themselves. The charm of the words made him forget the horror of the situation.

The emotion his play aroused in everyone who read it encouraged him to try to have it produced by one of the major companies. He began to negotiate with the actress Savina. On 27 January 1887 Stakhovich, the man who had read the play to the muzhiks before, read it at a party in the home of the court minister Vorontsov-Dashkov, in the presence of Alexander III, the empress and the grand dukes and duchesses. His second audience grasped the torments of the peasant soul more clearly than the first had. The tsar found Tolstoy's play an admirable work of art and said that in order to ensure its success it should be acted by a joint company from both the Moscow and St Petersburg imperial theatres. He even promised to attend the opening night. But on 18 February Pobyedonostsev, minister to the Holy Synod, wrote to Alexander III to say that he was so upset after reading *The Power of Darkness* that he was unable to 'recover his spirits'. According to him, the entire play was nothing but 'negation of the ideal', 'degradation of the moral sense' and 'an offence to good taste'.

'To my knowledge there is nothing like it in any literature', he went on. 'Even Zola never reached this level of vulgar and brutal realism. ... It is a catastrophe, that at this minute enormous numbers of copies of Tolstoy's play have already been printed and are being sold for ten kopecks in cheap booklet form by pedlars on every street corner.'[27]

Unnerved by this furious outburst, Alexander III changed his mind and said, in his reply to Pobyedonostsev, that he had admired the play but had been 'disgusted' by it at the same time. 'My opinion,' he added, 'is that the play cannot be performed because it is too realistic and its subject too horrible.' A few days later, in March, he sent a note to his minister of the interior saying, 'This ignominious L. Tolstoy must be stopped. He is nothing but a nihilist and non-believer. It would be well to prohibit the publication of the play in book form, for the author has already sufficiently spread about and sold his rubbish among the people.'

However, the Alexandra Theatre in St Petersburg was going ahead with its plans to produce the play. Rehearsals were under way and enthusiasm among the actors was at fever pitch when, on the eve of the first night, the play was prohibited.* Shortly afterwards the censor also prohibited its sale in printed form. Faithful to his principles, Tolstoy had already announced through the newspapers that anyone might reproduce his text without paying royalties to him.

* *The Power of Darkness* was not produced until 1895, in Petersburg, by the Alexandra Theatre, and in Moscow the same year, by the company of the Skomorokh People's Theatre. It was produced in France by the Théâtre Antoine, however, in 1888.

[23]

The Kreutzer Sonata

FOR Tolstoy and his wife, the winter of 1886-7 was relatively happy. After a few arguments that resounded like muffled echoes of the great scenes of 1885, each decided, willy-nilly, to put up with the peculiarities of the other. Tolstoy continued to philosophize as he chopped wood and stitched boots, while Sonya made the rounds of the drawing-rooms, entertained and sold her husband's books at a stiff price. 'He has changed a great deal and takes everything quietly and tolerantly,' she wrote on 6 March 1887. 'Sometimes he even plays *vint* with us, or sits down at the piano. City life no longer drives him to despair.' Months later, 'He seems contented and happy and often exclaims, "How good it is to be alive!"'

In fact these moments of felicity were rare. Most of the time Tolstoy was 'mild and spiritless'. Especially when he returned to a vegetarian diet after more solid fare. Sometimes he ate nothing but vegetables, sometimes nothing but meat, and sometimes he drank only rum diluted with water, but his digestive troubles continued as before. One evening at table he complained that Sonya was 'a woman of money'. She retorted that she was selling the twelve volumes of his *Complete Works* for eight roubles, whereas he had sold *War and Peace* alone for twelve. He raged, but found nothing to say. Looking at him, a man nearing sixty, with a wrinkled face, whitening hair and sharp grey eyes lurking under bristling brows, Sonya yearned for her free, strong, happy companion of old, the writer and artist of 1865.

He had started to work again, but was producing nothing but moralizing articles, including one very big essay, *On Life and Death*, which he was trying to write in a style that would be simple enough for a peasant to understand. 'Continued association with professors leads to prolixity, love of long words and confusion,' he wrote, 'but with muzhiks, to conciseness, beauty of language and clarity.'[1] As usual, Sonya began to recopy the manuscript, but as soon as she had transcribed a few pages, Lyovochka would rewrite them completely. 'What patience and what perseverance!' she cried, half annoyed and half admiring.

Now that her children were grown or growing up, she had to fight on several fronts at once to maintain her authority. In every one of the Tolstoys she discerned some trait inherited from Lyovochka. At the table she sat with a half-dozen facets of her husband grouped around her, behind masks ranging from infancy to young adulthood. In a conflict, some sided with their father, others with their mother. But since she had raised them all, it offended her to see any of them on the other side.

Tolstoy, on the other hand, complained that he was a stranger in his own family. He was especially disappointed by his two older boys. 'Among my children there will be no one to carry on my work,' he said to Strakhov. 'If I were a carpenter, my sons would be beside me at my bench. ... Alas, it is exactly the opposite. One of my sons [Sergey] is finishing his studies at the University and wants to be a civil servant. The other [Ilya] will be a soldier, and his head is already turned by shoulder bars. The third – but what is the good of talking about them? ... Neither the third nor the fourth nor my daughters will follow the same path as I. ... It would have been better for me to have had no children at all!'

Naturally, he held his wife responsible for Ilya and Sergey's failure to understand him. Wasn't she the one who had brought them up as aristocrats? He was forgetting that he had not chosen to interfere while there was still time. Moreover, it was inevitable, once the boys were removed from the family atmosphere and involved in Moscow university life, that they would be tempted to compare their father's strange ideas with the more commonly held opinions of fellow students and professors. They unconsciously opposed the university world to the Tolstoyan world. Sergey, the eldest – rough, taciturn, music-minded – did not conceal his irritation, when he entered the house to find it teeming with obsequious disciples. He also thought it unfair of his father to hold his mother to blame for the luxury he himself enjoyed. 'Leo Nikolayevich,' he wrote, 'demanded that the family simplify its way of life, but failed to lay down any limits and seldom supplied concrete details. The questions of where and how the family was to live, how the property was to be disposed of, how the children were to be brought up, etc., were left unsettled.'[2] Although he venerated his father, he also regretted the extremes he was led to by his doctrine. 'How were we to reconcile life according to God, the life of the pilgrims and the life of the peasants, with the intangible principles that had been instilled in us from the cradle?' he wrote. 'We children often felt that it was not we who didn't understand our father, but he who did not understand us, because he was always busy with "personal affairs".'

After an erratic career at the University, Ilya had fallen in love with a poor girl, Sofya Philosofov, and made up his mind to marry her. Tolstoy hesitated a long time before asking his twenty-two-year-old son the question that was burning his lips. Finally, one evening, he slipped into the young man's room and went behind a screen, then said in a low voice:

'Now nobody can hear us, and we will not be embarrassed because we can't see each other. Tell me, have you ever had intercourse with a woman?'

'No,' Ilya replied.

Then, behind his screen, Tolstoy sobbed with joy. 'I began to weep with him,' Ilya wrote. 'With that screen between us, quite unashamedly, we cried heartily for a long time.'

Later, Tolstoy wrote a pastoral letter to his son on marriage:

'The goal of our life should not be to find joy in marriage, but to bring more love and truth into the world. We marry to assist each other in this task. The most selfish and hateful life of all is that of two beings who unite in order to enjoy life. The highest calling is that of the man who has dedicated his life to serving God and doing good, and who unites with a woman in order to further that purpose.'

Before sending the letter, Tolstoy read it to his family. The girls found it sublime, but were surprised that it made no mention of 'the love of man for woman and the blessings of procreation'. The recipient's feelings were in no way altered by this cold shower and on 28 February 1888 Ilya married Sofya Philosofov, with the uneasy blessing of Leo and Sonya Tolstoy.

Leo, the third son, born in 1869, was a restless, change-able boy who, after a brief flirtation with the Tolstoyan doctrines, soon derided them. For the present, acute inertia was the only noteworthy feature of Andrey and Michael, the youngest boys, really no more than children.

Disappointed in his sons, Tolstoy took what comfort he could in his daughters. Tatyana (Tanya), the eldest, was a light-hearted, obedient, bright girl with mannish features and a brusque manner. Painting was her passion, but she also wanted to elevate her soul. At first she was attracted by society, but quickly abandoned it in favour of her father's precepts. In 1885 he had written: 'It is far more important for you to take care of your own room and cook your own soup than to make a good marriage.' This sentence domi-nated her for the rest of her days. With the zeal of a neo-phyte, she forced herself to wash her own linen, care for the poor and follow a vegetarian diet. Her private diary bears witness to her strivings after perfection. If she saw Mikhailo the tailor and his apprentice Sergey sewing a 'sleeveless bolero' for her, she immediately loathed herself for her selfishness and uselessness: 'The money I give them cannot compensate for the fact that two human beings have bent their backs and laboured for me all day, whilst I did nothing for them.' If a few days passed without her meeting any beggars, she deplored the fact as a guilty respite for her conscience: 'Everything is hidden from us, even this living reproach, so that it may be impossible for us to remember that there are men who are starving and naked.' She thought of death, and calmed her fears by recalling her father's words: 'If you regret the loss of your body, think that every gram of it will surely serve some purpose and nothing will be lost. Nor will your spirit die.' If the coachman caught cold waiting for her while she played cards with friends, she asked herself, in shame, 'When will these poor people cease their servile obedience to those who pay them?'[3]

Nevertheless, in spite of her desire to be worthy in all respects of the great man whose name she bore, she could not always stifle nature. She loved the theatre, she liked young men to pay court to her, and found it both 'odious and enjoyable' to order pretty new dresses and shoes. Also, she understood her mother, although she did not agree with her, and pitied her and endeavoured, by a constant display of affection, to make life bearable for her at home. 'Maman is torn apart,' she wrote. 'She works hard for the money that we, that is, Ilya, Masha and I, consider superfluous; and yet we insist on having it, in clothes and all sorts of other things, and she is continually irritated by our inconsistency. It hurts me so to see her fighting against the good, that is, what Papa believes to be good, and is good indeed; to see how intolerant she is with anyone who makes an effort to improve his life. ... I am talking nonsense. I sound as though I am judging her, when in fact all I feel for her is love, tenderness and compassion.'

She wanted to be her father's favourite, and was hurt because he seemed to take more interest in Masha. She secretly observed her younger sister and found her deceitful, obsequious and intriguing. 'She licks Father's boots!' she wrote in disgust. Out of pride, in order not to be like her, she forced herself to disagree with the great man when all the time she was wanting to say he was right. After she chanced upon Masha's diary, she vented her spleen in her own: 'It is a great misfortune to have a nature like hers: lying, scheming and, at the same time, sensuous and ostentatiously lofty and noble.' And later, 'When she is away, Papa is much sweeter to me. Comparing us, he must naturally see that she models herself after him more than I do, is more attentive to him, believes in him more blindly than I do.'

If the thought of marriage occasionally crossed her mind, she thrust it out of sight. No husband could ever measure up to her father's knee. 'Why marry, as long as he is there? If I were to get married I should be terribly afraid of losing contact with him,' she wrote. Besides, she was horrified by her mother's description of the sexual relations between couples. 'I am very happy to think that I am a virgin and have not had to undergo that fearful humiliation all married women suffer, as Mother's remarks have made so clear to me; she was so ashamed the morning after her wedding that she did not want to leave her room. She hid her face in the pillow and cried. I am proud not to have known that and I wish I may never know it!'[4]

On this point Masha agreed with her older sister. For her, too, the ideal husband was Papa. She looked like him, moreover; she had his penetrating little grey eyes, his too high forehead, his thick nose and high cheekbones. Six and a half years younger than Tanya, she was less easy-going, less sociable, more tormented and possessive than her sister. She had felt her father's moral isolation at a very early age, and resolved always to remain by his side. Putting 'Tolstoyan Christianity' into practice, she, like Tanya, but even more than Tanya, followed a vegetarian diet and went in for manual labour and deeds of charity. She wanted to become a schoolteacher and devote her life to the muzhiks. Sonya, who had scant affection for her, disdainfully replied, 'You were born counts and countesses and counts and countesses you will remain.' But Tolstoy was touched by his daughter's noble aspirations, and wrote in his diary, 'I feel great tenderness towards her. Her only. She makes up for the others, I might say.'

Gradually, he began to give her his correspondence to file and his manuscripts to copy, and dictated his letters to her. Every time Masha entered the paternal study, Sonya choked with jealousy. After serving him faithfully as secretary for twenty-five years, she could not bear to see her own daughter take her place beside Lyovochka. It was as though her husband were being unfaithful to her with the child. She would probably have suffered less had he hired an outsider, if only because adultery is easier to accept than incest. 'I used to be the one who copied everything he wrote,' she recorded on 20 November 1890. 'It was my joy. Today he assiduously hides everything from me and entrusts his manuscripts to his daughter to copy. He is systematically killing me, cutting me off from his personal life, and it hurts me dreadfully. ... I would like to commit suicide, run away, fall in love with someone else.' Less than a month later, observing that young Paul Biryukov, Chertkov's friend and Lyovochka's disciple, had become sufficiently enamoured of Masha to contemplate marriage, she was at first offended by his impertinence and then took a malicious delight in it: 'I'd like to get rid of Masha. Why keep her here? Let her marry Biryukov. Then I shall have my old place next to Lyovochka, I shall copy his manuscripts and keep his affairs in order.'[5] A short while later came this dreadful cry: 'Masha is a cross God has given me to bear. From the day of her birth she has given me nothing but trouble. She is a stranger in the family.'[6]

The stranger remained in the family despite the young man's sighs, and Sonya was both relieved and disappointed. In fact, Masha's departure would not really have cleared the air in the house. It was impossible, in the same time and place, to lead the social life Sonya delighted in and the communitarian existence Lyovochka dreamed of. At Yasnaya Polyana the countess continued her custom of entertaining extensively, neighbours, friends and relatives, all people of good breeding, polished by culture and dressed with discrimination, who rolled up with their servants in tow. There were picnics, bathing parties, croquet and tennis matches, concerts, amateur plays. But in addition to these distinguished guests, there were what the servants called 'the Dark Ones'. They came to look at the master, tell him how much they admired him, extort some piece of advice or money from him and help with his manual labours. Sonya wrinkled up her nose in their presence, for many of them gave off an unpleasant smell. She perceived the same smell on her husband's clothes after he had been with them, and would light her perfume burner; and he would say, with a laugh, that she was 'chasing away the evil spirits with incense'.

Among the spirits were individuals of all ages and conditions, earnest idealists and adventurers, the inquisitive and the insane, university students and illiterates, popes and muzhiks, officers who had left the army, passing foreigners. Their devotion to Tolstoy was equalled only by their lack of consideration for him. The more they admired the master, the less compunction they felt about importuning him. And he made no protest, believing that he did not have the right to withhold his word from the faithful. He was the lay equivalent of starets Ambrose, the sage of Optina-Pustyn. There was no pilgrims' inn at Yasnaya Polyana, but this did not stop some of them from staying on for days, sleeping in a shed, isba or cupboard in the servants' rooms. Although most of these people were worthless, Tolstoy did not lose heart. 'One more, and another and another,' he sighed. 'And it always seems to me that the next one will be someone new and rare who will know what the others do not and live better than the rest. But it is always the same, always the same weaknesses, always the same low level of thinking.'[7] When one of his visitors was manifestly a scoundrel he said to his wife, to excuse himself for having let him come, 'If he really is a wicked man,

I can be more useful to him than to those who are no better than he.'

Sonya was not satisfied with this edifying explanation: 'How unattractive they all are, the followers of Leo Niko-layevich's doctrines,' she wrote. 'Not one normal man among them. As for the women, most of them are hysteri-cal.'[8] She cited the example of Marya Schmidt, a former schoolteacher who was now devoting her time to copying Tolstoy's censored books; she followed him along the paths like a shadow and burst into tears whenever she parted from him. Then there was Feinermann, a Jew converted to Tolstoy, who had left his pregnant wife and child to receive the master's light and, even more, his hospitality; and But-kevich, son of a Tula landowner, who had been imprisoned twice for revolutionary activities and considered himself to be a spiritual brother of Tolstoy on that account. He ate at his table, but never uttered a word – he just sat, with sleepy face and eyes hidden behind blue-tinted spectacles; and there was Ivanov the copyist, who had a nimble pen and aspirations to saintliness, but punctuated his periods of labour with long rambles on the highroads and vodka binges; and the peasant Osipov, who spent all his time reading in the orchard and did not even bother to look up at the master's approach; and the blind Old Believer who reproached Tolstoy for not living according to his doctrine and cried out 'Liar! Hypocrite!' at the sound of his foot-step; and the seventy-year-old Swede who went around bare-foot preaching moral and vestimentary 'simplicity', and had to be turned out because he was beginning to be in-decent; and the two eccentric Americans who had set out around the world, one to the east and the other to the west, and had chosen the home of the author of *What Then Must We Do?* as their rallying point; and the morphine addict who provided mathematical proof of Christian dogma; and big, dumb Khokhlov, who followed Tanya around out of love of Tolstoyism; and all the rest, the talkers, the lazy, the ignorant, the failures, the servile ...

Maxim Gorky said later, after spending a day at Yasnaya Polyana, 'It is most curious to see Leo Nikolayevich among his Tolstoyans. He is like a great steeple whose bell is heard throughout the world, and all around him scurry contemptible, cringing little curs who try to bark in tune, casting anxious, jealous glances at each other to see who yapped the best, who has made the best impression on the master. To my mind these people are polluting the atmosphere of Yasnaya Polyana in a miasma of cowardice, hypocrisy, sordid intrigue and speculation on his inheritance.'

Tolstoy's voice did not, however, draw only the dregs of mankind. A few intelligent and sincere figures towered over the flea-bitten rank and file Tolstoyans: such were Chertkov and Biryukov, who were handling the Intermediary publications, or the delightful painter Gay, who was called 'Grandad' by the children, or the faithful Strakhov, or Rayevsky the surgeon, or Kern, the forestry inspector, or Syutayev's son, a conscientious objector recently released from the Schlüsselburg Prison, or Wilhelm Frey, who had gone to America as a communist, been naturalized there and come back spreading propaganda for the ideas of Auguste Comte, or young Prince Khilkov who, without ever meeting Tolstoy, had followed his precepts and distributed all his land to the peasants, keeping only eight acres for himself. ... Here and there in Russia and in the provinces of Tver and Smolensk in the Caucasus, little Tolstoy communities were springing up to confront their precarious destinies.

Abroad, Tolstoy's word was also gaining a hearing among the intellectuals in quest of a new faith. In 1887 young Romain Rolland, a student at the École Normale, wrote to the sage of Yasnaya Polyana to convey his high regard and ask for particulars regarding the importance of manual labour in educating the spirit. Tolstoy replied on 4 October 1887, in a long letter in French:

In our depraved society – the society of so-called civilized people – manual labour is essential solely because the chief defect of that society has been and still is that the people make every effort to avoid working themselves, and exploit the labour of the poor, ignorant and unhappy classes who are their slaves, just like the slaves in antiquity, giving them nothing in return. ... I shall never believe the sincerity of the Christian, philosophical or humanitarian pretensions of a person who sends a servant to empty his chamberpot. The simplest and shortest ethical precept is to be served by others as little as possible and to serve others as much as possible. ... This is what involuntarily drives a moral and honest man to prefer manual labour to the sciences and the arts: the book I write, for which I need the work of the printer; the symphony I compose, for which I need the work of musicians; the experiments I perform, for which I need the labour of the people who manufacture laboratory instruments; the picture I paint, for which I need the work of those who manufacture pigments and canvas – all these things can be useful to men, but they can also be – and are, for the most part – utterly useless and even harmful. And while I am doing all these things whose usefulness is highly questionable and to produce which I must, in addition, make other people work, there are an endless number of things to do right in front of me, all of which are indubitably useful to others and for which I need no one but myself: a burden to carry for someone who is tired, a field to work for its owner who is ill, a wound to dress; not to mention those thousands of things within our immediate reach, for which we need no one's help, which give instantaneous pleasure to those for whom we do them: planting a tree, raising a calf, cleaning a well are actions which are incontestably useful to others and an honest man cannot fail to prefer them to the dubious occupations which are proclaimed by our society to be man's highest and most noble callings.

The year before, 1886, Paul Déroulède had been in Russia to begin negotiating a Franco–Russian alliance, and had gone to Yasnaya Polyana out of curiosity. Paradoxically, the meeting between the apostle of non-violence and the author of *Chants du soldat* was most cordial. Tolstoy found that this 'revengist' had his attractive side; but at table, when the guest said he hoped another war would soon return Alsace and Lorraine to France, nobody supported him. Then, at his request, Tolstoy took him out to the fields and questioned the muzhiks to see whether, in case there was a war, they would be willing to fight the Germans as allies of the French. 'What for?' answered Prokopy, one of the peasants. 'Let the Frenchman come work with us, and bring the German along with him. When we've finished we'll go for a walk. And we'll take the German with us. He's a man like all the rest.' Tolstoy was jubilant, but Déroulède took a disgruntled departure.

Other foreigners followed: scientists, authors, philosophers, travellers – Masaryk, professor of philosophy and future president of the Republic of Czechoslovakia; Loewenfeld, director of the Schiller Theatre; Stockheim, specialist in tocology; the physiologist Charles Richet ... Tolstoy saw them all. 'It is the price of Lyovochka's greatness and the fame of his doctrine,'[9] commented Sonya.

This already numerous court of adulators and tourists swarming around Tolstoy did not lessen his preference for the iron-willed Chertkov. Even in his absence, the master's thoughts were filled by this man. He had just married Anna Konstantinovna Dietrich, a thin, pale student with unhealthily dilated eyes, who adored philosophy, worshipped her husband's ideas even more fervidly than he himself and dreamed only of becoming his collaborator. She helped Chertkov to transform their estate at Lizinovka into a centre for neo-Christian propaganda. From his headquarters, the disciple sent missives to the master in which hymns of praise alternated with pious admonitions. Their intimacy was so complete that Tolstoy confided all his family troubles to him, in addition to his metaphysical torments. One day Chertkov wrote how fortunate he was to have married such a peerless spiritual companion and how he pitied Tolstoy for being deprived of this blessing. The letter fell into Sonya's hands and she flew into a rage: 'That obtuse, scheming, false man, who has managed to ensnare Leo Nikolayevich, would like (no doubt in the name of Christian principles) to break the ties that have bound us so closely for twenty-five years,' she wrote on 9 March 1887. 'All relations with Chertkov must cease, he is nothing but deceitfulness and evil.' Fortunately, Chertkov's visits were rare; he operated long-distance, distilling his poison through the mail.

On 3 July 1887 the children arranged a little concert, featuring Liassotta, a pupil at the Moscow Conservatory of Music who had been engaged to give violin lessons to the third Tolstoy son. Liassotta and Sergey, playing the violin and piano respectively, gave a performance of the *Kreutzer Sonata*. Tolstoy, who was very fond of Beethoven, listened with tears in his eyes; then, during the presto, unable to control himself, he rose and went to the window where, gazing at the starry sky, he stifled a sob. Sonya received the benefits of his transports later that same evening, when they were alone: as she wrote immediately afterwards in her diary, under the influence of the music he had become 'the affectionate and tender Lyovochka of old'. A few weeks later she discovered that she was pregnant. On 23 September 1887 it was a mother-to-be whom Tolstoy kissed on both cheeks in front of his entire family, assembled to celebrate the couple's silver wedding anniversary; but Sonya was too embarrassed to announce her condition yet. And Lyovochka, looking back over his long wedded life, commented laconically in his pocket notebook, 'It could have been better!'

That summer a painter, Repin, came to stay at Yasnaya Polyana and painted two portraits and a large number of sketches of the master. Alexandra Tolstoy also came, and did her best to avoid arguments with Lyovochka over his anti-Orthodoxy. In spite of all the comings and goings in the house, and his worries about some of his peasants who had been ruined by a fire, Tolstoy worked steadily on a number of important articles, until he returned to Moscow with the family on 26 October 1887. While writing *On Life and Death*, he began planning a soul-staggering, 'definitive' novel against sensuality. But perhaps his faithful flock would reproach him for cursing the evils of the flesh with his wife in an advanced stage of pregnancy; to parry their thrusts, he reminded them that procreation in the state of wedlock was lawful and even recommendable.

'It is not licentiousness,' he wrote to Chertkov on 20 March 1888, 'but the will of God. ... If no more children were born, we could not go on hoping that the kingdom of God on earth will ultimately arrive. We are already corrupt, and it is a struggle for us to purify ourselves, whereas in the new generation pure souls are coming to light in every family, and they remain so. The river is cloudy and full of filth, but many springs flow into it and there is still hope that one day the water will all become clear.'

Eleven days later, on 31 March, in Moscow, after two hours of agonizing pain, Sonya gave birth to her thirteenth child, a boy, who was baptized Ivan (Vanichka). When the sixty-year-old father picked up the baby in his arms and bent his grey beard over it, the mother could not restrain her tears of gratitude. 'It is a miracle from Lyovochka!' she wrote to her sister, on 11 April. 'He is so glad it is a boy and is full of tenderness for it. I can't say whom he looks like. He is long-limbed and has cloudy eyes and dark hair, but it seems to me it's always the same baby, just a continuation of the previous ones, not a new person.'

Two weeks after his wife's confinement, the proud father decided that he needed to stretch his legs and set off to walk to Yasnaya Polyana with a pack on his back, accompanied by the young son of Gay, the painter. The hikers covered the hundred and thirty miles in five days, through rain, wind and sun. Arriving at Yasnaya Polyana, Tolstoy felt twenty years old. When Sonya wrote, 'Little Ivan is too thin, he is not developing well and I am terribly worried about him,'[10] he replied with sublime confidence:

'Don't worry too much about Ivan, dear heart, God has given us a little one, and will provide nourishment for him too. ... I feel so good, so light and simple and affectionate towards you, as you towards me, I hope.'[11]

Back in Moscow, he heard the *Kreutzer Sonata* again, played by Liassotta and Sergey at a gathering of friends in the family drawing-room. Repin, the painter, and Andreyev-Burlak, an actor, were among those present. Subjugated anew by Beethoven's music, Tolstoy proposed that they interpret the feeling the music inspired in them, each using the tools of his own art. He would write a story called *The Kreutzer Sonata*, and the actor would read it in public in front of a picture painted for the occasion by the artist. The previous summer, at Yasnaya Polyana, the painter had told him about a stranger he had met in a train one day, who had recited the tale of his conjugal woes with tears in his eyes. Tolstoy seized upon this, combined it with one of his own unfinished short stories – *The Man Who Murdered His Wife* – and felt he had hold of an awesome, profound, challenging subject, the kind he liked these days. Since the story was to be recited by Andreyev-Burlak, he thought it would heighten the tragic tone to write it in monologue form. But Andreyev-Burlak died in May of that year, Repin forgot his promise to paint a picture and Tolstoy alone carried out his project.

Between March and May 1888 he sketched out the novel in which, for the first time, the character of the musician appears. Then he put the manuscript aside, but continued to think about this strange fable in which sexuality and family life were the villains. As always, when he had found an idea that seemed right to him, he needed to carry it to the extreme. The further his deductions led him into absurdity, the more strongly he believed he must be inspired by God. He, who had once written to Chertkov in praise of procreation in wedlock, suddenly began preaching the necessity for conjugal abstinence to the same correspondent. According to St Matthew (xix, 12), Christ had said, 'For there are some eunuchs, which were so born from their mother's womb: and there are some eunuchs, which were made eunuchs of men: and there be eunuchs, which have made themselves eunuchs for the kingdom of heaven's sake. He that is able to receive it, let him receive it.' All this meant, affirmed Tolstoy, was that in order to live in accordance with God's word it was necessary, if not actually to mutilate oneself, at least to forget that one had an instrument for sex. To this end, it was advisable for husband and wife to sleep in separate rooms. If they were unable to resist temptation and, by mishap, a child be born of their commerce, they must refrain from all further intercourse so long as the mother was nursing her offspring. 'Otherwise, the woman may perhaps become a good mistress, but she will certainly become an overworked mother and a sick, irritable, hysterical person,' wrote Tolstoy on 6 November 1888 to Chertkov. 'Therefore let everyone try not to marry and, if he be married, to live with his wife as brother and sister. ... You will object that this would mean the end of the human race? ... What a great misfortune! The antediluvian animals are gone from the earth, human animals will disappear too. I have no more pity for these two-footed beasts than for the ichthyosaurus.'

In March 1889, during a visit to his friend Prince Urusov, he took up his manuscript again and revised it. 'I read [*The Kreutzer Sonata*] to Urusov,' he noted. 'He liked it very much. It is true that it is something new and powerful.' Upon his return to Moscow, he received a package of books and pamphlets from America on the Shakers, a sect that preached the abolition of sexual relations. This coincidence struck him as a sign of divine approbation. 'I read the writings of the Shakers,' he wrote on 9 April 1889. 'Perfect. Total chastity. Odd to receive them just when I am concerned with the question.' The next day he wrote to Chertkov: 'I do not agree with the solution advocated by the Shakers, but I cannot deny that it is far more reasonable than that which results from our universally accepted institution of marriage. I shall not overcome this problem in a hurry, because I am a dirty, libidinous old man!'

The idea of innocence was so appealing to him that he wrote in his notebook, 'Must propose the Shaker arrangement to [Sonya].' But he did not dare speak to her about it yet. If she had accepted, which of the two would have been more cruelly punished?

All summer long he worked on the book with grim passion. For the love of God he had given up property, hunting, meat and tobacco, one after the other. Now he wanted to give up sex. For him, the enemy was woman; and the reason was that he was too strongly sensual not to be continually led into temptation. In physical pleasure he abandoned some part of himself; when the act was over he hated the woman who had gained that moment of power over him and he scurried back into his shell, determined not to come out of it again, for he was truly happy only in the solitary recital of his aspirations towards Christ and his grievances against his family, his literary projects and the gurgles of his stomach. Impenitent old Narcissus, eternally preoccupied with himself, he blew on his image in the water for the sheer pleasure of seeing it come back again when the ripples died away.

Superficially, there was nothing in common between Leo Tolstoy and Pozdnyshev, the hero of *The Kreutzer Sonata* who tells his fellow passenger in the train compartment how he murdered his wife out of jealousy. But the theories propounded by this character are so exact a copy of the author's convictions that, apart from the murder, the entire story might be autobiographical. A great deal of water had flowed under the bridge since Tolstoy propounded his views of love leading to domestic felicity in *War and Peace*. In *Anna Karenina*, he condemned adulterous passion while still glorifying marital affection, but the Levin/Kitty couple is already being undermined by malaise. In the third phase – *The Kreutzer Sonata* – even conjugal bonds are accursed. As coldly as he previously analysed the death agony of Ivan Ilich, he now analyses the death agony of the Pozdnyshev marriage. In passing, women in general and Sonya in particular are hauled over the coals. To give a touch of plausibility to his indictment, the author is continually enriching it with details from his own experience. Like Tolstoy, Pozd-nyshev also shows his private diary to his fiancée: 'I re-member her distress, followed by alarm and despair, when she learned those facts. I saw her almost on the point of breaking off. Would she had only done so!' Elsewhere, Pozdnyshev-alias-Tolstoy tells how his wife refused to nurse her baby: 'In this way she was deprived of her sole weapon against coquetry. A wetnurse took the child; in other words, we took advantage of a woman's poverty, need and ignor-ance to tear her away from her own baby and give her ours and, in return for this service, put a beribboned cap on her head.' And here is the old grievance of the move to Moscow: 'Really, there are some curious coincidences: just when the parents cannot bear to live together a moment longer, it becomes essential to go to the city for the child-ren's education.' Or, better still: 'When the children began to grow up and have definite personalities, they became allies which each of us tried to draw into his camp. They suffered dreadfully, poor things, but in our unending battle we had other things to consider besides their feelings.'

It is hard not to imagine the irritation Tolstoy must have felt in Sonya's presence when Pozdnyshev says, speaking of his wife, 'I watched her pouring out her tea, putting the spoon in her mouth and swinging her foot, noisily sucking on the liquid, and found myself loathing her as though she were committing some hideous crime. I did not notice, then, that these periods of animosity occurred with perfect pre-dictability and corresponded to the other periods, which we call of love. Period of love, period of hate; period of violent love, prolonged period of hate; more feeble manifestation of love, shorter period of hate.... We were two convicts serving life sentences of hard labour welded to the same chain, we hated each other, we were making each other's lives hell, and trying all the time not to see it. At that time I had not yet learned that this hell is the fate of ninety-nine per cent of all couples.'

And how Pozdnyshev's quarrels with his wife echo those

of the author with Sonya. 'I shout at her, "Be quiet!" or something of the sort; she rushes out of the room and runs to the children. I want to hold her back and finish my explanation, I catch her by the arm. She pretends I have hurt her and screams, "Children, your father is beating me!" I go back to my study, lie down and begin to smoke. ... I think of running away, hiding, going to America. ... Around eleven o'clock her sister arrives as emissary. It begins as usual: "She is in a dreadful state. What is the meaning of this?"'

The virtuoso's arrival on the scene, his playing of the Kreutzer Sonata, the birth of jealousy in Pozdnyshev's heart, and the murder, are all imaginary, of course. But from beginning to end, every line of the book reveals the author's disgust with marriage – nothing but 'legalized prostitution'; his hatred of women – 'who take revenge upon us by playing on our senses'; his conviction that in order to obey the will of God, man must refrain from reproduction – 'The strongest passion of all, the most perfidious, the most stubborn, is sexual passion, carnal love. ... As long as mankind shall endure, it has an ideal to strive for and its ideal is certainly not that of rabbits and swine, which is to multiply as often as possible, nor that of apes and Parisians, which is to enjoy sexual pleasure with the highest possible degree of refinement. . . .' Or, 'Will the human race be wiped out because a dozen or a score of individuals refuse to behave like pigs?'

Novel of manners? Propaganda pamphlet against society? Confession? Profession of faith? *The Kreutzer Sonata* is all these. Violent, heart-rending, grotesque, tragic, admirable – it is a powerful book because of its fervent sincerity. Once again, the author has indulged in breast-beating; but this time he has added a final touch of refinement by dragging his wife through the mud with him. He unhesitatingly offers up to the public the secrets of his periods of rut, his quarrels, his loathing; he flings open their bedroom door. And he knew perfectly well that his readers, who were accustomed to the autobiographical element in his writing, would identify Sonya with the victim, and that some would pity her and others mock her. How was it that he, who professed to be filled with loving kindness for his fellow creatures, who was continually afraid of inadvertently hurting anyone's feelings, did not imagine what an unspeakable humiliation he would inflict upon his life-partner by publishing this book?

Whether unwittingly or out of conscious cruelty, he did more than merely publish it: he gave the manuscript to her to read and copy in her own hand. On 4 July 1889 he wrote in his diary, 'Sonya is copying it and is very much affected by it!' Singular gift for a silver wedding anniversary. She read, cursed, wept. After twenty-five years of preaching to all Russia that woman's most noble calling was marriage and childbirth, how could this man publicly deny his ideal? How dared he tell others to be chaste when, at sixty, he had got her with child for the thirteenth time? She tried to reason with him, but he swelled out his chest and spoke of his mission on earth, and she bowed to the majesty of the written word.

As soon as it had been copied the book was taken to Moscow, and on 29 October 1889 Koni read it to a small group of writers gathered in the Kuzminsky home; a second reading took place the next day in the editorial offices of the Intermediary; during the night, unpaid scribes made copies of the text and in less than a week nearly eight hundred lithographed copies were circulating in St Petersburg; their numbers doubled, tripled, invaded the provinces. Before the book was even printed, before the censor had given its decision, the case was being hotly debated all over Russia. According to Strakhov, people no longer greeted each other in the street with 'How are you?' but with 'Have you read *The Kreutzer Sonata*?' Some hailed it as a work of genius, others as a scandal; the Church fulminated, and so did the partisans of free love, and single women, and mothers! ... A large number of articles appeared and even literary works, the most noteworthy of which is a story by Leskov, On 'The Kreutzer Sonata'.

In the midst of this turmoil, Sonya felt as though waves of mud were spattering her from head to foot. 'Everyone feels sorry for me,' she wrote, 'from the emperor down. ... But why consult the opinions of others? Deep in my own heart, I always felt that the book was directed against me, mutilated me and humiliated me in the eyes of the whole world, and was destroying everything we had preserved of love for one another. And yet never once in my entire married life have I made a single gesture or given a single glance for which I need feel guilty towards my husband.'

Her sole obsession now was not to become pregnant again. What a howl of derision would rise from the public then! For, need it be said, after stigmatizing all fornicators Tolstoy had been unable to abstain himself. Upon leaving his wife's arms, he wrote in his diary, 'And what if another baby came? How ashamed I should be, especially in front of my children! They will compare the date [of conception] with that of publication [of The Kreutzer Sonata].'[12] To remove temptation, he wanted Sonya to sleep alone. But she refused. So he must rely on his own willpower. When he reached out for her, she had mingled feelings of triumph and disgust. 'The coldness and severity melted,' she wrote, 'and the end was the same as always! ...' And, 'He is being charming, cheerful and affectionate again. It is, alas, always for the same reason. If those who have read and are reading The Kreutzer Sonata could have one glimpse of Lyovochka's love life, if they could see what makes him so gay and kind, they would hurl their idol down from the pedestal they have put him on.'[13]

At the beginning of 1890 the censor still had not announced its decision. Pobyedonostsev wrote, 'A powerful work. If I ask myself whether I must condemn it for immorality, I cannot bring myself to say I should.'[14] Emperor Alexander III found it a magnificent work, but the empress was shocked. In the end, under pressure from ecclesiastical

circles, the minister of the interior forbade the publication of
The Kreutzer Sonata both as a separate volume and in the
Collected Works.

Tolstoy was not unduly incensed by this. He had said
what he wanted to say. It was no more concern of his
whether the book was printed or circulated in manuscript
form. He was more disturbed, however, by the criticism he
was receiving from a large body of readers. His mail had
tripled. From all sides strangers were begging him to tell
them whether he really desired the extinction of the human
race. Chertkov himself was pestering the master: 'In its
present form,' he wrote to Tolstoy, 'this book [*The Kreutzer
Sonata*] can only sow doubts in the public mind and fail to
clear up its uncertainties, whereas you might have settled
them by emphasizing a few Christian concepts.'

Goaded by all this misinterpretation, Tolstoy undertook
to write an afterword to the book. On a much smaller scale,
it gave him as much trouble as the novel itself. How could
Chertkov, who knew his master so well, imagine that in
elucidating his thesis he would tone it down? Once he was
well in his stride, Tolstoy made straight for the goal, mowing down everything in his way. Starting with the idea that
in order to live a Christian life it was necessary to dominate
the appetites of the flesh, his afterword recommended physical exercise, which diverted the mind from impure
thoughts, and criticized gastronomy, which was conducive
to sensuality. Continence, he affirmed, was indispensable outside marriage and desirable within. Besides, marriage was not
a creation of Jesus but an invention of the Church. 'There
has never been and never can be a Christian marriage, just
as there never has been and never can be a Christian religious ritual or Christian professors or Christian fathers or
Christian property or a Christian army, court or state.'

While he was pounding out this diatribe, Sonya again became terrified of having been fecundated by her champion
of sterility. 'I am very much afraid I am pregnant again,' she
wrote on 25 December 1890. 'Everyone will hear of this

ignominy and they will al! be maliciously repeating the
joke that is making the rounds in Moscow, "That is the real
postscript to *The Kreutzer Sonata*."'

She felt she needed to understand her husband better, and
decided to recopy the diaries he had kept in his bachelor
days. Some of the pages still offended her as they had done
when she first read them. 'Today I was copying Lyovochka's
diaries,' she wrote, 'and stopped where he says, "Love does
not exist, there is only the body's need of physical communion and the reason's need for a companion in life." Had
I seen that sentence twenty-nine years ago, I would never
have married him.'[15] 'The connexion between those old
notes in Lyovochka's diary and *The Kreutzer Sonata* is so
obvious! And I am the fly buzzing in the spider's web and
the spider is sucking my blood.'[16]

When Lyovochka found out that she was ferreting about
in his papers, he became angry. 'Why stir up all that old
trash?' he said. She retorted, with vindictive glee, 'Suffer for
it, since you've lived so badly!' Then he forbade her to continue copying. 'I am very much annoyed,' wrote Sonya, 'because I had already finished a large part of it and had only a
little more to do in the notebook I was working on. But I
shall continue in secret, and I shall finish, whatever happens.'[17] She had lost all respect for him, she laughed at his
virtuous poses, she even dared to question the virtues of a
new vegetarian diet he had found in a German review: 'No
doubt the person who advocates this diet follows it as closely
as Lyovochka, who preaches chastity in *The Kreutzer
Sonata* and yet behaves like . . .'[18]

Not content with contradicting him whenever she could,
she wanted public absolution for the indignity he had inflicted upon her in *The Kreutzer Sonata*. By way of riposte,
she wrote an autobiographical novel entitled, *Who Is To
Blame?* Using the subject of *The Kreutzer Sonata* but arranging it to suit her own purposes, she described a man of
the world, Prince Prozorovsky, a sensual brute who, at the
age of thirty-five, marries a girl of eighteen, Anna, pure,

mischievous, noble and pious. While they are still engaged, he is already casting lewd glances at her hips. After the wedding ceremony he cannot even wait to get inside the house, but takes the poor girl like an animal, in the carriage, in spite of the bumps and jolts. She is humiliated by this for the rest of her life. Later, a consumptive young painter falls in love with her – platonically – and the dreadful Prozorovsky, a violent-tempered man reeking of tobacco, is unable to control his jealousy and kills the woman who had done no wrong.

Sonya was very proud of her story and read it to anyone who would listen.[19] Her friends had some difficulty persuading her not to publish it. If she heeded them, it was only because more serious threats against her husband were looming on the horizon. She was ready and willing to attack him *en famille*, but would not tolerate anyone else attacking him from outside, and even though she hated *The Kreutzer Sonata* she was infuriated because the censor had prohibited the publication of Volume XIII of the *Complete Works*, which contained it. Friends in good standing at court advised her to try a personal appeal to the tsar to have the decision reversed. 'If I liked *The Kreutzer Sonata*, if I believed Lyovochka would write any more *artistic books* in the future, I would go,' she wrote.[20]

Two things helped her to overcome her reluctance. One was the fact that the prohibition of Volume XIII would represent a substantial financial loss, and the other was the fact that by openly militating for the book she would prove to the world that there was no connexion between her married life and the abominable tale recounted by the author. 'Vanity is pushing me, more than anything else,' she wrote in a moment of truthfulness. When he heard what she intended to do, Tolstoy tried to dissuade her. He did not want to owe anything to the emperor. Besides, that edition of his *Complete Works* was nothing but a low commercial enterprise, he said, completely at odds with his theories. His opposition tipped the scales for Sonya.

She set off for St Petersburg on 28 March 1891, went to stay with her sister Tanya, contacted a few influential persons and, on 31 March, wrote to the emperor:

I humbly implore Your Imperial Majesty the favour of an audience, so that I may make a request of Your Majesty concerning my husband, Leo Nikolayevich Tolstoy. With Your Majesty's kind permission, I shall state the conditions in which my husband might resume his former artistic and literary activities. I would also point out to Your Majesty the inaccuracy of certain allegations being made with respect to the present activities of Leo Nikolayevich Tolstoy, which are painful to him and are undermining the creative powers of a Russian author whose health is already beginning to fail but who might yet add to his contribution to the glory of his fatherland.

I am,

Your Imperial Majesty's loyal subject,
Countess Sofya Tolstoy.

Twelve days later her request for an audience was granted and, on 13 April, decked out in ceremonial attire – black dress and hat with a black lace veil – she left the Kuzminsky home for the Anichkov Palace on the Nevsky Prospect. On the threshold she lost all contact with reality. All that marble, those plants, those purple azaleas, those wax-faced lackeys, those Negroes dressed in Egyptian costumes! A young messenger wearing a red uniform trimmed in gold and a plumed three-cornered hat led the caller up a wide staircase and into a little drawing-room, and disappeared. She was so excited and her heart was pounding so hard that she almost fainted. 'Very cautiously, so that no one should see me,' she wrote, 'I unlaced my corset and sat down to massage my chest.' The messenger came back and announced, 'His Majesty asks Her Excellency Countess Tolstoy to come this way.' In a dizzy haze, she made her curtsey to the emperor. In spite of her agitated state, she observed that he was 'tall, rather stout', had 'hardly any hair' and that 'his temples were too narrow'. Some things about him reminded her of Chertkov. He received her cordially.

When she had told him, without a blush, that her husband was about to give up his philosophical activities and settle down to write a book in the style of *War and Peace*, he exclaimed:

'Ah, how wonderful that would be! How he can write! How he can write! ...'

She was emboldened to speak of *The Kreutzer Sonata*, presenting it as a highly moral work.

'The story does exaggerate,' she said, 'but the basic idea is that the ideal can never be attained. If total chastity is accepted as the ideal, then only in marriage can one remain pure.'

This specious reasoning brought a smile to the tsar's lips. In the end he authorized the publication of the novel, but only in the *Complete Works*, as the relatively high price of those volumes would be a curb to their wide distribution. Then he expressed concern at the negative influence the Tolstoyans were having on the peasants, and Sonya passionately defended her dear Lyovochka, and even the hated Chertkov. In order to break down the sovereign's last defences, she asked him to be the first to judge her husband's literary productions in the future. He willingly accepted, asked after Sonya's children and invited her to pay her respects to the empress – a tiny woman with dark-brown hair plastered to her skull as though glued to it, waspwaisted, squeezed to bursting-point inside a black woollen gown – who held out her hand, bade Sonya be seated, and spoke in a guttural voice that contrasted sharply with the affability of her remarks. Leaving the palace, glowing and relieved, Sonya could hardly keep from running.

That same day she took the train back to Yasnaya Polyana at three in the afternoon. She would have liked to be met as a conquering heroine, but Lyovochka greeted her as a defaulting ally. He reproached her for going too far, for making promises that he could not keep. Motionless, she listened to him storm, and he soon grew ashamed of his outburst. How could he criticize her, after letting her go?

And fifteen days away! Too long! The infamous desire he denounced in *The Kreutzer Sonata* began to burn in his veins once again. '... I spoke to her angrily,' he wrote in his diary, 'but eventually it all worked out, particularly since, under the influence of a culpable impulse, I was glad to see her back.'[21] A few days later, fresh violation of the principle of chastity – this time, recorded by Sonya: 'Lyovochka has sent Tanya to tell me that he is in bed and has put out the light. Innocent lips transmit these anything but innocent words. I know what they mean and I don't like it. ...'[22]

Soon afterwards, she received a ministerial letter confirming her authorization to publish *The Kreutzer Sonata* and the afterword to it in the *Complete Works*. When she read the official document, her pride overflowed: 'Deep in my heart, I exult to think that I braved them all and went to the tsar and obtained from him – I, a mere woman – what no one else could have obtained,'[23] she wrote.

I wanted to show myself in public so they could see how little I resemble a victim; I wanted people to talk about me; I did it instinctively! I was sure my appeal to Alexander III would be successful; I have not yet used up all my talent for arousing sympathy in others, I conquered the tsar with my words and the intensity of my feelings. But for the public, I also needed the authorization to publish *The Kreutzer Sonata*. ... If the book had been inspired by me, if it did portray my relations with Leo Nikolayevich, I should certainly have done nothing to further its circulation, anyone who thinks for a moment will realize that. The tsar speaks of me in the most flattering terms. ... According to Princess Urusov, who had it from Zhukovsky, the emperor said I was simple, sincere and engaging; he had not supposed I was still so young and good-looking. All this is highly flattering to my woman's vanity and revenges me upon my husband who, far from trying to make me attractive in the eyes of society, has constantly sought to debase me.[24]

While she was trumpeting her triumph all by herself in her corner, he was piling up stores of hostile notes about women: 'To say that a woman has as much strength of character as a man, or that one can find in women what one can expect to find in men, is to deceive oneself.' (17 June 1891.) 'A pretty woman says to herself, "He is learned, intelligent, virtuous and he does what I say, therefore I am superior to learning, intelligence and virtue."' (August 1891.)

He was not pleased with what he had written during the last few years. Now, even *The Kreutzer Sonata* did not satisfy him: 'To stir up so much mud, there must have been something culpable in my reasons for writing it,' he said to Chertkov. For relaxation, he had put together a pleasant little comedy in the meantime, called *The Fruits of Enlightenment*, which Tanya produced at Yasnaya Polyana at the end of December 1889,* then played at Tula and Tsarskoye-Selo in April 1890, as the tsar had authorized the performance of the play by amateurs only. He had also written, or rather tossed off, a large number of articles and tales of the early Christians, such as *Walk in the Light*, and a long story, *The Devil* – yet another illustration of the negative influence of women, in which, through the diabolical workings of sensuality, a simple peasant girl drives a married man to suicide.†

But the work by which he set most store in this period was *On Life*. Originally, the essay was to have been entitled *On Life and Death*, but as he progressed, the author came to the conclusion that death did not exist. Throughout the thirty-five chapters of the essay he explains that true life does not begin inside a man until his animal, individual conscience is no longer supreme, in short, until he stops thinking about himself. Rebirth is dictated by love of one's neighbour. Seen in this light, even pain is useful because it opens the way to a higher existence. As to death, man fears it because he mistakes the demands of his animal instincts for the funda-

---

*Tanya had just returned from a trip through France and Italy with her brother Sergey and the Olsufyevs.

†*The Devil* was suggested to Tolstoy by the story of Friederichs, an official in Tula who had assassinated his peasant-mistress Stepanida, and by his own affair with a serf before his marriage.

mental disposition of his soul. At the close of his meditation, thus, Tolstoy had acquired the same certainty as Ivan
Ilich breathing his last: 'Where is death? What death? He
was not afraid any more because there was no death any
more. Instead of death, there was light.'

Sonya was so fond of *On Life* that, with the help of Professor Tastevin, she translated it into French. Earlier, she
had written in her diary, 'I am copying Lyovochka's study
On Life (and Death). When I was young, very young, before
my marriage, I aspired to the good described in it with all
my heart and soul, the fruit of total self-denial and the gift
of oneself to others. I aspired to the ascetic life. But fate
gave me a family and now I live for that.' [25]

She was so happy every time her ideas approached those
of Lyovochka. Why was she forever having to look after a
thousand material details, the household accounts, the children's education, Michael's nightshirts, Andrey's shoes,
meals for the teachers and servants, while he forged ahead
unfettered, his head in the clouds, heedless of everyone
and everything? Sometimes she raged at her husband, striding far ahead of her, in such a hurry, and sometimes at her
family, who were holding her back and preventing her from
catching up with him.

[24]

Famine and Strife

AFTER the flare-up over *The Kreutzer Sonata* the couple's relations were poisoned by resentment, in spite of all their conciliatory efforts. As Tolstoy's audience grew, he suffered increasingly from the conflict between his principles and his instincts. He continually saw himself in a false position, because he was eating, because he was loving, because he was breathing, because he could not forget that he had a body. After proclaiming the necessity for chastity in marriage, he held Sonya to blame for the fact that at the age of sixty-three he still desired her. And although she was very glad to have preserved at least this power over him, she despaired because she no longer had any place in his thoughts. He seldom spoke to her about his plans, did not share his work with her, listened in irritation when she presented some domestic problem to him, often upbraided her grossly, even in front of the children, and went out of his way to avoid being alone with her, except when in the grip of a sudden need of affection. In his eyes she personified two dreadful sins: lust and cupidity. All the money in the house passed through her hands, she was soiled by it; whereas he longed to have no possessions at all. True, he had turned over the supervision and management of the estate to Sonya, but he was still its legal owner. Everything in the deeds and abstracts, both land and buildings, was in his name. How was he to square that with his vow of poverty? While he was posing as a martyr to riches and comfort, Sonya complained that the family was dumping all the dirty work on her shoulders and then sniffing contemptuously at her for doing it. 'I feel as though I am caught in a vice and cannot get out,' she wrote on 11 December 1890 in her diary. 'This business of managing the property, which has been imposed upon me in the name of Christian principles, is the heaviest cross God has given me. If saving one's own soul means damning that of others, then Lyovochka will be saved. But isn't that perdition for both of us?'

An incident that same winter of 1890 shattered the last vestiges of harmony between them. For some time, muzhiks had been cutting down the birch trees in one of the Tolstoy forests and taking the wood. Sonya, losing patience, decided to lodge a complaint with the district chief. It was her intention – approved by Lyovochka – to release the culprits as soon as they had been judged. They were sentenced to six weeks in prison and a fine of twenty-seven roubles. But when Sonya requested their release, she was told that this was a criminal case and it would be quite impossible either to withdraw the complaint or to change the sentence. Tolstoy promptly had an attack of remorse. Once again, property had engendered evil. And it was he, the apostle of abandonment of all worldly goods, who was responsible for a conviction for theft! He ought to have given all his trees to the poor wretches, since they needed them, instead of which he had delivered them into the hands of justice, whose utility he denied in his writings. Naturally, he had acted at the instigation of his wife! He rebuked her vehemently. She retorted that it had been his idea in the first place to give the muzhiks a scare by sending them up before the police.

He could not sleep. He paced up and down in his room, with drooping beard and moistened, tragic eye. 'What astonished me is that he has continually sought to arouse my sympathy for him,' she wrote, 'but has not made the slightest effort to put himself in my place or understand that I never had any intention of doing any harm to anyone, not even to thieving muzhiks. That self-worship of his comes across on every page of his diary. It is amazing to see how people simply do not exist for him except in so far as they concern him directly.'[1]

Until five in the morning he sighed, wept and inveighed

against his wife, while she, exhausted, momentarily contemplated suicide: 'Tell them all good-bye and go lie down peacefully on the railroad track.' She was haunted by the memory of Anna Karenina. The author's wife, even in death. It relieved her to write this resolution in her notebook, and she dropped off to sleep. The next day the argument pursued its course in the rest of the family. The two older daughters thought their mother was wrong, but Tanya wrote in her diary, 'I feel more sorry for Maman than for Papa ... because she does not believe in anything. ... And then she loves Papa more than he loves her. She is as overjoyed as a child at the smallest word of kindness from him.' Meanwhile, Tolstoy was writing, 'It has become more than I can bear. My heart ached all day long. I should go away.'[2] The next day, 'I think I should inform the government that I am giving up my property rights and let it do what it will.'

During the ensuing weeks, this idea ripened in his mind. He decided that it was no longer enough to leave the management of his property to his wife. If he wanted to suit his action to his thoughts, he should refuse to own anything at all in his own name. The best thing would be to distribute all his land to the peasants. But Sonya and the older sons were opposed to this. After lengthy confabulation, they reached a compromise: Tolstoy would bequeath all his goods and chattels to Sonya and the children, who would divide them up among themselves. The evaluation of the property and the contents of each share gave rise to heated debate around the family table. The apostle of dispossession now sat and listened in dismay as the true nature of his wife and children became apparent: they were haggling over a few roubles or an acre of ground. 'Now one is not satisfied with something and the other is afraid of heaven knows what,' wrote Sonya. 'It is most trying. As for Lyovochka, his only contribution to the discussion is indifference and sulkiness.' Tanya observed that her father, aghast at the turn events had taken, looked like 'a condemned man who cannot wait to put his head through the noose'. Sometimes he could stand no more and fled, shutting himself up in his workshop to make boots. Then Sonya would sigh, 'I would so like to see him in good health, but he is ruining his stomach, even the doctor says so, eating things that are no good for him. I would like to see him doing an artist's work, but all he writes is sermons. I would like to see him tender, sympathetic, friendly, but whenever he is not being grossly sensual, he is indifferent.'

The decision to divide up the property was made at Easter, but the actual bequest to the living heirs was not signed until over a year later: 7 July 1892. The bargaining continued bitterly until the last moment. The entire estate was evaluated at 580,000 roubles.* It was divided into ten shares, and a legal document was drawn up allocating the first to Sonya and the others to the nine surviving children. Nikolskoye (the Tolstoy homestead) was divided among Sergey, Ilya, Tanya and Masha; Ilya also received Grinevka; Leo had the Moscow house and a part of the Samara farm; Tanya and Masha received Ovsyanikovo and 40,000 roubles in cash; Andrey, Michael and Sasha were each given 3,400 acres of fallow land in Samara; and Yasnaya Polyana went to the mother and Vanichka, the last-born, 'for the children cannot take this estate away from their father,' Sonya wrote, 'and wherever I am he will be too'.

Of the entire family, only the two eldest daughters wondered whether, out of loyalty to their father's ideas, they should not refuse any part of this wild scramble. Tanya, who was more sensitive to worldly attractions, ultimately yielded: 'I still need so many things and am so useless that in the end I shall have to be supported by somebody else,' she wrote, to excuse her adherence to the plan; but Masha the violent, the sectarian, came forth with a lofty refusal. Her father was moved to tears; her mother, brothers and sisters said she was only doing it to put them in a bad light.

* Or $1,642,300.

Yesterday, a really amazing conversation among the children [noted Tolstoy on 5 July 1892.] Tanya and Leo were trying to prove to Masha that it was a low, evil trick on her part to give up her share of the estate. Her attitude forces them to face the fact that theirs is truly base, and since they must needs be right at all costs, they invent explanations to prove that what she is doing is wicked and vile. Disgusting! I can't write. I have already wept and I feel like crying some more. They say, 'We thought of doing it ourselves, but it wouldn't have been right.' My wife tells them, 'Leave it all to me!' That silences them. Horrible. I have never seen more obvious and more clearly motivated hypocrisy. Sorrow, sorrow, what weight, what torture!

Masha held her ground against the whole pack of heirs, in spite of their concerted baying. Her farsighted mother decided to keep back her share, however, and let the income from it accumulate, just in case her daughter should change her mind one day. 'The poor girl,' she said, 'cannot see things clearly, or imagine what her life would be like if, after living as she has, she were suddenly to find herself penniless.'

There remained the ticklish question of royalties. Tolstoy meant to give them up too, but Sonya opposed him once again. 'She doesn't understand, and the children do not understand,' he wrote, 'that every time they spend a rouble from the sale of my books they are causing me shame and suffering. The shame I could bear, but why lessen the impact that proclaiming such a truth as this might have? I suppose it must be so. The truth will prevail without my help.'[3]

On the following day, 15 July, Sonya surrendered, and consented to her husband authorizing anyone and everyone to publish his later works. But when, a week later (21 July), he announced that he had written a letter to the press explaining the implications of his decision, she flew into a rage. White with anger, she screamed that she needed that money to keep the family going and that by giving up his rights he was making a public scandal of his dispute with

his wife and children, that it was just one more indignity
inflicted on those who bore his name; that, moreover, he
was not acting out of real conviction but for the sake of his
own fame and glory, that he would stoop to anything to
attract attention to himself. The apostle winced and retorted that his wife was 'the most stupid and greedy creature' he had ever met and that she was perverting the children 'with her roubles'. Then, pointing to the door, he
shouted, 'Get out! Get out!' Sonya, racked by sobs, ran into
the garden and hid in the apple orchard so that the caretaker should not see her in tears; she sat down, panting, on
the edge of a ditch. There she pencilled a few words in her
notebook, explaining that death was the only solution to the
discord between herself and Lyovochka. Decidedly, Anna
Karenina's example was contagious. This time, for sure, she
would throw herself under a train. She got up and ran,
stumbling in her skirts, towards the Kozlovka station. Her
head ached painfully, 'as though clamped in a vice'.

In the twilight, she saw a man dressed in a peasant blouse
coming towards her. She thought it was her husband and
there would be a reconciliation. A surge of joy drove her on-
ward. But she was mistaken: the man in the peasant blouse
was her brother-in-law Kuzminsky. Seeing the state she was
in, he questioned her, tried to calm her and pleaded with
her to return to the house. She walked a little way with him,
then left him to bathe in the Voronka, hoping to drown
herself. But the dark, chilly water frightened her. She went
back to the forest. Suddenly she thought she saw an animal
charging at her. Dog? Fox? Wolf? She screamed. Nothing,
nobody. The animal had vanished in the evening mist. She
told herself that she had gone mad. Then, feeling better,
she returned to the house and went to see Vanichka in his
bed. She loved him so, her frail little boy whose grace and
gentleness and intelligence consoled her for the brutality of
the others. Sometimes she feared he was too perfect for this
world. She wrote, 'What an exquisite child! I am afraid he
will not live.'[4] She smothered him with kisses. Outdoors, on

the terrace, Tolstoy was chatting and laughing with his big sons and daughters and their guests. 'He will never know how close I came to killing myself,' she thought, 'and if he does find out, he won't believe it.'[5]

Late that night, after the guests had gone away, Lyovochka came to find his wife, took her in his arms and spoke to her tenderly. 'I begged him to publish his statement and not to speak about it any more,' she wrote. 'He told me he would not publish it until I understood that it had to be. I replied that I could not lie and would not lie and that it was impossible for me to understand that. Scenes like the one today are hastening the hour of my death. Let them strike, but let them finish me off quickly!'

The ensuing days brought more arguments followed by more reconciliations in bed. After these embraces, in which there was no real love, both repented in their respective diaries.

'Terribly displeased with myself,' wrote Sonya on 27 July. 'Lyovochka woke me early in the morning with passionate caresses. ... Then I took a French novel, *Un coeur de femme* by Paul Bourget, and read in bed until eleven-thirty, a thing I never do. This stupor that is creeping over me is unforgivable at my age. ... What a strange man my husband is! The day after this quarrel began he made me a declaration of his passion and love, assured me that I had great influence over him and that he would never have believed so strong an attachment possible. But that is all purely *physical*. It is the secret of our division. I, too, am dominated by his passion, but in my heart of hearts that is not what I want or ever have wanted. I have always dreamed of a platonic relationship, a perfect spiritual communion.'

And he was writing, in despair, 'I live not purely but by my senses. Help me, my God. I have lost my way, I am suffering, I cannot go on.'

Paradoxically, he began to be afraid of death again, just when he professed to be growing increasingly detached from material things. For some time he had begun every entry in his diary with the initials i.I.l. (if I live). He was wavering between heaven and earth. Nevertheless, this painful business of his royalties had to be settled. In order not to upset Sonya further, he resorted to the compromise he had adopted a few years before, whereby only the works subsequent to his 'rebirth' would immediately become public property.

On 16 September 1891, he sent a letter to the most important Russian newspapers: 'I hereby grant to all who wish it the right to publish, without payment, in Russia and abroad, in Russian or in translation, and to produce on the stage, all the works written by me since the year 1881 and published in Volumes XII (1886) and XIII (appearing this year, 1891), as well as those which have not yet been published in Russia or are to appear in the future.'

He would have liked Sonya to sign the letter abdicating his rights, to make it quite clear that the measure was not directed against her. But that was presumably asking too much of such a coarse-natured woman! She let him assume full responsibility for his action. What irked her most was that, as a bonus with his present to mankind, he was giving away *The Death of Ivan Ilich*, which she admired enormously and which he had offered to her on her birthday in 1886 for inclusion in Volume XII of the *Complete Works*. After reading the fateful announcement in the papers, she fumed: 'Everything he does comes from one source: vanity, thirst for fame, the need to be talked about as much as possible. Nobody can change my mind about that.'[6] She reproached him for his eternal talk about a Christian life, 'when he does not have one drop of love, either for his children or for me or for anyone except himself'.[7] She claimed, not without reason, that the people to benefit from his absurd renunciation would not be the poor and needy – far from it – but the publishers, that is, the rich themselves!

Tolstoy was too glad to be rid of his possessions to pay

any attention to her nagging. Now, in theory, he was delivered from the evils of property, legally a pauper, hypothetically divested of all means of subsistence. Ah, the pleasures of utter destitution! But how was he to live? To be consistent, he should leave his handsome home, retire to some abandoned isba and earn a bit of bread by the sweat of his brow, or set off with the pilgrims on the highroad to Kiev, preaching the truth and begging his bread from door to door. But he could not bring himself to make such a radical change. As always, he contented himself with half-measures, and dug himself into an ambiguous position whose ludicrous side did not escape him. He affected semi-starvation and peasant dress, he drew the water from the well himself and cleaned his own room, but he did not give up his library or his saddle horses or his piano or the big drawing-room in which his admirers congregated. Poor as Job on paper, he nevertheless continued to profit from his fortune, which had simply changed from his hands into those of his wife and children. Believing that he owed nothing, he was still living on them. Around him were the same chairs and tables, chandeliers, white-gloved lackeys as before; seated at the master's vast table and served by bowing attendants, he watched the disciples flocking in. The more there were, the greater his fame, and the more difficult it became for Sonya to feed them all.

In the village, Tolstoy often saw Timothy, the child he had had long before by his peasant mistress Axinya. A crude muzhik with steely eyes, a shapeless nose and heavy brows, he resembled him more closely than any of his legitimate children. He was a coachman on the estate. Tolstoy suffered occasional twinges of conscience at this reminder of his wayward youth. But, after all, it was the rule for a great noble to keep a few bastards on the premises, to prove his past virility. According to the custom of the time, the master's real children – those fortunate enough to bear his name – were not at all hostile towards Timothy and treated him as a brother who had lost out in his dealings with the law.

Only Sonya still became indignant, now and then, at the thought of this left-handed descendant.

The spring and summer of 1891 brought an unusually large crop of visitors to Yasnaya Polyana. Fet and his wife spent a few days in May. The old poet was more charming than ever, with his plunging nose and greying beard in his long goat's face, and his small hands with their well-manicured nails. He was bubbling over with juvenile enthusiasm, but Lyovochka was too preoccupied with God to have any taste for such purely human lyricism.* 'Fet read us some poems,' wrote Sonya. 'Love and more love ... His feverish inspiration awakens poetical, ambiguous ideas and feelings in me, and I am too old for them.'

The poet was succeeded by guests of lesser repute. As usual, the warm weather brought a new wave of admirers of every kind, professors, students, visionaries, opera singers, defrocked priests, repentant revolutionaries and government spies disguised as disciples. There were never fewer than fifteen at table. Stasov, a bearded giant with a leonine mane who was director of the St Petersburg Public Library, set the tone of praise of the master of the house with his endless ranting about 'Tolstoy the genius' whom he also called 'Leo the Great'. In the timeworn tradition, Sonya organized picnics and walks or rides, programmes of charades, amateur concerts, readings. She bustled from drawing-room to pantry, the overworked servants complained, the children's governesses quarrelled, and still more people wrote announcing their arrival ...

Tolstoy devoted his afternoons to his guests. In the morning he was, in principle, invisible. He withdrew at dawn to the vaulted ground-floor chamber in which he had made his study. The walls were fortress-thick and kept out all outside noises. Light fell softly from two high, narrow barred windows. The furniture was composed of one large table, a few old chairs covered with imitation black leather, a simple bookcase and a hard, narrow divan. A scythe and saw

* Fet was to die the following year.

leaned against one wall. A basket of cobbler's tools lay on the floor. In this lair Tolstoy wrote or made boots, depending on his mood. Just then, he was working on a story, *Father Sergey*, making notes for a future novel (entitled, for want of anything better, *Koni's Story*, after the friend who had supplied the subject) and composing religious articles such as *The Kingdom of God Is Within You*. He admitted into his inner sanctum an occasional artist, who had begged permission to see him at work, pen in hand; Repin painted a portrait of him writing, and Ginzburg sculpted a bust. Both were aware of the honour that had been conferred upon them. Repin also painted Tolstoy standing barefoot in the grass. The model did not like this picture. 'Why not paint me without my pants, while he's at it?' he grumbled.

Towards midsummer, alarming news reached Yasnaya Polyana: an unusually prolonged period of drought had brought famine to some of the central and southwestern provinces of Russia. A number of people, including the author Leskov, came to ask Tolstoy whether he did not think something should be done to help the suffering peasants. The master was annoyed by this appeal to charity – to begin with, because he had not had the idea first, and then because, together with the muzhik–philosopher Syutayev, he had long condemned private charity as a cheap means for the wealthy to ease their consciences, and lastly because, according to him, the principle of 'non-resistance to evil' should apply to natural disaster as well. His reply to his colleague was sententious:

There are crowds of customers for operations of this type [aid to the starving]: people who have lived all their lives without a thought for the common people, often disgusted by and disdainful of them, and who, at the drop of a hat, are consumed by solicitude for their inferior brothers. ... Their motives are conceit, vanity and fear of the people's anger. ... To fight famine, all that is necessary is for men to do more good deeds. A good deed does not consist in giving bread to feed the famished, but in loving the famished as much as the overfed. Loving is more important than giving food. ... Therefore, since you ask me what must be done, I reply: awaken, if you can (and you can), the love of men for one another, not now when there is a famine, but always and everywhere.[8]

Excerpts from this letter were published and aroused a storm of indignation in other newspapers. Tolstoy was called a 'heartless doctrinarian'. He himself, upon learning that the famine was growing worse, felt his paper turn to ash in the heat of reality. On 19 September 1891 he decided he would take his daughter Tanya and go to his brother's place at Pirogovo to investigate the extent of the damage and seek a remedy. In response to Sonya's ironic smile at his sudden devotion to a cause erstwhile held in contempt, he snapped, 'I beg you not to imagine I am doing this in order to get talked about; the fact is that I simply can't stop thinking about it!'

She let him go, noting, 'If he were doing it because his heart bleeds at the sufferings of the starving, I would fall on my knees before him, no sacrifice would be too great. But I didn't feel and do not feel that his heart was in it. I only hope he may move others by his pen and his cleverness.'

He toured the villages around Pirogovo, realized the extent of the disaster and planned an article on the famine. In October he decided to leave his wife in Moscow and return, taking his daughters Tanya and Masha – this time to the Province of Ryazan where his friend Rayevsky was struggling heroically to organize emergency relief. Sonya was horrified when he told her of his plan : 'To spend the whole winter separated from them, and to think of them twenty miles from the nearest station, Lyovochka with his stomach-aches and intestinal pains and the two little girls completely on their own! ...' The 'little girls' were not overjoyed either, but for different reasons. As good Tolstoyans, they considered – especially Tanya – that after condemning philanthropy, their father should not begin to champion it. 'We are about to leave for the Don,' wrote Tanya on 26 October 1891. 'I am not looking forward to this trip and am feeling completely unenthusiastic about it, because this action of Father's is inconsistent; it is not right for him to handle funds, take in gifts and ask Mother for the money he has just turned over to her. ... He says and he writes (and I agree with him) that the people's hardships stem from the fact that they are robbed and exploited by us, the landowners, and that the whole point is not to rob them any more. That is right, and Papa did what he said, he stopped robbing them. In my opinion, there is nothing more for him to do. ... He is too much in the public eye, he is too severely judged, to settle for *second best* when he has already reached *first best*.'*

Despite this lack of spirit in the 'troops', the father, his two daughters and his niece Vera Kuzminskaya went to Begichevka, the Rayevsky property in the government of Ryazan. When they arrived, after a tiring two-day train and sledge trip, they were overwhelmed by the misery they saw. Many peasants had died of starvation. Others had fled to seek work elsewhere. The survivors, dull-eyed skeletons, were too weak to move. Tattered children with swollen stomachs, their faces blue with cold, dozed on heaps of rags inside glacial isbas. There was no wood, so they burned the thatch off the roofs. Further rationalization was impossible in the face of such privation. Tolstoy and his daughters went to work alongside Rayevsky.

Tolstoy bought firewood with the first money Sonya advanced, and organized the baking of brown bread. Then he set up free kitchens in the villages. 'The mothers bring their children and feed them, but eat nothing themselves,' Tanya wrote on 2 November 1891. 'If those who are giving money to this cause could see their gifts going directly to help the victims, they would be amply rewarded for their sacrifices.'

The kitchens multiplied rapidly. Tolstoy made his headquarters at Begichevka, in the Rayevsky home. From there he set out every day on horseback to visit the surrounding

*In English in the original.

hamlets, make lists of the needy, supervise the fair allot-
ment of supplies, clothing and firewood. His daughters
helped him unstintingly. His sons, too, joined the relief
workers in other districts: Sergey and Ilya were in Chern,
Leo in Samara.

Every evening when he returned to Begichevka, freezing
and exhausted, Tolstoy commented on the day's incidents
to his daughters and the team of volunteers he had assembled. Some, like Tanya, reproached him for compromising himself by accepting gifts from persons who were
part of the 'System' and therefore despicable. He admitted,
with tears in his eyes, that his present activities were not in
harmony with his principles. But at the same time he said
he could not stand by and do nothing when the people were
in such a plight.

From afar, Sonya herself began to be affected by this
compassion that had outweighed personal interest in her
husband. In Moscow, where she was detained by her four
younger children – Vanichka, Andrey, Michael and Sasha –
her throat ached as she read her husband's letters from the
front and the searing articles he was writing for the newspapers. After finding it unthinkable that he should leave her
alone 'for the whole winter', she now began to wish she could
help him. Seated at the dining-room table with her own
children, she imagined those of others in rags, dying of
hunger, and felt the injustice of her own good fortune. 'We
have no contact with the people,' she wrote. 'We share in
none of their misery, we help no one. ... I feel sorry for
myself and my children, who are being morally stifled in
this atmosphere and are deprived of all spiritual activity.
What can I do?' For the first time in her life she felt
tempted to convert to Tolstoyism. One sleepless night she
resolved to make an appeal to public charity. She wrote her
letter in a rush of emotion, showed it to a few friends, who
liked it, and took it in person to the editors of the *Russian
News*. On the following day, 3 November, it appeared in
full in that newspaper:

My whole family has separated and gone to help in the relief effort for the starving people. . . . Compelled to remain in Moscow with my four young children, all I can do to help is send money and supplies. But the needs are immense and isolated individuals are powerless to satisfy them. And yet, if we think of all the people who are dying of hunger in this moment, every hour we spend in a well-heated house and every piece of bread we eat are living reproaches. We all live in the lap of luxury here, we cannot tolerate the slightest discomfort for our own children : would we be able to endure the sight of exhausted, heartbroken mothers who must watch their children die of hunger and cold, or of old people who can find nothing to eat? Thirteen roubles will see one person through to the next harvest. . . . If each of us, according to his means, could feed one, two, ten or a hundred people in this way, our consciences might be eased. . . . Therefore I have decided to turn for help to all those who can and will contribute by their gifts to the work begun by my family.

Sonya's letter was reproduced in every paper in Russia, and translations appeared in a few in Europe and America. The money immediately started to pour in. The astonished Sonya saw a poor woman come into the room and cross herself before handing her one silver rouble; a young socialite sniffling beneath her veil and holding out an envelope full of banknotes; a child clenching a few kopecks in his fist. . . . 'I do not know what you will think of my idea,' she wrote to her husband, 'but I had had enough of sitting still and doing nothing to help you. . . . Since yesterday, I feel better, I keep accounts, hand out receipts, say thank you; I am speaking to the public and I am happy to be able to support your effort, even with other people's money.'

In two weeks she collected over thirteen thousand roubles. One of the first to subscribe was Father John of Kronstadt. Soon she was sending whole wagonloads of wheat, rye, peas and cabbage to the relief workers, as well as clothes and medicine. This dealing in money and goods entailed a huge amount of correspondence, which she performed without a murmur. At Begichevka, Tolstoy was flabbergasted. Was Sonya at last going through the 'rebirth' he had experienced ten years before? In his tiny, chilly room, in which there was neither rug nor curtains, furnished with one rickety table and a cramped iron bed, he thanked God for this miraculous reunion. In a letter he wrote to his wife on 14 November, he inserted a sentence in French: 'I am sure you cannot imagine how lovingly we think and speak of you.' And later: 'Every night I see you in my dreams, my sweet friend.'[9]

He was preparing to return to Moscow when his friend Rayevsky, worn out by his long cross-country chases, caught a chill and took to his bed. He died of influenza after two days of high fever. Tolstoy was hard-hit by this loss, coming on top of another, the previous month – his childhood companion Dyakov.

Rayevsky's death left him alone at the head of the relief effort; he would have to give up all thought of quitting now. In one month he had opened thirty kitchens supplying free food to fifteen hundred people. But he knew they were not enough. Some people were saying with a sarcastic smile that he was the 'thirteenth apostle'. He himself continued to complain that his present activities were contrary to his principles. 'There is a great deal to be said against all this,' he wrote to Gay. 'There is that money from my wife, and the other contributions; there is the problem of the relations between those who eat and those who give food. Sin is everywhere. But it would be impossible for me to stay home and write.'[10] Yielding to Sonya's pleadings, he returned to her at the end of November to rest for a few days. Their reunion was suffused in tenderness and gratitude. 'Went to Moscow,' he noted. 'Joy of relations with Sonya. Have never been more warm. I thank you, Father. I had prayed to you for this. Everything, everything I asked for has been given to me. I thank you. Suffer me to become still more closely united with your will. I want only what you want.'[11] Ten days later he was back at Begichevka resuming his struggle against hunger.

On 23 January 1892, Sonya, who decidedly seemed to have

been touched by grace, joined him on the battlefield. She moved into the little curtainless room and was appalled at its filth and disorder. In a twinkling the entire Rayevsky house was swept and aired and put in order. Then she toured the kitchens.

When I arrived [she wrote in her diary], I found ten people inside the isba. But they kept coming and soon there were forty-eight. All in rags, their faces emaciated and sad. They come in, cross themselves and sit down on long benches in front of the tables which are placed end to end. The woman in charge offers each in turn a tray full of rye bread cut in pieces, then sets a big soup tureen full of cabbage soup on the table. There is no meat in it, and it has a mild taste of hemp oil. . . . After the soup there is potato mash or peas, kasha, beet greens or barley porridge. Two dishes at noon, two at night. . . . In the second kitchen I visited, I saw a young peasant woman with pale grey skin who looked at me so mournfully that I almost burst out crying. It was clearly very hard for her, as well as for an old man and several others among the group who were there, to come and accept this handout.[12]

With a determination that compelled the admiration of all who saw her, Sonya tackled the bookkeeping, which had hitherto been kept in a state of utter chaos, and, with the help of the tailor's apprentice, cut out clothes, including thirty coats for the neediest children, from bolts of cloth sent from town. She stayed for ten days, and then returned to Moscow to her younger children, whom Tanya had been looking after in her absence.

Meanwhile, the government's uneasiness was mounting as Tolstoy's campaign gathered steam. More than anything else, it was the fever aroused abroad by the incorrigible author's articles that it found prejudicial to the Russian honour. He was becoming an international figure, denouncing his country's failings and waging his war on famine as though he himself were the government. These packages arriving from the four corners of Europe, the seven boatloads of corn being sent by the United States, the promise by the Minnesota millers to provide free flour for the muzhiks – they might all enhance the renown of the promoter of the campaign, but they cast public discredit on the imperial administration. To put a stop to the alarming reports being circulated, the government had already issued one communiqué: 'There is no famine in Russia. Some localities have had a poor harvest; that is the truth.' But this euphemism could not stand up to Tolstoy's broadside. Then the reactionary newspapers launched an invidious slander campaign against him; Pobyedonostsev submitted a report to the emperor accusing the writer of seeking to foment a peasant revolution.

Upon her return from Begichevka, Sonya learned that a new threat had sprung up during her absence. In November 1891 Tolstoy had written an article entitled 'Help for the Hungry' for a publication called *Philosophical and Psychological Questions.* 'The people are starving because we eat too much. This has always been true, but this year's poor harvest has proved that the rope is stretched to breaking point. ... The privileged classes must go to the people with the attitude that they are guilty.' This text, of Christian inspiration, had been so disfigured by the censor that Grot, the editor-in-chief, pronounced it unprintable, but at Tolstoy's request, he sent the uncensored proofs to French, German and English translators. On 14 (26) January 1892 the London *Daily Telegraph* published the article in full. Thereupon, an ultra-reactionary newspaper, the *Moscow News*, protected and directed by Pobyedonostsev, reproduced extracts of Tolstoy's message in a faulty Russian translation exaggerating its revolutionary tenor. A violent commentary accompanied this truncated and falsified version: 'Count Tolstoy's appeal is based on the most rabid, wild-eyed form of socialism in comparison to which the pamphlets of the clandestine agitators are milk and honey. ... He openly preaches social revolution. Using the overworked, lame-brained catchwords of the Western socialists, which the ignorant mob is always so eager to lap up, he affirms that the rich subsist on the sweat of the people, consuming everything they possess and produce. Can we remain deaf to this propaganda, which is invisible only to those who have no eyes or refuse to see?'

Durnovo, minister of the interior, investigated the matter and submitted a report to Alexander III. Rumour in the palace had it that the tsar was very annoyed by Tolstoy's attitude, and had even said in public, 'To think that I received his wife! A thing I have done for nobody else!' In a panic, Sonya wrote to Lyovochka on 6 February 1892: 'You'll be the death of us all with your provocations. Where are your sacred love and "non-resistance"? You have nine children; you have no right to ruin their lives and mine.'

With her customary courage, she fought back. All her connexions in St Petersburg were alerted. She asked for an audience with Grand Duke Sergey, the governor general of Moscow, who advised her to publish a letter from Tolstoy in the *Official Herald* disclaiming the distorted version of his article on the famine. Tolstoy grumblingly consented to write it, but the director of the *Official Herald* refused to publish the letter on the ground that he was responsible for a government organ and did not have the right to become involved in journalistic quarrels. Sonya then had hundreds of copies of the letter lithographed and distributed in Russia and abroad. Too busy giving relief to the muzhiks to be concerned about intrigues going on behind his back, Tolstoy ingenuously wrote to his wife, on 28 February 1892:

For the love of God, do not trouble your head over such things, my dear. . . . I write what I think – things that could not conceivably be acceptable to the government and upper classes – and have been doing so for the last twelve years; I do not write that way by accident, but on purpose; and not only do I have no intention of justifying myself, but I trust those who believe I should will, if not justify their own conduct, then at least clear themselves of the crimes they have committed; it is not I who am accusing them of these crimes, but life itself. . . . Please don't *you* begin to take the defensive: that would be reversing the roles.

In the meantime, State and Church continued their attacks upon Tolstoy. Informers watched his every move. One of them reported: 'He arrived here with a secretary and a confidential agent. ... None of them eat meat, and when they sit down to table they do not say grace. This has caused the peasants to think that Tolstoy must be working for the devil, not God. ... Surveillance has been carefully organized, so that every move he makes will be brought to my attention.' Obeying orders from their superiors, some of the popes in the disaster area preached a similar message to their parishioners and ordered the muzhiks to refuse relief under pain of damnation. One day a peasant woman flung herself at Tolstoy's feet and entreated him to give her back her child, who was being fed in one of the kitchens.

'Be it on my head only,' she whimpered. 'There is nothing to eat at home, but I do not want to send my child to perdition!'

In Moscow and St Petersburg people were saying that the 'thirteenth apostle' would soon be confined to his estate or sent abroad or even locked up in the Suzdal Monastery, reserved for disobedient clergy.

Seeing danger so near at hand, the pious Alexandra Tolstoy forgot her differences with her renegade nephew and decided, without telling him, to plead his cause to the tsar. Having obtained an audience with Alexander III, the old maid of honour said, in a trembling voice:

'Sire, they are preparing to ask you to imprison the greatest genius in all Russia in a monastery.'

'Tolstoy?' asked the tsar.

'Yes, Sire.'

'Would he be plotting an attempt on my life?' murmured the sovereign with a smile.

Alexandra left reassured. A little while later, receiving his minister of the interior, the tsar said, 'I will ask you not to touch Tolstoy. I have no desire to make a martyr of him and provoke a general uprising. If he is guilty, so much the worse for him!'

And the storm blew over, without a moment's pause for thankfulness from Tolstoy. Perhaps, at heart, he was sorry for his state of comfortable impunity. The blows were always for others; but there are people for whom the worst punishment is no punishment at all.

A second year without rain forced him to continue his work among the underfed peasants. His mind was at peace there, as at Sevastopol years before, when the proximity of death had kept him from thinking about himself. Also, it made him happy to feel that he had Sonya's support in his crusade. He was almost prepared to treat her as a fellow believer. 'Yesterday,' he wrote her, 'reading over your letters, I wanted with all my heart – the heart you say I don't have – not only to see you, but to be with you.' Between tours of the kitchens, he continued writing *The Kingdom of God Is Within You*, which was to be the keystone of his entire ethical structure. 'No book has ever given me so much trouble,' he confided to Chertkov.

Naturally, the book, which was completed in April 1893 after three years of work, was prohibited by the censor, but typed copies sped across Russia, leaped the frontiers and were immediately translated in Germany, France, England and the United States. In this essay Tolstoy claimed that the kingdom of God was within reach of every man and that to enter it he need only consent to dominate his animal nature. But, he added, 'the doctrine of Christ could only be interpreted as a negation of life by mistaking for an absolute rule what is merely a guide to an ideal. It is in this sense that Christ's precepts seem irreconcilable with the necessities of life, whereas, in fact, they are the only means of living a just life.' Having dealt with the critics who reproached him for not having sufficiently liberated himself from his own instincts, he moved on to define spiritual perfection, which was, for him, 'the asymptote of human life'. 'Mankind is always reaching towards it and can approach it, but can reach it only in infinity.' He held that the teachings of the Church had deformed the simplicity of the Sermon on the Mount. As the ally of the State, it had become the chief obstacle to human happiness on earth. Therefore any fundamentally Christian mind should refuse all laws, both religious and secular, and adhere to the following precept: 'Do not do unto others what you would not have them do unto you.' Inspired by the American Adin Ballou's books on non-resistance, Tolstoy now produced his famous theory of non-resistance to evil.

However, although he refused to resist evil by violence, he believed it his duty to denounce it whenever he encountered it in the world. His campaign against famine had given him a taste for public action. Now that he was certain of his convictions at last, he made up his mind to speak out every time the government overstepped its prerogatives. He had protested against the persecution of the Jews in 1890. In 1893 he wrote to Alexander III because Prince Khilkov, a disciple of his who had been exiled to the Caucasus, had been deprived of legal custody of his children.* Other 'cases' were in the offing, over which he was prepared to do battle with his wife at his side.

Unfortunately, their period of unison did not outlast the food shortage. As soon as the harvest improved and Tolstoy, 'demobilized', returned to his home and habits, the conflict between them flared up again. After the cold shower of privation from which he had just emerged, his reaction to the ease and comfort of his family's way of life was even gloomier than before. On 22 December 1893 he wrote, 'I feel oppressed, sick at heart. I cannot contain myself. I desire to perform some great deed. I should like to devote the rest of my life to God. But He does not want me. Or else He does not want to encourage me in the direction I have chosen. And it makes me so irritable! Oh, this luxury! This commerce in my books! This ethical morass! This empty agitation! ... I want to suffer, I want to trumpet forth this truth that is consuming me!'

* The letter was posted on 2 January 1894.

And a few days later, on 24 January 1894:

Lord, help me! Teach me to bear my cross. I have unceasingly prepared myself to bear the cross I know: prison and the gallows; now I see before me a completely different cross, a new cross, one I do not know how to carry. What is new and different about it is this: I am placed against my will in the position of a spiritual weakling and by my way of life I am compelled to destroy the very things I live for. . . . I am unable to tear myself free from these awful cobwebs in which I have become entangled. Not for want of strength, but because my conscience will not let me; I feel sorry for the spiders that have spun them.

The chief 'spider' was Sonya, of course. However hard he laboured to live the life of an ascetic, eating vegetables and porridge, drinking nothing but water, fleeing his wife's guests, chopping his own wood, drawing his own water, he still felt the pernicious warmth of the house around him. He was so happy to escape from horrid Moscow to spend a few days at Yasnaya Polyana, where at least there were some peasants in sight! In March 1894, with his daughter Masha, he also went to visit his disciple Chertkov, with whom he felt a communion of thought so intense that he could not refrain from writing to Sonya: 'I am very glad I have come. . . . He and I are so close spiritually, we have so many interests in common and we see each other so seldom, that both of us are very happy.'[13]

Nothing could have hurt Sonya more than that declaration. She had long considered Chertkov as her real rival in Lyovochka's affections. By pretending to serve the great writer's philosophy, this cunning, puritanical man was really trying to ensnare him, detach him from his family, encourage his most subversive tendencies, and appropriate his works for himself. He was the ringleader of that abominable gang of 'dark ones', the spoil-sport, the preventer of new novels! As long as Lyovochka was in his power, there would be no more *War and Peace* or *Anna Karenina*. He had even begun writing to Masha and Tanya. He would finish the job of weaning them away from their own mother. In

August 1893 she learned that most of Tolstoy's manuscripts, which she had entrusted to the Rumyantsev
Museum, had been removed by Chertkov and taken 'for
safekeeping' first to his home and then to that of one of his
friends, Colonel Trepov, in St Petersburg.* Lyovochka,
when informed of this underhanded appropriation, had no
comment to make. He was subjugated, bewitched. The following summer he even had the nerve to propose that
Chertkov and his wife should be invited to Yasnaya Polyana. Sonya indignantly refused, whereupon Tolstoy wistfully wrote to his great friend:

'She is afraid of you because you are the one who helps
me to preserve all the things she hates in me. If you ask,
"Does she want me to come?" I would answer, "No." But
if you asked whether it is necessary for you to come I
would answer, "Yes, it is necessary." I repeat to you what
I told her: if there is bad feeling between you, you must
both use all your strength to destroy it so that true love may
grow in its place.'[14] Only a few days before, on 21 April
1894, he had written in his diary, 'I am happy with Sonya.
... What a mother and, in a sense, what a wonderful wife!
Fet may have had something when he said that every man
married the wife he needed.' Was she going to force him to
change his mind by her stubborn hostility towards the man
he loved most? Once again, he called upon all his self-
control, mastered his anger and behaved like a Christian
husband. 'I have been feeling ill for a week,' he noted in his
diary on 15 May 1894. 'It began, I think, when I was so upset by Sonya's shameful outburst over Chertkov. It is all
very understandable, but depressing, especially as I had lost
the habit of this kind of incident and was so happy to have
recovered my profound affection and good-will for her. I
was afraid she had destroyed everything, but no; it is over,
and my affection has returned.'

* The same Trepov who later became an implacable governor general of St Petersburg. At that time, he was relatively tolerant of
liberals.

A fortnight later he was saddened by the death of his friend Gay, the painter: 'He was a delightful, gifted, grown-up child,' he said. Gay's last painting, a Crucifixion, had been removed the previous March from its room in St Petersburg because the tsar, offended by the stark realism of the canvas, had said, 'What carnage!' Whereupon Tolstoy had written to Gay, 'What a triumph!'

The man who had considered Gay's work an insult to religion did not long outlive him: on 20 October 1894 Tsar Alexander III succumbed to nephritis and complications. His death gave rise, in Tolstoy as in all the enemies of autocracy, to renewed hopes of reform in Russian domestic policy. Nicholas II, the deceased emperor's eldest son, was only twenty-six; he was about to marry a German princess, Alix of Hesse, whose name after conversion became Alexandra Fyodorovna; he was said to be mild, conciliatory and sensitive; surely he would endorse the liberal ideas of the intelligentsia and give the country a constitution. But in fact, Nicholas II was a weakling filled with superstitious respect for his father and ruled by the reactionary minister to the Holy Synod, who had been his tutor. When he received the representatives of the zemstvos on 17 January 1895, he wanted to make a show of strength and declared, as a dutiful pupil of Pobyedonostsev, 'I have heard that voices have recently been raised in zemstvo meetings, of men carried away by the mad dream of electing representatives to participate in the internal administration of the country. Let it be known to all that I, dedicating all my strength to further the happiness of my people, shall defend the principle of autocracy as unswervingly as did my late father.'

Despair was all the blacker as hope had been so high. Tolstoy wrote in his diary, 'Important event. Insolent speech by the tsar. ... I'm afraid this may have consequences for me.' But, faithful to his principle of denying the legality of all temporal authority, he refused to sign his colleagues' petition to abolish the censor. He said, 'This is what you should say to the monarch: "You can do nothing as long as you are emperor. The only thing you can do for the people and for yourself is to abdicate."'

Already concerned for the future of his country, he was beginning to be concerned for the future of his marriage as well. After a few months' respite, Sonya's jealousy of Chertkov had flared up again; she saw him as the cause of all her troubles. She had just turned fifty, and her disposition was growing worse. It seemed to her that the whole world was conspiring to contradict and thwart her. Her children gave her nothing but trouble; Leo's nerves were very bad, he had to have 'electrical treatments'; Vanichka, poor, sweet Vanichka, was so delicate that she feared the worst at every sniffle; Sergey was living in sin; Ilya had made a bad marriage and was spending too much money; Tanya and Masha were completely obfuscated by their father's ideas and spent all their time with the 'Dark Ones'; they never even thought of starting a family. 'They are utterly lacking in moderation or judgement and have no sense of duty,' wrote Sonya. 'They take after their father there. But he at least has struggled all his life to improve himself, whereas they simply let themselves go.'[15]

Day after day, she poured out the same old grievances into her notebook. Everything about Lyovochka irritated her, beginning with his aspiration to a simple life, which simply complicated hers. 'This vegetarian diet means that two menus have to be prepared, which adds to the cost and makes twice as much work. The result of his sermons on universal love is that he has lost all feeling for his own family and shares his private life with anyone and everyone. His – purely verbal – renunciation of earthly goods has led him to criticize and condemn others.'

And elsewhere:

He pushes everything off on to me, everything, without exception: the children, the management of his property, relations with other people, business affairs, the house, the publishers. Then he despises me for soiling my hands with them all, re-

treats into his selfishness and complains about me incessantly.
And what does he do? He goes for walks, rides his horse, writes
a little, goes wherever he pleases, does absolutely nothing for
the family and takes advantage of everything: his daughters'
help, the comfort and adulation that surround him, my submis-
siveness and my sufferings. And fame; that unquenchable thirst
for fame to which he has sacrificed everything and is continuing
to sacrifice everything . . .[16]

If she heard some pertinent criticism of him, she ran to
note it down, to strengthen her case: 'Today Chicherin
said that there were two men in Leo Nikolayevich, one
writer of genius and one mediocre thinker who impressed
people by talking in paradoxes and contradictions.'[17]

Physically, she was increasingly repelled by him. She said
he was slovenly. Was it in order to become one with the
peasants that he went around unwashed like them? He used
to be so particular, and now he smelled like a goat. 'It's
like pulling teeth to get him to wash!' she wrote. 'He told
me his feet are caked with dirt and sores have formed
underneath and are beginning to cause him pain. ... My
aversion to my husband physically these days is making me
very miserable, but I cannot, I simply cannot get used to it,
I shall never get used to the dirt and the bad smell.'[18]

Or sometimes, in a towering rage, her pen racing across
the page, she would plead her cause, no longer to her family
and contemporaries, but to posterity. With what passion she
justified herself to the judges of generations to come! 'His
biographers will tell how he went to draw water for the
porter, but no one will know how he never gave his wife
one moment's rest or one drop of water to his sick child;
how in thirty-five years he never sat for five minutes by a
bedside to let me have a rest or sleep the night through or
go for a walk or simply pause for a moment to recover my
strength.'[19]

It is true that she had added grounds for resentment at
the time she consigned this grievance to paper. It was
January 1895. Lyovochka had just completed a story, *Master*

and Man, telling the adventures of two men of different
social conditions who were caught in a blizzard and compelled by their impending death to discover the Christian
truth within themselves, that is, their equality and depen-
dence. Sonya greatly admired this straightforward, stern
morality tale, in which human warmth and sympathy stood
out in sharp contrast with the impersonal whiteness and
cold of the snow. She was surprised to learn that instead of
giving it to Chertkov's Intermediary or to her own *Complete Works,* Lyovochka had promised it to a review called
Northern Herald. The editor of this publication, Lyubov
Guryevich, was 'a scheming half-Jew', who must surely
have inveigled him by flattery. This time, he had offended
both wife and publisher at once. She insisted that her husband break his promise and honour his double obligation
to her. In the middle of the night the big house in Moscow
resounded with her screams and sobs. Goaded beyond endurance, Tolstoy threatened to leave her for good if she did
not stop. Then she began to suspect him of wanting to abandon her for the woman editor. Completely beside herself,
she rushed out of the house in her bathrobe and bedroom
slippers, with her hair flying about her face.

The snow lay deep on the ground. Not a living soul. Sonya
wanted to die, never mind how, but quickly. Tolstoy, in
vest and trousers, came running after her, caught up with
her, seized her by one arm and dragged her back to the
house. 'I remember that I was sobbing and crying that I
didn't care what happened, that they could take me to the
police station or lock me up in an asylum,' she wrote.

The next afternoon she tried to obtain by sweetness what
she had failed to obtain by force: permission to copy the
story and priority to publish it. Once again he balked, stubborn, bad-tempered and irrational, and once again she took
to the street. But this time she put on a warm coat and hat
and galoshes over her boots. As usual, her suicide attempt
was inspired by her husband's books. Before, she had
planned to throw herself under a train like Anna Karenina.

After reading *Master and Man*, death by exposure now struck her fancy. 'In the story, I had liked the death of Vasily Andreyevich,' she noted ingenuously, 'and I wished to meet my end the same way.' Thus, stumbling through the snow, she made her way towards the Sparrow Hills, where she was sure no one would come in search of her. But Masha had picked up her trace and finally brought her back to the fold.

After two days of total prostration her obsession returned. She hailed a sledge in the street and asked to be driven to the Kursk station. Sergey and Masha took off in hot pursuit. She saw them coming just as she was paying the driver. No choice but to turn around and go back again, with one of them on either side. She had caught cold and the children forced her to go to bed. The doctors came running. One prescribed bromide, another Vichy water, and a third – who was a gynaecologist – alluded to her change-of-life 'in cynical terms'. Lyovochka, however, alarmed by this series of runaway attempts, had become more tractable. He came into the room where she was resting and knelt down to beg her pardon. On 21 February 1895 she was able to record, with pitiful pride, 'The Intermediary and I have won *Master and Man*, but at what cost!'

By a diabolical coincidence, the very day she wrote those words in her diary, Vanichka, who had been sick once the previous month, fell ill again. Rash, sore throat, diarrhoea; Dr Filatov diagnosed scarlet fever. A premonitory silence settled down inside Sonya. She had always known that she would lose Vanichka before long. Not a week went by without some mention of him in her diary: 'The bonds uniting me to him are so close! ... He is a weak child, delicate, and so sweet-tempered.' 'The spark of life is about to go out in my poor darling Vanichka.' In the rare moments when she was not trembling for his health, she was explaining how he was destined for greatness, even more, perhaps, than Tolstoy himself. She was not alone in thinking so. 'The first time I set eyes on that child,' said the Russian scientist

Mechnikov, 'I knew he must either die a premature death or prove a greater genius even than his father.' And Tolstoy marvelled to hear the little boy of seven, so small, so gentle, with his skin the colour of milk, saying to his mother when she told him that the house and trees and land at Yasnaya Polyana would one day belong to him, 'You mustn't say that, Maman. Everything belongs to everyone.'

Vanichka's fever had begun in the morning; towards evening he was burning and delirious; but as always, his thoughts were all for others: 'It's nothing, Maman,' he murmured. 'It will soon be over. Don't cry, Nanny!' Thirty-six hours later he was dead. A sepulchral silence fell upon the house, suddenly shattered by a woman's sobs. Cowering in the children's room, little Sasha thought it was a wounded bitch screaming, with a voice like her mother's. On 23 February 1895 Sonya wrote in her notebook, 'My darling little Vanichka died this night at eleven. My God! And I am still alive.' She did not touch her diary again for two years. For once, Tolstoy was as stricken as she. 'For the first time in my life, I feel caught in a situation there is no way out of,' he stammered.

Looking at him on the day of the funeral, Sonya was alarmed: an old man. Bent, wrinkled, grey-bearded, the light gone from his eyes. With his sons' help he lifted the light coffin – open, in the Russian manner – on to a big sledge. Then he sat down with his wife among the flowers, near the dead child, and the horses moved off at a walk. The road to Nikolskoye cemetery where little Alyosha already lay buried was the same road he used to take thirty-three years before, when he went courting his fiancée at the Behrs' home outside Moscow. He reminded Sonya of this, and she was terrified at the distance that separated the carefree girl of those days and this aged, disillusioned mother going to bury her child. Was that what they called a full life?

During the entire service she held Vanichka's icy head between her hands and tried to warm it with her kisses. The real separation came when the coffin lid was nailed down.

No more Vanichka. She wrestled and fought against the hard fact. Back in the house Tolstoy murmured, 'And I, who was hoping Vanichka would carry on God's work after me!'

The next day he tried to ease his pain by sublimating it; while Sonya wandered through the house like a demented soul, caressing the dead child's toys and clothes and looking for his ghost behind the doors, he wrote in his diary, 'We have buried Vanichka. Terrible – no, not terrible : great spiritual event. I am grateful to you, Father, I am grateful to you.' [20] Days later, 'Vanichka's death has been like the death of Nicholas for me;* no, not the same, but to a far greater degree the manifestation of God, of the force of attraction of God. Thus, not only can I deny that this event was sad or painful, but I can say without hesitation that it was, if not happy – that is not a fitting word – at least merciful, coming from God, revealing the lie of life, bringing us closer to Him. Sonya cannot see it that way. For her the almost physical pain of loss has hidden its spiritual value.' [21] He enlarged upon his idea to Aunt Alexandra: 'I feel his loss cruelly, but by no means as cruelly as Sonya, because I had – because I have – another, spiritual life.'

He wanted to persuade himself that Vanichka had not died in vain, that God had sent him into the world with a message, that he was the 'harbinger swallow', herald of the melting snows and opening-up of hearts. ... In obedience to the desires of this evanescent angel, he redoubled his demonstrations of affection for his wife. 'Never have I felt such a need to love in Sonya and myself, and such a hatred of everything that separates and hurts,' he wrote in the same letter to Alexandra. 'Never have I loved Sonya as I love her now. It is doing me much good.' [22]

But Sonya was still too deadened by sorrow to appreciate this new wave of warmth. She went to the church, questioned the priests, had strange dreams and saw absolutely

* His brother, who had died at Hyères thirty-five years earlier.

no reason to go on living. Once she remained in the Ark-hangelsky Cathedral praying, for nine hours, and came home through a driving rain. To jar her out of her apathy Tolstoy sent her to visit a prison, tried to interest her in the misfortunes of the political convicts. In vain. She responded to nothing but her own unhappiness. 'The new feeling that has brought us together is strange,' he told her. 'It is like the setting sun. From time to time the little clouds of our quarrels, some coming from your side and some from mine, veil its rays. But I still hope that they will blow away before the night and the sunset will be radiant.'²³ Listening to him, Sonya would shed tears of joy; but the next minute she sank back into her morbid brooding. Then, gradually, he gave up. Was it his fault if he still had something to live for? His faith in God, first. Then, his writing. On 12 March 1895, two weeks after little Vanichka's burial, he wrote in his diary: 'I feel like writing something literary.' He listed a dozen ideas, including *Koni's Story* (later *Resurrection*) and concluded, 'Enough there to last me for eight years!'

The enormous success of *Master and Man* surprised and annoyed him, but it also encouraged him to take up his pen again. The Intermediary sold fifteen thousand copies in four days. And Volume XIV of the *Complete Works*, which contained the story, was in its tenth thousand! Praise rained down upon him. 'What can I say to you?' wrote Strakhov. 'The cold clutched at my skin. ... The mystery of death, that is the inimitable thing about you. ... The precision and purity of every stroke are prodigious!' And Tolstoy noted, 'Since I hear no criticism, only compliments, about *Master and Man*, I am reminded of the anecdote of the preacher who, surprised by a storm of applause at the end of one of his sentences, stopped short and asked, "Have I said something wrong?" My story is no good. I should like to write an anonymous review of it.' To the young writer Ivan Bunin, who came to see him about this time, he reiterated his aversion for his latest work:

'It's unspeakable! It's so bad that I am ashamed to show myself in the street.'

Then, referring to the recent death of Vanichka, he exclaimed:

'Yes, he was a delightful, wonderful little boy. But what does it mean to say he is dead? There is no death; he is not dead because we love him, because he is giving us life.'

Bunin was deeply impressed; he noted that at that time the master's face was 'gaunt, his complexion dark, his features severe, as though cast in bronze'. After a brief conversation, the two men went out into the night together. A sharp wind stung their faces and fluttered the flame in the lamps. They walked diagonally across the snow-covered Virgins' Field. Bunin could hardly keep pace with the old man, who had broken into a run and was leaping the ditches and repeating in a jerky, savage voice, 'There is no death! There is no death!'[24]

A few days later, reading that his colleague Leskov, who died in the same month as Vanichka, had left a literary testament, he decided he would also make a will. In this document, dated 27 March 1895, he began by stating that he wished to be buried in a cheap coffin, without flowers or wreaths and without speeches or announcements in the newspapers. He left his unpublished papers to Sonya and Chertkov, both deeply devoted to his work, to sort and classify together. His daughters, Tanya and Masha, were not to have any part in this work. Still less his sons; although they loved him, their views were too far removed from his. The faithful Strakhov, on the contrary, was to be allowed to collaborate with Sonya and Chertkov if any help were required. Tolstoy also asked that the private diaries he had kept before his marriage be destroyed, except for the few pages that were 'worthy of preservation', and that everything that might cause embarrassment in the later notebooks be deleted. 'Besides,' he added, 'Chertkov has promised to do this while I am alive. In view of his great and utterly undeserved affection for me and his unique moral intuition,

I am certain he will acquit himself irreproachably of this task.'

How could he fail to understand, writing those lines, what an affront he was inflicting upon his wife by allowing an outsider to decide what should and should not be published among all the things he had written on the subject of his marriage? How could he fail to foresee the dreadful struggle that would ensue between wife and disciple, each bent on securing possession of the master's private manuscripts? With the boundless naïveté of the man of letters, he must have imagined that the posthumous labour he was commissioning them to perform would lead them to a reconciliation rather than discord. However, upon reflection, he returned to his original idea: 'No, let my private diaries stay as they are. That way, at least, it may be seen that in spite of the degradation and shamelessness of my youth, God had not forsaken me and that – late in life, it is true; on the very threshold of old age – I did begin to understand him a little, and to love him.' He also urged his heirs to relinquish their rights to his early works, but without making this an absolute order. There followed some lofty considerations on man's relations with God: 'Do not use the soul to preserve and cultivate the physical being, but use the physical being to preserve and cultivate the soul.' 'To live for God means to dedicate one's life to people's happiness.' The entry concluded abruptly on a different note: 'It is one o'clock, I am going to dinner.'

The day after this solemn interrogation of his conscience, one month after Vanichka's death, Leo Tolstoy, aged sixty-seven, took his first bicycle lesson. His brand-new machine was a present from the Moscow Society of Velocipede Lovers. An instructor came to teach him, free of charge, how to keep his balance. What could Sonya be thinking, on 28 March 1895, as she watched her husband pedalling awkwardly along the snow-edged garden paths? She was probably shocked to see him enjoying a new sport so soon after their bereavement. Was it callousness, selfishness or the reaction of a prodigiously vital organism against the creeping fear of doom? She envied and hated him for being so strong. That evening, Tolstoy's entry in his diary consisted of the three ritual initials – 'i.I.l.' (if I live) – and nothing else.

25

Sonya's Folly;
What Is Art?

THE summer after Vanichka's death, Tolstoy went back to work in the fields, rode horseback, played tennis and pedalled his bicycle. His skill at the latter provoked the admiration of his children and the shocked disapproval of his disciples. The prudish Chertkov soberly noted, 'Tolstoy has learned to ride a bicycle. Is this not inconsistent with his Christian ideals?' Tolstoy, however, convinced himself of the utility of his project by reading the *Scientific Notes on the Action of the Velocipede as Physical Exercise*, by L. K. Popov. He also noted in his diary, 'I don't know why I like it [riding a bicycle]. N. [Chertkov] is offended and finds fault with me for this, but I keep doing it and am not ashamed. On the contrary, I feel that I am entitled to my share of natural light-heartedness, that the opinion of others has no importance, and that there is nothing wrong in enjoying oneself simply, like a boy.' However, he refrained from showing off his new accomplishment in the presence of distinguished visitors, of whom there were a bumper crop that year – scholars, journalists, sycophants, busybodies ... and a thirty-five-year-old Russian author, whose name was beginning to be known: Anton Chekhov.

In those days Chekhov admired Tolstoy as a writer but did not accept his philosophy. He came of a modest family and had muzhik blood,* and he thought the 'old wizard' of Yasnaya Polyana was wrong to want those at the top to bring themselves down to the level of the people in order

---

* His grandfather, Egor Chekh, had been a serf on an estate belonging to none other than the father of Tolstoy's disciple Vladimir Grigoryevich Chertkov.

to drink the sacred truth at its source; on the contrary, he thought it was the level of the people that should be raised, through education. 'The devil take all the philosophies of all the great men,' he wrote. 'Every great sage is as despotic as a general and as devoid of consideration, because he knows he is safe. Diogenes spat in people's faces, knowing that no one could touch him; and Tolstoy says all doctors are scoundrels and shows no respect for major issues because he too, like Diogenes, cannot be hauled into a police station or attacked in the newspapers.'[1] Elsewhere: 'I was subjugated by the Tolstoyan philosophy ... for some seventeen years. But now something in me has protested; reason and a sense of justice have convinced me that there is more love in electricity and steam than there is in chastity and the refusal to eat meat.'[2]

When he first came to Yasnaya Polyana, one bright August morning, he encountered an old peasant in a white linen blouse walking along the birch drive with a towel over his shoulder. It was Tolstoy, on his way to bathe in the stream. When the caller stated his name, the master's face lighted up. He put his young colleague at his ease with a few friendly words and invited him to come along to the bathhouse, where he undressed and plunged into the water up to his neck. The ripples hid the nakedness of his body, and his beard floated on the surface while he chatted away. Chekhov was entranced by such unaffected simplicity.

The next day Tolstoy arranged a reading of passages from *Resurrection* for Chekhov and a few friends. Chekhov found the book moving and fascinating, but could not admire it unreservedly, as he had Tolstoy's other books. Every time the characters stopped living their own lives and became the protagonists of Tolstoyan theories, he was disturbed by their double personalities. After he left, Tolstoy, very favourably impressed, defined him as follows: 'He is full of talent, he undoubtedly has a very good heart, but thus far he does not seem to have any very definite attitude towards life.'[3] Chekhov said, in return, 'Talking with

Leo Nikolayevich, one feels utterly in his power. I have never met a more compelling personality or one more harmoniously developed, so to say. He is almost a perfect man.'[4] But he still could not forgive him his ideas about religion, progress and non-resistance to evil.

That summer Tolstoy had the great joy of seeing his most cherished disciple, Chertkov, move with his wife into a little house less than three miles from Yasnaya Polyana. Thus they were able to meet every day. Chertkov urged Tolstoy to keep working on *Resurrection*, applauded him when he dashed off a virulent article against corporal punishment,* poked his nose into his diary and, when he caught the master straying from the 'doctrine', called him to order with respectful sternness. Sonya, still sore and bruised in her mourning, did not even have the energy to protest this appropriation of her husband by the 'outsider'. 'She is exhausted,' wrote Tolstoy, 'she is mentally ill, it would be a sin to hold it against her. What a pity she will never admit her mistakes!'[5] And he gave the following analysis of the suffering woman's condition to his son Leo: 'She offers a striking example of the grave danger of placing one's life in any service but that of God. She is no longer alive. She is making herself miserable but cannot lift herself up into the sphere of the divine, that is, the spiritual. She would like to return to her former interests in life and her other children, but she cannot because her relationship with Vanichka, who was so young and so gifted, had elevated her, softened and purified her. ... How easy it would have been for her, however, especially since she loves me! The trouble is that she loves me as I have not been for many years now and does not recognize me as I really am; I am a stranger to her, frightening and dangerous.'[6]

One summer day his disciple Alyokhin, who was cutting hay at his side, advised him to leave his wife. He shrugged, but when the other man insisted, he flew into a rage and made a threatening gesture with his scythe. The next mo-

*Entitled *Shame!*

ment he threw the instrument away and fell sobbing to the ground. The witnesses of this scene, all confirmed Tolstoyans, looked at each other in dismay.[7]

In September, he had difficulty concealing his pleasure when he learned that Tsar Nicholas II, reversing his father's decision, had at last authorized the performance of *The Power of Darkness* in the imperial theatres. He was immediately caught up in a whirl of activity – casting, setbuilding, discussing the director's reflections on the meaning of the play. Returning to Moscow, he read it to the Art Theatre company and sat in on rehearsals, but did not appear on opening night. The play was a triumph. The public rose to acclaim the missing author. Students rushed out to look for him, gathered in front of his house, demanded to see him, deafened him with their ovation.

This roar of approval reawakened Tolstoy's interest in the theatre. He began to attend performances, less to admire other dramatists than to confirm his suspicions of their shortcomings. Shakespeare was still his pet hate; after seeing the Italian actor Rossi in *King Lear* and *Hamlet,* he announced that he was revolted by 'such affectation'. On 18 April 1896, he walked out of a performance of Wagner's *Siegfried* before the end of the second act, muttering, 'Fit for a circus, idiotic, pretentious!' He later explained to his intimates that German folklore was 'the most stupid and tedious' of all and that the composer's music was utterly shapeless. 'You listen,' he said, 'but you cannot tell whether the orchestra has already started to play or is still tuning up.'[8] Excited by all the clumsy mistakes he found in the world's most famous dramatists, he set to work on a play of his own, *The Light Shines in the Darkness.* It was a semi-autobiographical analysis of the conflict between a man animated by a fervent sense of Christianity and those around him, especially his wife, who wants to go on living according to the law of the world. Curiously, when writing these four acts Tolstoy unconsciously exaggerated his hero to the point of caricature. After a few weeks he may have realized that his argument was in danger of blowing up in his face, and he put the play away unfinished. Or, unable to find the right ending for it, he may have decided to wait until his life provided material for a denouement.

Death was all around him. Nagornov, his niece Varya's husband; Strakhov the critic, who had been his admirer and friend. ...[9] Funerals alternated with baptisms and weddings. Some of the latter, he thought, were as sad as the former. The year before (10 July 1895), his son Sergey had married a Miss Rachinsky; this year it was the other son, Leo, who married a Miss Westerlund (15 May 1896); his daughter Tanya was in love with Sukhotin and to Sonya's great displeasure was compromising herself by seeing him too often. What was it made them all run like lunatics after common terrestrial love? He seemed to be the only person who was capable of denying himself a pleasure. On 2 May 1896 he suddenly decided not to touch his bicycle again. 'I have stopped riding my bicycle,' he proudly wrote. 'I cannot understand how I could be so carried away [with this sport]!'[10] Tanya, guessing the real reason for his sacrifice, wrote in her diary, 'Papa has given up his bicycle. I am happy for him *because I know how much he loves to deny himself things*;* and for myself as well, because now we will not need to worry about him all the time or wait up all evening while he is out in the rain or send people out looking for him everywhere, etc.'[11]

In May 1896, Tsar Nicholas II came to Moscow for his coronation, and Tolstoy thanked heaven he was at Yasnaya Polyana during these festivities, which he could not condone. Nothing seemed more absurd to him than the revelry among the common people which always accompanied the official installation of a tyrant on his throne. 'The inanity and ignominy of this ritual make me unspeakably miserable,' he wrote.[12] The tsar had commanded all his subjects to take part in the celebrations, so a fair was planned for 18 May on the Khodanka parade-grounds outside Moscow.

* Author's italics.

It was huge. The police were soon overwhelmed; the crowd that milled back and forth between the candy and vodka stands was so enormous that over two thousand persons were killed in the crush. This catastrophe was universally hailed as a bad omen: the reign had been baptized in blood. Nevertheless, that same evening Nicholas II attended the ball at the French Embassy. 'Dreadful occurrence in Moscow on the Khodanka parade-grounds,' wrote Tolstoy. 'Three thousand persons crushed to death. I do not know how to react to this event. I am not in condition, I am losing my grip.'[13]

A few lines earlier the same day he had noted, 'Tanayev annoys me with his air of moral self-satisfaction, his artistic obtuseness (deep-seated, not just superficial) and his position as cock-o'-the-walk in this house.' A burst of spleen, quickly repressed. Sergey Ivanovich Tanayev, pianist and composer, was a friend of the family of long standing. He had already come to Yasnaya Polyana the previous year. In 1896, wanting to spend the summer with the Tolstoys, he rented the pavilion in which the Kuzminskys usually stayed, for one hundred and thirty roubles, and thus became part of the master's daily life.

He was a little man of forty, chubby and awkward, who wore his clothes too tight, had tiny eyes, a pug nose and a falsetto voice. A limp beard encircled his puffed-up doll's cheeks. Absent-minded and bashful, he was utterly lacking in poise. Young women intimidated him, especially if they were pretty. An old nanny lived with him, brushed his clothes and made his morning tea. He played with the children on the croquet lawn, went on walks and picnics, dined joyously at the big table with twenty other guests, played chess with the master of the house, charmed everyone with his simple manners and kindliness and, in the evening, never refused when asked to give a little concert. He had a very light touch on the piano and an unaffected sensitivity that delighted his audience. Even Tolstoy, who was increasingly coming to suspect music of being in league with the devil, could not suppress his emotion when he heard certain pieces. Annoyed with himself, he pooh-poohed Tanayev's favourite composers, said that Bach and Beethoven were overrated and wondered whether art in general were a necessary part of experience. Impassioned debates ensued, involving the whole family.

It was Sonya's opinion that life was not worth living without music and poetry. When Tanayev played Mendelssohn's *Songs Without Words* she clasped her hands to her bosom and had to choke back her tears. Vanichka's death had left such a void in her heart that she had an unconscious need to transfer her excess affection to someone else. By a natural reflex of self-defence she clung to whatever was still able to give her pleasure: music, which she had always loved, and the company of a man younger than herself, refined, discreet, reassuringly ugly. The consolation she had been unable to accept from her husband – a genius, to be sure, but so excessive, obstinate, sectarian, so selfish and sententious – she found in the company of this artist, whose opinions on every subject coincided with her own. She delighted in their serious, high-minded, poetic conversations; when he looked at her, she felt younger; when his fingers touched the piano, her feet left the ground; sometimes it seemed to her that Vanichka was encouraging her in this newfound affection; perhaps, if he had lived, he would have been like Tanayev. ... She was so certain of the innocence of her feelings that she did not even try to hide them. Her daughters, from youngest to eldest, looked on with disapproval. Tanya (thirty-two) observed that her mother pinned a rose on her blouse before the musician's arrival. Sasha (twelve) was horrified to hear her reciting, with beatific gaze, a poem by Tyutchev that began with the lines:

> Oh, how much more timid and tender love grows
> As our days draw on towards their close.

The girl thought these lines must surely be connected in her

mother's mind with that disgusting Tanayev. She was delighted to learn that Papa, who was always right, considered
that this decadent poet's glorification of 'senile, toothless'
love was 'repulsive'. In fact, Tolstoy had long been aware of
Sonya's pitiful attempts at coquetry. Although he loudly
proclaimed his indifference to public opinion, he could not
stand the idea of being made a fool of by his wife. He was
willing to accuse himself of the most heinous crimes, revile
and ridicule himself and her for the love of Christian self-
mortification, but not to be mocked at behind his back.
Strange coincidence, that his final downfall should come at
the hands of a musician, just like that of the criminal hero
of *The Kreutzer Sonata*. Had he been giving voice to a premonition when he wrote the book? Was this the price of
the humiliation he had inflicted upon Sonya five years before when he published it? But there was nothing of Truk-
hachevsky in Tanayev. Oh, his colleagues would have a good
laugh at his expense! Sentences from the book leaped up
before his eyes: 'The moment his gaze crossed my wife's I
saw the hidden beast in them thumb its nose at their position and all our social conventions.'

Exasperated by the languishing airs assumed by Sonya,
who was living a teen-age romance at the age of fifty-two,
he became increasingly impolite to Tanayev: 'Morning.
Did not sleep all night. Heart bothering me. ... Unable
to overcome my pride and indignation. ...' (26 July 1896.)
'I console myself with the thought that I ought to pity her,
that she is suffering and that I am infinitely to blame. We
talked of the Gospels. Tanayev tried to prove to me, *in jest*,
that Christ was in favour of castration. I lost my temper.
Am ashamed of myself.' (30 July 1896.)

When summer was over Tanayev left, and the helpless
Sonya remained alone to face her husband's recriminations.
She protested that he was insane to imagine she had fallen
in love with a man twelve years her junior, that they were
just good friends, that music was the only thing that prevented her from losing her mind. But she confided her true

feelings to Mrs Annenkov, a family friend, in a letter written in September 1896:

As to my attitude towards the man who has disrupted my married life, against his will and without his knowledge, I can only say that I try not to think about him any more. It is hard for me to sever my friendly relations with him and to offend such a fine person and good and gentle man; but I am obstinately compelled to do so. He left Yasnaya Polyana a month ago and I shall undoubtedly see him [in Moscow] in a few days. I do not know what I shall feel when I see him again. Joy, perhaps nothing at all. Sometimes my heart rebels and I refuse to abandon the artistic, musical happiness he gave me; I do not want to live without this relationship, so simple and tender, which has given me so many shining hours in the past two years. ... But when I think of my husband's sufferings and his insane jealousy, I feel deeply bitter and ashamed and I don't want to go on living; it is better for me to die than to hear such offensive accusations made against me, who have always taken care to behave so that neither my husband nor my children should have any cause to blush for me. And it is ludicrous, now, to have suspicions of any kind about a woman at my time of life – over fifty-two years old. Anyway, that's not what I mean to say: there are no *suspicions*, nor can there be; there is only his demanding, tyrannical nature and his possessive love of himself and his family, and I must try to submit to it. The future looks terribly bleak to me. ... I continue to pine and seek comfort in new interests, totally different from those I had when my sweet little boy was alive. Where will all this lead me? I have no idea.

When she returned to Moscow at the beginning of winter she immediately resumed her relationship with Tanayev. She took piano lessons to please him and deafened the house practising scales. He appeared almost every evening before supper, with his paunch, red-tipped nose and honeyed smile. Or else she, meaning no harm, would drop in on him after running her errands in town. She was dressed to the teeth, in fur-lined velvet cloak and otter toque. Gliding along in the sledge with her daughter Sasha, she would suddenly raise her head with a bright smile, tap the coachman on the back with her tortoise-shell lorgnette and call out:

'Take us round to Mertvy Street!'

Tanayev, seeing the mother and daughter come in, would leap up from his piano, beaming to hide his confusion while Sasha sputtered with fury. Sometimes the child defied her mother and refused to go out driving or come into the drawing-room because she did not want to meet the musician.[14] As for Tolstoy, he had to muster all his willpower and all his faith in God to accept such a humiliating situation. When he reached the boiling point, he, spurner of the flesh, denier of earthly passions and sworn enemy of human love, rushed to his diary to relieve himself:

'i.I.l. I am still as upset as ever. Help me, Father. Dwell in me, subjugate me, drive out, abolish the base urges of the flesh and everything I feel through the flesh. Talking of art a while ago, saying one could only create when thinking of the loved one. And the way she tries to conceal it from me! It does not make me laugh, it does not make me feel sorry for her, it hurts. ... When one is in prison in irons, at least one can take pride in one's humiliation, but in this situation there is nothing but pain, unless I look at it as a trial ordained by God. Yes, teach me to bear it with equanimity, joy and love.' (20–21 December 1896.) 'Sonya came in a moment ago. She spoke to me. It merely added to my pain.' (21 December.) 'What is bad is that I want to feel sorry for myself and my last years, which are being ruined for nothing.' (22 December.) 'My hands are cold, I want to weep and love. At dinner, my sons' vulgarity was most trying.' (26 December.)

At the beginning of 1897, he thought his patience would come to an end, with 'these games of all kinds, this continual eating and this *senile flirtation*'. 'I write it so that it will be known, even if only after my death,' he fumed. 'For the moment I cannot talk about it. She is ill, it's true, but her illness is being treated as a form of health and encouraged instead of fought. What will become of all this, how will it end? I pray all the time, accuse myself and pray!'[15]

He wrote to his daughter Masha and to Chertkov, making veiled allusions to his woes. Then, after a night of bad dreams in which he clearly saw 'the same offence, over and over', his old desire came back to him: to go away, avoid having to look on any longer at 'the life of degrading madness' to which his wife was subjecting him. She still glanced occasionally into her husband's diary and was infuriated by his comments about her improper conduct. In tones of outraged innocence she asked him what right he had to treat her in this manner in pages which strangers might read one day. Did he want posterity to put her down as a strumpet? From accuser, he somehow found himself turned into accused. In self-defence he assured her that no one who had seen them together could believe she was unfaithful. But a few pages later he wrote, 'If she wants to come looking in this diary again, then she must take the consequences. I can't write if I must be thinking all the time of her and the readers of the future, trumping up a sort of clean bill of health for her. All I know is that last night I imagined that she died before I did, and I was terror-stricken.'[16] The moment he had told Sonya that he believed she was incapable of being unfaithful to him, she went tearing off to St Petersburg where Tanayev was giving a concert. Aghast, Tolstoy also left, with his daughter Tanya, for the Olsufyev estate at Nikolskoye, from which he wrote to his wife:

'It is infinitely sad and humiliating that an utterly useless and uninteresting outsider should now be ruling our life and poisoning our last years together; infinitely sad and humiliating to be obliged to inquire when he is leaving, where he is going, when he is rehearsing, what he will be playing. It is horrible, horrible, base and shameful! And it had to happen just at the end of our lives, which had been honest and clean until then – and at a time when we were drawing closer and closer together in spite of all the things that had divided us. ... And suddenly instead of the good, healthy, happy ending of thirty-five years of life together, there comes this sordid nonsense, leaving its abominable imprint on everything. I know you are miserable too, because you love me and you want to behave decently; but thus far you haven't been able to, and the whole thing is making me ill; I am ashamed, I feel deeply sorry for you because I love you myself, with the best love in the world, not the love that comes from the body or the mind, but the one that comes from the soul.'[17]

In a postscript he entreated her to awaken from her 'sleepwalking' state and resume 'a normal life'. It must have seemed to Sonya that by taking her friendship with Tanayev so seriously, her Lyovochka was displaying a state of mental derangement at least as acute as the one he alleged her to be suffering from. Recriminations, explanations and exhortations between the two continued by letter and – for a novelty! – by telephone.

Tanayev, however, was oblivious to the upheaval he had caused in the master's life. Vague, good-humoured and naïve, he thought of Sonya as an elderly, respectable lady whose affection flattered him. She invited him to spend a few days at Yasnaya Polyana again that summer, and he ingenuously accepted, certain that he would be welcomed by all. When Sonya, with an air of false detachment, announced this news at table Tolstoy told her in no uncertain terms that if the musician set foot in the house again he, Tolstoy, would leave it forever. She took this for a passing fit of pique and tried to argue with him, but after five sleepless nights and five days of deadlock he went to his brother Sergey's home to find some peace, and from there, on 18 May 1897, he wrote a furious and desperate letter to Sonya:

'I am disgusted to see you taking up with Tanayev again. I cannot go on living with you in these conditions; I am shortening and poisoning my existence. ... If you cannot put an end to this situation, let us separate.'

During the night he went back to his pen, to state the four solutions he saw to their conjugal plight:

1. The best is for you to break off all relations with him, not gradually but all at once, and never mind what he may think,

in order to release us once and for all from the nightmare that has been tormenting us for a whole year. No meetings, no letters, no portraits, no mushroom-gatherings. 2. Another solution is for me to go abroad, after separating entirely from you, and each of us would live his own life. 3. The third solution is, in order to break with Tanayev, for us both to go abroad and remain there as long as necessary for you to be cured of the cause of your torment. 4. The fourth and most terrible, which I cannot envisage without a shudder, is for us to try to make ourselves believe that things will get better by themselves, that there is nothing irremediable in this, and go on living as we have done the past year.

The fourth solution was the one he ultimately adopted. On 25 May, weary, sick at heart and red-eyed, he returned to Yasnaya Polyana. Betrayed and not betrayed, unable to break away and unable to accept, he, the giant, felt 'bound to earth by the tiny fine hairs of Lilliputians'. Sonya was touched by him, but more concerned about how he would receive Tanayev. 'Am I guilty?' she wrote on 2 June 1897. 'I do not know. When I first grew friendly with Tanayev I thought it would be pleasant for me to have a friend like him in my old age, calm, kind, gifted.' And the next day, 'The morbid jealousy displayed by Leo Nikolayevich when he heard that Tanayev was coming has hurt me deeply and filled me with dread.'

At last Tanayev appeared, chubby and amiable, drummed a few songs with his little sausage-fingers, and was tactful enough to go away again forty-eight hours later, leaving a trail of music and gratitude behind him in Sonya's heart: 'Sergey Ivanovich [Tanayev] left today, my husband is calm and cheerful again. I am calm, too, because I have seen Tanayev. If my husband insists that I have nothing more to do with Sergey Ivanovich, it is only because he is suffering. But it would be torture for me. I feel so little guilt and such a peaceful joy in these pure and simple relations with someone else that I could no more give them up than I could prevent myself from seeing, breathing or thinking.'

With increasingly morbid pleasure, she associated her

little dead boy with the living musician. In her dreams she saw Vanichka sitting on Tanayev's knee. Or they would be standing side by side holding out their arms to her in questioning supplication. She often went off by herself under the grape arbour to talk to the dead child, tell him her troubles and ask his advice. 'I asked Vanichka whether my feelings for Sergey Ivanovich [Tanayev] were impure,' she wrote on 5 June 1897. 'Today, Vanichka tried to draw me away from Sergey Ivanovich, probably out of compassion for his father. And yet, I know my child cannot blame me and does not want to deprive me of Sergey Ivanovich, because he sent him to me in the first place.'

A month later, yielding to her obsession, she invited Tanayev back to Yasnaya Polyana without consulting anyone. Her dread at the thought of her family's scathing disapproval only added to the delight with which she anticipated the encounter: 'Fearing my husband's anger, I have not told him yet. Could he be jealous again? If Sergey Ivanovich were to imagine such a thing, he would be so shocked! As for me, I cannot hide my joy at the thought of playing music again and having someone pleasant and cheerful to converse with.'[18]

The next day Michael (age seventeen), who knew of Tanayev's impending arrival, made a reference to it at the dinner table in front of his father. Tolstoy scowled and snapped, 'First I've heard of it!'

Tanayev remained at Yasnaya Polyana from 5 to 13 July. Again there was a festival of music. Mozart, Chopin, Beethoven and Schubert joined forces to send Sonya into a swoon: 'His playing tears me asunder. I was inwardly shaken with sobs as I listened to the *Polonaise*.' She photographed her idol from every conceivable angle and developed the plates herself while Lyovochka, seething, climbed back on to his bicycle and pedalled grimly off across-country to work off his anger. It ended, however, without any major explosion, and Sonya concluded that her husband had resigned himself. But what she did not know was that on 8 July he had again decided to run away from home and had written her a farewell letter. He did not go, but neither did he tear up the letter. In it, he justified his decision by his desire to live in accordance with his principles, yet it could not have been plainer that it was his wife's behaviour that had actually driven him to such a state:

My dear Sonya, the inconsistency between my life and my beliefs has long been tormenting me. And I have been unable to compel you to change a way of life and habits for which I myself am responsible. Nor could I leave you before, fearing to deprive my children of what little influence I may have had upon them in their youth and not wanting to wound you. But now I am equally unable to go on as I have done these past sixteen years, either struggling and irritating you all or succumbing in turn to the temptations that surround me and that I have ultimately grown used to. Therefore, I have now decided to do what I have been wanting to do for some time: leave. . . . The chief reason is this: just as the Hindus retire to the forest at the age of sixty, so any elderly religious man hopes to devote the last years of his life to God and not to pleasantries, punning, gossip and tennis matches; and so I, on the eve of my seventieth year, aspire with all my heart and soul to peace and solitude and, if not a perfect harmony between my life and conscience, at least something other than this howling clash between them. . . . I ask you all to forgive me, should you be hurt by my decision; but you, Sonya, you above all, accept my going, do not come looking for me, do not feel resentment towards me, do not condemn me. The fact that I am leaving you does not mean I am not satisfied with you. I know that you literally *could not*, and cannot, see and feel as I do, and that it is impossible for you to change your way of life and make sacrifices for a cause that means nothing to you. I accordingly do not blame you. On the contrary, I think back with gratitude over our thirty-five years together, especially during the first period when you performed what you considered to be your duty in life with the maternal self-denial and energy that abound in you. You have given us, the world and myself, everything you were able to give, a great deal of love and maternal devotion, and you are to be revered for that. But in the later phases of our life together, the past fifteen years, we have drawn apart from each other. I do not believe it is my fault, for I know that I did not change either for my personal pleasure or for fame and glory, but because I could not do otherwise. Nor can I hold it against you that you did not follow me; I think of you; I remember and always shall remember what you gave me with love. Farewell, dear Sonya.

Tolstoy hid this letter under the imitation leather upholstery of his desk chair. A few years later, when told that the chair was to be recovered, he removed the letter from its hiding place and gave it to Obolensky, with instructions to hand it to Sonya after his death.*

After giving up the idea of going into retreat like a Hindu, he rushed to the opposite extreme and, the moment his rival was out of sight, yielded to the 'urges of the flesh' in his wife's arms. She, however, continued to feel herself a virgin, after her thirteen children. There was a lavender haze drifting through her head. All the gossip about Tanayev left her quite unconcerned: 'I am proud to have my name associated with that of a man who is kind, upright and gifted. My conscience is clear before God, my husband and my children. I am as pure in soul, thought and body as a newborn child.'[19] After giving Tolstoy the animal satisfaction he claimed, she watched in amused astonishment as he revelled, at the age of sixty-nine, in his manly prowess. Her disrespect even went as far, on occasion, as to call him an 'old man' in her diary. She wrote, 'We women cannot live without someone to worship. ... I have uncrowned Leo Nikolayevich who is no longer my idol. I am still profoundly attached to him. ... But happiness, true happiness – he can no longer give to me.'[20] On 1 August her daughter Sasha observed, 'How cheerful Papa is this morning!' Sonya's wry comment in her notebook: 'If she knew that Papa is always cheerful for the same reason – the love that he denies!' That day, Papa, who

---

* After Tolstoy's death, Sonya found not one but two letters: she tore up the first as soon as she had read it, and the second is the one quoted here.

was decidedly 'his old self' again, played tennis for three hours non-stop, rode over to Kozlovka on horseback and, on his return, was sorry he could not give his calves a little workout on the bicycle, which was being repaired. No more 'old man' now! 'What a vigorous nature!' sighed Sonya. 'Yesterday, not without regret, he told me I had aged lately. I shall be worn out before him, in spite of my good health and youthful looks and the fact that I am sixteen years younger than he.'[21]

Since she felt nothing but loathing for the physical act of love, she thought wistfully back to the delights of her sentimental conversations with Tanayev: 'I am doing my duty towards my husband,' she wrote on 3 August 1897, 'and there is some satisfaction in that, but I am often very sad and then I have other desires.' At the end of the summer, 'Soon I shall be going to Moscow, I shall rent a piano and play, and I hope that Sergey Ivanovich will come and play with me. That would be so lovely! The mere thought of it restores me to life!'

In the autumn the couple separated, Tolstoy staying on at Yasnaya Polyana while his family returned to Moscow. After rebuking her husband for not coming too, Sonya immediately began to invent pretexts for seeing Tanayev. She attended his concerts, invited him to tea, called on him at his home if he happened to say he was feeling unwell. When there were obstacles, she thought – pious soul – 'God will help me, somehow. And if He doesn't, never mind!' But she was not above taking help from the devil too: a gypsy read her palm and offered to cast a spell on her aspirant and drive him mad with love. She hesitated before saying no. 'I was terribly frightened,' she wrote in her diary. 'I suddenly wanted to buy her potion.'

Upon joining his wife Tolstoy soon realized that she was more infatuated than ever with her pianist. The stormy scenes resumed, absurd, grotesque. At last a quarrel broke out that was so violent Tolstoy consigned it verbatim to paper and entitled it *Dialogue*. They were lying in bed one night when it began. At first a murmur, then the voices began to rise, a candle was lighted. Summoned by her husband to confess that she was still enamoured of Tanayev, Sonya protested her innocence.

'All I ask,' she whimpered, 'is the right to have him here once a month! To come in and sit down and play the piano for me, like any other friend could do!'

'That's just the point, what you just said proves that your feelings towards the man are out of the ordinary,' retorted Tolstoy. 'I don't know of any other person whose monthly visit could give you such joy. If that's the case, you would find it that much more agreeable to see him every week, or every day! ...'

He finally called her a 'concert hag', which made her wild with rage. Screaming, laughing, sobbing and hiccoughing, she became hysterical.

'My head is splitting!' she stuttered. 'There! ... Right there! ... Cut open the vein in my neck! ...'

'I held her at arm's length,' wrote Tolstoy. 'Knowing that it usually helps, I kissed her on the forehead. It took her a long time to get her breath back. Then she began to yawn and sigh, and fell asleep. She is still sleeping now.'

This crisis was followed by a long truce. Sonya's passion for the pot-bellied pianist began to wane. And Tanayev, who must finally have become aware of Tolstoy's resentment, began to space his calls.

But Tolstoy had not seen the last of love's devastations. That year, 1897, it seemed to him that every female at Yasnaya Polyana had been bitten by the devil. 'They are scampering about in every direction like cats on a hot tin roof,' he wrote. 'What a blessing to be married, but how good it would be to be rid of this galloping and miaowing on the rooftops!' When it wasn't the wife who had to be called to order, it was the daughters. He would never have believed that Masha and Tanya, his two darling girls, who had his teachings in the very marrow of their bones, could turn away from him, one after the other.

It began with Masha – noble, uncompromising, industrious, vegetarian, saintly Masha – who had given up her share of the inheritance out of respect for her father's principles. Of course, she had had boyfriends, but all of them were harmless little Tolstoyans like Biryukov, and not for one moment had the master dreamed that his favourite daughter might desert him for a mere disciple. Now, all of a sudden, here she was crazy about young Prince Nicholas Leonidich Obolensky, a distant relative and a handsome, lazy, affable and irresponsible boy with empty pockets and polished fingernails. His only affinities with Tolstoyism were that he did not drink or gamble and would not have hurt a fly. In grieving wonder, Tolstoy watched as Masha melted in admiration of the playboy from Moscow. Even Sonya, deep in the toils of her intrigue with Tanayev, observed that the 'child' had lost her wits. To disenchant the poor girl, her father sent her a solemn letter enumerating the pecuniary difficulties she would have to face when she set up housekeeping:

'You are going to exchange your peace of mind and independence for the most agonizing and complicated sufferings. ... Does he want to enter the service, and where? Where and how will you live? ... Do you intend to claim your share of the inheritance? ...'[22]

And a few days later:

'You must have guessed that your decision means failure to me; you know it full well; but on the other hand I am glad to think that it will be easier for you to live after abandoning your ideal, or rather after mingling your ideal with baser aspirations, by which I mean having children.'[23]

In spite of this double warning, Masha stood her ground, announced her engagement and, since Nicholas Obolensky had not a kopeck to his name, came forward twisting her skirts and hanging her head to reclaim her share of the inheritance she had previously disdained. Tolstoy clothed his disappointment in a dignified silence. But Masha's brothers and sisters protested vehemently, because they had

been counting on dividing up her share among themselves.
And Sonya exulted, with a bitter smile: she alone had
known all along what would happen. You had to be crazy
like Lyovochka to imagine that any normal woman could
forget she had a womb.

Another obstacle arose when the time came to set the
wedding date. Masha had stopped confessing and taking
communion long ago, so the Church would not bless her
marriage. Prince Obolensky suggested they bribe a priest,
which would cost only one hundred and fifty roubles. Tolstoy indignantly replied that any such monkey-business as
that would be performed over his dead body. Since his
daughter had decided to return to the common herd she
must abide by its rules, even the most ludicrous ones, and
in particular its religious ceremonies. It was a question of
integrity. Weeping at her relapse, she yielded, confessed,
took communion and, on 2 June 1897, in the presence of
her family and dressed in her everyday clothes, married
Nicholas Obolensky, the 'sponger', the 'long-eared lazy-
bones', as Sonya called him. 'Masha is married,' wrote Tolstoy on 16 July. 'I feel all the compassion for her I
would feel for a pure-bred racehorse put to work hauling
water.'

His grief at Masha's departure was sharpened by his
suspicion that his gentle, high-spirited Tanya was also about
to elude him. After rejecting quantities of suitors out of
devotion to the Tolstoyan ideal, she had fallen wildly in
love with a man much older than she, Michael Sukhotin,
who was married and the father of six children; he was in
his fifties, had a middle-aged paunch and was both charming and witty. Tanya carried on a kind of platonic romance
with him, met him secretly, suffered from the falseness of
the situation but could not bring herself to break it off. 'I
am ashamed when I think of Sukhotin's wife and children,'
she wrote, 'although he assured me that I am depriving
them of nothing and although I know his wife stopped loving him long ago.' [24] And also, 'Papa is the great rival of

all lovers and none has been able to vanquish him yet. But this love of mine is competing more strongly than any other has done so far.'[25]

Sukhotin's wife was very ill, and Tanya was sometimes horrified to catch herself hoping she would die, which, with admirable tactfulness, she did soon afterwards, and on 9 October 1897 the thirty-three-year-old virgin wrote to her father announcing her desire to marry her widower. This was the last straw. His hatred of the ties of the flesh revived. With the fierce selfishness of an old man who cannot tolerate happiness in others except on his own terms, he replied to his daughter on 14 October:

I have received your letter, dear Tanya, and I simply cannot give you the answer you would like. I can understand that a depraved man may find salvation in marriage. But why a pure girl should want to get mixed up in such a business is beyond me. If I were a girl I would not marry for anything in the world. And as far as being in love is concerned, for either men or women – since I know what it means; that is, that it is an ignoble and, above all, an unhealthy sentiment, not at all beautiful, lofty or poetical – I would not have opened my door to it. I would have taken as many precautions to avoid being contaminated by that disease as I would to protect myself against far less serious infections such as diphtheria, typhus or scarlet fever. Just now it seems to you that life is not possible without it. This is also true of alcoholics and smokers, except that when they break the habit they discover life as it really is. You have not managed to avoid this intoxication, and now you feel it is impossible to live without it. And yet it is possible! After saying this, without any real hope of convincing you or inciting you to change your way of life and rid yourself of your addiction, and without any hope of avoiding the other diseases that will infect you later, I shall proceed to tell you how I view your state.

Uncle Sergey told me that one day (I was not there) he went to see the gypsies with our brother Nicholas and some other people he hardly knew. Nicholas had had too much to drink. Whenever he went drinking with the gypsies, he would begin to dance, badly, hopping about on one foot and flapping his arms convulsively in a way that was meant to be bold and reckless, and suited him about as well as a saddle on a milch-cow. He, a quiet, sober man, awkward, modest and homely, would suddenly begin to fling himself into contortions while the people around him laughed and seemed to be encouraging him. It was a dreadful spectacle.

It happened that this particular day, Nicholas wanted to dance. Sergey and Basil Perfilyev begged him not to but he wouldn't listen, and, sitting on a chair, began gesticulating incoherently and awkwardly. They beseeched him; but when at last they saw he was too drunk to hear what they were saying, Sergey simply told him, in a defeated and mournful voice, 'Then go dance!' And, heaving a sigh, he put his head down in order not to see this humiliating spectacle which seemed to the drunken man (and to him alone) an admirable exhibition, joyful and delightful to all.

That is how I see your desire. All I can say to you is, 'Then go dance!' I take comfort in the thought that when you have finished dancing you will become as you were before, and ought always to be. 'Dance!' If it has to be, I can but repeat it. But I cannot fail to see that you have become irresponsible; your letter proves it. I cannot see what interest and importance there can be for you in the fact that you will be seeing him one hour more. By way of explanation, you tell me that you are thrilled at the mere thought of receiving a letter from him. This is confirmation of my opinion that you are acting with the total unconsciousness of one possessed. I might have understood that a thirty-three-year-old virgin should choose to love a man past his prime, who is good, honest and not a fool, and should determine to unite their destinies. But then she would not attach such a price to one more hour of conversation or the approach of the moment when she might receive a letter, because she would know that neither the continuation of the conversation nor the contents of the letter could give her anything more. If there is this emotional strain, that means there is also an artificial stimulus, in other words, that the soul is not at ease. And when the soul is not at ease, the thing to do is not to bind oneself to someone else, but to lock oneself up in a room and throw the key out of the window.

This time Tolstoy's aim was better. Wounded, Tanya bowed to her father's will. But she returned to the charge a few months later – she must have Sukhotin, she wanted to be his wife for better or for worse, she begged her parents to let her go. The marriage took place on 14 November 1899. Tolstoy sobbed as he led his eldest daughter to the church. On 20 November he wrote in his diary:

'I am in Moscow. Tanya has gone away – God knows why – with Sukhotin. It is pitiful and humiliating. For seventy years my opinion of women has done nothing but sink steadily, and yet it must go lower still. The problem of women? One thing is sure! It is not solved by allowing women to run one's life, but by preventing them from destroying it!'

During 1897 Tolstoy was wrestling simultaneously with the follies of his wife and daughters and with a book by which he set great store: *What Is Art?* He had long felt the need to explain the tragic contradiction between the prophet and the writer in him. In his essay *What Then Must We Do?* he had already said that artists who neglected their vocation as educators were prostituting their talent. The older he grew the more self-evident this principle seemed to him. He defended it so vehemently to his family and friends that, in Sonya's words, 'everyone's sole wish was that he would stop talking as soon as possible!' The advent of Tanayev at Yasnaya Polyana had strengthened his hatred of 'immoral and idle' art. His attacks upon music, painting and literature as entertainment were so many kicks in the pants of this weakling Sonya had the effrontery to pretend she was in love with. He added the recriminations of the jealous husband to the vaticinations of the apostle. Sonya, who was recopying the essay, noted on 25 June 1897, 'So much fury and meanness, even in this text. I feel clearly that he is attacking an imaginary foe (would it be Sergey Ivanovich [Tanayev] he is jealouse of?) and that his one and only purpose is to destroy him.'

The truth was that Tanayev had simply precipitated a reaction prepared long before. It was inevitable that after condemning the pleasures of the senses Tolstoy should be brought to reject all forms of art that were not useful to the people. He might have qualified his verdict, attached a few judicious concessions to it, but it was not in his nature to be diplomatic. Just as he strove to reproduce every shade in a landscape or the expression of a face or state of mind, so, when it came to philosophical ideas, he saw everything in black and white. Starting out from premises that seemed sound to him, he lumbered ahead looking neither right nor left, preferring to end in an impasse rather than to swerve by so much as a hairsbreadth from a straight line. If he happened to change his mind on the way, he did not gradually shift his course but tacked about all at once, proclaimed the opposite of what he had said the previous day, and called his about-face a conversion or rebirth. 'Why talk in subtleties,' he wrote in his diary, 'when there are so many flagrant truths to be told?'

In aesthetics, the first of the 'flagrant truths' was embodied in the statement that 'art must not be regarded as a means of procuring pleasure, but as an aspect of social life'. Therefore, for Tolstoy, the artist's duty was not to give form, colour and rhythm to his flights of fancy, but amuse the workers after their hard day of labour, and give them 'rest, as refreshing as in their sleep. When an artist begins to say, "I am not understood, not because I am incomprehensible (that is, bad) but because my listeners-readers-spectators have not yet reached my intellectual level,' he has abandoned the natural imperatives of art and signed his own death warrant by ignoring the mainspring of creation.' The criterion of quality was, hence, the approval of the masses, however ignorant and illiterate they were. The notion that a work might be beautiful and have no meaning for the masses was an invention of the wealthy, who, out of pride and perversity, had encouraged the artists to work for a narrow circle of so-called connoisseurs. And thanks to them, modern art was running to rack and ruin. 'The artist of tomorrow will realize that it is more important and useful to compose a tale, a touching little song, a *divertisse-*

ment or sketch or light interlude, or draw a picture that will delight dozens of generations, that is, millions of children and adults, than a novel, symphony or painting that will enchant a few representatives of the wealthy classes and then be forgotten for ever.'

Carried away by his theory, Tolstoy furiously set about demolishing the alleged geniuses of the race. French literature fared worst at his hands, not only because its authors positively indulged themselves in the study of amorous passion, but also because its poets had so refined and polished their style that their products were no more than puzzles in code. Down with Charles Baudelaire, that convoluted, unclean versifier! Down with Verlaine the drunkard, incapable of expressing a thought clearly, recommending – heavens above! – 'that grey song where Precise and Vague join hands!' Down with Mallarmé, who was proud of being so obscure when he ought to have been ashamed! And all those manufacturers of verse, Jean Moréas, Henri de Régnier, Maeterlinck. ... What aberration had led the French to abandon their last great poets – Leconte de Lisle and Sully Prudhomme?

Things weren't much better in the field of painting: Monet, Manet, Renoir, Sisley, Pissarro, all compounders of fog, splitters of the sable hairs on their brushes, intellectuals refusing all contact with the people to wallow in an art for the initiated! Were there any blue faces, or landscapes composed of hordes of multicoloured dots? There were not, right? Then into the wastebasket with the Impressionists! But they were not the only guilty ones. Those painters whose sole occupation was to represent 'the pleasures and graces of a life of leisure and idleness' must also be scrapped, along with those whose paintings had 'a symbolical meaning comprehensible only to people of a certain class', and whose pictures were 'full of feminine nudity, such as are to be seen in galleries and exhibitions'.

The same depravity prevailed in the music of Beethoven, Schumann, Berlioz, Liszt and Wagner – 'dedicated to the expression of sickly states of nervous emotion'. All works that departed from the traditions of the people (folk dances or songs) were to be banished, except possibly 'Bach's famous air for violin, one of Chopin's nocturnes and a dozen pieces or passages in Haydn, Schubert, Beethoven and Chopin ...' One must not be afraid to denounce the public's blind veneration for certain taboo titles, such as Beethoven's Ninth Symphony, which was thought to be so admirable; Tolstoy did not believe it deserved its reputation, and to prove his point he asked two questions: 1. 'Does the work give birth to elevated religious feelings?' Answer: 'No; because no music of any kind can produce such feelings.' 2. 'If the work does not belong to the category of religious art, then does it have another characteristic of good modern art, i.e., does it unite people in a community of feeling?' There again, the answer was negative. And the author adds, 'Not only do I fail to see that the feeling expressed by the Ninth Symphony is capable of uniting people who have not been especially trained to enter into this complicated form of hypnosis, but I cannot even imagine how a crowd of normal beings can be touched by this interminable, muddled and artificial work, in which only one or two short passages manage to emerge from an ocean of incomprehensible sound.'

When he contemplated all the perversions of art, he felt sorry for the millions of good souls working twelve or fourteen hours a day printing books, or wearing themselves out shifting the scenery of amoral plays in theatres, or those who had devoted their entire lives from the age of ten to suppling their fingers so that they could play some musical instrument, or those who did acrobatics and risked their lives in circuses. ... According to him, the muzhiks were right to express surprise at the sight of a monument to Pushkin, who was not a saint, had been killed in a duel and 'whose sole merit was to have written some frequently improper love-poetry'. Similarly, he approved of the peasants in Brittany and Normandy who were offended by the tributes paid to the depraved Baudelaire or the drunken Verlaine. He said the artists of tomorrow must give up mystification, go to the people and revive their jaded inspiration through contact with them. With what pride this latter-day inquisitor watched the flames leaping at the stakes on which he had flung all the decadent and false works of those little Western witches!

The final version of *What Is Art?* is actually relatively mild: his true feelings were expressed in his diary of the period:

'Yesterday, I glanced through Fet's books – novels, short stories and poetry. I recalled the time we spent together at Yasnaya Polyana, our interminable four-handed sessions at the piano, and I plainly saw that all this music and fiction and poetry is not art, that men do not have the slightest need for it, that it is nothing but a distraction for profiteers and idlers, that it has nothing to do with life. Novels and short stories describe the revolting manner in which two creatures become infatuated with each other; poems explain and glorify how to die of boredom; and music does the same. And all the while life, all of life, is beating at us with urgent questions – food, the distribution of property, labour, religion, human relations! It's a shame! It is ignoble! Help me, Father, to serve you by destroying falsehood.' [26]

Or:

'The aesthetic is merely one expression of the ethical. ... If feelings are fine and noble, art will be fine and noble too, and vice-versa.' [27]

And:

'How relieved all those people would have been who spend their time shut up in a concert hall listening to Beethoven's last symphony if the orchestra had played them a trepak or a czardas or something of that order instead!' [28]

When *What Is Art?*, mutilated by the censor, came out at the beginning of 1898, it aroused a storm of protest. Most artists were simply dismayed by this profession of faith by the most illustrious author in Russia, confusing art with pedagogy and talent with right-mindedness. Abroad, translations soon appeared and indignation rose even higher: Tolstoy was called a renegade, an iconoclast, the enemy of freedom of thought. In the *Revue des Deux Mondes* René Doumic wrote, 'Tolstoy absolutely refuses to acknowledge the value of form, through which the language of art differs from any other. The artist is the man who knows better than anyone else how to express feelings which anyone else may experience more deeply than he.' 'When Tolstoy speaks of French literature it is clear that he is speaking of what he knows not,' observed J. K. Huysmans. 'His weakness is to give art a moral purpose,' noted Camille Mauclair. Rémy de Gourmont went one better: 'Art is its own purpose and goal.' Mallarmé explained: 'It seems to me that the illustrious apostle is assigning a quality to art as a principle which is actually more its consequence.' The soft-hearted Henri de Régnier sputtered and fumed, 'These are the ideas of an old man!' 'Tolstoy has always got his muzhik in his pocket,' André Suarès later said. 'Schopenhauer and Rembrandt are worthless because the muzhik doesn't understand them!'

Tolstoy was not displeased by this commotion. If they were all shouting so loudly then he must have hit the mark. Besides, the painter Repin, who had so often done his portrait, thought he was right. And so did all his friends and disciples. The truth was that he could not be mistaken because he was inspired by God, whereas those scribblers in France, England and Germany were all in league with the devil.

Now that he had defined the role of art in society, he felt like writing a piece of fiction. *Resurrection*, perhaps – he had been working on it for a long time, but rather half-heartedly; or the adventures of Hadji Murad – that would take him back to his youth in the Caucasus. In any case, his next novel must be an illustration of his theories. Would he himself be able to live in accordance with what he taught others? Suddenly, he wasn't so sure! This lust for life, this love of nature, this need to expend his energies in the open air, or in bed, this childish desire to tell stories. ... Was it moral? Was it necessary? At seventy, Tolstoy the philosopher began to have suspicions of Tolstoy the author.

PART VII

THE APOSTLE OF
NON-VIOLENCE

26

Resurrection;
the Dukhobors

As though by design, every time Tolstoy was about to become engrossed in some fictional characters, a real-life injustice or calamity would strike his compatriots, tear him away from his dream world and thrust him back to his post of protester. Such vast numbers of people saw him as the incarnation of the conscience of the times that he was compelled, under pain of losing face, to adopt an unequivocal stand on every event. His sincerity, moreover, was always absolute, and his courage owed nothing to his impunity.

Early in 1895, there was renewed talk in Russia of an old religious sect known as the Dukhobors, or 'spirit-wrestlers', which Tsar Alexander I had exiled to the Caucasus long before. Their doctrine resembled that of Tolstoy: like him they advocated chastity, vegetarianism, abstinence from tobacco and alcohol, pooling of all goods and property and non-resistance to evil. As a consequence of the latter, they refused to serve in the army, and this led to very harsh disciplinary measures against some of their members. When Nicholas II acceded to the throne, the government's reactionary tendencies increased, and the Dukhobors were placed under strict surveillance. In the spring of 1895 those in the Caucasus, who had been accustomed to carrying arms to defend themselves against marauding hillsmen, determined, at the instigation of their spiritual leader Verigin, to destroy their daggers, pistols and rifles and publicly proclaim their refusal to serve in the army. The auto-da-fé took place during the night of 28–9 June 1895, in all the lands held by the Dukhobors. The sectarians gathered to pray and sing hymns around the huge bonfires in which their instruments of death were melting, crackling and exploding. Cossacks were sent to 'restore order'; they arrived at a gallop, circled the unfortunate worshippers and beat them with *nagayki* whips until they had disfigured them. Then, by administrative order, the Dukhobors' lands were confiscated and their houses pillaged, four thousand of them were exiled to the mountain villages, and their leaders were put in prison.

Tolstoy was horrified when he heard of this brutality. No doubt it was his books that had given these poor folk the courage to proclaim their faith. His disciple Biryukov left for the Caucasus on 4 August to investigate the matter at first hand. He returned with an article of such virulence that it could not conceivably be published in Russia. But Tolstoy had it printed anonymously (wise precaution) in the London *Times*, under the title *The Persecution of Christians in Russia in 1895*.[1]

The following year, having learned that of the four thousand Dukhobors sent to live in the mountains, four hundred had already died of privation, he encouraged Chertkov, Biryukov and Tregubov, another of his disciples, to write a manifesto to attract public attention to the sufferings of these innocent people. The manifesto was called *Give Help!* and was followed by a postscript by Leo Tolstoy; this time the text was signed, adding to its moral weight. Large numbers of typewritten copies were made and sent to all the influential figures in the administration. The tsar himself received a copy through the mail. Retaliation was swift: the police searched the homes of Chertkov and Biryukov and confiscated masses of papers relating to the religious sects, destroying any that might compromise Pobyedonostsev; and shortly thereafter, in February 1897, Biryukov was exiled to a little town in Kurland, and Chertkov, who still had friends in court, was given the choice of accompanying his 'accomplice' or leaving the country. He decided to go to England.

Tolstoy made a special trip to St Petersburg to bid his

disciples farewell. He was not to see them again for many years. He felt sorry for them and envied them too: they, at least, were suffering for a just cause. When would he, too, be allowed to become a martyr? Speaking of Biryukov and Chertkov, he wrote, 'The joy of spiritual communion ... was so much stronger than the sorrow of separation that even now I cannot produce in myself that state of affliction which is considered proper in such circumstances. They are (both) so full of light, so happy and simple that they inspire absolutely no pity. What is going on inside them is far more important than an enforced change of residence.' [2]

Sonya, who had accompanied Tolstoy to St Petersburg, was so incensed at the punishment inflicted upon her husband's followers that she even forgot her hatred of Chertkov. Since he was leaving, she began to see all his fine qualities. 'The place Tolstoy and his partisans will occupy in history because of this,' she proudly wrote to her sister, 'will be far more enviable than that of Pobyedonostsev and company.' She confided to her friend Mrs Annenkov: 'I wept a great deal, for I regard the men who have just been banished as our best and most devoted friends, and it is very hard for us to be separated from them.' At this time she was still in the throes of her platonic infatuation with Tanayev; her husband, Chertkov, the children, the music, all swam together more or less harmoniously in her mind. But Tolstoy was grateful to her for siding with him on behalf of the Dukhobors.

Moreover, throughout his stay in the capital, he felt that public opinion was on his side. In the street, young people recognized him from his portraits, spoke to him, told him how they admired him; Koni's neighbours broke off in the middle of a party and came out to watch the great, taciturn writer go by in his muzhik dress; the day he left, he was acclaimed by a crowd at the station and had to come to the doorway of his compartment to bow, like a politician or an actor. The only person to give him a cold shoulder in Petersburg was his *babushka* Alexandra. He could not resist telling her all the ill he thought of the tsar and his clique, any more than she could resist upbraiding him for his religious waywardness. They parted unreconciled. Tolstoy found her 'lifeless, utterly lacking in kindliness, pitiful' and 'possessed of boundless pride'.[3] And she wrote, 'It is sad to say, but he has no need of Him who is the only Saviour. How is one to understand the merits and inconsistencies of this remarkable and mystifying character? On the one hand, love of truth, love of mankind, love of God and of the Master whose glory he will not or cannot admit; and on the other, pride, obscurity, lack of faith, the abyss.'

After his Petersburg experiment, Tolstoy went through a period of discouragement and doubt. It had become clear to him that the government was cunningly contriving to exempt him from all punishment and prosecuting only his partisans. That was the best way to give him a guilty conscience and discredit him in the eyes of the public. They said – and it was probably true! – that when a minister suggested that Tolstoy should be exiled, the new tsar, Nicholas II, had taken the same line as his father: 'I do not intend to add a martyr's crown to his glory.' Frustrated, Tolstoy wrote to Gastev, one of his followers, 'You probably know that Chertkov and Biryukov have been sent into exile. That is all very well and good. The sad thing is that they won't lay a finger on me. They (the people in authority) are defeating their own purpose, however, for by leaving me free to speak the truth, they are compelling me to speak it. And I have the impression that much remains to be said.'[4]

In his eagerness to compromise himself irretrievably, he seized every opportunity to defend his 'dear brothers suffering for the doctrine of Christ'. All the little religious sects being persecuted by Pobyedonostsev had no more loyal ally than he. When, on police order, the children of the Molokhans were removed from their parents' custody under pretext that they were not taught to respect the official Orthodoxy, he wrote to the tsar in protest:

'Majesty, for the love of God make an effort and, instead

of avoiding the matter and referring it to commissions and
committees, decide, without asking anyone's advice, you
yourself, acting on your own initiative, that these religious
persecutions, which are causing the shame of Russia, must
cease; the exiles must be sent back to their homes, the prisoners released, the children returned to their parents, and,
above all, the whole body of administrative laws and regulations be abolished, as they are so complicated and obscure
that they are just so many pretexts for illegality.'

The Molokhans, who were supposed to send this letter to
the emperor, were alarmed by its violence and destroyed it
instead. But Tolstoy overrode their fears and rewrote it, and
the second copy was handed to Nicholas II by Alexander
Olsufyev,* a member of the emperor's military staff. Tolstoy
never heard of it again. On 19 September 1897 he wrote
another. To no avail. Four months later he instructed his
daughter Tanya, who was not married at the time, to make
another attempt. On 27 January 1898 she was granted an
audience with Pobyedonostsev and dutifully described the
sufferings of the Molokhan parents who had been separated
from their children. 'Yes, yes, I know,' muttered Pobyedonostsev. 'The bishop of Samara has gone too far. I shall
write to the governor right away.' He was as good as his
word. The Molokhan children were returned to their families, and Tolstoy was so flabbergasted that he forgot to rejoice.

Besides, other injustices were already claiming his attention. Some of his friends were urging him to join a group
of Russian liberals who were signing a manifesto soliciting
a reprieve for the French officer Dreyfus, charged with high
treason. Tolstoy became angry. Was Dreyfus a man of the
people, a muzhik, a sectarian? No; he was an officer, that
is, one of the worst possible sort. Guilty or not, he was unworthy of consideration. 'It would be a strange thing that
we Russians should take up the defence of Dreyfus, an

* The brother of Adam Olsufyev, whom Tolstoy often visited in
the country.

utterly undistinguished man, when so many exceptional ones have been hanged, deported or imprisoned here at home,'[5] he exclaimed.

He was keenly interested, though, when he heard from a supposedly well-informed source that the recently founded Nobel Prize Committee in Sweden was considering him for the award. The grant was rumoured to amount to one hundred thousand roubles.* Seizing the opportunity, Tolstoy sent a letter to the director of the Swedish newspaper *Stockholm Dagbladet*, suggesting that the sum be given to the Dukhobors, who had contributed far more than he to the cause of peace by refusing to bear arms. His advice was not followed, and indeed, the Swedish Academy seemed to be in no hurry to choose its first prizewinner. Then Tolstoy, with his old propagandist's zeal, multiplied his appeals to public charity, launched a campaign in the foreign press, wrote personal letters to the highest officials in the Caucasus and Siberia exhorting them to give the sectarians more humane treatment, and sent his son Sergey to England to make contact with a relief committee there.

However much sympathy Sonya may have had for the Dukhobors, she was terrified by the enormous risks Lyovochka was taking by defending them. Would he not be deported too, along with his wife and children, to teach him a lesson for provoking the tsar? Unless the dreaded autocrats had some worse fate in store for him! He had recently been receiving anonymous threatening letters, 'because he was offending Our Lord Jesus Christ and setting himself up as an adversary of the tsar and the fatherland'. Some of them even mentioned a date: the beginning of 1898. If he had not mended his ways by then, he would be executed. 'More letters threatening my life,' he wrote on 28 December 1897. 'I am sorry that there are people who hate me, but I am scarcely interested and still less concerned.'

There were no attempts upon his life, but his mail soon began to bring criticism from friends as well as enemies.

* Or $283,100.

The purest Tolstoyans were complaining that he had betrayed his principles by begging money from the rich to save the poor. He had been faced with a similar conflict when he joined the relief work for the peasants during the great famine, and he had settled it the same way, with the same sense of guilt: 'Adopting this solution [giving aid to the unfortunate] means acting contrary to one's ideas,' he wrote to Gastev, one of his fiercest critics. 'But not adopting it means withholding the word and the deed that might relieve present suffering.' He accused himself of 'spinelessness' because he had yielded to pity. One week he wrote twelve personal letters to people who were known to have vast fortunes, and six more another week.[6] All the 'moneybags' answered his appeal, some with ten thousand roubles, some with five thousand. Tolstoy contemplated the money with a mixture of loathing and joy.

Meanwhile, in London, Sergey had succeeded in interesting the Quakers in the fate of the Dukhobors, whose doctrines were closely allied with their own; and in St Petersburg, the government, exasperated by the stir being made over the affair both in Russian society and in the foreign press, authorized the sectarians to emigrate to Canada where tracts of uncleared land were being placed at their disposal by the State. It then remained to find the balance of the amount required for the transport and resettlement of nearly seven thousand emigrants. Despite Tolstoy's efforts, the subscription did not yield enough. Then, once more violating his own principles, he decided to retain his rights to the books he was then writing, sell them at the highest possible price to both Russian and foreign publishers and use the money to help the sectarians. Even though this infringement of his own rules was being made to further a humanitarian undertaking, he was aware of its gravity and apologized to Chertkov: 'Although these writings do not satisfy my present aesthetic requirements (they were not accessible to all in their present form), there is no harm in their substance and they may even be of some use to readers.

Therefore I think it would be good to sell them at the highest possible price, publish them without waiting for my death and transfer the money to the Dukhobors' emigration committee.'[7]

In this charitable design he hurried *Father Sergey* to completion and returned to his long novel, *Resurrection*. Before it was finished he had sold it to the publisher Marx for his review *Niva*, for the 'exorbitant' (in Sonya's own words) sum of one thousand roubles* per sixteen-page sheet.

There are scores of entries in his notebooks to prove that he cared enormously about *Father Sergey*. Prince Kasatsky, a brilliant lieutenant of the cuirassiers, becomes engaged to the very beautiful Marya, a young lady of the highest society who is a great favourite with the court, only to learn that, the previous year, she had been the mistress of Tsar Nicholas I. Horrified, Kasatsky leaves her, takes holy orders and becomes something of a saint – Father Sergey, whom pilgrims come to see in his hermitage. In spite of his apparent serenity, Father Sergey must wrestle with two temptations: concupiscence, and a sort of 'monastic ambition' or pride in saintliness, which prevents him from finding true salvation. One night, a pretty woman from the neighbouring town who has had a little too much to drink makes a bet with some friends that she can seduce the anchorite. She enters his retreat, brushes against him, excites him. And Father Sergey, about to fall, cuts off one of his fingers with an axe. Having punished his flesh, he now believes he will be freed of the demon forever. But later he succumbs to the advances of a sensual and stupid merchant's daughter. Then, horrified at his sin, he runs away and loses himself among the masses of the humble, poor and nameless. Convicted of vagabondage and deported to Siberia, he finds happiness at last in his physical debasement: 'He works his employer's vegetable garden, gives lessons to the children and nurses the sick.'

---

* Or $2,830.

After writing this story, which combines elements of *The Kreutzer Sonata* and *What I Believe*, Tolstoy could not make up his mind to publish it.* It is brutal, disconcerting, provocative; it may be taxed with absurdity and it is not exempt from melodrama; but by transcending them, the tale achieves greatness. How often was Tolstoy himself tempted to cut off a finger in order to stifle his burgeoning desire? How many times did he dream of finding release from the burdensome glory of apostlehood by running away and living like a muzhik? From Father Sergey to Father Leo, there is only the thickness of a sheet of paper.

And it was himself again that he featured in *Resurrection*, under the name of Nekhlyudov. Himself – or, at least, the ideas that disturbed him, the remorse that gnawed at him, the indignation that rose up in him at the world in its present state.

The idea for this novel came to him in June 1887 when his friend Koni, who was visiting Yasnaya Polyana, told him the most singular case of his career on the bench. He was representing the State at the St Petersburg court when a young aristocrat came to him with a complaint against the prison administration, which refused to give a sealed letter to a woman convict, Rosalie Oni, on the ground that all letters must be read before being distributed. Koni explained to his client that those were indeed the prison regulations and, his curiosity aroused, made an inquiry into the woman's case. He learned that Rosalie, a sharecropper's daughter, had been taken in at her father's death by the owner of the estate, who had kept her on as a house-servant. At sixteen she had been seduced by the son of her benefactress, and when she became pregnant she was driven out of the house. Forced to make a living somehow, she soon became a prostitute of the lowest sort. One of her clients accused her of stealing a hundred roubles from him, and she was arrested and put on trial. It so happened that one of

* It was not published until after his death.

the members of the jury was the very man who had seduced her and brought about her downfall: Koni's young visitor himself! He had recognized his victim in that faded, abandoned woman and, overcome by remorse, offered to marry her to atone for his error. But before the marriage could take place, Rosalie Oni died of typhus in prison.

Listening to this tale, Tolstoy felt himself half-sick with emotion. He, too, had seduced a servant in his youth – Gasha. He, too, had a bastard child by a peasant woman, at Yasnaya Polyana. He, too, was a swine, like the young aristocrat Koni was telling him about. He asked the judge to write out the cruel tale for the Intermediary. In the spring of 1888, Koni still had not done so and Tolstoy spoke to him again, asking him to cede the rights to the story, which Koni was more than willing to do. However, it was not until December 1889 that Tolstoy began what he first called 'Koni's story'. Then he put it aside for nearly five years. In 1895, in a burst of energy, he wrote a full but relatively short first draft. As with *War and Peace*, he wanted to build his work on a foundation of unimpeachable documentation. Through the offices of his friend Davydov, State representative at the court of Tula, he was able to visit the prisons, question the prisoners, study the machinery of the law courts. After revising his first draft during the summer months he read it to some friends, and his confidence faltered: 'I am now convinced that it is no good,' he said, 'the centre of gravity is not in the right place, the agricultural question weakens the story. I think I am going to abandon it.'

And for another three years he did not touch the manuscript. His scheme to help the Dukhobors sent him excitedly back to his characters, and this time he stuck to them throughout the summer and autumn of 1898. As he progressed, the story expanded. He introduced all the great guiding principles of his life and wrought them into one virulent whole, one scorching testament. 'I thought it would be very good to write a long novel in the light of my present opinions,' he had noted a few years earlier. Now he was sure the book would be good. A cargo of dynamite. Enough to blow up the whole rotten old world. Remember to thank God who had enabled him, at the age of seventy (i.I.l.) to carry out this strenuous undertaking! He wrote to his disciples Shkarvan and Abrikosov: 'I am very busy ... with my novel *Resurrection*. I am so taken up with it that I can think of nothing else, day and night. I think it will be important.'[8] And to Chertkov: 'As a projectile gathers speed nearing the earth, so I, as the end of my novel approaches, can think of nothing else – absolutely nothing else – but that.'[9]

The following year he revised the book from the printed proofs, changing everything, as usual – crossing out whole pages and filling the margins and reverse sides with innumerable additions. At their wit's end, the publishers begged him to forgo some of his revisions; the book was coming out in a weekly review and the slightest delay in sending his copy might hold up publication. Letters and telegrams rained down on the desk of the overscrupulous author. To help with the revision he enlisted Sonya, his daughters, Obolensky and the alcoholic scribe Ivanov. Visiting friends occasionally joined the family team. One of them, Goldenweiser, described the work in the following terms: 'The corrections of the proofs revised by Leo Nikolayevich, which are used as a rough draft, must be copied over on to a clean set of proofs, in two copies. The "draft proofs" stay in the house, the "clean proofs" are sent to Marx, for *Niva*, and to Chertkov in England. It is interesting work, but exacting and difficult. To replace one sheet of proofs it is sometimes necessary to copy over three or four long pages. Leo Nikolayevich's corrections are often written so close together that they can only be made out with a magnifying glass.'[10]

The publication of *Resurrection* in *Niva* began on 13 March 1899, while Tolstoy was still retouching and expanding the final pages of his manuscript. The imperial censor worried the book like a bone, but even in its amputated and watered-down form, its impact on the public was overwhelming from the very first issues.

In the story of Nekhlyudov, who recognizes the prostitute Katyusha Mazlova as the young peasant girl he seduced long ago and is then impelled by guilt to follow her to Siberia, Tolstoy is indicting the whole of modern society. But whereas in *War and Peace* and *Anna Karenina* the pace of the novel was slowed by philosophical and historical digressions, here the author rushes straight ahead, without pausing once to become entangled in secondary plots. As we move from chapter to chapter we see only Mazlova and Nekhlyudov, at grips with the iniquity, poverty and squalor of the world. They form a pair of 'reporters' whom we follow into the hell of criminal justice – 'reporters' who are the victims of the universe they unmask. This universe – a place of stench and darkness – begins just on the other side of the panelled walls of drawing-rooms, the gilded triptychs in the churches and the marble halls of the law courts. In denouncing the filth camouflaged by this opulent stage-setting, Tolstoy employs a technique of pitiless observation and a brutal style in which every word is calculated to sting the reader to the quick.

First of all, he wants to open his contemporaries' eyes to the preposterousness of the imperial institutions. Seen from the wings, the hearing in the court of assizes is enough to finish off the magistracy. 'The president of the court was a big, heavy man who wore long, grizzled side-whiskers. Although married, he lived in a very dissolute fashion, as did his wife. They did not interfere with one another. That morning he had received a message from a Swiss governess who had spent the previous summer with them and was passing through town on her way to St Petersburg, informing him that she would expect him between three and six at the Italian Hotel. He was accordingly anxious to begin the hearing without delay.' To limber up a little before going into court, he does a few turns on the bar in his office. One of his assistants has just quarrelled with his wife, the other is worried about his stomach complaint. And yet when they come into the courtroom, these dregs of humanity, propped up by their stiffly starched robes, are supposed to intimidate both prisoners and public. The comedy continues with the parade of jurymen before a 'little old priest with a swollen yellow face, wearing a brown cassock and a golden cross on his breast and some other little decoration pinned on one side'. This holy man, who has been officiating for forty-six years, is proud to be working 'for the good of Church, State and family; to his own family he was planning to leave a capital of thirty thousand roubles in stocks and bonds, in addition to a house'. 'His task,' the author continues, 'consists in administering oaths upon the Gospels, which expressly forbid it.'

Still more ruthless is his description of the divine service in a prison : 'The mass consisted of the following procedure : the priest, having decked himself out in a special brocade costume, odd-looking and highly uncomfortable, cut some bread into little pieces which he arranged on a plate, before dipping them into a goblet of wine as he uttered various names and prayers. The sacristan, meanwhile, read and sang, alternating with the choir of prisoners, numerous orisons in Slavonic, which were hard enough to understand in themselves and were rendered totally unintelligible by the breakneck pace at which he recited them. The chief object of these prayers was to ask God's blessing upon the emperor and his family.' Here is the communion : 'The priest lifted the napkin covering the plate, cut the central piece of bread into four parts, dipped it in the wine and then put it into his mouth. He was supposed to be eating a piece of the body of God and drinking a mouthful of his blood.' After distributing 'this bread' and 'this wine' among the faithful congregated in front of him, 'he carried the goblet behind the partition where he proceeded to eat up all the little pieces of God's body and drink the remaining blood; then he carefully sucked on his moustache, wiped his mouth, cleaned the cup and, feeling very cheerful, the thin soles of his calf-skin boots creaking smartly, strode resolutely forth.'

Sonya was so offended by this passage that after correcting the proofs she wrote in her diary, 'I am revolted by his intentionally cynical description of the Orthodox mass. For instance, the place where the priest holds up a gilded cross to the people, "representing the gallows on which Jesus Christ was executed". For him, the communion is nothing but bread crumpled into a cup. It is all absurd and cynical, in my opinion, it is nothing but a crude attack on those who have faith, and it disgusts me.'[11]

Naturally, neither priest, deacon, prison governor, wardens nor prisoners would dream of supposing that what goes on in church is 'monstrous and sacrilegious', 'a practical joke played on Christ'. For the priests, the ritual hides the truth – just as civil servants have regulations in place of a heart. In his efforts to alleviate the sufferings of Katyusha Mazlova and the other convicts, Nekhlyudov comes into conflict with every possible representative of bureaucracy. Count Charsky, ex-minister, is a perfect example of a parasite, always on the lookout for some unearned preferment or perquisite. 'He had been convinced from earliest childhood that just as it is natural for a bird to eat worms, bear feathers and fly, so it was natural for him to feed on costly dishes prepared by famous cooks, dress in elegant and luxurious clothes and have the most handsome and swiftest horses.' General Kriegsmuth, commander of the St Peter and St Paul Fortress, has been decorated twice, the first time in the Caucasus 'because he had killed thousands of natives who were defending their freedom, their homes and their families' and the second time because he had facilitated the crimes of the Russian peasants in Poland. 'Nekhlyudov listened to the rasping old voice, stared at the stiff limbs and lifeless eyes beneath the white eyebrows, the pendent shaven jowls supported by the military collar, and the white cross in which he took such evident pride because he had earned it for massacring people in particularly gruesome circumstances, and he realized that it was utterly use-less to make any answer to this old man or to explain the meaning of his words.' The chief attraction in this gallery of monsters, however, is Toporov, a caricature of Pobye-donostsev, the minister for religious affairs. Shown here with his big skull, blue-veined hands, and lips folded into an ingratiating smirk, he is cold, narrow-minded, hypocritical and cruel, encouraging superstition while feigning to defend the faith.

In the administrative hierarchy, the subordinates are no better than their masters. At every level, the 'function' transforms the man into a monster. This rogues' gallery is reminiscent of that in Gogol's *Dead Souls*. Like Gogol's Chichikov, on each successive occasion Tolstoy's Nekhlyu-dov discovers some new facet of human baseness, lechery, stupidity, cruelty or malpractice. Gogol had wanted to con-trast the black creatures in the first part of *Dead Souls* with white ones, who would incarnate the hopes of the human race in the second part, before emerging as virtually full-fledged angels in the third part of his Russian *Divine Comedy*. But try as he would, he could not add a Purgatorio or a Paradiso to the Inferno he had so masterfully por-trayed. Tolstoy chose to combine his figures of light and darkness in the same story. Opposite the repulsive gang of authorities – ministers, judges, priests, police, prison warders – he aligns the people, simple and resigned. In his previous novels, the labouring masses had been represented only by peasants, but in *Resurrection* there are, in addition to the muzhiks on Nekhlyudov's estate, cobblers, masons, house painters, factory hands, laundresses, servants and common criminals. For these underlings, the victims of a misbe-gotten society, the author has nothing but esteem and affec-tion. He describes them with the same realism as he does persons of high degree, but is never sarcastic towards them. How could he sneer at them, the salt of the earth? He paints their external filth in the blackest of hues, but sees nothing but light in their souls. There is Fyodosya, with her 'gentle voice' and 'limpid eyes', and Taras, who has 'kindly blue eyes', following his unjustly sentenced wife to Siberia; and the peasant Menshov, who also has eyes full of light and a heart of gold. Even the drunkards and brutes have the excuse of their immense poverty. Hundreds of silhouettes file past the reader – mere sketches, but when superposed, they form a single collective character whose presence dominates the book. A 'barefoot peasant in a torn caftan, holding the tatters of his hat with dignity in the crook of his arm'; a 'muzhik dressed in rags and bark shoes, with a beard that had never been combed'; Anisya, 'a gaunt woman with a bloodless but smiling face'. Further on Nekhlyudov sees, in a sort of hallucination,

those cobblers he had watched working behind a basement grille; those thin, pale, unkempt laundresses with bare bony arms, ironing in front of gaping windows from which thick scrolls of soapy steam poured out; those two dyer's boys in aprons whom he had recently met, shoeless, wearing only linen rags wrapped around their feet, stained with dye from head to toe. With their shirtsleeves rolled up to the elbow, they were carrying dye pails that were too heavy for them, making the big veins swell out on their scrawny arms, and snapping incessantly at each other. Their sullen faces showed profound lassitude. The same expression could be seen on the dusty, black faces of the wagoners lurching about on their carts, the bloated faces of the men and women begging alms at the street corners with their children, the features of the drinkers glimpsed through café windows. There, around tiny tables cluttered with bottles and glasses of tea, in the ceaseless bustle of the waiters in white aprons, sat creatures with brutish faces, inflamed by alcohol, covered with sweat, shouting and singing.

Between the grey horde of the victims and the glittering little clan of their executioners stand those who want to overthrow the established order: the revolutionaries. Tolstoy studies them here for the first time. As a partisan of non-violence, he should have felt nothing but aversion for them. And yet he draws and animates them with compassion. Among them are aristocrats, bourgeois intellectuals, civil servants, a peasant, a labourer who is a great reader of Karl Marx. The more fanatical of these agitators are mistaken, to be sure, when they proclaim that one must 'work for the masses and expect nothing from them', overthrow the government by force, impose a constitution upon an ignorant people to make them happy in spite of themselves. But their motives are never base. They are ready to suffer and die for others. Therefore they are entitled to the author's respect. Katyusha Mazlova herself admits that she 'never knew or could imagine men more wonderful than those with whom she was walking now'.

Nekhlyudov had tried to carry out a bloodless revolution among the peasants on his own estate. Thus, after lending his agricultural theories of one period to Levin in *Anna Karenina*, Tolstoy now bestows his latest views on the subject upon the hero of *Resurrection*. Inspired by the American socialist Henry George, Nekhlyudov favours a single land tax, high enough to compel the large owners to cede their land to the State. The tax would abolish private property and the State would redistribute the nationalized land among all the peasants who cultivated it. It is odd that Nekhlyudov (alias Tolstoy) should have been so hypnotized by this pseudo-communistic utopia that he failed to realize that in order to carry out such a redistribution it would first be necessary to change the government, or in other words, to make a radical and presumably bloody political reform. When Nekhlyudov finally decides to abandon his land to the peasants in return for a token rent, he has to struggle with their scepticism. With his usual honesty, the author recognizes the gulf between even the best-intentioned landowner and the people. 'It all seemed perfect and yet Nekhlyudov had misgivings. He saw that in spite of the profuse expressions of thanks uttered by some of them, the peasants were in fact dissatisfied and expected something more from him. ... He climbed into the steward's troika with a disagreeable sensation of having left the job unfinished.' Moral: the lord's half-measures are useless and even harmful; as long as he has not given his muzhiks everything, he has given them nothing; one day he will give up all his possessions, less in order to make them happy than to appease his own conscience. Then, without money, attachments or worries, he can set out, illuminated, for Siberia with Katyusha Mazlova at his side.

Most of Tolstoy's novels are dominated by the idea that a man's real life begins when the spiritual forces in him triumph over his animal nature. But in *War and Peace* and *Anna Karenina* this quest for perfection was not the only mainspring. The movement of those stories and their highpoints of interest were in the love affairs that swept the main characters along (Prince Andrey and Natasha; Pierre Bezukhov and Elena, then Natasha; Nicholas Rostov and Sonya, then Princess Bolkonsky; Lenin and Kitty; Anna Karenina and Vronsky, etc.). In *Resurrection* Nekhlyudov's love for Katyusha Mazlova is the preface to the novel, rather than the substance of it. Their love is the past. It is seen through mirrors. But since the reader does not have to follow several intermingled plot-lines at once, as in the great works that preceded it, the story gains in unity and drive. The action of the book actually begins when Nekhlyudov, looking at the prostitute being tried for theft, recognizes the little servant-girl he had seduced in his youth. Later, he never feels involved with her in the ordinary way. He follows her out of pity, not passion, and out of a need to expiate, a desire to elevate himself by joining forces with those who are most lowly. It is not sentiment that gives rhythm and warmth to this couple's story, but the denunciation of social injustice and the search for a remedy that will cure mankind's ills.

And therein, perhaps, lies the weakness in this beautiful book. All that is 'reporting' – the courts, prisons, convicts' travels, life in a prison colony – is compellingly convincing, but the saga of Nekhlyudov and Katyusha Mazlova seems rather trite alongside it. Like Nikolenka Irtenyev in *Childhood, Boyhood* and *Youth*, Nekhlyudov in *A Landlord's*

Morning, Pierre Bezukhov in *War and Peace* and Levin in *Anna Karenina*, the Nekhlyudov of *Resurrection* is Leo Tolstoy. But the gap between protagonist and author has widened with age. The writer has put the ideas of a solitary thinker of seventy-two into the head of a hale and hearty man of thirty-five, high-living, lusty and frivolous. As Romain Rolland points out, one feels here 'the juxtaposition of one very real person going through the moral crisis of another one, and the other one is the aged Tolstoy'. To be sure, a moral crisis of this sort is conceivable at any age. But here there has been nothing in what we know of the hero's character and life to prepare for it; it arrives on command, more, it would seem, at the author's will than as the consequence of the psychological impulses of his spokesman; and once it has begun, it proceeds with mechanical regularity.

To hide his uneasiness at this arbitrary aspect of the revelation, Tolstoy makes lavish use of overdramatic expressions. When he first sees Katyusha Mazlova at the court hearing, Nekhlyudov 'feels he is *a dog* who should be ashamed to look people in the face'. Later, 'he felt all the *cruelty and indignity* not only of that one deed, but of his entire *idle, debauched, spiteful and arrogant* existence'. Returning home after the trial, he repeats to himself, '*Shame and loathing! Loathing and shame!*'* And when he sees a portrait of his mother in a black gown with shoulders bared and swelling bosom, he chokes with revulsion for all that is 'flesh'. He remembers that he had seen Missy, his fiancée, similarly revealed a few days before. 'I shall tell Missy the truth: that I am a *profligate*, that I cannot marry her and have troubled her for nothing. ... I shall tell Katyusha that I am a *filthy wretch*, that I am guilty towards her and shall do everything in my power to lighten her burden.' Having made this decision, nothing can move him from it. He is wealthy, enjoys a good reputation and is about to marry Missy – but he abandons everything to atone for an error made in the distant past; and not for one moment

* Here and in following quote, Troyat's italics.

during the months of his calvary with Katyusha Mazlova, a care-worn woman with a vicious tongue and foul breath, does he question the choice he has made. Even when he learns she is about to relapse into sin, he does not entertain one moment of regret or discouragement.

How is it that Tolstoy, whose own convictions and feelings fluctuated so wildly, did not try to 'shade' his hero a little? Nekhlyudov would have seemed so much more plausible to us had he been a little less sure of himself! Moreover, he and Katyusha Mazlova follow different paths to illumination. Katyusha is reborn when she places herself at the service of a political prisoner whom she does not love; she abandons Nekhlyudov, who has given up everything to save her, perhaps because she senses that a man like him must find his salvation alone. And so it is: Nekhlyudov, feeling that 'his dealings with Katyusha are at an end', opens the New Testament and chances upon a passage that enlightens him. In a matter of minutes he is turned inside out, renewed, cleansed. For the reader, this conversion *in extremis* is hardly convincing. It does not follow naturally from the story and it bears the mark of Holy Scripture less than that of the fatigue of an author who is in a hurry to dispose of his characters. After reading the book, Chekhov wrote to Menshikov, on 28 January 1900, 'An admirable work of art! The most interesting parts are the passages on the relations between Nekhlyudov and Katyusha, and even more, those on all those princes and generals and aunts and muzhiks and convicts and guards. The scene with the spiritualist general in command of the St Peter and St Paul Fortress took my breath away, it is so powerful! And Mrs Korchagin in her armchair, and Fyodosya's peasant husband ... the one who said his wife was *clutching*. It's Tolstoy's pen that is *clutching*. But the novel has no end, or rather what ends it cannot be called an ending. To write and write, and then suddenly to throw it all away on a piece of scripture, is a little too theological!'

In fact, the end of *Resurrection* is astonishingly like that of *Father Sergey* and also like that which Tolstoy, in his diary, hoped would be his own: the departure, the break with society to mingle with the hordes of the lowly and be lost in the flood.

His refusal to live in the world is even more singular when one thinks that his perception of it has never been sharper. It is not loss of appetite that drives him away from the table, but fear of his own gluttony. At seventy as at twenty, he writes with nostrils flaring, eyes alert and ears pricked; he told Sergeyenko, 'No detail must be neglected in art, for a button half-undone may explain a whole side of a person's character. It is absolutely essential to mention that button. But it has to be described in terms of the person's inner life, and attention must not be diverted from important things to focus on accessories and trivia.' [12] Applying this principle, he notes the physical peculiarities of his people in passing, characterizes old Korchagin by his 'bull's neck', Mazlenikov by his 'white, fat fist', Katyusha Mazlova by her eyes as dark as wet black currants and her slight squint, Missy by her tapered thumbnail. He gives to each his own way of speaking: socialites, high public officials, muzhiks and guards, revolutionary theoreticians and convicts. For the latter, he uses the pungent expressions he noted during his prison tours. Even the inner monologues are in keeping with the characters' physical type and social rank. All in all, he never wrote with greater violence and less 'artistry'. He takes even less pains than usual with his style because he is not trying to tell a story: he is trying to stigmatize those who are responsible for the present plight of society. The crudeness of naturalistic detail is intended to convince the reader of the extent of the evil that must be remedied: the gabbling woman squatting over the garbage trough, the old man with a huge grey louse crawling across his cheek, the convicts' wrangling around the tap during their washing-up period. ... The reminiscences of Nekhlyudov's and Katyusha's distant past are the only moments that contain any poetry. There is the unforgettable snowy Easter night, the church filled with peasants in their best finery, Katyusha looking so pretty with a red ribbon in her hair; and the thaw, the white fog; and the vision of the girl sitting quietly behind a window; and the swell of desire in Nekhlyudov's veins, while, 'from the stream, strange snortings and cracklings came to him, the rattle of breaking ice' and the crow of the cock leaps out of the mist. All the grace and loveliness of the long-ago time of innocence merely deepen the squalor of the present. Tolstoy colours his drawing with his adjectives. His brush skims, adding a stroke here and there, deepening a shadow, encircling a silhouette: 'There were four judges: Nikitin, the president, a *waxen, smooth-shaven* man with *steel grey eyes* in a *narrow* face; Wolff, with lips *tightly compressed*, leafing through the brief with his *little white hands*; then Skovorodnikov, *tall* and *heavy* with a *pockmarked* face, a learned jurist; the fourth, Bey, wearing a *patriarchal* air, came in last. The clerk and the State representative, a *young* man of *medium* height, *dry* and *close-shaven* with a *swarthy* complexion and *black, mournful* eyes, had come in at the same time as the judges.'

There is one set of words that recur whenever Nekhlyudov is among people of the upper classes: 'satiated', 'fat', 'scrubbed', 'idle', 'smug', 'contemptible'. ... But when he goes among the people, everyone becomes 'gaunt', 'pale', 'hairy', 'worn', 'querulous', 'swollen', 'wretched'.... Tolstoy's love of the adjective is boundless. He would not cross out a single one to lighten his sentence or avoid a clash of vowel sounds. Little he cared whether he wrote well, so long as what he wrote was true! To an anonymous young poet who sent him a sample of his work around that time he replied, 'I do not like verse and I think poetry is a pointless occupation. When a man has something to say he must try to say it as clearly as possible, and when he has nothing to say it is better for him to keep quiet.' [13]

If Tolstoy is so scornful of the music of words, it is because the only thing that matters to him is the thought behind them. His sentences, badly built, strung together with 'who', 'what', 'which', 'the latter', 'the one who' and 'as a result', express what he thinks all the better. After criticizing the old master's style, Chekhov wrote, 'You read on and between the lines you see an eagle soaring in the sky, and the last thing in the world he cares about is the beauty of his feathers.' True; Tolstoy's style is total freedom, absolute sincerity. He is the enemy of mystery in literature. His world is lighted full-face, brutally. Every shadow is defined by the position of the sun. No mirages, no phantoms, no sham. He bedevils his style for love of the truth as he bedevils his friends for love of the truth. If he could, he would live and write like a peasant: hammer words the way you hammer wooden wedges into a shoe sole. Make them stick, make it work, make it last for generations.

Written with a propagandist's vehemence, *Resurrection* shocked Russia into silence. Even the authorities did not dare to make an open attack upon this indictment of the vices of the régime. And all the money went to the Dukhobors. 'Your novel is more than literature,' Nemirovich-Danchenko wrote to Tolstoy on 10 July 1899. 'I, at any rate, cannot recall ever reading anything in the least like it. I read and it seems to me that I am not reading but walking about, and I see these people, these cells and rooms, this piano and sidewalk. . . .' Four days later Stasov confirmed this opinion: 'Ah, what an amazing miracle it is, your *Resurrection*. All Russia is living and feeding on this book. ... You cannot imagine the conversations and debates it is provoking. I think there are only a few imbecilic and decadent degenerates against you in all of Russia. ... Such as those poor wretches Merezhkovsky, Minsky et al. . . .'[14] And on 2 January 1900: 'This event has had no equal in the literature of the nineteenth century. It is far greater than *Les Misérables* because there is not one shred of idealism or invention or literature in you, only flesh, living meat!'

Tolstoy, however, was sceptical. As usual, it seemed to him that his work was not polished enough. And then, he was rather ashamed of this success, which was addressed more to the novelist than to the philosopher. His excuse was that the Dukhobors would benefit greatly by it – he had paid the eighty thousand roubles * he received for the book into their fund. With coquetry he feigned self-belittlement to Prince Khilkov: 'I suppose that, just as nature has endowed certain men with a sexual instinct for the reproduction of the species, she has endowed others with an artistic instinct, which seems to be equally absurd and equally imperious. ... I see no other explanation for the fact that an old man of seventy who is not utterly stupid should devote himself to an occupation as futile as writing novels.'[15]

Tolstoy celebrated his seventieth birthday at Yasnaya Polyana on 28 August 1898. There were forty people around the table, singing and making speeches. Tolstoy, with patriarchal beard and misty eyes, was aglow. But Preobazhensky cast a chill over the gathering when he proposed to drink a glass of white wine to the master's health, for, as Sonya was forced to explain, 'One may not drink to the health of Leo Nikolayevich because he belongs to a temperance league.' He was at the height of his fame, and was alternately delighted and disgusted by his physical prowess. When was he sincere – glorying in the fact that he could still cut hay for three hours at a stretch, or regretting the impure thoughts that passed through his mind at the sight of a farm girl? 'Lyovochka made my bed himself,' wrote his wife, 'and after riding over twenty miles still had enough energy to manifest his passion. I note this as proof of his remarkable vitality at the age of seventy.'[16]

His fame brought an ever-increasing number of letters and visitors. All foreigners of note who were travelling in Russia came to see him, from the criminologist Cesare Lombroso ('A naïve, narrow-minded little old man,' said Sonya) to the poet Rainer Maria Rilke, who seems to have made no impression at all. When Lombroso tried to explain to Tolstoy his theory of the 'delinquent man' whose responsibility

* Or $226,500.

was attenuated by heredity, illness and environment, the author of *Resurrection* scowled, glared at him and burst out, 'It's insane! All punishment is criminal!'[17]

The sculptor Paolo Trubetskoy was given permission to come into the master's presence, and made a life-size bust of him, with arms crossed and beard awry and a discontented expression on his face. Later, he sculpted him on his mare Délire: the patriarch's shoulders are squared, his feet thrust home in the stirrups, his blouse bouffant, the reins in his hands. His face is rough, wrinkled and hairy, like a hunk of earth, crazed and moss-grown in patches. His cheekbones are high, his ears large. Under the protuberant brow, his eyes – black holes – stare into the distance: away! The 'second tsar of Russia', as some called him, had not given up his scheme. His need for asceticism and vagabondage was most intense just after he had dazzled Sonya with his virility. On 17 July 1898, he wrote to his Finnish translator Jernefeld, whom he had never seen, announcing in covert terms that he would like to come and live with him. Then he recoiled at the thought of the scandal that would follow his flight. 'My whole soul reaches out,' he told one of his friends, 'but I cannot tear myself away from here. Do you know why? I am afraid I should have to step over a pool of blood, a corpse in the door. That would be so horrible that I prefer to go on with my hateful life, however burdensome!'[18] To Chertkov he wrote, on 21 July 1898: *'Do not let anyone read this. ... I am a poor excuse for a man. I teach others and cannot live as I ought myself. For how many years have I been asking myself, must I go on as I am or must I go away? And I cannot make up my mind. I know that everything is decided by renunciation, and when I succeed it all becomes clear, but those moments are few and far between.'*

He might have found another reason for indecision that year, in addition to his fear of hurting his wife. Hundreds of peasants needed him: famine was threatening again, even in the richest provinces. The district of Chern, where both

Nikolskoye and Grinevka – the estates of his eldest son Sergey and his second son Ilya – were located, was particularly hard-hit. He went there and, with Sergey and Ilya, set up relief kitchens and clothing distribution centres and wrote an article, *Famine or No Famine*. And yet he felt no communion of thought with these strapping young men, so deeply entrenched in their class privileges. 'They make such a strange and unpleasant impression upon me, my children who own land and force other people to work,' he wrote. 'I feel guilty for them. In me it was not the result of reasoning, but of a very powerful emotion. Was I wrong not to give the land to the muzhiks outright? I don't know.' [19]

After trying his hand at a few vague administrative jobs, Sergey had settled on his share of the estate in 1891. He was a gruff, tender-hearted, solitary man, and his marriage was not a success. Although a son had been born, he was already contemplating divorce. Ilya was also living a retired and idle existence on his land, and he, too, did not get along with his wife, by whom he had had several children. But while Sergey gave vent to his emotions at the piano, Ilya consoled himself with the bottle. Looking at him, Tolstoy's pain became all the sharper because this 'muzhik' with the grey eyes, shapeless nose and broad shoulders resembled him so closely. Riding side by side on their horses, they toured the most destitute villages of the district. On several occasions the police tried to prevent them from opening relief kitchens. They had to telegraph to the minister of the interior for permission to feed people who were starving.

One day Tolstoy wanted to revisit Spasskoye, Ivan Turgenev's home, which was only seven miles away from Ilya's. As he went through the abandoned grounds, he recalled the elegant old author with the white beard and woman's voice, with whom he had quarrelled so bitterly and whose importance he now appreciated more fully. But he did not grieve long over this ghost at his heels: the forest was so beautiful and calm in the light of the setting sun that it positively beckoned one to eternal rest. He wrote to Sonya, 'Cool grass underfoot, stars in the sky, the perfume of flowering laburnum and limp birch leaves, trills of the nightingales, buzzing of beetles, the cry of the cuckoo, the solitude, the easy movement of the horse beneath me and a sensation of physical and moral health. As always, I thought of death. It seemed clear to me that everything would be just as good – although in another way – on the other side, and I understood why the Jews imagine paradise in the form of a garden.'[20]

On his return to Yasnaya Polyana, already bitterly disappointed by Sergey and Ilya, his two older sons, Tolstoy ran foul of the third, Leo, the highly-strung intellectual who suffered from being only the pale copy of a great father, and who also wanted to write. At every opportunity he openly opposed his father in the press, but thus far his undistinguished articles had attracted little attention.

Now, however, he had written a novel, entitled *The Prelude of Chopin*, no more nor less than an insolent retort to *The Kreutzer Sonata*. Was it Leo's recent marriage to Miss Westerlund that had given him the impudence to defend marriage after his father had condemned it? Did he pretend to balance his insignificant personal experience of married life against that of the patriarch of Yasnaya Polyana? And he was proposing to publish this balderdash! At the risk of making the author of his days look ridiculous! It was one thing to preach Christian meekness, indifference to the gossip of the world and respect for the opinions of one's fellow man; but there were some forms of attack, coming from a son, that were not to be tolerated. Stung in both his paternal dignity and his author's pride, Tolstoy fumed with rage. Some very strong words were exchanged between the two Leos. On the evening of 22 June the father wrote in his diary: 'Leo spoke to me of his novel. I told him in no uncertain terms that what he had done was not only extremely ill-bred (his favourite expression) but also stupid and devoid of talent!' Disregarding threats and pleas, Leo decided to publish his prose, and two years later, he did so. But *The Prelude of Chopin* sank without a ripple.

At the end of the year, however, the much-maligned Sergey gave proof of unexpected devotion when he agreed to accompany the Dukhobors to Canada. On 21 December 1898 he embarked at Batum on the steamship *Lake Superior* with two thousand sectarians. Two more shiploads had already left during the previous weeks, making a total of six thousand persons. The crossing took twenty-four days. Tolstoy could tell himself that this monumental migration had been made possible by him, through the collections he had organized and, above all, the money from *Resurrection* which he had contributed to the Dukhobors' fund. There was proof of the power of mind over matter: one little idea was enough to feed the masses and stoke the engines of steamships; he was touched. And he confessed in his diary, 'Sergey is very close to me, because he is trying and because he has feeling.'

If only his two younger sons would make an effort to imitate their brother. But Andrey and Michael were strangers to their father's world. Besides, he had to admit that he neither understood nor loved them. Andrey even claimed that during one entire year his father had spoken to him only once, and then to say, 'Go home.' Both, after half-hearted and fitful studies, had joined the army. Indolent and spend-thrift amateurs of the gypsies, they turned up at Yasnaya Polyana only to demand money from their mother. To the astonishment of all, however, Andrey suddenly decided to settle down and, on 8 January 1899, married Countess Olga Dietrich, Chertkov's sister-in-law. After serving as a volunteer in Sumsky's regiment, Michael married a Miss Glebov in 1901.

Unions and separations, flirtations and quarrels, presentations of fiancées and arrivals of daughters-in-law, births; Tolstoy took increasingly little interest in all this flurry. Since his double disappointment over Tanya's marriage to

Sukhotin and Masha's marriage to Obolensky, he expected nothing more from his daughters. The first was living the life of a provincial dame at Kochety, her husband's estate; the second had moved to Pirogovo with her husband. One-time priestesses of the Tolstoyan cult, they were now slaving to satisfy the whims of their imbecilic spouses. He was still glad to see them, however; but they no longer belonged to him, there were impure smells clinging to them. After he visited Kochety, Tanya wrote in her diary, 'I am ashamed to have let Papa down, yet I cannot feel guilty about it. We did not have much serious conversation; I was afraid he would tell me that my marriage was a disappointment to him.' [21] And he: 'Tanya's frivolity disturbs me; she has embarked upon a purely selfish love. I hope she will come back.' [22]

Wrapped up in his grief at the loss of his two older daughters, he paid little attention to the youngest, Alexandra, aged fifteen, who never took her eyes off him and drank his every word. Sensitive, wilful and jealous, she had felt nothing but contempt for her mother ever since she had watched her sighing over Tanayev at the piano, and she wanted to become closer to her father. For her, he was an awesome and omniscient god, the master of all Russia, the only writer in the world. One day – just before Palm Sunday – Sonya came to her husband in his study and announced, her eyes sparkling with anger, that Sasha (Alexandra) refused to go to church. Tolstoy summoned his daughter. Alone with her, looking deep into her eyes, he asked why she had made such a decision.

'Because it's all lies!' cried Sasha between her sobs. 'It is all false! I can't!'

A breath of fresh air wafted through the old warrior's heart. Just when he believed he had been abandoned by his entire family, here he was witnessing the birth of a new disciple, under his own roof. The least likely, the most delightful of disciples! A little girl with a stubborn forehead and braids, wearing a stiff skirt over her starched Sunday petticoats. 'My father's face softened,' Alexandra Tolstoy later wrote. 'His eyes became gentle and loving.'

'Go to church anyway, today,' he said.

And he leaned over to kiss her. With pride and joy she bathed in the perfume of his harsh grey beard. From that day forward, she felt bound to her father by a loving conspiracy, and her sole desire was to take her mother's place at his side, her mother who – that she was sure of! – did not understand him.

27

Excommunication;
the Crimea

AFTER a year's residence under surveillance in the government of Kurland, Biryukov was allowed to go to Switzerland. As soon as he reached Geneva he arranged with Chertkov, who was living in London, to found a Tolstoyan review, *Free Thought*. All the master's works that were forbidden by the censor in Russia were brought across the frontier, where his two disciples saw to their translation and publication. He had virtually ceased to write for anyone else. Orchestrated by them, his fame was assuming ecumenical proportions. The figure of the noble old man with the white beard, suffering, thoughtful countenance and knotted limbs, dressed in a linen blouse and Turkish trousers stuffed into soft leather boots, spread throughout the world in cheap picture-books. And in the opening days of the century he began, for the first time, to feel the weight of his years. He still rode his horse, hiked for miles cross-country and did the work of ten in his study, but he seldom touched his bicycle any more, played hardly any tennis and often complained of pains in the stomach. He had even been forced, reluctantly, to give up gymnastics. And yet it seemed to him that as his strength waned, his soul only rose higher. 'The moral progress of mankind is due to the aged,' he wrote in his diary. 'The old grow better and wiser.' And, 'I am moved to tears by nature: the meadows, woods, wheat fields, the ploughed earth, the hay. I tell myself: "Am I living through my last summer?" If I am, so much the better.'

Unlike some old people, for whom the approach of death brings greater indulgence towards themselves, his need to submit to a stern moral code was stronger than ever. The years had not weakened his love of perfection. Every evening without fail he would shut himself up in his study, open a notebook and, by the light of a single candle, without glasses, his nose buried in the page and his hand steady, record his good resolutions, his failures, his resentments, his weaknesses and victories, and lay down rules of conduct as he had done when he was twenty. In addition to his diary, he had a notebook that never left his pocket, in which he jotted down candid impressions and thoughts. Very often the notes from it were expanded and enlarged upon in the diary. Everything he read, saw and heard was food for thought.

On 23 March 1900, his daughter Tanya, who was suffering from a frontal abscess, had to have her skull trepanned. Von Stein, the surgeon, thought he was doing the right thing when he invited Tolstoy who was waiting in the next room to watch the operation. He entered apprehensively, took one glance between the white-coated men at his daughter, who lay stretched out, livid, her skull bared and her face covered with blood, and nearly fainted. As he was being helped from the room Sonya aroused the whole hospital with her cries of indignation. But it was neither the horror of the sight nor the surgeon's tactlessness that had affected Tolstoy: it was the injustice, he said, all the care lavished upon a privileged few like his daughter, while so many died because they could not afford treatment. The next day, 24 March, he wrote in his diary: 'Yesterday, dreadful operation on Tanya. I saw clearly that all these clinics, built by merchants and manufacturers who have grown rich exploiting and continuing to exploit tens of thousands of lives, can only be evil. The fact that they heal one rich man after causing the death of hundreds if not thousands of poor ones, is abominable. It is also abominable that they are learning, so they claim, to lessen suffering and lengthen life – for the means they employ in doing so are such (they say "for the time being" and I say "by their very nature") that only a chosen few can be saved or comforted; and that is because medicine is less concerned with preventing – through hygiene – than with healing.' His hatred of the wealthy had grown so intense that he added: 'I cannot rejoice at the birth of a child into the wealthy class; it is the proliferation of parasites.'[1]

Despite his age, physical love was still a source of torment to him, and he classified the attitudes that a man could take towards desire as follows: 'The best thing one can do with the sexual drive is (1) to destroy it utterly in oneself; *next best** (2) is to live with one woman, who has a chaste nature and shares your faith, and bring up children with her and help her as she helps you; *next worse*† (3) is to go to a brothel when you are tormented by desire; (4) to have brief relations with different women, remaining with none; (5) to have intercourse with a young girl and abandon her; (6) worse yet, to have intercourse with another man's wife; (7) worst of all, to live with a faithless and immoral woman.'[2] The list ended with the following sentence, encircled: 'This page must be torn out.'

However, if he considered it preferable not to divulge his opinions on this subject, he made no secret of his views on domestic and foreign politics. The quelling of the Philippine uprising by the United States, and the British expeditions against the Boers in the Transvaal shocked his sense of justice. 'They are horrible, these wars that the English and Americans are waging in a world in which even schoolchildren condemn war!'[3] he wrote. And he told a friend: 'Above all else I place the ethical motives that impel and mould the course of history. ... If Poland or Finland were to rise [against Russia] and succeed, my sympathy would be with them, as oppressed peoples.'[4] After watching the factory hands and freight gang at the Moscow–Kazan freight station, he flew into a rage against this exploitation of man by man, and wrote *The Slavery of Our Times*. The assassination of King Umberto of Italy inspired him to appeal to

* In English in the original.
† In English in the original.

universal conscience: *Who Is Guilty?* And there were other occasional pieces: *Letter to the Canadian Dukhobors, Patriotism and Government, Which Way Out?, Is It Necessary?* He even started a *Message to the Chinese.** He had been fascinated by them for some time, considering them to be the possessors of supreme wisdom. He devoured Confucius ('Everything else seems so trivial by comparison' [5]), meditated upon the paths to moral perfection proposed by 'the king without a kingdom' and despaired at being unable to read his precepts in the original. Fortunately, there were less obscure languages; having heard that the best version of the Bible was that used in the Netherlands, he set out to learn Dutch. He made fairly rapid progress and marvelled to rediscover the Sermon on the Mount as he felt his way along in his translation.

That year his religious convictions were confirmed by his indignation over Nietzsche's *Thus Spake Zarathustra.* 'It is perfectly clear to me,' he wrote in his diary on 29 December 1900, 'that Nietzsche was quite mad when he wrote it, not in any figurative sense but in the most literal and direct sense: his incoherence, leaping from one thought to the next, making comparisons without telling what he is comparing, his beginnings of reasonings that have no end ... and all against a positively demented background, with this obsession that by denying the most noble principles of life and thought the author is demonstrating his brilliant superiority! ... But what kind of a society are we living in, where a man as mad as that, dangerously insane, can pass for a teacher?'

In contradiction to Nietzsche, who sang hymns to the will-to-power and wanted to elevate man into 'superman', Tolstoy felt a profound joy in debasing himself before God. He called himself 'foul scum' [6] and affirmed that, whatever he did, he would never know for sure why he was born or where he was going, as the Lord alone held the key to the mystery. Now, every day, he prayed to God in his own

*Subsequently abandoned.

way, and conversed with him in his diary: 'Lord, thou who art within me, give me light, give me love ...'[7] However, while confessing his impotence and unworthiness, he was still convinced that his purpose on earth was to teach his fellow men. At times the 'foul scum' lifted its head, and a breath from on high blew over him. With the tranquil assurance of the visionary, he stated his role: 'I must remember that I am not an ordinary individual, but an emissary, and my vocation is as follows: (1) never to prostitute the dignity of him whom I represent; (2) always to act according to his prescriptions (love); (3) always to work to accomplish the mission I have been given (kingdom of God); (4) whenever its interests conflict with mine, to sacrifice mine.'[8]

While he was thus preparing himself for an ever wider ministry, the dignitaries of the Orthodox Church were discussing how best to combat his influence. As early as 1886, Mgr Nikanor, archbishop of Kherson and Odessa, preached against 'this latter-day heretical master'; in 1891, Butkevich, archpriest of Kharkov, called him an 'impious infidel'; in 1892, during the great famine, the priests of the country churches exhorted the muzhiks to refuse the renegade's bread; in 1896, Pobyedonostsev tried in vain to persuade the tsar to imprison him in the Suzdal monastery. And now at last, in 1900, Mgr Anthony, president of the Holy Synod and Metropolitan of St Petersburg, furious at his attacks against the Church in *Resurrection*, determined, at Pobyedonostsev's instigation, to excommunicate the culprit. A confidential pastoral to the clergy was drafted, declaring Leo Tolstoy an outcast from the ecclesiastical community and forbidding the celebration of requiem masses, should he die impenitent. But after a few months of reflection, the members of the Holy Synod, meeting in plenary session, deemed it prudent to moderate the terms of the circular. On 22 February 1901 they adopted an official decision and ordered it to be posted on the doors of every church. It was signed by three metropolitans, one archbishop and three bishops:

'God has permitted a new false prophet to appear in our midst today, Count Leo Tolstoy. A world-famous author, Russian by birth, Orthodox by baptism and education, Count Tolstoy, led astray by pride, has boldly and insolently dared to oppose God, Christ and his holy heirs. Openly and in the sight of all, he has denied the mother who nurtured him and brought him up: the Orthodox Church; and he has devoted his literary efforts and God-given talent to spreading doctrines which are contrary to Christ and the Church, and to undermining their fathers' faith in the minds and hearts of the people – the Orthodox faith, which upholds the universe, in which our ancestors lived and were saved and in which Holy Russia has remained strong until this day. In his works and letters, circulated in great numbers throughout the world by himself and by his disciples, and especially within the frontiers of our beloved fatherland, he preaches the abolition of all the dogma of the Orthodox Church and of the very essence of the Christian faith with fanatical frenzy; he denies the living and personal God glorified in the Holy Trinity, Creator and Providence of the universe; he refutes Our Lord Jesus Christ, God made Man, Redeemer and Saviour of the world, who suffered for us and for our salvation, and who has been raised from the dead; he refutes the Immaculate Conception of the human manifestation of Christ the Lord, and the virginity, before and after the Nativity, of Mary, Mother of God, most pure and eternally virgin; he does not believe in the life hereafter or in judgement after death; he refutes all the Mysteries of the Church and their beneficial effect; and, flaunting the most sacred articles of faith of the Orthodox community, he has not feared to mock the greatest of all mysteries: the Holy Eucharist. ... Therefore the Church no longer recognizes him among her children and cannot do so until he has repented and restored himself to communion with her.'

Immediately after its publication, the pastoral of the Holy Synod aroused protest throughout Russia. Even those who

disapproved of Tolstoy's ideas deplored this archaic procedure unearthed by the priests in the hope of discrediting
Russia's greatest living author. What would other countries
say to such medieval practices? And the moment for publishing the anathema could not have been more ill-chosen:
for some time the Moscow University students had been
agitating on behalf of some of their comrades in Kiev who
had been sent into the army as common soldiers after a riot.
The whole city was in a ferment. Groups were forming at
every street corner. On Sunday 24 February 1901, the day on
which the excommunication was published in the *Ecclesiastical News*, Tolstoy was coming home from a visit to his
doctor when he collided with a crowd of a thousand workers
and students on Lubyanka Square. Someone recognized him
and shouted:

'There he is, the devil in human form!'

Within seconds, he was surrounded and was being jostled
and deafened by a joyful roar:

'Three cheers for Leo Nikolayevich! Hail, the great man!
Hurrah!'

He was losing his balance in the pushing, surging crowd,
and a student helped him into a sledge. But the crowd would
not let it move. Admirers seized the horse's bridle, and a
mounted policeman had to clear a path for the apostle. Exhausted and delighted, he returned home in triumph. Hundreds of telegrams and letters of congratulations were
already piling up on his desk. So many people came to the
house that a book had to be put in the hall for them to sign.
Delegations appeared bearing baskets of flowers. Little hectographed poems passed from hand to hand: 'The Lion*
and the Asses', or 'Pobyedonostsev's Dream'.

Processions were organized during the days that followed,
groups of students flocked to the house to manifest their
attachment to the 'outcast'. The authorities forbade the
publication in the newspapers of any 'telegrams or other

---

* The Russian word for both lion and Leo is 'Lyov', which lends
itself to an easy play on words.

expressions of sympathy for Count L. Tolstoy, excommunicated by the Church'. But it was impossible to smother the news or stifle reaction to it. At a travelling art exhibition in St Petersburg on 25 March, the crowd congregated in front of Repin's portrait of Tolstoy, burst into applause and sent a message to the writer bearing three hundred and ninety-eight signatures. 'For several days,' wrote Sonya, 'a curiously festive atmosphere has reigned in the house. A steady stream of visitors from morning to night. Whole crowds of them ...'[9]

Although a fervent Orthodox herself, she was nevertheless extremely vexed at the sentence passed against her husband. As usual, while criticizing him herself, she would shield him with her own body against any blows from anyone else. She was swept along by the general enthusiasm: in a burst of bravura, she even wrote a letter of protest to Mgr Anthony, the metropolitan of St Petersburg – which was, of course, prohibited by the censor; but innumerable copies of it circulated in Russia:

Having read in the newspapers yesterday of the cruel decree of the Holy Synod exiling my husband, Count Leo Nikolayevich Tolstoy from the Church, I cannot remain silent. My indignation and grief have no bounds. ... If I put myself in the place of the Church, to which I belong and from which I shall never separate, which was founded by Christ to bless in God's name all the great moments of life (birth, marriage, death, sorrow and joy), and the duty of which is loudly to proclaim love and the forgiveness of sins, the opening of our hearts to our enemies, to those who hate us, and the necessity to pray for them – from the viewpoint of the Church, I say, the resolution of the Holy Synod is incomprehensible to me. Those who are guilty of betraying the faith are not those who go astray in their search for truth, but those who stand haughtily at the head of the Church and, instead of practising love, resignation and forgiveness, transform themselves into religious executioners. God will sooner pardon those who give up their earthly possessions to live a life of humility and charity outside the Church than those who wear glittering mitres and decorations and who condemn and excommunicate.

Reproduced abroad, this remonstrance created such a furor that Mgr Anthony was compelled to reply. His letter was suave and unctuous, quoting Scripture, arguing that the Church could not bless blasphemers and pointing out that it was not the Holy Synod which had turned the count out of the Church but the count himself who had cut himself off from the communion of the faithful: 'Priests were instituted by God and have not set themselves, as you say, at the head of the Church out of pride. Their glittering mitres and decorations are of no consequence in divine worship. ... May God bless and keep you, and your husband the count.'

This soft-spoken retort made no impression upon the addressee. 'Everything he says is true, but cold,' wrote Sonya in her diary. 'My letter was written from the heart, it has gone around the world and moved people by its sincerity.' [10]

Tolstoy was both touched and embarrassed by his wife's generous impulse. He thanked her for the ardour with which she defended him, but he would have preferred her to keep still and do nothing. For him, a woman lost her best quality the moment she left the sidelines: the incorrigible misogynist confided to his diary on 19 March: 'When religious feeling wanes in a society, it means that woman's power is waxing.' And: 'Women have only two emotions: love of their husband and love of their children, and, as consequences of these two, love of dress on account of the husband and love of money on account of the children. All the rest is artifice, imitation of men, tools for seduction, coquetry, fashion.' He wrote to his daughter Masha, 'Maman's letter to the metropolitan has had a very good effect upon her. Nothing is predictable in a woman. In man, thought precedes and determines action; but in woman (especially very feminine women), action determines thought.'

His own reaction to the excommunication had been a feeling of deep content. This measure gave him an inexpensive martyrdom, and he deprecatingly told the callers who came to congratulate him that he took no interest in these absurd ecclesiastical rantings. However, after thinking it over for more than a month, he determined to reply to his judges, in order to silence the materialists and atheists who were overjoyed at his falling-out with the Church and were already trying to claim him as their own. In a letter of 4 April 1901, he condemned the decree of the Holy Synod as unlawful and slanderous, reaffirmed that the dogma of the Holy Trinity and Immaculate Conception were incomprehensible to him, disposed of the sacraments as 'base, crude magic' and taxed the ecclesiastical hierarchy with deforming the word of Christ. Then he stated his own credo:

I believe in God, whom I conceive of as the Spirit, Love and Principle of all things.

I believe He is in me as I am in Him.

I believe that the will of God was never more clearly expressed than in the doctrine of the Christ–Man; but to regard Christ as God, and to pray to him, are to my mind the greatest possible sacrilege . . .

I believe that the intention of our individual lives is to augment the sum of love for Him.

I believe that this added measure of love will secure daily increasing happiness for us in this life, and in the other, a felicity all the more perfect for our having better learned to love before.

I believe that there is only one means of progressing in love: prayer. Not public prayer in temples, which was explicitly condemned by Christ (Matthew, vi, 5–13), but prayer as he himself has taught us, solitary prayer, which consists in restoring and strengthening, within oneself, an awareness of the meaning of our life and a belief that we must be ruled by the will of God.

As soon as it reached the public, this noble affirmation released a new wave of fervour. A flood of typed and handwritten copies poured into the big cities. Even young Sasha, aided by a cousin, was secretly hectographing her father's credo. Alexis Suvorin, director of the *New Times*, noted: 'We have two tsars, Nicholas II and Leo Tolstoy. Which is the stronger? Nicholas II is powerless against Tolstoy and cannot make him tremble on his throne, whereas Tolstoy is incontestably shaking the throne of Nicholas II and his whole dynasty. He is anathematized, the Synod publishes a decree against him. Tolstoy replies, and his reply circulates in handwritten copies and is published in the foreign press. Let anyone lift a finger against Tolstoy and the whole world will be up in arms and our administration will turn tail and run!'[11]

At the beginning of summer, Tolstoy's enemies hoped he would soon relieve them of his unwelcome presence without necessitating any police action: for some time he had been losing weight, suffering from rheumatism and pains in the stomach, complaining of hot flushes in his head. In June 1901 he suffered an acute attack of malaria. The family came running. The doctors were so alarmed that the minister of the interior began flashing coded telegrams to every provincial governor and chief of police instructing them to forbid all demonstrations in the event of the author's death.

He realized his situation, however, and contemplated the ordeal ahead with equanimity. 'I am at a crossroads,' he murmured to Sonya. 'I would be just as glad to go forward [to death] as backward [to life]. ... And yet, I still have so much to tell them!' Then, moved to tears by the devotion of his wife, who was nursing him like a baby: 'Thank you, Sonya. Don't believe I am not grateful to you, or that I don't love you.' She kissed his hands, told him it was a joy for her to take care of him, and reproached herself for having inadvertently caused him so much pain. ... Ten days later, on 16 July he began to feel better, smiled to see the glad faces around him, asked for his diary and ruthlessly penned: 'Woman's chief talent is to guess the role that pleases every person and then to play that role.' Now that he was out of danger, he regretted, for the future of his doctrine, that his martyrdom had not been more spectacular. 'If one wants to be heard,' he wrote the same day, 'one must speak out from the top of Golgotha, affirm the truth by suffering and, better yet, by death.' His daughter Masha also showed a sudden and intense concern for the future of Tolstoyism – the will her father had written in his diary in

1895, giving all his copyrights to the public, had never been made legal. There were three copies, kept by herself, Sergey and Chertkov. In order that his will might not be contested after his death she asked Tolstoy, without telling her mother, to sign her copy of the document. As was to be expected, Sonya soon discovered her daughter's action and, on 28 August, a scene of unprecedented violence broke out between the two women. Disfigured by fury, Sonya screamed that Masha was nothing but a hypocrite and a Pharisee, that she had been quite capable, when the time came, of demanding her share of the estate in order to support her 'sponger of a husband' and that she had no right to come playing the disinterested onlooker now. And she entreated Lyovochka to destroy the paper he had so rashly signed. His wife's screaming and sobbing upset him so that he began to have palpitations. Fearing to aggravate his condition, the two rivals calmed down. Masha gave the will to her mother, but warned her that if her father's provisions were not respected, she would send the exact text to the newspapers.

A week later, urged by his doctors, Tolstoy agreed to go to the Crimea to convalesce in the sun. The immensely wealthy Countess Panin, a friend of the family, offered the patient her magnificent villa at Gaspra. Sonya would accompany Lyovochka, as would his daughter Sasha, the Obolenskys, P. A. Boulanger – the 'nice Tolstoyan' – Dr Bertenson, a court physician, and the pianist Goldenweiser. A half-dozen servants completed the retinue of the apostle of poverty. He was so feeble that he had to be lifted into the carriage.

The Tula station was eleven miles away. They started out at night, in driving rain, over muddy roads. The groom lighted the way with a kerosene lamp. Tolstoy, exhausted by the bumps and jolts, nearly lost consciousness at Tula. Sonya wondered whether it would not be better to turn back. But Boulanger, who worked for the railroad company, reassured everyone by showing them the magnificent private car he had reserved for the party. Each person had his own room and toilet; there was a kitchen, a dining-room and a drawing-room with a piano. Tolstoy was too weary to protest against such lordly splendour, and resigned himself.

He slept well and felt strong enough next day to look out at the countryside. When they came into Kharkov he was surprised to see an excited crowd thronging the platform, composed almost exclusively of students. How had they heard of his departure for the Crimea? Feverish acclamations rose up to him as he cowered in the car, alarmed and unhappy, and muttered, 'Oh, my God! ... Why? That is all superfluous!' Nevertheless, he was forced to receive one delegation after another, and reply to the compliments of the overexcited young people. Then the crowd demanded that he show himself at the window.

'He can't. He's ill,' said Sonya.

'Just for one minute, for heaven's sake! Let him only show himself!'

As the train was about to pull away, Tolstoy came to the window. Every head was bared.

'Hurrah, Tolstoy! Leo Nikolayevich! Good health! Bon voyage!'[12]

The train moved away and the students came running after it. Their ranks soon thinned, and the last of them disappeared, waving their arms, in clouds of smoke. Tolstoy, worn out, blew his nose, lay down and had another attack of fever.

At Sevastopol, fortunately, the public had not been told the day of his arrival, so there were only a few wild-eyed ladies at the station, who had been relaying each other for forty-eight hours, to welcome him with shrill wails and fluttering handkerchiefs. He rested there for a day, toured the city in a coach, dragged himself, groaning and wheezing, to the 4th Bastion where, as a boy, he had fired on the enemy, and went back to the hotel, his head burning with memories.

The next day two heavy coaches, each drawn by four

horses, carried Tolstoy and the rest of the party towards Gaspra. The narrow road zigzagged along the rock face. At every turn the changing landscape drew cries of admiration from Sasha. Tatar villages with smoking chimneys, exuding a strong smell of *kizyak* and tallow, men in round sheepskin caps, veiled women with lacquered nails, forests, rushing streams, promontories and, suddenly, through a gap in the foliage, the sea.

Towards evening the coaches entered a dream garden and rolled along a flower-bordered drive. A huge castle in the Scottish manner, flanked by twin towers, stood waist-deep in wistaria. Behind, the rocky walls of Mount Ai-Petri, and before, an esplanade of roses, statues, copses, marble benches and a fountain splashing into a pool full of fish.

Countess Panin's servants were lined up before the door, and the German steward held out the traditional bread and salt of hospitality to the travellers. Tolstoy looked long and disapprovingly at the marble staircase, the carved doors, high frescoed ceilings, precious furniture and dark paintings with crazed varnish surfaces. His daughters were dismayed by so much luxury. But all was forgiven and forgotten when they reached the floor above and stood on a terrace looking out to sea. Beyond the lawns planted with cypress, walnut and rose laurel, sparkling waves reflected the transparent blue of the sky. Trellises loaded with ripe grapes stretched out beneath the veranda. The air was warm, fragrant, sweet. Unfamiliar birds called back and forth to each other, before going to sleep in the trees.

Stimulated by the change of air, Tolstoy promptly recovered. At the end of two weeks, he hired horses and went out a few times with his daughter Sasha into the surrounding countryside. He also resumed work on an essay he had started, entitled *What Is Religion?*, began writing his diary again, turned out dozens of letters to catch up with his correspondence, and began to receive callers, some with joy and others with annoyed reluctance. In the first category were a group of Russian authors of the younger generation:

Balmont, Korolenko, Chekhov, Gorky; in the second, Grand Duke Nicholas Mikhailovich, uncle of the tsar.

The grand duke's estate lay not far from Gaspra; it was guarded by sentinels. He came to pay a neighbourly call, strolled through the garden with the sworn enemy of the monarchy, disarmed him by his simplicity and even told him to come to him if he had any trouble with the local authorities. 'I am like the measles, I'm an outcast,' Tolstoy told him. 'I may make trouble for you; they'll be suspicious of you and criticize you for being seen with a man who is politically compromising.'[13] In spite of this warning the grand duke – who, although a traditionalist, bemoaned the fact that the tsar was so badly counselled – remained friendly with Tolstoy. And the author took advantage of this to ask him, as early as January 1902, to give a letter to the emperor which could, he believed, help to save Russia. The grand duke passed on the letter and informed Tolstoy that Nicholas II had promised to read it himself and not show it to any of his ministers. 'You see,' he concluded, 'how good our sovereign is, how sensitive to the sufferings of others; all the harm is done by his associates.'

In his letter to the tsar, Tolstoy exhorted him to give the nation its freedom, in order to avert a civil war. 'Autocracy,' he wrote with breathtaking audacity, 'is a superannuated form of government that may suit the needs of a Central African tribe, remote from the rest of the world, but not those of the Russian people, who are increasingly assimilating the culture of the rest of the world. That is why it is impossible to maintain this form of government, and the orthodoxy that is attached to it, except by violence, or, in other words, by the methods being used today – by doubling the size of the Guards, by administrative expulsions, executions, religious persecutions, prohibitions of books and periodicals and all bad and brutal measures in general.' Then, after summarizing the errors of the latest government, from 'the exactions in Finland' to the 'vodka monopoly', not forgetting 'the restriction of provincial autonomy', he observed: 'You could not have performed these acts had you not been pursuing, on the ill-considered advice of your counsellors, an impossible goal: not merely to halt the progress of the Russian people, but to drive it back to a completely retrograde, even more primitive condition.'

There was, of course, no reply to this letter. But additional spies appeared around the house. Whenever Tolstoy set foot outside the grounds a shadow fell into step behind him. The comings and goings of his family were also under observation. Setting off for a walk, young Sasha often amused herself by 'shaking' the spy assigned to follow her.

Police surveillance did not prevent the master's friends from calling upon him often. One of those he was most glad to see was Anton Chekhov. After a long bachelorhood, Chekhov had just married a young and charming actress, Olga Knipper. But his health was too poor to permit him to take part in the busy whirl of his wife's life, so he had withdrawn to the Crimea to conserve his failing strength in the sun. Consumed by tuberculosis, he looked upon men and things with the equanimity of one who knows he must soon part from them.* He had seen Tolstoy several times before, at Yasnaya Polyana and in Moscow, and had never swerved from his scepticism of the Tolstoyan philosophy. Everything he had learned of life had convinced him that it was not by 'putting on bark shoes' and 'going to sleep on the stove next to the labourer' that one would save the people from their moral and physical indigence, but by building more schools, hospitals, means of communication, by raising their educational level and giving them important work to do in the State. But although he opposed the doctrines of his illustrious colleague, he respected the nobility of his purpose and his talent. At Gaspra his fondness for Tolstoy increased enormously, when he saw how the old man had aged. 'His worst disease is age, which has now infected him completely,'[14] he wrote to Maxim Gorky. And to his wife,

---

*He died three years later, on 2 July 1904, in Badenweiler, Germany.

'If – God forbid! – what I fear should happen, I'll notify you by telegram. But I would call him "grandfather" in the text, otherwise I don't think it would reach you.'[15] The year before, he had expressed his filial affection for the great man in a letter to Menshikov: 'I am afraid of Tolstoy's death. It would leave a great void in my life. In the first place, I have loved no man as I have him. ... In the second place, when there is a Tolstoy in the world of literature, it becomes a fine and easy thing to be a man of letters. And even if one knows one has done nothing and is still doing nothing, it is not too terrible because Tolstoy is creating for us all, and his work justifies all the hope and faith we put in literature. In the third place, Tolstoy's position is solid, his authority is immense, and as long as he is alive literary bad taste – pretentious and sentimental vulgarity, and all the frustrated little egos – will remain out of sight, hidden in the shadows. His domination alone can raise the different literary currents and trends to any height. Without him, there would be only a flock without a shepherd.'[16]

On the terrace at Gaspra, looking out to the blazing sea, the two men had long talks together. Chekhov, dressed like a schoolmaster, with a mournful beard, dangling eyeglass and hollow chest, struggled with his soft voice to contradict his host, as he drummed with his fingertips on the felt hat he had parked on his knees. Tolstoy sat beside him behind a cup of tea, looking shrunken in his peasant blouse, with a broad panama hat pulled down over his forehead, his legs encased in boots and his beard white and flowing, hardly listening to what the other man was saying; he talked on and on, condemning this and approving that, passing judgements without appeal. He liked Chekhov – 'an atheist's head, but a heart of gold', he said; he was pleased by his 'modest, gentle young lady's manner'; and he thought him very talented. He even said: 'His language is extraordinary. I remember that it seemed most peculiar and "awkward" to me the first time I read him, but when I began to pay closer attention, I was utterly captivated by it. ... With no false modesty, I maintain that Chekhov is technically far superior to me.'[17] Chekhov was dead, it is true, when Tolstoy gave him this *satisfecit*; at Gaspra, the master took a harder line towards his junior's work. Yes, of course, his stories and tales were admirable, although he greatly deplored the absence of any mystical principle motivating them; but he could not stomach his plays, which the Russian public devoured so eagerly. 'He has so much talent,' he said, 'but in the name of what does he write? It is not so much that he has no overall view of the world, but that he has a wrong one, base, materialistic, self-satisfied.'[18] *The Sea Gull* was nothing but rubbish, he had not been able to force himself to read *The Three Sisters*, he was revolted by *Uncle Vanya*. One evening, he put his arm around Chekhov's shoulders and said, with brutal frankness:

'Shakespeare's plays are bad enough, but yours are even worse!'[19]

And on another occasion, somewhat more gently:

'My dear friend, I beg of you, do stop writing plays!'[20]

Chekhov bowed his head, smiled and choked back a dry little cough, but kept his temper. Then Tolstoy expounded his own idea of the theatre:

'In my opinion, modern writers have lost the sense of what a play should be. A drama is not meant to tell us a man's whole life, but to place him in a situation and tie up his destiny in such a way that his entire being will be clear from the manner in which he unties the knot! Yes, I have criticized Shakespeare. But at least, in his plays, every character acts, and it is clear why he acts as he does ...'

Chekhov went on listening, motionless and courteous, to this demolition of his entire dramatic production, which was compounded of mystery and half-intentions, acting on the spectator by some undefinable charm, inconclusive, devoid of any moral, utterly lacking in 'utility'. 'It is my impression,' wrote Sergey Tolstoy, 'that my father would have liked to be more intimate with him, to draw him into his circle of influence, but he felt an unspoken refusal, an uncrossable frontier, that prevented complete understanding.' And in the end Tolstoy, disappointed, grumbled:

'Chekhov is not a religious man!'

No more so was Maxim Gorky. But at least he had the makings of a 'genuine man of the people'. He was tall and ungainly, with a round head, hair swept back, a drooping moustache and turned-up nose, Mongol cheekbones and blue, luminous, childlike eyes. The first thing that struck one about him was an air of unsophisticated goodness. The government had exiled him for his Marxist affiliations, and he lived a little over a mile from Gaspra. A friend of the 'barefoot ragamuffins', he had plied every trade – errand boy, baker's helper, dishwasher, gatekeeper, barman – educated himself by reading everything he could lay hands on, and astonished the public with the earnestness and drive of his first stories. Tolstoy appreciated his storytelling powers and conceded that he did not lack substance, but found his characters 'contrived', 'manufactured', their psychology artificial and the style weak in places. 'There is much that is juvenile, unripe in your thinking,' he said, 'but you know life.' Although he liked this authentic plebeian, he could not prevent himself from treating him with condescension and the curiosity of someone from another world. 'Suddenly,' Gorky wrote, 'the old Russian lord, the arrogant aristocrat would spring up behind the stage costume of muzhik beard and rumpled blouse, and then the friends and partners in conversation would feel a chill down their spines and turn pale.' Neither of them was at ease in this confrontation of the official representatives of two classes of society. The nobleman who aspired to be a peasant feared the mocking eye of his visitor, who had known true poverty; and at every word the visitor felt the intellectual superiority of his muzhik-clad host. They chatted away, however, about literature, music, God, politics and women. On the latter subject, Tolstoy always expressed himself, in Gorky's words,

'with the crudeness of a Russian muzhik'. One day, out of
the blue, he asked Chekhov:

'Were you very profligate in your youth?'

Chekhov, embarrassed, did not answer. The author of
Resurrection glared out to the far-off sea and added:

'I was insatiable!'

He gave details. Coarse words tumbled out of his mouth.
Gorky, who was present, was shocked at first, but then
realized that 'by calling a spade a spade' Tolstoy was simply
striving to be accurate. His vulgarity was merely the result
of his aversion to prettifying. In his speech as in his books,
he wanted above all else not to lie.

A short time later he told Gorky:

'Man can endure earthquake, epidemic, dreadful disease,
every form of spiritual torment; but the most dreadful
tragedy that can befall him is and will remain the tragedy
of the bedroom.'

And to prove that he was qualified to speak, he gave his
young colleague his own diary to read. Rare mark of confidence to a stranger! Or senile self-indulgence, in showing
off his scars to the whole wide world. Everything about
himself, so he imagined, was fascinating, instructive, essential. By opening his heart, he encouraged others to do as
much. But Gorky remained on the defensive, more inclined
to observe than to put himself on display. 'His interest in
me is ethnographical,' he wrote. 'In his eyes I am a specimen of a little-known tribe and nothing more.' In the end,
this reserve tried Tolstoy's patience and, after a low-pitched
altercation, Tolstoy suddenly cried out, drilling him with his
eyes:

'I am more a muzhik than you are and my feelings are
more like a muzhik's than yours!'

Copying this sentence into his notebook, Gorky added,
'Oh, God! He must not brag of that, no, he must not!'

Alternately irritated and dazzled by the incorrigible old
man, he went to see him day after day, followed him on his
walks through the countryside or along the seashore,

listened, contradicted, and returned home bewitched, a mountain of images whirling in his head. Here is Tolstoy, bristling his heavy eyebrows, screwing up his eyes and sighing, as he stares out to the open sea, 'Ah, how well I feel! If only I could suffer a little!' Or jogging along under a grey mist, leaping ditches, shaking the drops of water from his beard, sniffing the earth and moss, tossing out moral aphorisms and literary pronouncements in all directions: 'The body must be the obedient she-dog of the soul. Wherever the soul goes, there the body must follow.' 'Chekhov would write even better if he weren't a doctor.' 'The French have three writers: Stendhal, Balzac, Flaubert, and then Maupassant, but Chekhov is better than him.' 'With no false modesty, *War and Peace* is like *The Iliad*.'

One evening, Gorky was taken aback by an abrupt question:

'Why don't you believe in God?'

'I have no faith.'

'That's not true; by nature you are a believer, you cannot live without God. Soon you will feel it. If you don't believe, it's out of stubbornness and spite, because the world isn't the way you would like it to be. Also, sometimes people do not believe because they don't dare. That happens to the young: they worship some woman but they don't want to let her see it, afraid she won't understand; they have no courage. Faith, like love, demands courage, boldness. You must tell yourself, "I believe," and everything will be all right.'

This conversation took place in Tolstoy's study. Seated on the sofa with his legs folded under him, he smiled all-knowingly, blinked, and added after a short pause, one finger raised in the air: 'You can't avoid that question by saying nothing.'

'And I,' wrote Gorky, 'who do not believe in God, I looked at him, I don't know why, with a great deal of circumspection and a little fear, too; I looked at him and I thought, "This man is like God."'

He also wrote:

'This little man's limbs had grown knotted together with I don't know what deep, powerful roots of the earth. ... He made one think of some very ancient personage, the owner of everything around him – owner and creator – returning after a hundred years' absence to the domain he had built. He strides along the roads and paths with the quick step of a connoisseur of the earth; not one pebble, not one pansy escapes his penetrating eyes that look everywhere, measure, weigh, compare.'

The 'old wizard' was unable to convert Gorky to Christianity, just as Gorky was unable to convert him to Marxism. As early as 1900 Gorky wrote to Chekhov: 'Leo Tolstoy does not love men; no, he does not love them. The truth is that he judges them, cruelly and too severely. I do not like his idea of God. Is that a God? It is a part of Count Leo Tolstoy and not God, this God without whom men cannot live. He says he is an anarchist. To some extent, yes. But although he destroys some regulations, he dictates others in their place, no less harsh and burdensome for men. That is not anarchism, it is the authoritarianism of a provincial governor.'

Later, he employed more vehement terms in a letter to Korolenko:

No man deserves more to be called a genius, no man is more complex, more contradictory, more admirable than he in all things, yes, in all things, in some broad and undefinable way. ... He is a man who envelops all men, a man-mankind. But I have always been repelled by his obstinate, despotic drive to transform the life of Count Leo Nikolayevich Tolstoy into the life of Our Father the Blessed Boyar Leo. You know, he spent a long time preparing to 'suffer'. ... He wanted to suffer, not only in order to measure his willpower, but with the manifest, despotic – I repeat the word – intention of increasing the authority of his doctrine, rendering it irresistible, dazzling the world with his pain, forcing – can you imagine, forcing! – people to share his ideas. ... All his life he has hated death, all his life the 'horror of Arzamas' has been quivering inside him. Living, trembling antennae reach out to him from China, India, America, everywhere. His soul belongs to all, forever! Why should not nature make an exception to the rule, by giving him, him alone, physical immortality, yes, why not?

Gorky returned to this impassioned portrait later, and elaborated upon it even further in a letter to Vengerov: [21]

Count Leo Tolstoy is an artist of genius, perhaps our Shakespeare. But although I admire him, I do not like him. He is not a sincere person; he is exaggeratedly self-preoccupied, he sees nothing and knows nothing outside himself. His humility is hypocritical and his desire to suffer repellent! Usually, such a desire is a symptom of a sick and perverted mind but in his case it is a great pride, wanting to be imprisoned solely in order to increase his authority. He lowers himself in my eyes, by his fear of death and his pitiful flirtation with it; as a rabid individualist, it gives him a sort of illusion of immortality to consolidate his authority.... What comic greed! Exactly, comic! For more than twenty years this bell has been tolling a paean from the steeple-top that is contrary to my beliefs in every respect; for more than twenty years this old man has been talking of nothing but transforming young and lovely Russia into a province of China and young and gifted Russians into slaves. No, that man is a stranger to me, in spite of his very great beauty.

However, at the first sign of faltering in the dreadful old wizard, Gorky was panic-stricken. Even his detractors could not do without him. His health suddenly took a turn for the worse in January 1902; pneumonia set in; his temperature soared; his heart was reacting badly; doctors came running from St Petersburg and Moscow to assist the local practitioners; the entire family was alerted and closed its ranks around his bed.

Reinstated in her role as chief nurse, Sonya spent every night by her husband's side until four, when she was relieved by Tanya and Sasha. Masha was on duty during the day. As soon as one centre of infection died out, another would flare up. For weeks, gaunt, livid and gasping, Tolstoy wrestled with death. Every breath tore his lungs. He could not remain prone without suffocating, and cushions were placed behind his neck and shoulders to raise the upper half of his body. Sasha performed his toilette. She wrapped cotton around the comb before drawing it through her patient's hair – white hair, very fine, curling at his neck 'like a baby's'. Then she brushed out his beard, which was long, curling and tangled; at the smallest tug, he moaned in pain. But a wan smile flitted across his lips when the girl soaped his hands and washed his face and neck with a sponge and dried him with a towel soaked in cologne water.

In moments of respite, he summoned all his strength and dictated his thoughts and letters to Masha in a voice that was scarcely audible. He was completely unmoved when he learned that the Nobel Prize, for which his name had been proposed, had gone to Sully Prudhommme. After all, in *What Is Art?* he himself had ranked Sully Prudhomme among the foremost poets of France. Swedish authors wrote to express their regret at this unjust decision. Between two bouts of fever, he replied, on 22 January 1902, in French:

'I was very pleased to learn that the Nobel Prize was not given to me. First, because it spared me the great problem of disposing of the money, which, like all money, can lead only to evil, in my view; and second, because it has given me the honour and great pleasure of receiving such expressions of sympathy from so many highly esteemed although unknown persons.'

Once again the government busied itself with preparations for Tolstoy's death. Should obituary notices be allowed or forbidden? How was the body to be conveyed to Yasnaya Polyana without any danger of public demonstration? Should booksellers be allowed to display photographs of the dead author? The Holy Synod, anxious to announce that the outcast had recanted, dispatched a priest to Gaspra, who solicited permission to speak to the dying man. Informed of this initiative by his son Sergey, Tolstoy murmured:

'So these gentlemen refuse to understand that even in the face of death two and two still make four!'

The metropolitan, Anthony, also wrote to Sonya privately, exhorting her to reconcile her husband to the Orthodox Church. She mentioned this offer of succour to Lyovochka, who said:

'There can be no question of a reconciliation. I die without resentment or hatred. But what is the Church? What reconciliation can there be with an indefinite object?' [22]

On his advice, she did not answer the metropolitan. The infection was spreading, both lungs were affected. He was given injections of morphine. He could hardly breathe, his pulse grew weaker. One night the doctors told the children that they had abandoned hope. Sonya, exhausted by her long nights of vigil, could not take her eyes off the face from which life was retreating with every breath. She wrote in her diary, 'The situation is almost (one might as well say totally) hopeless. Sleepless night. Pain in the liver. Anguish. Sudden burst of energy, the effect of valerian and champagne. ... Dear Lyovochka, the only time he dozed off at all was when I lightly massaged his stomach and the area around his liver. He thanked me and said, "Darling, you must be worn out."' [23]

That night no one in the house got any sleep. Three doctors were installed in the dining-room and tiptoed to look at the sick man from time to time. At dawn loud moans were heard, but they came from another room: Olga, Andrey Tolstoy's wife, was pregnant and had been fearing a miscarriage after a recent fall. The first pains came, just when her father-in-law was at his worst. At seven in the morning a child was born, dead. As one of the doctors carried the tiny corpse away, the old man was still clinging to life, and, as though this sacrifice of young flesh had appeased the angry gods, Tolstoy's agony abated. He mumbled, 'There, everything is in order. You will give me a shot of camphor and I shall die.' Then he dozed off. The crisis was over. The next day, the infection began to retreat. He said to Dr Volkov:

'Well, I see I must go on living!'

'Do you mind?' Sonya asked.

'What do you mean? Not at all! It's fine with me!' he retorted gaily. 'An excellent thing, a long illness! It allows one to prepare for death. ... I am ready for anything: life or death ...'

Soon he was able to go out on to the balcony and breathe the sea air. To Sonya's surprise and irritation, after begging for death, he became much engrossed with the state of his health: 'From morning to night,' she noted, 'every hour on the hour, he is worrying and nursing his body. ... He used to speak of death, prayer, his relations with God and eternal life. Now I observe with horror that he has lost every trace of religious feeling. With me he is demanding and unpleasant.'[24] She felt utterly alone, abandoned and slightly ridiculous now that her nurse's work was over. If at least he were still able to desire her! But now he was too weary and old for her to hope that spark would ever rekindle in him again. A few months before, she had noted in her diary, 'With Leo Nikolayevich things have happened exactly as I predicted. When his old age compelled him to give up sexual relations with his wife (which happened just a little while ago!), I did not see rising up to replace them the thing I had always so ardently desired: a tranquil and tender friendship. Instead, there was a total void.'[25]

Unconcerned by Sonya's anguish, Tolstoy was gratefully digging his way back into life. He was full of plans: articles on the religious question, a message to the young, a commentary on Henry George's theories of agricultural reform. ... Once again he became completely engrossed in the events of the world he had been so close to leaving. He was stunned by a student's assassination of Sipyagin, the minister of the interior who had quelled an uprising with such a heavy hand the previous year. He wrote to Grand Duke Nicholas Mikhailovich: 'This is an awful thing, because of the anger, hatred and thirst for vengeance it will stir up, but it had to happen, and it is a precursor of still more dreadful things to come, as long as the government does not change its policy.'[26] On the other hand, when Chekhov asked him to join in protest against the tsar's decision to veto Gorky's election to the Academy he growled: 'I don't consider myself a member of academies!' and plunged back into the book he was reading.

When he seemed definitely out of danger, the family dispersed. Even Sonya left Lyovochka to the charms of his convalescence and took the train to Moscow to settle a few publishing matters and, so Sasha claimed, make the rounds of the concerts. Upon her return, on 1 May 1902, she thought she was being punished for her sins: Lyovochka had a relapse – typhoid fever. Once more into the breach. A fresh batch of telegrams was fired off in all directions, the family returned to mass itself around the patriarch, the doctors reappeared, devoted and anxious, and Sonya remorsefully immersed herself once again in the atmosphere of vigils, medicine and presentiments. The eldest son, Sergey, was more help than the others. Tall and strong, he guessed the sick man's every wish in advance and could pick him up in his arms like an infant. Ilya too was full of consideration. Only Leo, the intellectual, was a disappointment to his father: once again he had taken it into his head to publish a book on the evils of Tolstoyism. What annoyed the old man was not so much that the upstart puppy should combat his ideas, but that he should do so with so little talent, and bear the name of Tolstoy! His daughters, on the other hand, gave him every satisfaction. Sasha, Masha and Tanya bent over him with angelic faces. It grieved them to see him failing. And in fact, he was feeling better. Was it possible? It was; for the third time in ten months, he was wriggling off the hook. Perhaps he really was immortal! His appetite returned, he sat up in an armchair, went into the garden, leaning on a cane, delighted in the almond trees and magnolias in bloom and the sun sparkling on the sea. But how he had aged! 'Poor dear!' wrote Sonya. 'I find it hard to look at this world celebrity, who is a skinny, pitiful little old man in his private life.'[27]

At last, on 25 June 1902, the Tolstoys left Gaspra for Yasnaya Polyana. They were to travel from Yalta to Sevastopol by boat and from there by rail. A crowd of onlookers was milling about in the port. Kuprin, the novelist, had managed to slip on board the ship, and saw a man climb out of a carriage wearing an overcoat that was too short for him, a bowler and boots. On the deck, someone introduced him to the master. 'I recall that I was staggered,' said Kuprin. 'Instead of a gigantic, venerable patriarch looking like Michelangelo's "Moses", I saw an old man, rather short, whose movements were precise and careful.' As Tolstoy moved towards the section of the ship in which the poor people were herded together, a passage opened up before him. 'He moved on as a king, who knows nothing can stand in his way.' Later, he was surrounded by friends wishing him a good crossing. 'Then,' continued Kuprin, 'I saw a different Tolstoy, a Tolstoy who was almost a coquette. In a moment, he was thirty years old: firm voice, keen eyes, elegant manners ...'

A Pullman was waiting for the prophet at Sevastopol. Flowers, ovations, women wailing and fainting, he was used to them now.

Back in his birthplace once more, he saw that the beauties of the Crimea, great as they were, could not do him one-tenth as much good as the scenery, silence, climate and peasants of his own home. The doctors unanimously advised him to live in the country all year round; to his great joy, the winter trips to Moscow were abandoned. At Yasnaya Polyana, he moved out of his damp, vaulted rooms on the ground floor into two sunny rooms upstairs. He no longer shared a room with his wife, but slept in a sort of monastic cubicle, furnished with a bed, a stool and a washstand. His study was next to it, giving on to the balcony.

Sonya had been so anxious during her dear Lyovochka's illness that she now lived in continual fear of a relapse.

Twenty times a day she felt his pulse, inquired into the condition of his stomach or throat, entreated him to keep well covered. Still opposed to his vegetarian diet, she secretly fortified his vegetable broth with meat to build up his strength. She knitted caps for him and cut and sewed warm shirts. Although somewhat annoyed by this oppressive solicitude, he was happy to be the centre of the family's attention. Every time he went out, his walk became a little longer. He cautiously resumed his gymnastics. Then, one morning, with Sasha's help, he heaved himself into the saddle and set out for a ride, aglow with satisfaction. 'It seemed that his capacity for loving life, flowers, trees, children, everything around him, had actually increased since his illness,' wrote Sasha. Back from a ramble, he came up to her with sunburned face, white beard and hair in a tangle and eyes shining with joy, his shirt collar open over his protruding collarbones, and thrust out his hat filled with mushrooms.

'Smell them,' he said. 'They smell so good!'

That day she knew he was well again.

He began to write, 'as though he were hurrying to do as much as he could before he died,' said Sonya.

The end of 1902 and the year 1903 were a time of peace and hard labour for him. He did not set foot outside Yasnaya Polyana. He produced an anthology of the major moralists entitled *Thoughts of the Wise Men*, a few short stories including *The False Coupon*, two plays (*The Light Shines in the Darkness* and *The Living Corpse*) and an essay, *Shakespeare*, in which he settled the English dramatist's hash once and for all. 'After reading, one after the other, the plays considered to be his most beautiful – *King Lear*, *Romeo and Juliet*, *Hamlet* and *Macbeth* – not only did I derive no pleasure from them, but I felt an overpowering repugnance, a boundless tedium, and I wondered whether it was I who was mad, to find empty and offensive these works that are held by all cultivated people to be the summit of perfection, or whether it was the cultivated people who were mad to attach such importance to Shake-speare's works.' He also wrote a few pages of reminiscences, at the request of Biryukov, who was diligently preparing his biography. And he continued to work on his novel *Hadji Murad*, the first draft of which dated from 1896; some passages were now in their fifth revision.

As always, he had embarked upon an enthusiastic period of preliminary documentation for this book. His own recol-lections of military life at the Starogladkovskaya *stanitsa* and Fort Stary Yurt did not provide a broad enough basis for the adventures of the Circassian chieftain. He collected over eight books on the subject – from Poltoratsky's *Memoirs* to those of Loris-Melikov, and including Vederev-sky's book, *Prisoner of Shamil* – read them, took notes, squeezed the juice from them. He asked his friends to ob-tain information from the chief participants in the Cauca-sian campaign. His concern for authenticity went to the extent of trying to find out the colour of the horses Hadji Murad and his escort rode on their last raid. At court, Alexandra moved mountains to satisfy his curiosity about the private life of Nicholas I. 'I absolutely must find the key to him,' he wrote on 26 January 1903. 'That is why I am collecting information, reading everything that relates to his life and personality. Mostly what I need are details of his daily life, what are called the anecdotes of history: his intrigues at a masked ball, his relations with Nelidova, his wife's behaviour towards him. ... Do not blame me, dear friend, for busying myself with such trivialities when I have one foot in the grave. These trivialities occupy my leisure time and give my mind a rest from the serious thoughts that fill it.'

Hadji Murad is historically irreproachable, and yet its form is that of a pure fantasy. It is a strange thing that Tolstoy should have written this tale, devoid of all religious considerations, whose extraordinary beauty alone is enough to content the reader, at a time when his thoughts were increasingly bent on the propagation of his faith and books intended for mere entertainment seemed pointless and even harmful to him. With the seventy-year-old fatuousness that Kuprin had observed on the ship deck, it is almost as though, after paying philosophy its dues, he wanted to prove to himself at the end of his career that the artist in him was not dead. Immediately, in recounting the adventures of Hadji Murad, the old man recovered the fresh, lusty love of life he had felt writing *The Cossacks* forty-five years before. But between his first and second Caucasian novels, the problem had gained in depth and the painting in dimension.

In *The Cossacks*, Tolstoy was studying the conscience of a young aristocrat attracted to the rough, free life of the mountaineers, wanting to become one of them and realizing that he was incapable of doing so. The main themes of *Hadji Murad* are the defeat and oppression of a free and proud people by the artificial Russian civilization, and the destruction of a man who tries to escape from his family, traditions and faith in order to satisfy his will to power. The action takes place around 1850. Hadji Murad, the hero, is a combination of bravery, integrity, cruelty, cunning and childlike candour. He is savagely opposed to colonization, but he so hates Shamil, the leader of the Moslem forces, that he decides to offer his services to the Russians in order to defeat him. He thinks that he will be allowed to govern the Caucasian tribes in the name of the 'white tsar' in return for his treason. At first, the Russians welcome this unexpected and distinguished ally with open arms, and lavish favours and promises upon him. But when he fled from his own people, Hadji Murad had left his family at Shamil's mercy. His one desire is to go back with an army and deliver his two wives and his son Yusuf, who are being held as hostages. The suspicious Russians are opposed to an operation in which they see no military or political advantage. As time passes, Hadji Murad feels himself more and more a prisoner. He is covered with honours, but is entangled in administrative machinery that hampers his every movement. Out of his native element, he grows bored, feels stifled, loses his sense of justification, like the lovely thistle-flower wrenched from its stalk and trampled underfoot, with which Tolstoy opens the book. To return to his family and the unrestricted life that was his natural environment, he eludes his Russian guards and sets out on a wild chase from which he knows he has no hope of emerging alive.

Tolstoy does not even try to excuse this traitor and renegade. But he makes him worthy of our pity, and consequently closer to us, by a mathematically precise analysis of his destruction by power. The thirst for power is a disease that corrodes the finest metal. Obsessed by his desire to supplant Shamil, Hadji Murad prepares the way for his own downfall. He is the victim of his own lust for power and of the people who possess it: Shamil on one side, and the tsar on the other. Allying himself with the former proves as disastrous for him as being the enemy of the latter. 'It is not only Hadji Murad and his tragic end that interest me,' Tolstoy said to Shulgin. 'I am fascinated by the parallel between the two main figures pitted against each other: Shamil and Nicholas I. They represent the two poles of absolutism – Asiatic and European.'

Of course, the despot with the greatest power also has the heaviest load on his conscience. To be tsar is to be, *a priori*, guilty before God and man. But, as portrayed by Tolstoy, Nicholas I is certainly more horrible than either his predecessor, Alexander I, or his successors Alexander II, Alexander III and Nicholas II. His icy face hides such depths of evil and conceit that there seems to be no possibility of communication between him and ordinary human beings. Intoxicated by the flattery of his court, he sees himself as a knight-errant in the modern world, but with consummate hypocrisy he writes an edict at the bottom of a report on a Polish student accused of striking his professor: 'Deserves death penalty. However, thank God, it does not exist here and I shall not be the one to reinstate it. Run him twelve times down the gauntlet between one thousand men.' As he knows, twelve thousand strokes mean certain and hideous death. But appearances will be saved! As benefactor of his people, the tsar orders all the peasants who refuse baptism to be judged by court-martial. As model husband, he has an official mistress and various affairs with young ladies of good society. As a practising Orthodox, his main belief is that he can get away with anything, from adultery to crime.

In his physical description of the emperor, Tolstoy emphasizes his 'gigantic stature', his 'big white hands', his 'long white face' which is 'exceptionally cold', his 'dull eyes', his 'lifeless' expression, meant to symbolize the destructive principle of despotism. And these outward signs of power are repeated in the autocrat opposing him. Like Nicholas I, Shamil is 'tall in stature, straight and powerfully built', giving 'an impression of strength'; like Nicholas I he has 'a pale face', 'carved out of stone, utterly immobile', and 'eyes that look at no one'; like Nicholas I he is vain of his 'big white hands'; and both of them play their part of all-seeing, all-powerful master to perfection. 'Chernyshev', we read, 'knew that whenever Nicholas I had an important decision to make, he required only a few moments of reflection, and then it was as if inspiration suddenly visited him; the best solution presented itself unsought, some inner voice dictated what he must do.' Here is Shamil: 'He closed his eyes and was silent. His counsellors knew that this meant he was listening to the voice of the Prophet within himself, dictating what he must do. After five minutes of triumphant silence, Shamil opened his eyes and said . . .'

In fact, Shamil is not a person and still less Nicholas I: they are both incarnations of a system. Their close associates are also contaminated by power – witness Prince Vorontsov, governor general of the Caucasus, who will stoop to any compromise or commit any massacre to further the policies of the government. Or Chernyshev, the minister of war, whom the tsar himself accounts 'a thoroughgoing scoundrel'. Or Loris-Melikov, notorious intriguer. . . . All these gentlemen carry their toadying to the point of imitating the monarch's dress and manners: Nicholas I wears 'a black dolman with shoulder straps but no epaulets', so we see Vorontsov 'dressed in his usual black military coat with shoulder straps, but no epaulets'. Prince Basil Dolgoruky, under-secretary of state at the war office, has 'a bored and doltish face adorned with side-whiskers, moustache and curls on his temples, like Nicholas I'. At the next level below, the aides-de-camp copy the ministers, and have 'little moustaches and locks of hair brushed towards their eyes, like the emperor Nicholas Pavlovich'.

Even though he is a traitor, Hadji Murad continues to command respect, in contrast with all these creatures who have lost sight of any meaningful form of life in their scramble to obtain power over the largest possible number of their fellow men. A refugee in the Russian camp, he dominates it by his physical charm, oriental courtesy and disdain for the flattery of the beribboned officials, young *arriviste* officers and coquettish and curious provincial ladies who would like to draw him into their nets. He is indifferent to the intrigues woven about him. He is surprised at nothing, even though this is his first contact with what it is customary to call civilization. Supported by the memories of his former primitive, independent existence, he achieves moral strength by refusing to live like his conquerors. To be sure, he is wide-eyed as a child when Vorontsov gives him his watch, but displays no interest at all in the scantily clad women he meets at the governor's ball. Tall and slender, with close-shaven head and black eyes 'set too far apart' and a limping stride, he is like a superb beast of the forest who has strayed into an artificial garden and knows no law but self-preservation. Without the slightest scruple he betrays Shamil and surrenders to the tsar's troops, and later kills the brave Cossacks assigned to serve as his escort.

Hemmed in on all sides, he defends himself to the death with irrational doggedness. He goes down sword in hand, as he had always hoped to do. And the author seeks no compassion for him.

But there is more to this book than just the story of Hadji Murad himself. Just as the candles in a chandelier light up one after the other at the touch of a flame running along a hidden wick, so in this book characters apparently very remote from each other receive and emit light because of a mysterious bond that unites them. Starting with a trivial incident of guerrilla warfare, Tolstoy demonstrates its repercussions at every level of the social hierarchy. From the lowliest to the most high, hundreds of people are affected by the decision of a single one. Guided by the author, we move from Hadji Murad to the tsar's intimate advisers discussing his case, to Nicholas I himself, whose cruel, cold heart is swiftly unveiled to us, to Vorontsov, who has his own problems, to the unyielding Shamil, to Hadji Murad's son in captivity, to the Cossacks, attacking, pillaging and burning enemy *aouls*, to Avdeyev, a simple soldier killed in a raid, to Avdeyev's village where they are threshing oats on the barn floor, to Avdeyev's wife who bursts into tears when she hears of her husband's death but is glad at heart because she is pregnant with the child of the clerk in whose house she is employed ...

The field of vision spreads beyond the Caucasus to envelop all Russia. In a few pages a whole vast panorama is presented to us. Who is the hero? Hadji Murad, Nicholas I or Avdeyev the soldier? Impossible to determine. Or to determine what the author was trying to prove. Setting all moral considerations aside, his creation remains a hymn to life, nature, the sap that rises in men and plants. Can one discuss the distinction between good and evil in relation to a beheaded thistle? Written in a language as spare and precise as that of Pushkin, without digression, without a trace of self-indulgence, compact, nervous, virile, this novel gives proof that Tolstoy's artistry had reached perfection. And

yet *Hadji Murad* was not published during his lifetime.*
The censor would never have passed this broadside against
the autocracy, war and the treatment inflicted upon the
Caucasian tribes by the Russians. After revising his manuscript for the last time in 1904, he put it away without regret. At his age, the opinion of generations to come
mattered more than that of his contemporaries.

He also refused to publish his third play, *The Living
Corpse*, in which he returned to a subject dear to his heart:
the failure of marriage and release through flight. Observing
that his wife does not understand him after ten years of
marriage, and actually prefers a man of 'the common
mould' to himself, Protasov feigns suicide, flees his family,
breaks all ties with society and sets up house with a gypsy,
Masha. The warmth and simplicity of his relations with
Masha are contrasted with the artificiality of love sanctified
by orthodox marriage. But his hideaway is discovered.
Trapped in the machinery of the law, his only escape this
time will be to make his suicide real. Once more Tolstoy
sets out to demolish marriage, human justice and society.
Protasov combines the features of the heroes of *The Kreutzer
Sonata* (hatred of the legitimate couple) and of *Resurrection* (attraction of life with a woman of lower estate,
need to reject the hypocrisy of society and vanish into the
crowd).

The author experienced all of these feelings, one might
say, on a permanent basis. But his pleasure in his work temporarily helped him to bear the guilt inspired by his comfortable surroundings. 'I have utterly abandoned myself to
the temptations of fate,' he wrote to Biryukov on 2 September 1903; 'I am living in luxury and physical inactivity.
And I therefore suffer continually from remorse. But I comfort myself with the thought that I am living on good terms
with all my family and writing pages which I think are
important.'

* The book was not published until 1912, two years after Tolstoy's
death.

Among these important pages were *Hadji Murad* and *The Living Corpse*, but also articles and short stories – *The False Coupon* and *After the Ball* – and letters to prominent people. There was a pogrom in Kishinev in August 1903, and he expressed his indignation in very sharp terms. A declaration he had composed was given to the governor of Kishinev:

'Profoundly shocked by the atrocities committed at Kishinev, we extend our heartfelt sympathy to the innocent victims of mob savagery and express our horror at the acts of cruelty perpetrated by Russians, our scorn and disgust with all who have driven the people to such a pass and have allowed this dreadful crime to be committed.'

In December of that year he learned that his aunt-*babushka* Alexandra Tolstoy was critically ill. His friendship for her had cooled considerably of late because of her insistent efforts to bring him back to the Orthodox Church. He had delighted in wrestling with her while she was robust and militant on her feet, but he could not restrain his sympathy when he knew she was on her deathbed. He wrote a tender letter to her on 22 December, thanking her for all the good she had done for him during their 'half-century of friendship'. Deeply touched, she answered that in reading his letter she had heard once again 'that note of utter sincerity' that had resounded between them in the days of their youth. A few months later, on 21 March 1904, the old maid of honour, aged eighty-six, passed away in her apartment in the Winter Palace at St Petersburg. With her disappeared the faithful friend and confidante, ever ready to do battle for the cherished nephew whose ideas she abhorred. However, Tolstoy was not as deeply affected by her death as those around him had feared. He felt his own end so close at hand that he no longer had any inclination to weep for others. In August 1904, another trial affected him more powerfully: at the age of seventy-eight, his brother Sergey was dying in agony, of cancer of the tongue. He, too, had become estranged from his younger brother when Leo began to preach his neo-Christian gospel, condemning him for exhorting others to practice abstinence and poverty while he lived on in sin and plenty. But family ties ultimately prevailed over ideological differences, and relations between the two old men had improved towards the end.

Although he hated the Tolstoyans, Sergey often came to Yasnaya Polyana. And Leo, who did not bear grudges, went to see him at Pirogovo. Sergey's estate, with its gravelled walks, neatly trimmed hedges and trees aligned in military precision, was the complete opposite of ragged and untidy Yasnaya Polyana, where the vegetation proliferated in defiance of any order or control. Unlike his brother, who dressed like a muzhik and made his own boots, Sergey lived as a lord in the old manner, authoritarian, aloof, elegant, hot-tempered. His peasants bowed to him from a distance and were afraid of him. His wife (the ex-gypsy Masha) did not dare raise her voice in his presence. His three daughters, unmarried and in their forties, never dreamed that a suitor might one day come along who would be bold enough to ask their taciturn, chilling father for their hands. Besides, they had all read their uncle's *Kreutzer Sonata* and saw marriage in the grimmest possible light – which did not prevent one of them from murmuring, in French, 'We are just a covey of old maids and our children will be a covey of old maids, too,' without noticing the inconsistency between the two terms of that proposition. Their father, otherwise a misanthrope, doted on them, but it was difficult for him to show his emotions. He shut himself up in his study for days on end, calculating the income from his property. Sometimes he was heard through the wall, uttering heart-rending sighs, 'Ah, ah, ah!' His wife was used to them: 'It's Sergey, thinking about something,' she said. When he came out of his study he hurriedly slammed the door behind him, to prevent any flies from entering it; he had a horror of flies and gnats. Also of artists, professors, tradesmen, favour-seekers, socialites and ostentatious people. He was eccentric and sardonic; his nephew Ilya compared him to old Prince Bolkonsky in *War and Peace*.

When the end drew near, Tolstoy went to Pirogovo to spend a few days. The gypsy and his three daughters wanted the dying man to confess and take communion, but they were afraid to suggest it because he had long since given up practising any form of religion. At their entreaty, the younger brother and excommunicated author undertook this mission for them, and, to satisfy his family, Sergey agreed to see a priest.

On the day of the funeral, in spite of his age, Tolstoy helped carry the coffin to the coach. When he returned to Yasnaya Polyana, he told Sonya how he had parted from his 'incomprehensible and beloved' brother. And in his *Reminiscences*, intended to fill the gaps in the biography Biryukov was writing he added: 'In his old age, towards the end, Sergey became fonder of me again and set great store by my attachment to him. He was proud of me, he would have liked to agree with me but he could not; and he remained as he had always been, utterly unique, utterly himself, very handsome, aristocratic, proud and, above all, a more upright and honest man than any I have ever known.'

28

The Russo-Japanese
War

ALTHOUGH deprived of the amusements of the big city, Sonya led a very active life at Yasnaya Polyana. She sorted her husband's huge correspondence, answered some letters for him, catalogued the books he received from publishers, compiled press clippings and glued them into albums, exposed, developed and printed her own photographs, picked up all the bits of paper lying about the house and burned them, weeded the driveway in front of the house. . . . She learned to type; then she developed a passion for painting, and copied the family portraits in the drawing-room; she also had a try at literature and published in the periodical *Life* a prose-poem she had written; it was entitled 'Moan' and signed, 'A weary woman'.[1] Her passion for music continued unabated: whenever she had an hour to spare, she sat down to play, badly, Beethoven, Mozart, Mendelssohn or Tanayev...

This round of secondary activities did not interfere with her masterful administration of the estate, nursing of her husband, keeping of her diary, and her duties as hostess to the guests who made pilgrimages to Yasnaya Polyana. After lunch, while Lyovochka was taking a nap, she sometimes turned guide, to show a group of sightseers through the house. It was as though the great man had already died and she were the keeper of his museum; as though a light were being reflected upon her, from the depths of the Beyond. How she loved him, how she admired him, when he was not there to disappoint her. But the moment she was face to face with him again, at the dinner table, in the drawing-room or outside in the grounds, she was irritated by everything he did. One day he jibed at the stupidity and smugness of the medical profession. Had he forgotten that she was a doctor's daughter, or was he offending her on purpose? 'It makes me furious,' she noted. 'Now, yes, he is in good health; but after the Crimea, where nine doctors struggled with such devotion and intelligence to save his life, he ought not – if he were a decent and honest man – to treat them in such a way.' Even so, she would have held her tongue had he not added that, according to Rousseau, doctors were all in league with women. 'At that, I exploded. If he doesn't believe in medicine, why did he call for the doctors and wait for them and do what they told him?'[2] When her anger subsided, she lectured herself: after all, her husband was a genius. Could she, with her tiny brain, understand and judge him? 'I must remember that his mission is to teach man, to write and preach,' she wrote in her diary four days later. 'His life and ours and those of all who are close to him must serve that end and it is therefore our duty to take the best care of him that we can. We must close our eyes to his compromises and absurdities and contradictions, and see only the great author, the preacher and master, in Leo Nikolayevich.'

This excellent resolution could not stand the test of everyday reality. It was a lamentable tug-of-war; whenever Lyovochka happened to be well-disposed towards his wife she was too busy to notice, and whenever she tried to draw closer to him she was cut by his indifference. These contretemps provided much material for the diaries of both. But Sonya, who had no other goal in life than to protect her marriage, was often the more bitter of the two. 'I go into Leo Nikolayevich's room,' she noted on 17 November 1903. 'He is getting ready for bed and before lying down he pulls up his nightshirt and massages his stomach with a circular motion. His scrawny old man's legs are pitiful to behold. "There," he said, "first I rub my stomach this way, and then that." I see I shall never have another word of comfort or tenderness from him. What I predicted has come to pass:

the passionate husband is dead; the friendly husband never existed; how could he be born now?'

A few weeks later these minor personal grievances paled before an event involving the entire country: on 27 January (8 February) 1904, after long diplomatic tension, hostilities suddenly broke out between Russia and Japan. Without declaring war, the Japanese torpedo boats attacked the Russian fleet lying at Port Arthur, and put seven big ships out of commission; the disaster touched off an explosion of patriotism in Russia. Tolstoy was alarmed by this return of violence. 'I am still not well,' he wrote the following day, 28 January, in his diary. 'Liver ailing, and a cold.... I have thought deeply about this war that is beginning. I would like to write that at the beginning of something as dreadful as war, everybody offers hundreds of suppositions as to the meaning or consequences of the conflict, but not one person thinks about himself. ... This is the best and clearest evidence that nothing can provide a remedy for evil, except religion.'

In the days that followed he could think of nothing else. Five continents were waiting for him to speak: he began a pacifist article entitled *Bethink Yourselves!* But he sensed that even his great authority was not strong enough to stop the bloodshed. He read the papers feverishly, questioned peasants returning from town, rode to Tula himself to see the dispatches from the front as soon as they came in. The villages resounded with accordions and weeping women. Drunken draftees staggered from door to door. The parents of those being sent complained to the master: one had been drafted illegally, another's papers were not in order. ... Tolstoy tried to remain calm, but he was sputtering with indignation.

'I cannot read these articles that glorify the grandeur and beauty of acts of bloodshed in order to excite the people's patriotism,' he growled.

But as soon as a guest arrived from Tula, he asked:

'Well? What? What news from the front?'

Sonya did not dissimulate her anger with the Japanese for having struck treacherously, without warning. The cook at Yasnaya Polyana was mobilized to serve in General Gurko's kitchen. Andrey, Tolstoy's fourth son, enlisted. His motives were not, it must be said, solely patriotic: he had just abandoned his wife and two children for another woman and, suddenly guilt-stricken, hoped to redeem himself through ordeal by fire. His brother Leo contented himself with loudly demanding a war to the death. Their father disapproved of both. But Sonya was proud to accompany Andrey to the recruiting station at Tambov. He looked so handsome in his non-commissioned officer's uniform, his cap tilted to one side and his chest and back tightly moulded in a sand-coloured shirt, cantering his horse stylishly at the head of his unit! However, when they had all been sandwiched into the cars and the train pulled out, she was overcome by despair. The crowd wept and moaned. There was no more talk of patriotism. In an effort to put some heart into the draftees and their families, a general called out, 'You show 'em what you're made of out there!' 'Those words,' Sonya wrote, 'rang out, vile, out of place, absurd.'

The *North American Newspaper* of Philadelphia had asked Tolstoy, which side he was on; he replied, 'I am for neither Russia nor Japan; I am for the workers of both countries who are being deceived by their governments and forced to take part in a war that is harmful to their well-being and in conflict with their conscience and religion.' Despite his pacifist attitude, however, the old veteran flinched at the blows being struck at his country. He confessed to Georges Bourdon, a French journalist who had come to interview him for *Le Figaro*, that he was not always able to rise above the battle, and felt every Russian defeat in his bones. The inferiority of the Russian army was apparent from the first engagement. The theatre, forty-five hundred miles away, was linked to the centre of the country by a single railroad which was unfinished and would have been inadequate anyway, so the expeditionary forces were necessarily ill-supplied with food and ammunition. After several setbacks, the stronghold of Port Arthur, besieged by land and sea, fell to the Japanese on 20 December 1904 (2 January 1905). Learning the news, Tolstoy mourned:

'Ah, that's not how they fought in my day! Surrendering a fortress when you have ammunition and an army of forty thousand men! It's a shame!'

And he wrote in his diary for 31 December:

'The surrender of Port Arthur has made me miserable. I suffer from it. Patriotism. I was brought up in that sentiment and I have not freed myself of it. Nor have I rid myself of personal selfishness or family and even class egotism. All these forms of selfishness are within me, but there is also within me a consciousness of the law of God and that consciousness holds the selfishness in check, so that I cannot yield to it completely. And, little by little, it atrophies.'

February 1905 brought the disaster of Mukden; in May of that year, after an exhausting seven-month toil across three oceans, the Russian Baltic fleet entered the straits of Tsushima and met the enemy fleet, whose ships were faster, better armed and better protected. There was an uneven battle during which the best Russian ships were sunk or captured, despite heroic resistance. Casualties rose above seven thousand. Filled with mortification and grief, Tolstoy was no longer able to keep the balance between Russians and Japanese. 'I care more for the Russians,' he told Makovitsky. 'My children, the muzhiks, are among them. The interests of one hundred million peasants are bound up with the army, and they do not want it to be beaten.' Trying to explain to himself the causes for this military disaster, he wrote in his diary on 19 May 1905: 'It has become plain to me that things could not and cannot happen any other way. No matter how poor Christians we are, we cannot avoid the fact that war is contrary to the Christian doctrine. Recently (during the last thirty years), this has become more and more obvious. That is why, in any conflict with a non-Christian people for whom the highest ideal is patriotism and military heroism, a Christian people must be defeated. ... I am not saying this to console myself for the fact that we have been beaten by the Japanese. The shame and humiliation are as sharp as ever.'

Pursuing this line of reasoning, he came to consider that his country's defeat was due to excessive materialism, the over emphasis on technology, and neglect of the great truths of the Sermon on the Mount. In his search for the guilty parties he even began sliding imperceptibly towards anti-Semitism. 'This débâcle,' he wrote on 18 June, 'is not only that of the Russian army, the Russian fleet and the Russian State, but of the pseudo-Christian civilization as well. ... The disintegration began long ago, with the struggle for money and success in so-called scientific and artistic pursuits, where the Jews got the edge on the Christians in every country and thereby earned the envy and hatred of all. Today the Japanese have done the same thing in the military field, proving conclusively, by brute force, that there is a goal which Christians must not pursue, for in seeking it they will always fail, vanquished by non-Christians.'

He later went so far as to declare that the entire tragedy of mankind resulted from a racial incompatibility between Christ and St Paul: 'I should like to write something to prove how the teachings of Christ, who was not a Jew, were replaced by the very different teachings of the apostle Paul, who was a Jew.'[3]

At last, thanks to the initiative of Theodore Roosevelt, negotiations began at Portsmouth and the peace between Russia and Japan was signed in August (5 September) 1905. Russia lost Port Arthur and the southern part of the island of Sakhalin, and abandoned all claims to Korea and southern Manchuria. Receiving a telegram with the news, Tolstoy's features darkened and he muttered:

'Great news that is. I'm ashamed of myself, but I must

confess that I have to struggle against my patriotism. I had always hoped the Russians would win.'[4]

As was to be expected, there was trouble in the country even before the war had ended. The reverses suffered by the Russian army were proof to all of the improvidence of the government, incompetence of the administration and general weakness of a regime that merely looked as though it were solidly established. The extreme conservatism of the authorities no longer corresponded to the needs of the people or the aspirations of the most advanced class. Student demonstrations, workers' movements, strikes in industrial centres were violently suppressed by the ill-advised tsar, but his measures for restoring order not only failed to intimidate the revolutionary movements, they positively incited them to intensify their struggle. Secret societies sprang up everywhere, universities and factories were flooded with anti-government propaganda and, now and then, some political assassination of stupefying boldness was brought off to prove the real strength of the enemies of autocracy: murder of the Grand Duke Sergey, the governor general of Moscow; murder of the minister Plehvey . . .

On Sunday, 9 January 1905, thousands of workers, led by a pope named Gapone, made an orderly march upon the Winter Palace to present a petition to the tsar demanding an eight-hour day and a constitution. They were savagely dispersed by the guards, leaving many dead and wounded behind, and were hunted down and fired upon until late at night. The result of Bloody Sunday was to precipitate into the opposition all the liberals who had still been hanging fire, unwilling to speak out openly against Nicholas II. Foreign indignation at this senseless massacre encouraged the revolutionary leaders to take immediate advantage of the general discontent. There were more strikes, in factories and printing presses and on railways; there were barracks mutinies and rural insurrections; a few homes were burned down by the peasants; and on 27 June 1905 the crew of the battleship *Potemkin* mutinied in protest against their unpalatable rations, killed several of their officers and steamed into Odessa, where striking factory workers were battling with the government troops. The left-wing revolutionary violence was echoed at the other extreme by the pogroms of the reactionary League of the Black Hundreds.

In October, the nation was paralysed by a general strike, which had spread from Moscow. No railways, no post, no telegraph, no newspapers, no public transport, no electricity. Under pressure of events, Nicholas II consulted Count Witte, the successful peace negotiator of Portsmouth, and on 17 October he published a manifesto granting his subjects freedom of conscience, speech and the press, freedom of assembly and freedom to form associations, and promising respect for human dignity and the individual. He also promised to liberalize the electoral system and announced that henceforth no law could become effective unless it was approved by a parliament elected by universal suffrage: the Duma. The public at large hailed this body of liberal measures with enthusiasm, but men of sharper political acumen greeted it with suspicion, and both arch-reactionaries and arch-revolutionaries were equally incensed by it, for opposing reasons. 'There is nothing in it [the manifesto] for the people,' wrote Tolstoy. And the disturbances resumed, more vehement than ever, with a round of strikes, mutinies at Kronstadt and Sevastopol, and police action to cripple the St Petersburg workers' union.

A second revolt broke out in Moscow in December, and there was renewed fighting in the streets; regiments of the guards stormed the barricades, drove the rebels into corners and cut them down. Count Witte was considered too temperate and was replaced at the head of the government by a strong man: Stolypin. Six months later, the first Duma was dissolved.

At Yasnaya Polyana the news of these fratricidal conflicts disturbed Tolstoy even more than the war with Japan. He was in favour of a certain amount of reform, but he condemned the violence of the left-wing terrorists and mocked

at those who claimed they could make all men happy by
removing the emperor and putting some equally ambitious
and insignificant republican leader in his place. 'All this
fighting, imprisonment, hatred – it all reeks of blood,' he
wrote on 4 September 1905.[5] But he had attacked tsar and
Church so often that he found himself, against his own will,
co-opted into the ranks of the revolutionaries whose bloodthirsty methods appalled him. Aware of this anomaly, he
struggled to justify himself at either end. After *Bethink
Yourselves!* he wrote an article entitled *Present Events in
Russia, a Letter to Nicholas II* and a *Letter to the Revolutionaries.* He told both that they were wrong to try to settle
their differences by a show of strength and that any social
reform that was not preceded by a spiritual reform was
doomed to fail. Neither oppressor nor oppressed paid any
attention to him. He was preaching in the desert, and he
did not really care. This was not the first time that being
the only man to believe as he believed gave him a feeling
of infallibility and supremacy. An aristocrat in revolt, a
well-endowed utopian, an anarchist capitalist, he was equally
at home lashing out against the partisans of the imperial
regime and the tsar's adversaries. For him, as he had so
often reiterated, all forms of government were suspect because they were all founded on the submission of the masses
to a pre-established order. The Marxists repelled him because their sole aim was to satisfy the people's material
needs, and they were not above recourse to violence in
achieving their ends; the monarchists infuriated him because they were defending social inequality and religious
dishonesty; the liberals drove him wild because they were
verbose intellectuals who claimed to be the peasants'
brothers and did not even know how to hold a scythe. He
stormed at his son Sergey, who supported the liberal, or
'young men's', party:

'You want a constitution, they want monarchy, the revolutionaries want socialism, and you believe you can fix
things for the people? Well, I can certify to you that the

lives of men in general will not improve until every single man strives to live well himself and not interfere in the lives of others!'[6]

His son-in-law Sukhotin had been elected to the first Duma; this provoked a caustic comment in his notebook: 'The subjects of a constitutional State who believe they are free are like prisoners who believe they are free because they have been allowed to choose their warden.'[7]

On another occasion he wrote:

'The intellectuals have brought a hundred times more harm than good to the people's lives.'[8]

Tolstoy solemnly repeated these phrases to the American, English, French, Swedish and German press correspondents who thronged to Yasnaya Polyana to seek the opinion of the seer of seers. They questioned him about politics, and he answered them with religion; they talked about the tsar, the ministers or the leading revolutionaries and he referred them to God; they spoke of the imperatives of the moment and he proclaimed that the true moment was that of the Beyond. Besides, at the mere sight of all these news-hungry foreigners, he felt himself turning more and more into a Slavophil. Russia had no use for the West. She must follow her own path, lighted by God. To him it was not beyond the realm of possibility that God was Russian. 'If the Russian people are truly uncivilized and barbarian, then we have a future,' he wrote in his diary. 'The Westerners are civilized barbarians, so they have nothing more to live for. It would be as aberrant for us to imitate them as for a stalwart, hard-working, healthy young man to envy a rich Parisian who is bald before thirty and sits in his town house moaning, "Ah, how tedious it all is!" He is to be pitied, not envied.'[9]

He predicted that if the Russian revolutionaries began to ape the West, they would be degraded by politics as soon as they came into power: 'Smugness, pride, vanity and, above all, contempt of their fellow men.'

This refusal to take sides was beginning to alarm the Tolstoyans themselves. In England, Chertkov received the text of the manifesto *The Government, the Revolutionaries and the People*, read it with astonishment and wrote to Tolstoy imploring him to tone down his derogatory remarks about the Marxists. Tolstoy paid no attention, feeling that he had divided his blows very equitably between the adversaries. The article was not published until later, with minor changes. With the same concern for equity, he decided to break off all relations with Grand Duke Nicholas Mikhailovich, whose amiability and broadmindedness he had found so congenial in the Crimea. 'There is something unnatural about our relationship and I think it is better not to go on with it,' he wrote to the grand duke on 14 September 1905. 'You are a grand duke, a rich man and a close relative of the tsar, I am a man who rejects and condemns the established order and the authorities and I make no secret of it.'

The grand duke replied on 1 October that he quite understood and indeed agreed wholeheartedly with Tolstoy but was compelled to keep silent because of his position at court. 'I suffer all the more from my silence,' he confessed, 'because every one of the government's flaws is so blindingly clear to me and I see no remedy except in a radical change from everything that now exists. But my aged father is still alive and, out of respect for him, I must be careful not to offend him by my views or my behaviour. ... Thus I shall say *au revoir* to you, dear Leo Nikolayevich, but not farewell.'*

Tolstoy was touched by this letter. Were there then good men in every station of society? Yet, back in the cities, the blood was still flowing. 'The revolution is in full swing,' Tolstoy wrote on 23 October 1905. 'They are killing on both

---

*Two years later Tolstoy changed his mind and wrote to the grand duke: 'I am ashamed, now, when I think of the letter I wrote in 1905. Today I would not have written it. You cannot imagine how one's views change as one approaches old age, that is, death. What matters most to me now is a loving communion with all men, be they tsar or beggar.'

sides. ... The contradiction, as always, lies in wanting to stop violence by violence.' A little later he confessed to Chertkov that he was weary of the battle and wished to extricate himself: 'The more savage this revolution becomes, the more I want to withdraw into myself and have no more part, whether by act, word or even opinion, in the whole dirty business.' [10]

In the thick of the social upheavals, an unhoped-for event occurred to gladden the hearts at Yasnaya Polyana. Since their marriages, both Tanya and Masha, dogged by ill-luck or some mysterious malformation, had had an uninterrupted series of miscarriages and stillbirths. But on 6 November 1905, to the stupefaction of one and all, Tanya – who was nearly forty – gave birth at the homestead to a living, normal girl child, who was given her mother's name.* When Sasha told him the news, Tolstoy snapped at her for seeming so affected: 'What an idiot you are!' he muttered. 'What are you crying about?' But then he had to blow his own nose to hide his tears. Shortly after, Michael Sukhotin, the baby's father, who had been ordered by his doctors to move to a warmer climate, left for Rome with Sasha, Masha and her husband Obolensky, the 'sponger'.

I advise you [Tolstoy wrote to Masha on 22 March 1906] to get the most you can from Europe. I personally don't want anything from it at all, despite the cleanliness and neatness that are its main features. To my great regret I observe that we are continually borrowing bits of it: political parties, electoral campaigns, blocs, etc. Abysmal! ... The only possible result of all these constitutions is to allow a different set of people to exploit the majority. The faces will change, as they do in England, France, America and everywhere else; and in their eagerness to make greater and greater profits from each other, men will come more and more to abandon the soil, which is the only basis for a rational and honest existence, and will hand over such drudgery to slaves from India, Africa, Asia, Europe or anywhere else. Materially, the European way of life is very clean; morally, very dirty.

*Tanya had five stillborn babies before this one.

A peasant named Voronin from the government of Kostroma wrote seeking his advice as to the best choice to make in the present political situation, and Tolstoy told him, mincing no words: 'I advise you to join no party, except the Tolstoyan party if there is one.'

He would have been happy to see his family's names on the roster of members of that party, but apart from his daughter Sasha, every single Tolstoy had rejected his doctrine. His sons Leo and Andrey (discharged after a few months in the army,* even had the nerve, one day, to declare to his face that the death penalty might be defensible in some cases. Carrying contrariness to such lengths was, Tolstoy felt, an insult to his grey head. 'I told them,' he wrote, 'that they had no respect for me and hated me. I left the room and slammed the door. And for two days I have been unable to forget it.'[11] Once again he was stifling in the atmosphere of Yasnaya Polyana and wanted to flee this easy, aristocratic life filled with deceit, idle talk, food and money. But he could foresee what would happen. 'It is plain to me,' he told his daughter Sasha, 'that after two days Sofya Andreyevna would come after me with her flunkeys and doctors and everything would begin all over again.'

In August 1906, while he was bemoaning his inability to get rid of his wife, she fell critically ill. She had long been complaining of pains in her stomach, and they suddenly grew worse. She took to her bed, the doctors diagnosed a fibroma and recommended surgery, but she was too weak to be taken to the hospital, so an eminent surgeon, Professor Snegirev, came to the house and brought his assistants, a nurse, even an operating table with him. Alerted by telegram, the family came running. When she saw all her sons and daughters around her bed, Sonya felt that she must be dying. After having nursed so many, it was something new for her to be nursed in turn; weakened by spasms, fever, hunger and thoughts of death, she became so tractable that

---

* Andrey was discharged for a nervous disorder and sent home in January 1905.

Tolstoy hardly knew her. She apologized for upsetting the household routine, murmured words of tenderness to the family and her old servants. When her husband came into the room she tried to smile reassuringly and sometimes, taking his wrinkled hand, she kissed it and begged him to forgive her for all the wrongs she had done him. Overwhelmed by this spiritual elevation, Tolstoy withdrew to wander tearfully through the house with hanging head, return to his study and scribble a few words. 'Sonya's condition is growing worse,' he wrote on 1 September 1906. 'I felt deeply sorry for her today. She has become so reasonable, sweet and considerate that she is touching. ... My three sons – Sergey, Andrey and Michael – are here, and my two daughters, Masha and Sasha. The house is full of doctors, which is very trying. Instead of submitting to the will of God in a sublimely religious state of mind, they all give way to selfishness, revolt, pettiness. . . .' He deplored his sons' determination to keep their mother alive. Didn't they understand that their tactless meddling might destroy the majesty of a such beautifully Christian leave-taking? 'Seen that way, death is not the end of something, but a complete revelation,' he added with a flourish of enthusiasm.

Sonya sent for a priest, confessed and took communion. Pointless mimicry, of course, all that, and Tolstoy would have preferred her to die in the pure Tolstoyan faith, but one must not demand too much of a poor weak woman, whose religious upbringing was reasserting itself at the last moment. He generously noted in his diary: 'Not only did I consent to this request, I helped her to carry it out. There are beings who cannot raise themselves to an abstract, purely spiritual communion with the principle of life. They need a cruder form.'

But the surgeon was still hesitating: peritonitis had set in. After explaining the danger, Professor Snegirev asked Tolstoy whether he gave his permission to operate notwithstanding. In a fresh burst of hatred for the medical profession, the old man refused.

'But if we don't operate, she will die!' cried the surgeon.

Tolstoy glared at him and growled:

'Do as you please.'[12]

Since Sonya's soul appeared to be saved, it little mattered to him whether her body was or not. If these fools were to heal her, with their scalpels and drugs, she might never regain her exemplary spiritual attitude. Perhaps this was the ideal moment for her to leave the world. ... His indignant sons stared at him uncomprehendingly. Then he seized his cherry stick and walked to the door, announcing that he was going to pray in the forest, and told them to ring the bell twice if the operation were a success and once if not. Then he changed his mind:

'No; don't ring at all. I'll come back when I'm ready to.'[13]

The vigil began. Now and then, Sasha stole over to the bedroom door, and peering through a crack, saw the scoured floor, white-coated figures and cotton wadding in a basin, heard the clink of metal instruments, inhaled the smell of ether, and went away, full of dread. Suddenly the door was thrown open and the surgeon appeared, sweating and red-faced; the nurse threw a blanket over his shoulders; he called for champagne, swallowed a few gulps, straightened himself and announced that all was well.

Sasha sped away to the forest. She found her father sitting in a clearing in the oaks, and called out:

'Papa! It's a success!'

'What a blessing! What a blessing!' he said.

'But,' wrote Sasha, 'what showed on his face was not joy, but great pain.'

He did not follow his daughter back to the house, but stayed on alone in the clearing. Alive, his wife no longer interested him. He was in no hurry to see her again. For the moment, his only dealings were with God. He prayed and dreamed on, to the murmur of the leaves. At last he went to see Sonya, who was regaining consciousness and whimpering with pain. He took one glance at her and hurried out of the room, horror-stricken:

'My God! What a dreadful thing!' he said. 'Why can't they let people die in peace! A poor woman lashed to her bed with her stomach cut open and no pillow! It's torture!'[14]

That very evening, hiding in his study, he recorded his disappointment at the reprieve the doctors had granted to Sonya, who had been so beautifully prepared to meet her maker. 'Sonya was operated on today,' he wrote. 'They say it was a success. It grieves me to think of it. This morning she was spiritually very beautiful. What composure in the face of death!' Further on: 'In dying, Sonya reveals herself to us.'[15]

The operation was indeed a success; the tumour was not malignant and Sonya quickly recovered. But it seemed to Tolstoy that her spiritual strength failed as her physical strength increased. Soon every trace of the gentle, happy woman on her deathbed had disappeared. The robust matron of sixty-two, round-cheeked, bright-eyed, eating with hearty appetite, once again bustled about the house scolding the servants and keeping accounts, playing the piano and sewing shirts. A few weeks after the operation, on 10 October 1906, a disheartened Tolstoy wrote in his diary, 'Our life here is too tawdry to be borne; they amuse themselves, they pamper themselves, they go off here and there, they study this and that, they quarrel, they worry about things that are no business of theirs; but they do not live because they have no duties. It is abominable!!!!'

The autumn rains and mud cut Yasnaya Polyana off from the world. That year the Obolenskys were staying in the pavilion. One evening, coming in from a walk, Masha, who had a delicate constitution, complained of chills and headache. She had caught cold, and went to bed shivering with fever. The doctors diagnosed double pneumonia. In a few days, racked by fits of coughing, she had become unrecognizable. Her eyes were fixed and glittering, her cheeks on fire, her mouth dry and discoloured, she could hardly lift her hand. Her pulse weakened. But she remained perfectly conscious.

When the doctors announced that they could not save her, Tolstoy seemed surprisingly resigned. As on the occasion of his wife's operation, he stifled any impulse to sorrow, thinking of the joy in store for the dying woman. 'Even though she is my best friend, the one I love best of all those around me,' he wrote to Chertkov, 'selfishly, I am not frightened or saddened by her death. ... Only, forgetting rational reactions aside, I suffer and I am sorry for her because, at her age, she would undoubtedly have preferred to live. ... Death has become so close to me lately that I no longer fear it, and it seems natural and necessary. It is not opposed to life but related to it, a continuation of it. And therefore although it is natural to fight death with one's instinct, one must not fight it with one's reason. Any reasoned, intelligent battle against death – such as that waged by medicine – is unfortunate and evil in itself.'[16]

On 26 November it was clear that Masha would not live through the night. Her husband, father, mother and Sasha were gathered by her bedside. The room was dimly lighted, by a single shaded lamp. In the deep silence the young woman's breathing became more and more irregular. Conscious to the end, she opened her eyes, took Tolstoy's hand, held it to her chest and whispered, 'I am dying.' A little later her breath stopped and her features stiffened. It was over. She was thirty-five years old. Tolstoy left the room, shut himself into his study and opened his diary.

'27 November. It is one o'clock in the morning,' he wrote. 'Masha just died. Strangely enough, I felt no horror, fear or sense of anything out of the ordinary occurring, or even pity or affliction. That is, I thought I was required to produce some special feelings of tenderness and grief in myself, and I succeeded; but in my heart of hearts, I was more at peace than if I had been witnessing some evil or unjust deed committed by someone else, or even more by myself. Yes, it is a physical event and therefore unimportant. My eyes never left her, all the time she was dying: amazingly calm. She was a human being reaching the highest point of her fulfilment, before it is my turn to do so. I watched this high point and rejoiced in it. But then it moved beyond the area that is accessible to me (life); that is, it ceased to be visible to me. But I know it was still going on. Where? When? These are questions that torment our understanding here on earth, and yet they have no bearing on real life, which is outside space and time.

On the day of the funeral he followed the coffin all the way to the little Kochaky cemetery in which his ancestors, and two of the children who had died in infancy – Nikolenka and Petya – were already buried. When the procession passed through the village, the peasants came out of their isbas and pressed coins into the priest's hand for a requiem in memory of the woman who had cared for them and loved them so well. The professional mourners were sobbing. The road was long and muddy. At the cemetery gate the procession came to a halt. Tolstoy would not go any further; he took his leave of the coffin and returned to the house. 'I watched him go,' wrote his son Ilya. 'He walked through the melting snow with his old man's gait, taking short quick steps, with his toes turned out. He did not look back once.' As soon as he reached the house Tolstoy opened his diary again and wrote, '29 November 1906. They have just taken her away, carried her off to be buried. Thank God, I am not depressed.'

Sonya displayed more grief than he, although she had never really cared for Masha-the-Tolstoyan; but she was made of simpler stuff, and was incapable of rejoicing in the loss of a child. She admired her husband for being able to return to his regular occupations so quickly: writing, going for walks, riding his horse. ... And yet, while he made an outward show of perfect serenity, sometimes, at nightfall, sorrow got the best of him, and he felt the absence of his favourite daughter like a craving. She had been the only one who had found the way to his heart, the only one in whom, now and then, he had seen a reflection of himself. 'I live on, and I often recall Masha's last minutes,' he wrote a month later. 'She is sitting up, her pillows all around her, I am holding her dear hand, so thin, and I feel the life going, going. ... Those fifteen minutes were among the most important and most serious of my whole life.'[17]

PART VIII

THE SOLUTION

[29]

Days Pass, and
a Birthday

AFTER Sonya's recovery and Masha's death, there was a long lull in Tolstoy's life. Even politics seemed to have calmed down, as though to spare the old patriarch's nerves. To continue meditating, writing, even living, at his age, he needed an absolutely rigid schedule: he felt that this routine was what kept him in good health. Up early in the morning, he washed with cold water, emptied his basin, straightened his bed and covered it with a crocheted blanket embroidered with a Greek key motif, swept the floor and, in the winter, carried logs and lighted a fire in the stove. Then he went for a short walk in the woods, sat on a bench to jot down some philosophical thought or literary project, and was back in his room at nine. He ate his breakfast alone (coffee and dry bread) and read the newspapers: two Russian dailies and the London *Times*.

In the meantime Philichka, a red-headed, grimy muzhik who wore an immense black cap and was nicknamed 'Tolstoy's mail clerk', had climbed on to his horse and gone to fetch the mail at the railway station. He returned with a sackful and poured out the contents on the master's desk. Tolstoy drank the last of his coffee as he opened envelopes – thirty or forty missives a day, from the four corners of the earth. Waves of writing, washing up at his feet, showing him the extent of his popularity and his powerlessness. How to help all these strangers who needed him? True: for every moving appeal there were dozens more from visionaries, autograph hounds, hysterics, unsuccessful authors, inventors of perpetual-motion machines and blinkered Tolstoyans asking whether it was right to kill microbes, eat honey produced by the labour of the bees or use glue manufactured from the bones of animals. Tolstoy initialled the envelopes 'N.A.' (no answer), 'S' (silly) or 'A' (appeal for help). Sometimes he wrote out a reply himself, but as his writing had become very poor he usually scribbled a few lines for his daughter Sasha to copy in legible form.

In the early days, Tolstoy's secretariat had been a rudimentary affair: Sonya, the two elder daughters, Ivanov the scribe and various guests all shared in the copying. Tanya, however, had bought a typewriter and begun to type some of her father's letters. Sasha also learned to type, and the Remington became the standard means of dealing with correspondence and manuscripts. All incoming letters and copies of replies were recorded and filed.

The only exception to this rule was made for Chertkov. Everything Tolstoy wrote was sent to him for publication in England, where, as guardian of the master's thought and defender of his fame, he saw that every new work came out simultaneously in the various languages; and if Tolstoy were rash enough to send an article directly to some foreign periodical, he received such an avalanche of reproof that he humbly begged pardon of the tyrannical servant of his glory. One day he said to Sasha with a sad smile:

'By the way, Chertkov asks that no one be allowed to read his letters and that they be returned to him immediately.'

When his daughter bristled at these high-handed ways, he entreated her, with a weary and embarrassed air, not to poison his relations with the exile.

After finishing his letters, he worked on his own projects until two in the afternoon. He still refused to wear glasses, so he sat on a chair that had been Tanya's when she was a child in order not to have to bend over so far to bring his eyes close to the paper. He gripped the pen in his fist, the forefinger bunched up with the rest instead of extended along the penholder. With a rubber pad under his seat, his head lowered and his elbows spread apart, he looked like some old bearded schoolboy labouring over his homework.

'When he wrote,' Sasha noted, 'he pushed his lips out as though he were blowing. Then he would put a full stop and raise his thick, beetling eyebrows.' No one was allowed to disturb him during his hours of creation. He demanded absolute silence, for the slightest noise, he said, prevented him from concentrating. If he needed anything, he rang a turtle-shaped bell or knocked on the wall with his big walking-stick. Most of the time he rang to tell them to drive away the dogs barking on the lawn or the hens cackling beneath his windows, and a servant was sent around the house waving a branch to scatter the animals. When silence was restored, Tolstoy went back to blackening of sheets of paper with his flowing hand. He usually filled only a quarter of the page, and often preferred to use scraps of paper torn from letters he had received. Sometimes, rather than change the order of the sentences in a difficult passage, he cut the whole manuscript into strips, marked them with tall, angular numbers, and gave them to Sasha with a sheepish growl:

'Careful! Don't lose any of the bits! I made a lot of noodles today.'

'He did not finish his words,' she said later, 'and wrote without punctuation; any he did put in was always in the wrong place. Sometimes he made grammatical errors.'

One imagines the pride with which Sasha, just turned twenty-three, bore off the precious scraps of paper to the 'Remington room', reserved for secretarial work. Behind the library and drawing-room doors, guests were laughing and exchanging trivial remarks; she, meanwhile, sitting bolt upright behind her typewriter, was the first to learn the new word of Leo Tolstoy. In addition to this routine work she also copied her father's diary, and thus she learned what he thought of his intimates and himself. Before, he had been more willing to share his secrets with everyone around him, but now it occasionally troubled him to think that a mere girl, his own child, should be following every twist and turn of his most private thoughts. But Chertkov had demanded that the diary be typed and a copy sent to him, and it was impossible to oppose that man's will. Pitifully trying to maintain the illusion that he was writing for himself, Tolstoy told his daughter:

'Take the diary without telling me, don't let me know it's being typed; otherwise, I wouldn't be able to write it!'[1]

At two o'clock a bell rang for lunch. With a brisk step, 'hopping a little', Tolstoy went into the big dining-room where the table was set. White cloth, silver, servants in livery and white gloves. When the master came in everyone stood and all talk ceased. Tolstoy made a pleasant remark to everyone present, and sat down to the right of his wife. In addition to the family, there were his secretary, his private physician Dushan Makovitsky, his grandchildren's tutors and governesses, friends, passing foreigners, neighbours. Some thirty persons in all. Two menus: one for ordinary people and one for the master, usually consisting of a soft-boiled egg, raw tomatoes, and macaroni and cheese. He ate rapidly, paying no attention to what was on his plate. His guests never heard him express any opinion of his food. As he had lost all his teeth, his cheeks wrinkled into deep folds as he chewed. On his bad days, he was aggrieved by the material comforts around him, cast murderous glances at the servants and the crystal, did not join in the conversation and hurried away from the table. When he was in a good mood, on the other hand, he charmed his guests with the vivacity of his conversation. Leaping from one subject to another, he stated his views on everything in simple, colourful language, flew into a rage at the slightest sign of disagreement, pressed his argument to the point of absurdity, apologized for speaking so sharply and, his features alert and his eyes darting around the room, basked in the wonderment of his audience.

After the meal he took a walk in the grounds. But before he could start, he had to cross a barrage of suppliants. They had been sitting for hours, in front of the house, on the bench, under the old elm, patiently waiting their turn. Pilgrims on the way to the monasteries of Kiev, muzhiks

from villages far and near, simpletons, professional beggars, a whole ragged tribe who bent down and murmured
words of blessing as the master drew near. He questioned
them, gratified them with a few evangelical words of counsel and gave them a few kopecks. A big jar in the upstairs
drawing-rooom was kept full of coins especially for the
purpose. Most of the visitors thanked him when they received their pittance. But some grumbled that he could give
more, since he was so rich.

'But they told me he was a kind man!' one woman exclaimed, looking with contempt at the palm of her hand.

In addition to the poor, there were callers of higher degree, who had come by coach from the Yasenki station.
They were all 'problem' people. They had souls, and they
intended to tell him about them. Sasha wrote, 'One is a
landowner who agrees that private property is a sin but does
not know how to expiate; one is a student wanting money
as a "revolutionary expropriation"; one is a lunatic who
wants Tolstoy to support her Esperanto propaganda campaign; one is a young man who has gone astray and wants
us to put him back on the path of righteousness; one is a
peasant who has refused to perform his military service on
religious grounds and wants to tell his tale of woe. ... And
then there are the sightseers, who simply come to look at
"the great writer of the Russian nation".'

For them all, Tolstoy was a national monument, and no
one had any right to prevent them from coming to look at
him. Some feigned a neophyte's admiration in his presence,
but others did not even trouble to do that: they asked impertinent questions of the author and his family and
snooped about the house in search of material for a 'feature'
story. Biographers, annalists, souvenir hunters, they all went
away with their notebooks full, and one subsequently heard
that they had known the master intimately and were writing their memoirs. Some came back once or twice and performed some small service, and although no one liked them,
they eventually edged their way into the little clan around

Tolstoy. One grew accustomed to their faces, one forgot to be careful what one said in front of them; and then one day, using what they had seen and heard, they might peacefully set about demolishing their host. 'Usually,' Sasha noted wistfully, 'people can choose their friends and acquaintances according to their tastes. This was not so with us. Because of my father's name, we saw many people who had no value, and were simply full of their own importance.'

After making his way through these groups, Tolstoy set off at last, on foot or on horseback, for the Zasyeka forest. Sonya worried about him during these rambles and had insisted that he be followed, at forty paces, by a servant or his secretary or some friend. He grumblingly resigned himself to this silent escort. He often paused to take notes and, during the warm months, to pick flowers. He was always the first to appear with violets, forget-me-nots and lilies-of-the-valley. Clutching his bouquet in his fist, he sniffed at it with a sly, voluptuous expression on his face: 'What a delicate fragrance! Like bitter almond!'

His companions on these jaunts through field and forest were amazed at his ability on horseback. At eighty, mounted on his faithful Délire, he clattered down the sides of ravines, leaped over ditches and galloped away beneath low-hanging branches. His daughter Sasha trembled with terror when he took her with him on these sylvan expeditions. From time to time he would turn back and cry out:

'You all right?'

'Yes, I'm still in the saddle,' she would gasp.

He laughed:

'Well, hang on!'

On these occasions he usually wore a peculiar white muslin hat, stretched on a wire frame. A canvas blouse, shapeless trousers and soft boots completed his attire. Sometimes he exchanged the muslin hat for a cap. From the distance, he looked like a young man disguised as an old one, with a false beard and eyebrows made out of cotton batting. One day Délire, who was very high-spirited, took fright passing by a foundry, shied and fell Without abandoning the reins, Tolstoy slipped his foot out of the stirrup, leaped to one side and landed on his feet, unhurt.

'Don't say anything to Maman!' he growled, turning to Sasha.[2]

When he returned from his outing, around five o'clock, he drank a glass of tea, shut himself up in his study and, lying on the leather couch, daydreamed, read, took notes or napped. But at the first sign of anything amiss – a cold or excess fatigue – this all changed. He wrapped himself up in his dressing-gown, covered his shoulders with a russet camel's-hair shawl, pulled a black silk skullcap down over his head and sat in semi-darkness, yawning cavernously, at such length and so noisily that when the windows were open he could be heard in the garden.[3]

Towards seven he reappeared, after the rest of the family had already sat down for supper. This time his meal was more copious: borscht, rice or potato dumplings, dessert, and, on very rare occasions, a drop of white wine in a large glass of water. After supper, the women sat sewing in the drawing-room under the big lamp with the pleated paper shade, while he played chess with one of his sons or a visiting friend. Writers came to see him: Dmitry Merezhkovsky and his wife Zinaida Hippius ('I would like to like them but I can't'), his translator Halperin-Kaminsky. ... Often, there was music. There were two pianos in the room and the *étagère* sagged under the weight of the sheet music of Haydn, Mozart, Chopin, Glinka and Beethoven. Most often, it was the pianist Goldenweiser, a close friend of the family, whose swift fingers swept the keyboard. Or some noted guest such as Wanda Landowska, who came in 1907.[*] However he bewailed the evil effects of music, Tolstoy could not resist its charms. When a melody pleased him, his face softened into an expression of gentleness and suffering. Seated in the old Voltaire armchair, his head to one side and his eyes closed, he sighed and wept, unable to restrain

[*] She had brought her own harpsichord.

his emotions. Under the blue light of the big paper lampshade, there was 'something immaterial and seraphic' in his profile with its white beard and hair. Once the spell was broken, he resented the composer and performer who had so unsettled him:

'My tears mean nothing,' he growled. 'So what? There is some music I cannot listen to without weeping, that's all, just as my daughter Sasha cannot eat strawberries without getting hives! Anyway, sometimes I weep when I laugh, too. It's nerves, nothing but nerves!'[4]

Tea was drunk, once again, around ten in the evening. At eleven, after wishing everyone a good night, Tolstoy withdrew. 'His handshake was very special,' noted Gusev. 'He held the other person's hand a long time and gave him a friendly look, straight into his eyes.' Alone in his study, he lighted his candle, sat down in his child's chair in front of the writing table and took out his notebook. Everything he had jotted down in it he now expanded in his diary, adding thoughts and impressions that had come to him in the meantime. Then he drew a line beneath his report and wrote the date of the following day, with the customary 'i.l.l.'.

Having thus examined his conscience, he went into the next room and took off his clothes, meditated, prayed, lay down on his little iron bed and calmly surveyed his surroundings. On the night table stood a little bell, a clock under a glass dome, a candle, matches; above his head, a portrait of his daughter Tanya; a washstand in one corner. More portraits: his father in uniform, Masha, who had died the previous year, Sonya. ... Everything was in order. He lay his cheek against the pillow, pulled up the blanket decorated with the Greek key design, closed his eyes and waited for sleep to come.

This uneventful life was being recorded on all sides. The most zealous chroniclers were the new secretary, Nicholas Nikolayevich Gusev, whom Chertkov had recommended to Tolstoy; Goldenweiser; and Dr Dushan Makovitsky, who had recently been hired as the master's personal physician. All three kept their diaries with scrupulous punctuality. Gusev, at twenty-five, was an impassioned Tolstoyan who wrote so fluently that Tolstoy allowed him to answer some letters and acknowledge consignments of books in his own name. Instead of restricting himself to a conventional expression of thanks, Gusev composed four-page epistles enthusiastically expounding the master's doctrine. In his capacity as disciple, he also received and conversed with callers. And yet, despite his admiration for Tolstoy, he had not read *War and Peace*. 'Tolstoy, as an artist, does not exist for me,' he said. 'Tolstoy himself repudiates his past works.' His major drawback was a resistance to hygiene. Sasha, who worked with him in the 'Remington room', said she could not stand the smell in hot weather.

At thirty, the pianist Goldenweiser, who lived near by and came to the house nearly every day, was a very different type. 'He was sad, as Tolstoyans nearly always were, and tall, and something dogged and ineradicably tedious emanated from him,' wrote Maurice Kues, the Swiss tutor of Tolstoy's grandson. The author liked to play chess, converse and go for walks in the woods with the pianist. Goldenweiser, a careful biographer, noted the most minute details of these occasions. He did not fail to record that Tolstoy had a faint lisp, that his toes pointed out and his heels touched the ground first when he walked, that he was miserly in small things (paper, candles) and had a very characteristic smell, 'reminiscent of cypress'.

A still more impressive observer was Dr Makovitsky. Although Tolstoy claimed to have nothing but contempt for medicine, he had been attended by a private physician since 1908. Dr Bertenson, who had accompanied him to the Crimea, was followed by Drs Nikitin and Berkenheim, and now by Dr Makovitsky, a Hungarian Slovak who had left his native land and come to live at Yasnaya Polyana out of love for the apostle of non-violence, whose entire opus he knew by heart. He was a puny little man, anaemic and bald, with a waxen face ending in a short little pepper-and-salt beard. But this unprepossessing envelope enclosed a soul of fire. He would willingly have laid down his life for his idol. Tolstoy said of him, 'Dushan is a saint. But since there are no true saints, God gave him one fault: hatred of Jews.'

True enough, the mild and pacific Dushan Makovitsky was so rabid an anti-Semite that his state sometimes bordered on insanity. He was endowed with a colossal memory and, on the slightest pretext, could rattle off statistics demonstrating the superiority of Slavs over Israelites. He scolded Sasha if he heard that she had shopped in a Jewish store.

'Oh, Alexandra Lvovna, aren't you ashamed of yourself? Why buy from the Jews, why? Why not support your own? Don't you see how the Jews hate you, how they lord it over you?'[5]

It pained him that Goldenweiser, who was a Jew, should be treated as a friend of the family.

He was amazingly active for a man of such puny appearance. Every morning he held consultations in the village at Yasnaya Polyana in an isba fitted out as an infirmary, after which he set off on his rounds in a telaga to see patients scores of miles away who could not come to him. Whenever he had a free moment he ran to Tolstoy's side and hearkened to catch the Word as it fell. No founder of a religion ever had a more fervent hagiographer by his side. The very idea of wanting to consider the doctrine objectively was sacrilege to him. His mission on earth was to record and witness, and in order to escape the notice of the master, who did not like people to write down every word he said, the doctor had devised an ingenious form of notation. He wrote on stiff cardboard squares inside his pocket, feeling his way along with a minute pencil sharpened to a very fine point. With practice, he had become a past master at this form of blind-writing. Often, at teatime, Sasha saw Makovitsky's left hand on top of the table, while his right was scratching away out of sight.

'Dushan,' she would say in a low voice, 'I'll tell Papa!'

'Oh, no, Alexandra Lvovna, don't do that,' he stammered, blushing and pulling his right hand out of his pocket.

A few seconds later he resumed his watchdog pose. His right hand disappeared, his eyes unfocused. His mind a-quiver, he was recording, recording for posterity.

'Thus we were deprived of the great joy of having a private life,' wrote Sasha, 'of talking nonsense, joking, singing, not having to be careful of everything. Instead, we knew that every word we spoke and every gesture we made would be recorded on the spot.'[6]

Dushan Makovitsky and Gusev helped Tolstoy to compile the texts of famous authors he wanted to use in his next book, *The Circle of Reading*. It was probably his work on this anthology that reawakened his taste for pedagogy. He wrote a brochure, *The Teachings of Jesus Explained to Children*, prepared a *Circle of Reading for Children* and suddenly started evening classes for the little muzhiks of Yasnaya Polyana. At first, fifteen of them came to the library where, this time, Tolstoy sought to teach, not science or history or grammar, but religious and moral principles, using the simplest methods possible. They listened, they appeared to understand. The old man was jubilant. 'Lately,' he wrote in his diary on 17 March 1907, 'I have been completely occupied giving lessons to the children. The farther I go the more clearly I see the difficulties of the task, and at the same time the greater the success I look forward to.'

Sonya shrugged. 'Leo Nikolayevich has a new hobby,' she said. 'He is droning away, teaching Christian truths to the children; they repeat after him like parrots. But they will turn into drunkards and thieves all the same!' Although he was offended by his wife's scepticism, Tolstoy had to admit that his pupils were not angels, despite their sweet faces and high piping voices. He would have liked to find a sort of fundamental innocence in them, the purity of souls preserved from civilization; but instead, he ran headlong into all the wicked impulses he had learned to recognize in the

adult. One afternoon he returned from his walk in a very
agitated state and said to his daughter, 'It's dreadful!
Dreadful! I am walking along, it is a gorgeous morning, the
birds are singing, the smell of clover is spreading through
the air ... and suddenly, I hear the most terrible swearing.
I come closer; there were some children behind an acacia
tending the horses, and they were hurling the crudest insults at each other. It brought tears to my eyes.'[7]

The number of pupils dwindled steadily. Tolstoy did not
know whether to attribute this loss of interest to the children themselves or to their parents, who did not like to see
them being indoctrinated by the master. Although the revolution had been smothered, the villagers still harboured
deep resentments against the landowners. Strikes and insurrections had given way to isolated acts of violence.
Sonya's own brother Vyachesla Behrs, chief works engineer
on a project near St Petersburg, was murdered by unem-
ployed workers. The peasants on Tolstoy's son Michael's
farm had set fire to the barns containing the farm machinery. Another fire was started by muzhiks on the Sukhotin
property. On the land of a neighbour, Mrs Zvegintsev,
prowlers shot and killed two house-servants sent to ask them
for their passports. At Yasnaya Polyana itself, marauders
often robbed the vegetable garden, and the night watchman
complained of being shot at while trying to catch them in
the act; and one hundred and twenty-nine of Tolstoy's beloved trees were cut down by the peasants, who appropriated
the wood. On the advice of her son Andrey, Sonya requested
official assistance from the governor of the province, D. D.
Kobeko. The police raided the village and arrested a few
peasants for possessing firearms. Only too happy to blow up
the case, the governor placed sentinels on the property and
even inside Tolstoy's house. Thus the apostle of non-violence found himself under uniformed protection. The situation was made all the more paradoxical by the fact that
Yasnaya Polyana was the only estate in the district to receive such official help. Now the enemies of Tolstoyism

could chortle to their heart's content, to see what a fool the prophet had made of himself. He fumed at his wife:

'Why can't you understand that the presence of police who arrest and imprison peasants is intolerable to me?'

'Then do you want them to shoot us here?' she retorted.

'This is hell. Pure hell. This is the worst possible atmosphere to create. To think that there are seven armed men on this property!'[8]

The wives and parents of the incarcerated peasants came to plead with the master to intercede on their behalf. No matter how often he told them that it had all been decided without consulting him, that in obedience to his ideal of poverty he had given all his rights to his wife and children and was no longer the owner of Yasnaya Polyana and therefore could do nothing to help, they did not believe him. 'They cannot accept the fact that I am not the master here – since I live here – and they hold me responsible for everything that happens,' he wrote in his diary on 7 September 1907. 'It is very hard.' In his notebook: 'The governor has just come, with all his suite. Revolting and pitiful.' Now two tall, heavy, coarse guards stood preening themselves in the entryway, revolver on hip. In their vicinity, Sasha detected an unpleasant odour of 'bad tobacco and male perspiration'. She begged her mother to send them away, to pardon the muzhiks and have mercy on her father. But Sonya was adamant. Then Tolstoy dispatched his daughter to Tula, to see Governor Kobeko and give him a letter. She was received by Deputy Governor Lopukin. After glancing over Tolstoy's appeal, he turned to Sasha and concluded with a smile:

'The countess, your mother, has asked us to protect your family at Yasnaya Polyana, and we are only obeying her orders.'

And he showed her a letter from Sonya asking that the guards be kept on the premises at all costs. When Sasha returned to the house, she ran to her mother and sobbed out:

'Even if we lose everything, everything, not just a few

old oak trees but Yasnaya Polyana itself, we can't put Papa in such a position!'

'I can expect nothing but trouble from you!' Sonya replied curtly. 'I know you don't care a rap whether Yasnaya Polyana is torn to rack and ruin. But I don't have the right to talk like that: I have children!'

The police remained at Yasnaya Polyana for two years, and Tolstoy suffered leaden remorse all the time they were there. 'If someone were to speak to me about myself as a stranger, living in the lap of luxury, surrounded by armed guards, despoiling peasants and having them thrown into prison while he preaches and practises Christianity and hands out fortunes in money and performs all these ugly deeds hiding behind his beloved wife, I should not hesitate to call that man a criminal,' he wrote.* Once again, he wanted to run away. But when the moment came to take the plunge, he hung back and invented excuses: 'However powerfully I desire to obey the call of my ideal, I do not feel capable of it; it is not that I so love fine food or a soft bed or the pleasure of riding horseback, but there are other reasons: I cannot be the cause of a woman's unhappiness, provoke the anger of a person who is convinced she is doing her duty ...'[9]

On 22 October 1907, Gusev was arrested as a revolutionary propagandist and Tolstoy wrote to Governor Kobeko and Count Olsufyev to obtain his release. When he was freed, at the end of December 1907, the old man embraced him and said, 'How I envy you! How I should like to be put into prison, a real prison, good and stinking! ... I see that I don't deserve such honour!'[10]

Badly shaken by these emotions, he had several slight strokes, accompanied by temporary loss of memory, during the winter of 1907–8. But his ardour for battle was undiminished. He anxiously followed the policy of Stolypin's new government, which had opted for strong-arm tactics. Before the 1905 revolution, the death penalty had hardly

* July 1908.

ever been applied in Russia, and ordinary criminal offences were punished by prison sentences or hard labour. But punitive action was intensified after the terrorist crimes began. Most of those charged with political murder were executed. Tolstoy looked in the papers every day for the notices on the executions. In this violent settling of accounts between the tsarist society and its adversaries, his compassion went equally to victims and executioners. He would have liked to write something on the subject. 'I should like to show in this book that no one is guilty,' he said. 'I should like to explain that the judge of the court who signed the order and the hangman who put the condemned man to death were both led to do so perfectly naturally – as naturally as we drink tea here together, while so many others are shivering with cold and soaked by rain.'[11] But a novel would not have enough impact on the public. The question was too serious to be argued by fictional characters. Professor Davydov, the lawyer Muravyev, the young Tolstoyan Biryukov were sending Tolstoy secret documents, photographs of the hanged men. ... So many mistakes! So much arbitrary action! So much violence! To abolish violence, one had to begin by abolishing private property. On 26 July 1907, Tolstoy had written to the prime minister, P. A. Stolypin, to warn him:

'Two courses are open to you. Either you will continue in the way you have begun, condoning and even directing the policy of exile, hard labour and capital punishment, and, without accomplishing your aims, leave a hated name behind you and, which is more serious, lose your soul; or, taking the lead among all the countries of Europe, you will strive to abolish the oldest and greatest injustice of all, which is common to all peoples: the individual ownership of land.'

At Tolstoy's request, Stolypin's brother, a reporter on the *New Times*, conveyed this letter to its destination, and also undertook to reply to the writer on behalf of the overworked minister:

'As regards the idea of abolishing private property, my brother said it would be utterly impossible to make such a transformation – particularly as he is now completely committed to the idea that he can put Russia on the road to prosperity by establishing and consolidating small holdings; that is, by following a course exactly opposite to yours. You know how children love property, what joy they derive from their first horse, their first dog. The only way the common people can experience this same thrill of joy is if they have their own land, around their own house, fenced in by their own stockade ...'[12]

Tolstoy wrote to the minister again in January 1908, but with no hope of being understood. In May of that year, opening the newspaper *Russia*, he read the following announcement: 'Today, 9 May on the Stryelbitsky Esplanade in Kherson, twenty peasants were hanged for armed trespassing upon a property in the district of Elizavetgrad.' He crumpled the paper and groaned:

'It's impossible! We can't go on living this way! No! No!'

That same day he decided to launch a fresh appeal to the government: *I Cannot Be Silent*. Early that year Thomas Edison had sent him a dictating machine from America, in token of his esteem. Until now he had not been able to use the machine: when the moment came to speak, he became nervous and rattled and could not find his words. This time, he determined to get the best of his stage fright and, standing in front of the machine, his voice blurred by tears, slowly began to dictate. The speech went well. Sasha typed it out on her Remington. On 31 May the revised and corrected text was ready for the press:

'People now talk and write of executions, hanging, murders and bombs, as they used to talk and write about the weather. Schoolboys, hardly more than children, go out to expropriate and kill as they used to go hunting. ... It is impossible to live this way, for me at any rate, and I shall not do it ...'

Further along, he called upon the government to stop the growing carnage and begged, as a special favour, to be persecuted for his opinions.

'Let me be put in prison,' he wrote, 'or better yet (so good that I dare not hope for such happiness), let me be dressed in a shroud like those twelve or twenty peasants, and pushed off a bench so that the weight of my body will tighten the well-soaped slipknot around my old neck.'

This manifesto was prohibited by the censor, but extracts appeared in the Russian press; the newspapers publishing them had to pay large fines. Innumerable printed, hectographed and handwritten copies were already circulating. Abroad, the full text was published simultaneously in several languages. All Europe was soon talking of the great Tolstoy's protest against the tsar's method of expediting justice. The mail at Yasnaya Polyana multiplied tenfold overnight. Most of the letters congratulated the author for his courage, some insulted him and called him destructive. A package arrived; when he unwrapped it Tolstoy found a little box containing a piece of rope as thick as his finger. There was a note with the package: 'Count, here is the reply to your message; you can do it yourself, no need to bother the government about it, it isn't so difficult! And you will be doing a favour to our nation and our young. – A Russian Mother.'

Tolstoy's admirers did not want to let the year 1908 go by without a full-scale celebration of his eightieth birthday. For some it would be a tribute to the greatest Russian author, for others a means of making money by publishing articles and photographs, and for still others a political manoeuvre calculated to discredit the government. An organizing committee was set up in St Petersburg in January. Response to its appeal was enthusiastic, in Russia and abroad; subscription lists went as far as England for contributions to a 'Tolstoy Fund'. All this fuss displeased the old man. 'All my life I have hated anniversaries of every sort,' he said. 'It's a ridiculous habit. At this advanced age, when there is nothing left to think about but death, they want to bother me with that!'[13]

The government was equally unhappy, for whenever Tolstoy's name appeared in the press, it could expect the worst. As usual, alarm in official circles took the form of an exchange of coded telegrams between the capital and the larger provincial cities. Old Princess Dondukov-Korsakov warned Sonya that Orthodox churchgoers would be outraged if religion's public enemy No. 1 were to be publicly honoured. There were grumblers in the opposite camp as well, for to a true Tolstoyan this form of manifestation could be nothing but trickery. Bodyansky wrote to Gusev that Leo Nikolayevich 'ought to be imprisoned for his birthday, which would have given him deep moral satisfaction'. Tolstoy replied to Princess Dondukov-Korsakov that he quite approved of her protest and that the festivities being arranged were 'more than painful' to him, and to Bodyansky he wrote, 'Indeed, nothing could have satisfied me as fully or given me as much happiness as to be put in prison: a good, proper prison that stinks, where people suffer from cold and hunger.'

Thus enlightened from both sides as to where his duty lay, he announced his refusal to Stakhovich, who was a member of the organizing committee: 'I have an urgent request to make of you; do everything you can to stop this jubilee and release me from it. I shall be eternally grateful to you.'[14]

The committee deferred to his request, but it was too late to silence the public, which was in a fine frenzy of anticipation over the celebration. So, even though the newspapers confirmed the announcement that all demonstrations were being cancelled at the request of Tolstoy himself, government and Church redoubled their precautions. The bishop of Saratov even issued an order forbidding his faithful to honour 'the anathematized infidel and revolutionary anarchist Leo Tolstoy', 'the Russian Judas, reviled and accursed', 'morally rotten to the core', 'intellectual murderer and corrupter of the young ...'

Just then, as it happened, the Russian Judas was in rather poor health. He had had more strokes, which had so muddled his wits that when he regained consciousness he could not remember what he had been doing when the attack came. Then he developed phlebitis, in July. The doctors forced him to stay in bed with his leg encased in ice and raised on wooden trestles. The date of his birthday was drawing near but he was thinking more and more of death. Too weak to write his diary, he dictated it:

'Difficult situation. Pain. The last few days continual fever and pain, it is hard for me to bear. I must be beginning to die. It is hard enough to live in the absurd and luxurious state in which I have been compelled to spend my life, but it is even harder to die in it: the fuss and bother, the medicine, the deceitful reassurance and rallying, when it is all impossible and useless, for the only result is a worsening of the state of the soul.' [15]

Just in case, he specified his last wishes: all his books to become public property, no requiem mass, a plain wooden casket and, for his last resting place, that spot in the Zakaz forest near the ravine, 'where the green stick was buried'.

Four days after making his arrangements to die, his temperature dropped. He realized that he had been spared once again. Was he happy? He said not – life was a burden, he had lost all desire to work. But on 17 August, he noted seven fresh themes for novels in his notebook, one of which concerned a young priest who, 'having read Tolstoy', has a sudden revelation of the great problems of mankind.*

On 28 August 1908, visitors began arriving early in the morning, although the celebration was supposed to be confined to the family. The horses' bells disturbed the old man, who was writing in his study as usual. The post office was submerged by letters, telegrams and packages from all over the world. At noon, Tolstoy appeared in an upholstered wheelchair to receive his family's birthday wishes. He was

* None of them was ever written.

wearing a snowy-white blouse, his carefully combed beard flowed across his chest and his hair had been cut very short, which made his ears look enormous. Except for Leo, who was in Switzerland, all his daughters and sons were there. Sonya, very excited, her face flushed and her back rigid, was scuttling about in all directions in a ruffled gown, seeing to the last-minute arrangements. Her head shook with a slight nervous tremor and she peered out at the world from misty, short-sighted eyes.

The old man was brought to see his presents. Boxes of candies, books, portraits of the author embroidered on handkerchiefs, an album of original drawings offered by the Russian painters Repin, Pasternak, Levitan. ... From France he received twenty bottles of *apéritif* bearing the motto, '*Le meilleur ami de l'estomac*'; the Ottoman tobacco company sent a chest of cigarettes with his portrait printed on them (he returned them immediately, with a letter stigmatizing smokers); a group of restaurant waiters in St Petersburg had taken up a collection among themselves and offered him a magnificent samovar ...

At last, the bell rang for dinner. More than thirty people sat down to the table, arranged in horseshoe shape. The sons read out a few of the one thousand and seven hundred messages of congratulation sent by scientists, authors, students, artists, shopkeepers, engineers, farmers, factory workers, prisoners, aristocrats and even clergymen. 'We wish you many more years of life in your struggle against the power of darkness,' signed: 'The faculty of the St Petersburg Polytechnical Institute.' 'The Art Theatre makes its bow to you today, great teacher,' signed: 'Stanislavsky and the company.' 'Do not be silent, old man inspired by God,' signed: 'A peasant.' 'May God prolong your life, strong sower of truth and love,' signed: 'A group of cartwrights.' 'To the seeker after God, greetings!' signed: 'A Catholic priest.' The English writers Thomas Hardy, George Meredith, H. G. Wells and Bernard Shaw sent a message of friendship. Similar missives continued to arrive, from

France, Germany, Australia. There were tears in Tolstoy's eyes. The noise of voices and clinking of glasses made him giddy. He was sitting at a separate table, his leg propped up in front of him. In his weary face the pale pupils glittered beneath the thick roll of his eyebrows. After the meat course, the servants brought in bottles of champagne wrapped in napkins. Corks popped; the guests assembled around the old man, glass in hand.

Meanwhile, more delegations kept arriving outside, and were assembling on the lawn. An open-air banquet had been arranged for them. Tolstoy rolled towards them in his wheelchair, working the rubber wheels with both hands. They surrounded him. How to quench the thirst of all these people, so avid to hear the word? The first disciples, listening to Christ long ago, must have worn just such expressions of naïve respect. They were waiting for the sage of Yasnaya Polyana to pronounce his Sermon on the Mount. But at his age, it was asking too much. Besides, he had never been able to speak in public. He muttered a few trivialities, thanked everyone, shook hands, kissed the children, smiled through his legendary beard for the numerous photographers. A brass band was playing under the lindens. A cameraman was filming the scene for posterity. Worn out, Tolstoy soon slipped away from his admirers and shut himself up to play chess with his son-in-law Sukhotin, who let him win – which made him very happy. To end the day, he asked Goldenweiser to play Chopin's Études on the piano. The music stirred him profoundly. He withdrew to his room. As his daughter Sasha was wishing him a good night he murmured:

'My heart is very heavy!' [16]

Then Sonya came to tuck him in, with the blanket with the Greek key design she had crocheted herself. The expression on his face when he looked at her was one of heart-rending tenderness. He resembled a child, in spite of his white hair and his wrinkles. The birthday was over, and there had been no toy fine enough to occupy his mind any longer. Sonya tucked the blanket under her aged husband's shoulders. He grunted with comfort:

'It's so good! It's so good! As long as it doesn't end with a catastrophe!' [17]

And he sent her away. Before going to sleep he wrote in his notebook: 'To eat when one is hungry, drink water when one is thirsty; those are great pleasures of the body; but to refuse food and drink and everything the body desires is more than a pleasure, it is the joy of the soul!' [18]

[30]

Re-enter Chertkov

ONE of the guests congratulating Leo Tolstoy most warmly on that 28 August was none other than Vladimir Grigoryevich Chertkov. The previous year he had been allowed to return to Russia, after ten years in exile. From his long residence at Christchurch in England he had brought back an unshaken confidence in the master's doctrine, an even greater measure of inflexibility than before, and a touch of British stiffness in his demeanour. Although his hairline was receding and he had put on a little weight, he still cut an imposing figure. His sufferings for the faith gave him unequalled prestige in the eyes of all the Tolstoyans and of Tolstoy himself. True, young Biryukov had also been forced to leave the country, but he had been returned to grace in 1904 and had been living with his family near Yasnaya Polyana ever since, so he had far less authority than the Christchurch exile.

Beyond the seas, Chertkov had campaigned energetically for the cause. His subjugated master had long since delegated virtually all his powers to him. Not one line by Leo Tolstoy could appear without his agent's imprimatur. Chertkov alone dealt with the publishers, both Russian and foreign, chose translators, supervised their work, decided publication dates. Sole minister of a pontiff too old and feeble to contradict him, his power was increased by his utter sincerity. If he sometimes differed with Tolstoy, it was always in the name of Tolstoyism. He regarded himself as the incarnation of the doctrine. He was Tolstoy, relieved of his temptations, but also of his genius: a caricature, a reflection in a deforming mirror. A perfect refutation of the thesis he imagined he was defending. One torrid day, Tolstoy saw a mosquito land on Chertkov's bald pate and smacked it. The disciple looked reproachfully up at his master:

'What have you done, Leo Nikolayevich? You have killed a living creature! You should be ashamed of yourself!'

'My father became embarrassed,' wrote Sasha, who was present, 'and there was a moment of general uneasiness.' To justify his meekness with the aggressive Chertkov, Tolstoy said, 'That man has sacrificed everything for me. Not only did he give up his wealth and his position in society, but he has devoted all his energies to the publication of my works, he has been deported . . .'[1]

Thus, with Chertkov's devotion inspiring Tolstoy to gratitude and his gratitude, in turn, feeding Chertkov's demands, the more rights Chertkov claimed to Tolstoy's work, the more Tolstoy felt obliged to him. This readiness to see himself as someone's debtor expressed the old man's eternal tendency to self-accusation. He had felt guilty his whole life long: to his wife, because he could not live according to his ideal and give her the life she desired; to the peasants, because they were poor while he had everything he could ask for; to his readers, because he preached virtue while living in vice; to his disciples, because they were sent into exile while he stayed on at Yasnaya Polyana.

And although the minor disciples did not question Chertkov's supremacy, the most important ones, such as Biryukov or Aylmer Maude, Tolstoy's English translator, criticized his tyrannical and scheming nature. 'It was very painful to me,' wrote Biryukov, 'to see how he [Chertkov] tyrannized Tolstoy and sometimes forced him to do things that were completely at odds with his ideas. Tolstoy, who was sincerely attached to Chertkov, visibly suffered from this subjugation, but resigned himself without a murmur because it served the principles most dear to him.'[2] Maude commented: 'I never knew anyone with such a capacity for enforcing his will on others. Everybody connected with him either became his instrument, quarrelled with him or had to escape. . . . [But] discarding physical violence seemed to leave him the freer to employ mental coercion, and he was expert in its use.'[3] As Maurice Kues, the Swiss tutor, portrayed Chertkov: 'Together with a profound and sincere faith, the kind that leads people to renounce the world for an ideal, he had all the essential attributes of a sectarian: the blind inflexibility in matters of doctrine, and the aridity, the stubbornness and crudeness, refusing to recognize any subtleties or shades, and the heartless indifference to human contingencies.'

Everything vague, uncertain, profound, sensitive and tragic in the master corresponded, in the disciple, to narrow, restrictive conviction, a total barrenness of heart and a lack of tact that was all the more inexplicable in a man who had received such an elegant education. A believer in non-violence, he nevertheless considered that every means of imposing the ideas he served, short of actual physical force, was fair play. He would have sacrificed Tolstoy's peace of mind without a qualm to ensure the fame and posterity of the Tolstoyan cause. Instinctively, he knew that true apostles are a nuisance, because their acts may at any moment belie their words. Therefore, he thought, it was his duty to keep watch over the old man, filter all his rash remarks and writings, transform him into a statue, a public monument, and appoint himself custodian of it.

He spent his first days in Russia with Tolstoy; then, after a short trip back to England where he had business to clear up, he settled in the neighbourhood of Yasnaya Polyana. Sasha sold him half of her property at Telyatinki, and on it, two miles from the Tolstoy house, he built a big, very ugly, two-storey wooden villa, in which the rooms opened off a long corridor as in a hotel. The upper floor was set apart for the 'collaborators', that is, those performing any form of work at the Chertkovs' – secretaries, gardeners or dishwashers. These collaborators, of whom there were a score, all practising Tolstoyans, disdained creature comforts and cleanliness and slept in their coats on straw pallets on the floor. Downstairs, however, Chertkov and his wife, his mother and his son Dima occupied more decently furnished rooms. When the disciple showed his old master around the new residence, Tolstoy leaned over to his daughter Sasha and murmured: 'It pains me. ... It pains me to see Chertkov build such a house, too big and too handsome, and spend so much money on it!'

At that time Chertkov began an enormous anthology: *The Collected Thoughts of L. N. Tolstoy*. Hunting through Tolstoy's fiction and philosophy, letters and private diaries, for the best phrases to define and illustrate his doctrine, he hired a team of avant-garde intellectuals and placed them under the supervision of the philosopher F. A. Strakhov.* This little band spent the whole of every day going through the patriarch's works with a fine-tooth comb to cull out the main ideas. The day's siftings were then examined by Chertkov, who decided what to accept and what to reject. Sometimes he fulminated against a suspect passage, accusing Tolstoy of some anti-Tolstoyan heresy and demanding the deletion of a line or the replacement of one word by another, and Tolstoy generally consented to his inquisitor's dictates.

At noon, all the inhabitants at Telyatinki, among whom there were also some ordinary labourers, farm hands and shepherds, gathered around the big refectory table. Forty famished people held out their bowls to the steaming cauldrons. In theory, this Tolstoyan colony was governed by the sacred laws of equality, mutual assistance and love. But Sasha Tolstoy, who often dropped in for a neighbourly call, observed that the 'brothers' were divided into three classes, like passengers on a train. At the top of the table sat Chertkov and his family; in the middle were the *Collected Thoughts* team – secretaries and typists; and at the far end, the labourers and peasants and laundresses and night watchmen. Those in third class, who were given nothing but 'porridge in oil', envied those in the first class who fed on pork

* No relation to Tolstoy's friend, the critic N. N. Strakhov, who died in 1896.

chops, stew and preserves. Strange remarks were heard among the humble:

'Look at Alyosha, he's trying to get into first!'

'What about you, have you finished ogling the cutlets?'

Chertkov's mother, an aristocrat accustomed to associating with the court, lived by herself at Telyatinki, took tea in her room and demanded starched white cloths, silver tableware and porcelain cups; and Chertkov himself always had an air of elegance about him, in spite of his coarse canvas blouse and heavy shoes. His only son, Dima, on the other hand, was revoltingly filthy and undistinguished; his Tolstoyism was confined to refusing to study and wash. Covered with vermin, he scratched himself as he talked and was always sprawling on the sofas in his muddy boots. To his father's mild remonstrances he retorted that in order to become one with the muzhiks it was necessary 'to live simply in everything'.

Chertkov usually arrived at Yasnaya Polyana in the morning, while Tolstoy was working. It was a rule that no one could enter his study during his hours of creative activity without an invitation from the master; but this injunction, which was all very well for the hoi polloi, could not, of course, apply to the great disciple. He entered, peered over the old man's shoulder, read what he was writing, approved, criticized:

'It would be better to change that passage.'

'Ah, you think so?'⁴ murmured Tolstoy. And, irritated and uncomfortable, he gave in once again.

Chertkov often brought a photographer with him, who interrupted the writer to take photos for the Tolstoyan propaganda campaign. Sonya, who adored photography, began by rebuking her husband for allowing her fewer 'shots' than the outsider. But she soon had more serious cause for complaint. She quickly came to realize that by taking root at the source, Chertkov was intercepting everything that flowed from Tolstoy's pen. Not only did he see Lyovochka's articles before anybody else, he even appropriated the manuscripts. He had access to the diary day and night. Sonya was revolted and frightened by this intimacy. She felt that her rights were being usurped and her loyalty betrayed. In the past, she had been able to tell herself that in spite of their quarrels and misunderstandings, her husband was attached to her by his desire. But now she was a withered woman of sixty-four with badly deranged nerves, and he an octogenarian no longer tormented by sexual desire. When he looked at her, all he saw were her wrinkles. His respect for her as the mother of his children must also have vanished, after the 'Tanayev affair'. The pianist had returned to Yasnaya Polyana in February 1908. He had played the *Songs Without Words* for the countess; she wept. What had Lyovochka thought then? She was sure he had told all to his beloved confidant. Chertkov was probably well aware that she was no longer either bedfellow or advisor to her husband, and he was exploiting her past mistakes to consolidate his own domination. But she was not going to give up without a fight. She had not lived forty-six years of her life with a genius, sharing his work, keeping his house, copying his manuscripts, giving him children, nursing him and loving him, to step aside now for some mere valet of Tolstoyism. Her life was meaningless unless she could remain the admirable and irreplaceable consort of the great man to the end. It was her very *raison d'être* she was defending against Chertkov. But Chertkov was also defending his *raison d'être* against her: he, too, considered that his sacrifice and his efforts had earned him the exclusive right to represent Tolstoy in the eyes of posterity. For him, too, nothing else mattered except his place at the master's right hand. Certain he understood the essence of the doctrine better than anyone else, he wanted to preserve it from all corrupting influences. To do that, he thought, the author must be kept from backsliding under his wife's influence, now that he had grown old and feeble.

In this struggle for supremacy, the two antagonists began recruiting allies. Sonya would have liked to see all her children lined up behind her. But Sergey and Tanya maintained a judicious neutrality and Sasha was beyond recall; and although Ilya, Andrey, Michael and Leo sided with their mother, they most often did so by letter, for they seldom came to Yasnaya Polyana. On his side, Chertkov had the pianist Goldenweiser, Varvara Feokritova, who was helping with the copy-work, Dr Dushan Makovitsky, and the Tolstoyan secretaries. Last and most important, he won Sasha's confidence.

When he left Russia, she was a mere child of thirteen to whom he attached scant importance. Now she was a young woman of twenty-three, solidly built, with a heavy chest, rough gestures and a boyish appearance, who loved horses and dogs. Her broad face was illuminated by an unflinching, loyal gaze. She had a violent temper, was incapable of deception and was equally extreme in her loves and her hates. Since she adored her father she might, like Sonya, have resented Chertkov's intrusion in the house, and in fact his high-handed ways had offended her at first. But since the fight had to be waged two against one, she preferred to join forces with Chertkov against her mother rather than with her mother against Chertkov. For one thing, her mother had never liked her. There was more than a lack of spiritual rapport between them; there was positive physical incompatibility. As soon as they were in the same room they infuriated each other, provoked each other in an electrically charged atmosphere. The servants had told the girl that when Vanichka died the grief-maddened countess had moaned, 'Why him? Why not Sasha?' and Sasha never forgot that fatal sentence. Later, she had seen her mother making a fool of herself over Tanayev and humiliating the admirable man whose reputation ought to have been dearer than life to her. She had witnessed heart-rending quarrels between her parents. A hundred times, she thought that if she had been in Sonya's place, she would have known how to make Tolstoy happy. Perhaps she even imagined herself as his wife. Certainly, her father's age, which she could not help observing every day, removed any trace of ambiguity from her fantasy. But her passionate wish to care for him, serve him and protect him – he, so weary and good! – nonetheless proceeded from an unconfessed desire to supplant the unworthy partner by his side. She showed no interest in young men. She had no wish to marry. Her sole desire was to become ever more closely united with the justice-loving patriarch whom she adored without reservation – his ideas, his white hair, his smell, his moments of weakness and his fame. She took his side at every opportunity. Her brother-in-law Obolensky wrote, 'She used all her will and tenacity, and her growing influence over her father, to inflame their hostility [between Tolstoy and Sonya].'[5]

Tolstoy tried to ignore this struggle for possession of him. To preserve his own peace of mind he did everything to avoid scenes with both Sonya and Chertkov. He wanted to devote the little life he had left to meditation. His country's future disturbed him: 'We are on the verge of a gigantic upheaval, in which the Duma will play absolutely no part,' he said. 'There are only two weapons to use against the Russian government: bombs or love.'

In January 1909, Parthenios, bishop of Tula, came to call on him and made another vain attempt to woo him back to Orthodoxy. As the frustrated prelate was about to depart, Sonya drew him aside and asked whether it was true that the Church would refuse her husband a religious burial. Parthenios uncomfortably answered that he would have to obey the instructions of the Holy Synod, but added, with a benevolent smile, 'Nevertheless, countess, do send word to me in case Leo Nikolayevich should fall seriously ill.'

When his wife informed him of the bishop's helpful attitude, Tolstoy immediately imagined that there was a plot between her and the clergy, became alarmed and wrote in his diary, on 22 January 1909, 'I hope they are not going to invent some scheme to make people believe that I "repented" before I died! For this reason, I declare, and I repeat, that I could no more return to the Church and take communion on my deathbed than I could use profanity or look at obscene pictures on my deathbed; consequently *any reference to my repentance and communion before death would be untrue.*'

He felt that his strength was failing, which made him worry even more; he had a second attack of phlebitis in March. Was this the end? He honestly believed it was. But his temperature dropped again a week later and he immediately began to curse his wretched body, whose use he was nevertheless grateful to regain. Lying between cool sheets in his bed, he felt himself powerless, in spite of his eighty years, to prevent a return of sexual desire, and the thought horrified him. On 15 March he was preparing to breathe his last, and on 16 March he wrote in his diary:

It would be a hundred times easier to struggle against physical desire if carnal relations and the feelings that lead to them were not made to look poetical; if marriage were not presented as an admirable institution that makes people happy, whereas in at least nine thousand nine hundred and ninety-nine cases out of ten thousand, if not in all, it ruins their entire lives; if, from childhood to adulthood, people were persuaded that the sexual act (merely imagining a loved person in that posture is enough!) is an ignoble and bestial one that is meaningless unless it is uppermost in the minds of both partners that they are going to assume the heavy and complex responsibility of bearing a child and raising it to the best of their ability as a result of their intercourse.

Copying over these lines, Sasha must have been relieved to have no love in life but her father.

When the mild weather came he began to feel quite well again. On 31 March he was able to shuffle through the snow-covered garden. He was thinking of his sins, and particularly the most glaring of all, personified by Timothy, the natural child he had had by the peasant woman Axinya. In later years, she had married a muzhik, Ermil, but that had done nothing to alleviate Tolstoy's guilt. Timothy was a walking reproach, grooming the horses, climbing up on to the driver's seat, taking the reins: 'Where am I to drive you, master?' And what about the legitimate children, who knew all? What must they think of their father? A fornicator, a swine, a devil! 'I looked at my bare feet,' he wrote, 'and I remembered Axinya. She is still alive. They say that Timothy is my son, and I have never even asked his pardon, I have not repented, I am not repenting every hour of the day, and I set myself up to criticize others!'[6]

His convalescence was saddened by the departure of Chertkov, who was expelled from the government of Tula for 'subversive activities'. Notified of the decree on 6 March, the disciple managed to postpone his removal until the end of the month. He went to live with one of his aunts, at Krekshino, near Moscow. Sonya, secretly rejoicing to be rid of her rival, protested loudly against the arbitrary decision to punish him, and the gullible Tolstoy was touched by his wife's generous impulses. 'Ah, if only she could rise above herself!' he wrote. But some of his friends were wondering whether Chertkov's eviction might not have been prompted by the very person who was now taking his defence. She sent a circular letter to Russian and foreign newspapers:

'A fresh act of violence has been committed in our neighbourhood, and has stunned the entire population of the region. ... Chertkov's crime is plain: it is his friendship for Tolstoy, and the fervour with which he serves his ideas. And what ideas? That it is wrong to kill, that we should love everyone, that it is wrong to oppose evil by violence, that the bloodshed of the revolution must be stopped, etc. Chertkov's expulsion and the punishment inflicted on all who dare to read and encourage others to read Tolstoy's books are expressions of petty resentment towards an old man, whose creations have contributed to the glory of Russia. Everyone knows how dearly Leo Nikolayevich loves Chertkov. ... I have carefully observed Chertkov's life and teachings and although I do not share the majority of his views or those of Tolstoy, particularly as regards the denial of the Church, I can affirm that the object of all Chertkov's efforts has been to communicate the love of one's fellow man and the need for moral betterment to all. More than once he has dissuaded young peasants from revolution and other acts of violence.'

Neither Sonya's expostulations nor the efforts of Chertkov's influential friends succeeded in having the decision against him repealed. 'I miss Chertkov,' Tolstoy sorrowfully noted in his diary on 15 April 1909. He began to languish, like an abandoned wife. Sonya worried about him. She had grown so nervous that she could not sit still for more than ten minutes, or listen to a conversation or concentrate on a book. Life seemed a tissue of insoluble problems, and if she were to stand idle for one minute, sickness and poverty would immediately descend upon the family. To occupy her mind, she developed photographs. Every window ledge was cluttered with basins full of chemicals. She ran from one to the other, her fingers yellow with acid stains, muttering:

'Of course, Lyovochka has an easy life. He doesn't care about anything. He just goes peacefully on his way.'

Silent, patient, his muscles taut, Tolstoy waited out the storm. Watching his wife flutter about the house, he was torn between pity and anger. He had so much to say to her! But if he opened his mouth she would contradict him, and their conversation would end in a fight. To get some of the weight off his chest and maintain his self-possession, he resorted to a system of posthumous letters. 'You will receive this letter after I have ceased to be,' he wrote to Sonya on 13 May 1909. 'Pardon me for all the wrong I have done you throughout our long life together, especially in the early days. I have nothing to forgive you. You have been as your mother made you, a good and faithful wife, and an excellent, admirable mother. But because you were the way your mother made you, and remained that way and did not want to change, because you refused to try to improve yourself, to move ahead towards greater goodness and truth, because you clung with a kind of obstinacy to everything that was worst and most contrary to what I considered desirable, you did a great deal of harm to others and to yourself, you lowered yourself more and more until you reached the lamentable state you are in now.' This letter did not get beyond the state of a rough draft.

In June, Tolstoy went to Kochety to visit his son-in-law Sukhotin, escorted by Sonya, Dr Makovitsky, Gusev and a servant. At the station, a coach was waiting to drive them to the estate. Along the road, Tolstoy noticed that the peasants took their caps off as they passed. 'In their place,' he said, leaning towards Gusev, 'I would spit at the sight of these horses and these huge estates, while they don't even have a post to prop up their collapsing shanty.' After a tour of the countryside he wrote in his diary, 'A painful sensation of poverty, no, not poverty, of debasement, of animal apathy in the people. The revolutionaries' cruelty and madness are excusable. ... Conversation in French and tennis, and alongside them starving slaves in tatters, limp from overwork. I cannot bear it, I feel like running away.'

But he did not run away, and he even found life so pleasant in his daughter's house, where he was petted and spoiled and respected, that he let Sonya return to Yasnaya Polyana alone. But what Tanya had not told her mother was that Chertkov, forbidden to live in the government of Tula, was looking for a house along the frontier of the government of Orel, near Kochety. 'My plans are indefinite,' Tolstoy wrote to Sonya on 28 June, 'because I don't know yet whether I shall be able to meet Chertkov, which I desire as intensely as he does himself, poor man!' At last, the beloved disciple located an isba for rent in the village of Suvorovo, two miles from Kochety. The moment Tolstoy heard the news, he climbed on his horse and rode through the woods with pounding heart, straight to the little house in which the man of his life was awaiting him. 'Radiant meeting,' he was to record in his diary. He went to Suvorovo several times, always in the same state of exaltation. 'I shall put off my departure,' he said. Sonya, however, was beginning to complain and reluctantly he set out for Yasnaya Polyana on 3 July 1909.

The homecoming was stormy. Sonya began by upbraiding Lyovochka for seeing Chertkov behind her back. Then she rebuked him for deciding to attend the World Peace Congress in Stockholm.

'I must use my position to speak up and say what no one else, perhaps, would dare to say,' he explained to his wife.

She replied that at his age he had no business going so far away. She was probably right to fear the fatigues of the journey, the official receptions and lectures, but, as always, she had no diplomacy. At the slightest sign of disagreement she began to threaten, whine and sob. Sonya was suffering from neuralgia in her shoulder and claimed that he was to blame because he was mentally torturing her.

'Promise me you won't go. What does it cost you to promise?' she wailed.

'I cannot give it up, Sonya! It's my duty to go,' he said.

'Ow, ow! You're trying to kill me! You are a cruel man, you have no pity!'[7]

'If she could only know, realize,' he wrote on 12 July, 'how she alone is poisoning the last hours, days, months of my life!'

Sasha encouraged him to stand fast, but perhaps she only did so in order to contradict her mother; if Sonya had been urging him to attend the World Peace Congress, his daughter might well have been indignantly opposed to the idea. He no longer knew what to think or whom to follow, and nevertheless, obeying the dictates of his conscience, he prepared his address to the Stockholm Congress on the incompatibility between the Christian spirit and military service.

The conflict over the trip had not yet died down when another arose, more complex and more serious. Chertkov had allowed *Three Deaths* and *Childhood* to be published without payment of royalties, and as both had been written before 1881, they were covered by the agreement between Sonya and her husband under which she retained the copyright. At the instigation of her sons Ilya and Andrey, who were hard up just then, she talked of suing the overenterprising publishers. But her nephew Ivan Denisenko, who was a magistrate, advised her that she could not be sure of winning the case, and Tolstoy threatened to revoke his power of attorney if she went to court. In a white fury Sonya screamed at him:

'You don't care whether your family is driven out to beg! You want to give all your rights to Chertkov and let your grandchildren starve to death!'[8]

One scene followed another, each more violent and absurd than the last. 'They came to wake me up,' Tolstoy wrote on 21 July. 'Sonya had not slept all night. I went to her. It was quite insane. She claimed that Dushan [Makovitsky] had poisoned her, etc. I am exhausted, I can't take any more, I feel absolutely sick. I see that it is impossible for me to preserve a reasonable and affectionate attitude, utterly impossible. ... I have given serious thought to going away. All right; show your Christian spirit, it's now or never. I have a terrible desire to run away. I doubt that my presence here is of any use at all. A costly sacrifice, that serves no earthly purpose to anyone. Help me, my God, guide me! All I want is to do thy will, not mine.'

Now Sonya was demanding, not only that he stay away from the Congress, but also that he make her the sole heir to all his work, whether written before or after 1881. As he would not yield on either point, she lost all self-control and pretended to poison herself with morphine. He tore the flask out of her hand and threw it down the stairway, while she burst out sobbing. Back in his room he forced himself to think calmly, and finally decided to decline the invitation to Sweden. 'I went to tell her,' he wrote. 'She is pitiful; I feel truly sorry for her. But how instructive. All I had to do was a little work on myself. The moment I had made

this effort to master myself, everything was straightened
out.'[9]

Sonya calmed down a little, Sasha reproved her father
for capitulating, and Tolstoy saw that the truce would be
short-lived. While Dr Makovitsky was massaging his leg,
he said, 'I speak to you as to a close friend. I should like
to leave home and go somewhere, abroad. How can I
manage a passport? No one must know about it, at least for
a month.' Dr Makovitsky told him that it was possible to
arrange travel on those conditions, but that he had heard
the countess say that she now intended to go to Stockholm
with her husband. The old man frowned and growled that
that was mere noise: 'I do not want to be dependent upon
a hysterical creature,' he concluded. 'Her illness is mental,
not physical, it is based on egoism.'[10]

Fortunately, the arrival of Lyovochka's sister Marya Tolstoy on 29 July succeeded in quieting Sonya, for she loved
and respected the pious old woman, a nun in the convent of
Shamardino. More guests came, as in other years, to spend
a few days or weeks at Yasnaya Polyana. Despite his fatigue
and ill health, Tolstoy took pleasure in discussing art with
the painters Botkin and Parkhomenko (the latter was doing
a portrait of him), land reform with the Assembly representatives Tenishev and Maklakov, and mathematics and
geometry with the Russian physicist Tsinger. One evening
in August he was playing chess with Goldenweiser when a
police commissioner and his men arrived at the house. By
order of the minister of the interior, he had come to arrest
Gusev, the author's secretary. White with anger, Tolstoy demanded to see the warrant. It was presented: Gusev was
ordered into exile for two years, to Cherdyn in the government of Perm, for 'revolutionary propaganda and circulation of forbidden books' While the dogs barked at the
police wagon, the inhabitants of Yasnaya Polyana gathered
around the unfortunate young man. Tolstoy helped him to
pack his bag and Sasha slipped a copy of *War and
Peace* into it, which the fervent Tolstoyan still had not

read. Sister Marya, the nun, did not understand what was
going on, shook her old head under her tall black head-
dress and spat in the direction of the commissioner:

'Pah! Pah! Why do they arrest such a good man?'

After the police had escorted their prisoner away, Tolstoy swallowed his tears and shut himself up in his study.
The next day, 5 August, he wrote in his diary, 'Yesterday
the bandits came for Gusev and took him away. The parting was perfect, both his attitude towards us and that of
everyone else towards him. Yes, it was all perfect. Today I
wrote a protest about it.'

This protest was published in a great many newspapers,
and the minister of the interior instructed the high commissioner of police to convey his dissatisfaction to the
governor of Tula at the way in which his subordinates had
handled the case: 'Instead of arresting Gusev at the police
station, where you might easily have summoned him, the
police decided to enter Count L. Tolstoy's property and allowed the accused only one hour in which to prepare for his
departure. This behaviour on the part of the local authorities – utterly unjustified by the circumstances – has merely
fanned the flames of Count L. Tolstoy's notoriety (which
was, of course, to be expected) and provoked a series of emotional articles in the press designed to cast the said Count
Tolstoy in the role of a victim of arbitrary government
action.'

After Gusev's arrest, Tolstoy's desire to see Chertkov grew
more intense. Sonya held out for a while, but finally re-
lented and made preparations herself for her husband's
departure for Krekshino,* where the exiled disciple was still
living. On 3 September 1909, Tolstoy set out, with Sasha,
Dr Makovitsky and Ivan Sidorkov, a servant, at his side.
Such was the patriarch's fame that Pathé-News had applied
for permission to film him leaving Yasnaya Polyana.
Despite his refusal, reporters and photographers had hidden
in the bushes. A camera had been set up on the station plat-

* Krekshino was twenty-four miles from Moscow.

form and the cameraman was cranking away. Furious, the old man stomped past the lens with his head hunched between his shoulders.

Upon reaching Moscow he had to withstand a fresh onslaught of journalists. The travellers stayed in the old family home on Khamovnichesky Street, which Sasha found ugly, dilapidated and gloomy in comparison with the palace of her memory. Her brother Sergey and sister-in-law Marya now lived in it. The next day Tolstoy wanted to look at the city he had not seen for eight years. 'He was amazed at the tall houses, trolleys and traffic,' wrote Goldenweiser. 'He was frightened by the immense human anthill, and every step brought fresh confirmation of his long-standing hatred of so-called civilization.'

He did admit, however, that civilization had its good points, when he was taken to Zimmermann's Music Shop to hear Chopin played by Paderewski on the mechanical piano. 'It's marvellous! A wonder!' he said. 'How does it work?' He was still talking about it on the train to Krekshino. The day after he arrived at the Chertkovs', the mechanical piano joined him: a gift from Zimmermann! He did not have the strength to refuse it, and the instrument was installed in the big drawing-room.

But people had not come all that way to hear recorded music. A brotherhood of the faithful had gathered about the Chertkovs' and was waiting for the sanctifying visit of the messiah. Peasants, country schoolteachers, neighbours. ... The first days were spent in philosophical or educational discussions. As always in the Chertkov household, masters and servants ate together at the same table, to the great discomfiture of Ivan Sidorkov, the manservant Tolstoy had brought with him.

Back at Yasnaya Polyana, Sonya was already sorry she had let her husband fly away to his tryst with his disciple. Nothing good could come of their meeting. Tolstoy had not been a week at Krekshino before she turned up herself, and was greeted with forced enthusiasm. She had twisted her ankle on the way and the pain made her particularly shrewish; nothing pleased her in this sordid phalanstery. She peered at her tablemates through her lorgnette and when her eyes came to rest on Sidorkov, the servant, the poor wretch tried to shrink into his bench, hoping to offer a smaller target for his mistress's displeasure. However, she controlled her ill-humour during the ensuing days and tried to fit herself into her hosts' way of life. She did not dream that Lyovochka, encouraged by his disciple and daughter, had just drawn up a will bequeathing everything he had written after January 1881 to the public and instructing that all his manuscripts be turned over to Chertkov, who alone would decide the terms of their publication.

Tolstoy would have preferred to go straight back to Yasnaya Polyana, but Sonya insisted on stopping off in Moscow. At the station, the old man was again terrified by the crush of journalists and photographers. But on the evening of his arrival he consented to go to a film showing in the Arbat district. It was his first experience of an event of this type and he marvelled at the moving shapes on the screen. But the programme was disappointing. 'Views of places, a melodrama, and something comical at the end.' Leaving the theatre he said, 'What a wonderful instrument this could be in the schools, for studying geography and the way people live. But it will be prostituted. Like everything else.' The next day Sasha, accredited by him and by Chertkov, made a secret call on Muravyev, the lawyer, to submit the will drawn up at Krekshino. Muravyev read the paper through several times and shook his head:

'At first glance I would say this has absolutely no legal validity. I don't see how one can bequeath one's property to the public. I shall have to think about it and do some research into the law. Leave the paper with me, I will write to you.'

News of Tolstoy's presence in Moscow had already got around; reporters and busybodies were telephoning constantly to ask what train he was leaving on. This surge of interest and concern flattered Sonya's vanity and worried her daughter.

On the morning of 19 September 1909, a large hired landau came to Khamovnichesky Street to pick up Tolstoy and the rest of the party and take them to the station. The author, Sonya, Sasha and Chertkov got into it. Sergey and his wife, Maklakov and other friends climbed into cabs behind them. Dr Makovitsky was out of the country, so Sonya had found another doctor, named Berkenheim, to make the trip with her husband. A small crowd had gathered in the courtyard. There was even an old general standing in front of the porte-cochère. He removed his cap and bowed low as the landau went by. Strangers were lined along the road. As the team moved forward, heads were bared. A murmur rose up to the old man, who had tears in his eyes.

When the coach reached the Kursk station, point of departure for the Tula train, Sonya and Sasha exchanged alarmed glances. A crowd of several thousand was milling in the square. University students, high school girls, factory workers, housewives, befeathered socialites, soldiers, townsmen in bowler hats. The horses shied at the dark sea in front of them, dotted with pink spots. A shout rose up:

'There he is! Glory to Tolstoy! Hail the great warrior! Hurrah!'

The coach could not move. They had to dismount. Tolstoy gave his arm to his wife, who was limping. Chertkov, wearing a white panama hat, tried to clear a passage to the platform. Maklakov and a broad-shouldered policeman walked on either side of the author. Students were shouting:

'A chain! Make a chain!'

They seized each other by the hands. Buffeted on all sides, Tolstoy, pale and staring, his features tense, moved forward between two rows of green-striped blue caps. Young eyes were fixed upon him in blind devotion. Unknown mouths were yapping his name. He felt faint with joy and with the fear that the scene would end in a monstrous crush, as at Khodanka. At the entrance to the station the pressure became so great that the chain broke. Caught up in the mass, Tolstoy, Sonya and Sasha were tossed about like corks.

'In the name of heaven! Hold them back! Protect him!' cried the girl.

'For the love of Leo Nikolayevich! I beg you! You're crushing him!' wailed Sonya.

The platform on to which the travellers erupted violently was even more tightly packed with people. They had climbed on to the wagon roofs and shinnied up the posts supporting the glass roof. Bouquets of flowers were passed from hand to hand. The police were utterly powerless to control the situation. However, thanks to their sergeant escort, who thrust out right and left with his elbows, Tolstoy and Sonya, clinging to each other, somehow managed to edge their way towards the train. The old man was bent and staggering, his lower jaw was trembling; he was summoning all his strength to hold out until the end.

At last everyone was inside the train, safe and sound. Tolstoy fell on to the seat and closed his eyes. Now that the danger was past, Sonya kept repeating, with shining eyes and scarlet cheeks:

'Like kings! They followed us like kings!'

Chertkov mopped his face and fanned himself with his hat.

The crowd outside was still shouting:

'Hurrah! Hurrah! Glory!'

On Chertkov's counsel, Tolstoy went to the window. The roar grew louder. Voices rang out:

'Silence! Silence! He's going to speak!'

'Thank you,' Tolstoy said, in a steady voice. 'I did not expect so great a joy. I am deeply stirred by this expression of sympathy.... Thank you.'

'Thank you!' replied the crowd. 'Hurrah! All hail to our good Leo Nikolayevich!'

Cameramen were filming the scene. The train began to move. Standing at the window, Tolstoy continued to wave at the crowd dwindling into the distance, its voice melting

into the harsh grating of the wheels. He was surprised at
the pleasure this ovation had given him, for he thought he
had long since become immune to the temptation of pride.
He sat down again, happy and weary. He was given some
oatmeal porridge to revive him.

Chertkov got off at Serpukhov; he was not allowed inside
the government of Tula and so could go no farther. When
the train started up again, Tolstoy lay down to rest and had
a stroke. His pulse was so weak that the doctor seemed
worried. When they reached Yasenki he opened his eyes
and tried to speak, but his tongue was paralysed and he
could only utter disconnected words. He was carried to a
coach that was waiting at the station. Throughout the trip
home he stared into space, drawing circles with his fingers
and muttering:

'Moses . . . Pygmalion . . . Moses, Moses, religion . . .'

Leaning against him, Sonya covered him with a carriage
rug, rubbed his hands to keep them warm and prayed
through her tears.[11]

He was still delirious when the coach pulled up at the
door of Yasnaya Polyana.

'Hot water bottles, wine, leeches, an icepack for his head,'
prescribed the doctor.

Then, with Sonya's help, he began to undress the patient.
Seeing her husband half-naked, staring wildly with his
mouth hanging open, Sonya thought the end had come.
Then she remembered all the enemies around her. With
Lyovochka gone, she would be stripped, trampled underfoot. They would use the dead man's diaries to make her
out a shrew. And the person who would work hardest to
ruin her would surely be her youngest daughter, who had
been bewitched by that Chertkov! Quick, quick, she must
prevent them from carrying out their dirty plot. Beside herself with fatigue and anxiety, Sonya paced back and forth
around the bed, casting hunted glances on all sides.

'Lyovochka! Lyovochka!' she burst out. 'Where are the
keys?'

'I don't understand. Why?' stammered the old man.

'The keys, the keys to the box you keep your manuscripts in.'

'Maman, leave him alone, for pity's sake,' said Sasha. 'Don't force him to try to remember things.'

'But I have to have those keys,' Sonya went on. 'What if he died and they stole the manuscripts! ...'

'No one is going to steal them. Leave him alone.'[12]

The doctor gave him a hot enema. Then he administered an injection. Sonya moaned:

'Now the end has come!'

But later in the night, Tolstoy regained consciousness, gave a weary smile and dropped off to sleep. The next morning he wrote in his diary: 'Trip. Almost crushed to death by huge crowd. Chertkov saved me. I was afraid for Sonya and Sasha. ... Reached Yasenki. I remember getting into a coach but what happened after that, until 10 a.m. on 20 September, I have no recollection. They tell me I began to talk nonsense, then I lost consciousness. How easy and nice it would be to die like that!'[13]

The next day he went horseback-riding. And a few days later he returned to his articles and correspondence. He had just received a letter from an unknown Hindu, calling him the 'Titan of Russia' and signing himself 'a humble follower of your doctrine'. The Hindu's name was Mahatma Gandhi. Tolstoy replied, asking him to convey his expression of fellow-feeling to his 'beloved brothers, the Indian workers of the Transvaal'.

Back in Moscow, Chertkov was not standing idle. At his behest, the lawyer Muravyev was drafting a new will. He drew up several versions, all legally valid, and Strakhov agreed to take them to Yasnaya Polyana and submit them to Tolstoy for approval. The basic idea in all was the same: the copyrights had to be left to some specific person, so that this person, designated by name, could, by his refusal of the inheritance, cause the signer's works to revert to the public domain. The conspirators chose a day when they thought

Sonya would be in Moscow, but Strakhov found himself face to face with her in the train taking him to Yasenki. Sonya stared at him in icy mistrust, and he had difficulty in hiding his discomfort. They reached Yasnaya Polyana together. Taking Tolstoy aside, Strakhov showed him the papers drawn up by the lawyer. But in the meantime, the old man had changed his mind. He wondered whether it would not be better to abandon the idea of a will. 'This thing is preying on my mind,' he told his caller. 'It is not necessary to adopt any special measures for the propagation of my work. Take Christ as an example – strange as it may seem that I should pretend to compare myself with him – he did not worry about people appropriating his ideas for themselves, he boldly offered them to all and he mounted the cross for them. And his ideas were not lost. Besides, no word ever disappears without leaving a trace, if it expresses some truth and the man who spoke it had faith in its truth.'

Then Strakhov explained that if he did not conform to the legal regulations governing inheritance, and if he did not provide otherwise, all his copyrights would be inherited by his family. What a storm that would arouse among the Tolstoyans, to hear that after condemning all property, their master had not had the courage to deprive his wife and children of the income from a work which, by its very essence, was destined to become public property. Shaken by this argument, Tolstoy withdrew to think it over. After a few hours, he announced to Strakhov that he had reached his decision. Trusting the integrity of his daughter Sasha, he would bequeath his copyrights to her, on condition that she turn them over at once 'to the people'. This decision would apply not only to works written after 1881, but also to those published prior to that date.

When these arrangements were explained to Sasha, she protested that she was unworthy, and that her mother, sister and brother would hate her for depriving them of the inheritance. But she yielded to her father's urging. At heart, she was proud to be the one chosen to carry out this great mission. The prospect of seeing her mother choking with jealousy was compensation enough for all the storms ahead. Tolstoy made her promise that after his death she would use the money from the sale of his posthumous works to repurchase the land at Yasnaya Polyana from Sonya and give it to the muzhiks. Strakhov left, satisfied.

On 1 November he came back with Goldenweiser and the new text, whereby Alexandra Lvovna Tolstoy (Sasha) became the sole heiress to her father's copyrights. The two men arrived during the night. Everyone in the house was asleep except Tolstoy. He received Chertkov's emissaries in his bedroom, read the document over and copied it out in their presence. But he kept starting up at every moment, listening. Sonya was a light sleeper. Wasn't she suddenly going to burst through the door in her nightgown with a lamp in her hand and unmask the conspirators? Several times he went to make sure no one was hiding behind the door. In spite of the reassurances of Goldenweiser and Strakhov, he felt he was doing something wrong. After he signed the paper, the two men witnessed it and Strakhov put it in his portfolio to take back to Moscow.

The next day, Sonya, suspecting nothing, behaved very cordially to the two guests. Strakhov had pangs of remorse; but he consoled himself with the thought that the night before he had, in his own words, successfully completed an undertaking destined to have historic consequences.

In January 1910, young Dorik Sukhotin – Tanya's stepson, who was staying at Yasnaya Polyana – came down with measles, and Sasha, who often went to see him in his bedroom next to the 'Remington room', caught them from him. But her case was complicated by double pneumonia. She began to cough blood. Tolstoy spent anguished hours by her side. When she asked for a drink, he held out the glass in his trembling old hand. 'The water spilled out and ran down my chin,' she wrote. 'I covered his dear hand with kisses. He sobbed and took hold of my long hand that had grown so thin. I felt the touch of his beard and my hand was moist.'

In March she was able to get out of bed. But the doctors, fearing consumption, advised her to convalesce in the Crimea. Two months, they said, should bring back her strength. She was terrified at the thought of being away from her father for so long: 'What if I were never to see him again?' They insisted. It was decided that her friend Varvara Feokritova would go with her. On 13 April, the day of departure, Tolstoy wept. 'I am sad, I don't know what to do with myself,' he wrote in his diary the next day. 'Sasha has gone. I love her, I miss her, not for the work she does but because of her soul. ... The tears came to my eyes, out of weakness. In the night, a physical oppression that affected my mind, too. ... I must not write any more. I think I have done all I can in that field. And yet, I want to write, I want terribly to write. ... It is midnight. Going to bed. Still in a bad frame of mind. Look out! Leo Nikolayevich, hang on!'

He soon found that with his daughter gone, the atmosphere of Yasnaya Polyana became more bearable. Sasha's absence and Chertkov's enforced removal restored Sonya to a semblance of balance. She still complained of her health (migraine, nervous fatigue, fear of losing her sight), kept producing shirts and hats which no one needed, wailed that her sons were spending too much of her money, wore herself out preparing an edition of her husband's *Complete Works* in twenty-eight volumes, wrote a story of her life and predicted that the entire family would end in the poorhouse; but as long as her agitation and lamentations remained within these familiar limits, Tolstoy did not suffer from them. Perhaps he would even have felt lost in more peaceful surroundings. He corresponded regularly with Sasha, told her everything he did and assured her of his affection.

'You are so near to my heart, dear Sasha, that I cannot help writing to you every day.' (24 April 1910.) 'No letter from you today, my dear friend Sasha, but I want to write to you anyway.' (25 April.) 'How are you spending your time? I would like to think that you are striving for spiritual improvement there, too. That is more important than anything else. Even though you're young, you can do it, and you must!' (End of April.)

As in every other year, the advent of the warm weather brought a flood of visitors to Yasnaya Polyana. Tolstoy wore himself out seeing them. Sometimes his old sense of social injustice welled up and he rushed to his study, seized his diary and wrote: 'No dinner. Aching pain caused by a sense of the shameful life I live surrounded by people who work and slave and only just manage to avoid dying of cold and hunger, they and their families. Yesterday, fifteen people gorging themselves on pancakes, and five or six fathers and mothers slaving away, breaking their necks to get all that swill ready and on the table. ... Also yesterday, riding past some stonecutters, I suffered the torments of a soldier running the gauntlet.' [14] Almost every day he found some pretext for being upset or miserable. One time it was a young guest in schoolboy uniform who confessed that he was a spy paid by the police to denounce terrorists; another time it was a real revolutionary, come to reproach him for not 'fighting with bombs'; another time it was a Tolstoyan accusing him of living on his family like a parasitic Croesus; another time it was two Japanese who, thinking it would make him happy, told him how much they admired the Christian civilization. One evening the Japanese accompanied him to the village, where he and his friends were going to show the peasants one of the wonders of the modern world, a phonograph. Men, women and children came out of their isbas and assembled on the green. From the box the joyful sounds of a balalaika orchestra issued forth. The muzhiks looked at each other in amazement. Then, urged on by the master, they began to dance a hopak. The Japanese were in ecstasy. Soon after they left, Chertkov's son and the writer Sergeyenko arrived. Rejoicing to see these two emissaries, reminders of his best friend, Tolstoy wrote in his diary, 'I felt a breath of Chertkov pass. It is very pleasant. Going to bed.' [15]

In spite of this steady stream of visitors, he worked hard. A story, *The Khodanka*, articles, the introduction to *The Ways of Life*, hundreds of letters. ... He was corresponding with Bernard Shaw, whose plays he considered 'crude and untrue'; with Gandhi, whom he deeply admired, 'except for his Hindu patriotism, which spoils everything'; with strangers, who criticized him or asked him for advice. To replace Gusev as his secretary, Chertkov had recommended Valentin Fyodorovich Bulgakov, a sensitive, cultivated young man whom the master liked for his integrity and gentle manner. Why, he even showed sympathy for Sonya's complaints! 'They' had told him she was selfish, devious and domineering, but he found her simple and understanding. His worship of Tolstoy did not prevent him from viewing the protagonists in the drama impartially. Of course, he, too, kept a diary. Before his departure for Yasnaya Polyana, Sergeyenko had supplied him with specially made notebooks and carbon paper to place between the pages. He was to write his daily notes in invisible ink, tear off the copy along the dotted line and send it to Krekshino; by this means, Chertkov hoped to be informed of Tolstoy's every word and deed by a reliable witness. However, Bulgakov soon lost patience with this form of amusement, which was altogether too much like espionage; he continued to keep his diary, but stopped sending secret reports to his 'chiefs'.

He liked Yasnaya Polyana, he found it 'an aristocratic place'. Every morning, when he saw Tolstoy in his rough white linen blouse, with his hands stuck through his belt, his broad white beard and keen eyes, he experienced a feeling of religious joy and awe. The master often took him along on his walks, and questioned him, eager to learn the opinions of a boy of twenty-four on the problems that were tormenting him. Although he despised 'novelty' and 'progress', the old man marvelled at the new technical inventions. Within a few months he had been introduced to the phonograph, the mechanical piano and the cinema. On a visit to Yasnaya Polyana, the author Leonid Andreyev spoke of the future of the latter device and Tolstoy said he would certainly write a scenario for a film. At dinner the following day, he returned to the subject, and said he had been thinking about it all night:

'Just imagine, with this technique one could reach huge masses of people, all the peoples of the earth! ... One could write four, five, ten, fifteen films.'[16]

A few days later he went out to the Kiev road to watch the Moscow–Orel automobile race. He had never seen these diabolical contraptions before, rumbling, coughing, spitting, shrouded in smoke and dust. The drivers, wearing their sporty caps and huge goggles, recognized him and cheered. One of them stopped to let Tolstoy peer into the motor; he shook his head and wished the driver good luck.

'I suppose,' he later said to Bulgakov, 'I will not live to see airplanes. But those fellows [pointing to the village children] will certainly fly. Personally, I would rather see them till the soil or wash clothes.'

And that same evening, he anxiously confided to Dr Makovitsky:

'Automobiles, in our Russian world. There are people who have no shoes, and here are automobiles costing twelve thousand roubles.'[17]

The next day he was to leave for his daughter Tanya's home at Kochety, with Bulgakov and Dr Makovitsky. Sonya, who was not going with them, helped him to pack. At the station a cameraman was grinding feverishly away. Although the party had bought third-class tickets, they had to travel in second class because all the third-class compartments were full. Tolstoy worried over this irregularity and mistakenly supposed that it was another plot of Sonya's, to spare him added fatigue.

'It's illegal, illegal,' he repeated irritably.

He protested so vociferously that one of the conductors

finally found him a seat in a third-class car. Once he was settled on the hard bench, he calmed down and began to stare out into the immensity of the landscape. Sitting opposite him, Bulgakov observed him with love. 'His head and the expression of his face and eyes and lips were strange and wonderful!' he wrote. 'The depth of his soul shone out of his features. It was not his wicker travelling hamper, not that third-class compartment that was the right setting for him – it was the whole vast pale blue sky which this great man sat staring out at unwaveringly.' [18]

[31]

Last Will and
Testament

THE first few days at Kochety were sheer delight. For Tolstoy, far from Sonya, nature was beautiful, people were kind and his cares light as air. His letters to Sasha, still convalescing on the shores of the Black Sea, were all variations on a new theme: the joy of living. 'I walk in the park, the nightingales are singing all around me, the lilies-of-the-valley are so lovely that I cannot refrain from picking some and my joyful soul is filled with good feelings, each better than the last.'

After this burst of light-heartedness, however, his old remorse came back to him: 'Once again I am painfully oppressed by the luxury and idleness of the rich,' he wrote. 'Everybody is working, but not I. Painful, painful ...'[1] And he would run to write a letter to Sasha: 'I feel an increasing need to describe all the folly and ignominy of our lives of luxury and brutality, surrounded by starving, half-naked people being eaten alive by vermin, living in chicken coops.'[2]

He was suspicious of the very kindness some masters showed towards their servants or peasants. It was merely a disguised form of domination, worse than outright despotism. The charms of Kochety were beginning to pall when – giving new life to everything – Chertkov arrived. The two men embraced tearfully. For eight days they engaged in a sweeping exchange of confidences, punctuated by the discreet click of camera shutters. Some of the master's photos were taken by Chertkov himself, others by a photographer he had chosen. They parted on 20 May, promising to meet again soon.

A week after his return to Yasnaya Polyana, Tolstoy had
the joy of welcoming Sasha back from the Crimea, completely cured, hale and hearty, with her hair cropped short
like a boy's (her head had been shaved during her illness),
and her faithful Varvara Feokritova by her side. At the sight
of these two minions of Chertkov, Sonya's anxiety welled up
again. While Sasha's big manly hands were moving over the
keyboard of the Remington, her mother prowled about the
house, scolding the servants and feeling an outcast in her
own home. She announced to one and all that she was exhausted, that nobody ever gave a thought to her, that the
management of the estate was too much for a woman of
sixty-six. 'Who's forcing you to do it?' said Tolstoy. He
recommended a trip, to take her mind off her troubles.
'You're driving me away!' she cried. 'You're trying to get
rid of me!' And she fled, uttering dire imprecations. People
were sent after her, on foot and horseback. They found her
some distance from the house, sitting at the bottom of a
ditch. She came back in a dogcart, relaxed and full of forgiveness.

A second incident followed immediately upon the first,
this time caused by the young Circassian guard, Akhmet,
whom Sonya had hired some months before to guard the
estate in place of the police agents furnished by the governor until 1909. Akhmet cut an imposing figure in his black
tunic decorated with cartridge belts, a sword at his side and
a Persian-lamb cap perched on his head. But he was a narrow-minded brute, who stopped the peasants from walking
on the 'lord's' woods and fields, terrorized them with threats
and occasionally beat them and molested their wives. On
4 June, he arrested a muzhik, Vlasov – a former pupil of
Tolstoy's – for stealing a sapling, and dragged him, tied to
his knout, all the way to the house to be reprimanded by the
countess. Hearing of this, Tolstoy felt 'a weight on his
heart'. He would not allow a savage Circassian in Sonya's
employ to interfere with a peasant he knew and loved, on
account of 'a branch he had picked up without permission'.

He asked Sonya to fire the guard, whose presence was, moreover, an insult to his theories on the evils of property. She refused, wept and wrote in her diary: 'He is torturing himself and he is torturing me.' He, meanwhile, was writing: 'Emotions, upsets. It's very painful. Keep wanting to cry.' The next day, feeling ill, he came home from his walk earlier than usual and lay down, his pulse weak and his memory uncertain. Seeing how feeble he had become, Sonya did not have the heart to try to prevent him from going to spend a few days in Chertkov's new home, at Meshcherskoye, near Moscow. This represented such a sacrifice for her that after making it she wondered what demon had induced her to give in.

He left on 12 June, with Sasha, Dr Makovitsky and Bulgakov. Varvara Feokritova stayed on at Yasnaya Polyana, ostensibly to keep Sonya company, but actually to guard her and see that she remained calm. Once again, on meeting Chertkov, Tolstoy felt ten years younger. The Meshcherskoye house was dirty and run-down and, to his satisfaction, full of Tolstoyans. With Chertkov and Sasha, he visited a nearby insane asylum, talked to the inmates, questioned the doctors and attended film projections for the patients. 'They were showing stupid melodramas on the screen,' wrote Sasha. 'In the darkness I could make out my father's white shirt and beard; I felt the hall around me full of crazy people and I wanted to run away as fast as I could. But my father was talking away to Chertkov, as calm as could be, and he did not even seem to sense the danger. I remember him saying on several occasions that madness is only an extreme form of egoism – the egoism of a person who concentrates all his thoughts and interest upon himself.' Perhaps he had Sonya in mind when he formulated that definition. But just then he felt so much at peace that the thought of his private life evoked nothing but forbearance and understanding. 'I must try to fight Sonya consciously, with kindness and love,' he wrote in his diary on 20 June. 'At a distance, it seems possible. I must try to succeed at close quarters.' And to her he wrote: 'How time flies! Only five days before we leave. We have decided to start out on the twenty-fifth. It is nice to be away visiting, but it is also nice to be at home. Farewell, dear Sonya, I embrace you!' Diplomatically, he served up the honey before the gall; in a postscript, he told his wife the 'good news' that the government was allowing Chertkov to return to Telyatinki – almost next-door to Yasnaya Polyana – to visit his mother for a few days.

Back at Yasnaya Polyana, meanwhile, Sonya was finding her solitude oppressive. Offended because Chertkov had invited her to Meshcherskoye in the vaguest of terms and had not even offered her a room of her own, she brooded over her grievances and orchestrated her ire. When she heard that 'the monster' would be in the neighbourhood again, she suddenly lost control. Her head on fire, she ordered Varvara Feokritova to cable her husband: 'Sofya Andreyevna's nerves in very bad state. Insomnia, weeping, pulse: one hundred. Please telegraph. Varvara.' Another telegram followed a few hours later, signed by Sonya herself, on the night of 22–23 June: 'Entreat you hurry back – on twenty-third.' Sasha, who guessed that her mother was not seriously ill, begged her father not to set their departure ahead, especially since they were expecting the cellist Erdenko that day. Tolstoy obeyed, and wired back: 'More convenient return tomorrow. But if indispensable will come tonight.' The 'more convenient' revolted Sonya. 'I recognize Chertkov's cold hand there,' she cried, and ordered Varvara Feokritova to reply immediately, with the command: 'Indispensable. Varvara.'

Then, in her nightgown, with hair undone and breast heaving with sobs, she flung herself upon her diary and poured out her despair.

What is the matter with me? Hysteria, attack of nerves, cramps in the chest, is it the beginning of madness? I don't know. . . . This depression came over me as a result of Leo Nikolayevich's long absence. He has developed a revolting, senile crush on

Chertkov (falling for men was more in his line as a boy!) and now he is absolutely at that man's beck and call. Chertkov is what is keeping us apart. He is an ingenious, despotic, heartless man, who has reached a far more advantageous and distinguished position in life as Tolstoy's intimate friend than he could have had as an insignificant, silly officer of the guards. I am wildly jealous of Chertkov where Tolstoy is concerned. I feel he has stripped me of the one thing that has kept me alive for forty-eight years. ... Every form of suicide has crossed my mind. ... I am thinking of going to Stolbova and lying down under the train on which it would be *convenient* for Leo Nikolayevich to come home. ... I have consulted Florinsky's book on medicine to see what the effects of opium poisoning would be. First excitement, then lethargy. *No antidote.* I must write to my husband who has just been to an insane asylum and ask him to find out all the details about the place, since Chertkov will undoubtedly find it *convenient* to have me committed to it.

But whether she killed herself or was institutionalized, all she really cared about was seeing that Chertkov was punished for his devilry. One of her sons would make sure that vengeance was done. 'You, Andryushka,' she went on in her diary, 'avenge your mother's death; you loved her, you saw through her enemy!'

When he reached home at ten o'clock that evening, Tolstoy found his wife in bed in a state of feverish agitation. He spent part of the night with her, and then went to write in his notebook. 'It's worse than I expected. Nervous breakdown and over excitement. Indescribable. I did not behave particularly badly, but not very well either, I was not kind.'

Despite Tolstoy's efforts to avoid further disputes, Sonya attacked him at every turn with his 'love' for Chertkov, and wept continually. One morning she was found on her knees behind a cupboard in the library with a vial of opium in her hand. She sobbed:

'Just one little swallow!'

'However,' wrote Sasha with pitiless objectivity, 'she waved the vial of opium around her mouth but did not drink any. At first I tried to take it away from her, then I suddenly felt disgusted.'

After being given a no-nonsense treatment by her daughter and admonished by Dr Makovitsky, she dried her tears and promised to control herself in future. The next day, 26 June, she asked her husband to show her what he had written about her in his last diary. He reluctantly consented. Opening the notebook, she came across the entry for 20 June: 'I must try to fight Sonya consciously, with kindness and love.' She immediately flew into a rage:

'Why do you say you want to fight me? What have I done wrong?'

Refusing to listen to Tolstoy's explanations, she demanded to know where the diaries of the previous ten years had gone. He was eventually forced to admit that Chertkov had them. She ordered him to tell her where Chertkov had put them and he answered that he had no idea. Then she rushed out into the garden, wandered about under driving rain and came back soaked to the skin. When her husband urged her to change her clothes, she cried:

'No, I shall stay like this, I'll catch cold and die! ... That's all they want! ... I'm going to have an attack this very minute! ...'

Tolstoy did not sleep at all that night, and the next day he consulted Dr Korsakov's treatise on psychiatry. On every page he seemed to recognize some trait of Sonya's. 'The insane are always better at achieving their purposes than the sane,' he noted on 27 June, 'because they have no morality to hold them back, neither shame nor truth nor conscience, nor even fear.' He dreaded the effect upon Sonya of the news that Chertkov would be in the neighbourhood for any length of time – even temporarily. He was expected at any moment. Returning from Telyatinki in the evening of the twenty-seventh, Bulgakov announced that the disciple and his mother had arrived. Sonya was terrified by the thought that the 'devil' had returned to his lair, and she determined to take Lyovochka away – anywhere, so long as he was removed from the sphere of evil radiation. In a few hours she persuaded him to go with her to Nikolskoye to visit their son Sergey, whose birthday it was. At the same time, she asked him to alter the description of the hero's wife in *By Mistake*, one of his stories, because she bore a physical resemblance to the author's wife. Tolstoy obediently changed a few words and the 'forceful black-eyed brunette' became a 'blue-eyed blonde'.

Their departure for Nikolskoye was set for the following day, 28 June. That morning, while everyone in the house was still asleep, Chertkov came gliding furtively through the mists to renew his acquaintance with his idol's haunts. He brought a letter, intended to placate Sonya: 'I have heard that you have recently been speaking of me as an enemy. I think this feeling can be attributed to a passing irritation, caused by some misunderstanding that a face-to-face conversation would soon dispel, like a bad dream. Leo Niko-layevich contains in himself so many things that represent life's most precious treasures for both you and me that a solid and indestructible bond must inevitably have been forged between us.' He was about to hand this letter to a servant when Tolstoy, catching sight of him through the window, came out of his bedroom, embraced him and led him away on tiptoe into the grounds. Walking and talking with his disciple, he suddenly noticed that they were headed towards Yasenki, and the family was to catch the train at Zasyeka. By the time they had returned to the house, Sonya had already left in a coach. He caught up with her in Chertkov's trap, excused himself like a guilty schoolboy, climbed up beside her and patiently bore her ill-humour. During the entire train trip, whenever he got out to stretch his legs at a station, Sonya got out with him.

'I am with you, I shall go with you every time,' she said, 'otherwise, you might stay behind on the platform on purpose.'

At Sergey's house at Nikolskoye there were too many people and too much noise, and the weary old man was sorry he had come. Sonya, however, who cared about appearances, put on a show of gaiety at her son's; but as soon as she returned to Yasnaya Polyana, on 30 June, she abandoned herself once more to her *idée fixe*: the private diaries of the last ten years. A visit from Chertkov on 1 July drove her into a frenzy. The sight of him affected her brain like an electric shock. Her blood boiled, her mind began to race, she lost all sense of propriety. His behaviour, however, was always icily correct. In the evening, after paying his respects to the mistress of the house, he withdrew with Tolstoy and Sasha into the author's study. Sonya was certain that the triumvirate was conspiring against her, and in effect, behind the closed doors, father, daughter and disciple were talking in hushed tones of the will and the diaries. After a moment, Sasha heard a rustle outside the balcony door: Sonya was there, in the dark, straining to hear. She had taken off her shoes to make less noise. She screamed:

'Another plot against me!'

Tolstoy was so upset by this nocturnal apparition that Sasha took him into the next room. Alone with Chertkov, Sonya, her eyes glittering with hatred, demanded to know where the diaries were and by what right he was keeping them. Unabashed, Chertkov counterattacked. His courtesy vanished. In a cutting voice he informed Sonya that she had no business interfering between master and disciple: 'What are you afraid of? That I shall use the diaries to unmask you? Had I wanted to, I could have ruined you and your family too, without the slightest difficulty. The only thing that has stopped me is my affection for Leo Nikolayevich.' Moving towards the door, he added, 'If I had a wife like you, I would have blown my brains out long ago or gone to America.'[3]

Sonya caught up with him and, in the presence of her husband and daughter, insisted that he at least promise to return the diaries when asked to produce them.

'Yes,' said Chertkov, 'but I will give them to Leo Nikolayevich, not to you.'

He wrote out the following note to Tolstoy:

'In view of your wish to resume possession of the diaries which you gave me to keep, asking me to delete from them the passages you had marked, I shall hasten to finish this work and shall return the diaries to you immediately thereafter.'

'And now,' said Sonya, 'I want Leo Nikolayevich to give me a paper promising to turn the diaries over to me!'

'That's all we need!' exclaimed Tolstoy. 'A husband signing papers to his wife.'

He muttered:

'I promised that you would have those diaries and you'll have them.'

He was so obviously insincere that Sonya wrote in her own diary, 'I know there is only one purpose behind all those notes and promises: to hoodwink me. Chertkov will drag out his imaginary work on the diaries and won't ever give them to anyone.'

But the following day, she played the gracious hostess to Chertkov's mother, 'a very handsome woman, not quite normal, and extremely aged,' who talked at length of her soul, her mourning, her land, and believed that Christ dwelled in her entrails. Sonya spent a pleasant day with her, but suffered agonies to see Chertkov sitting on a low sofa next to Lyovochka. They were whispering away, their knees were almost touching. 'They were so happy in their intimacy together,' she wrote, 'and I was in torments of spite and jealousy.'[4] And that evening, to top off all her other sufferings, the conversation turned to suicide and madness. Sonya interrupted:

'Can't we change the subject?'

'Really, Sonya, I don't understand you,' said Tolstoy. 'We're talking about my article!'

'You did it on purpose! I wasn't in the room a minute before you brought up the subject again. You might have a little more consideration!'

She could not sleep that night, she was haunted by the

vision of Chertkov sitting so close to Lyovochka. Her over-wrought imagination produced pictures of the white-bearded old man and his corpulent disciple united in a monstrous intercourse.

In spite of her fatigue, by dawn she had determined to continue the battle. Oozing duplicity, she made a formal re-turn call on Chertkov's mother, but went on afterwards to see Mrs Zvegintsev, who had a great deal of influence in St Petersburg, and asked her to persuade the authorities to banish Chertkov from the government of Tula again. Out of ten tries, she thought, one at least would have to work. Also, her son Leo, who had recently arrived at Yasnaya Polyana, was some consolation to her. He was an anti-Tol-stoyan of long standing, who had already put Chertkov in his place once and even called him an imbecile for trying to preach to him. The moment seemed propitious for a direct attack.

During the night of 10–11 July, Sonya again demanded that Lyovochka give her the diaries Chertkov was keeping. She swept up and down the balcony outside her husband's bedroom, threatening and pleading until he begged her to go away and let him get some sleep. Then she accused him of wanting to drive her away, cried out, 'I'll kill Chertkov!' and rushed half-naked into the grounds. After some time passed without any sign of her, the old man began to worry; in his nightshirt, candle in hand, he went to wake his son Leo and Dr Makovitsky and sent them out in search of the poor woman. They found her lying full length in the wet grass. She told them she had been driven away 'like a dog' and would kill herself unless her husband came in person to ask her to go back to the house. Leo, who was always spoiling for a fight, ran to tell his father that he had no right to lie in his warm bed indoors while his abandoned, insulted wife was threatening to kill herself. Dragged along by his forty-year-old son, Tolstoy reluctantly trailed into the grounds. After soothing Sonya and bringing her back to the house, he wrote in his diary, 'Only just alive, only just.

Dreadful night. Until four in the morning. Leo was the
worst of them all. He shouted at me as though I were a boy
and ordered me to fetch Sonya back from the garden.' The
couple went to sleep, shattered, each in his own room.

To offset Leo's pernicious influence on his mother, Chertkov sent an urgent appeal to the calm and equable Tanya,
who arrived with her husband on 12 July, and was horrified
to see how far relations between her parents had deteriorated within a few weeks. Sonya, looking old and haggard,
stared about her like a madwoman; Tolstoy was bent and
shrivelled, and whenever he wasn't paying attention, his
face assumed an expression of childish bewilderment.
Tanya, who was twenty years older than Sasha, urged her to
be more tolerant, but could not alter the girl's inflexible
determination to treat their mother as a fake. And indeed,
once the crisis was past, Sonya quickly became her old self
again. The very day of the Sukhotins' arrival, she was trying
to win the secretary, Bulgakov, to her side. After offering to
drive the young man over to the Chertkov home in her trap,
she suddenly turned a tear-stained face to him and begged
him to make them give her back the diaries.

'Let them copy them all,' she said, 'every word. But at
least, let them give back Leo Nikolayevich's original manuscripts to me. I used to be the person who kept the diaries.
Tell Chertkov that if he gives them back to me, I shall
grow calm again. I will like him again, and he can come to
see us as he used to do and we will work together to serve
Leo Nikolayevich. Will you tell him? For the love of God,
will you tell him? . . .'

Although a staunch Tolstoyan, the boy was shaken.
'There was absolutely nothing fake about her tears or her
emotion,' he wrote. 'I confess I was deeply moved. At any
price, even if it meant returning the manuscripts to Sonya
Andreyevna, or by any other means, I wanted peace to be
restored to Yasnaya Polyana.'

When they reached Telyatinki, Sonya was ceremoniously
received by the great disciple's mother, while Bulgakov re-

tired with Chertkov and his advisor Sergeyenko and explained that, in all fairness, they must consent to the countess's request.

'What?' cried Chertkov, rolling his eyes. 'Have you told her where the diaries are?'

He stuck out his tongue in fury. His handsome, regular features were distorted into a gargoyle's mask. Bulgakov protested that he was unable to tell anything because he didn't know anything. Reassured, Chertkov told him, 'Go, now. Go have tea next door. You must be hungry.' He pushed him out and closed the door behind him. After consultation, he and Sergeyenko decided to hold their ground. But Tolstoy was beginning to weaken. 'She is suffering, poor thing,' he wrote on 12 July, 'and it is no effort for me to feel sorry for her and love her at the same time.'

Was he merely battle-weary, or was this an attempt to conform to his doctrine of non-resistance? In all probability, his philosophical principles were conveniently summoned to cover up his wavering will. He wanted peace and quiet so badly! Two days later it was decided: he would take the diaries back from Chertkov; but, instead of giving them to Sonya, he would deposit them in a bank in Tula, where they would remain until his death. To make sure his intentions were clear, he wrote a long letter to his wife:

1. I shall give no one the diary I am now writing, and shall keep it with me.

2. I shall take back my earlier diaries from Chertkov and shall keep them myself, probably in a bank.

3. If you are worried lest future biographers who may be unfriendly to you should make use of the pages in my diary which were written in the heat of the moment and record all our conflicts and quarrels, I would remind you, first of all, that such expressions of fleeting emotion, in my diary as in yours, cannot pretend to give a true picture of our relations; but if you are still afraid, I shall be happy to take this opportunity to say, in my diary or in this letter, what my true relations with you are, and my view of your life.

My relations with you and my view of your life are as follows: as I loved you when I was young, so I never stopped loving you in spite of the many causes of estrangement between us, and so I love you now. Leaving aside the cessation of our conjugal relations (a fact that could but add to the sincerity of our expressions of true love), those causes were as follows: first, my increasing withdrawal from society, whereas you neither would nor could forgo it, because the principles which led me to adopt my convictions were fundamentally opposed to yours: this is perfectly natural and I cannot hold it against you. ... In recent years, you have grown more and more irritable, despotic and uncontrollable. This could not fail to inhibit any display of feeling on my part, if not the feelings themselves. That is the second point. And in the third place, the principal, fatal cause, was that of which we are both equally innocent: our totally opposite ideas of the meaning and purpose of existence. For me property is a sin, for you an essential condition of life. I forced myself to accept the painful circumstances of our life in order not to leave you, but you saw my acceptance as a concession to your views, and this only deepened the misunderstanding between us. ... As for my view of your life, it is this:

I, a debauched man, profoundly depraved sexually, and no longer in his first youth, married you, a girl of eighteen, pure, good and intelligent, and in spite of my wicked past you lived with me for almost fifty years, loving me, living a life full of care and pain, giving birth to children, bringing them up, caring for them and nursing me, without succumbing to any of the temptations to which a woman like you, beautiful, solid and healthy, is always exposed; and your life has been such that I can have absolutely nothing to reproach you with. As for the fact that you did not follow me in my moral development, which is a unique one, I cannot hold that against you, either, for the inner life of any human is a secret between himself and God, and no one else can call him to account in any way; I have been intolerant with you, I was mistaken and I confess my error ...

4. If my relations with Chertkov are too trying for you now, I am ready to give him up, although I must tell you that it would be more unpleasant and painful for him than for me; but if you ask it of me I shall do it.

5. If you do not accept these terms for a peaceful and good life, I shall take back my promise not to leave you; I shall go

away. And not to Chertkov, you may be sure! In fact, I would even lay down as an absolute condition that he must not come and settle near me. But go I certainly shall, for I cannot continue living like this. I might have gone on with this life had I been able to look at all your sufferings unmoved, but I am not capable of that. . . . Stop, my dove, tormenting not only others but yourself, for you are suffering a hundred times more than they. That is all. July 14, in the morning. Leo Tolstoy.'

He immediately showed this letter to Sonya, who was both delighted and disturbed by it. She feared some manoeuvre designed to fetter her still more tightly. To reassure her, Tolstoy sent Sasha to Chertkov with instructions to bring back the diaries in exchange for a note signed by him. The girl set out, furious with her father for yielding on this capital point, and soon came back empty-handed, for in his troubled state he had forgotten to mention the return of the diaries in the note he had given her for Chertkov. He at once drafted another: 'I was so upset when I wrote to you this morning that I mistakenly supposed I had told you the most important thing, which is that you are to give the diaries to Sasha immediately. I ask you to do it. Sasha will take them to the bank. I am loath to do it, but so much the better. Be brave and steadfast for the good, you also, dear friend.'

Sasha set out again, with an ugly smile on her face, while her father wrote, 'I am not sure this is right, and I may have been too weak and conciliating, but I could not do anything else.'

When the girl reached Telyatinki, the Tolstoyan general staff was already assembled around a table, with Chertkov presiding: in addition to the master of the house, there were the two Goldenweisers, Sergeyenko, and Olga Dietrich, Andrey Tolstoy's ex-wife and Chertkov's sister-in-law. Hypnotized, Sasha took her place in their midst. They distributed the seven notebooks and went through them looking for any passages that were derogatory to Sonya, who would be sure to destroy them if she ever got her hands on the diaries. Every time they spied a criticism, confession of depression or disgust, or description of a quarrel, they avidly copied out the paragraph. When this anthology of hatred had been compiled, the editors lay down their pens and looked at one another with the satisfaction of men who have done their duty. Then the diaries were tied up, wrapped in heavy paper and, as Sasha was getting back into the coach, Chertkov derisively made the sign of the cross over her head three times with the package.[5] He also gave her a letter for her father in which he deplored that the master's true friends were prevented from coming to his assistance, as were the disciples of Christ on Golgotha on an earlier occasion: 'The thought of the death of Christ came to my mind today with strange intensity. I thought of the insults, offences and gibes heaped upon him and the long, slow death to which he was subjected; I saw his closest friends and relatives, powerless to approach him, compelled to witness the tragedy from afar; and I thought of his words, in the depth of his agony: "Forgive them, for they know not what they do."'

While this was going on, Sonya, twitching with impatience, had stationed herself at the window on the top floor of the house at Yasnaya Polyana, from which she could watch all the roads at once. Her son Leo was mounting guard at the entrance to the estate. But Sasha, guessing that they would be lying in wait for her, took another road back, entered through a ground-floor window and gave the diaries to her friend Varvara Feokritova, who handed them to Tanya. Too late! Sonya, alerted by Leo, came bearing down upon her eldest daughter, tore the package away from her and hugged it to her breast like a mother who has found her long-lost child. Then she unwrapped the seven notebooks bound in black oilcloth and feverishly began to read them. Hearing Sasha's outraged cries, Michael Sukhotin, Tanya's husband, came running; he reasoned with his mother-in-law, took the diaries away from her, put them into an envelope and sealed it and put it away in a cupboard.

Two days later he deposited the manuscripts in the name of Leo Tolstoy at the Tula branch of the national bank.

Still suspicious, Sonya demanded that her husband give her the key to the strongbox containing the diaries. He refused and left the house. As he passed beneath her windows, she cried out:

'Lyovochka! I drank a vial of opium!'

He rushed up the stairs, reached the landing gasping for breath, opened the door and fell upon his weeping wife:

'I said it on purpose,' she whimpered, 'but I didn't drink it.'[6]

Heartsick, he went to find Sasha and told her:

'Go to see Maman and tell her that her behaviour is forcing me to leave. I shall certainly go if she continues. As for the diaries, tell her I shall give the key to Michael Sergeyevich [Sukhotin].'

After a sharp scolding, Sonya calmed down sufficiently to tolerate, at least in theory, an occasional visit from Chertkov at Yasnaya Polyana. But as soon as she caught sight of him, she lost all self-control. True, the diaries were no longer in her rival's possession, but neither did she have the right to look at them. She had won only a half-victory. 'He shies and snorts, knowing I have my eye on him and have seen through his self-righteous posing. He would like to get even with me. But I'm not afraid of him,'[7] she wrote. Then she turned on her husband: 'By obstinately refusing to let me have those notebooks he is keeping a weapon ready to wound and punish me with. Ah, this sham Christian life, this meanness towards his fellow men, instead of the simple goodness and loyal openness that would hurt no one!'[8]

Life in the house was becoming so difficult that, with the approval of Sasha and Tanya, Tolstoy sent for medical help. On 19 July, the famous psychiatrist Rossolimo, and Dr Nikitin, a friend of the family, arrived at Yasnaya Polyana. Leo growled, 'My mother isn't the one who needs treatment; her health is fine; but my father has gone into his second childhood.'[9] Courteous and disdainful, Sonya allowed the two men to examine her. They stayed overnight and concluded the following day that the countess was not suffering from a mental illness, but from 'double degeneracy: paranoiac and hysterical, chiefly the former'. For treatment, they recommended baths, walks and, above all, the separation of the couple. Sonya adamantly refused to leave Lyovochka, because she was sure that Chertkov would arrive within the hour to take her place beside him. The doctors yielded. While they were getting back into their coach, she stood, imperturbably repeating, 'I shall stop being ill when the diaries have been returned to me!' And Tolstoy, filled with his old mistrust of medical men, wrote in his diary that evening, 'Rossolimo is astonishingly stupid, in the way of scientists: absolutely no hope!'

The truth was that he had a guilty conscience. Two days before, on 18 July, he had made a secret trip to Chertkov's house to rewrite his will, the final version of which was proving extremely ticklish to draft. After they thought everything had been provided for, Chertkov, alarmed by Sasha's recent illness, asked Muravyev to draw up a new will whereby, if she were to die before her father, the copyrights would go to her elder sister, Tanya. This was the version Tolstoy had recopied and signed in the the presence of three witnesses on the day before the psychiatrist's visit. He hoped he had seen the last of this distasteful affair, when Chertkov informed him that the words 'of sound mind and in full possession of his memory' had been omitted from the final draft, which might enable the heirs to break it on a point of form. So it had to be done over again. Anxious to avoid arousing Sonya's suspicions, Tolstoy decided not to go back to Telyatinki, but to arrange a meeting with the witnesses on 22 July, in the forest. Sergeyenko – Chertkov's friend and adviser – his secretary Radinsky and Goldenweiser set off on horseback to meet the patriarch. They saw him waiting for them, on his faithful mare, the glossy-coated Délire. Wearing a broad white hat, his white beard fanning out over his white blouse, he stood out, magnificent in his age and dignity, against the background of quivering leaves. The group rode on a little way under the trees, looking for a suitable spot. Then they dismounted. The old man sat on a tree stump and unscrewed the top of an English fountain pen he had brought with him. Sergeyenko handed him a blotter pad and a big sheet of paper. Radinsky held the paper he was to copy over, word for word.

'We look like conspirators,' said Tolstoy as he braced the pad on his knees.

And he began to write, slowly and carefully. It was cool beneath the branches. Sunspots flickered across the white page. The tethered horses swished their tails to drive away the flies. Far away, birds chattered, and furtive feet scampered through the underbrush. When he had finished, the old man signed his name, and the three witnesses followed suit. He thanked them, gave them the will and murmured, 'What a trial all this has been,' remounted his horse and rode home.

When he reached the house, Sonya's piercing glare made him fear she had guessed everything. Curiously, she had insisted that Chertkov come to the house that evening, but as soon as she saw him she lashed out, 'He won't give me one day's rest!' forgetting that she had asked him to come. 'There he is again!'

When Chertkov turned up at Yasnaya Polyana again the next day, her temper plunged from bad to worse. She caught him talking to Tolstoy in hushed tones, and they refused to tell her what they had been whispering about. With good reason: Tolstoy had just announced to his disciple that, in a letter appended to the will, he was giving Chertkov sole authority to revise and publish his work after his death. Furious at being left out of their secret, Sonya proffered some vague threats, went to her room and melancholically stroked her opium vial, but decided against suicide: 'I don't want to give them all – Sasha included – the satisfaction of seeing me dead,' she wrote in her diary. Transferring her fury to the 'devil', she added, 'I feel like killing Chertkov, or sticking something into his bloated body to release the soul of Leo Nikolayevich from his deleterious influence.'

Too excited to sleep, she then decided to leave the house the next day for good, and began to pack her bags. When her suitcases were all shut and strapped, she wrote a farewell letter to Lyovochka: 'I have tried to make the best of my misery, and to go on seeing Chertkov, but I can't do it. Cursed by my daughter, rejected by my husband, I am abandoning my home because my rightful place in it has been usurped by a Chertkov, and I shall not return to it unless he goes away.'

An extraordinary event has just come to pass at peaceful Yasnaya Polyana. Countess Sofya Andreyevna has left the home in which, for forty-eight years, she affectionately cared for her husband, having devoted her entire life to him. Her decision was prompted by the fact that Leo Nikolayevich, in the weakness of his extreme old age, has now come completely under the pernicious influence of Mr C . . . ; he has lost all will of his own, allowed C . . . to speak in crude and vulgar terms to Sofya Andreyevna and has continually maintained mysterious relations with him. The countess, who has been suffering from a nervous illness necessitating the consultation of two specialists from Moscow, is no longer able to tolerate the presence of C . . . , and, heartbroken, has abandoned her home.

After preparing this version of the facts for the public, she spent the morning of 25 July in her travelling suit, looking solemn and sullen. Her son Andrey was to arrive that afternoon; a trap had been ordered to fetch him at the station. At two o'clock Sonya got into the trap and said good-bye to her family. Tolstoy, thinking she was going for a drive, offered to go with her. But she refused, and left alone. In her handbag she carried her passport, a revolver and the vial of opium. At seven o'clock she was back: her son Andrey, whom she had met at the station, had persuaded her to return home. At the sight of her husband she fell into his arms, apologized for the fright she had given him and immediately demanded to know what he and Chertkov had been plotting. He changed the subject. To Sasha, he said mournfully, 'She's a pitiful old woman, one has to feel sorry for her, she was laughing and crying.' More deeply touched than he cared to admit, he thought once again of asking Chertkov to remain away from Yasnaya Polyana for a time. 'I think I need not tell you how I suffer, for you as much as for myself, at the thought that we will not be seeing each other any more,' he wrote on 26 July; 'but we must give up our meetings, it is necessary. . . . For the time being, let us write to each other. I shall not hide my letters or yours, if I am asked to show them.'

Chertkov immediately replied that he would abide by this resolution, but regretted it as a compromise on the part of the mystical spirit:

'I fear that your desire to appease Sofya Andreyevna may lead you to go too far, and cause you to renounce the independence that is essential to anyone seeking to obey, not his own will, but the will of the Master. ... The danger threatening you is that you may make your actions dependent upon the wishes of another human instead of upon the voice of God, which resounds in our souls at every moment. And that is why I am prepared without a murmur never to see you again if you are sure you are obeying the voice of God; but it would be unspeakably hard and painful for me to forgo a single opportunity to meet you if it is only because of a promise binding you to some human being.'

Tolstoy humbly accepted this lesson in Tolstoyism, but stood his ground. This was not the moment to add fuel to the fire. With Andrey's arrival, Sonya had gained a considerable ally – now there was a boy who had his feet on the ground! He enjoyed the good things of life, favoured the established order and was opposed to all philosophers, and he was determined to protect his mother against those who were claiming she had lost her mind.

'In spite of his non-resistance, all Papa can manage to do is hate people and hurt them!' he shouted. 'I don't care a damn about the opinion of an old man in his dotage!'

On 27 July he entered his father's study and challenged him: 'Nasty things are going on in this family. Maman is in an awful state. We want to know whether you have made a will.'

Tolstoy's heart missed a beat, but he controlled himself, returned his son's insolent stare and said in a steady voice:

'I do not see any reason to answer that question.'[10]

Andrey went out, slamming the door. Since he could not force his father to talk, he tried his sister, but Sasha pretended not to know anything about anything. It may have been easy and even pleasant for her to lie to her exasperated brothers and her mother, but Tolstoy was sick at having to feign innocence within a ring of inquisitors.

The diary in which he ordinarily gave vent to his feelings was no longer enough, as every single person around him now claimed the right to read it. On 29 July, he began a new diary, entitled *Diary for Myself Alone,* which no one knew about and which he hid in his bootleg or under his shirt. This need to record his most intimate thoughts coincided with a fresh attack of conscience. Increasingly often, he was wondering whether he had been right to disinherit his family and had not betrayed his own teachings by acting in accordance with a law system to which he was theoretically opposed. To justify himself in his own eyes, he invoked his sons' mediocrity. 'I can be completely sincere in my love of Sonya, but it is impossible with Leo,' he wrote in his *Diary For Myself Alone* on 29 July. 'Andrey is simply another of those men about whom it is hard to believe they have a God-given soul (yet it exists, we must not forget). . . . But one cannot deprive millions of people of what is certainly necessary to their souls . . . in order that Andrey may drink and carry on, and Leo scribble books.' But the following day he confessed how deeply torn he was: 'Chertkov has involved me in a conflict that is painful and repellent to me.'

His feelings of guilt increased after a conversation on 2 August with his biographer and friend Paul Biryukov, who was visiting Yasnaya Polyana. He was counting on his dear 'Posha' to congratulate him upon leaving his opus to mankind. But Biryukov criticized the secrecy with which the whole affair had been handled, and thought Tolstoy should have called the family together and openly stated his intentions. Wasn't he big enough to brave the opinion of his own family? Shaken by this admonishment, the old man wrote that evening, 'I see my mistake very clearly. I should have called all my heirs together and announced my decision to them instead of acting in secret. I am writing Chertkov to the same effect.'

But Chertkov wouldn't hear of it: a series of letters was brought to Yasnaya Polyana by Goldenweiser or Bulgakov, explaining how it would have been impossible to make the document public without giving his wife a fatal shock: 'She has spent so many long years taking so many precautions and exercising such care in conceiving, forming and preparing her plan to obtain control of all of your works after your death that a disappointment during your lifetime would be a blow too great for her to bear; she would spare no one and nothing, and I am referring not only to you and your health and your life, but to herself.'

Turned about-face once again, Tolstoy answered his disciple:

'I am writing you on this scrap of paper because I am walking in the forest. I have been thinking about your letter since yesterday evening, and all morning too. It aroused two feelings in me: disgust at the manifestations of vulgar cupidity and selfishness that I had either not noticed or had forgotten; and sorrow and remorse for the pain I caused you by my letter saying I regretted what I had done. The conclusion I drew from all this is that Paul Ivanovich Biryukov was not right, nor was I right to agree with him, and I fully approve of your reaction; however, I am still not pleased with myself. I feel that we might have done better, although I don't know how.'

Sonya was exasperated by this steady stream of emissaries between Yasnaya Polyana and Telyatinki. She called Bulgakov and Goldenweiser 'walking post offices'. One day, stung by jealousy, she said to her husband: 'You and Chertkov are writing secret love letters to each other.' When he rebuked her, she triumphantly brandished a copy of a passage from one of his earlier diaries, dated 29 November 1851: 'I have never been in love with a woman ... but I have quite often fallen in love with a man. ... For me the chief symptom of love is the fear of offending the loved one or of not pleasing him, or simply fear itself. ... I fell in love with a man before I knew what pederasty was; but even after I found out, the possibility never crossed my mind. Beauty has always been a powerful factor in my attractions; there is D ... [Dyakov], for example. I shall never forget the night we left P ... [Pirogovo] together, when, wrapped up in my blanket, I wanted to devour him with kisses and weep. Sexual desire was not totally absent, but it was impossible to say what role it played, for my imagination never tempted me with lewd pictures. On the contrary, I was utterly disgusted by all that.'

After reading the paper, Tolstoy turned pale and shouted, 'Go away! Get out of here!' Sonya did not budge, so he rushed into his own room and locked the door behind him. 'I stood there petrified,' Sonya wrote in her diary. 'Where is love, then? Where non-resistance? Where Christ? ... Is it possible that old age can so harden the heart of man?' When Dr Makovitsky, alerted by Sasha, came to examine the old man, he found him prostrated, his heartbeat irregular, his pulse over a hundred.

'Tell her that if she's trying to kill me, she'll soon succeed,' murmured Tolstoy.

Far from subsiding, Sonya continued to repeat her wild accusations of homosexuality, to Dr Makovitsky, Sasha or anyone else within earshot. She found out that Tolstoy occasionally met Chertkov in the pine woods during his walks, and began to follow him, spying on him from behind the trees and questioning the village children to discover whether the count had been alone or with another man. At home, she waited until he left his study to search through his papers. She was looking for evidence of his betrayal, his wickedness and his immorality. Sometimes she realized that she was going mad and thought with horror of her brother Stepan, who had died in an asylum the year before. Then, needing a moment of respite, she wrote, 'I wondered whether I might not make peace with Chertkov. ... Perhaps I will end by no longer hating him. But when I think of actually *seeing* his face again, and when I think of the joy that would be written on Leo Nikolayevich's face to see him again, then my heart fills with agony, I feel like weeping, and a desperate protest cries out within me. The spirit of evil is in Chertkov, that is why he frightens me and makes me suffer so.'[11]

Andrey and Leo were seriously contemplating having their father declared feeble-minded, in order to invalidate the will they suspected him of having made despite his protestations to the contrary. Hated by some, ill-treated by others and spied on by all, Tolstoy looked upon his divided tribe in horror. No matter what he did now, he infuriated either his family or his disciples. He preached universal love, and had become the apple of discord in his own family. What a failure his life was, in spite of the great principles he professed to follow. He made one last attempt to deceive himself: unable to reach any decision, he wrapped his cowardice in a cloak of religion.

'In my position,' he told Bulgakov, 'inertia is the lesser evil. Do nothing, undertake nothing. Answer every provocation with silence. Silence is so powerful! ... One must reach the point, as it says in the Gospels, of being able to love one's enemies, to love those who hate one.'

Thinking of Chertkov and Sasha, he added:

'But they go too far, they go too far.'

'No doubt you regard this as a challenge, useful to your spiritual progress?' asked Bulgakov.

'Yes, yes, of course! I have thought a good deal lately. But I am still a long way from being able to act, in my position, like Francis of Assisi.'[12]

He wrote in his *Diary for Myself Alone*, on 6 August, 'I think I would like to go away, leaving a letter, but I'm afraid for Sonya, although I think it would be best for her too.' A few days later, 'Help me, Father, universal Spirit, source and principle of life, help me, at least in these last days and hours of my life on earth, help me to live before Thee, serving Thee alone.'

Tanya returned to Yasnaya Polyana in the midst of this nightmare, and in an unguarded moment Tolstoy told his eldest daughter about his will. She was not surprised, and even approved of it; but a little while later, she said she was sorry he had felt it necessary to give up the rights to the books written before 1881. In any event, one glance was enough to tell her that if he remained at Yasnaya Polyana much longer in that atmosphere of spying and hysteria, he would die of a heart attack. She invited him to come, alone, for a rest at her home at Kochety. He accepted enthusiastically, but Sonya insisted upon coming with him. She preferred to make him miserable by her company, rather than know he was happy somewhere else. On 15 August he left, with his wife, Sasha, Tanya and Dr Makovitsky.

Their first days at Kochety were so enjoyable that Sonya forgot all about her grievances. She began to relax, basking in the solicitude of her son-in-law and spoiled by her grandchildren. But on 18 August, she read an item in the newspapers which her family had been hiding from her for the past four days: the minister of the interior had just given Chertkov permission to settle permanently in the government of Tula. 'It's my death warrant!' she cried. 'I shall kill Chertkov! I'll have him poisoned! It's either him or me!'

And she took her pulse: 'One hundred and forty! ... My chest hurts, my head hurts!'

To quiet her, Lyovochka had to promise that he would not see Chertkov any more, or let himself be photographed by him 'like an old coquette ... in the woods and ravines'. While she was proudly recording this victory in her diary, he was writing in his: 'I have had a conversation with Sofya Andreyevna and, although it was an error, have consented not to allow any more pictures to be taken of me. One should not make such concessions.' But he told her the same day that he would continue writing to his disciple, and she immediately scented another danger: 'I could not sleep all night for thinking that henceforth it is not his diary that will be filled with nasty remarks about me and evil schemes against me (under cover, of course, of Christian humility), but his correspondence with Mr Chertkov (Leo Nikolaye-vich has cast himself in the role of Christ and given the part of his favourite disciple to Chertkov).'

Driven by her obsession, she hunted through every word Tolstoy had ever written in search of passages revealing his penchant for men. Perhaps the most significant was that paragraph in *Childhood* where the author goes into raptures over the beauty of Sergey. 'You can't teach an old dog new tricks,' she wrote in her diary. 'Falling for a little boy in childhood and having a crush on Chertkov-the-fair-inamorato in old age are one and the same thing.' When she looked in the mirror she could not understand how Lyovochka was able to prefer that obese balding bearded man to herself. Gone were the days when her amorous, impetuous husband came to take her by surprise, as she stood undressed for her bath on the edge of the stream.[13] 'My birthday,' she wrote on 22 August 1910. 'I am sixty-six years old and have as much vitality, intensity of emotion and, so people tell me, youthfulness as ever.'

Tolstoy's birthday followed, six days later. Eighty-two years old. He hoped that this day, at least, would bring a lull in the storm. But a quarrel broke out between them because he maintained in her presence that celibacy and chastity were the Christian ideals. She remarked that he had no business talking that way after fathering thirteen children. One thing led to another, and the venerable couple, quivering with rage, were soon digging up all their old resentments: the division of the estate, the copyrights, Chertkov; they didn't overlook a single one. The ensuing reconciliation was sincere on her side, but inspired on his by a profound sense of pity. 'My relations with Sonya are becoming more and more difficult,' he wrote that day. 'What she feels for me is not love, but the possessiveness of love, something that is not far from hatred and is being transformed into hatred. The children saved her before. An animal love, but full of self-denial. When that was over, there remained only immense egoism. And egoism is the most abnormal state of all, it is insanity. ... Dushan Makovitsky and Sasha refuse to admit that she is ill. They are wrong.'

Two days later Sonya, furious at being treated 'like a Xantippe' by everyone, determined to leave Kochety and return to Yasnaya Polyana. At her father's request, Sasha went with her. The moment Sonya entered the house, she took down the photographs by Chertkov and Sasha and replaced them with her own. Then she sent for a priest, to exorcise the disciple's diabolical spirit from Lyovochka's study. The pope appeared at four in the afternoon of 2 September, wearing his sacerdotal garb and accompanied by a sacristan who carried a little chest. He sprinkled the room with holy water, swung his censer towards the four corners and intoned a series of purgative prayers in a cavernous voice, including one rather strange one celebrating His Majesty the emperor's victories on the battlefield, which shocked Sonya's Tolstoyan pacifism. Sasha left again the following day, and reported these aberrant goings-on in the house to her father. He was much saddened to hear of them and his sorrow increased at the news that Sonya was already restless and threatening to return to Kochety.

On 5 September she was back, and their quarrel flared up again. Reproaches, curses, imprecations, nocturnal flights into the garden. The old man lumbered after her as she howled, 'He's a monster! A murderer! I never want to see him again!' Between rounds in their match, he tried to read and write a little. He was disappointed by the new novels. Charles Salomon had brought him Gide's *Retour de l'enfant prodigue*, which he found 'empty and bombastic'.[14] Nor did he care for Gorky's *Mother* ('Worthless!'). On the whole, he remained faithful to the literary preferences of his youth and adulthood. Among foreign authors, he continued to revere his beloved Rousseau, for the unqualified, agonizing sincerity of his confessions; Pascal, whose mystical writings reminded him of his own; Molière, because his theatre was accessible to all; Stendhal, who had taught him to see and portray war; Hugo, the giant, who, like himself, proclaimed that art must be useful; the bantering Anatole France; Zola, the champion of social rights; Dickens, friend of the weak and poor, whose genius was tinged with humour and melancholy; and Maupassant, 'the only one to have understood and expressed the negative side of relations between men and women'.[15] Gorky and his friend Posse once asked Tolstoy how he could have any esteem for that 'virtually pornographic' author, to which the old man replied: 'True talent always has two shoulders: one is ethical, the other aesthetic. If the ethical shoulder hitches itself up too high, then the aesthetic shoulder dips down to the same degree, and the talent becomes misshapen.'[16] Curious statement from a man who maintained elsewhere that the artist should be a professor of morality before all else.

On 6 September 1910 he sent a poignant letter to Gandhi, then a lawyer in Johannesburg in the Transvaal, explaining that there was a monstrous inconsistency between the law of love professed by Christian nations and the violence they practised, in the guise of government, army, courts and all administrative institutions. With one foot in the grave, he continued to exhort his Asian brethren not to resist evil with evil. Perhaps they would succeed where the Christians had failed. Sometimes he wondered what his far-off correspondent, who took him for a seer, would have thought had he been able to observe the master's struggles with a half-demented wife and children wallowing in materialism. Chertkov had just sent him an extract from the diary of Varvara Feokritova, who had made a note of one of Sonya's rash threats uttered in her presence: 'Even if my husband made everything over to Chertkov I would not give up my rights to his unpublished works, because they are not dated. Everybody will believe me if I say they were written before 1881. Besides, I don't care what he does, because my sons and I will surely try to break the will (if there is one); our case is very strong; we shall prove that he [Tolstoy] had become feeble-minded towards the end and had a series of strokes, which is no more than the truth and the whole world knows it, and we will prove that he was forced into writing that will in a moment of mental incapacity and that he himself would never have wanted to disinherit his children.'

While thus plunging Tolstoy into a state of anguish, Chertkov was also writing to Sonya, in an attempt to return to her good graces: 'I am convinced that so unexpected and sudden a change in your attitude could not have come about through your own volition. It seems to me that it must be due in part to a few most regrettable misunderstandings which we have been unable to clear up, and in part to the calumny of third persons who have transmitted to you their feelings of hostility towards me.'[17] She haughtily replied that she could not forgive him for appropriating her husband's diary:

His diary is the most intimate reflection of his life and therefore of my life with him; it is the mirror of his soul, which I had grown accustomed to feel and to love, and it should not fall into the hands of an outsider. And the notebooks were removed by stealth, unknown to me, by persons whom you sent to take them, and they remained with you in a wooden house exposed to all the dangers of fire or confiscation, long enough to be copied ten times. . . . How many times have I asked you what arrangements you have made with regard to Leo Nikolayevich's papers and manuscripts in the event of his death? You have always maliciously refused to answer. You love neither truth nor light. . . . You published the works of Leo Nikolayevich, that is your claim to merit. But why do you always insist upon having all his manuscripts in your possession? I see it as a proof of your cupidity, not mine! You will tell me that he gives them to you himself. But it is by that action and many others that I recognize your growing ascendancy over a man whose will is steadily weakening, an old man who has already ceased to care for most of the things of this world. Your despotic personality has subjugated him (in a conversation I had with your mother, she shared my opinion regarding your tyranny). Your pernicious and insidious influence and my husband's excessive regard for you have estranged him from me. . . . You are the one who has given him the idea that one should either run away from a wife like me or kill oneself . . .[18]

On 12 September, after refusing to eat for two days in order to punish Lyovochka for treating her so harshly, Sonya left, alone, for Yasnaya Polyana. During her short stay at Kochety she had managed to antagonize even placid Michael Sukhotin, who had shouted at her, 'Your only claim to fame, which is to be Tolstoy's wife, will be destroyed if he leaves you! Tolstoy has run away from his wife, they'll say, because she was making his life hell!' Now that she was gone, her adversaries, led by Sasha, tried to consolidate their authority over the old man. 'What I want is for my father not to give in to my mother,' Sasha wrote to Bulgakov. Chertkov, tearing his hair because he could not talk to his master in person at such a critical moment, wrote letter after letter exhorting him to be firm. 'Received a letter from Chertkov who joins in the chorus of advice telling me I must not give in, but I don't know whether I shall be able to hold out,' wrote Tolstoy on 19 September. 'I plan to return to Yasnaya on the twenty-second.' 23 September was their forty-eighth wedding anniversary and he had promised to be with her on the great day: 'Twenty-second, morning. Leaving for Yasnaya, in terror at the thought of what awaits me there. Do what you must. ... And above all, say nothing, do not forget there is a soul-God in her.'

Sasha and Dr. Makovitsky returned to Yasnaya Polyana with him. The meeting was ominous and awkward. But the next day Sonya appeared in a white silk dress with a party smile on her face, ordered hot chocolate for breakfast and asked Bulgakov to photograph her with her husband. Lyovochka could not refuse this one favour, she said, after posing for Chertkov so often. The picture, appearing in the newspapers, would put an end to the rumours of conflict between the author and his wife. Tolstoy unwillingly consented to pose for the camera. A screen was put up to concentrate the sun's pale rays on the couple. With his head under the black hood and the rubber pear in his hand, Bulgakov timidly suggested that his models move right and left, face each other, look happy. But Tolstoy, exasperated by this farce, paid no attention. The photographs were no good, and had to be taken over again the next day, in the same clothes and pose. It was cold, a sharp wind was blowing. Bulgakov took forever to arrange his camera. At last, he counted: 'One ... two ... three.' Standing before him, with ravaged features, staring fiercely into space, one hand in the pocket of his blouse, Tolstoy seemed unaware of his wife, who was clutching his arm in her white dress, supplicating and imperious, devouring him with her eyes. The shutter's click fixed for all time the tragic image of these two disunited beings, one trying to restrain the other.*

Sasha, of course, was furious at her father for consenting to have his picture taken with her mother, as though they formed some sort of model couple; and even more because he had not replaced the photographs by his daughter and Chertkov that had formerly adorned his study. In the angry amazon with the blazing eyes, Tolstoy sorrowfully recognized the bellicose spirit of his wife.

---

* This is the last portrait taken of Tolstoy alive.

'How you resemble her,' he sighed.

In his *Diary for Myself Alone*: 'They are tearing me apart. Sometimes I feel like leaving the lot of them.'

Later, when a repentant Sasha came to him with pencil and paper in hand, he murmured:

'It isn't your shorthand I need, but your love.'

Whereupon father and daughter wept and made up. The next day Tolstoy returned the portraits by Sasha and Chertkov to their former places. And it was Sonya's turn to perform. As it happened, Sasha had just left with Varvara Feokritova to visit Olga Dietrich, Andrey's ex-wife, at Taptikovo, and Lyovochka had gone for a walk in the forest. Brandishing a child's cap pistol, Sonya stormed into the study and fired at Chertkov's picture, then tore it up and threw the pieces down the toilet. When her husband came back from his walk she fired a second time into the air, to frighten him. Then, as he showed no sign of alarm, she ran sobbing into the garden. In turn, Dr Makovitsky, Bulgakov and old Marya Schmidt went out to admonish her. She eventually consented to go back to the house and Marya Schmidt, who was worried by her state, sent a servant on horseback to inform Sasha that her mother had gone raving mad. Sasha returned from Taptikovo in the night of 26–7 September to find her father dropping with exhaustion and her mother astonished at all the fuss being made over such a trifle.

'You crazy girls, why have you come back so soon?' she said.

Sasha retorted sharply. Sonya resented their impertinent insinuations. In the heat of the argument, she banished Varvara Feokritova like a thieving servant and screamed at her daughter:

'I'll throw you out of here as I did Chertkov!'

Sasha, about to leap upon her mother like a wildcat, managed to control herself and went into her father's study to announce that she was going to spend a few days with Varvara Feokritova at Telyatinki, where she had a little house not far from Chertkov's, in order to restore peace and quiet in the family. She was certain her father would come with her. But he only said, wearily:

'Yes, do go.'

She and her friend left the next morning. With relief, Sonya watched the 'two pests', as she called them, retreating into the distance with their 'horses, dogs and parrot'. Tolstoy wrote: 'I am in a comical and contradictory position. Without false modesty I may say that I formulate and express the most important and significant ideas, and at the same time, I spend the best part of my life yielding to or resisting the whims of women. As far as moral perfection is concerned I feel like a youngster, a schoolboy, and a not very assiduous schoolboy as yet.'

Chertkov was sending a complete correspondence course to the schoolboy: 'You have allowed yourself, on my account, to be forced into an ambiguous and to a certain extent false position, unconsciously, no doubt, and trying all the while to do right.' On the other side, Sonya was deafening him with a stream of words in which the same vindictive allusions and the same protestations of love recurred again and again. 'We have been left alone, the two old folks,' she noted with satisfaction. 'He is flabby, and his intestines are out of order.' And: 'When the others aren't there he becomes the way he used to be, kind and coaxing with me and, I think, *mine*.' But he was irritated beyond words by these attentions that were mingled with so much mistrust. After reading Maupassant's story *En famille*, he conceived a desire to write a novel 'demonstrating the triviality of existence', the central figure of which would be 'a man who is spiritually alive'. He waxed enthusiastic: 'Oh, it will be fine!' But he drooped at the thought of such a tremendous undertaking. 'Impossible to work because of her [Sonya], because of the feeling that obsesses me about her, because of my inner struggle. And of course that struggle and the possibility of victory are more important than any work of literature could be.'

On 3 October, he was much agitated by the arrival of his son Sergey and daughter Tanya, who had decided to convince their mother to separate from him. They accused her of torturing their father and threatened to have her put under surveillance by a board of guardians if she would not consent either to leave or to mend her ways.

To escape from their screaming and shouting, Tolstoy went out for a ride with Dr Makovitsky. When he returned, after a seven-mile canter, he lay down fully dressed on his bed, without pulling off his boots. At seven in the evening, when he had not appeared for supper, the countess served the soup and then, apprehensive, went to his room. He was lying unconscious on the bed, his jaws jerking and emitting a muffled mooing noise at intervals. Sonya's cries brought the whole household on the run; the Sukhotins, Sergey, Biryukov, Bulgakov, Dr Makovitsky. They undressed him. He was mumbling, 'Society ... society ... reason,' and slowly waggling his sluggish fingers across the blanket as though trying to write. With remarkable presence of mind Sonya, following Dr Makovitsky's instructions, put hot-water bottles on her husband's feet and a compress on his forehead, made him drink coffee and rum and waved smelling salts under his nose. Suddenly he went into convulsions. His legs thrashed so violently that three men – Biryukov, Bulgakov and the doctor – could not hold him down. His head slid off the pillow, his features contracted, his eyes were glassy and his throat filled with a gurgling rattle. Kneeling before him, Sonya clasped his feet in her arms and prayed aloud, 'Not this time, my God, not this time! Spare him!'

Alerted by the coachman, Sasha came speeding over from Telyatinki. Chertkov came too, defying orders. But he did not dare to let the countess see him, and installed himself in Dr Makovitsky's room downstairs. His secretary, Belinsky, reported to him every fifteen minutes. No doubt Chertkov had worked out a plan of action in case the master died: produce the will, thrust the widow aside, get his hands on the last manuscripts.

In spite of her anguish, Sonya, too, was thinking how to protect her rights. Taking advantage of the confusion around her, she seized a little portfolio of papers, and it required the intervention of Tanya, who had seen her in the act, to make her put it back. Sasha was more skilful, and managed, without her mother's notice, to steal a little notebook she found inside her father's blouse. The patient had five convulsions, each lasting for three minutes. At eleven o'clock that night he resumed consciousness, asked what had happened and dropped off to sleep.

The following day he was out of danger, but very weak, and was forced to stay in bed. Her husband's survival could only be the result of divine grace, Sonya thought, requiring a compensatory act of contrition on her part. Just as Sasha was about to return to Telyatinki, a servant came to tell her that the countess was waiting for her on the front steps. She found her mother standing, coatless and red-eyed, her head shaking from side to side.

'Forgive me!' said Sonya. 'I give you my word of honour I shall never offend you again.'

She also promised her daughter that she would cease tormenting Lyovochka and entreated her to come back, with Varvara Feokritova, and live at home. She looked so pitiful that even Sasha – tough, suspicious Sasha – burst into tears. The two women exchanged moist kisses and sighs of endearment. A great hope dawned over Yasnaya Polyana. Sasha returned to the fold with Varvara Feokritova, and Sonya, pushing her spirit of sacrifice to sublime heights, invited Chertkov to call on 7 October, as though nothing had happened.

She had presumed upon her powers. When she heard the springs of the disciple's carriage in the drive, her heart began to pound so wildly that she nearly fainted. Snatching her binoculars, she watched out of the window, to make sure that her husband did not show too much joy at his approach. He came out on to the steps. She had made him promise not to embrace the villain. Did the two men know they were being watched? They shook hands. Hiding, Sonya spied on them all day. That evening she wrote, 'Impossible! That creature is the devil in person! I shall never be able to bear him!'

In view of Sonya's agitation after Chertkov's departure Tolstoy wrote to his disciple's wife that it would be better, in the interests of all, not to repeat the experiment. He was particularly unwilling to provoke Sonya just then, having noticed a few days before that one of the notebooks of his *Diary for Myself Alone* had disappeared. Had he mislaid it or had someone taken it without his knowledge? He suspected his wife; and he was not mistaken. She had found it in the boot in which he always hid it, and had made off with it while he was asleep. Naturally, she said nothing to him about her find. But her perusal of his notes confirmed the existence of a plot against her concocted by her husband and Chertkov. Now she was sure a will had been made, excluding her from the inheritance, and she had special reason to find this intolerable at that particular moment: a publishing company, Prozveshenye, had just offered her the fabulous sum of one million roubles for exclusive rights to publish the works of Leo Tolstoy after his death. A million roubles!* Enough to provide for her sons and daughters and twenty-five grandchildren for life! Well; that will, whatever it contained, had to be destroyed. She explained this to her husband on 12 October, but he would not listen. Then she wrote a letter, which she left on his desk on 14 October:

Every day you inquire after my health with a compassionate air and ask how I have slept; and every day you are merely driving so many fresh nails into my heart, shortening my life and subjecting me to unendurable torture, and I can do nothing to lessen my own pain. Fate has decided that I should learn of this new blow, this evil deed you have perpetrated by depriving

*Or $2,831,600.

your numerous offspring of your copyrights – although your partner in crime has not done as much to his own family. ... The government that both of you have slandered and maligned in your pamphlets will now *lawfully* take the bread out of the mouths of your heirs, and give it to Sytin* and other rich publishers and businessmen, while Tolstoy's grandchildren will starve as the result of his malevolence and vanity. And it is the government, again – in the form of the State Bank – that receives Tolstoy's diaries for safekeeping, so that his wife may not have them ... I am aghast (supposing that I should survive you) to think what evil may grow up out of your grave, and in the memories of your children and grandchildren.

When, trembling with apprehension, she went to her husband's study to hear his reaction to this, he coldly remarked, 'Can't you leave me in peace?' She tried kind words and tears. He was immovable. How was he to confess that he had dispossessed her of her rights not only to the works written after 1881, but to *War and Peace* and *Anna Karenina* and *The Cossacks* as well? 'When she rhapsodizes to me about her love and kneels down before me and kisses my hands, it is very hard for me,' he wrote. After she left, he felt his pulse (an automatic reflex among the Tolstoys) and noted: 'Ninety.' Then he corrected his article *On Socialism* and went for a ride. Every time he went into the forest alone, Sonya was sure he was going to meet Chertkov. On 16 October she set out on foot across the fields towards Telyatinki, lay down in a ditch a little way from the entrance to the estate and trained her binoculars on the house. She was watching for the tryst. But Lyovochka did not come. At nightfall, chilled to the bone, she made her way back to Yasnaya Polyana and sat down on a bench beneath a pine, where she was found by a servant with a lantern. When she told Lyovochka what she had done and begged him to swear he would never see the 'disgusting' Chertkov again, he growled: 'I do not want to obey your whims and fancies. I want freedom; at eighty-two years of age I refuse

* A well-known publisher of the time.

to be treated like a little boy, tied to my wife's apron strings!
I retract all my promises.'

Shortly afterwards a Tolstoyan peasant named Novikov
came to see him, and, feeling in a mood for confidences, he
told this 'Dark One' how difficult his wife was making life
for him. 'Among us,' said Novikov, 'we settle quarrels with
our womenfolk more simply, and you never see any fits of
hysteria. I am not a partisan of the stick and have never
had recourse to it myself, but even so, one can't do everything a woman wants!' Tolstoy gave a hearty laugh and
told the anecdote to Dr Makovitsky and Sasha; and,
with just a touch of malice, Sasha in turn told him how
Ivan, the coachman at Yasnaya Polyana, criticized the
master for overindulgence and told everyone that, 'In our
village, when a woman starts acting up, her man gives her
a good hiding with the reins and she turns soft as a glove!'

After Novikov left, Tolstoy could not stop thinking about
the simple, rough life the peasant had described to him.
Oh, to go out there, plunge into the world of the common
people, earn his living sewing boots, and live on kasha. ...
To prove that he had not used up all his strength, he took
up gymnastics again. One day, hanging from a clothes
cupboard, he pulled it over on to his back, was bent double
and nearly collapsing beneath the weight. 'Wearing myself
out needlessly! Eighty-two-year-old fool!' he wrote after
this incident. However, he was convinced that the time
had come for him to begin his new way of life: if a man
can hold up a clothes cupboard single-handed, no obstacle
can stand in his way. On 24 October he found a letter in
his mail from a St Petersburg student named Alexander
Barkhudarov, reproaching him for the inconsistencies between his theory and his practice, on the basis of quotations from Merezhkovsky's book, *The Life and Works of
Tolstoy and Dostoyevsky*, published the previous year.
There was a second letter, merely abusive, from a German
woman in Breslau. How strange that these two criticisms
should reach him just when he was wondering whether

he ought not to break away and seek rebirth. He wrote to Novikov forthwith:

'Couldn't you find me an isba in your village, never mind how small it is, as long as it is by itself, and warm, so that I will disturb you and your family no longer than absolutely necessary? If I were to send you a telegram I would not sign my own name, but T. Nikolayev. I await your answer. ... I warn you, this must be kept between ourselves.'

The next day he wrote in his *Diary for Myself Alone*: 'Suspicions, espionage, desire that *she* should furnish me with a pretext to go; and when I think of the state she is in I feel sorry for her and cannot.' He told Sasha of his plan and proposed that she come with him.

'Oh, yes!' she said, flushing with pleasure. 'But I wouldn't want to get in your way. In the beginning, it might be better if I let you go alone.'

'Yes, yes; besides, I keep telling myself that your health is not good enough, you will catch a cold, you'll start coughing . . .'

'That's nothing!' said the girl. 'I will feel much better living in more simple surroundings.'

'If that is true, then it will be very pleasant for me to have you with me, as a helper. Here is how I plan to proceed; I shall buy a ticket to Moscow, send somebody over to Laptevo* with my things, and get off the train there myself. If I am discovered, I'll go on farther. There, now; for the moment, this is nothing but dreams. I shall certainly worry myself to death if I leave her, her condition will torture me. But then, the atmosphere here is becoming harder for me to bear every day.' [19]

He also wanted to know what Dr Makovitsky thought of his plan. The doctor saw no objection to it, either as disciple or as physician. But old Marya Schmidt, whom he also took into his confidence, reacted very differently.

* Station on the Moscow–Kursk line, a few versts from the village in which Novikov lived.

'My dear Leo Nikolayevich, you'll get over it, this is only a passing weakness,' she said.

And Tolstoy sadly realized that his conscience would not allow him to take such a brutal and selfish step.

That day there was a large gathering at Yasnaya Polyana. One of the guests was Mrs Almedingen, an author of children's books, who had actually come on behalf of the Prozveshenye publishing company to try to persuade the countess to sell her rights to the posthumous publication of her husband's complete works. Although neither Mrs Almedingen nor Sonya alluded to the scheme in front of Tolstoy, he guessed at it and was annoyed by it.

On 26 October, the arrival of Andrey, followed by Sergey, destroyed his last trace of good humour. Andrey particularly – that narrow-minded reactionary – was a bane to him; and as for Sergey, a neighbour in the country had just challenged him to a duel, after some absurd quarrel; very probably, nothing would come of it, but Sonya sighed and moaned and made a great display of maternal anguish. 'It is very painful for me to find myself in this madhouse,' the old man wrote. But he put on a smiling countenance for his sons the next day, which cost him a considerable effort. The dinner-table conversation touched on every subject except Chertkov and the will. Sonya, in her Sunday best, sat in state between her two tall bearded sons. Tolstoy soon slipped away from his guests and went for a ride with Dr Makovitsky.

A light snow was falling from the grey sky. The ground was frozen and slippery, and the riders had to dismount to cross a gulley. Dr Makovitsky took both horses by the bridle and forced them to jump the stream with him. Tolstoy, tucking up the flaps of his short cloak, slithered down the slope, clinging to the branches of the pine trees, and then toiled up the opposite bank on all fours, grunting with effort.[20] After a ten-mile ride he returned home exhausted and stooping, his eyes blank and his beard damp with snow.

In the meantime, Bulgakov had brought a letter from Chertkov. Sonya wanted to know what was in it. Tolstoy refused to tell her, 'on principle'. A quarrel broke out. Once again, with her head shaking from side to side and her eyes bulging, Sonya demanded that her husband tell her whether it was true that he had signed a will disinheriting her and her children. Once again, his only answer was equivocal and cowardly silence. She was making him feel permanently guilty, yet he could not turn against Chertkov. Caught between the woman who personified his life and the man who personified his doctrine, he himself no longer knew which way to turn.

Towards eleven that evening he withdrew to his study with his mind in a whirl, and wrote in his diary, 'It looks bad, but at bottom it is good. Our relations are weighing upon me more and more.' Then he read a few pages of *The Brothers Karamazov* – the chapter dealt with Dmitry Karamazov's hatred of his old father. Which of the two families, Karamazov or Tolstoy, was the more horrible? His thoughts began to stray, full of obscure unease, and he laid the book down open on the round table. No doubt about it, he did not like that book : 'I cannot overcome my repulsion for all I find in it that is anti-artistic, superficial, attitudinizing, irrelevant to the great problems,' he had written to Mrs Chertkov a few days before.[21] No, no, Dostoyevsky was not one of the great writers. How could critics presume to talk about the author of *The Brothers Karamazov* in the same breath as the author of *War and Peace*, even if only to oppose them? Merezhkovsky's book was ridiculous! Besides, Tolstoy couldn't care less what they said about his writing. His life was what mattered. Would he ever find a way out of his present predicament? He prayed to God for help, lay down and, at half past eleven, blew out his candle.

[32]

Flight

On 28 October 1910 at three o'clock in the morning Tolstoy awoke with a start. A door creaked open, footsteps approached, a gown rustled as it brushed against a piece of furniture. From his study, a ray of light shone beneath the closed door. Sitting up in bed, the old man held his breath and listened. Soon he heard a shuffle of paper, and knew that Sonya was going through his desk drawers. 'So, day and night, she has to know my every word and deed, and have everything under her control,'[1] he thought with a shudder of disgust. Motionless, he waited until his wife went away and then tried to go back to sleep, but he could not: his overwrought brain refused. He lighted his candle and sat on the side of his bed, with his legs hanging down. Drawn by the light, Sonya came into his bedroom. Was he ill? Did he need anything? At the sight of his solicitous jailkeeper, in her nightgown, with her hair undone, her pasty face and her black, sharp eyes, a fresh wave of anger rose up in him. However, he controlled himself, reassured her and advised her to go back to bed.

After she left, his heart was pounding so wildly that he was afraid he would have an attack. Automatically, he felt for his pulse: ninety-seven. Suddenly, it was clear to him that he could not go on living like this, under the double surveillance of Sonya, demanding that he act for the good of the family, and Chertkov, demanding that he act for the good of his soul.

All the inconsistencies of his entire life spread before his eyes and his mind reeled in horror. He preached universal love – and made his wife miserable; poverty – and lived in luxury; forgetfulness of self – and recorded his every twinge;

fusion with God – and wasted his life in domestic bicker-
ings; contempt for fame – and curried his celebrity with
correspondence, receptions, photographs; the worship of
truth – and was driven every single day to the shabbiest
dissimulation. How many times had he wanted to get
away, since that 17 June 1884 when he had walked for
hours down the road to Tula, trying to escape from his conjugal inferno? But he had always come back, unhappy and
contrite. Today he would have the strength to carry it
through to the end. Yes; flight was the only way to resolve
this painful conflict between his ideas and his action. Once
he had broken out of the circle, left both friends and
enemies behind and recovered his solitude, he would find
that peace of mind he needed to prepare for death. There
was not a moment to lose! He struggled into his dressing-
gown and put on his slippers; then he went into his study
and wrote a farewell letter to Sonya, based on a draft he
had prepared the previous evening. He dated the letter
28 October 1910, 4 a.m.:

My departure will cause you pain, and I am sorry about that;
but try to understand me, and believe that I could not do otherwise. My position in the house is becoming – has already become
– intolerable. Apart from everything else, I cannot go on living
in the luxury by which I have always been surrounded, and I am
doing what people of my age very often do: giving up the world,
in order to spend my last days alone and in silence. Do understand this, I beg of you, and do not come rushing after me, even
if you should learn where I have gone. Your coming would only
make things worse for yourself and for me, and would not alter
my decision.

I thank you for the forty-eight years of honourable life you
spent with me and I ask you to forgive all the wrongs I have done
to you, just as I forgive you, with all my heart, those you may
have done to me. My advice is that you should reconcile yourself to your new situation resulting from my departure, and not
bear me any ill-will because of it. If there is something you want
to tell me, tell it to Sasha, who will know where I am and will
see that the message reaches me. But she cannot tell you where

I am because I have made her promise not to tell anyone. – Leo Tolstoy.

I have instructed Sasha to get my things and my manuscripts together and to forward them to me. – L.T.

After completing his letter, he tiptoed away to wake up Dr Makovitsky:

'I have decided to leave. Come with me. We will not take much with us, just the bare essentials.'[2]

Makovitsky showed no sign of surprise. Not for one moment did it occur to him that his eighty-two-year-old patient, who had had several serious strokes, was endangering his life by setting out on such a journey. He was an ideologist first, and a doctor afterward. What an honour for him to assist the patriarch in his flight! Instead of enjoining Tolstoy to be calm and go back to bed, he gratefully prepared to follow him. The old man returned to his bedroom, dressed warmly, put on his boots, went back downstairs and knocked on Sasha's door. When she saw him standing there in his peasant blouse with a candle in his hand and a businesslike expression on his face, she immediately understood. But neither did she make a move to restrain him. Her joy at his decision, which would give her mother such a blow, silenced all her fears for her father's health.

'I'm leaving now,' he told her. 'Come help me pack.'

She alerted Varvara Feokritova, and the two went up the stairs, light as shadows, to join Dr Makovitsky in the study. Tolstoy quietly closed the doors to Sonya's room. Fortunately, she had gone back to sleep. But what if she woke up and came in and demanded explanations? Straining to hear every sound, his hands trembling, Tolstoy himself tied up his bundles, showed Sasha what was to go in the trunk, urged his accomplices to move quietly and keep their voices down.

After half an hour, the preparations were still unfinished; he became impatient, announced that he could wait no longer, put on his heavy blue coat and brown wool cap and mittens and started off to the stable to order the horses harnessed. But it was so dark outdoors that he strayed off the path, collided with a tree trunk and fell on to his knees. He spent minutes hunting for his headgear, which had fallen off in the wet grass. Then, not having found it, he went back to the house bareheaded and distraught. Sasha gave him another cap and he set out again, carrying an electric torch. A few minutes later, Makovitsky, Sasha and Varvara Feokritova followed him to the stable, carrying packages and dragging his trunk. Heavily laden, they struggled through the black mud; halfway, they saw the gleam of a lamp. It was Tolstoy coming back to light their way. Taking the lead, he flashed his pocket lamp on and off, which made the night seem even blacker.

In the stable, he tried to help Adrian Pavlovich, the coachman, harness the second horse to the shaft. He took the bit and held it up to the horse, but his hands were weak and refused to obey him; in despair, he sat down on his trunk and dropped his head.

'I'm sure we will be caught,' he mumbled. 'Then all will be lost. I won't be able to get away without a scandal.'

At last, the coach was ready. He heaved himself inside with Makovitsky.

'Wait, Papa,' cried Sasha. 'Let me kiss you!'

'Good-bye, darling,' he said hurriedly. 'We'll meet again soon.'

He told the driver to start. The groom mounted a horse, holding a lantern to show the way. The coach jolted along in the ruts; the night was chilly and damp; they circled the house, where Sonya was still sleeping. Dawn was breaking as they reached the village. There were lights in a few isbas; the first curls of smoke were rising skyward. Tolstoy was still afraid his wife would come after them and kept turning around to look. It was very cold and Dr Makovitsky made him put on a second cap. 'Where to go?' murmured Tolstoy. 'Where to go, the farthest possible?' Dr Makovitsky suggested Bessarabia, where they could stay with the

Muscovite labourer Gusarov, a genuine Tolstoyan. But the trip would be long and tiring. The old man said nothing. He had told Sasha he would stop off to see his sister Marya first, at the Shamardino convent. Afterwards, he would trust to inspiration, or circumstance.

At the Shchekino station they had to wait an hour and a half for a train. His fear that Sonya would catch him grew greater with every minute. Who would get there first, she or the locomotive? The locomotive won. He heaved a sigh of relief. He and Dr Makovitsky went as far as Gorbachevo in second class, but there they had to change trains and they continued in third class. The car was filled with passengers, more than half of whom were smoking bad tobacco. The smell and the stuffiness of the car bothered him and he went out on to the rear platform, only to find five more smokers; finally he took refuge on the front platform, where he turned up his overcoat collar and leaned back on his walking-stick, which was equipped with a folding seat. 'What can Sofya Andreyevna be doing?' he muttered. 'I pity her.' A little later he added, 'How good it is to be free!' The wind blasted across the platform. A stream of icy air whipped the old man's face. Cinders seared his eyes. It required all Dr Makovitsky's urging and authority to bring him inside the car after three-quarters of an hour.

He was soon identified by his fellow passengers: peasants, factory workers, a surveyor, a high-school girl. ... Flattering notoriety, which he forbade himself to enjoy. The surveyor drew him into a discussion of Henry George's single tax scheme, Darwinism, non-violence, science, education. After that, a muzhik said, 'What you need, Father, is to get away from the affairs of this world, go into the monastery and labour to save your soul!' Tolstoy answered with a smile of complicity. Behind him, a worker began to sing, accompanying himself on the accordion. The train inched along. The old man's features were sharpened by fatigue; now and then his mind began to wander.

At last, at ten minutes before five, they reached Kozelsk, the closest station to Optina-Pustyn. Tolstoy immediately wrote two telegrams, one for Sasha and one for Chertkov, announcing his arrival: 'Spending night at Optina. Shamardino tomorrow.' Both were signed with the code-name, Nikolayev. He also wrote a letter to Sasha, telling her about the trip and asking her to send him the books he had been reading (Montaigne's *Essays*, the second volume of *The Brothers Karamazov, Une Vie* by Maupassant), a pair of small scissors, some pencils and his dressing-gown. As for the scene she must inevitably have with her mother, he gave her a piece of advice: 'I beg you, my darling: few words, but be gentle and firm.'

The travellers hired a carriage to the Optina monastery. The roads were full of potholes, the wind glacial, the sky black, the moon glimmering intermittently through the clouds; they had to ferry across a river. Dr Makovitsky watched Tolstoy apprehensively. At the convent hostelry they were received by the head monk, an affable man with a flamboyant beard and a mane of red hair. A vast room with two beds, clean and well heated, was made ready for them. Tolstoy drank tea with honey but ate nothing, asked for a glass to hold his fountain pen during the night, wrote a long entry in his diary and, around ten in the evening, undressed for bed, worn out and happy. When Dr Makovitsky moved to help him take off his boots, he growled:

'I wish to take care of myself!'

But he had difficulty pulling them off. As he struggled and puffed, bending double, he added:

'I want to live with the utmost simplicity, spend money parsimoniously ...'[3]

Then he stretched out and closed his eyes, thinking of those he had left behind in the old white house at the end of the birch drive.

At Yasnaya Polyana on that 28 October, Sonya rose at eleven and, as soon as she was dressed, went to her husband's bedroom. Empty! Alarmed, she ran into the Remington room and asked Sasha:

'Where is Papa?'

'Gone,' answered the girl drily.

'Where?'

'I don't know.'

'What do you mean, you don't know? Has he gone for good?'

'He left a letter for you. Here.'

Sonya jerked upright, snatched the letter out of her daughter's hand, tore open the envelope and read the first few lines, moaned, 'My God, what is he doing to me?' and ran out into the garden. Sasha, Bulgakov, who had just arrived from Chertkov's, and a few servants rushed off in pursuit. In the distance they caught glimpses of her grey dress weaving between the trees. She was running towards the pond as hard as her old legs would carry her. When she reached the planks of the laundry-raft she slipped and fell, dragged herself to the edge and rolled off into the water. She was already going under, her arms beating weakly, when Bulgakov and Sasha splashed in after her, seized her and pulled her on to the bank. She was brought back, soaked and shivering, to her room.

'Wire your father that I drowned myself,' she begged.

Sasha had just finished changing her clothes when she saw her mother come out of the house in a bathrobe and turn back towards the pond. Once again Bulgakov and the servant stopped her. She was delirious with grief all day long; she could not be left alone, she cried and beat at her breast with a paperweight or a hammer, jabbed herself with scissors, a knife, pins, threatened to throw herself out of the window or down the well. Seriously alarmed, Sasha called a doctor from Tula, who merely diagnosed a fit of hysterics, 'without the least trace of mental derangement'. Sasha telegraphed an urgent summons to her brothers and sister. Andrey arrived that evening and immediately lay the blame on his father. Bulgakov and old

Marya Schmidt took turns sitting up with Sonya, who wandered about the house all night talking to herself, sobbing and threatening: 'I'll find him, I'll get out of here, I'll jump out the window, I'll go to the station! ... Just let me find out where he is and I'll never let him go again! ... I'll lie down in his doorway! ...'

While she was wailing on, Sergeyenko was on his way to Optina-Pustyn bearing instructions from Chertkov. He reached the monastery at seven in the morning of 29 October. After a bad night (there were caterwauling cats galloping down the halls, a woman was weeping in the next room), Tolstoy welcomed the emissary apprehensively. What was happening at Yasnaya Polyana? When he learned that Sonya had tried to kill herself he was horror-stricken, yet everything he knew about his wife should have prepared him for just such an eventuality. He was also upset when Sergeyenko told him that Sonya and his sons might be tempted to put the police on his trail. Fortunately, the traveller brought good letters, one from Sasha counselling her father not to lose heart and one from Chertkov, rejoicing as though on the morn of a personal victory.

'I can find no words,' the disciple wrote, 'to express my joy at your departure. I feel with my whole being that this is what you should have done and that it would have been wrong for you to continue living at Yasnaya Polyana with things as they were. I only think you waited too long, fearing to act out of self-interest; but now there was no selfishness in the force that impelled you to take your decision. To be sure, at times you will inevitably find your new life more peaceful and pleasant, and simpler, but you must not let that trouble you. I am convinced that your action will be a source of relief to all, and to Sofya Andreyevna first of all, however she may react outwardly.'[4]

Tolstoy immediately answered both letters. Sasha first:

It is difficult. I cannot help feeling a great burden upon me. ... I am relying on the good influence of Tanya and Sergey. The main thing is for them to understand and to try to show her that this spying, these eternal reproaches, this way of treating me as an object, this perpetual checking-up on me, this hatred of the man who is closest and most useful to me (Chertkov), this obvious hatred and simulated love for me – that this entire life is worse than disagreeable to me, it is utterly impossible, and if someone has to drown himself it is I and not she, and that I desire only one thing: to free myself from her, from the lying and hypocrisy and malice that fills her whole being. Naturally, they cannot make her understand that, but they can tell her that not only does her behaviour towards me fail to express her love, but its evident object is to kill me, and that she will succeed, for I hope that the third attack that is now threatening me will release us both from the dreadful atmosphere in which we have been living and to which I will not return.[5]

To Chertkov he wrote more briefly, but with no less determination:

'A return to my former life has become difficult if not impossible, for now I would incur yet more reproaches and less good-will. As for accepting some form of compromise, I cannot and will not. Come what may; so long as I do not commit too many sins.'[6]

Relieved by his double confession, he dictated some reflections on the death penalty to Sergeyenko and went for a walk in the monastery gardens where he, the renegade, banished from the Church, felt the peace of the place as a blessing from God. He chatted with a few simple-minded brothers in tattered frocks, and went up to the hermitage wall, intending to have a conversation with the starets, but changed his mind just as he was about to cross the threshold. Returning to Dr Makovitsky, he said:

'I shall not go to see the starets of my own accord. But if they were to send for me, I would go.'

It was certainly not a desire to become reconciled with the official Church that attracted him to the solitary monks; it was a need to discuss his thoughts on God, the soul and death, with men whose high degree of morality he esteemed, while continuing to deplore their beliefs. Also, he would have liked to learn more about the ascetic lives they led, find out to what extent they really had given up the world, compare their experience with his own. After all, was not he, too, a truth seeker? Ah, if only he could have gone to live in one of those white cells, far from his wife and sons and disciples, to meditate on the great problems at his leisure, while still repudiating the dogma of the Church!

At one o'clock he sat down to dinner with a hearty appetite. He was served the monastery menu: cabbage soup and kasha with sunflower oil and he was delighted with this plain fare.

That afternoon he went to Shamardino convent, nine miles away, where his eighty-year-old sister Marya lived as a nun. Her daughter Elizabeth was visiting her at the time. The two women received the old man affectionately, listened to his tale of his disputes, his dilemma and his flight, and succeeded in pacifying him. From the moment he left Yasnaya Polyana, he had been counting irrationally on this meeting. For him, Marya was the sole survivor of his happy past, and in going to her, he was travelling back through time to inhale the fresh air of their childhood. Was it a sign of approaching death, this need to immerse himself in his infancy?

'My sister,' he told her, 'I have been to Optina. How pleasant it is there. I should be so happy to live there, performing the most menial and strenuous tasks. I would lay down only one condition: that I be exempt from church service.'

That evening he ordered his baggage brought to the Shamardino convent inn and, the following morning, began to look for an isba to rent in the village. He found one, whose owner, a widow, would let him have it for three roubles a month. Why go farther? He would end his days at Shamardino. Beneath this glorious sky, occasionally punctuated by the clang of bells and muffled chanting of monastery choirs, his personal heresy and the Orthodox faith would get along very well together. A bargain was struck, and he promised his landlady to move into the isba on 31 October.

While he was nursing this dream of a contemplative old age in the shadow of the monastery walls, a family council was in session at Yasnaya Polyana. All the Tolstoy children – except Leo, who was in Paris – had arrived at the homestead on 29 October in response to their youngest sister's summons. Assembled in her bedroom, they were debating their parents' respective wrongs. Sergey and Sasha alone stood up for their father; the others considered that he had been wrong to forsake their mother after preaching a Christian faith his whole life long, and that it was his duty to come back to her.

'If you try to make him come back, you'll be throwing the whole burden on the shoulders of a man of eighty-two!' cried Sasha.

But the pro-return party would not be deterred. They wrote to their father to recall him to the paths of duty.

'I know,' said Ilya in his letter, 'how difficult your life is here. But you regarded that life as your cross and so did all who knew and loved you. I bitterly regret that you did not have the patience to bear your cross to the end. You are eighty-two and Maman is sixty-seven. Your life is behind you, but you still have to die honourably. I don't say you must come back, but for Maman's peace of mind, do not break off all relations with her, write to her, help her to get her emotions under control again, and afterwards, may God be your guide.'

Andrey was more gruff:

'It is my duty to inform you that by taking this decisive step you are killing our mother.'

Sergey gave an altogether different opinion:

'I think that if something were to happen to Maman, which does not seem likely, you would not have to take any blame for it. The situation was hopeless and I think you chose the best way out.'

As usual, the gentle Tanya qualified her opinion:

'I will not condemn you; as for Maman, I will only say that she is pitiful and heart-rending. She cannot live any other way, and it is probable that she will never change fundamentally.'

While this debate was going on between her grownup children, Sonya wandered blindly through the house, clutching to her bosom a little pillow which her husband used to put under his cheek. 'Dear Lyovochka, where is your thin little head lying now?' she mumbled. Or hissed between clenched teeth, 'A savage beast! He tried to kill me!'

At last, she wrote an anguished letter to her husband:

Lyovochka, my darling, come back home, my beloved, save me from turning to suicide again. Lyovochka, companion of my whole life, I'll do anything, everything you want, I'll give up every kind of luxury, your friends will be mine, I will take care of myself. I will be mild and gentle. My darling, my darling, come back, you have to save me. You know it is written in the Gospels that a man must not abandon his wife under any pretext. My darling, my beloved, friend of my soul, save me, come back, come back, if only to say good-bye to me before we part forever. Where are you? Where? Are you in good health? ... Lyovochka, my darling, do not hide from me, let me come to see you again. I won't disturb you, I give you my word of honour, I will be humble and gentle with you. All my children are here but they can do nothing to help me, they are so intolerant and so self-assured. There is only one thing I need – your love. ... Farewell, Lyovochka, I am looking for you, calling for you every moment ...

But how was she to get her letter to him? She did not know where he was, although she suspected that he had gone to Shamardino. Once more, she had no alternative but to turn to her children. They had just finished their discussion upstairs. It had been decided that Sasha, the only one who knew where their father was hiding, would go to him with the eternal Varvara Feokritova. How proud she

was, with her weighty secret locked inside her head. The
envy of the others incited her to become tyrannical: let
the entire family grovel at her feet, she would not betray!
She collected her brothers' and sister's and mother's letters
and promised to place them in the fugitive's own hands.
After reading them, he would decide what to do.

That night, Sasha packed her suitcase and left, cloaked in
mystery, with Varvara Feokritova. The next morning, 30
October, she reached Shamardino, went to the monastery
and was received by her aunt Marya and cousin Elizabeth
in the old nun's cell. Shortly afterwards Tolstoy arrived,
and froze in the doorway at the sight of his daughter.

'Well, what's going on back there?' he asked in a toneless
voice.

She told him everything and handed him the letters; he
read them, and his body seemed to shrivel up.

'Is it possible that you are sorry for what you did or that
you think it's your fault if something should happen to
Maman?' asked Sasha severely.

'No, of course not. Can a man feel remorse when it was
impossible for him to act otherwise? But if anything were to
happen to her, I should be very, very unhappy.'[7]

Feeling him wavering, Sasha threatened him with visions
of his wife coming after him in hot pursit, the police discovering his hiding place and hustling him ignominiously
home. With the bullying authority of a nurse, she explained
that he must not linger there, he must move on.

'Yes,' he stammered, 'I found an isba to rent. But I mustn't
think of that now.'

He was dejected and upset; his sister ordered tea for him
and calmed him by saying:

'If Sonya comes here, I shall be the one to see her.'

Late that evening Tolstoy went back to his room at the
inn, opened the transom because he was too hot, asked to be
left alone and began to write a long letter to Sonya in reply
to the one he had received. Twice Sasha asked him to close
the transom, but he refused:

'Leave me alone, I'm hot!'
The girl anxiously said to Varvara Feokritova:
'Papa looks as though he is already sorry he left.'
He, however, was writing:

A meeting, and still more my return, is now completely out
of the question. For you, from what they tell me, it would be
extremely harmful, and for me it would be terrible, for in view
of your nervousness and excited state and morbid condition,
matters would, if possible, become even worse than before. I
urge you to make the best of what has come to pass, try to adjust
to the new situation in which you have been temporarily placed
and, above all, take care of yourself. I have spent two days at
Shamardino and Optino, and I am now leaving. I am not telling
you where I am going because I feel that separation is essential
for you as well as for me. Do not suppose that I went because I
don't love you. I do love you and I pity you with all my soul, but
I have no choice. ... Farewell, dear Sonya, may God help you.
... Perhaps the months that are left to us to live are more important than all the years before; we must live them well.

Letter in hand, he went to Dr Makovitsky's room and
found the physician, Sasha and Varvara Feokritova seated
around a table with a map spread out in front of them.
'If we go, we have to know where we're going,' said the
doctor.
Tolstoy joined in the discussion of alternative routes:
Novocherkassk and then Bulgaria, Turkey. ... If they could
not get a passport to cross the frontier, they could always
settle in the Caucasus, in a Tolstoy colony. Tolstoy had
brought only thirty-two roubles with him, but Sasha had
two hundred. As the discussion was growing heated, the old
man lost his patience:
'That's enough! We must not make plans! We'll see tomorrow!'
He had always had a superstitious fear of long-term planning. He liked to live from day to day, like the simple folk
and animals whose innocence brings them closer to God.

Suddenly, he said he was hungry. The young women had brought eggs and dried mushrooms; they quickly warmed some barley soup on a spirit lamp. He ate hungrily, then his eyes dimmed and he heaved a sigh:

'My soul is heavy.'

He soon went to bed. But he was too restless to sleep. More and more, he felt hunted by his family. The whole pack, with Sonya in the lead, was about to encircle him. He must leave immediately. Go south, settle somewhere in the Caucasus, as Makovitsky and Sasha advised. The mountain air would be ideal for the girl, who had a delicate throat. He, too, had a fondness for the region, it reminded him of his youth. He went back to his letter-writing; one to Sergey and Tanya, thanking them for being so understanding, another to Chertkov requesting him to keep a close watch on events at Yasnaya Polyana and to notify him by telegram in case of emergency.

At four in the morning he awoke Dr Makovitsky, Sasha and Varvara Feokritova and called for horses and a carriage: he wanted to leave for the station at once. The next train stopped at Kozelsk at seven forty. While Sasha was packing, he scribbled a note to his sister and niece:

'Dear Mashenka, dear Lizenka, do not be surprised and do not be angry with me for going off like this without a proper good-bye. I cannot tell you both, and especially you, my dear Mashenka, how grateful I am for your love and your share in my tribulations. ... We are leaving without warning, because I'm afraid that Sofya Andreyevna may find me here.'

Shamardino was nine miles from Kozelsk. The old man and his singular physician set out in the lead. Crowded into the ramshackle trap, Tolstoy moaned at every jolt. His calvary lasted over two hours. The girls joined him at the Kozelsk station with the baggage, and all four took the train for Rostov-on-the-Don. According to the plan of flight, Novocherkassk was the first stop, where they would

stay with a nephew of the author, Denisenko. But Novocherkassk was over six hundred miles away, which meant,
at the pace at which the train was crawling along, a trip of
thirty hours. Trusting to his patient's robust constitution,
Dr Makovitsky apparently did not consider the idea insane,
and Sasha excitedly felt as though she were living a novel.
To cover their tracks, she decided to buy tickets that had
to be renewed at every major station. Tolstoy, at the end
of his tether, lay down on the bench. His head wobbled
with every lurch of the train. He could not relax. He
wanted to read the morning papers. At the next station,
they were bought for him. The news of his departure was
splashed across every front page. He was dismayed.

'They know everything already,' he sighed.

Sasha covered him with a blanket, urged him to sleep and
went out of the compartment into the main section of the
car. There, passengers were reading the papers and commenting on the news. Two young men dressed with provincial elegance – looking extremely pleased with themselves,
cigarettes dangling from their lips – were talking louder
than the rest. Sasha heard:

'The old boy's played her a pretty trick! It must not have
made Sofya Andreyevna very happy to see him skip out like
that in the middle of the night.'

'And after she spent her whole life taking care of him.
Probably her nursing wasn't the right kind!'[8]

They burst out laughing. But the news soon got around
that Leo Tolstoy was on the train and they fell into an
embarrassed silence. Others grew bolder. A crowd formed
in the passageway. Curious faces were continually pushing
open the door to gawk at the patriarch asleep on his bench.
Sasha had to call a conductor to send them away. When
her father awoke, she gave him some of the barley soup
she had warmed up on her spirit lamp. He emptied the bowl
with pleasure and went back to sleep. Towards four in the
afternoon, he complained that he was not feeling well. He
was shivering and his teeth chattered. Recalled to his sense

of duty, Dr Makovitsky insisted that he take his temperature: it was 100·1.

The train was travelling slowly, with a crashing and squealing of metal; the floor creaked, the windowpanes vibrated; a smell of hot soot filled the compartment; Sasha uneasily watched her father's colourless face. At Gorbachevo, two suspicious-looking strangers climbed aboard and posted themselves in the corridor. An employee of the railways confessed, in answer to the girl's questions, that they were plainclothes policemen. Meanwhile his fever was mounting, he was moaning weakly. 'I cannot describe our distress,' Sasha later wrote. 'For the first time, I felt that we had no house, no home. We were in a smoke-filled second-class railroad car with strangers all around us, and not a single corner in which to lay a sick old man.'[9] Even Makovitsky was losing his blithe confidence.

'Courage, Sasha, everything is fine,' Tolstoy whispered, squeezing his daughter's hand.

But he himself was plainly worried. The train had just left Dunkov: the fugitives decided to get off at the next stop. At six thirty-five, the lights of a tiny unknown station swam out of the night: Astapovo. Dr Makovitsky jumped on to the platform and returned a moment later with the stationmaster. As there was no hotel in the hamlet, this cooperative man, whose name was Ozolin, offered the travellers a room in his cottage, set in its little garden across the tracks, facing the station. It was a common little house, all on one floor, with a tin roof and walls painted red. The doctor and stationmaster helped Tolstoy out of the car, and he went to sit in the ladies' waiting-room while his bed was being made.

When everything was ready, they came back for him. Supported by Sasha and Makovitsky, he walked unsteadily, his head wobbling. As he passed, the people fell back and took off their hats. He returned their salute. The stationmaster had cleared his living-room and installed a small iron bed for the sick man. As he lay down, his mind was beginning to wander; he thought he was at Yasnaya Polyana and could not understand why things were not in their usual places.

'Do as you always do,' he said. 'Put the night table and chair by the bed. ... A candle, matches, my notebook, my lamp.... Everything as at home ...'

He lost consciousness, had mild convulsions, then grew quiet and dropped off to sleep. The next day his temperature had dropped and he wanted to continue the journey. He even dictated a telegram to Sasha, for Chertkov: 'Ill yesterday. Passengers saw me leave train in weak condition. Fear publicity. Going on. Make arrangements. Give news.' But he soon admitted that he was too weak to get up. Sasha urged him to be patient, and asked whether he wanted her to notify the family if his illness were to last for some time. Terrified at the thought of being besieged by his narrow-minded, money-grabbing sons, he begged her to do nothing of the sort. However, he humbly requested:

'I would like to see Chertkov.'

She immediately wired the disciple:

'Left train yesterday at Astapovo. High fever. Lost consciousness. This morning temperature normal. Chills. Impossible to leave. Expressed desire to see you.'

That morning, as he continued to feel better, her father asked her to write down a few thoughts on God that had come to him during his delirium. When he spoke, his voice was hoarse and gasping: 'God is that infinite whole of which man is conscious of being a finite part. Man is his manifestation in matter, space and time.'

Then, worried by the thought that Tanya and Sergey might be angry with him for not having told them of his illness, he dictated a letter for them:

'I hope and trust that you will not hold it against me if I do not ask you to come now. To call for you and not for Maman would cause her great sorrow, and your brothers as well. You will both understand that Chertkov, whom I have asked to come, has a very special position in relation to me.

He has devoted his life to the cause I myself have served for the past forty years. That cause is dear to me, but it is my strongest belief, right or wrong, that it is essential to all men, including the two of you. ... Farewell, try to calm your mother, for whom I feel the most sincere consideration and love.'

His hand shook as he signed the sheet of paper Sasha held out to him. He murmured, 'Give them that letter after my death,' and began to cry.

Then he saw Ozolin, thanked him for his hospitality and talked to him about his family. The obliging man had vacated the two best rooms in his house to lodge Tolstoy and his 'suite'; and had relegated to one tiny bedroom the stationmaster's three children who were laughing and singing with their high voices. 'I listened to that gay, innocent singing,' Sasha said, 'and it only added to my grief, for the contrast between those glad, heedless melodies and the anguish in our hearts was so sharp.'

For a while, Tolstoy was entertained by the tumble and chatter of the children at play; he was about to say he felt quite well when he began to shiver again. Excruciating pains shot through his head. His fever rose and his ears began to hum. At four o'clock, his temperature was 103.5. Dr Makovitsky, assisted by the station doctor, examined him with his stethoscope and detected a characteristic wheeze in the left lung. The patient was coughing and spitting bloodstained mucus. No doubt about it: he was in the first stages of pneumonia. Realizing the gravity of the situation, Sasha overrode her father's recommendations and telegraphed Sergey to bring Dr Nikitin to Astapovo post haste. The night of 1–2 November was agitated. Tolstoy's heartbeat was erratic, he had difficulty in breathing, he was tormented by an unquenchable thirst. In the morning he took his own temperature, looked at the thermometer and said:

'That's bad. It's going up.'

While Sasha was nursing her father at Astapovo, a doctor and nurse, sent for by Sergey, were looking after the distraught Sonya, who refused to eat. 'These strangers only make things harder for me,' she wrote in her diary, 'and all my children want is to avoid responsibility.' However, on 1 November she saw a priest, confessed, took communion and ate, 'for fear of being too weak to go to Leo Nikolayevich should he fall ill.' That morning she received his letter from Shamardino. Unjust, unfair, but even so, it was his writing, it was a little of himself. Overjoyed by this first sign of life after four days of total silence, she replied: 'Do not fear that I shall come hurrying in search of you; I am so weak I can scarcely move; and besides, I do not want to use any form of coercion; do what you feel is best. Your departure was a terrible lesson to me – such a lesson that, if I do not die as a result of it, and you come back to me, I shall make every effort on earth to ensure your felicity. But I have a strange presentiment that we are never to meet again. ... Lyovochka, awaken the love that is in you, and you will see how much love you will find in me. ... I embrace you, my dear, my old friend, who loved me once. ... Well, God keep you, take care of yourself.'

The next morning she got up at dawn and wrote a second letter to her husband, trying, in the intensity of her love, to justify herself for all the trouble she had caused him:

If I watched through the balcony door while you played solitaire in the evening, or followed you when you went riding, or tried to find you when you were out walking, or ran into the big hall when you came in or were dining alone there, it was not because I didn't trust you, but because of a feeling towards you that had grown to be madly passionate of late. ... Every day I meant to tell you that I wanted you to see Chertkov again, but something restrained me from giving you any sort of permission for the second time. And you became more and more gloomy and morose; you completely ignored me, you held out your cup to somebody else and asked them to pour your tea or strawberry water; you avoided talking to me. ...

Continuing her defence, she arrived at the circumstances that had motivated Lyovochka's departure in the night of 27–8 October. At this point the most far-fetched falsehoods flowed naturally out of her pen:

As far as your diary is concerned, I had a stupid habit of feeling in the dark as I went by to see that it was still on the desk; but I never made any noise; that awful night. . . . I glanced into your study on my way downstairs with some letters and, according to my stupid habit, I *touched* the notebook with my hand. I did not *rummage* around, I did not search for anything, I did not read anything; and at that very moment I felt that I was doing something wrong and silly. Besides, you would have left anyway, I was sure you would and I was dreadfully afraid of it. . . . Don't be afraid, I won't come to you without your permission; I must get back my strength; don't be afraid of me: I would rather die than see the horror on your face at the sight of me.

She had hardly finished this letter when a telegram was brought to the house from someone named Orlov, a correspondent for *The Russian Word,* who, without consulting anyone, had taken it upon himself to alert the family: 'Leo Nikolayevich ill at Astapovo. Temperature 104.'

After the first moment of stunned shock, Sonya determined to start at once, with Tanya, Ilya, Michael, Andrey, the doctor-psychiatrist and the nurse at her heels. In spite of her anxiety she supervised preparations with extraordinary clear-headedness, forgetting nothing that might be useful or agreeable to her husband. When the travellers reached Tula station, the only train of the day for Astapovo had just left. With majestic authority, the countess ordered a locomotive fired up, and formed a special train.[10]

At ten on the morning of 2 November, Tolstoy, fighting for breath and burning with fever, joyfully greeted Chertkov, who had been alerted by telegram and had travelled all night with Sergeyenko to join him. The disciple took the master's thin, wrinkled hand and kissed it reverently.

They wept as they gazed at each other. Girding himself, Tolstoy inquired after Sonya, the children, his friends, and asked Chertkov to read out the letter he had written to the newspapers explaining Tolstoy's departure.

'Perfect!' he murmured when Chertkov had finished.

At eleven his temperature was over 103. His heart was showing signs of weakness, so Dr Makovitsky gave him some champagne to drink. Everyone put on slippers before going into the room, to make less noise. Early in the afternoon Ozolin, the stationmaster, rushed into the room in alarm and whispered to Sasha that a telegram had just come from his colleague at Shchekino: a special train bearing the countess and her family had left Tula and would reach Astapovo around nine that evening.

After a moment of panic, the accomplices pulled themselves together and sat down for a council of war. It was decided that a meeting between Tolstoy and his wife could have the worst possible consequences and that Dr Makovitsky should exert all his professional authority to dissuade the countess and her children from approaching the patient. Sasha was particularly fanatical in her determination to keep her mother out: 'I decided not to let her in unless my father asked for her,' she wrote afterwards, 'and to pay no attention to the opinion of the doctors or the family.' Now she even regretted having sent for Sergey and Dr Nikitin. Just in case, she sent her brother a telegram countermanding the first one: 'Father asks you not to come. Letter follows. No immediate danger. Will inform you otherwise.' But it was too late. Sergey reached Astapovo at eight that evening.

He would have liked to go to his father at once, but at first he agreed with the others that the old man might be extremely annoyed to see that one of his sons had discovered his hiding place. In the end, he decided to take the risk and pushed open the door. A kerosene lamp lighted the half-empty room. On a narrow iron bed against the far wall lay a thin shape with a waxen face and white beard; eyes

closed, nostrils pinched, the patient was breathing jerkily.
Dr Makovitsky whispered that Sergey was there. Tolstoy
opened his eyes, an expression of animal fear crossed his
face and, as his son kissed his hand, he asked:

'How did you find out I was here? How did you find
me?'

'As I was passing through Gorbachevo I happened to
meet the conductor of the car you were in,' answered Sergey.
'He told me where you had got off.'[11]

This fib calmed the sick man's fears. He wanted to know
what was happening in the family. Sergey told him that he
had come from Moscow (which was true), that his mother
had not left Yasnaya Polyana (which was false), that a
doctor and nurse were taking care of her (which was true)
and that she seemed completely reconciled to the situation
(which was false). When his son had left the room, Tolstoy
said to Sasha:

'I was terribly happy to see him. He ... he kissed my
hand!'

He burst into sobs.

A little before midnight the train bringing the rest of the
family entered the station. Dr Makovitsky rushed on to the
platform to tell the countess she must not come into the
house. Sasha stood with her forehead pressed anxiously
against the window frame; through the black mist punc-
tured by blurred points of light, she made out her mother's
stooped figure, leaning on one of her sons. Mute phantoms
gesticulated behind the pane for a long time, then the entire group drifted away and melted into the night.

Dr Makovitsky returned and triumphantly reassured
Chertkov, Sonya, Sergeyenko and Varvara Feokritova, the
true Tolstoyans, the qualified guardians of the master's
thought and life: duly sermonized, the family had agreed
that it would indeed be dangerous to allow the countess to
approach her husband. Sonya herself had accepted the
harsh decree. Her special train had been put on a siding
and the passengers were preparing to stay in it, for want of

any other accommodation. They would remain as long as necessary but would not try to see the sick man.

On the morning of 3 November, Dr Nikitin arrived from Moscow, examined Tolstoy and said his pulse was weak and his bronchia inflamed, but his temperature had gone down to below normal and all hope was not lost. Suddenly reanimated, the old man joked with the doctor, explained his art of living to him and demanded permission to get up as soon as possible and continue his journey. Upon hearing that he would have to stay in bed for two or three weeks, he became gloomy again.

Now and then, Tolstoy's sons came prowling around the forbidden house like pariahs. They knocked at the window, Sasha opened the transom and gave them a whispered account of their father's condition. Then they went back to their mother, who was raving with grief in her blue first-class railroad car on the siding. If only the doctors had forbidden *everyone* to see her husband! But there was a positive procession of outsiders filing in and out of his room: Chertkov, Goldenweiser, Gorbunov the publisher. ... The last two had just arrived and Tolstoy had asked to see them at once. He scolded the pianist for cancelling a concert to come to his bedside:

'When the muzhik is ploughing his land and his father is dying, he does not leave the field,' he said. 'The concert is your land, and so you must plough it.'

Then, turning to Gorbunov, who was publishing the Intermediary series:

'We are united not only by work, but also by love.'

'All the work we have done together is filled with love,' replied Gorbunov. 'May God grant that you and I may continue our fight for the good cause.'

'You, yes, but it's over for me,' whispered Tolstoy.

He went on to speak of the next volumes in the series, and in particular of the final chapters of his work *The Ways of Life*. But his voice was growing weak. Gorbunov withdrew to let him rest; instead of resting, however, Tolstoy summoned, in rapid succession, Sasha, Varvara Feokritova, Chertkov, Dr Nikitin. He thought he saw Sonya spying on him behind the glass-paned bedroom door:

'I clearly made out two women's faces watching me from behind the glass.'

To pacify him they had to put a blanket over the door. Then began a phase of feverish intellectual activity; he had the papers and his letter read to him, and outlined replies to each correspondent. He dictated a letter to Chertkov in English, for his translator Aylmer Maude, and a telegram to his sons, not knowing they were at Astapovo: 'Condition improved, but heart so weak that meeting with Maman would be dangerous.'

'You understand,' he said to Chertkov, 'if she wants to see me I can't refuse, but I know the encounter will be fatal for me.'

Delighted with this definite statement, Sasha transmitted the message to her mother, whom she found furious with the entire world and 'lacking in any feeling of repentance'.

'Does he know I tried to drown myself?' the poor woman demanded.

'Yes, he knows.'

'Well?'

'He said that if you committed suicide it would grieve him greatly, but he would not consider himself responsible because he could not have acted any differently.'

'I had to come running out here in a train that cost five hundred roubles!' exclaimed Sonya.

She poured out a torrent of reproach against her husband, affirming that he was a monster but that she would never leave him again if he got well.

That day she begged Makovitsky to slip the little embroidered pillow Tolstoy was so fond of under his head; she had brought it specially from Yasnaya Polyana. The doctor saw no harm in her request and carried it out, but Tolstoy immediately recognized the pillow and demanded an ex-

planation. At a loss, the doctor told him that it was Tanya
Sukhotin who had asked him to give the pillow to her
father. Hearing that his eldest daughter had just arrived in
Astapovo, the old man was overjoyed and called her to his
bedside.

As soon as she came in he questioned her about Sonya.
Tanya forced herself to say as naturally as possible that her
mother had stayed behind at Yasnaya Polyana. And when
he plied her with more questions ('What is she doing? How
does she feel? Is she eating at all? Isn't she going to come
here?'), she tried to change the subject. Then he burst out,
with tears in his eyes:

'Tell me! Tell me! What can be more important than
that?'[12]

Tanya, shaken, murmured something evasive and fled
from the room. In spite of her resolute air, her conscience
was not at ease.

What made this family tragedy still more odious was the
publicity around it. Access to the station was already
blocked by journalists. They stopped everyone coming out
of the stationmaster's little red cottage to beg for fresh
copy. Sonya, having nothing else to do, was glad to talk to
them and, with tragic countenance, related her version of
the story. Mr Pathé cabled his cameraman, Meyer: 'Take
station, try to get close-up, station name. Take family, well-
known figures, car they are sleeping in. Send all to Tula to
be forwarded here.' But in Russia it was forbidden to photograph a railway station without special permission. Protest
from the journalists: 'We are being prevented from doing
our work!' The captain of the local police consulted Moscow. Permission finally arrived, by telegram. The little
station came alive with the clicking of shutters. The rabid
picture-hounds snapped the platforms, the crossing gates,
the little garden, the snowy, muddy landscape under a
sodden sky. Sergeyenko stood guard at the door and allowed
no one to enter except the chosen few approved by Chertkov
and Sasha. The telephone rang non-stop. The telegraph

operators, submerged by the flood of messages, sent a distress call for reinforcements to the capital of the province. In the afternoon of 3 November the doctors issued their first health bulletin: 'Inflammation of the lower part of the left lung. Generalized bronchitis.' Fearing public demonstrations, the ministry of the interior sent a stream of coded telegrams to local authorities: 'Take measures. Mobilize sufficient units of mounted police in neighbouring communities; stand by.' A detachment of county police moved into Astapovo.

Oblivious to the immense turmoil around him, Tolstoy called for his diary – a notebook bound in black oilcloth – opened it to page 129 and, with unsteady pencil, set down on the ruled paper a few almost illegible words:

'3 November. Difficult night. Two days in bed with fever. Chertkov came on the second. They say Sofya Andreyevna. ... The third, Tanya. Sergey came during the night. I was very touched by him. Today, the third, Nikitin, Tanya, then Goldenweiser and Ivan Ivanovich.* And here is my plan. *Fais ce que dois adv* ...† It is all for the good of others and mostly for my own.' ‡

In the evening he had a painful attack of hiccups, which Dr Makovitsky and Dr Nikitin tried to stop by giving him sugared milk diluted in Seltzer water to drink. While his bed was being made up, he muttered:

'What about the muzhiks? How do the muzhiks die?'

In the midst of a fit of tears, he became delirious. He wanted to dictate something important, but his tongue had thickened and the words that came out of his mouth made no sense; he became angry with his daughter for not writing them down. To calm him, she began to read passages from

---

* Gorbunov.

† Written in French. The complete sentence, which Tolstoy left unfinished, is *Fais ce que dois, advienne que pourra* (Do as you must, come what may).

‡ This is Tolstoy's last entry in his diary.

the *Circle of Reading*. When she grew faint with fatigue, Chertkov took the book out of her hand and began where she had left off. All night long they took turns reading by the side of their patient, who dozed, woke up, said he had not heard the last sentence clearly and asked to have it repeated.

In the morning of 4 November he whispered:

'I think I am dying, but maybe not.'

He fretted, wheezed, twisted the corner of the blanket around his fingers, frowned, clutching at an idea, and whimpered plaintively when he could not express it.

'Don't try to think,' Sasha told him.

'How can I not think? I must, I must think!'

He fell asleep with his mouth open, his lips thin and pale, his features sharpened by pain; then he shook himself and began to pronounce more disconnected words in a staccato voice:

'Seek! Keep seeking! ...'

His fingertips made writing motions, moving swiftly and gracefully across the sheet. Tireless labourer, lost in the mists of fever; what new novel or philosophical treatise did he think he was composing? Towards evening, Varvara Feokritova came into the room, and, mistaking her for his dead daughter, the old man raised himself on his bed, his eyes shining with unearthly joy, stretched out his arms and cried in a mighty voice:

'Masha! Masha!'

Then he fell back:

'I am very tired. Do not torment me any more.'

Meanwhile Sonya was chafing and fussing in her railroad car, surrounded by her baffled sons and her suspicious nurse. Four times she slipped away from them and went over to the red cottage, trying to catch a glimpse of her husband through the window. But each time, a hand pulled the curtain in front of her nose. Then she ran to the door and collided with the implacable Sergeyenko. No admission. She fumed. By what right? Lyovochka might be dying! She had lived with him for forty-eight years, and now strangers were trying to prevent them from coming together. If he knew she was there, loving and repentant, he would order the doors of his room opened wide! Her voice began to rise, as she argued with the watchdog outside, and her sons came running and escorted her back to her railroad car by force. Dressed all in black and wearing a fur hat covered by a light veil tied under her chin, she passed in front of the newspaper reporters.

The following day, 5 November, the patient's condition grew worse. Summoned from Moscow by a rush call, Dr Berkenheim came to the rescue. He brought a new, softer bed, digitalin and oxygen balloons. But after examining the old man he did not hide his concern. The heart threatened to give way at any moment. Tolstoy refused every form of medication, dozed, talked incoherently, mixed up names and faces. In a moment of lucidity, he said to Tanya:

'Much has fallen upon Sonya.'

Not understanding what he meant, Tanya asked:

'Do you want to see her? Do you want to see Sonya?'

But he did not answer, his eyes were blank and he was wheezing heavily. A little later, he said to his son Sergey:

'I cannot seem to get to sleep. I am still composing. I am writing. Each thing moves on smoothly to the next.'

The number of press correspondents, photographers and cameramen grew with the arrival of every train. Where were they to go? The Ryazan-Ural Railroad Company housed them in railway cars until they were all full, and then opened up a new building, that had to be heated to dry the plaster. Company cables poured out in a steady stream: 'Please rush ten or fifteen most sturdy model table lamps Astapovo ...' 'Please send mattresses, blankets, pillows by baggage car ...' The railway employees contrived to maintain a zone of relative quiet around the sick man. They kept their brakes from screeching any more than necessary, muffled the couplings, held back their steam valves. When a convoy went through the station, faces lined the windows. Locomotives stopped and started without blowing their whistles. In the snowy streets of Astapovo, however, ordinarily so placid, every tongue on earth could be heard. The station restaurant was besieged by busy, brash men, drinking vodka, munching salt pickles and loudly voicing their opinions of the dying man. His temperature, pulse and rate of breathing were announced to the whole world. All his life, he had noted the clinical manifestations of his slightest disorder with care: now every newspaper in the world was doing it for him. By a grim twist of fate, his private diary was being fed straight into the mass-circulation press and the man who had fled in search of silence and oblivion was the subject of the noisiest publicity ever given to an author.

Seeing the world-wide impact of the affair, the ministry of the interior decided to take drastic action. The governor of the province arrived on the scene on 4 November, along with the chief of the Ryazan police. On 5 November the deputy director of the national police turned up incognito. Were they afraid of a proletarian uprising? The order was given to distribute ammunition to the constabulary. Plain-clothes spies mingled with the journalists. Nor was the Church standing idly by: on the previous day, the metropolitan of St Petersburg sent a telegram to the patient exhorting him to repent 'before appearing for judgement at the throne of God'. But Chertkov refused to show him the message. On the evening of 5 November, an emissary of the Holy Synod, Father Varsonofy, starets of the Optina-Pustyn monastery, arrived in Astapovo and reported directly to the captain responsible for keeping order. This holy man had instructions to see Tolstoy and try, by every means in his power, to bring him back to the Church. What a victory it would be for religion, if the old outcast should admit the error of his ways on his deathbed. But family and physicians alike categorically refused to let the monk approach the sick man. He remained at Astapovo, however, creating a monumental housing problem for the captain of the police, for waiting-rooms, offices, railway cars – everything was filled to overflowing. Father Varsonofy had to content himself with a bed installed in a closet in the ladies' restroom. He still hoped against hope that Tolstoy's guardians, touched by grace, would make some last-minute concession. The archbishop of Ryazan, less optimistic, reminded local clergy that the miscreant was not entitled to religious burial or services. Other prelates sent messages attempting to persuade the dying man, but they were not given to him.

On 6 November Drs Usov and Shurovsky arrived at the behest of Tolstoy's children. The number of doctors around him increased in proportion as their ability to save him declined. Now there were six of them: Usov, Shurovsky, Nikitin, Berkenheim, Semenovsky, Makovitsky. With this new detachment of important personages, the stationmaster decided to abandon his entire house to the 'gentlemen', and moved himself and his family into the switchman's cabin. Tolstoy's temperature was only 99·2, but he was so weak that all hope seemed lost. Tanya and Sasha never left his bedside. He said to Tanya:

'So this is the end! … And it's nothing …'[13]

Then, when Sasha moved to arrange his pillows, he half-rose and said in a firm voice:

'I advise you to remember this: there are many people on earth besides Leo Nikolayevich and you are taking care of no one but him.'[14]

He sank back and his head dropped, exhausted by his effort. His nose and hands turned blue. They thought the end had come. Sonya and her sons were already gathering outside the red cottage. But the doctors gave him an injection of camphor oil and oxygen to inhale, and once more the three brothers and their mother were thrust back into their railway car. After twenty minutes Tolstoy regained consciousness. He struggled and moaned. Bending over him, Sergey heard him murmur:

'Ah, what a bother! ... Let me go away somewhere ... where nobody can find me. ... Leave me alone! ...'

Suddenly he shouted, tough and crude as an angry peasant:

'Clear out! ... Got to clear out!'

Towards evening he had another attack of hiccups. Sixty a minute. With every jerk his old body shook from head to heel. He wanted to sit up at the side of the bed in order to get his breath, but he couldn't move his limbs. A shot of morphine calmed him.

Learning that the patient's condition was hopeless, hope returned to Father Varsonofy. He asked to see Sasha, whose youth, he thought, should betoken sensitivity. She sent back a laconic note, virtually a refusal:

'I cannot leave my father now, he may need me at any moment. I can add nothing to what our whole family has told you. We have all decided, regardless of any other considerations, to respect my father's will and desires, whatever they may be.'

Tolstoy had clearly stated his will and desires in his private diary, on 22 January 1909: 'I could no more return to the Church and take communion on my deathbed than I could use profanity or look at obscene pictures on my deathbed.'

But he had also written in the same diary on 29 November 1901, when he was critically ill at Gaspra:

'When I am dying I should like to be asked whether I still see life as before, as a progression towards God, an increase of love. If I should not have the strength to speak, and the answer is yes, I shall close my eyes; if it is no, I shall look up.'

Although everyone present had read and reread his diary, no one thought of asking him the question. For the Tolstoyans, it was essential that Leo Tolstoy should not deny his creation in a moment of weakness. The monk sent a letter to Sasha in reply to her note, in which he cunningly alluded to a vow which the dying man had allegedly made but was virtually unverifiable:

'You know that the count had told his own sister, your aunt, who is a nun, that he wished to see us and talk to us for the peace of his soul, and that he deeply regretted that his wish could not be satisfied. I therefore respectfully beg you, countess, not to refuse to inform the count of my presence in Astapovo; if he wishes to see me, if only for two or three minutes, I shall hasten to his side. If the count's answer should be negative I shall return to Optina-Pustyn and allow God's will to be done.'

Sasha did not think of answering. Her father was dying. The old man's bony hands were crawling across the blanket, climbing up to his chest, parting invisible veils. The blue spots had come back to his ears, lips and nails. At ten in the evening he began to choke:

'I can hardly breathe,' he said.

The doctors gave him more oxygen and decided to inject camphor oil to reactivate his heart. He muttered:

'This is all foolishness! ... What's the point of taking medicine? ...'

But he felt better after the injection, and called for Sergey. When his son was by his side, he opened his eyes wide and, his face contorted by the importance of what he was about to say, he feebly uttered:

'The truth ... I care a great deal. ... How they ...'

Those were his last words. He dozed off, relaxed, relieved. It looked like a turn for the better. The room was plunged in darkness. A single candle burned on the night table. An occasional murmur of voices, a sigh, a creaking of springs came from the next room, which was full of people. The glass door opened, a doctor entered on tiptoe, approached the patient, listened to his laboured breathing and went out again shaking his head. The minutes dragged on, weighted down with silence and the night. Sasha was exhausted, she undressed and went to lie down on a couch, while Sergey and Chertkov took turns sitting up.

They woke her a little after midnight. The end was coming. He was thrashing about and mouthing noises, unable to articulate. At two in the morning his pulse grew still feebler, he began to rasp and pant. Lying on his back, with his eyes closed, he seemed to be wrestling with some knotty problem. After consulting the other doctors, Dr Usov suggested that Sasha might call in her mother. This time neither the girl nor Chertkov had any objections to make: they did not think he would recognize his wife.

Leaning on her sons, Sonya left her railway car and hurried through the darkness towards the red cottage with the dim light shining in its windows. She stopped short, swaying, in the doorway of the room, not daring to go near her husband in front of all these people who hated her. From the doorway she looked at the skeletal little old man with the cavernous cheeks and white beard, who was all the love of her life. At last she made up her mind and walked straight up to the bed, kissed her Lyovochka on the forehead, kneeled and said, 'Forgive me, forgive me.' But he did not hear. He was suffocating. She went on talking to him in a low voice, incoherently, mixing together her vows and words of tenderness and reproof. She was beginning to lose control of herself and the doctors asked her to go into the next room.

Despite renewed injections of camphor oil, Tolstoy did not regain consciousness. But when a lighted candle was held up to his face, he frowned. Dr Makovitsky called out in a loud voice:

'Leo Nikolayevich!'

His eyes opened on to a glassy stare. The doctor held out a glass of water tinged with red wine. He docilely swallowed a mouthful. It was five in the morning. Shortly afterwards, he stopped breathing. A long silence.

'First stop,' said Dr Usov.

The breathing began again, whistling, irregular. There was a death rattle. Everyone in the house was there, around the bed. Sonya knelt down in front of her husband and began reciting prayers. How he battled against death! After every breath she waited in agony for the next one. Suddenly a great calm spread through the room. Dr Makovitsky leaned over and gently closed Leo Tolstoy's eyes. It was five minutes past six in the morning.

Sergey and Dr Makovitsky undressed the dead man, washed him and put on the coarse white linen blouse he always wore, grey trousers, woollen stockings and slippers. Another telegram, among the hundreds, went out from the Astapovo station: 'Order coffin polished oak 2 arshins and 9 vershoks,* with zinc casing.' Sonya, meanwhile, back in her railway car, wrote in her diary.

'November 7. Astapovo. Leo Nikolayevich died at six this morning. I was not allowed in until his last breath. I was not allowed to say good-bye to my husband. Cruel people.'

She returned to his side, sat down by the bed and did not leave him again all day. At eight thirty the doors of the stationmaster's house were opened to the crowd. Friends, acquaintances, railroad employees, journalists, peasants and factory workers filed past the body with its folded hands. Not one icon in the room, not one crucifix. A kerosene lamp cast a dim light on the peaceful features of Tolstoy and on Sonya's face, red-eyed, her chin quivering, her lips distorted by a tic.

Parfeny, the bishop of Tula, who had taken the train the night before, reached Astapovo at eight thirty that morning and was exceedingly vexed to learn that the author was already dead. Losing no time, he convened the members of the family one by one to ask them if there had been anything in the attitude of the deceased to indicate that he might have wished for a religious burial. All answered no. Andrey Tolstoy even told the bishop:

'Monsignor, I am a practising Orthodox and I would have liked to see my father reconciled with the Church, but I cannot lie.'

---

* About 5′ 11″.

Thereupon the deputy director of the police sent a coded telegram to the under secretary of state of the interior: 'The mission of His Excellency Parfeny was not successful; no member of the family was able to affirm that the dying man expressed a desire to return to the Church.'

Father Varsonofy, fearing criticism from his superiors, had a certificate signed for him by the governor of Ryazan:

'In spite of his pressing requests to the members of the family of Count Leo Nikolayevich Tolstoy and the physicians attending him, Father Varsonofy was not allowed to see Count Tolstoy and the deceased was not even informed of his presence during the two days he was in Astapovo.'

After this, the frustrated clerics withdrew, but not before reminding Father Nicholas Gratsyansky, the local priest, that it was forbidden to say a mass for Tolstoy's soul. There remained the police. They observed the reactions of the crowd filing past the body of the enemy of autocracy, whose numbers increased as the news spread through the countryside. The railway employees decorated the bed with juniper boughs and placed the first funeral wreath, bearing the inscription: 'To the apostle of love.' The second, made of paper flowers cut out by children, was laid at the foot of the deathbed by the granddaughter of the poet Delvig: 'To our glorious grandfather, from his young admirers,' read the band. Muzhiks from neighbouring villages pushed forward, mingling with schoolchildren. A peasant woman said to her son:

'Remember him, he lived for us.'

Women sobbed, prostrating and crossing themselves, strangers kissed the hands of the champion of the underdog, the hands that would never move again. It was as though the dead man's family had grown to embrace all the humble of Russia. Towards noon, they spontaneously began to sing the funeral chant, 'Eternal Memory'. If the Church refused to say a mass for the dead man, then the people would say one for him in their own way. Beneath the low ceiling of the little room, their rough, untaught voices rang out, commending unto God the soul of his servant Leo. The police on duty in the next room, who had been instructed to see that the decree of the Holy Synod was obeyed, could not tolerate such a manifestation of piety, and rushed in with their swords at their sides, shouting:

'Enough of that singing!'

Everyone fell silent, but soon a few voices timidly resumed the chant, and continued until the police returned a second time.[15]

On the whole, however, the authorities were not displeased. At one o'clock in the afternoon the captain of the police telegraphed – in code – to his headquarters:

'By authorization of the governor of Ryazan the placing of wreaths has been permitted, but without provocative inscriptions that might incite demonstrations. There are no signs of an attempt to make use of the event for reprehensible purposes. The strength of the detachment has been increased. Order has been established outside. All measures have been taken to ensure the rapid transfer of the body in order to avoid too great an influx of spectators.'

A medical student injected formaldehyde into the dead man's veins, the sculptor Merkurov modelled his death mask, and a painter, Pasternak, who had come from Moscow with his son Boris,[16] set up his easel near the bed, but the crowd was continually in his way. Impossible to paint under such conditions; he simply made a sketch. Then a railway worker drew a circle on the wall around the shadow of Tolstoy's profile, and journalists and onlookers photographed him from every angle and in every light, and he was laid on the bier.

All day and all night the telegraph rattled non-stop, bringing expressions of sympathy for the Tolstoy family from all over the world. In twenty-four hours the weary operators recorded eight thousand words.

On 8 November, four of Tolstoy's sons – Sergey, Ilya,

Andrey and Michael – carried the plain dark-yellow coffin, bearing no cross or ornamentation, out of the house and placed it in a freight car on a pedestal covered with black cloth. Photographers pushed and shoved to get as many shots as they could, and cameramen cranked away feverishly. The interior of the car was decorated with shocks of straw and pine boughs. It was hooked on to the first-class car in which Sonya and her family had been living. Another car containing twenty-five press correspondents wound up the convoy. At one-fifteen in the afternoon, the funeral train pulled out of Astapovo and headed for Kozlov-Zasyeka. Tolstoy himself had said where he wanted to be buried: at Yasnaya Polyana, on the edge of the ravine in Zakaz forest where his brother Nikolenka used to say the secret of universal love lay buried, engraved on a little green stick.

At the last moment, the ministry of the interior forbade the departure of special trains for Yasnaya Polyana, the Holy Synod refused to allow the celebration of religious services in memory of the infidel, the police were given orders to keep an eye on flower shops selling funeral wreaths, to prevent the inscription of any revolutionary sentiments on the bands, the troops quartered in the major cities were told to stand by, newspaper censorship doubled overnight; and nevertheless, all Russia communed in mourning. Edged in black, the writer's portrait spread across the front page of every newspaper; a few theatres closed, St Petersburg University declared a holiday and the tsar in person, the Duma and the Imperial Council sent telegrams of sympathy to the family. There were strikes, too, and student demonstrations, quelled by the army – a whole sea of agitation surging about a withered old man nailed inside a box, rolling along behind a freight car.

At six thirty in the morning of 9 November 1910 the train steamed slowly into the station at Zasyeka. There was a large crowd on the platform and around the station:

peasants from Yasnaya Polyana and the neighbourhood of Tula, students who had made a special trip from Moscow, delegations of all sorts, intimate friends and unknown followers. When the car doors opened, every head was bared and the crowd broke into 'Eternal Memory'. Once again the four sons lifted the oak coffin. The procession set out down the main road Tolstoy had so often travelled with his rapid stride. It was grey and cold, patches of snow lay here and there on the brown earth.

Two muzhiks walked at the head of the procession, waving a banner: 'Dear Leo Nikolayevich, the memory of your goodness will not die among us, the orphaned peasants of Yasnaya Polyana.' Behind them came the coffin, the bearers taking turns carrying it, then wagons heaped high with wreaths, then a murmuring cohort of three or four thousand people, teams of horses, police in plain clothes. They passed between the two entrance towers. Police were patrolling the grounds. The number of photographers increased as they neared the house.

On Sergey's orders, the coffin was placed on a table between the doors of the study, one of which led to the entry-way and the other on to a terrace. The lid was raised, revealing the dead man. His family stayed alone with him a few minutes. At eleven the crowd began to file past, and went on until a quarter to three. Occasionally, a voice grumbled somewhere:

'Move along, move along, don't hold up the line.'

The floor groaned as though it would give way beneath the weight of so many people. The visitors' dark clothes made the face of the man lying there between the bare sides of his varnished wooden shell seem even whiter by contrast. Bending over him in the crush, people leaned into the table, sometimes jarring the dead man's head, which shifted imperceptibly to one side or the other. He had grown even thinner in the past two days, his nose was longer, his skin diaphanous. Lying there with his hands crossed, at rest after all their labours, he was nothing more than a bit of wax, with tufts of white silk on the brow and under the chin, a construction of mist and snow, a phantom that would dissolve at a puff of wind, someone out of a book, the Platon Karatayev of *War and Peace*.

At two forty-five, the funeral began. A host of people had assembled outside on the steps. The cameras began to roll while other photographers stood on tiptoe to shoot the scene. The dead man's sons and friends took turns carrying the coffin. The crowd, larger now, followed them, singing 'Eternal Memory'. They stumbled along the path full of deep, frost-hardened ruts. A chilling wind streamed through the bare branches. The grave had been dug at the edge of the wood in accordance with Tolstoy's wish. Peasants lowered the coffin on ropes. Swelling out of a thousand throats, the hymn of farewell rose and swept through the forest. Between the tree trunks, as far as the eye could see, men and women knelt in prayer. In such a large gathering of people, the eyes involuntarily sought the embroidery of some ecclesiastical vestment or the glitter of a cross; this was the first public burial in Russia that was not attended by any priest. But the fervour of the people could not have been greater if the metropolitan of St Petersburg had come in person to bless the author's remains.

The family requested that no speeches be made at the grave. There was only some unknown old man, who said a few words about 'the great Leo'; and Sulerzhitsky, a Tolstoyan of long standing, explained why the dead man had wished to be buried in that spot. Suddenly a few policemen appeared to see what was going on. Someone shouted:

'On your knees! Take off your hats!'

After a moment's hesitation, they knelt down too, and removed their caps. The sky was beginning to darken when the first clods of frozen earth thudded dully on to the coffin. Dazed by grief, Sonya was no longer even crying now. When it was all over, the crowd dispersed in silence. The police climbed on to their horses and trotted away, their mission accomplished. The family turned back to the house.

At the end of the drive the old white house rose up, surrounded by the shivering trees. A few close friends stayed on after the burial. So many people in the big room. And yet, it was so empty. All that was left of Leo Tolstoy was a name on the cover of a long row of books.

Post Mortem

THE day after the funeral Sonya, who had caught cold, fell ill: temperature 104. She was bedridden for two weeks. As soon as she was strong enough to walk, she went back to her husband's grave. She was shattered by her sudden solitude and her guilt over Lyovochka's flight and death. On 29 November 1910 she wrote in her diary: 'Unbearable depression, remorse, weakness, aching regret for my husband. How he suffered, these last months! I cannot go on living.' And on 13 December, 'I did not close my eyes all night. Oh, these awful nights of insomnia, with my thoughts, the tormenting of my conscience. Darkness of the winter night and darkness of my heart.' To sleep, she took massive doses of veronal that left her drugged during the day. Even religion, on which she had been relying, could not pull her out of her depression. What was to become of Yasnaya Polyana? The government had been approached as a possible buyer, but had declined, not wishing to honour the memory of a writer who had been an enemy of State and Church. However, two years later Sasha, the sole heir, received one hundred and twenty thousand roubles for the publication of her father's posthumous works and was able to buy back the estate from her mother and brothers. Then, according to Tolstoy's wishes, she gave the land to the peasants. Sonya kept the house and orchard. The Moscow house was bought by the city, but did not become a museum until long afterwards.*

As for the manuscripts, the struggle for their possession and use continued, with Sonya and her sons on one side and Sasha and Chertkov on the other. Not one line of Leo Tolstoy's writing appeared without the approval of his

*In 1920.

youngest daughter and favourite disciple. They regarded themselves as the continuators of his work. In their pious aim of remaining loyal to his memory, they refused all collaboration from the other members of the family, who were judged to be impure. Some even suspected the Chertkov–Sasha tandem of 'correcting' the texts before delivering them to the printer. Sergeyenko, a confirmed Tolstoyan, accused Chertkov of deleting all the passages in Tolstoy's letters that were favourable to his wife. Tanya herself, who had succeeded in preserving a judicious neutrality in the fight between her parents, now became incensed at the lengths to which Chertkov was going. 'If my father could put a stop to the activities of Sasha and Chertkov, he would surely do so,'[1] she wrote. And she added, speaking of a Tolstoyan society founded by her sister, 'Nothing good can come of it. ... Everything said and done there is far removed from the spirit of my father's ideas.'[2]

Sonya undertook to write an autobiography, to counter the malevolent insinuations of the Tolstoyans. It took her back to a time of agitation and violence which she had formerly cursed and now regretted. It made her happy to write about her life as the wife of an exceptional man, whose fame was growing steadily after his death. But now her role was limited to poring over her memories. She lived on a pension, paid by Tsar Nicholas II. Every day she went to pray at Lyovochka's grave. Many pilgrims came, some reverent, others indifferent or derisive. Greasy papers littered the mound, stupid inscriptions were carved on tree trunks. ... 'I see clearly that Yasnaya Polyana will never be our home again,' Tanya wrote. 'Our house has become public property of its own accord.'

In 1914 Sonya was dismayed to see her husband's pacifist dreams shattered by the first cannonball. She said to her daughter Sasha, who wanted to enlist as a nurse on the Turkish front, 'Why are you going to the war? Your father would not have approved.' She was even more distressed by the revolution of 1917. She remembered Lyovochka preaching 'non-violence' to the revolutionaries, and was glad he had died before this fratricidal fury was unleashed.

From one end of the country to the other, peasants were pillaging and setting fire to the estates of the nobility. Warned that the men from the neighbouring villages were marching on the house behind the red flag, Sonya, her daughter Tanya and granddaughter Tanichka made preparations for flight; but at the entrance to the estate the 'expropriators' were met and repelled by the muzhiks of Yasnaya Polyana, armed with axes, pitchforks and scythes, and so Yasnaya Polyana was one of the few homes to be spared. Transformed into a State farm, it was placed under the administration of Sonya's son-in-law Obolensky,[3] and this enabled the great man's widow to stay on in the family home, in which a few rooms were set aside for her use.

In 1918 Sasha went to Yasnaya Polyana and found, in the place of her enemy, a bent little old woman with a quavering chin, lifeless eyes and a broken voice. Falling into each other's arms, mother and daughter were reconciled. It was the beginning of the great famine. A decrepit servant officiated, in patched white gloves. As before, silver and crystal glasses gleamed on the damask tablecloth. But in the centre of the platter were nothing but boiled beets and chunks of black bread mixed with chopped straw.[4] The following year the situation became so acute that in order to support her mother, aunt[5] and daughter, all of whom were living at Yasnaya Polyana, Tanya was reduced to knitting scarves and selling them at the Tula market. The civil war was approaching. Bolshevik soldiers were quartered in the house. At the beginning of October 1919, a red flag was hoisted on the rooftop. As guardian of the premises, Tanya protested: 'To what extent can the presence of soldiers be tolerated in the home of Tolstoy?'[6] The red flag came down again.

A few days after this incident Sonya caught cold and fell ill. Pneumonia. Like Lyovochka. Tanya, who was nursing her, asked:

'Do you often think about Papa?'

'I never do anything else,' she answered mildly. 'I have never stopped living by his side and I torment myself because I was not good. However, I was always faithful to him, body and soul. I was only eighteen years old when I married him and I never loved anyone else.'[7]

Her condition grew worse; the doctors held out little hope. Tanya wrote to Sergey, who was living in Moscow. Yasnaya Polyana was in a military zone, so he had to apply to the Kremlin for a pass. The paper was signed by V. Ulyanov (Lenin), head of the Soviet of People's Commissars. Sergey arrived in time to witness his mother's last minutes. She recognized him, blessed him and told him she wanted to be buried in the Church. Then, turning to Sasha, she murmured:

'Sasha, my darling, forgive me. I don't know what was going on inside me in those days.'

'Forgive me, too,' Sasha replied through her tears. 'I have greatly wronged you.'[8]

Sonya died, clear-headed and calm, after receiving extreme unction, on 4 November 1919, nine years after Leo Tolstoy. She was buried in the little Kochaky cemetery beside her daugher Masha. In digging the grave, the men unearthed some bones and the copper buttons of a uniform which, judging by the engraving on them, must have belonged to an officer in the days of Alexander I – one of those whose memory Lyovochka had immortalized in *War and Peace*.*

---

*After Countess Tolstoy's death, her sons and daughters soon scattered. Tanya, director of the Tolstoy Museum in Moscow from 1923 to 1925, emigrated to France and finally settled in Italy, where she died in 1950. Ilya emigrated to the United States, where he had a difficult life, worked in the cinema (chiefly on the film of *Resurrection*) and died in 1933. Leo, the tormented intellectual, travelled widely, lived in the United States, Italy and France and suffered until the end of his days (1945) from being the son of the great Tolstoy who could not write or accomplish anything that did not appear trifling in comparison with the work of his father. Michael lived in France until 1935, then settled in Morocco, where he died in 1944. Andrey died in 1916 during the First World War. Sasha, Tolstoy's sole surviving child, made an unsuccessful attempt to carry on her father's teachings in the Yasnaya Polyana school. She came under suspicion by the Soviet regime and left Russia late in 1920, first emigrating to Japan and then settling in the United States. She is president of the Tolstoy Foundation, which cares for displaced persons; its funds are used to maintain a home for the aged, a church, school, library, etc. Sergey remained in the USSR, had one leg amputated after an accident and died in 1948. Together with Tanya, he contributed greatly to research into and publication of his father's work. Twenty-one grandchildren of Leo Tolstoy are now living in Europe and America, all of whom have children of their own.

Chertkov remained in the USSR, was associated with the publication of the Soviet Government edition of the *Complete Works* of Leo Tolstoy in ninety volumes, and died in 1936 at the age of seventy-six.

APPENDIXES

Biographical Notes

BRIEF biographical notes on some of the people mentioned in this book are given below.

AKSAKOV, IVAN SERGEYEVICH (1823–86).
   Slavophil publicist.
AKSAKOV, KONSTANTIN SERGEYEVICH (1817–60).
   Slavophil publicist, brother of the above.
ALEXEYEV, VASILY IVANOVICH (1848–1919).
   Tutor of Leo Tolstoy's children from 1877 to 1881. Before that, he spent two years on a farming community in the United States.
ALYOKHIN, ARKADY VASILYEVICH (1854–1918).
   Disciple of Tolstoy; member of several Tolstoy colonies.
ANDREYEV, LEONID NIKOLAYEVICH (1871–1919).
   Author of tormented and morbid imagination, noted chiefly for *The Abyss* (1902), *In the Fog* (1902), *The Red Laugh* (1904), *The Governor* (1906), *Darkness* (1907), *The Seven That Were Hanged* (1908) and *He Who Gets Slapped* (1914).
ANDREYEV-BURLAK, VASILY NIKOLAYEVICH (1843–88).
   Actor.
ANNENKOV, PAUL VASILYEVICH (1812–87).
   Literary and art critic; published the important *Pushkin in the Reign of Alexander I* in 1875, and some interesting literary reminiscences.
BARTENYEV, PETER IVANOVICH (1829–1912).
   Bibliographer, editor-in-chief of *Russian Archives*.
BIBIKOV, ALEXANDER NIKOLAYEVICH (1822–86).
   Landowner in the government of Tula; Tolstoy's neighbour.
BIRYUKOV, PAUL IVANOVICH (1860–1931).
   Tolstoy's friend, secretary and biographer; nicknamed 'Posha' by the author's family.
BOTKIN, VASILY PETROVICH (1811–69).
   Publicist and literary critic, partisan of 'art for art's sake' movement.
BOULANGER, PAUL ALEXANDROVICH (1865–1925).
   Tolstoy's friend and admirer; worked for the Moscow–Kursk Railroad Company.

BULGAKOV, VALENTIN FYODOROVICH (1886–   ).

Employed as Tolstoy's secretary in 1910 (he was then 24). Wrote one book: *Leo Tolstoy in the Last Year of His Life.*

BUNIN, IVAN ALEXEYEVICH (1870–1953).

Author, fled to France in 1918; chiefly noted for *The Village* (1910), *The Cup of Life* (1914), *Brothers* (1914) and *The Gentlemen from San Francisco* (1915). Bunin won the Nobel Prize in 1933, the second Russian author to do so before Pasternak and Sholokhov.

BUTURLIN, ALEXANDER SERGEYEVICH (1845–1916).

Revolutionary, knew Tolstoy from 1870 on.

CHALIAPIN, FYODOR IVANOVICH (1873–1938).

Famous bass; his best-known roles were Boris Godunov, Mefistofele and Basilio.

CHEKHOV, ANTON PAVLOVICH (1860–1904).

Born at Taganrog; his childhood was spent in poverty and misery. He grew up in terror of a fanatical and brutal father, and followed his family when they moved to Moscow to escape their creditors. There, living in a slum, he somehow managed to continue his studies and entered the School of Medicine. To earn money, he began writing stories, for which he was very badly paid. Received his medical degree in 1884, but his health was too poor to allow him to practise and he had to abandon all professional activity. However, thanks to Grigorovich and Suvorin, who had singled him out, his literary career looked promising. In 1888 he published his first important story, *The Steppe*, which was a success. It was followed by a series of charming, poignant stories of matchless sincerity: *A Dreary Story* (1889), *The Duel* (1891), *Ward No. 6* (1892), *An Anonymous Story* (1893) and *The Black Monk* (1894). His plays, *The Sea Gull*, *Three Sisters* and *Uncle Vanya* consolidated his reputation. But his increasingly poor health – he had tuberculosis – prevented him from fully enjoying his good fortune. In 1898 he fell in love with a young actress from the Moscow Art Theatre, Olga Knipper, who had acted in *The Sea Gull*. They were married in 1901, and this marked the beginning of a difficult time for the couple – the wife bursting with vitality and ambition, the husband dying by inches. Olga Knipper continued to act in Moscow and Petersburg, while her husband, who had taken refuge in the Crimea, coughed blood; it was in this lonely and forsaken condition that he wrote *The Cherry Orchard*. The play was completed in October 1903 and the Moscow Art Theatre production opened on 17 January 1904; it was a triumph, to the profound joy of the author. Six months later he died at Badenweiler, a little German spa where he had gone to rest.

CHERTKOV, VLADIMIR GRIGORYEVICH (1853–1936).

Tolstoy's secretary and disciple, and executor of his will.

DANILEVSKY, NICHOLAS YAKOVLEVICH (1822–85).
Publicist of the Slavophil school.

DOSTOYEVSKY, FYODOR MIKHAILOVICH (1821–81).
Deeply marked in early childhood by the violent death of his father, who was murdered by his peasants; muddled through a course at the St Petersburg School of Engineering and obtained immediate fame in 1845 with his first novel, *Poor Folk*. About the same time, he joined a group of young liberals led by Petrashevsky, who were opposed to the tsarist regime and favoured the abolition of serfdom. Denounced by a spy and arrested with his companions in 1849, he was imprisoned, sentenced to death and led before the firing squad. Just as he was being bound to the stake, he was informed that his sentence had been commuted to four years' hard labour in Siberia; but he was not allowed to return to Russia until 1859. His health had been destroyed, but he was endowed with superhuman willpower, and published, in rapid succession, *The Insulted and Injured*, *The House of the Dead* – a realistic account of his sufferings as a convict – *Notes from Underground*, *Crime and Punishment* and *The Gambler*, based on his unlucky experience at cards and roulette. Over his head in debt, he fled abroad with his second wife to escape from his creditors; and there, notwithstanding privation, fatigue and anxiety, he wrote his most powerful masterpieces: *The Idiot*, *The Eternal Husband* and *The Possessed*. He returned to Russia at the age of fifty, wrote and published his *Diary of a Writer*, in which he adopted a nationalist and fervently orthodox attitude towards the major issues of the day. This herculean labour did not prevent him from producing two more major works: *A Raw Youth* and *The Brothers Karamazov*. His status was confirmed in the eyes of literate Russia by his speech at the unveiling of the monument to Pushkin in 1880. He died shortly afterwards, without having met his great contemporary, Leo Tolstoy.

DRUZHNIN, ALEXANDER VASILYEVICH (1824–64).
Publicist, literary critic, novelist and translator. One of the first people Tolstoy met when he arrived in St Petersburg in November 1855.

DUDYSHKIN, STEPAN STEPANOVICH.
Literary critic, one of the first to praise Tolstoy's novel *Childhood*, in *Fatherland Notes*.

DYAKOV, DMITRY ALEXEYEVICH (1823–91).
Boyhood friend of Leo Tolstoy.

FEINERMANN, ISAAC BORISOVICH (1863–1925).
Schoolmaster, disciple of Tolstoy; began writing late in life under the pseudonym of Teneromo.

FEOKRITOVA, VARVARA MIKHAILOVNA (1875–1950).

Friend of Sasha (Alexandra Lvovna) Tolstoy, worked as secretary in the Tolstoy home.

FET, AFANASY AFANASYEVICH (1820–92); real name Shensin.
Poet of the 'art for art's sake' school. Lived a quiet and retired life and was a friend of both Tolstoy and Turgenev. A poet of love and the night (or so he has been called), he was known chiefly for a series of slight volumes of lyrical poetry published in the 1880s under the collective title *Evening Lights*, and two volumes of memoirs. In later years Tolstoy cooled towards Fet, in spite of his great fondness for him, because of the poet's unwaveringly human lyricism and reactionary political views.

GASTEV, PETER NIKOLAYEVICH (1866–   ).
Disciple of Tolstoy.

GAY, NICHOLAS NIKOLAYEVICH (1831–94).
Well-known painter and friend of the Tolstoy family.

GOLDENWEISER, ALEXANDER BORISOVICH (1875–1960).
Gifted pianist and close friend of Tolstoy; professor at the Moscow Conservatory of Music, author of a book of recollections: *Talks with Tolstoy*.

GONCHAROV, IVAN ALEXANDROVICH (1812–91).
Author, a realist, with an exceptionally polished style. His chief works are *Oblomov* (1859), an admirable portrait of a dilettante, and *The Precipice* (1869).

GORKY, MAXIM; pseudonym of Alexis Maximovich Peshkov (1868–1936). Born at Astrakhan; his father died when Gorky was an infant. He was brought up by grandparents in Nizhny-Novgorod, which was renamed Gorky after the Bolshevik Revolution (in Russian, *gorky* means bitter). To escape his grandfather's brutality, Gorky went to work as cook's helper on a Volga steamboat when little more than a child. Worked at various trades, lived as a vagabond and tramp, and educated himself as he went along. The direct and colourful style of his first works attracted critical and public notice. He quickly became famous; was elected to the Russian Academy in 1902, but his revolutionary views were frowned upon in high quarters and his election was vetoed by a government order, whereupon Chekhov and Korolenko resigned in protest. Gorky then entered the political scene, took part in the Moscow uprisings of December 1905, was arrested and then released, left the country and settled in Capri, where he established a colony for revolutionary writers. Returned to Russia in 1914, was a pacifist during the war; joined forces with the Bolsheviks and supported them during the 1917 revolution, although he condemned their violent tactics. Founded his own review and fought for the preservation of historical buildings and sites, but after a falling-out with the Soviet authorities he emigrated to Germany in 1921 and then to Italy again.

Already suffering from tuberculosis, he returned to Russia in 1928, recanted and ended his days crowned with honours. His most noteworthy works are autobiographical. *Childhood* (1913–14), *In the World* (1915–16), *My Universities* (1923) and *Reminiscences of My Literary Life* (1924–31). Other works worth mentioning are *Foma Gordeyev* (1899), *Twenty-six Men and a Girl* (1899), *Mother* (1907), and his plays, which include *The Lower Depths* (1902).

GRIGOROVICH, DMITRY VASILEVICH (1822–99).
Author; Tolstoy first met him in 1856. His short stories and novels denouncing the poverty of the Russian peasants paved the way for the emancipation of the serfs. Tolstoy was particularly impressed by his short story *Anton Goremyka* (1847). For a time both men were contributors to *The Contemporary*. Grigorovich was the first to call attention to Dostoyevsky, by recommending the manuscript of *Poor Folk* to Nekrasov and Belinsky.

GROT, NICHOLAS YAKOVLEVICH (1852–99).
Idealistic philosopher, professor at the University of Moscow and good friend of Tolstoy.

GUSEV, NICHOLAS NIKOLAYEVICH (1882–   ).
Tolstoy's secretary from 1907 to 1909. Author of numerous biographical studies of the author.

HERZEN, ALEXANDER IVANOVICH (1812–70).
Author and revolutionary, exiled to Siberia for his subversive ideas, then permitted to leave Russia in 1846; lived in Paris and Nice and finally settled in London. There he published his periodical *The Bell* (*Kolokol*) denouncing the abuses of the Russian government. Later, moved to Geneva and published the same review in French.

HIPPIUS, ZINAIDA NIKOLAYEVNA (1869–1945).
Novelist and poetess, wife of Dmitry Merezhkovsky; emigrated to France.

KATKOV, MICHAEL NIKIFOROVICH (1818–87).
Publicist and publisher of reactionary tendency.

KHILKOV, DMITRY ALEXANDROVICH (1858–1914).
Prince, and at one point officer in the Guards, who resigned from the army in obedience to Tolstoy's ideals.

KHOMYAKOV, ALEXIS STEPANOVICH (1804–60).
Author and poet of Slavophil persuasion; however, welcomed technical progress and the emancipation of the serfs. With Kireyevsky, Samarin and Aksakov, founded the small clique whose aims were to defend Russia, Russian religious tradition and Russian history.

KIREYEVSKY, IVAN VASILYEVICH (1806–56).
Philosopher and co-founder, with Khomyakov, of the Slavophil movement.

KIREYEVSKY, PETER VASILYEVICH (1808–56).
Brother of the above. Slavophil publicist, collected and did research on Russian folk songs.

KONI, ANATOL FYODOROVICH (1844–1927).
Reputed jurist and judge, wrote memoirs; friend of Tolstoy, to whom he furnished the story for *Resurrection*.

KOROLENKO, VLADIMIR GALAKTYONOVICH (1853–1921).
Author of Ukrainian origin. Arrested for associating with revolutionaries, exiled to Siberia, then allowed to return to Russia; published a number of works defending the downtrodden, such as *Makar's Dream*, *The Blind Musician* and *The Murmuring Forest*.

KORSH, EUGENE FYORODOVICH
Publisher of the periodical *Athenaeum*.

KRAMSKOY, IVAN NIKOLAYEVICH (1837–87).
Artist and friend of Tolstoy; was the first to paint a portrait of him.

KRAYEVSKY, ANDREY ALEXANDROVICH (1810–89).
Publicist, publisher of the journal *Fatherland Notes*.

KUPRIN, ALEXANDER IVANOVICH (1870–1938).
Author; wrote a large number of realistic novels and short stories, the most famous of which are *The Duel* (1905), *Captain Rybnikov* (1906), *Sulamith* (1908), *The Garnet Bracelet* (1911) and *Yama* (1915). After the Russian Revolution, settled in France, but became homesick and returned to his country, where he died.

LEONTYEV, KONSTANTIN NIKOLAYEVICH (1831–91).
Author, essayist and critic, ended his life as a monk at Trinity Monastery near Moscow. Especially noted for a remarkable study: *Analysis, Style and Atmosphere in the Novels of Count L. N. Tolstoy* (1890).

LESKOV, NICHOLAS SEMYONOVICH (1831–95).
Author; a realist, excelling in the portrayal of ecclesiastical circles and common people, as in *Lady Macbeth of the Mtsensk District* (1865), *The Amazon* (1866), *Cathedral Folk* (1872), *The Sealed Angel* (1873) and *The Enchanted Wanderer* (1873).

LOEWENFELD, RAPHAEL (1854–1910).
German author, pro-Slav, literary critic; wrote several books about Tolstoy, whom he visited in 1890 to obtain material for a biography he had begun.

MAKLAKOV, VASILY ALEXEYEVICH (1870–1957).
Lawyer, member of the imperial Duma and friend of Tolstoy; at the time of the Kerensky government in 1917 he was ambassador to France, and remained there after the Revolution.

MAKOVITSKY, DUSHAN PETROVICH (1866–1921).
Tolstoy's personal physician from 1904 to 1910.

MAYKOV, APOLLON NIKOLAYEVICH (1821–97).
Son of a painter; at first, wanted to paint himself, but showed such striking talent for poetry at twenty that he decided to shift to literature. A trip to Italy produced *Roman Sketches* (1847). Later, classical Rome inspired him to write tragedies in verse, such as *Two Worlds* (1882). He also published *The Princess* (1877), another long narrative poem. After a period in Paris, where he attended the Sorbonne and defended a thesis on ancient Slavic law, returned to St Petersburg, was appointed librarian of the Rumyantsev Museum and became Chairman of the Foreign Works Censorship Committee. His idylls on nature show a delicate touch; he was an 'imagist' poet and an avowed partisan of 'art for art's sake'.

MECHNIKOV, ILYA ILICH (1845–1916).
Russian zoologist and biologist; lived in Paris, where he was appointed assistant director of the Institut Pasteur. Visited Yasnaya Polyana with his wife on 30 May 1909. Nobel Prize 1908.

MEREZHKOVSKY, DMITRY SERGEYEVICH (1865–1941).
Author; deeply concerned with religious and historical questions, he wrote *Julian the Apostate* (or *The Death of the Gods*) (1896), *Leonardo da Vinci* (or *The Forerunner*) (1901), *Peter and Alexis* (1905), and several critical studies, among them *Tolstoy and Dostoyevsky* (1901–2). After the Revolution, fled to France with his wife, Zinaida Hippius.

NAZHIVIN, IVAN FYODOROVICH (1874–1940).
Writer, friend of Tolstoy. Emigrated after the Russian Revolution.

NEKRASOV, NICHOLAS ALEXEYEVICH (1821–78).
Great poet and courageous publicist; in 1846, purchased *The Contemporary*, the review founded by Pushkin and Pletnyov in 1836. Assisted by Ivan Panayev, he soon transformed it into Russia's foremost literary review of progressive and liberal tendency. Its publication was banned by the authorities in 1866. Affirmative and atheistic, his best-known works (*Who Can Be Happy in Russia*, *Frost the Red-Nosed* and *Vlas*) described the miseries of the common people and their aspirations, and helped to prepare public opinion for the abolition of serfdom.

OGARYOV, NICHOLAS PLATONOVICH (1813–77).
Liberal-minded poet; banished from the capital in 1834 by administrative order. After travelling about Europe, left Russia for good in 1856 and settled in London, where he collaborated with Herzen. Wrote a collection of poems of intense sincerity.

OSTROVSKY, ALEXANDER NIKOLAYEVICH (1823–86).
Dramatist, excelling in the portrayal of the lower middle-class and trades people. Wrote some forty plays, including *The Bankrupt* (1849), *The Poor Bride* (1853), *Poverty Is No Crime* (1854), *The Ward* (1859), *The Thunderstorm* (1860) and *The Forest* (1871).

OZMIDOV, NICHOLAS LUKICH (1844–1908).
Good friend of Tolstoy; shared his ideas.

PANAYEV, IVAN IVANOVICH (1812–62).
Author and co-publisher, with Nekrasov, of *The Contemporary*.

PISEMSKY, ALEXIS THEOFILAKTOVICH (1820–81).
Novelist and dramatist. His first novel, *The Boyars* – a plea for free love – was banned by the censor, circulated in manuscript form and was published in 1858. In 1852 he had already obtained a resounding success with *The Hypochondriac* and in 1858 with a novel, *A Thousand Souls*, depicting Russian society before the abolition of serfdom. Also worth mentioning are *Troubled Sea* (1863), and a few realistic dramas such as *Bitter Fate* (1859). Pisemsky was a first-rate observer of provincial life.

POBYEDONOSTSEV, KONSTANTIN PETROVICH (1827–1907).
Tutor of Tsarevich Alexander, who reigned as Alexander III, he gained considerable ascendancy over him and led him towards absolute autocracy. He became the tsar's representative to the Holy Synod and held this position for nearly fifty years under Alexander III and Nicholas II; to the last, he remained a sworn enemy of liberal ideas.

POLONSKY, YAKOV PETROVICH (1819–98).
Poet of pleasing and elegant manner.

RAYEVSKY, IVAN IVANOVICH (1835–91).
Landowner in the government of Ryazan; friend of Tolstoy, who lived on his estate in 1891 while organizing relief during the great famine.

REPIN, ILYA EFIMOVICH (1844–1930).
Famous painter, known for his colourful renditions of historical events and famous persons and his genre paintings. Major works include 'The Volga Boatmen', 'The Procession', 'The Nihilist', 'Back from Siberia', 'The Cossacks', 'The Death of Tsarevich Ivan' and a few portraits and sketches of Tolstoy, whom he often visited in his home in Moscow and at Yasnaya Polyana.

RUSANOV, GABRIEL ANDREYEVICH (1846–1907).
Friend of Tolstoy, member of the Kharkov district court.

SALTYKOV-SHCHEDRIN, MICHAEL EVGRAFOVICH (1826–89).
Author, impassioned liberal. Exiled in 1848 for his first novel, *A Mixed-Up Affair*; returned to St Petersburg in 1856 and joined the civil service. Became vice-governor of Ryazan and then of Tver, while continuing to publish savagely satirical stories, entitled *Provincial Sketches* (1856) in the *Russian Herald*. In 1868 he resigned from the civil service to devote all his time to writing, and published a series of mordant books whose sharp wit left no class of Russian society unscathed: *Pompadours and Pompadouresses* (1867–73), *The History of a Town* (1869–70), *Innocent Tales*

(1869–86) and, most important of all, *The Golovlyov Family* (1876–80), an admirable sombre novel with a haunting tragic quality.

SAMARIN, PETER FYODOROVICH (1830–1901).
Landowner, Marshal of Nobility of the Tula district, friend of Tolstoy.

SERGEYENKO, ALEXIS PETROVICH (1886–   ).
Man of letters; Chertkov's secretary from 1906 to 1920. Wrote a book of recollections.

SERGEYENKO, PETER ALEXEYEVICH (1854–1930).
No relation to the preceding. Man of letters, admirer of Tolstoy, whom he first met in 1892. Published a large number of articles about him, and a book entitled *How Leo Tolstoy Lives and Works*.

SHKARVAN, ALBERT (1870–1926).
Initially, a military doctor of Slovak origin; disciple of Tolstoy.

SOLLOGUB, COUNT VLADIMIR ALEXANDROVICH (1814–82).
Abandoned a diplomatic career for literature, joined the staff of *The Contemporary*. Wrote *Tarantass* (1845), The Pain of a Heart and *Two Minutes*.

SOLOGUB, FYODOR KUZMICH. Pseudonym of Tyetyernikov (1863–1927).
Poet and novelist; with Bryusov, Blok, Balmont and others, an outstanding exponent of the Russian symbolist school. In addition to his poems, written in a language of great beauty, he produced an important autobiographical novel, *The Little Demon* (1907).

SOLOVYOV, VLADIMIR SERGEYEVICH (1853–1900).
Theologian and philosopher; taught at Universities of Moscow and Petersburg, provoking violent reactions in rationalist circles. Preached the reconversion to Christianity of the lower classes; forced to resign after the assassination of Alexander II, for giving a lecture on the necessity of abolishing the death penalty. Barred from the classroom, he returned to his cause via the pen. At first, disgusted by the money-corrupted West, he joined the Slavophils. But he soon discovered that the government identified absolute power with Orthodox Christianity, and he did not agree that Russia should become a 'third Rome', as Dostoyevsky advocated. Towards the end of his life his sole preoccupation was the achievement of Christian union through the reconciliation of the Roman and Eastern Churches. His writings include *The Justification of Good* (1898), *Russia and the Universal Church* (1889), originally written and published in French, and his most important literary works, *Three Conversations* and *The History of Anti-Christ* (1900).

STAKHOVICH, MICHAEL ALEXANDROVICH (1861–1923).
Landowner, member of the imperial Duma and Council of 1907, close friend of Leo Tolstoy.

STASOV, VLADIMIR VASILYEVICH (1824–1906).
Art and literary critic. Librarian of the St Petersburg Public Library, where he met Tolstoy. Grew to be an admirer, more exactly a worshipper, of the man he called 'Leo the Great'.

STASULEVICH, MICHAEL MATVEYEVICH (1826–1911).
Liberal publicist, publisher of the *European Herald*.

STOLYPIN, PETER ARKADYEVICH (1862–1911).
As minister of the interior in 1904, he dealt energetically with the uprisings; but in 1906 he attempted to reconcile the peasants to the tsarist regime by enacting agricultural reforms. A sworn enemy of the revolutionaries, he was murdered by one at the Kiev Theatre.

STRAKHOV, FYODOR ALEXEYEVICH (1861–1925).
Author of a few philosophical essays inspired by Tolstoy, whose intimate friend he was.

STRAKHOV, NICHOLAS NIKOLAYEVICH (1828–96).
Literary critic and idealistic philosopher. A close associate of Dostoyevsky on the staff of the periodicals *The Times*, *The Age* and *The Citizen*, and author of the first biography on Dostoyevsky, published in 1883. A great admirer of Tolstoy, he laboured devotedly on his behalf and, in particular, helped with the proofreading of *War and Peace*, *Anna Karenina* and the *Readers*. His correspondence with Tolstoy is fascinating.

SULERZHITSKY, LEOPOLD ANTONOVICH (1872–1916).
Director of the Moscow Art Theatre; Tolstoy's friend and admirer.

SUVORIN, ALEXIS SERGEYEVICH (1834–1912).
Grandson of a serf. First schoolmaster, then journalist; became the director of the largest Russian daily newspaper, the reactionary *New Times*. An autodidact, he had a keen sense of business, built up a great publishing house and obtained a concession to operate newspaper stands in every railway station in Russia. Author and playwright, with a passion for literature.

SYTIN, IVAN DMITRYEVICH (1851–1934).
Famous publisher.

TANAYEV, SERGEY IVANOVICH (1856–1915).
Composer, professor at the Moscow Conservatory of Music, close friend of the Tolstoys. Sonya was very partial to him and Tolstoy took offence at this.

TCHAIKOVSKY, PETER ILICH (1840–93).
Famous composer. Met Tolstoy in December 1876.

TRETYAKOV, PAUL MIKHAILOVICH (1832–98).
Founder of the Tretyakov Galleries in Moscow.

TRUBETSKOY, PAUL PETROVICH (PAOLO) (1867–1938).
Russian sculptor, born and died in Italy; a portrait-artist of considerable talent, also sculpted family groups. His works in-

clude the statue of General Cadorna and the monument to Alexander III.

TURGENÉV, IVAN SERGEYEVICH (1818–83).

Studied in Moscow and St Petersburg, later in Berlin; his first prose composition, *A Sportsman's Sketches* (1847–52), strongly criticized serfdom. Confined to his estate because of an obituary notice he had written after Gogol's death; pardoned in 1854. He spent most of the remainder of his life abroad, in France, where he was more or less adopted into the family of Pauline Viardot-Garcia, the sister of Malibran and herself a well-known singer. Turgenev's talent, wit and culture won him the friendship of George Sand, Mérimée, Flaubert and others. He became a sort of ambassador of Russian literature in France, and of French literature in Russia. Translated Flaubert's *Saint Julien l'Hospitalier* and *Hérodias* into Russian; Mérimée translated his *Smoke* into French. Although an expatriate, Turgenev invariably dealt with Russia in his novels of great psychological subtlety and highly polished style: *Rudin* (1856), *A Nest of Gentlefolk* (1859), *Fathers and Sons* (1862), *Smoke* (1867) and *Virgin Soil* (1877).

TYUTCHEV, FYODOR IVANOVICH (1803–73).

After thirty-two years in the imperial diplomatic service and chancellery, he published a single volume of poetry. Influenced by the eighteenth-century poets Lomonosov and Derzhavin, he was first published in Pushkin's journal, *The Contemporary* (1836–7). He was noted in politics for his pan-Slavic views and in literature for an extremely pure style, a constant concern for the melody of words and a pronounced penchant for romanticism. At the end of the century, his poetry influenced the Russian symbolists.

URUSOV, ALEXANDER IVANOVICH (1848–1900).

Lawyer and author; specialized in aesthetic questions.

ZHEMCHUZHNIKOV, ALEXIS MIKHAILOVICH (1821–1908).

Poet, of whom Tolstoy said that he 'had no spark' and 'drank out of other people's cups'. (Diary, 1857.)

ZHUKOVSKY, VASILY ANDREYEVICH (1783–1852).

Russian poet of romantic and mystical temperament; encouraged Tsar Alexander II, whose tutor he had been, to emancipate the serfs.

Notes to the Text

Part I, Chapter 1

1. Leo Tolstoy used this incident in *War and Peace*: Marya Bolkonsky begs her brother, who is going off to war, to wear a little
   icon to protect him from the shells. The exploits of the Volkonsky
   family, moreover, do not stop there: one of the prince's relatives
   (Nicholas Grigoryevich Volkonsky) covered himself in glory during the Napoleonic wars, while another (Sergey Grigoryevich)
   was sent to Siberia in 1826 for his part in the Decembrist plot,
   and spent thirty years in exile.
2. Letter (in French) to T. A. Ergolskaya.
3. Tolstoy used this episode in *Resurrection*. He also noted, in his
   Reminiscences, that 'Mishenka often came to beg help of us, his
   brothers, when we had grown up. I remember the feeling of helplessness and dismay that would overcome me when this brother,
   who had become a beggar, and who resembled my father more
   closely than any of the rest of us, would ask for help and be
   thankful for the ten or fifteen roubles we gave him.'
4. In *War and Peace* the servants carry a black sofa to Princess
   Marya when she is about to give birth; the same black leather
   divan appears in the Levin home in one version of *Anna Karenina*.
5. Vlasov: *Reminiscences of Tolstoy*, a manuscript quoted by Gusev.

Part I, Chapter 2

1. Diary, 10 January 1908.
2. Written on a loose sheet of paper, dated 10 March 1906.
3. *Reminiscences* of Leo Tolstoy.
4. ibid.
5. ibid.
6. From a rough draft of *Childhood*.
7. *The Old Horse*, an autobiographical story for children (1872).
8. From an unfinished autobiographical sketch, *Notes of a Madman*.
9. ibid.
10. *Childhood*, Chapter 7.

Part I, Chapter 3

1. Written in French.
2. *Childhood*, Chapter 28.
3. Scene reported in a sketch for *Childhood*.
4. *Boyhood*, Chapter 15.
5. ibid.
6. *Childhood*, Chapter 24. And on 27 November 1903, when Tolstoy was seventy-five, he wrote to Biryukov: 'My greatest love was a childhood love – for little Sonya Koloshin.' And as early as 1890 (24 June), he wrote in his diary, 'Thought of writing a book about love, like for Sonya Koloshin – a love that would preclude the transition to sensuality, that would be the best possible protection against sensuality.'
7. *The Cossacks*, Chapter 22.
8. *War and Peace*, Volume II, Book IX, Chapter 12.
9. *Childhood*, Chapter 19.
10. Told by Leo Tolstoy to Biryukov, his biographer.
11. *Boyhood*, Chapter 23.
12. Unfinished autobiographical story: *What I Am*.
13. *Boyhood*, Chapter 1.
14. ibid.
15. ibid., Chapter 19.
16. Letter written (in French) in February 1840; preserved in the Manuscripts Department of the Tolstoy Museum.

Part I, Chapter 4

1. Turnelli, assistant at the University of Kazan.
2. *Youth*, Chapter 1.
3. ibid., Chapter 31.
4. ibid., Chapter 2.
5. ibid., Chapter 5.
6. ibid., Chapter 13.
7. Letter from Mrs Zarnitsin to Mrs Molostvov, dated 13 January 1906.
8. The *Kazan Government News*, 1845, No. 11.
9. *Boyhood*, Chapter 26.
10. ibid., Chapter 27.
11. ibid.
12. ibid.
13. ibid., Chapter 6.
14. ibid.
15. N. N. Gusev, *Tolstoy in His Youth*.

16. *Youth*, Chapter 45.
17. ibid., Chapter 28.
18. ibid., Chapter 32.
19. ibid.
20. ibid.
21. *Complete Works*, Volume 1, p. 233.
22. *Youth*.
23. *Complete Works*, Volume 46, pp. 262–72.
24. Remark by Tolstoy on Biryukov's book. *Complete Works*, Volume 3, p. 398.
25. Note, 4 January 1857, in a notebook. *Complete Works*, Volume 47, p. 201.
26. Diary, 17 April 1847.

Part I, Chapter 5

1. *A Landlord's Morning*, Chapter 19.
2. ibid.
3. Letter from Tolstoy to Grigorovich, 27 October 1893.
4. Draft of the article 'The Slavery of Our Times'.
5. Written (in French) in late February–early March 1849.
6. Letter to Sergey, 11 May 1849.
7. Letter of June 1846.
8. Draft of a letter, quoted by Gusev.
9. Dunyasha died in 1879. Entry in Tolstoy's diary dated 14 October 1897.
10. Diary, 10 August 1851.
11. *Reminiscences* of Leo Tolstoy.
12. Diary, 17 January 1851.
13. Letter from Tolstoy to his sister, 3 March 1851.
14. Letter, 24 December 1850.
15. Cf. Biryukov.
16. Diary, 1 January 1851.
17. Leo Tolstoy: *The Four Readers*.
18. Letter (in French), 8 May 1851.
19. *The Cossacks*, Chapter 2.
20. Letter (in French), 8 May 1851.

Part II, Chapter 6

1. Diary, 30 May 1851.
2. Letter (in French), 22 June 1851.
3. Diary, 10 August 1851.
4. ibid., Stary Yurt, 11 June 1851.

5. Letter to Aunt Toinette, 22 June 1851. Tolstoy described Captain Khilkovsky, under the name of Khlopov, in *The Raid*.
6. Diary, 4 July 1851.
7. *The Raid*, Chapter 4.
8. ibid., Chapter 9.
9. ibid., Chapter 9. This very early work (*The Raid* was written in 1852) contains the seed of Tolstoy's bitter animosity towards the French army.
10. First draft of *The Raid*.
11. Diary, 3 July 1851.
12. ibid., 8 June 1851.
13. *Childhood*.
14. Diary, 22 August 1851.
15. *The Cossacks*, Chapter 4.
16. ibid., Chapter 6.
17. ibid., Chapter 11.
18. Rough draft of *The Cossacks* (Variant 12).
19. *The Cossacks*, Chapter 14.
20. ibid., Chapter 12.
21. Diary, 25 August 1851.
22. ibid., 26 August 1851.
23. ibid., 4 May 1853.
24. ibid., 25 June 1853.
25. ibid., 20 March 1852.
26. *The Cossacks*, Chapter 25.
27. ibid., Chapter 33.
28. Letter (in French), 6 January 1852.
29. ibid.
30. ibid.
31. Diary, 28 March 1852.
32. The district was inhabited by descendants of German colonists who had emigrated from Württemberg to Russia in 1818.
33. Letter of 10 December 1851. (Original in French.)
34. Letter (in French) to Aunt Toinette, 15 December 1851.
35. Letter (in French), 12 November 1851.
36. Which furnished him with the material for his short story, *Memoirs of a Billiard-Marker* (1853).
37. Hadji Murad, chief of the Avar tribe, became the hero of Leo Tolstoy's famous novel *Hadji Murad*.
38. Letter (in French) to Sergey Tolstoy, 23 December 1851.
39. Letter (in French), 12 January 1852.
40. ibid.
41. *The Cossacks*, Chapter 2.
42. Sergeyenko: *How L. N. Tolstoy Lives and Works*; and Golden-weiser, *Talks with Tolstoy*.

43. Letter (in French), 26 June 1852.
44. Letter (in French) to Aunt Toinette, 2 October 1852.
45. Letter (in French), 30 May 1852.
46. Letter to his brother Sergey, 24 June 1852.
47. Diary, 31 May 1852.
48. ibid., 18 April 1852: 'Horribly lazy and apathetic. Do not feel well. Have Alyoshka beaten.'
49. ibid., 2 June 1852.
50. ibid., 13 July 1852.
51. ibid., 3 August 1852.
52. ibid., 17 August 1852.
53. ibid., 29 August 1852.
54. Letter, 27 November 1852.
55. *Reminiscences* of Leo Tolstoy.
56. *Childhood*, Chapter 23.
57. ibid., Chapter 27.
58. *Boyhood*, Chapter 5.
59. N. N. Gusev, *Material for a Biography of Leo Tolstoy*, p. 396.
60. Letter by Dostoyevsky, 19 January 1856.
61. Diary, 6 January 1853.
62. ibid., 7 January 1853.
63. Draft for an unpublished letter (in French). Quoted by Gusev in *Material for a Biography of Leo Tolstoy*, p. 431.
64. Diary, 8–15 May 1853.
65. ibid., 30 April 1853.
66. ibid., 23 June 1853.
67. ibid., 25 June 1853.
68. Tolstoy's servant. This was not the first time his master had had him punished, cf. note 48 above.
69. Letter (in French), 27 December 1853.
70. This work was not completed; a fragment of it was published under the title *A Landlord's Morning*.
71. Diary, 19 January 1854.

Part II, Chapter 7

1. This short story, *The Snowstorm*, was published in 1856.
2. Makovitsky, *Notes from Yasnaya Polyana* (1922), quoted by N. N. Gusev.
3. Letter, 6 February 1854.
4. Letter (in French) to Aunt Toinette, 13 March 1854.
5. Letter (in French) to Aunt Toinette, 17 March 1854.
6. Letter (in French) to Aunt Toinette, 24 May 1854.
7. Diary, 15 June 1854.
8. Letter (in French), 24 May 1854.

9. Letter (in French) to Aunt Toinette, 5 July 1854.
10. ibid.
11. ibid.
12. ibid. Tolstoy was thinking of Gorchakov when he painted the portrait of Kutuzov in *War and Peace*.
13. ibid.
14. ibid.
15. Letter, 29 November 1854.
16. Unpublished letter, quoted by N. N. Gusev in *Material for a Biography of Leo Tolstoy*.
17. Letter (in French), 17 October 1854.
18. Diary, 4–5 October 1854.
19. Letter, 3 July 1855.
20. Diary, 2 November 1854.
21. *Sevastopol Sketches: Sevastopol in December*.
22. Letter, 20 November 1854.
23. Letter to Nicholas Tolstoy, 3 February 1855.
24. Diary, 26 November 1854.
25. Letter to Sergey Tolstoy, 20 November 1854.
26. *Recollections of Tolstoy*, compiled by Zhirkevich.
27. Told by Krylov.
28. Letter to Valerian Tolstoy, 24 February 1855.
29. Diary, 21 April 1855.
30. ibid., 8 May 1855.
31. Reminiscences of Colonel Odakhovsky, approved by Tolstoy.
32. Diary, 19 May 1855.
33. Letter, 31 May 1855.
34. Letter, 10 July 1855.
35. Letter, 28 August 1855.
36. Letter, 4 August 1855.
37. Letter (in French), 4 September 1855.
38. *Sevastopol in August*. These are the final sentences of the third and last part of Tolstoy's account of the Crimean War.
39. *Some Words About 'War and Peace'*.

Part II, Chapter 8

1. Diary, 27 July 1853.
2. Letter to his sister Marya, 20 November 1855.
3. Letter, 9 December 1855.
4. Letter, 24 November 1855.
5. Letter, 27 November 1855.
6. Fet, *Reminiscences of Tolstoy*.
7. Reported by Fet, as told to him by Grigorovich, in his *Reminiscences of Tolstoy*.

8. Letter, 8 February 1856.
9. Diary, 8 May 1856.
10. 'Literary intriguing revolts me like nothing else has ever done.' (Diary, 22 November 1856.)
11. Memoirs of Mme Golovachov-Panayev.
12. Turgenev's expression, according to Eugene Garshin (Memoirs).
13. Letter, 10 May 1856.
14. *Reminiscences* of Leo Tolstoy.
15. ibid.
16. Reminiscences of Countess A. A. Tolstoy (correspondence of L. N. Tolstoy and A. A. Tolstoy). Quoted by Gusev.
17. *Reminiscences* of Leo Tolstoy.
18. *Anna Karenina*, Part V, Chapter 17 ff.
19. Diary, 15 May 1856.
20. ibid., 25 May 1856.
21. ibid., 11 May 1856.
22. ibid., 9 June 1856.
23. ibid., 10 June 1856.
24. Letter, 9 June 1856.
25. Diary, 28 May 1856.
26. ibid., 6 June 1856.
27. ibid., 30 May 1856.
28. ibid., 31 May 1856.
29. Letter of 13–25 September 1856.
30. 14 October 1856.
31. This letter of Tolstoy's has never been found.
32. Letter from Turgenev to Tolstoy, 16–28 November 1856.
33. Letter from Turgenev to Tolstoy, 3–15 January 1857.
34. Diary, 15 June 1856.
35. ibid., 18 June 1856.
36. ibid., 26 June 1856.
37. ibid., 28 June 1856.
38. ibid., 1 July 1856.
39. ibid., 2 July 1856.
40. ibid., 12 July 1856.
41. ibid., 25 July 1856.
42. ibid., 25 July 1856.
43. ibid., 24 September 1856.
44. ibid., 29 September 1856.
45. ibid., 28 October 1856.
46. Letter, 2 November 1856.
47. Diary, 16 November 1856.
48. ibid., 19 November 1856.
49. ibid., 22 November 1856.
50. Letter, 1 December 1856.

51. Letter (in French), 5 December 1856.
52. Letter, 12 December 1856.
53. Diary, 3 February 1857.
54. *Complete Works*, Volume 47. Notebooks, entries of May and June 1856.
55. *Youth*, Chapter 14.
56. ibid., Chapter 23.
57. Diary, 3 February 1857.

Part III, Chapter 9

1. Cf. *Lucerne*, by Leo Tolstoy.
2. Letter, 24 March (5 April) 1857.
3. ibid.
4. Diary, 23 March (4 April) 1857.
5. ibid., 6 (18) March 1857.
6. Cf. the reminiscences of Tolstoy's son Sergey, and Leo Tolstoy's letter to Valerya Arsenyev, 4 March 1857.
7. Diary, 4 (16) March 1857.
8. ibid.
9. Notebooks of Leo Tolstoy, 13 (25) February 1857.
10. Diary, 11 (23) February, 23 February (7 March), 2 (14) March, 20 March (1 April) 1857.
11. Letter, 20 February (4 March) 1857.
12. Letter (in French), 10 (22) February 1857.
13. Diary, 18 February (2 March) 1857.
14. Letter (in French), 30 March (11 April) 1857.
15. Letter to Botkin, quoted earlier, of 24–5 March (5–6 April) 1857.
16. Cf. Diary, 19 (31) March 1857.
17. ibid., 27 March (8 April) 1857.
18. Letter, 15 April 1857.
19. Letter, 18 April 1857.
20. Reminiscences of Alexandra Andreyevna Tolstoy.
21. Diary, 22 October 1857.
22. Reminiscences of Alexandra Andreyevna Tolstoy.
23. Diary, 29 April (11 May) 1857.
24. ibid., 21 May (2 June) 1857.
25. Travel Notes, 1857.
26. Diary, 22 June (4 July) 1857.
27. Letter, 26 June (8 July) 1857.
28. ibid.
29. ibid.
30. Diary, 25 June (7 July) 1857.
31. Letter to Botkin, 27 June (9 July) 1857.

32. Diminutive of Ivan. Diary, 20 July (1 August) 1857.
33. Letter, 18 August 1857.

Part III, Chapter 10

1. Letter, 18 August 1857.
2. Cf. Diary, 27 November 1858 and 9–10 October 1859.
3. ibid., 19, 20 and 21 October 1857.
4. Letter, 22 November (4 December) 1857.
5. Letter, 4 January 1858.
6. Diary, 21 March 1858.
7. Letter, 16 December 1857.
8. Cf., in particular, reviews by Almazov in *Morning* and by an anonymous critic in *Northern Flowers*.
9. Diary, 17 August 1857.
10. ibid., 15 September 1858.
11. ibid., 30 January 1858.
12. ibid., 14 January 1858.
13. Letter to Alexandra Tolstoy, 1 May 1858.
14. Notebooks of Leo Tolstoy, 20 April 1858.
15. Diary, 1 February 1860.
16. Letter, 1 May 1858.
17. Letter, 3 May 1859.
18. Letter, 1 May 1858.
19. ibid.
20. Letter, 14 April 1858.
21. Fet, *Reminiscences of Tolstoy*.
22. ibid.
23. Makovitsky, *Anecdotes of M. N. Tolstoy*, quoted by Gusev.
24. Fet, *Reminiscences of Tolstoy*.
25. Diary, 16–19 June 1858.
26. ibid.
27. ibid., entries of May 1858.
28. ibid., 4 September 1858.
29. Letter, 12 April 1859.
30. Letter, early October 1859.
31. Letter, 9 October 1859.
32. Article by Leo Tolstoy: *The Yasnaya Polyana School in November and December*.
33. Letter, 30 January 1860.
34. Letter, 15 February 1860.
35. Letter, 22 February 1860.
36. Diary, 25–6 May 1860.

Part III, Chapter 11

1. Diary, 16 July 1860.
2. Cf. Auerbach: *A New Life.*
3. Peter Vasilyevich Morozov.
4. Diary, 11 (23) August 1860.
5. ibid., 12 (24) August 1860.
6. Letter, 24 September (6 October) 1860.
7. Letter (in French), 6 January 1852.
8. Letter, 24 September (6 October) 1860.
9. Diary, 13 (25) October 1860.
10. Letter to Fet, 17 (29) October 1860.
11. Diary, 29 October (10 November) 1860.
12. Letter from Marya Tolstoy to Delvig, 9 November 1860.
13. Letter, 24 November (6 December) 1860.
14. S. Plaxin, *Count L. N. Tolstoy and Children.*
15. Article by Tolstoy, '*On Popular Education*'.
16. Article by Loewenfeld on Tolstoy, quoted by Gusev.
17. Letter, 9 April 1861.
18. Related by Tolstoy in his article *On the Meaning of Popular Education.*
19. Proudhon, *Correspondance*, Volume 10. Letter, 7 April 1861.
20. Diary, 2 (14) April 1861.
21. ibid., 5 (17) April 1861.
22. ibid., 9 (21) April and 10 (22) April 1861.

Part III, Chapter 12

1. Letter to Alexandra Tolstoy, 14 May 1861.
2. Diary, 6 May 1861.
3. In Russian, *samo* = self, and *son* = sleep, dream.
4. Sergeyenko, *Contemporary Views of Tolstoy.*
5. The scene is recounted in A. Fet's *Reminiscences of Tolstoy* and repeated by Biryukov in his *Biography of L. N. Tolstoy.*
6. Diary of Countess Tolstoy.
7. ibid.
8. Letter from Turgenev to Tolstoy, late September 1861.
9. Letter from Turgenev, 8 November 1861.
10. Told by Loewenfeld.
11. Letter, 26 January 1862.
12. From an article by Leo Tolstoy: 'Who Should Teach Writing and to Whom?'
13. First article on 'The Yasnaya Polyana School in November and December'.

14. Poem by Pushkin (1825).
15. Third article on 'The Yasnaya Polyana School in November and December'.
16. ibid.
17. Peterson, *Notes of a Former Schoolmaster.*
18. *Reminiscences of Leo Tolstoy,* by a pupil at the Yasnaya Polyana school.
19. Letter to Alexandra Tolstoy, 7 August 1862.
20. Peterson, *Notes of a Former Schoolmaster.*
21. Markov, *The Living Mind at School.*
22. Letter, 7 August 1862.
23. Letter (in French), 18 August 1862.
24. Letter to Alexandra Tolstoy, 7 September 1862.

Part IV, Chapter 13

1. In *Childhood,* Sofya Alexandrovna Zhdanov is 'la belle Flamande'.
2. Tatyana Andreyevna Kuzminskaya (née Tatyana Behrs), *My Life at Home and at Yasnaya Polyana.*
3. In her *Memoirs,* published as the first part of Countess Tolstoy's Diary.
4. *Memoirs* (Diary of Countess Tolstoy).
5. ibid.
6. All these incidents have been related by Sofya Andreyevna Tolstoy in her memoirs, and by her sister Tatyana Andreyevna Kuzminskaya in her book, *My Life at Home and at Yasnaya Polyana.* Leo Tolstoy also used the lovers' conversation-by-initials in Chapter 13, Part IV of *Anna Karenina* (conversation between Kitty and Levin).
7. Diary, 20 September 1862.
8. Memoirs of Countess Tolstoy.
9. ibid.

Part IV, Chapter 14

1. Diary, 19 December 1862.
2. Diary of Countess Tolstoy, October 1862–March 1863.
3. Diary, 2 June 1863.
4. Diary of Countess Tolstoy, 24 April 1863.
5. ibid., 23 November 1862.
6. Diary, 8 February 1863.
7. Diary of Countess Tolstoy, 17 October 1863.
8. ibid., 10 April 1863.

9. Diary, May 1858 and May 1860.
10. Diary of Countess Tolstoy, 16 December 1862.
11. Lyovochka or Lyova, diminutives of Leo.
12. Diary of Countess Tolstoy, 14 January 1863.
13. ibid.
14. ibid., 22 May 1863.
15. Presumably *The Cossacks*.
16. The editors of the diary have prudishly censored what follows. (Entry of 5 January 1863.)
17. Diary of Countess Tolstoy, 24 December 1863.
18. ibid., 11 October 1862.
19. ibid., 23 November 1862.
20. ibid., 11 January 1863.
21. ibid.
22. ibid., 15 January 1863.
23. Diary, 8 January 1863.
24. Diary of Countess Tolstoy, 17 January 1863.
25. ibid., 29 January 1863.
26. *Kholstomer* was finished in 1885 and published in 1888.
27. Diary of Countess Tolstoy, 29 April and 8 May 1863.
28. ibid., 22 May 1863.
29. T. A. Kuzminskaya, *My Life at Home and at Yasnaya Polyana*.
30. Diary, 5 August 1863.
31. Diary of Countess Tolstoy, 3 August 1863.
32. Letter, 1 May 1863.
33. *War and Peace*, Book I, Chapter 6.
34. ibid., Chapter 8.
35. Diary of Countess Tolstoy, 22 September 1863.

Part IV, Chapter 15

1. Diary, 16 September 1864.
2. ibid., 26 September 1865.
3. Diary of Countess Tolstoy, 31 July 1868.
4. ibid., 12 November 1866.
5. Tatyana, born 4 October 1864.
6. T. A. Kuzminskaya, *My Life at Home and at Yasnaya Polyana*.
7. Letter, 23 January 1865.
8. Letter from Turgenev to Botkin, 4 (16) February 1865.
9. S. L. Tolstoy, *Sketches of the Past*.
10. Diary, 30 September 1865.
11. ibid., 23 September 1865.
12. Letter, 16 May 1865.
13. Letter from Dr Behrs to Tolstoy, 31 May 1865.
14. Letter, 4 February 1866.

15. Diary of Countess Tolstoy, 12 March 1866.
16. Letter to Biryukov, 24 June 1908.
17. Letter, 4 April 1866.
18. Letter, 8 December 1866.
19. *War and Peace*, Volume II, Book VII, Chapter 7.
20. Letter, 14 November 1866.
21. Letter, 15 November 1866.
22. Letter, 31 March 1867.
23. Letter from Bartenyev to Tolstoy, 12 August 1867.
24. Letter from Tolstoy, written in the second half of August 1867.
25. Letter to Bartenyev, 8 December 1867.
26. Diary of Countess Tolstoy, 31 July 1868.
27. One of Tolstoy's notebooks, *Complete Works*, Volume 48, p. 116.
28. Letter, 10 May 1869.
29. Letter, 21 October 1869.

Part IV, Chapter 16

1. Letter from Botkin to Fet, 9 June 1869.
2. Letter from Goncharov to Turgenev, 10 February 1868.
3. Letter from Dostoyevsky to Strakhov, 24 March (5 April) 1870.
4. Letter, 13 (25) April 1868.
5. Vyazemsky, 'Recollections of 1812', *Russian Archives*, 1869.
6. Norov, 'On War and Peace', *The Military Review*, 1868.
7. *Minayev's Poetry*, quoted by Gusev.
8. Countess Tolstoy, Miscellaneous notes for documentation.
9. Diary, 19 March 1865. He also wrote, in a letter to Ertel dated January 1899, 'No matter what they do [the French] to swell his glory, this obtuse and wretched individual with his fat stomach and his hat, marching around his island and feeding on memories of his former quasi-greatness, is a pitiable and ignoble figure.'
10. ibid.
11. 'For a Bust of the Conqueror', poem by Pushkin (1829).
12. Cf. *Tolstoï sans tolstoïsme*, by Nina Gourfinkel.
13. *War and Peace*, Volume I, Book III, Chapter 14.

Part IV, Chapter 17

1. Diary of Countess Tolstoy, 14 February 1870.
2. Notebooks of Leo Tolstoy, 4 December 1865.

Part V, Chapter 18

1. Letter to A. A. Fet, 16 February 1870.
2. Letter, 17 November 1870.

3. Letter, December 1870.
4. Letter, 25 November 1870.
5. Diary of Countess Tolstoy, 27 March 1871.
6. ibid.
7. Letter, 9 June 1871.
8. Letter, end of May 1871.
9. Letter, 18 June 1871.
10. Letter, 28 June 1871.
11. Letters from Strakhov, 4 December 1872, 15 March 1873, 17 May 1873.
12. Letter to Strakhov, 7 April 1872.
13. Letter, 3 March 1872.
14. Letter, 12 January 1872.
15. Letter, 1 October 1872.
16. Letter, 14 June 1872.
17. Letter, 15 September 1872.
18. Letter, 19 September 1872.
19. Letter, 20 November 1872.
20. Letter, 10 December 1874.
21. Diary of Countess Tolstoy, 13 February 1873.
22. Ilya Tolstoy, *Reminiscences of Tolstoy, by His Son*.
23. Letter, 26 October 1872.
24. Ilya Tolstoy, *Reminiscences of Tolstoy, by His Son*.
25. Diary of Countess Tolstoy, 16 January 1873.
26. Letter, 1 March 1873.
27. Letter, 10 November 1873.
28. Letter, 18 November 1873.
29. Letter, December 1874.
30. Letter, 10 May 1874.
31. Tolstoy's *Reminiscences* and *Sketches of the Past* by Sergey Tolstoy.
32. Letter, 23 June 1874.
33. Letter, 15 August 1874.
34. Letter from Strakhov, 13 February 1875.
35. Letter, 16 February 1875.
36. Letter, 22 February 1875.
37. Letter, 9 November 1875.
38. Sergey Tolstoy, *Sketches of the Past*.
39. Letter, March 1876.
40. Letter, 21 February 1876.
41. Letter to Golokhvastov, March 1876.
42. Letter, 9 April 1876.
43. Letter, 8–9 November 1875. Twenty-seven years later, however, he looked back on this period of his life with envy, as shown by his conversation with Elpatyevsky on the deck of a ship in

1902. ' "How old are you?" he suddenly asked,' wrote Elpatyevsky in his *Literary Reminiscences*. 'I replied that I was forty-eight. To my great surprise his expression became serious, almost forbidding, he looked up at me with envy and, turning aside, muttered sadly, "Forty-eight. I was doing my best work. I never worked as well as then." He remained silent for a long time; then he said, less to me than to himself, "I was writing *Anna Karenina*." '

44. Letter to Strakhov, 8 June 1876.
45. Diary of Countess Tolstoy, 3 March 1877.
46. S. A. Behrs, *Reminiscences of Tolstoy*.
47. Letter, 5 April 1877.
48. Letter, 21 April 1877.
49. *Anna Karenina*, Part VIII, Chapters 15, 16 and variants.
50. Diary of Countess Tolstoy, 12 September 1877.
51. Ilya Tolstoy, *Reminiscences of Tolstoy, by His Son*.

Part V, Chapter 19

1. Obolensky, *Two Meetings with L. Tolstoy*.
2. Letter to Strakhov, 26 April 1876.
3. *Literary Heritage*, Nos. 37–8, p. 426. Meetings between Zhirkevich and Tolstoy.
4. Letter, 13 June 1877.
5. Letter, April 1877.
6. Letter, 25 January 1876.
7. Article in *Russian World* for 1877 (No. 28). To this day it has been impossible to discover who wrote these lines.

Part V, Chapter 20

1. *Confession*.
2. ibid.
3. ibid.
4. Notebooks of Leo Tolstoy, entry of 12 March 1870.
5. *Confession*.
6. Letter, March 1876.
7. Starets Ambrose was Dostoyevsky's model for starets Zossima in *The Brothers Karamazov*.
8. Tolstoy was born three years after the Decembrist uprising, which took place on 14 December 1825.
9. Letter, 27 January 1878.
10. Diary, 1 November 1878.
11. As told by Stepan Behrs in his reminiscences – an unpublished

passage quoted by Gusev in Volume III of his *Material for a Biography of Leo Tolstoy.*

12. Loose note, 6 December 1881.
13. P. Sergeyenko, *Contemporary Views of Tolstoy.*
14. Letter, 27 October 1878.
15. Letter, 15 (27) November 1878.
16. Letter, 22 November 1878.
17. *La Guerre et la Paix, roman historique. Traduit par une Russe.* Paris, 1879, 3 volumes.
18. Letter, 28 December 1879 (9 January 1880).
19. Notebook No. 10 (1880).
20. ibid.
21. Letter, 4 October 1879.
22. Notebook No. 7.
23. Letter, 23 January 1880.
24. Letter, 2 February 1880.
25. *Reminiscences* of Ivakin, in *Literary Heritage*, Volume 69.
26. Letter, 8 January 1880.
27. Letter, 14 February 1880.
28. Sergey Tolstoy, *Sketches of the Past.*
29. Letter, 28 May 1880.
30. Letter, early February 1881.
31. Rusanov, *Visit to Yasnaya Polyana.*
32. Said by Tolstoy, as quoted by Maxim Gorky.
33. Letter from Dostoyevsky to his wife, 7 February 1875.
34. Letter to Tolstoy, 28 November 1883.
35. Letter, 30 November 1883.
36. Ilya Tolstoy, *Reminiscences of Tolstoy, by His Son.*
37. Letter, 15 June 1881.
38. Sergey Lvovich, Tolstoy's eldest son.
39. Letter, 22 April 1881.
40. Diary, 15 May 1881.
41. Letter, 11 June 1881.
42. Arbuzov, *Reminiscences.*
43. Polonsky, *Reminiscences.*
44. Letter from Turgenev to Urusov, 1 December 1880.
45. Letter, 24 July 1881.
46. Letter, 30 July 1881, quoted by Biryukov.
47. Sergey Tolstoy, *Sketches of the Past.*

Part V, Chapter 21

1. Diary of Countess Tolstoy, 27 October 1878.
2. ibid., 5 November 1878.
3. ibid., October–November 1878.

4. ibid., 16 October 1878.
5. ibid., 25 October 1878.
6. ibid., 19 November 1878.
7. Letter, 15 November 1881.
8. Sergey Tolstoy, *Sketches of the Past*.
9. Quoted by Biryukov.
10. Letter, 30 January 1882.
11. Letter, 3 March 1882.
12. Stasov, *The Life and Work of N. N. Gay*.
13. Quoted by Sergey Tolstoy in *Sketches of the Past*.
14. According to the *Reminiscences* of Sergey and Ilya Tolstoy.
15. Letter to Alexeyev, 7 November 1882.
16. Letter, 15 January 1883.
17. Diary, 22 December 1882.
18. Letter, 1 May 1882.
19. Letter, 31 October–12 November 1882.
20. Letter, 25 May 1883.
21. Sergey Tolstoy, *Sketches of the Past*.
22. Letters to Sergey Tolstoy, 29 September 1865, and to Fet, 7 October 1865, on *Enough!*
23. Letter, 9 October 1883.

Part VI, Chapter 22

1. Diary, 16 and 23 March 1884.
2. Ilya Tolstoy, *Reminiscences of Tolstoy, by His Son*.
3. Diary, 31 March 1884.
4. Told by Alexandra Tolstoy's nanny, and retold in Alexandra's book, *Tolstoy, A Life of My Father*.
5. Diary, 6 April 1884.
6. ibid., 12 July 1884.
7. ibid., 14 July 1884.
8. Letter, 23 October 1884.
9. Letter, 26 October 1884.
10. Letter, 27 October 1884.
11. Letter, 28 October 1884.
12. Letter, 24 February 1885.
13. Letter, 21 February 1885.
14. Letter, 22 February 1885.
15. Note of 5 April 1885.
16. Letter, 9 December 1884.
17. Letter, mid-December 1885.
18. Sergey must not have been in the house. Masha – diminutive of Marya.
19. *Recollections of the Death of My Father*, in *Europe*, 1928.

20. Letter, 22 December 1885.
21. Letter, 18 January 1886.
22. Letter, 23 January 1886.
23. Letter, 2 September 1886.
24. Letter, also written on 2 September 1886.
25. Stakhovich, *Fragments of Reminiscences*.
26. Letter, 28 April 1886.
27. *The Power of Darkness* had just come out in the inexpensive Intermediary series.

Part VI, Chapter 23

1. Letter to Countess Tolstoy, 13 April 1887.
2. Sergey Tolstoy, *Sketches of the Past*.
3. Diary of Tatyana Tolstoy.
4. ibid., 1878 to 1891.
5. Diary of Countess Tolstoy, 10 December 1890.
6. ibid., 2 January 1891.
7. Alexandra Tolstoy, *Tolstoy, A Life of My Father* (New York).
8. Diary of Countess Tolstoy, 19 July 1887.
9. ibid., 19 August 1887.
10. Unpublished letter by Countess Tolstoy, 26 April 1888.
11. Letter, 28 April 1888.
12. Diary, 6 August 1889.
13. Diary of Countess Tolstoy, 17 December 1890 and 21 March 1891.
14. Letter from Pobyedonostsev to Feoktistov, 6 February 1890.
15. Diary of Countess Tolstoy, 14 December 1890.
16. ibid., 19 January 1891.
17. ibid., 15 February 1891.
18. ibid., 6 March 1891. The words that follow have been deleted by the editors.
19. V. Lazursky, *Reminiscences of Tolstoy*, p. 4 ff.
20. Diary of Countess Tolstoy, 15 February 1891.
21. Diary, 18 April 1891.
22. Diary of Countess Tolstoy, 23 April 1891.
23. ibid., 15 May 1891.
24. ibid., 1 June 1891.
25. ibid., 3 July 1887.